CENTERSTAGE

CENTERSTAGE

American Diplomacy since World War II

EDITED BY
L. CARL BROWN

HOLMES & MEIER   New York   London

Published in the United States of America 1990 by
Holmes & Meier Publishers, Inc.
30 Irving Place
New York, NY 10003

BOOK DESIGN BY DALE COTTON

The paper used in this publication meets the requirements
of the American National Standard for Permanence of Paper
for Printed Library Materials, Z39.48-1984.

Library of Congress Cataloging-in-Publication Data

Centerstage : American diplomacy since World War II.

    Includes bibliographies references.
    1. United States—Foreign relations—1945-
I. Brown, L. Carl (Leon Carl). 1928-
E744.C38   1990   327.73   89-24676
ISBN 0-8419-1265-3
ISBN 0-8419-1270-X (pbk.)

Contents

v

Preface

Centerstage: American Diplomacy since World War II first began to take shape in the last months of 1986 when a small working group at Princeton University planned a series of public lectures to review the broad sweep of American diplomatic history since the Second World War.

This resulted in the Peter B. Lewis lecture series sponsored by the Center of International Studies during the fall semester 1987 with one public lecture presented during each of the twelve weeks of the teaching period. These weekly public lectures were given by four members of the Princeton faculty, two visiting professors then at Princeton and six specialists from other institutions.

Since 1987 marked the passing of four decades after the eventful year of 1947 it was decided to label the lecture series "Forty Years of American Diplomacy, 1947–1987." The announcement introducing this lecture series read, in part, as follows:

> 1947 brought the Truman Doctrine, George Kennan's celebrated "Mr. X" article enunciating the strategy of containment, the beginning of the Marshall Plan, and the establishment of a more centralized military/diplomatic bureaucracy with the creation of the Department of Defense, the Central Intelligence Agency and the National Security Council.
>
> Forty years have now passed. It is time to consider these two generations or the greater part of eight American presidencies by asking how these years fit into the larger fabric of American diplomatic history or—to change the perspective—of global international relations.
>
> . . . Does the period since 1947 represent a sharp break with America's past or merely an intensification of venerable American practices and ideologies? How effectively has rhetoric fit reality in American foreign relations? Is the American governmental machinery attuned to international relations requirements of the nuclear age? Is American foreign policy too bipolar, too concerned with the Soviet threat, or is it—on the contrary—not sufficiently linked to the major problem of relations between the two superpowers? These are among the questions to be pondered. . . .

Such was the broad interpretative mandate given those asked to deliver these public lectures. The lecture series also formed the basis of a special Woodrow Wilson School undergraduate class. The twenty-five students selected to participate in the class attended the public lectures, read the written paper sent in advance by each lecturer as well as other readings assigned by each lecturer and the two faculty members directing the course. These students also met the morning following the afternoon public lecture with that week's lecturer for a session of follow-up questions and discussion.

Thereafter the lecturers were urged to revise their contributions in a form suitable for publication in a multi-authored work treating American diplomacy since the end of World War II (as planning continued throughout 1988 and 1989 there was no longer the occasion to commemorate the passing of precisely four decades from 1947 to 1987, and all agreed that the most appropriate starting point was clearly 1945, the end of the Second World War).

The twelve public lectures provided an excellent basis for the comprehensive treatment being sought. Even so, there remained several obvious gaps in coverage. This is why the original twelve public lectures, later rewritten as chapters, were joined by six additional chapters subsequently commissioned. These eighteen different subjects treated in separate chapters plus the Introduction, the Conclusion and the chapter providing a bibliographical essay now constitute *Centerstage: American Diplomacy since World War II*.

In addition to the twenty contributors themselves, who have sought to work as a team throughout this project, many other individuals and groups have helped in different ways. It is a pleasure to acknowledge with gratitude here this support.

The planning, research and writing of this book have from the very first days been under the sponsorship of Princeton's Center of International Studies. Important support came as well from the Woodrow Wilson School of Public and International Affairs, the Council on Regional Studies, the Program in Near Eastern Studies and the Department of Near Eastern Studies.

At Princeton Professors Kenneth Oye and Richard Ullman were especially helpful in planning both the subjects to be treated and the specialists to be recruited for this book.

The Carnegie Endowment for International Peace graciously granted permission to use the Chronology that originally appeared in *Estrangement: America and the World*, edited by Sanford J. Ungar (Oxford University Press, 1985). And for the years since 1985 the Council on Foreign Relations granted permission to select portions of the Chronologies that appear each year in the issue of the journal, *Foreign Affairs*, entitled "America and the World."

Contributions of political cartoons from the following cartoonists and newspapers or magazines are gratefully acknowledged:

Gene Basset, Gib Crockett, George Fisher, Bill Graham, Sandy Huffaker, Bill Mauldin, Paul Szep and John Trever.

Albuquerque Journal, Arkansas Gazette, Chicago Sun-Times, Chicago Tribune, The Detroit News and *Newsweek*.

The graph of U.S.–USSR Strategic Offensive Warheads, 1946–1986, was reproduced with the permission of the Natural Defense Resources Council.

Lou Presti and Jeff Riesley of New Jersey Network helped by locating many useful photographs available from the National Archives.

Jens Heycke, Peter Crowley and Jonathan Katz, Princeton University graduate students, all used their research and editing skills in many useful ways. Katie Palmer (Princeton '89), the editor's undergraduate assistant, proved invaluable with her computer and editorial skills, and Justin Harmon used his expertise to accommodate computer systems, something well beyond the ken of the editor and his generation.

The staff of the Center of International Studies under the supervision of Gladys Starkey were unfailingly prompt, accurate and cheerful in helping prepare the various drafts of this book. And Judy Gross willingly, indeed enthusiastically, accepted an extremely broad definition of her duties (as Program Assistant to the Program in Near Eastern Studies) in order to monitor and actively participate in all aspects of this project.

CENTERSTAGE

1

Introduction

L. CARL BROWN

CENTERSTAGE: It would be difficult for either friend or foe to deny that in the decades following 1945 the United States played a predominant role in world affairs. This country emerged from the Second World War with an economy not only intact but greatly strengthened. Wartime America became, in Franklin Roosevelt's ringing phrase, the "arsenal of democracy." This massive tooling up for total war left an America in 1945 with a gross national product (GNP) roughly fourfold what it had been a decade or so earlier in the depths of the 1930s depression.

By contrast, the other great powers—whether victors or vanquished—had been devastated. Estimates of Soviet casualties, military and civilian, reach as high as 10 percent of the country's total population. German military casualties were ten times those of the United States, and the Japanese military dead outnumbered the American by more than three to one.

To this must be added the enormous numbers of civilian deaths and displacements resulting from Hitler's genocidal policies, the most dramatic in its horror being the deliberate destruction of six million Jews. On the other side of Eurasia, an enormous number of civilian deaths and displacements occurred in East Asia in a war that had begun well before 1939.

Germany and Japan were totally defeated and at the mercy of the victors. Italy and France had each in different ways been reduced in power and influence by having been forced out of the war earlier—France in 1940 and Italy in 1943.

The British Empire seemed superficially intact in victory, but it was only the afterglow of an imperial sunset. Britain after 1945 had neither the material

1

resources nor the desire (diehard imperialists might say "the will") to maintain a globe-girdling hegemony. British India, "the jewel in the crown," was given up as early as 1947. Thereafter, the British effort to regroup what remained in Asia and Africa amounted to a sustained rearguard action against inevitable "winds of change."

A quick roll call of the other possible power centers reveals at best latent potential not soon to be realized. The world's most populous country, China, was in the last years of its civil war that would bring victory to the Communists in 1949. Thereafter, the tightly centralized political control and the weight of millions of inhabitants did give China some regional influence (witness the Chinese entry into the Korean War), but it was an influence severely limited by that huge country's woeful economic underdevelopment.

Another potential power center, if measured in terms of common culture and huge numbers, was the Indian subcontinent, but British India emerged as three states, India, Pakistan, and Sri Lanka. Moreover, the combination of economic and agricultural underdevelopment generalized throughout the subcontinent and the antagonism between the two largest successor states, India and Pakistan, undermined any chance that a unified strong voice in international politics would emanate from South Asia.

In the rest of the world—Africa, the Middle East, Latin America—most of the contenders for even limited regional influence were either not yet independent or not sufficiently well organized politically and economically, or were neutralized by neighboring rivals of roughly equivalent power. A partial list of such potential "regional influentials," to adapt to this earlier period the later phrase of Zbigniew Brzezinski, suffices to make the point: Brazil, Argentina, Nigeria, Turkey, Egypt, Iran, Indonesia, or Vietnam.

In the immediate postwar period, the United States accounted for an incredible 40 percent of the estimated gross world product. This country, alone, possessed that awesome new weapon—the atomic bomb. And only the United States among all the countries of the world that can be ranked as major powers, potential or actual, enjoyed the advantage of having borders facing open seas and friendly, nonthreatening neighbors. At no previous time in history had one state possessed the combination of assets held by the United States in 1945.

There have been, of course, many states in times past whose dominance for a while permitted them to fix the rules of the international politics game. Until modern times, however, no candidate for hegemony had the technological wherewithal to extend its power and influence virtually to all parts of the world. If the measure is organized power (human and material resources) that can be brought to bear where needed, then the America of 1945 makes the earlier states of Alexander, Caesar, Harun al-Rashid, Genghis Khan, Sulayman the Magnificent, or Charles V appear almost provincial.

All of which is to say the United States was not only centerstage in 1945. It was at the center of a greatly enlarged stage, one that embraced the entire world. This movement toward a genuine world politics had been in the process of development for a long time, it is true. One can rightly trace the roots to the age of discoveries as long ago as the sixteenth century. The later industrial revolution slowly at first but then with increasing acceleration brought into existence a world economy. Even so, the more complete development of a single world political arena emerged only following the Second World War.

It has often been pointed out that the First World War was the last great European war, and the Paris Peace Conference produced the last great European postwar settlement (this was even more the case retrospectively, given the subsequent American abandonment of Wilsonian internationalism).

The Second World War, by contrast, was truly worldwide in scope with major battles in Asia and Africa as well as Europe. Two of the principal powers involved, Japan and the United States, were not European states at all and had been only loosely linked to the classic European state system. Moreover, the United Nations represented a world-embracing international organization to an extent that the League of Nations had never achieved. That two permanent members of the Security Council were non-European powers (China and the United States) symbolized the dethroning of Europe as the arbiter of world politics. Decolonization of the western colonial empires and the entry en masse of the newly independent states completed the process.

This concatenation of developments—the breakdown of the Eurocentric system of international relations, its replacement by a still inchoate new system of international relations much more worldwide in scope than any previous system known to human history, and the amazing rise to preeminence of the United States—will surely be singled out by subsequent generations of historians as marking a major milestone in human history.

Such, in brief, was the point of departure in 1945, and the amazingly pivotal role of the United States since the Second World War is best interpreted in this larger, global context. The "American age" in international relations (which is now winding down) should rightly be viewed neither as the fulfillment of America's rightful destiny nor as a terrible aberration. It has been the result of a complex of forces, some but by no means all "Made in America."

At the same time, the focal point of attention throughout this book is the United States. This is not intended to be a survey of international relations since 1945 but rather a study of the United States in international relations since 1945.

This still leaves an intimidating range of subjects to consider. The approach chosen for this book is to be comprehensive but selective. What this amounts to can be clarified by reviewing in this Introduction certain major themes, any one of which might have provided the organizing framework for such a work. Instead, all of them, and others, have been integrated here in the hope that the result will be an interpretative study that clearly reveals United States diplomacy in the truly global context that emerged after 1945.

• • •

Perhaps the most important single organizing framework for the study of American diplomatic history since 1945, certainly in terms of sheer quantity of writings, has been that of the Cold War or the continuing rivalry of the two superpowers, the United States and the Soviet Union. Many of the more

The domino theory or the idea that vulnerable states will fall to aggression one after the other like a row of dominoes unless the United States provides support has been often advanced since 1945. As this 1983 George Fisher cartoon indicates, the domino theory was not uniformly accepted after the American experience in Vietnam. (George Fisher, 1983. Reprinted with permission of the *Arkansas Gazette*.)

significant terms, often neologisms, that have come into common use among scholars and commentators on international relations since 1945 are lexical children of the Cold War. These would include both the significant and the frivolous, e.g., containment, superpower, detente, massive retaliation, "eyeball-to-eyeball," flexible response, linkage politics, the domino theory, and of course the term, Cold War, itself.

Simplifying a complex body of writing, it might be said that two diametrically opposed Cold War interpretations have dominated the American scene. The first can be labeled the "heroic" or "establishment" view, and the second that of the "revisionists."

The first interpretation depicts a United States that had placed no demands on the international community and sought only to facilitate the achievement of a secure and prosperous world. To do this the United States was obliged to "contain" the expansionist Soviet bid for hegemony. American actions after 1945 revealed that we had learned the bitter lessons of the interwar years. We could no longer afford to be isolationists, to let the rest of the world go by. Moreover, we had come to realize that facing up to the aggressor (or to use more nuanced language—the would-be disturber of the international power balance) sooner rather than later would be more effective and less painful in the long run. Postwar American strategy, according to this interpretation, was a realistic blend of three elements:

1. Resisting the expansion of international communism under Soviet guidance (the Cold War context of the Truman Doctrine, the subsequent variations of containment strategies, and the implementation of collective security policies with the creation of NATO and other multiparty pacts).
2. Helping restore international economic stability and growth (Bretton Woods, GATT, the Marshall Plan and subsequent bilateral and multilateral aid programs, and a willingness to work for the economic reconstruction of yesterday's enemies—Germany and Japan).
3. Facilitating the evolution of a new worldwide international system not based on European domination, by supporting an orderly decolonization in the areas once under western imperial control, even at the risk of disturbing relations with America's oldest allies, as well as by actively participating in the United Nations.

The revisionist interpretation suggests, instead, that the United States at worst caused the Cold War and at best must share the blame with the Soviet Union for the rise of the Cold War. In this latter view, both the United States and the Soviet Union are depicted as two clumsy giants who bumbled their way into an avoidable great power rivalry, fostered a dangerous bipolar system of world politics by each lining up as many clients as possible, and then proceeded to confront each other through clients and proxy wars.

In this interpretation, the United States was actually quite sluggish in championing decolonization, usually lining up in support of independence only after the issue was no longer in doubt. Or, alternatively, the United States supported decolonization largely in order to better place the newly independent Third World countries under an American informal protectorate controlled by means of American economic and military power. (This is a thesis often held by a strange coalition of Third World leftists and diehard European imperialists.)

According to many embracing the revisionist interpretation, the United States has always been an expansionist power, driven by the impetus of acquisitive laissez-faire capitalism. Even the period of presumed isolationism was marked by hegemonic control in this hemisphere plus adamant insistence on the international economic policy of the "Open Door." Accordingly, so this argument goes, the only substantive change that took place after 1945 was the temporary weakness and disarray among America's actual or potential rivals, which gave the United States the opportunity to throw its weight around more openly.

Two points can be made concerning these polar opposite interpretations of the Cold War. First, even the more sophisticated and nuanced interpretations in either of the two camps can be faulted for advancing a form of fighting history, of advocacy scholarship. Indeed, both interpretations show telltale signs of what has come to be called the notion of American exceptionalism. The first interpretation comes close to assuming that the United States has consistently been a positive influence in the world and is somehow better than the rest of the world. The second, equally extreme, simply reverses the formulation.

Henry Kissinger, admittedly not a dispassionate source, put it well in commenting on his difficulties with public opinion while holding high office, "whereas in the 1920s we had withdrawn from the world because we thought we were too good for it, the insidious theme of the late 1960s was that we should withdraw because we were too evil for it."[1]

A second point, more encouraging, is that the tough dialectic of the American scholarly debate on the Cold War has discredited the more extreme positions of either the heroic or establishment interpretation on the one hand or the revisionist interpretation on the other. No serious scholar today places the blame for the Cold War solely on the United States. No serious scholar today completely exonerates the United States from having at times seriously misread the capability or intentions (or both) of its adversary, the Soviet Union, or from having taken steps that unnecessarily exacerbated international tensions.

Within this narrower and more realistic range of interpretations strong differences of opinion still hold sway, but considerable progress has been made in developing a scholarly discourse that eschews American exceptionalism. This country is not to be seen as a monument to all that is good (or all that is bad) in international politics. Today's preferred American scholarly appraisal of America's Cold War diplomacy is that of a people and their leaders who are neither gods nor devils and who, just like other peoples, are necessarily bound by their heritage, their ideals, their fears, and their geopolitical circumstances. Also, just as with other peoples, Americans are to some extent the prisoners of their diplomatic failures and their successes, which is to say that a people necessarily carry with them into the future both the burdens and the boons of the past.

It cannot be said, alas, that this same measure of moderation prevails in today's American public rhetoric, but it is to be hoped that here, too, a change away from "exceptionalism" will come.

Even at its best, however, Cold War historiography can be faulted for forcing a complex world onto the procrustean bed of superpower confrontation. It is worth pointing out that the two superpowers together account for just slightly more than 10 percent of the total world population. Moreover, the tendency to interpret in Cold War terms regional issues stemming from regional causes distorts reality, often with painful consequences. From the 1957 Eisenhower Doctrine, ostensibly directed against international communism but actually designed to shore up western interests in the Middle East that were believed to be threatened by Egypt's Nasser, to the tragedy and trauma of the American

1. Henry Kissinger, *White House Years* (Boston: Little, Brown & Company, 1979), pp. 56–57.

intervention in Vietnam, one can trace a persistent pattern of American bipolar thinking distorting the reality of a multipolar world.

Yes, the Cold War has been the principal concern since 1945 of both politicians and the public, and this book will not stint in giving the durable bipolar Soviet-American rivalry the careful attention it deserves. Even so, sound diplomatic history seeks to do more than record what the major players in the game of international politics thought and what they did on the basis of that thought. That much is clearly necessary, but it is not sufficient. An important next step in sophisticated historical interpretation is to bring to light major developments that contemporaries ignored, discounted, or misread. Certainly, one important theme in diplomatic history since 1945 has been decolonization and the emergence of a new international relations system (still in process of development, or so it would seem to us contemporaries).

• • •

In today's world there are over 170 sovereign states. In 1945 there were sixty. Africa in 1945 had exactly four independent states—South Africa, Liberia, Egypt, and Ethiopia, the last two still more independent in name than in fact. Today Africa boasts a total of over fifty independent states.

It was not just paternalistic European colonial administrators who insisted in 1945 and for a number of years thereafter that this or that colonial territory would require at least fifty (or more) years before it could be seriously considered for independence. Instead, the post–World War II generation witnessed a "scramble for decolonization" that in its haste and confusion evokes memories of the equally untidy "scramble for colonies" among European states in the last years of the nineteenth century.

When it comes to considering the American role in this massive decolonization, surely one of the most dramatic changes in world politics since the rise of the nation-state system, there is nothing like the same corpus of scholarly writing as pertains to Cold War historiography. Even the literature of the Cold War debate pitting the establishment school versus the revisionists addresses the issue of decolonization only sporadically.

Indeed, the study of decolonization is fraught with its own form of bipolarism. To a large extent, the issue is seen almost exclusively in bipolar terms of colonizer/colonized (e.g., Britain and India, France and Algeria, the Netherlands and Indonesia, Portugal and Mozambique, and so on). Another complicating factor is that the study of decolonization, as of Third World studies in general, tends to be confined to regional specialists. An Africanist, for example, may know quite a bit about decolonization in Africa but precious little concerning other parts of the world. The same usually holds for specialists on the Middle East or South Asia or East Asia.

Added to this is yet another problem: Most so-called nonwestern area specialists have felt the need to change the earlier scholarly focus that viewed the colonized Third World largely as inert clay in the hands of the colonialist potter. The area specialist seeks instead, and rightly, to emphasize the indigenous culture and the view from within. Such specialists, still developing these new fields of study, look askance at diplomatic history as partaking of the older, Eurocentric view of the world.

There are, happily, certain exceptions to this general description; but it is perhaps more to the point to note that Rupert Emerson's classic study, *From Empire to Nation: The Rise of Self-Assertion of Asian and African Peoples*, appeared almost three decades ago in 1960, and those academicians inspired by such works as Emerson's have tended to confine their studies to much narrower topics.

This being the case, it is not so much a matter of classifying opposing interpretations among scholars who share a common scholarly specialization and agree on the definition of the subject under review—as with Cold War historiography. Rather, the problem is to construct a global perspective, one that takes into account the many different colonial situations and the many different patterns of decolonization while seeking to reach a satisfactory general interpretation of the major systemic change underway.

For example, the word "colonialism" is revealed to be a very crude taxonomic tool if used to cover both the roughly dozen years of the British mandate over Iraq (from the end of the First World War until 1932) and the British raj in India (beginning in the late eighteenth century and lasting until 1947). Equally, "decolonization" becomes entirely too protean a term when used to describe both Libyan independence, granted by the contending great powers largely because they could not agree on any other solution, and the Algerian independence that resulted from a brutal eight-year war (1954–62), and which, moreover, provoked a domestic crisis in France leading to the demise of the Fourth Republic and the rise to power of Charles de Gaulle.

Turning to the American role in decolonization, the development of Cold War historiography offers a model for what may be suggested as the most accurate interpretation. On the one hand, the argument that the United States consistently championed decolonization even at the risk of immediate security interests in NATO or elsewhere cannot be accepted. Equally unacceptable are the two arguments at the other end of the interpretative spectrum: (1) that the United States offered only *pro forma* pressure on its European allies and usually after the issue was virtually decided or (2) that the United States sought only to gain influence with the newly independent states at the expense of the former colonizer.

The United States does have an anticolonial tradition and self-image. There was a fairly consistent championing of the goals of independence for the colonized peoples. These goals were usually translated into policy pressures on the colonial powers, even at the risk of disturbing ongoing western security arrangements. This, however, was only consistently the case to the extent that U.S. officialdom could foresee an orderly transition. Moreover, the official American notion of "orderly" implied, among other things, a leadership in the newly decolonized states willing to continue working with the western bloc of states.

The United States was throughout the decolonization period especially vulnerable to the blandishments of those charging that the colonial nationalists were communists or under communist influence. The American fear of a possible disorderly transfer of power plus the persistent phobia of chaos-driven communist infiltration managed in a number of cases to dampen down if not indeed to completely reverse the more dominant American preference for decolonization.

As for the colonial nationalists, virtually all of them attempted to enlist the support of the United States in their struggles. They saw just as clearly as did the colonial powers that the United States had a central part to play on the enlarged world arena. The colonial powers, in the process of accepting American economic guidance as epitomized in the Marshall Plan as well as American military/ strategic leadership (NATO), also attempted to influence American policy regarding each decolonizing issue.

And the Soviet Union viewed the dismantling of the western colonial empires as a means of weakening the camp of the enemy. Moreover, after the death of Stalin in 1953, the USSR actively attempted to lure the leaders of these fledgling states into at least informal ties with the communist bloc. Stalin, perfectly prepared to sow dissension among his enemies, nevertheless had dismissed most Third World leaders as bourgeois nationalists who under a facade of formal independence would remain subservient to the West. Khrushchev, in particular, realized that the nonaligned movement formalized at the April 1955 Bandung Congress amounted to a clear Soviet gain, because it would undermine any western effort to link these recently decolonized peoples to western alliances.

The United Staes, in short, was a major player in the many-sided diplomatic game that led to decolonization and the ensuing major structural changes in the international order. The American position was neither that of a Metternich or a Garibaldi. Instead, to continue the parallel analogy with nineteenth-century diplomatic history, the American position can be compared to the diplomacy of such British statesmen as Canning and Palmerston. Just as our British predecessors had, we encouraged the new world aborning—usually. At the same time, the United States as a rising "have" power with many assets to protect did oppose those forces that seemed bent on challenging the world order we favored and were instrumental in producing. Our ideals were genuinely held and not simply a cover for naked self-interest. At the same time, if we—as with the British earlier—set out to do good in the world, we often managed to do well. Time after time when the dust of decolonization had settled in this or that part of Africa or Asia, the American economic and political standing in the former colony emerged greatly enhanced, just as that of the former colonial overlord declined.

Decolonization, coming at the time of America's unparalleled position of strength, thus served to accelerate American commitments and, for a time at least, to increase American assets in the four corners of the globe. Whether the United States is now overinvolved in too many parts of the world is among the pressing questions American statesmen must now face, but then perhaps the complex (and still in part unwritten) history of America's role in post–World War II decolonization can offer insights into how states expand and contract their commitments and interest in response to their changing standing in the international power balance.

In any case, this book does take the phenomenon of decolonization seriously as a major development in the latter half of the twentieth century. Equally, it offers due attention to the emergence of what has come to be called the Third World. Indeed, as the Table of Contents illustrates, an effort has been made to include, if not all countries and regions of the world, at least representative examples from all world regions. This, it is to be hoped, does stimulate us to keep in mind the global context of contemporary international relations.

• • •

Writing soon after the end of the Second World War, Bernard Brodie asserted that the atomic bomb had introduced an irreversible revolution in conventional military strategy. In a striking statement that has been often cited since, Brodie began with what seemed to be a reassertion of conventional strategic thinking, "The first and most vital step in any American security program for the age of atomic bombs is to take measures to guarantee to ourselves in case of attack the possibility of retaliation in kind."

What followed, however, made it clear that to Brodie the old rules of warfare no longer applied, for he continued: "The writer in making this statement is not for the moment concerned about who will WIN the next war in which atomic bombs have been used. Thus far the chief purpose of our military establishment has been to win wars. From now on its chief purpose must be to avert them. It can have almost no other useful purpose."[2]

Here in a pithy paragraph was presented a revolutionary new strategic maxim: Nuclear war offers an especially macabre example of the non-zero-sum situation, one in which all sides gain by avoiding a nuclear confrontation and all sides lose—lose in an unimaginably horrible fashion—should they plunge into nuclear war.

Total war, according to this view suggested by Brodie and advanced by many since, is unthinkable in the nuclear age. Or, to be more precise, total nuclear war is an option that is—and must remain—unthinkable to any rational strategist. To those strategists of this persuasion, the nuclear age has obliged mankind to confront radically new rules of warfare: A military planner must seek a status of preparedness that ensures not victory in a nuclear war but avoidance of a nuclear war.

In other words, there is, as never before, a clearly demarcated threshold in military escalation that simply must not be crossed. In subsequent trials of strength between states the gamut of options must be restricted at the upper end of the scale if civilization is to continue. While great powers can afford to engage

---

2. Bernard Brodie, ed., *The Absolute Weapon* (New York: Harcourt Brace, 1946), p. 76.

The awesome mushroom-like cloud created by a nuclear explosion. Total war became "unthinkable in the nuclear age." (National Archives)

in certain forms of adversarial relations as in times past—cold wars, proxy wars, conventional wars—a general nuclear war must be ruled out.

Accordingly, one major organizing theme for any study of the United States in international relations since 1945 is that of the new strategic realities imposed by the nuclear age. It is an even more significant theme for purposes of this book because the American move to centerstage in world affairs and the advent of the nuclear age were concurrent.

Even so, a few clarifications and reservations are in order. The idea that unlimited escalation in warfare can be self-defeating has been around, and rightly so, as long as warfare itself. Witness the much-used expression "Pyrrhic victory." Its origin lies in the words attributed to the victor in a battle won over two millennia ago. Pyrrhus, aware of his great losses in the battle of Asculum (279 B.C.), turned aside congratulations with the bitter retort, "Another such victory and I shall be ruined." Examples abound throughout the history of warfare of those who actually lost by pushing on to achieve overly costly victories.

By this logic nuclear warfare represents a major quantitative increase in the vulnerability of humans in war, not a qualitative change in the rules of warfare. Seen in this light, the nuclear weapon is yet another significant expansion in the modern tendency to make total populations, and not just military forces, the targets in warfare. It thus continues the sad trend in modern total war that has largely obliterated the distinction between combatants and noncombatants. Moreover, it could be argued that the terrible concept, and reality, of total war has been around for a long time. Earlier examples include French Marshal Bugeaud's campaigns against Algerians in the 1830s and 1840s, the American Civil War, and then the aerial bombardments of cities during World War II.

Certainly, not everyone accepted Bernard Brodie's argument that in the nuclear age the mission of those in charge of national security shifted from assuring victory in nuclear war to avoiding just such a war. Indeed, the notions of limited nuclear war and of so-called theater nuclear combat soon evolved among American strategic planners. Moreover, these ideas have by no means been laid to rest.

What can be said, however, is that with the nuclear age Americans began to consider matters of warfare as too serious to be left to the generals and the admirals. Americans had perhaps never been especially prominent in the roster of the world's strategic thinkers. If challenged to name American equivalents of modern European grand strategists such as Clausewitz, Jomini, Moltke, Mackinder, or Liddell Hart, the typical American before the nuclear age might well have hesitated after naming just one admiral—Alfred Thayer Mahan. Or, thereafter the list of names would likely have concentrated on military practitioners rather than theorists, especially the Civil War greats such as Lee and Grant and perhaps Pershing in World War I.

Since 1945, however, strategic planning has ceased to be the preserve of military professionals and become as never before a subject in which physicists and political scientists play a leading role. In universities and in think tanks, in government and outside, a new order of specialists has appeared on the American scene. They often speak the abstruse language of higher mathematics appropriate to theoretical physics or advanced games theory. Only a few of the names of these specialists have become "household words," even to the small percentage of the American public who follow foreign policy carefully. Those names—Bernard Brodie, Herman Kahn, and perhaps one or two more—might evoke a flicker of recognition among "political establishment" Americans. Others tend to be known only to their fellow specialists. Yet this small group is bringing about changes in the field of grand strategy no less significant than those initiated in their time by Adam Smith or John Maynard Keynes in economics.

This new school of thought includes in its numbers both hawks and doves, both those who insist on the necessity of an American nuclear superiority (however defined) and those who scoff at "superiority" among adversaries with the awesome capacity to destroy each other and the earth several times over. Yet, for all the many policy differences dividing them, they have developed a common language of analysis, which, just as with other innovative scientific terminology (as Keynesian economics, Freudian psychology, Weberian sociology, and the like), has since filtered down to usage among the larger public.

Among these words coined or given new meanings since 1945 that are now in common currency, the most significant perhaps is "deterrence." It is, after all, rather easy to see how the need to avoid nuclear war, as Brodie announced, could spawn a word that indicates the need to stop unacceptable military action. And in the nuclear age, the stress on deterrence rather than, say, on retaliation or punishment or victory is surely more than word play. It conveys a significant change in strategic thinking.

Perhaps second only to deterrence in this new vocabulary of strategy is "credibility" and its adjective, "credible." A show of force or will designed to deter unacceptable behavior must of course be of the sort that the adversary or adversaries to be deterred find believable and realistic—in a word, credible.

Going hand in hand with the new nuclear age strategic thinking has been a heavy dose of games theory, which seeks to reduce to mathematically precise formulae the choices likely to be made by "players" in "games" ranging from commercial bargaining to nuclear confrontation.

This pattern of strategic thinking produced for the nuclear age is based, as any scientific theory must be, on certain assumptions, one of the most important being the "rational actor model." That is, individuals or states will make the logically correct choice that best advances their self-interest to the extent that information available to them makes that possible. This type of thinking makes little allowance for individual or group irrationality and it thus downplays some rather basic human drives, such as altruism, hatred, revenge, group solidarity, religious zeal, and the like. In the same manner, this kind of strategic thinking remains close to equally rational, if not even at times mechanistic, forms of reasoning that one associates with cost-benefit or input-output analyses.

All of which would seem to suggest that this new breed of American strategic thinkers uses a concept of "strategic man" analogous to the "economic man" of the classical economists. Moreover, just as economic thought has never been the same since the revolution begun in the time of Adam Smith, it is most likely that strategic thought will henceforth be shaped by these new ideas here epitomized in the terms "deterrence" and "credibility."

To the tangible reality of awesome new weaponry—nuclear bombs—and the conceptual reality of new strategic thinking there has been added since 1945 the moral and political reality that concerns the question of what society's response should be to nuclear power. Acute moral or political dilemmas are often deftly summed up in slogans, and "better red than dead" (or the opposite) will suffice to suggest the problem. Since the beginning of the nuclear age, some Americans have wanted to ban the bomb. Others have insisted that one cannot put the genie

"It's Really More Of A 2-Power Conference, Ain't It?"

Nuclear weapons brutally changed the rules of the diplomatic game. Herblock, *Here and Now* (New York: Simon & Schuster, 1955).

back in the bottle. Some demand unilateral nuclear disarmament. Others insist that greater safety lies in superpower nuclear parity. Added to these sharply differing options are the problems of nuclear proliferation, of nuclear weapons getting ultimately into the hands of men or states who, whatever else might be said, do not conform to the "rational actor model."

That we now ineluctably live in a nuclear age clearly changes certain aspects of contemporary international relations so radically as to require completely new strategic thinking. At the same time, however, other aspects of international relations continue substantially in ways that have characterized human history since the beginnings of diplomacy and war. The approach taken in this book toward the nuclear dimension seeks to strike a balance between these two, the old and the new.

• • •

This book, then, takes due note of the Cold War and the bipolar relationship between the United States and the Soviet Union that has persisted since the end of the Second World War. It charts the course of decolonization, the rise of the Third World, and the resulting enlarging of international relations to embrace the entire world. The importance of the nuclear factor is never lost sight of. Even so, no one of these three major themes has been permitted to serve as the single, or even preeminent, organizing framework.

The same can be said for other themes that have rightly loomed large in the study of American diplomatic history since 1945. These would include the rapidly changing role of the United States in the world economy, or the institutional changes in American foreign policy machinery, or the ideological changes from isolationism to world involvement.

Instead, all of these approaches are given their due attention in the chapters that follow. The ensuing risk of trying to do too much is, we sincerely hope, more than offset by the resulting wide-angle lens view of an especially critical turning point in American diplomatic history and in world history—a period when for better or worse the world became a single large stage with the United States, for a time, at the center.

PART I

THE NEW WORLD OF SUPERPOWERS AND BIPOLARITY

2

Was 1947 a Turning Point in American Foreign Policy?

MELVYN P. LEFFLER

To CONTEMPORARIES the events of 1947 appeared electrifying. The Truman Doctrine, the Marshall Plan, and the containment strategy seemed to portend a revolution in the United States' peacetime relations with the rest of the world. Newspaper and magazine editors proclaimed that the foreign policy principles followed by the American government since Washington's Farewell Address were being scrapped. Hereafter, America's involvement in world affairs would not be episodic but continuous, not merely economic but political and military, not focused on the Monroe Doctrine in Latin America and the Open Door policy in East Asia but on the ideological, socioeconomic, and geopolitical crosscurrents of the Old World from which the United States had always shrunk except in times of global conflict.

This essay, therefore, seeks to place the dramatic events of 1947 in the context of a new conception of national self-interest that emerged in the decade following Hitler's conquest of Europe and Japan's quest for hegemony in East Asia. As a result of these momentous developments, the traditional ideological and economic impulses in American foreign policy, as embodied in the Open Door policy, were fused with a new set of geopolitical and strategic imperatives. Thereafter, neither in peacetime nor in wartime would the United States permit the preponderant resources of Eurasia to fall within the grasp of a potential adversary or coalition of adversaries. While these concerns with the Eurasian balance of power had influenced aspects of American diplomacy before and especially during the era of the First World War, the subsequent defeat of Germany and improvement in Japanese-American relations in the 1920s had ushered in an era of unprecedented safety for the American people. Until the international upheavals of the late 1930s sent shock waves across the Atlantic and Pacific, American officials carried on their economic, political, and diplomatic relations with the rest of the world with little sense that vital interests, fundamental institutions, or the physical safety of the nation could be endangered by developments abroad.

All of this changed after June 1940. My thesis is that the decade from June 1940 to June 1950 constitutes the crucial decade in the history of American foreign policy. Within that decade, the speeches, programs, and policies outlined in 1947 highlighted the direction of America's new relationship to the rest of the world, a relationship that was shaped by Axis domination of Eurasia, by Axis aggression against the United States, by Axis war-fighting capabilities, and by the fear that communist victories and revolutionary nationalist upheaval might enable the Kremlin to gain a similar ascendancy over Eurasian resources. As will become evident, American officials were acting in accord with this new conception of national security before 1947. But the full magnitude of the changes inherent in this new conception unfolded piecemeal during 1948, 1949, and early 1950. In the spring of 1950, Paul Nitze, the director of the Policy Planning Staff (PPS) in the State Department, authored the famous report, NSC 68, a guide to the future that was riveted in the perceptions, attitudes, and goals of the preceding decade. Just as the events before June 1940 were prologue, those after June 1950 have been epilogue. The real transformation of American foreign policy occurred within the confines of that decade, and, as a result, 1947 continues to deserve a special place of importance.

1947 as a Turning Point

It might well be appropriate to begin with a fuller description of the significant events and developments of 1947, a year that began with frigid temperatures, heavy snows, and terrible food and fuel shortages throughout Europe. Under tremendous financial pressure, the British government announced its withdrawal from Greece and Turkey; exchange shortages also forced the French and Italians to contemplate cutbacks in raw material and grain purchases abroad. As the financial crunch was accompanied by socioeconomic turmoil and by decisions to exclude the communists from the governing coalitions of Belgium, France, and Italy, American officials worried that the type of civil strife beleaguering Greece might spread elsewhere. The military aid to Greece and Turkey embodied in the Truman Doctrine and the economic aid envisioned in the Marshall Plan were efforts to defeat communist insurgencies, bolster noncommunist governments, and forestall communist political victories that might bring additional countries within the Soviet orbit, an area already enlarged by the defeat of Nazi armies and by the Russian occupation of much of Eastern Europe and the Balkans. The creation of the Cominform in September 1947, the bitter Soviet

Secretary of State George Marshall and President Truman. Architects of an activist and global American role. (UPI/Bettmann Newsphotos)

attacks on the Marshall Plan, and the ensuing strikes and protests gave credence to American apprehensions.

At the same time that American officials were calling for aid to Greece and Turkey and promoting a European Recovery Program (ERP), they launched a host of other initiatives that constituted part of the containment strategy. Most important were the changes in American policy toward the western zones of Germany. After the fruitless discussions at the Moscow Conference of Foreign Ministers in the spring of 1947, Secretary of State George C. Marshall decided that the western powers had to revive coal production in the Ruhr, boost industrial output in the British and American zones, undertake currency reform, allocate to the Germans themselves more control over economic production, and establish political institutions of self-government in Germany. The overall goals were to win the loyalty of the German people and to thwart the possibility of a future Soviet-German alignment. These objectives put an end to any serious American effort to bring about a four-power accord on Germany. In the summer of 1947, the Americans and British raised the permissible level of German industrial production and determined that the western zones of Germany must participate in the ERP. Marshall and his advisers ruled out the possibility not only of reparations from current production but also of Soviet participation in any international scheme to control the Ruhr. These attitudes contributed to the failure of the London four-power conference in November–December 1947, created the context for exclusively western agreements and initiatives on the future of the western zones of Germany, and culminated in the Berlin crisis of June 1948.

Marshall and British Foreign Minister Ernest Bevin realized the significance of their actions in Germany. Even had they wanted to escape the ramifications of their initiatives, the French would not let them. French Foreign Minister Georges Bidault was so alarmed by the short-term and long-term dangers of Anglo-American initiatives in Germany that he threatened to delay the ERP, resisted trizonal fusion, and questioned the wisdom of currency reform. The French feared that if Germany were reconstructed economically, it would use its coal to reemerge as the dominant industrial power in Europe. With its industrial infrastructure revived, Germany once again would have great latent military abilities that could be used either alone or in conjunction with the Kremlin. As for the short-term threat, the French worried that the Kremlin might react to initiatives in the western zones in ways that would elicit further Anglo-American countermeasures, generate a major crisis, and lead to war. However certain the French were that the Soviets did not want armed conflict, they believed that if war occurred from accident or miscalculation, Russian armies would overrun the continent, occupy France, and carry out mass deportations and executions.

French fears, however exaggerated they might have been, were understood by American policymakers. Marshall, Under Secretary of State Robert Lovett, and other State Department officials sought to allay French anxieties and thereby elicit French cooperation on German matters. In December 1947, Marshall and Bevin discussed measures that might reassure the French against the possibility of internal strife and external aggression. In these conversations, one can see the early beginnings of what was to be the North Atlantic Treaty Organization (NATO) with military assistance, coordinated strategic planning, and moves toward European unity. As these talks evolved in January and February 1948, Marshall emphasized that American occupation troops would remain indefinitely in Germany. He also stressed that a western security framework, however much it needed to be alert to a recurrent threat from Germany, also had to envision the incorporation of Germany into a western bloc that had the capability of deterring and, if necessary, defeating Soviet aggression.

At the same time that American policies toward Europe boded so much that would be new and permanent, the Truman administration was reappraising policies in other parts of the globe, studying new options, and preparing to launch new initiatives. With regard to Latin America, there was the Rio Treaty, the first regional defense agreement that included American participation; with regard to the Middle East, there were the talks at the Pentagon with the British to iron out military responsibilities and national missions; with regard to the Far East, plans for a quick peace treaty with Japan were scrapped, the liberal reformist impulses of occupation policy were squelched, and the so-called "reverse course" policy was conceived. As American officials decided to distance themselves from the incompetence and corruption of Chiang Kai-shek's regime in China, the new goal of American policy in Asia was to rehabilitate Japan economically, preserve its domestic stability, ensure its security, and gain access to its bases. As reconstruction and reintegration became the hallmarks of American policy toward Germany and Japan in 1947, American officials also resumed their efforts to win universal support for commercial multilateralism. At conferences in Geneva and Havana, American diplomats and State Department economic experts worked indefatigably to gain support for the General Agreement on Tariffs and Trade and to establish the International Trade Organization. And while American diplomats labored abroad in behalf of these goals, Marshall, his cabinet colleagues, and their subordinates endeavored to engender a new spirit of bipartisanship at home. In particular, they tried to gain the support and solicit the help and advice of the Republican majority leader in the Senate, Arthur Vandenberg.

The changes in American foreign policy envisioned in all these efforts exhilarated State Department officials. Dean Acheson subsequently called his memoirs *Present at the Creation,* a title that accurately conveys the spirit with which the men at Foggy Bottom perceived their efforts to remold and refashion American foreign relations. Humiliated by President Franklin D. Roosevelt's disregard for their advice in wartime and demoralized by Secretary of State James F. Byrnes's administrative ineptness in peacetime, State Department officials felt an entirely new sense of elan after Marshall was appointed secretary of state in January 1947. Although the former army chief of staff traveled

Dean Acheson, Truman's Secretary of State following George Marshall. The title of his memoirs, *Present at the Creation,* indicated that he and his generation of foreign affairs specialists believed they were setting the American ship of state on a new course. (AP/Wide World Photos)

frequently, tired easily, and was no longer at the peak of his abilities, his penchant for orderliness, his stature within the administration, his desire to plan and to allocate responsibility, his ability to influence (if not always determine) the actions of powerful proconsuls abroad (like Generals Lucius Clay in Germany and Douglas MacArthur in Japan), and his overall capacity to exert leadership and inspire loyalty infused a new sense of purposefulness into the State Department.

Moreover, Marshall took office as the legislation for restructuring the apparatus of decision making for foreign and military policy was reaching its concluding stages. Fearing, as did many of Truman's closest advisers in the White House, that Navy Secretary James Forrestal might be seeking to cast a military hue over foreign policy issues, Marshall insisted that the secretary of state chair the newly created National Security Council (NSC) in the president's absence. The establishment of the NSC itself, along with the National Security Resources Board, the Central Intelligence Agency, and many other coordinating bodies, however, was testimony to policymakers' realization that a better job needed to be done to harmonize diplomatic, economic, and foreign policies, to integrate logistical planning with strategic designs, and to reconcile budgetary resources, political commitments, and military capabilities.

Continuities in Goals

Notwithstanding the magnitude of the substantive and administrative changes outlined above, there were important elements of continuity in the way American policymakers defined their objectives. In many respects, the Truman Doctrine and containment strategy were part of the long-term American effort to effectuate a liberal capitalist world order that would be responsive to American economic needs and receptive to the dissemination of American ideas, values, and institutions. The containment strategy, after all, was conceived not in 1947 but in 1917 when Robert Lansing, Wilson's secretary of state, looked contemptuously upon the Bolshevik Revolution and reacted negatively to the Bolsheviks' withdrawal from World War I. Wilson and Lansing intervened in the Russian civil war, aided Kolchak and other white Russians, refused to establish diplomatic relations with Lenin, and approved the establishment of a *cordon sanitaire* of large eastern European states. For sixteen years the United States refused to recognize the Bolshevik regime. But during this time span the State Department did establish a Russian bureau that was imbued with an anti-Bolshevik outlook; it continued to welcome foreign service officers whose social backgrounds predisposed them to view the Soviet experiment with hostility; and it did train an elite corps of diplomats, like George Kennan, Charles Bohlen, and Elbridge Durbrow, whose knowledge of Russian history, culture, language, and traditions was heavily influenced by the white Russian émigrés with whom they often studied and by the anti-Bolshevik atmosphere of Riga where they spent considerable time reporting on Soviet developments. Many of these men were the first to staff the American Embassy in Moscow when diplomatic ties were established in 1933.

Not only did anti-Bolshevism have a long history, but so, too, did the struggle against Soviet-directed world communism. From the time of Wilson's Fourteen Points speech, American officials saw themselves locked in a battle to win the hearts, minds, and stomachs of the oppressed and toiling masses of Europe. The Red Cross, the YMCA, the American Federation of Labor were mobilized by the Wilson administration to combat the propaganda of the Comintern, while Herbert Hoover and his technocratic relief experts dispensed food and supplies to antirevolutionary forces throughout the continent. During the 1920s and 1930s Wilson's Republican and Democratic successors waged a quiet yet persistent struggle against communists in Latin America, in Spain, and elsewhere. In newly emerging revolutionary nationalist movements in China and in Mexico, Wilsonian and Republican policymakers thought they saw communist instigators and feared the influence of the Kremlin. In the Near East, the turbulent forces of nationalism seemed so foreboding in the early 1920s that Secretary of State Charles Evans Hughes recast America's traditional support for colonial self-determination, came to appreciate aspects of British colonialism that safeguarded western access to critical raw materials, and reshaped the Open Door policy to allow for collaboration among Anglo-American private multinational corporations. Confronted with mass suffering and the resurgence of the Left during the depression years of the 1930s, many of the same foreign service officers, whose antipathy to Bolshevism was reinforced by the firsthand observations of the brutality of Stalinist Russia, had little difficulty accommodating authoritarian and fascist regimes so long as the latter seemed capable of preserving order and stability, protecting private property, and thwarting the spread of communism.

In addition to the continuities in the struggle to stem the growth of Soviet power and to contain communism, American desires to reconstruct western Europe after World War II did not differ from American aspirations after World War I. The Marshall Plan had its roots in the stabilization policies of the 1920s. After World War I, Democratic and Republican officials alike had recognized the importance of rehabilitating Europe in order to provide markets for American exports, to promote peace, and to contain the spread of radicalism. Far from turning their backs on European affairs, Republican officials tried to bring about a reasonable agreement on reparations (the Dawes Plan), accepted reductions in interest payments on the war debts, encouraged private loans for developmental purposes, and, most important, promoted cooperation among central bankers (especially the efforts of the Federal Reserve Bank of New York) to stabilize European currencies. Like their successors in the Truman administration, Republican officials in the 1920s also grasped the importance of integrating Germany into a flourishing economy and feared a prospective Soviet-German alignment like the one portended at Rapallo. They prodded the French to abandon punitive measures, championed the idea of equal commercial opportunity for German goods in allied markets, and supported regional political pacts of nonaggression and arbitration, like the Locarno treaties.

Republican officials sought to achieve their goals by depoliticizing incendiary issues, enlarging the purview of international law, and allocating responsibility to quasi-governmental officials, financial experts, and the private sector. Informal mechanisms of collaboration were cultivated between the public and private sectors, the aim of which was to foster stability at home and abroad by promoting economic growth, class cooperation, and international peace. American champpioning of arbitration treaties and arms limitation agreements complemented American efforts to safeguard property rights, support the free flow of private capital, especially into raw materials industries, and expand trade according to the principle of nondiscrimination. The legalism that was so evident in the peace movements of the 1920s was not naive and innocent but was an integral part of the mind-set of a capitalist creditor nation increasingly cognizant of the interdependent nature of the modern international economy and of America's own proliferating interests in trade, raw materials, and overseas investments.

The depression simply accentuated trends already underway. After a brief flirtation with nationalist and domestic solutions to internal economic hardship, President Roosevelt decided to look abroad to overcome persistent domestic economic stagnation. Secretary of State Cordell Hull's affinity for reciprocity, nondiscrimination, and the good neighbor; Roosevelt's opening of diplomatic ties with Bolshevik Russia; the creation of the Export-Import Bank; the Treasury's attempts to effectuate tripartite stabilization agreements with Britain and France; and the administration's mounting dislike for Britain's Ottawa agreements, for Japan's co-prosperity sphere, and for Nazi autarchism were all attributable to policymakers' growing frustration with their incapacity to regenerate sustained economic growth at home. A small number of prominent businessmen like those represented in the Commerce Department's Advisory Business Council and on the Committee for Economic Development not only shared the administration's view that domestic rejuvenation depended on reviving and restructuring capitalism abroad but also believed that the private sector needed to collaborate with public officials in fashioning new instruments for promoting economic growth at home and abroad. Accepting a larger yet carefully delimited role for government and welcoming the insights and tools afforded by the Keynesian analysis of economic cycles, these businessmen (like Averell Harriman and Paul Hoffman) not only supported aid to the Allies but were ready to join the administration, eager to defeat the Axis, and intent on creating new institutions like the International Monetary Fund (IMF), the World Bank, and the United Nations that would bring peace and prosperity to the world while rejuvenating the wellsprings of liberalism, capitalism, and free enterprise at home.

Many of the dollar-a-year men who flocked from Wall Street banking firms and law offices to Washington to organize the victory over Axis aggression in 1940 and 1941 remained (or returned) after the war to implement the containment strategy. Men like Robert Lovett, James Forrestal, John McCloy, Robert Patterson, Ferdinand Eberstadt, Averell Harriman, and Dean Acheson had been familiar with or had vivid recollections of the defeat of the League of Nations and the failed financial efforts of the 1920s. They were intent on avoiding previous errors, averting a new depression, sustaining economic growth, and preventing the rebirth of totalitarian aggression. The goals they sought after World War II were not new. Their ideas were shaped by the economic tribulations of the thirties and by the views of prominent individuals whom they knew well from their experiences in the private sector, men like Elihu Root, Russell Leffingwell, Thomas Lamont, Dwight Morrow, Owen Young, S. Parker Gilbert, Charles Evans Hughes, and, most important, Henry L. Stimson.

Discontinuities in Tactics

The continuities in the way American policymakers defined their objectives after both world wars should not obscure critical differences over tactics. These tactical differences assume great qualitative significance because they reveal the growing importance that American policymakers attributed to the goals of disseminating liberal and capitalist institutions abroad, promoting open markets and equal access to raw materials, and containing communism and revolutionary nationalism.

After World War I, American officials generally eschewed political or military efforts to achieve international stability along liberal capitalist lines. Rather quickly Wilson evacuated American troops from Soviet Russia. Although Wilson's Republican successors abhorred radicalism and revolutionary nationalism, they generally refrained from utilizing military force, even in Central America. Alhough they wanted to foster stability in Europe, reassure the French, allay German grievances, and thwart the spread of Bolshevism, they rejected the political obligations implicit in the Treaty of Versailles and the League of Nations. They shunned political embroilments and strategic commitments and refused to guarantee French security. They withdrew American troops on the Rhine. The idea of a military assistance program never entered their minds, and they generally scorned the utilization of the proceeds of private loans for military purposes.

These tactics need only be compared to those measures adopted after World War II to visualize the magnitude of change. Joining the United Nations, of course, was among the least important shifts. But it symbolized a willingness to accept the risks of becoming embroiled politically and even militarily in the affairs of the entire world, and most particularly those of the Old World. Far more important than support for the United Nations was the fact that from the onset of the post–World War II era, Truman administration officials as well as former isolationists like Senator Vandenberg were ready to accept embroilment in European political affairs, as evidenced by their willingness to guarantee Germany's disarmament and demilitarization. While Roosevelt had thought that American troops would remain in Europe only briefly after victory had been achieved, as had been the case after World War I, American occupation forces stayed in Germany. By 1947 Marshall was promising to guarantee French security; by 1948 he was negotiating a North Atlantic Treaty, granting military assistance, and endorsing strategic collaboration. By this time, of course, the administration also had supported a military assistance program and regional alliance for the Western Hemisphere; had sent military aid to Greece, Iran, Turkey, China, and the Philippines; and had authorized American military advisers to work with Greek army officers on the divisional level.

The global military posture of the United States after World War II bore little resemblance to its posture after World War I. Unlike the naval competition that frayed Anglo-American relations in the 1920s, close military collaboration between American and British military officers continued after World War II and quickly became a hallmark of the second postwar era. In contrast to Harding, Hughes, and Hoover who accepted naval parity with the British and who acquiesced in Japanese superiority in the western Pacific, Truman and Forrestal intended to retain American military supremacy over any adversary. Notwithstanding the huge demobilization that immediately occurred and the budgetary retrenchment that persisted until 1950, American naval and air capabilities were unrivaled. American officials hoped to retain their monopoly over the atomic bomb as long as possible; while this monopoly lasted the United States could deter or strike an adversary in an unprecedented manner. American officials also negotiated for overseas bases that would provide the United States with the ability to project its power almost everywhere. Merely to mention these developments is to underscore the vast differences between political and military policies after both world wars. Moreover, the initiatives of the Truman administration, including the quest for overseas bases, the maintenance of strategic superiority, the acceptance of political obligations, the granting of military assistance, the participation in regional alliances, and the use of military advisers presaged much that would become commonplace in the four decades after 1947.

If the initial post–World War II years constituted a critical divide in political/military tactics, they also constituted an important, albeit not quite so decisive, turning point in foreign economic and financial policies. Although Republican officials in the 1920s endorsed the nondiscrimination principle and although the Democrats in the 1930s accepted reciprocity, Hoover continued to believe in protectionism and Secretary of State Cordell Hull lacked the courage to fight for large-scale reductions in customs duties. Hence true multilateralism, meaning both nondiscrimination and low tariffs, was adopted and implemented only after the Second World War (and even then with much congressional opposition). Similarly, although American policymakers after both world wars endorsed moderate reparations payments and emphasized Germany's importance in postwar reconstruction, the efforts to guarantee European access to the resources of the Ruhr and to oversee the integration of the industrial sectors of European nations through multinational instruments of control like the Committee on European Economic Cooperation, the American Economic Cooperation Administration (ECA), and the International Authority for the Ruhr were entirely new initiatives for the United States. Likewise, whereas after World War I Wilsonian and Republican officials were prepared to postpone or adjust interest rates on the war debts in order to accommodate international commercial flows, Roosevelt's decision to offer lend lease meant that the war debt issue would not poison America's postwar relations with the Allies. Qualitatively different from the piecemeal, informal, and quasi-official efforts to rebuild a modified gold exchange system in the 1920s, comprehensive and official attempts were designed to frame a new, more flexible, and enduring postwar financial system based on the agreements laboriously negotiated at Bretton Woods, on new international

The Truman administration used prominent businessmen in its ambitious economic
diplomacy. From Left: President Truman and Secretary Marshall conferring with
Paul Hoffman, former president Studebaker Corporation who headed the agency
administering the Marshall Plan for European recovery, and Averell Harriman.
(National Park Services—Abbie Rowe, Courtesy Harry S Truman Library)

institutions like the IMF and the World Bank, and on the $3.75 billion govern-
mental loan to the United Kingdom. And unlike the post–World War I years
when Wilson and Hoover restricted government aid for relief and relied on the
voluntary cooperation of the private sector for rehabilitation, Truman and his
advisers transformed relief into reconstruction assistance and acknowledged the
incapacity of the private sector to provide the requisite funding in the critical
transition years. While the Truman administration's use of prominent businessmen to administer the ECA bore some resemblance to the private-public
linkages of the 1920s, its decision to allocate billions and billions in public monies
to finance European reconstruction and to rehabilitate the German and Japanese
economies broke entirely with earlier precedents and constituted a real turning
point both in the role of the public sector and in the relationship of the United
States to Europe.

A New Conception of National Security

The challenging question is what caused these changes in tactics that not only
demonstrated a willingness to assume great political and military risks, to incur

substantial financial costs, and to forgo popular tax reductions but that also reflected a totally new degree of importance attached to international stabilization. To some extent, the changes can be attributed to the impact of the depression, the influence of Keynes, and the latent problems wrought by the huge expansion of America's physical plant and production capabilities during World War II. The nightmare of depression continued to haunt American officials throughout the war years. Policymakers feared that the American economic system would not be able to adjust to the closed economic blocs of the Axis powers, to the autarchical controls of the Soviet Union, to the imperial preferences of the British, or to the revolutionary nationalist practices of anticolonial movements.

The problem with this economic interpretation is that it focuses too much attention on market considerations, isolates them from other variables, and obscures the interlocking web of considerations, of which economic factors formed an important but not the decisive thread. Although the depression drastically reduced American exports (and imports), most businessmen did not see overseas trade as the most important means of redressing their problems. With the notable exception of the automobile industry, even during the prosperous 1920s the largest and most rapidly growing sectors of the American economy had not become especially dependent on foreign markets. In fact, the proportion of manufactured goods exported in relation to their total production decreased from a little less than 10 percent in 1914 to just under 8 percent in 1929. When the speculative bubble burst in 1929 and when the contraction of American lending was accompanied by proliferating exchange restrictions and commercial impediments abroad, American businessmen primarily looked inward rather than outward for solutions to their declining profits. They talked about curtailing production, ending price-cutting, suspending the antitrust laws, balancing the budget, and augmenting domestic purchasing power. Neither Hoover in the early 1930s nor Roosevelt in the late 1930s acted or spoke as if he believed that domestic economic well-being was dependent primarily on the international marketplace.

Yet the Nazi conquest of Western Europe in the spring of 1940, the movement of Japan into Indochina in July, and the consummation of the Tripartite Pact in September altered Roosevelt's priorities and transformed American foreign policy. Almost immediately the State Department, renowned private foundations like the Council on Foreign Relations, and the media elite started to assess the meaning and ramifications of an Axis victory. How would the global economy function, based as it had been on triangular patterns of trade, if it were now severed into economic blocs? Would the United States be able to trade on acceptable terms or compete with a Nazi-dominated Europe? How would Japan's co-prosperity sphere affect American (and British) access to Far Eastern markets and raw materials? More worrisome still was the problem of thwarting Nazi inroads into Latin America, given the great dependence of some Latin American economies on European markets and the alleged affinity of Latin American peoples for authoritarian modes of political leadership and for corporatist models of economic development. And even more ominous was the question of what would happen if the British signed an armistice, accepted a compromise peace, or handed over their navy to the Nazis. Planning for peace in the post–World War II era actually began with such scenarios in mind.

And the results of these projections were disheartening. The American economy, if properly managed and regulated, might adjust. But the American free enterprise system would be altered radically; the political economy would be transformed; the role of the government would become omnipresent; and political freedom would be jeopardized. American officials immediately agreed that domination of the European marketplace afforded Germany great leverage over the countries in the southern cone of South America, countries that traditionally sold their grain, meat, and raw materials to European purchasers. Mechanisms had to be designed and monies appropriated in order to buy up Latin American surpluses and to prevent Argentina, Brazil, Chile, and Uruguay from caving in to Nazi pressure and falling within the Nazi orbit. These instruments necessitated a greatly enlarged role for the government, cartel-like practices, joint market agreements, and infringements on free market mechanisms.

Because Europe also was the major market for American goods, American officials and businessmen had to consider how they would bargain commercially with the Nazis should Hitler win the war and consolidate his hold over the continent. This topic was of major concern, for example, at the 1940 convention of the National Foreign Trade Council. Because the German government carefully regulated trade for political and strategic purposes, would the American government have to exert similar controls? Might it have to take over the export sector altogether? Might it have to organize the producers of the Western Hemisphere and the British Empire (if the latter survived) into powerful cartels capable of negotiating on equal terms with Axis counterparts? There was the prospect, then, of unprecedented interference with free market mechanisms, interference dictated by geopolitical as well as economic considerations.

Such schemes were anathema to Roosevelt. "The logic of such implications," he emphasized, "would lead us to embark upon a course of action which would subject our producers, consumers, and foreign traders, and ultimately the entire nation, to the regimentation of a totalitarian system. For it is naive to imagine that we could adopt a totalitarian control of our foreign trade and at the same time escape totalitarian regimentation of our internal economy."[1] With great fervor and eloquence Roosevelt insisted that the United States could not become "a lone island in a world dominated by the philosophy of force. Such an island represents to me . . . a helpless nightmare of a people without freedom—the nightmare of a people lodged in prison, handcuffed, hungry, and fed through the bars from day to day by the contemptuous, unpitying masters of other continents."[2] Roosevelt's opposition to the Axis and his support of aid to the Allies, therefore, was inspired by his recognition that Axis domination of Eurasia would demand a reconfiguration of the American and Western Hemisphere economies, an unprecedented role for government, a huge increment in defense expendi-

---

1. National Foreign Trade Council, *Report on the Twenty-seventh National Foreign Trade Convention* (New York: National Foreign Trade Council, 1940), pp. 346–47.

2. Samuel Rosenman, ed., *The Public Papers and Addresses of Franklin D. Roosevelt, 1940* (New York: Macmillan, 1941), p. 261.

tures, and eternal vigilance against internal threats from Fifth Columnists as well as against external aggression from the Axis powers themselves. In such a context, personal freedoms and individual liberties would have difficulty surviving.

American officials could not contemplate coexistence and accommodation with the Axis powers. Roosevelt suspected that Hitler would not be satisfied with domination of Europe and Hull did not believe the Japanese would comply with any agreements they signed regarding China and Southeast Asia. Like the experts who pondered the consequences of Nazi hegemony over Europe and who assessed the prospects of a British surrender, Roosevelt and Hull believed that Hitler would use his economic leverage to wedge his way into South America. The president worried about the enormous growth in Nazi war-fighting capabilities if they should gain control of the British fleet. He was aware of the advantages that would accrue to Hitler's military machine if it should move into French North Africa and West Africa. He was concerned about safeguarding Dakar, protecting the bulge of Brazil, and controlling the Atlantic. He was attuned to and perhaps even exaggerated the potential of Fifth Columnists in Brazil and Argentina. Even if the Nazis had no immediate ability to attack the United States, as most experts agreed, the task was to prevent Germany from gaining the time and opportunity to develop those capabilities. Roosevelt had excellent reasons for distrusting Nazi intentions. Hitler anticipated that after a number of years his victories in the Old World would culminate in a military clash with the United States.

The physical safety of the United States required that Hitler be defeated before he had the capacity to assimilate the resources of Europe or to acquire bases in Northwest Africa or take over the British fleet or gain sustained access to the petroleum of the Caucasus and the Near East or the breadbasket of the Ukraine. Time was not necessarily on the side of the United States unless Germany's enemies remained in the conflict, wearing down German energies and complicating the task of absorbing the new resources falling within the German orbit. For with the defeat of each nation and the cooperation of others, Germany was gaining the raw materials and developing the potential for unprecedented military and industrial strength. From France, it could secure iron ore, railway equipment, cast-iron pipe, and machinery; from Bohemia and Moravia it obtained arms, chemicals, and iron and steel plants; from Poland, it could get coal, zinc, timber, and meat; from Belgium came iron, steel, industrial equipment, and railway supplies; from Rumania, petroleum; from Hungary, bauxite; from Yugoslavia, copper and chrome. And as it vanquished its enemies, Germany also gained extended leverage over neutrals like Sweden and Switzerland. Germany was gaining strength, not losing it. Unless Great Britain and the Soviet Union could be given the wherewithal to persevere in the struggle and to shun a compromise peace, Roosevelt had every reason to think that the nation's physical safety as well as its political institutions and economic welfare would be endangered.

Policymakers and military officials in all nations grasped that modern warfare demanded huge resources. Roosevelt and his chiefs of staff assigned priority to defeating Germany because Germany appeared to be on the brink of defeating

Britain, penetrating Latin America, and integrating the raw materials and granaries of the Near East, Eastern Europe, and North Africa with the industrial infrastructure, technological know-how, and skilled manpower of northwestern Europe and Scandinavia. The Japanese gambled on attacking Pearl Harbor because they hoped that a successful assault would provide the time to consolidate their hold over the natural resources of Southeast Asia and to augment their strength so substantially as to convince the Americans that it was not worthwhile to contest Japanese supremacy in East Asia. The Japanese assessment of American determination was terribly flawed. But their capacity to wage war for such a protracted period of time was made possible by their previous imperial acquisitions, by the assimilation of Manchuria, Korea, and Taiwan into the Japanese economic orbit, and by the growth of Japanese heavy industry in the 1930s, a development made possible, at least in part, by previous successful aggression and aggrandizement.

For American officials, the most decisive and most lasting legacy of the wartime experience was the notion that potential adversaries must never again be allowed to gain control of the resources of Eurasia through autarchical economic practices, political subversion, or military aggression. The acquisition of such resources allowed potential foes to augment their military capabilities, encouraged them to penetrate the Western Hemisphere, tempted them to attack the United States, and enabled them to wage a protracted struggle. Postwar peace and stability had to be constructed on the foundation of nonaggression, self-determination, equal access to raw materials, and nondiscriminatory trade. When these principles were violated, nations used military power and autarchical practices to accrue strength disproportionate to their size and stature. This was dysfunctional to the international system and dangerous to the physical security of the United States. Faced with such realities, American officials had to take defensive measures and had to contemplate substantial changes in the political economy of the United States, including huge increments in national defense expenditures and in the powers of the federal government, infringements on free market mechanisms, and the curtailment of individual liberties. Axis aggression and military successes in 1940 and 1941 demonstrated that the traditional principles of self-determination and the Open Door, principles that heretofore had been geared to American economic needs and ideological inclinations, now had profound implications for the national security, physical safety, and political economy of the United States. Once this fusion of geopolitical, economic, ideological, and strategic considerations occurred, traditional foreign policy goals were transformed into national security imperatives. Then, self-imposed restraints on political commitments, military guarantees, and the use of force were eroded and the economic costs of global embroilments became less important than their alleged geopolitical and strategic benefits.

Postwar Containment and the New Vision of National Security

This orientation was immediately apparent as the war against the Axis reached its concluding stages. In 1945, most American officials were still vacillating in their attitudes toward the Soviet Union. Harriman, Forrestal, and Admiral William Leahy, the chief of staff to the president, were advocating a tougher policy; but Byrnes, Acheson, Marshall, Henry Wallace, and many other officials still hoped to keep the alliance together. Truman himself was ambivalent and wavered back and forth. Everyone was dismayed by Soviet actions in Eastern Europe, but hardly anyone wanted an irrevocable rift. Yet even among those who looked benignly on Soviet intentions, there was great apprehension that the Soviets might capitalize upon the pervasive economic dislocation, political ferment, social unrest, and revolutionary nationalist upheavals to gain direct or indirect control over resources heretofore beyond their control. If communists won or seized power or if former colonial areas drifted beyond the reach of the West's grip, the Kremlin's actual and latent strength might grow significantly. If at the same time the penchant of the British for imperial preferences and the sterling bloc divided the noncommunist world into autarchical blocs, which would stifle growth and encourage destructive competition, the will and capacity of the West to contain Soviet-directed world communism would be weakened.

The balance of power was endangered, then, not by the prospect of Soviet aggression but by the instability of postwar governments, the volatility of the international system, and the vacuums of power left by the defeat of the Axis powers. The joy of victory was tarnished from the very moment of triumph by the fear of chaos. In April 1945 Assistant Secretary of War John McCloy returned from a trip to Europe and submitted a report to his good friend and boss, Henry Stimson. "He gave me a powerful picture of the tough situation that exists in Germany," Stimson noted in his diary. It "is worse than anything probably that ever happened in the world. I had anticipated the chaos, but the details of it were appalling."[3]

Less than two months later Assistant Secretary of State Acheson presented an equally vivid account of the portentous international situation. "There is a situation in the world," Acheson told the Senate Committee on Banking and Currency, "very clearly illustrated in Europe, and also true in the Far East, which threatens the very foundations, the whole fabric of world organization which we have known in our lifetime and which our fathers and grandfathers knew." All of Europe and Asia were ripe for revolution. "You find that the railway systems have ceased to operate; that power systems have ceased to operate; that financial systems are destroyed. Ownership of property is in terrific confusion. Management of property is in terrific confusion. Systems of law have to be changed." The industrial and social life of Europe had "come to a complete and total standstill." Europe could turn in upon itself using bilateral agreements, exchange controls, and other tactics of economic warfare. Acheson reminded his listeners that this is what had happened under Hitler. Germany had organized a system that had turned Europe inward "and with perfectly amazing skill made that system work and work so effectively that the Germans were able to fight all the rest of the world and support reasonably well the people of Europe."[4]

3. Diary entry, 19 April 1945, Henry L. Stimson Papers (Yale University).
4. Acheson testimony, 12 June 1945, Committee on Banking and Currency, *Bretton Woods Agreements* (Washington: Government Printing Office, 1945), especially pp. 19–21, 48–49.

Some Day They'll Come Crawling Back to Her

Not all Americans were happy with the new internationalism. The *Chicago Tribune* was a powerful advocate for what it dubbed "Americanism" and its opponents deplored as "isolationism." (Joseph Parrish, *Chicago Tribune*, 29 June 1949. Reprinted by permission of the Chicago Tribune–New York News Syndicate. All rights reserved.)

Acheson did not hold the Soviet Union responsible for these developments. But prudence impelled officials to fill the void before the Kremlin might be tempted to capitalize upon conditions beyond the sphere of Soviet occupation armies. Containment, therefore, began in 1945; it was not prompted primarily by animus toward the Kremlin nor by fears of postwar depression. It was inspired by the lessons of 1940–41, by the realization that a potential foe could not be allowed to gain direct or indirect control of the preponderant resources of Eurasia.

This policy was manifested in many ways. The United States government dispensed billions in relief in 1945–46; it loaned $3.75 billion to the British government; it began immediately to revive German coal production. The thread that tied these actions together was the conviction that economic suffering had to be relieved, avenues of trade unclogged, and the productive capabilities of Europe released in order to inspire hope in a better way of life before the communists made their own successful appeal to the dispirited peoples of Europe. American officials did not doubt that communist leaders would bring their countries immediately into the Kremlin's orbit, signing treaties with Moscow akin to those already consummated between the Soviet Union and Rumania, Poland, and Hungary, and perhaps offering strategic bases as well. In July 1945, Truman made the production of twenty-five million tons of coal by April 1946 the number-one goal of American occupation policy in Germany. At the Potsdam conference, Byrnes successfully rebuffed Soviet desires to participate in the international supervision of the Ruhr; he also made reparations from the western zones contingent upon conditions that the Soviets could not influence. Neither sympathy for Germany nor hatred of Russia dictated these decisions. Enlightened self-interest and a new conception of national security made it imperative for American officials to mobilize German resources for European reconstruction before suffering and unrest translated themselves into communist rule and indirectly into Soviet aggrandizement.

Similar efforts were made in the Near East to shore up British power and to stymie prospective Soviet gains. After extensive studies in June and July 1945, the War Department, the Joint Chiefs of Staff (JCS), and the State Department agreed that Soviet demands for a substantial influence in the Dardanelles could not be accepted, lest the Kremlin use that position to project its influence into the Middle East and the eastern Mediterranean, gain control of the region's petroleum, disrupt the British Empire, and maneuver to achieve a preponderant position in Eurasia. For similar reasons, Byrnes pressed Soviet officials to withdraw their troops from northern Iran even while he decided to keep America's own military advisory missions in place in Tehran. At the same time he complained not at all about Britain's retention of a hundred thousand troops at its base in the Suez canal zone, a number that vastly exceeded the quantity permitted in Britain's 1936 treaty with Egypt. Concern for the security of the region impelled Forrestal to begin deploying warships to the eastern Mediterranean in 1946.

America's containment policies in East Asia in 1945 and early 1946 were even more dramatic. From the outset, American officials decided to retain full control of the occupation of Japan. In August 1945, Truman approved the insertion of troops into Korea with the explicit purpose of thwarting a prospective Soviet takeover of the peninsula. In September, two divisions of marines were sent to northern China for the ostensible reason of repatriating Japanese soldiers but for the real purpose of guarding coal mines, securing the railroad lines, transporting Kuomintang forces, and limiting the territory under Chinese Communist control. At the same time Truman agreed to offer a huge package of military assistance to Chiang Kai-shek and to establish military advisory missions. All these initiatives were prompted by a concern that the presence of Soviet troops in Korea and Manchuria combined with Communist victories in northern China might enable the Kremlin to coopt the resources of Northeast Asia, much as the Japanese had done. In the autumn of 1945 Truman, Marshall, Forrestal, and Patterson explicitly envisioned the danger in this manner. Likewise, the State Department acquiesced in British, French, and Dutch attempts to resume their control over their former Southeast Asian colonies for fear that nationalist insurrections might place this region in unfriendly hands and bar western access to the markets, raw materials, and investment earnings of this region.

Globalism and Military Superiority

Globalism inhered in American policies from the very onset of the postwar era. The persistence of social and political turmoil and the economic setbacks arising from bad harvests and the ensuing frigid winter of 1946–47 prompted Truman administration officials to make Western Europe their number-one priority. But the Marshall Plan actually accentuated American interests in other parts of the globe as well. Middle Eastern oil, for example, became even more important once the United States had committed itself to European reconstruction. If the United States invested rather few resources and abjured strategic commitments in this area, it was because Soviet-directed world communism posed no immediate threat there and because the British still had a major presence in the Middle East, a presence that American officials encouraged the British to maintain. Similarly, because the Marshall Plan's major objective was to make Western European nations and Great Britain self-supporting by 1951 and because their payments deficits constituted a key source of their need for outside assistance, American policymakers came to believe that it was more important than ever for the former colonial powers to have access to the markets, investment earnings, and raw materials of their former colonial areas. The State Department believed it was essential to coopt and placate moderate nationalist movements before they were captured by radicals who might excise western influence or look to the Kremlin for guidance.

This kind of thinking continued to influence the approach of the United States to Asia. The decision to disengage from Chiang Kai-shek did not signal any diminution of U.S. interest in the Far East. In fact, the gradual withdrawal of support from the Chinese nationalists was inspired primarily by the realization that Chiang's cause was hopeless and by the calculation that China was not a critical region; indeed it was likely to be a drain upon rather than a contributor to the resources of any great power. Even more significant for the long run was the fact that the Truman administration increasingly aligned the United States against the Viet Minh and on the side of the French in Indochina. As American officials committed themselves to the reverse course in Japan in 1948–49 and as they realized the likelihood of a Communist victory in China, they dedicated themselves to containing communism and revolutionary nationalism in Southeast Asia. This area, in fact, had to be preserved as a market for Japanese exports and as a source of raw materials for Japan's economic rejuvenation (as well as for the success of the Marshall Plan). Decisions to safeguard the region and to provide aid were made in the months preceding the eruption of hostilities in Korea.

Indeed the decision to intervene militarily in Korea is understandable only in the context of America's continuous attempts after the end of World War II to block the Kremlin's position of preponderance in Northeast Asia as well as to limit its opportunities for mischief and insurrection in Southeast Asia. Notwithstanding the JCS view that Korea was strategically inconsequential in time of global war and notwithstanding the withdrawal of American occupation forces in 1948–49 (after the Soviets pulled out their troops), American efforts to contain the revolutionary nationalist Left in South Korea and to maintain the credibility of its interests there never ceased. Truman's decision to reinsert troops in June

1950 was not then a new departure, but an action consonant with American goals since the president first ordered troops to the peninsula in August 1945.

Nor was the Korean War a turning point in American strategic policy. It is true that the huge increments in defense expenditures came after June 1950. But the significance of this fact is often misunderstood. The United States did not spend more on defense prior to 1950 because American officials were confident of their military superiority. Notwithstanding the Soviets' alleged ability to overrun the European continent in wartime, the Kremlin could not effectively strike the United States. Nor was the Kremlin thought capable of assimilating the resources of Western Europe in a time of armed conflict. Eventually, then, the industrial superiority, air capabilities, and atomic weapons of the United States would constitute the decisive margin of victory. American initiatives in 1947, 1948, and 1949, especially regarding Germany, were premised on the belief that Soviet leaders were not likely to opt for a war they knew they could not win. Although it is now fashionable to stress that America's atomic arsenal and air power prior to the Korean War were a "hollow threat," Marshall, Forrestal, Clay, and Air Force Secretary Stuart Symington certainly did not think the Kremlin viewed American capabilities that way.[5] If the tables had been reversed in the late 1940s and if the Kremlin had possessed the American air force and atomic arsenal, American officials would not have deemed the threat a hollow one. They would have been alarmed by the disparity in capabilities.

In fact, as soon as the Soviets exploded their atomic device in August 1949, policymakers accelerated the development of American atomic capabilities. The number of bombs in the arsenal and the number of planes capable of delivering atomic weapons had been growing rapidly since early 1948. In February 1950, moreover, Truman decided to build the hydrogen bomb. A few months later Paul Nitze wrote NSC 68, a plea for a major arms buildup, both in conventional and nuclear forces. Although NSC 68 had not been formally approved by Truman at the time of the outbreak of hostilities in Korea and although the Budget Bureau was waging a battle against it, Acheson already had accepted it as a guide to policy. In other words, as soon as American military superiority appeared to be jeopardized by the Soviets' acquisition of the atomic bomb, the Truman administration scrambled to keep the lead.

American officials did not increase defense expenditures between 1947 and 1950 because American military superiority had not been threatened and because the real objectives of American diplomacy, of which the arms race was only an instrument of policy, were to control resources, retain allies, and preserve a favorable correlation between economic, technological, and geopolitical forces on the Eurasian landmass. These goals were as evident in NSC 68 as they had been apparent in every major American national security document and foreign policy program since Truman took office. Illustratively, at the beginning of NSC 68, Nitze emphasized that "Soviet efforts are now directed toward the domination of the Eurasian land mass." If the Soviets were to incorporate any substantial new

---

5. See, for example, Harry R. Borowski, *A Hollow Threat: Strategic Air Power and Containment Before Korea* (Westport, Conn.: Greenwood Press, 1982).

areas into their orbit, it "would raise the possibility that no coalition adequate to confront the Kremlin with greater strength could be assembled." Even with the atomic bomb, Nitze did not think that the Soviets would believe that they had the strength to win an armed conflict against the United States. What he truly feared were the diplomatic shadows cast by that military strength. Soviet atomic capabilities might "neutralize" America's own arsenal because Europeans might doubt the credibility of American commitments to defend Europe if the United States were vulnerable to atomic retaliation. "Our allies and potential allies . . . [might] drift into a course of neutrality eventually leading to Soviet domination. If this were to happen in Germany the effect upon Western Europe and eventually upon us might be catastrophic."

Nitze emphasized that what was fundamental ("cardinal") to American policy was that "we possess superior overall power in ourselves or in dependable combination with other like-minded nations." Otherwise the American system would be jeopardized. Nitze stressed that American officials had the responsibility "to create conditions under which our free and democratic system can live and prosper." He claimed that the system was endangered by the fundamental redistribution of power that had occurred over the past generation and by the Kremlin's fanatic determination "to impose its absolute authority over the rest of the world." He spoke hardly at all about overseas markets, profits, or investment opportunities, but he did consistently discuss the nation's national security in terms of its political economy.[6]

There was considerable continuity between the thinking that influenced Truman, Acheson, and Nitze in the spring and summer of 1950 and that which had influenced Roosevelt and his advisers a decade earlier. Like the Axis powers in 1940, the Kremlin's intentions could not be trusted; like the Nazis in 1940, the Kremlin's capacity to inflict physical harm on the United States was mounting; like the Axis in 1940, the Soviets' greatest challenge would evolve either if they had the chance to absorb additional regions into their war potential or if they succeeded at fragmenting the opposition into emasculated economic units. If these contingencies should arise, American vital interests would be jeopardized, even without a direct assault on American territory, because in order to safeguard the nation's security the American government would be compelled to assume unprecedented controls over the economy and to allocate unprecedented resources to defense expenditures. The power that totalitarian adversaries derived from squashing the self-determination of nations and coopting their resources constituted a threat to the political economy of the United States in peacetime and to its physical safety in wartime.

Conclusion

The fusion of traditional economic and ideological goals with geopolitical and strategic imperatives is what constitutes the great divide in the history of

6. For Nitze's quotations in NSC 68, see Thomas H. Etzold and John Lewis Gaddis, eds., *Containment: Documents on American Policy and Strategy, 1945–1950* (New York: Columbia University Press, 1978), pp. 386, 387, 414.

American foreign policy. The shocks of 1940, the strength and boldness of the Axis, the magnitude of the war effort, and the fear of another conflict under even more adverse conditions left lasting repercussions. It should not be forgotten that many of the men who were in charge of mobilization and procurement during the war (Forrestal, Lovett, Patterson, Byrnes, Clay, Marshall) were the same individuals who took charge of waging the cold war. They wanted to ensure that Soviet Russia should never find itself in the same position that the Axis powers had been in to control the resources of Eurasia and to endanger American security. Moreover, like so many Americans, they believed that stability, prosperity, and individual freedom in postwar America depended on expanding productivity, ending redistributive struggles, and promoting full employment without too greatly aggrandizing the role of the government in the domestic political economy. The functions of the federal government were likely to become too intrusive and too threatening to free enterprise and individual liberty if the world fell into autarchic blocs or if an adversary gained preponderant control of Eurasian resources, developed the capacity to wage war against the United States, and forced the American government to mobilize its economy for war and to be forever vigilant against external assault and internal subversion.

In this quest to ensure a favorable balance of power no developments were more important than the announcement of the European Recovery Program and the decision to integrate a revitalized western Germany into a western bloc. And it is noteworthy that in their testimony before congressional committees justifying these initiatives, Marshall, Lovett, Forrestal, Harriman, and Lewis Douglas emphasized that Western Europe (including western Germany) constituted an industrial core of such great magnitude that if it should be absorbed into the Soviet orbit, the balance of power would irrevocably shift in the Kremlin's direction and the capacity of the United States to prevail in wartime or for the American political economy to operate in peacetime (as it always had functioned) would be jeopardized. This emphasis on thwarting the Kremlin's ability to coopt another major industrial center also constituted the core of George Kennan's thinking during the apex of his directorship of the PPS in the State Department. Germany's and Japan's industrial potential, he warned, must not be combined with the military and economic assets already possessed by Soviet Russia. But to achieve this objective required unprecedented initiatives in the political-military realm as well as in regions of the world, like the Middle East and Southeast and Northeast Asia, where before 1940 American activity had been meager indeed.

In their special report to the president on European recovery in the fall of 1947, Secretary of Commerce Harriman and the elite group of businessmen, politicians, economists, and labor leaders who worked with him beautifully wove together the ideological, geopolitical, and institutional factors that had come to undergird American foreign policy. They emphasized that they regarded "as nonsense the idea . . . that we need to export our goods and services as free gifts, to insure our security." But then they went on to warn that "the deterioration of the European economy . . . would force European countries to resort to trade by government monopoly. . . . The United States would almost inevitably have to follow suit. The resulting system of state controls . . . would soon have to be

Churchill, Truman and Stalin at Potsdam, July 1945. The war, and war-time collaboration, comes to an end. The Cold War begins. (National Archives)

extended into the domestic economy to an extent that would endanger the survival of the American system of free enterprise." If this sounded remarkably similar to Roosevelt's concerns in 1940, the rest of the rationale behind the Harriman report also resonated with the memories, fears, and lessons of World War II. "If the countries of middle-western and Mediterranean Europe sink under the system of despair and become Communist," the Harriman committee insisted, "Scandinavia will follow into the same camp. The strategically and economically vital North African and Middle-Eastern areas will follow. The transfer of Western Europe, the second greatest industrial area of the world . . . would radically change the American position. If it should prove that a weakened United Kingdom could not resist . . ., then the shift would be cataclysmic." The domestic consequences in America would be intolerable: "The swift and complete conversion to a military footing . . .; the abrupt but necessary change in our relations with the rest of the Western Hemisphere; the immediate and sweeping limitation of our economic and political life, perhaps extending to our very form of government."[7]

The belief that the violation of self-determination and the Open Door policy actually posed real and immediate dangers to the nation's physical safety and to its domestic political economy was what was new in 1940 and was what persisted in the postwar years. Because of these new apprehensions, American officials were willing to offer unprecedented government aid and to risk unprecedented political embroilments. These departures were most apparent in 1947, when the United States declared its readiness to defend Greece and Turkey from internal subversion and external aggression, embarked upon the ERP and German integration, and prepared to accept the strategic obligations, political commitments, and global responsibilities that inhered in these actions. That is why 1947 remains a critical year in the decisive decade in the evolution of American foreign policy.

But while focusing on 1947, one should not ignore the way officials in the Truman administration defined American interests in other parts of the globe and the way they began protecting those interests even as World War II was closing. The peacetime embroilments in Northeast Asia, Southeast Asia, and the Near East that have become a hallmark of our lives had their origins in the experiences and lessons of World War II, ripened in the calculations that underlay American foreign policy in the first postwar months, and flowered in the year preceding the eruption of hostilities in Korea. Nor should one forget that during these same postwar years, no matter how small the American defense budget was compared to its subsequent dimensions, the United States possessed the capacity to launch an attack against the Soviet Union with atomic weapons, while it remained virtually impregnable to any effective retaliation. That, too, was new and unique; but unlike much else that characterized the decade, the atomic monopoly was to prove transitory. Indeed, after 1940, Americans, like other peoples, would be unable to escape the insecurities and vulnerabilities of a nuclear age and an interdependent world.

7. U.S. President's Committee on Foreign Aid (Harriman), *European Recovery and American Aid* (Washington: Government Printing Office, 1947), especially pp. 3, 18–22.

3

Risks, Costs, and Strategies of Containment

JOHN LEWIS GADDIS

ONE OF the more ironic consequences of World War II is that it persuaded Americans of the need for strategy in peacetime.[1] Until then, to the extent that they thought about the matter at all, most Americans would have assumed that one required strategies only to fight wars; the idea that one might need a strategy when not at war would have seemed odd indeed. But then neither did Americans until 1940–41 see their security as likely to be threatened in peacetime. Throughout most of its history the United States had enjoyed what C. Vann Woodward has called a tradition of "free security,"[2] a luxury sustained, to be sure, more by geographical distance from potential adversaries than by geopolitical wisdom in Washington. But because maintaining security in peacetime had required so little effort, strategies, it appeared, could be left undefined until wars created the need for them.

Pearl Harbor wrecked that complacent assumption forever. The Japanese attack made it clear in the most emphatic way that in an era of aircraft carriers and fighter-bombers, distance alone no longer guaranteed security. The war that followed multiplied and reinforced the point: no one concerned about postwar

1. This essay was published, in a slightly different form, as "Containment and the Logic of Strategy" in the Winter 1987/88 issue of *The National Interest*, and appears here by permission.
2. C. Vann Woodward, "The Age of Reinterpretation," *American Historical Review* 66 (October 1960): 2–13.

interests could ignore what wartime developments in long-range bombers, ballistic missiles, and, ultimately, atomic weapons implied for the old and comfortable American view that security came free. Insecurity, it now appeared, had become a permanent feature of international life for the United States, just as it had always been for most of the rest of the world.

That expectation of insecurity made it necessary to have a strategy not just for winning the war, but also for ensuring security after victory; the postwar world, it was clear, was likely to be a dangerous place. The strategy Washington eventually embraced began to emerge, while the war itself was still going on, from a sudden shock of recognition: the discovery that the United States had in fact been practicing a consistent approach to world affairs since the earliest days of the republic, but without being fully aware of it.

The assertion was put forward most clearly in the scholarly writings of Nicholas John Spykman of the Yale Institute of International Studies and in their more widely read popularization, Walter Lippmann's 1943 book, *U.S. Foreign Policy: Shield of the Republic*.[3] Its basic proposition was that the United States had always depended for its security upon the maintenance of a balance of power on the Eurasian continent. Should Europe and Asia ever fall under the permanent domination of a single hostile state, the resulting concentration of power would be so great as to make it unlikely that the United States could, over time, retain its independence. It followed that Americans should cooperate with like-minded states to maintain the balance; indeed, Spykman argued, they had done this throughout most of their history, first through tacit cooperation with the British to keep Latin America off-limits to further European colonization during the nineteenth century; then through explicit cooperation with Britain and France in 1917, and again with Britain in 1941, to turn back German bids for world domination; and finally through a simultaneous but mostly unilateral effort to resist the Japanese bid for hegemony in East Asia.

With the help of their World War II allies, Americans did succeed in restoring the balance of power both in Europe and Asia in a remarkably short period of time, and—at least as far as they and the British were concerned—with a remarkably low expenditure of lives. But in contrast to the situation that followed World War I, it did not appear likely that the post–World War II balance would maintain itself without assistance from the United States; even more important, technology had proceeded so far in overwhelming distance that Americans would no longer enjoy the luxury of rearming themselves only after threats to international stability had manifested themselves. It is interesting to note that this sense of vulnerability preceded identification of any specific source of threat: not until 1944–45 would concern over Soviet behavior begin to manifest itself within the context of this more general anxiety about postwar security.[4]

3. See Nicholas John Spykman, *America's Strategy in World Politics* (New York: Harcourt Brace, 1942) and *The Geography of the Peace* (New York: Harcourt, Brace, 1944); also Walter Lippmann, *U.S. Foreign Policy: Shield of the Republic* (Boston: Little, Brown, 1943).

4. John Lewis Gaddis, *The Long Peace: Inquiries into the History of Cold War* (Oxford University Press, 1987), pp. 25–29.

When this specific concern did arise, however, it did so in a big way, not least because of the Soviets' own lack of sensitivity to the security interests of their allies. By early 1947, most Americans saw the Soviet Union as posing almost as great a threat to the international balance of power as Germany or Japan ever had. The combination of an abrupt and apparently inexplicable breakdown of wartime cooperation, together with the Soviet Union's status as the only truly "Eurasian" power, created the apparent need for immediate countervailing action if the global balance of power, restored at such great cost during World War II, was not again to be endangered. There evolved in Washington from this concern an unprecedented preoccupation with strategy in peacetime, together with a new set of new institutions for formulating it.

The strategy that emerged, of course, was "containment"; the institutions that developed it were the Policy Planning Staff in the State Department, a unified national military establishment, the Central Intelligence Agency, and, at the level of the White House, the National Security Council, the body through which strategy was presented to the president and, with his approval, conveyed to those responsible for implementing it. Having written at some length about the various manifestations, permutations, and reincarnations of containment,[5] I do not propose to trace here in great detail the historical evolution of that strategy over the years since the end of World War II. What I would like to do, instead, is to try to place containment within a larger analytical perspective: to pinpoint a particular dilemma that has very much affected the evolution of American views on containment over the years, and to relate the dilemma to what seems to me to be a more general problem in the shaping of strategy itself. My purpose in doing this is twofold: to suggest some ways in which we might apply lessons of the past to improve our own future foreign policy performance, but also, I hope, to stimulate thinking about a still more difficult problem, which is how we know what the criteria for success in strategy are in the first place.

Strategy, as I understand it, is nothing more than *the calculated relationship, by states, of ends and means.* I should add that I mean this to be a generic definition, applicable to any situation in which states face the task of getting from where they are to where they want to go, on the basis of the resources and the determination they have available, but in the face of resistance in some form. I should also emphasize that this definition refers to ends and means in general, not exclusively to military means and military ends. It therefore encompasses— and indeed can hardly be separated from—considerations of politics, economics, psychology, law, and morality; these dimensions of strategy are every bit as important as its military components. I should stress, finally, that the inclusion of the adjective "calculated" is meant to imply a deliberate as opposed to an accidental, inadvertent, or fortuitous connection between ends and means; luck may enhance or impede the attainment of strategic objectives, but it is not strategy itself.

What, then, is "success" in "strategy"? I confess to being a good deal less

5. John Lewis Gaddis, *Strategies of Containment: A Critical Appraisal of Postwar American National Security Policy* (Oxford University Press, 1982).

certain of that. At the level of the battlefield, the criteria are simple: one either wins, loses, or produces a stalemate. But when one widens the realm of strategy to include both war *and* peace, defining "success" becomes much more difficult. One has to consider, for example, the question of time: Bismarck's efforts to make a unified Germany the pivot of European diplomacy certainly succeeded during his lifetime, but they had disastrous effects after his death. One has to consider geographical limits: The United States clearly failed to achieve its strategic objective in Southeast Asia—a viable, noncommunist South Vietnam, Laos, and Cambodia—but its overall influence in East Asia today is probably greater than at any time in the past four decades. One has to consider the question of means: "Victory" in World War I came at such great cost to both victors and vanquished alike that it soon became difficult to distinguish between them; the same would almost certainly be true, today, of a war waged with nuclear weapons.

Questions related to time, space, and means all suggest criteria by which we might evaluate "success" in strategy, but when we consider how frequently these standards intersect with one another, and in what confusing ways, it becomes clear that thinking about them in isolation will not get us very far. The better approach is to try to identify certain dilemmas that tend to recur in strategy, and then see how policymakers deal with them. There are several such dilemmas: How, for example, do you expand interests without expanding threats? How do you surprise an adversary without getting into situations that surprise yourself? How do you balance the need for security in the world against the need to preserve the ideals you stand for at home?

All of these are generic dilemmas, as applicable to strategy today as they were when Thucydides described all three of them 2,400 years ago. But there is one dilemma in particular that occurs with such frequency, and that presents such difficulties to those who seek to cope with it, as to make one wonder whether it is not an inherent structural problem in the formulation of "strategy" itself: it is the difficulty of balancing the risks against the costs of securing vital interests.

Anyone who has ever tried to devise a strategy will recognize the problem: you will want to do everything possible to minimize the *risks* of defeat, or humiliation, or embarrassment; but you will also want to minimize the *costs* of doing so, lest in the process you destroy what you are trying to defend. Destruction, after all, can come *either* from the actions of adversaries or from what you do to yourself. These two priorities compete, because unfortunately the things you do to minimize risks tend to drive up costs; but the things you do to minimize costs tend to drive up risks.

Let me first cite some examples from pre–Cold War military history to illustrate this "risk vs. cost" paradox; I will then attempt to apply it to the historical evolution of "containment" as a "grand strategy" since 1947.

General Grant's strategy of attrition during the American Civil War emphasized not so much sophisticated generalship as a slow wearing down of the Confederacy, designed to ensure a Union victory no matter how much it cost or how long it took. It was a strategy that minimized risk, but at great expense. So too did the strategies followed by the Germans, the British, and the French in the trenches on the Western Front during most of World War I; there both sides locked themselves into repeated attempts to wear each other down across a broad front, with little regard for manpower or material costs and with no clear indication of how long it would take. American naval strategy against Japan during World War II probably fits into this conception as well; it concentrated on the systematic elimination of the Japanese fleet and Japanese merchant shipping through surface and submarine warfare, and it anticipated forcing a surrender through blockade and eventual starvation, a strategy advocates of amphibious warfare and strategic bombing ultimately rejected. Eisenhower's slow and steady "broad-front" advance into Germany in 1944–45 was also a "risk-minimizing" strategy, selected in preference to Patton's call for quick and deep blitzkrieg-style attacks in an effort to force a rapid German surrender. Finally, Ridgway's strategy in Korea after MacArthur's relief in 1951, which involved holding the line against North Korean and Chinese Communist attacks until the latter simply wore themselves out, also sought to minimize risk, but without any assurance as to what ultimate costs would be or how long one would be required to sustain them.

These "risk-minimizing" strategies had several things in common: they placed a premium on massive military presence as opposed to maneuver, thus implying less of a role for surprise or for brilliant military leadership; they relied heavily on technology as a means of sustaining that military presence and wearing down the other side, but not for making dramatic breakthroughs; they operated under no particular deadlines by which objectives had to be met; and above all else they assumed *unlimited resources* and *steady political support*, regardless of the costs incurred.

Examples of "cost-minimizing"—but therefore "risk-maximizing"—strategies would include the war of maneuver that Lee and Jackson conducted against the North during the American Civil War, using skillful generalship to compensate for the Union's advantages in manpower and industrial strength, but running great risks in the process, as Gettysburg showed. Germany's pre–World War I Schlieffen Plan also illustrates the pattern: it had been intended to minimize costs by knocking France out of the war before the Soviet Union could mobilize, but it accepted the risk of bringing Great Britain in by violating Belgian neutrality. German blitzkrieg operations in 1940–41 also qualify as "cost-minimizing" but "risk-maximizing" strategies: there the objective was to compensate for the adversary's probable long-term superiority in manpower and resources by achieving surprise and exploiting new techniques of land warfare. Britain's "peripheral pecking" strategy against Germany during World War II sought to minimize costs as well through the exploitation of naval superiority and an insular geographical position, but at such dangerous risks as attempting to defend places like Narvik, Suez, and Singapore when the Germans were just across the Channel. American "high technology/low manpower" strategies in that same conflict also sought to minimize costs: notably the original "arsenal of democracy" concept and its subsequent variation, lend-lease, which were designed to leave the bulk of actual fighting to allies; strategic bombing, also seen as a way to avoid manpower commitments on the ground; and of course the development of the atomic bomb, the chief objective of which really was to save lives on both sides. Likewise MacArthur's Korean War strategy—which involved using American naval and air superiority to compensate for ground force inferiority, achieve surprise at Inchon, and make possible a blitzkrieg advance into North Korea—minimized costs but at risks that soon became painfully obvious.

What did these cost-minimizing strategies have in common? They sought to exploit the benefits of maneuver, of surprise, of imaginative military leadership; several of them relied heavily on technology to avoid prolonged stalemates or debilitating losses of manpower; most of them operated out of a sense of urgency to conclude the wars in question quickly; and above all else they assumed *limited resources* and *limited political support*, and so saw no alternative but to run risks.

This distinction between "cost-minimizing" and "risk-minimizing" strategies is hardly original with me. Clausewitz himself pointed out the costly nature of offensive strategies and the risky nature of defensive ones. Liddell Hart's advocacy of the "indirect approach" in strategy grew largely out of what he saw as its advantages in minimizing costs. Russell Weigley's interpretation of the two traditions in American military strategy has become widely accepted. And the distinction is implicit in recent work by Edward Luttwak, John Mearsheimer, and Richard Betts as well.[6] But the "risk vs. cost" dilemma does, I think, provide a hypothesis from the realm of war that may extend to that of geopolitics. It may also provide a basis by which we might begin to approach the tricky problem of judging strategic "success."

• • •

"Strategy," I argued earlier, encompasses more than what happens on battlefields. If there had ever been any doubt about that, the onset of the Cold War quickly resolved the matter, because its effect was to combine a perpetual state of insecurity requiring "strategic" thinking with unprecedented constraints on the actual use of military force. Americans responded by devising the various strategies of containment; these primarily defensive approaches to the problem of international insecurity have had obvious political, economic, and psychological as well as military dimensions. But just because the realm of strategy had expanded out to incorporate these nonmilitary considerations, the classic dilemma of balancing risks against costs did not disappear. Indeed, it became all the more central to determining the strategies actually chosen.

The first of the postwar approaches to containment, that of George Kennan as implemented within the Truman administration between 1947 and 1950, was a "cost-minimizing" strategy because it proceeded from the assumption that the United States could never provide the manpower or military equipment neces-

---

6. Carl von Clausewitz, *On War*, ed. and trans. Michael Howard and Peter Paret (Princeton University Press, 1976), especially pp. 381–83; B. H. Liddell Hart, *Strategy: The Indirect Approach* (New York: Praeger, 1954); Russell Weigley, *The American Way of War: A History of United States Military Strategy and Policy* (New York: Macmillan, 1973); Edward Luttwak, *Strategy: The Logic of War and Peace* (Harvard University Press, 1987); John Mearsheimer, *Conventional Deterrence* (Cornell University Press, 1983); Richard K. Betts, *Nuclear Blackmail and Nuclear Balance* (Washington, 1987).

sary to safeguard all exposed interests against all perceived threats; pressures of demobilization, budgetary limitations, and the lingering influence of isolationism were thought to preclude attempting anything like that. Instead, Kennan's approach to containment sought to accomplish its objectives in an asymmetrical manner: by being selective about where vital interests lay in the first place; by being parsimonious in the identification of adversaries; and by being flexible about the means chosen with which to act, with preference given to those forms of competition where we were could reasonably expect to prevail. This meant, in Kennan's mind, focusing containment primarily upon the defense of Western Europe, Japan, and the lines of communication that connected them to the United States. The strategy relied heavily upon inducing self-confidence through economic rehabilitation; it also sought to exploit adversary vulnerabilities, notably the unlikelihood that the Soviet Union could continue to dominate the international communist movement, together with the probability that, in time, internal changes would moderate its own external behavior as well.

But minimizing costs meant maximizing risks, or at least appearing to. Kennan's strategy provided no mechanisms with which to counter a Soviet military attack on Western Europe or Japan, should the Soviets have chosen to launch one. NATO, which came into existence in 1949, originated as an initiative taken by nervous Europeans, and was embraced by the Truman administration over Kennan's strong objections. Kennan also argued against any permanent American military presence in Japan. Nor did Kennan's strategy provide safeguards against the possibility that successive losses of peripheral areas to Soviet control might cause psychological demoralization in more vital ones. That is why Kennan himself, in apparent defiance of his own strategy, supported American military assistance to Greece in 1947 and to South Korea in 1950. There was little short-term reassurance in his argument that the "loss" of China to communism in 1949 constituted no long-term "gain" for the Soviets; no one could say how long Sino-Soviet differences might take to develop. Nor did his insistence that the Soviets would eventually change their morbidly suspicious approach to the outside world seem very persuasive while Stalin was still alive.

In the end, Kennan proved to be right on every one of these points: The Soviets did not launch a direct military attack; the Chinese did split with them; Stalin died, was buried, and quickly repudiated; the Soviet Union in time became a very different place from what it had been under his rule. But there could be no guarantee at the time that any of this would happen. Kennan's strategy appeared to its critics to be running dangerous risks with the nation's security in a misguided effort to keep down costs.

NSC-68, the reformulation of "containment" that took place during the first half of 1950, primarily under the direction of Paul Nitze, can be seen as a "risk-minimizing" strategy, because it proceeded from the assumption that the United States had the resources to defend its interests wherever they existed; hence there was no need to run the risks involved in differentiating those that were vital from those that were not. Nitze and the other authors of NSC-68 sought to minimize risks: by increasing American and allied military capabilities across the board, both in nuclear and conventional weapons; by making it clear that

Secretary of State Acheson signing American adherence to the NATO alliance (April 1949) as Vice President Barkley and President Truman look on. (UPI/Bettmann Newsphotos)

wherever threats to the international balance of power manifested themselves, the United States would respond; by calibrating response to offense, so that the act of countering such threats would not create new risks either by spreading the conflict or by allowing aggression to succeed; and by insisting that the nonmilitary instruments of containment—particularly economic assistance and the search for a diplomatic resolution of outstanding issues—would come into play only after what Dean Acheson called "situations of strength" had been created.

But if this approach to containment minimized risks, it also, as one might have expected, increased costs. The determination to respond wherever aggression took place but not to go beyond the level of provocation encountered placed the United States at the mercy of its adversaries in determining how and under what circumstances it would expend its resources—loss of initiative is always a costly business. As growing public frustration with the Korean War showed, the prospect of indefinitely high expenditures of men and material was costly in terms of domestic political support as well: the administration was unable to say how long such expenditures would be necessary or when a favorable resolution of difficulties with the Soviets might be expected. Finally, the strategy of placing diplomacy on the back shelf until "situations of strength" had been created precluded taking advantage of nonmilitary opportunities to resolve outstanding issues: the most important of these, many historians now agree, was the intriguing offer the Soviets made in March 1952 that might—one cannot say for certain because Washington refused to explore the proposal—have allowed free elections throughout Germany and the formation of a unified but neutral German state.

The architects of NSC-68, in short, played it safe. But in the process they relinquished the initiative to the other side, saddled the nation with expenses it was not prepared to sustain, narrowed the range of instruments available with which to deal with the Soviets, and in the process neglected what may have been opportunities to lower Cold War tensions.

Subsequent approaches to containment reflected either these "cost-minimizing" or "risk-minimizing" approaches. The Eisenhower-Dulles "New Look" strategy fell into the first category, as was clearly acknowledged at the time. Its basic premise was that although the United States had vital interests throughout the world, it possessed only limited resources with which to defend those interests, and hence had to regain the initiative over how and where it did so, even if this entailed increasing risks. An explicit willingness to run risks became the hallmark of the "New Look," with its conspicuous reliance on the deterrent effect of nuclear threats, together with its relative deemphasis on conventional military forces and a shift toward what would later become known as a doctrine of "sufficiency" in calculating the desired military balance with the Soviets. Predictably, criticisms of the Eisenhower approach centered around its risk-taking: Was it responsible to inflate minor crises like Quemoy and Matsu into situations that might require the use of nuclear weapons? Was it prudent to respond to apparent Soviet breakthroughs in missile technology by holding the line on defense spending? Was not all of this carrying the cause of economy too far?

The Kennedy-Johnson "flexible response" strategy in its turn responded to the perceived deficiencies of the Eisenhower approach with a renewed emphasis on minimizing risk, regardless of cost. Proceeding from NSC-68's original assumption that the United States had undifferentiated global interests but also unlimited capabilities for defending them, it reintroduced the idea of calibrating response to offense, thereby avoiding the twin dangers of escalation and humiliation. To sustain this strategy, it increased both nuclear and conventional military capabilities at a time when it perceived no comparable increases on the part of the Soviets, while at the same time enthusiastically building up the resources for unconventional warfare as well. The Vietnam War demonstrated even more painfully than Korea had the costs of this approach: once again loss of initiative and mounting casualties eroded domestic support for the war effort; the Soviets quickly exploited Washington's resulting distraction by attaining, almost unnoticed and within a remarkably short period of time, approximate nuclear parity with the United States.

The Nixon-Kissinger strategy of "detente" shifted the emphasis back to taking risks in order to minimize costs. This was the central purpose of the Nixon Doctrine, which sought to impose at least part of the burden of containment on allies; but the administration's participation in strategic arms limitation talks with the Soviets, the opening to the People's Republic of China, the use of "linkage" to facilitate negotiations, and the effort to build great power mechanisms for managing Third World crises all proceeded from a determination to lower the costs of containment, even if this meant taking risks. Again, though, some risks soon became apparent: the strategy failed to save Southeast Asia from communism, and as a consequence appeared to create new vulnerabilities in other Third World areas for the Soviets to exploit. Negotiations on arms control produced as many problems as solutions, with the result that by the mid-1970s some of its former supporters had come to see it as a more dangerous process than a continued arms race. The technique of "linkage," upon which much of Kissinger's strategy depended, became ensnarled in domestic politics; and of course Nixon himself felt obliged, in defense of his foreign policy, to take certain risks with constitutional procedures at home that ultimately ensured the collapse of his presidency.

The Carter administration's actions appear to fit the "cost-minimizing" model as well, for despite conspicuous superficial departures from the Nixon-Ford-Kissinger foreign policy—the campaign for human rights, the attempt to stress "North-South" over "East-West" issues, the preference for openness rather than secrecy in conducting its affairs—the continuities linking Carter and his advisers to their predecessors appear, in retrospect, to have outweighed the differences. Like them, the Carter team believed that the United States was operating from a position of relative weakness that would not allow vastly increased expenditures for defense: the emphasis then, as it had been since 1969, would have to be on minimizing costs.

The Carter administration therefore continued earlier Nixon-Ford-Kissinger efforts to secure a strategic arms limitation agreement with the Soviets, and indeed finally attained that goal with the unratified SALT II treaty of 1979. Nor did it modify Nixon's policy of *rapprochement* with the People's Republic of China, to which it in fact extended formal diplomatic recognition that same year. In keeping with the objectives of the Nixon Doctrine, the United States under Carter remained cautious about intervening in Third World countries, even where favored clients—as in Iran and Nicaragua—were on the verge of collapse. And the administration continued to work for cooperation with the Soviets in managing Third World crises.

But the risks that had been inherent in the Nixon-Ford-Kissinger approach became all the more striking under Carter. The Soviets after 1975 appeared to have abandoned whatever interest they might have had in joint Third World crisis management, opting instead for an opportunistic—and, as it turned out, profoundly shortsighted—effort to exploit perceived American weakness in the wake of the Vietnam defeat. Angola, Somalia, Ethiopia, and of course Afghanistan can all be seen as part of that pattern. Arms control efforts continued to appear to produce Soviet military buildups rather than Soviet restraint. Revolutions in Nicaragua and Iran resulted in significant losses of American influence; and with the 444-day Tehran hostage crisis, events in the latter country brought about a humiliating American loss of face as well. Compounding all of these difficulties was one painfully clear departure from the Nixon-Ford-Kissinger foreign policy: Carter's apparent inability to enforce consistency or coherence upon his quarreling subordinates.

The Reagan administration, I believe, will be seen in contrast as having pursued a "risk-minimizing" strategy that has maximized costs. Fundamental differences of viewpoint distinguished the new administration from its immediate predecessors when it came into office in 1981. The president and his advisers rejected any assumption that one could expect cooperation from the Soviets in limiting strategic arms, managing Third World crises, or anything else that might help cut the costs of containment; indeed, an excessive concern with costs, they asserted, had got the nation into the dangerous position of lacking sufficient military power to make itself respected, whether in Moscow or in the world at large. As had been the case with NSC-68 and the Kennedy-Johnson "flexible response" strategy, the Reagan administration assumed the nation's capacity to rearm without bankrupting itself. Economic growth—this time in the form of "Reaganomics"—would provide the means.

The chief elements of the Reagan "risk-minimizing" strategy were as follows: an impressive buildup in both nuclear and conventional warfare capabilities, with the greatest emphasis going to the six-hundred-ship navy; an uncompromising position on strategic arms control that made progress almost entirely dependent upon Soviet concessions; the Strategic Defense Initiative (SDI), a striking attempt to use the *prospect* of superior American technology either to induce

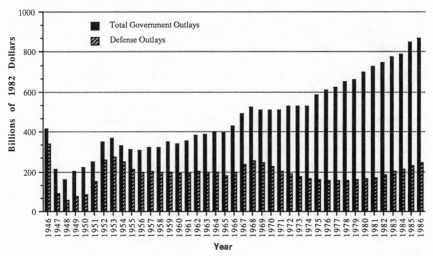

Defense and Total U.S. Government Spending in Constant (FY 1982) Dollars

Source: Office of Management and Budget, *Historical Tables: Budget of the United States Government, Fiscal Year 1989* (Washington, D.C.: 1988), pp. 122–40.

such concessions or to weaken the more primitive Soviet economy by exhausting it in an arms race; the Reagan Doctrine, which sought to counter Soviet Third World intervention wherever it took place, but by aiding local resistance fighters instead of by sending in American troops; and, finally, negotiations with the Soviets, but only from Acheson's favored "situations of strength," situations to be created by the combination of American rearmament, American technological prowess, and the weaknesses the Soviet Union could be expected to create for itself in attempting to sustain at home and to impose on others a defunct economic and political system.

How well did it work? With regard to the Soviets, it appears, remarkably well. Blatant Third World "adventurism" akin to what happened in the late 1970s did not recur; and unlike some of its predecessors, the Reagan administration succeeded in resisting more subtle forms of Soviet influence in such areas without costly direct military interventions and without relinquishing the initiative. The Soviets took SDI far more seriously than anyone else did (excepting of course the president himself), with the consequence that actual *reductions* in nuclear weapons on both sides became a realistic possibility; "negotiation" even from apparent "strength," it seemed, had produced results. And, most important, profound changes had taken place inside the Soviet Union itself since 1981. But whether these favorable developments occurred because of or in spite of Reagan's strategy is difficult to say: his incumbency coincided with a long period of internal disarray and introspection from which the Soviet Union is only now emerging; how well his strategy would have held up had there been energetic, sophisticated, and biologically functional Kremlin leadership throughout his first term is not at all clear.

In terms of management, the Reagan strategy was a good deal less successful. Massive military budgets failed to increase military effectiveness, as events in Beirut, Grenada, and the Persian Gulf have painfully demonstrated. Indeed, the very generosity of military appropriations since 1981 may well have induced lack of coordination, duplication of effort, and an unwillingness to assume responsibility for making tough decisions; similar difficulties afflicted the Strategic Defense Initiative, where the assumption seems to have been that if one threw enough money at the program, crossed one's fingers, and wished hard enough, it would all work, laws of physics, economics, and mathematics to the contrary notwithstanding. And, of course, the Iran-Contra affair demonstrated just how shallow—adolescent, even—the administration's management skills were at the level of the National Security Council. It could only be chalked up to President Reagan's remarkable luck that these problems did not produce much more serious consequences than they did.

The Reagan administration's greatest failure, however, is what one would have expected from the workings of the "risk vs. cost" dilemma. In its effort to minimize risks, the administration almost totally neglected the problem of costs. It is worth making the point again that defeat in strategy can come in two ways: from what one's adversary does, to be sure, but also from what one does to one's self in the process of countering that adversary. Here there were serious reasons for concern.

Consider, first, the problem of efficiency. What inducement was there, in an era of budgetary plenty, to use one's resources wisely? Why go through the unpleasant business of establishing priorities at all when one had the luxury of expandable means? Why close off ineffective or unworkable programs when appropriations for them continued to flow? Profligacy, after a certain point, can become the enemy of effectiveness, and stringency its ally.

This leads, in turn, to the question of solvency. "Reaganomics," after all, was supposed to be Keynesianism for conservatives: tax cuts to stimulate economic activity, thus generating the means to sustain economic growth without increasing the deficit. But that did not happen. What kept economic growth going—and, therefore, until recently, the military buildup—was a cheerful toleration of budget deficits that more than doubled the national debt in the course of a single administration.

Experts differ on the implications of this debt. As a percentage of total gross national product, it does not seem all that alarming, but when one considers the fact that the nation now owes more abroad than is owed to it, and that much of our economic future depends, as a result, on decisions that Americans will not be making, then the question has to arise: Did not our lack of concern about solvency compromise our sovereignty? Did we not, in our effort to remain a superpower, neglect one of the chief determinants of superpower status, which is self-reliance?

This leads to a still more basic question: If the effect of our short-term strategy has been to induce such long-term changes, and if the effect of those changes is, as it very well might be, to weaken our capacity to act effectively as a world power, then what is it that we have gained? Self-destruction, in such a situation, can be about as effective as destruction by adversaries. It is a fundamental requirement of an effective strategy, Dwight Eisenhower used to remind his subordinates, that it not destroy what it is attempting to defend.

● ● ●

In his recent and very interesting book on this subject, Edward Luttwak pointed out that "the entire realm of strategy is pervaded by a paradoxical logic of its own," which appears to confound what we would normally consider to be straightforwardly logical action, and to reward its opposite.[7] What this suggests is that "success" in strategy comes more from managing the inescapable paradoxes that reside within it than from attempting to meet some predetermined and arbitrary criterion of judgment. The "risk vs. cost" dilemma—the probability that strategies seeking to minimize costs, as did those of Nixon, Ford, and Carter, will run risks, but that strategies seeking to minimize risks, as Reagan's did, will increase costs—is just such a paradox. Costs and risks are inherent in any situation in which one needs a strategy in the first place, that is, any situation in which one is seeking to attain objectives in the face of resistance. Some expenditure of effort will always be required, some dangers will always have to be

7. Luttwak, *Strategy,* p. 4.

faced, and somebody will always have to make the decision as to which of these unpleasant alternatives one most wants to minimize. An "optimal" minimization of both risk and cost may exist in decision-making theory, but it is apt to be elusive in the extreme in the real world.

What we can do, though, is recognize that costs can become risks, and that risks can become costs: Too exclusive a concentration on minimizing one is almost certain to produce the other. This fact places a premium on the skill with which one can learn at least to *balance*—if not optimally minimize—costs *and* risks. And one of the best guides to doing this is to learn from the experiences of one's predecessors. There are occasional instances in which this has been done.

Despite the fact that they embraced what was in general a "cost-minimizing" strategy that was prepared to run risks, and despite having campaigned on a platform that called explicitly for this, Eisenhower and Dulles never attempted to "liberate" Eastern Europe from Soviet domination. Their judgment, in the end, was what Truman's had been: that the existence of injustice was not in itself sufficient justification for risking a third world war, even if we were certain to win it. The costs of this particular risk in a nuclear age would have been too great.

Despite the fact that he embraced what was in general a "risk-minimizing" strategy that placed a considerable premium on building military strength, Kennedy saw that to avoid negotiations with the Soviets altogether could in itself be a risk. Building on important precedents set by Eisenhower, he was willing to take the short-term risk of signing a Limited Test Ban Treaty with the Soviets, a decision all but the most extreme observers now acknowledge minimized risks over the long term as well.

Despite the fact that they embraced what was in general a "cost-minimizing" strategy, Nixon and Kissinger were unwilling to reverse immediately the Johnson administration's overcommitment of manpower and resources in Southeast Asia. Instead, they sought a gradual withdrawal from the war in a way that would not weaken American "credibility" as a great power. One can argue about whether the costs thereby incurred were worth it or not, but it is the case that the nation got out of Vietnam without anything like the long period of self-flagellation that followed the more abrupt collapse of our much less extensive efforts in China in 1949.

Despite the fact that the Reagan administration opted in general for a "risk-minimizing" strategy—and, again, despite its high anticommunist rhetoric—it was willing to accept the risks, as had Nixon, Ford, and Carter also, of dealing on a friendly basis with the world's most populous communist state. It even went beyond that point in its gradual realization that the Soviet political and economic example is that country's own worst enemy; at its end it seemed on the verge of accepting—although still with many qualms—the once-risky proposition that the Soviets could be counted on to defeat themselves through their own combination of arrogance and incompetence, provided we are wise enough to avoid deflecting to ourselves—through many of those same characteristics—the hostility their effects are bound to produce.

More often, though, administrations—whether out of pride, politics, or simple negligence—tend to ignore the experiences of their predecessors, with the result that they fail to maintain the critical "risk vs. cost" balance. Kennedy and Johnson failed to learn what the experience of Korea could have taught them, which was to avoid relinquishing the initiative to adversaries. The Nixon, Ford, and Carter strategies failed to give sufficient attention to a problem that had plagued Eisenhower and Dulles, which is how to provide the reassurance that must accompany risk-taking strategies if they are to be sustained. The Reagan administration learned little from the experiences of Johnson and Nixon about the unwisdom of centralizing intelligence assessment and operational control in the White House staff (especially if one lacks a Kissinger to do it), or from Carter's experience with the dangers of letting emotion govern responses to hostage crises, which after all are created for no other purpose than to exploit emotions.

Theory, Clausewitz said, does not hold you by the hand and tell you what to do at every moment in every crisis you are likely to encounter. The last thing I would want to claim, therefore, is that an understanding of the strategic dilemma I've identified here provides any guarantee of strategic success. The realm of strategy, like the fog of battle, is too unpredictable an environment for that.

But an awareness of such dilemmas beats trying to find your way through such an environment blindfolded. It can provide warnings about the pitfalls that are likely to lie ahead—a kind of "intellectual minesweeper," if you will. It can function as a checklist, reminding you to make sure the flaps are in the proper configuration before you proceed at full power down the runway. And if one considers them in their proper historical context, these dilemmas can extend one's own range of experience to incorporate that of others who have had to deal with comparable situations. The effect may therefore be to make you think more critically than you might about just what "success" in strategy is in the first place, and how you recognize it once you get there. Beyond that, I would not want to claim too much.

4

United States National Strategy since 1945

AARON L. FRIEDBERG

GRAND STRATEGY customarily refers to the ways in which states seek to coordinate all the instruments available to them—military, political, economic, and psychological—so as to achieve their political objectives in wartime. I propose to analyze the way in which the United States has pursued its broad strategic aims over the last forty-plus years of what might loosely be called "peace." Instead of reviewing all the possible instruments of "grand" or, as it ought to be called in peacetime, "national" strategy, I will concentrate on the military component of that strategy. I will focus on the ways in which the United States has developed, deployed, maneuvered, and to a far lesser extent actually used its armed forces to support its overall policies in the period since the Second World War.

The Long-Term Competition

Whatever one thinks about its causes, course, and likely consequences, it is apparent that since 1945 the United States has been engaged in an ongoing military competition with the Soviet Union. Such competitions between pairs of hostile powers are certainly not without precedent, but this one seems to be taking on an unusual and arguably an historically unique form. The two participants eye one another suspiciously, they build up and deploy their forces, largely in the hope of countering, circumventing, or defeating the deployments of the other side, but they do not go (or at least they have not yet gone) to war. With the passage of time and the progress of technology, the forces that the two sides would bring to bear against one another if they were ever to clash openly grow more and more different and removed from those last used in a global war. It is for this reason that the Third World has become such an important laboratory for American and Soviet equipment and for their operational concepts. And it is one reason why, at any given moment, there must be considerable uncertainty about the state of the military balance between East and West.

The superpowers have sometimes been compared to two scorpions in a bottle. That is too static an image. They are really more like two duelists who watch each other practicing, who experiment with and then discard one weapon after another, but who never come to blows for fear that both would die as a result. The geopolitical and ideological sources of Soviet-American animosity are, I would argue, potent and persistent. But under the constraints imposed by the existence of nuclear weapons, a new and peculiar breed of arms race has developed, which neither peters out nor ends in war but instead seems likely to go on indefinitely.

That "race" or competition is in one important sense an expensive and wasteful shadow game. Yet it would be a grave mistake to dismiss it as only that and to imagine that it can therefore be easily terminated or safely ignored. In fact, the condition of the military competition matters and it may at times matter a great deal. If war were ever to come, the balance of real capabilities would almost by definition determine its outcome. It is also possible that under certain, highly pressurized conditions, the state of the balance (or rather its perceived state) could influence the probability of war breaking out in the first place. Believing that its vital interests were at stake and calculating, rightly or wrongly, that it was capable of defeating its opponent, a nation might prefer aggressive action to compromise or to, perhaps, humiliation. Short of such drastic decisions, the course of the competition (or again, its perceived course) may provoke one side or the other or both into undertaking concrete and costly defense programs. Finally and perhaps most important, the unfolding of a competition in armaments can have real political consequences.

That the dynamic flow of economic processes can erode and eventually transform the political arrangements within which they operate is demonstrated in other chapters, especially that by Robert Gilpin. Something similar can be said of military processes. This is certainly true in wartime and it can also be the case during protracted periods of relative peace. Over sufficiently long lengths of time, the course of an ongoing military competition can eat away at existing political structures, rendering them rickety and eventually unsafe.

Although the record is mixed, I would argue that the general direction of the military competition since 1947 has been unfavorable to the United States or at least unfavorable to the continued maintenance of the political structures that it sought to establish in the wake of the Second World War.

The Course of the Competition

The Soviet-American competition has in fact gone forward simultaneously in several parallel arenas. The first of these is what the Soviets call the "transoceanic

The Shock of Sputnik. Would it render U.S. air defenses "impotent and obsolete"?
(Herblock, Herblock's *Special for Today.* New York: Simon & Schuster, 1958, p. 83.)

theater of operations" and what we usually think of as the "strategic" or intercontinental theater. The second encompasses what were once called the "rimlands" of the Eurasian landmass, those areas that directly abut the lands under Soviet control, primarily Europe in the west and northern Asia (including Japan) in the east. The third arena might simply be labeled "the periphery." It includes all those areas of superpower contention that are not directly contiguous to the borders of either state. A brief review of each of these arenas follows.

The Strategic Theater

The direction of events in the strategic theater can be summed up quite simply. In 1947 the Soviet Union had not yet tested an atomic weapon and had only just begun to deploy the sorts of long-range bombers that might have been capable of reaching the continental United States. The United States was essentially invulnerable to direct Soviet attack. Forty years later the Soviets could detonate tens, hundreds, or even thousands of nuclear weapons on American soil within minutes. The United States is today essentially defenseless against attack with weapons of mass destruction.

This is not something that happened all at once, nor is it a change that has been easily accepted by American strategists and decision makers. From the late forties to the late fifties there was growing concern over the possibility of an attack on the United States by Russian bombers carrying first atomic and then even more destructive thermonuclear weapons. Several steps were taken to meet this threat directly, including the deployment of an extensive early warning radar network backed by a force of jet fighter interceptors and surface-to-air antiaircraft missiles.

Just as the problem of a possible Soviet bomber attack (which, as things turned out, did not develop as quickly or as massively as many American intelligence analysts had feared) seemed to be coming within reach of a solution, a new and even more worrisome threat began to emerge. In 1957 the Soviets launched the first earth-orbiting satellite and seemed suddenly to be on the brink of deploying a force of intercontinental-range ballistic missiles that would, to borrow a phrase from a later period, have rendered existing American air defenses "impotent and obsolete."

Like the bomber threat before it, the missile menace took time to reach maturity. Over the course of the next decade (and especially from the mid-sixties onward), the Soviets were able to build increasing numbers of land- and sea-based missiles.

The U.S. response to these developments was mixed, even schizophrenic. On the one hand there was a predictable upsurge of interest in ballistic missile defense programs. (These tended to be supported by high-ranking military officers and their allies in Congress.) At the same time there was growing skepticism in some quarters (and especially among civilians in the Defense Department) about the utility of the proposed antimissile systems and indeed about the possibility of any effective defense against nuclear attack.

These contradictory trends culminated in 1967 with the announcement by Secretary of Defense Robert McNamara (by that time the leading critic of nuclear defenses) that the United States intended to build a "thin" ABM system, good enough to provide some protection against the virtually nonexistent danger of Chinese attack but essentially useless against the real and growing Soviet threat. This proposal satisfied no one. The system was never deployed.

From the late forties to the late sixties, the best and perhaps the only effective defense against nuclear attack was widely assumed to be a good offense. We now know that throughout this period American strategy allowed for, and because of the existing balance of capabilities American forces would probably have been able to carry out, a massive preemptive attack on the Soviet Union that would have disabled or destroyed its budding offensive force.

The period from the late 1960s to the late 1970s saw the full flowering of Soviet offensive capabilities. Between 1967 and 1977 the Russians tripled the number of ICBMs they had deployed in hardened concrete silos and expanded their fleet of submarine-launched missiles from around thirty to almost nine hundred. [1]

As Soviet forces grew in size and diversity, the possibility of their being destroyed in a single swift attack dwindled and then disappeared. Even if the United States struck first, there was henceforth no doubt that the Soviets would still have been able to launch hundreds, perhaps thousands, of nuclear weapons in retaliation. Given the growth in American capabilities, the same was of course true of a possible Soviet first-strike attack on the United States.

While the strategic forces of the two sides were becoming less vulnerable to preemptive attack, their populations were becoming more vulnerable than ever. The American interest in bomber and missile defenses, already wavering in the late 1960s, all but disappeared during the 1970s. With the signing of the 1972 ABM treaty the Soviets also accepted strict limitations on their missile defenses, although they appear to have continued to invest heavily in ABM research, active bomber defenses, and passive civilian defenses.

The mid-seventies marked the peak, in the United States at least, of the belief that what was called "parity," mutual societal vulnerability coupled with the mutual invulnerability of retaliatory forces, would reduce the risk of war and the hope that this condition would also permit a slow stabilization and perhaps even an eventual termination of the competition in strategic arms.

Over the last ten years these hopes have proven largely empty. First one and then the other of the two supposed preconditions for stability have been shaken, if not completely shattered, by the continued forward movement of the strategic arms competition. Following the signing of the SALT I treaty, the Soviets proceeded, within the terms of the agreement, to increase the size, accuracy, and destructive potential of their strategic offense forces. What this meant was that by the late seventies and early eighties a large fraction of American land-based forces had become susceptible, at least in theory, to a preemptive Soviet attack. The perception that this condition was emerging provoked a flood of schemes for reducing the vulnerability of U.S. ICBMs essentially by increasing their mobility. To date none has proved acceptable and the problem has simply been left unsolved. Meanwhile, the Soviet buildup gave new impetus to U.S. force modernization programs, which have in due course begun to eat away at the invulnerability of Soviet fixed land-based missiles, forcing them to respond (although more expeditiously) with mobile ICBMS of their own.

Even though it seems unlikely to give either side a decisive advantage (assuming that both behave prudently), the competition in offensive forces continues. The mutual invulnerability of retaliatory capabilities has not been established once and for all.

In the last decade the continued mutual vulnerability of civilian populations (the other purported foundation of stability) has also been called into question.

1. See Lawrence Freedman, *U.S. Intelligence and the Soviet Strategic Threat* (Princeton University Press, 1986), pp. 102, 156; also John M. Collins, *American and Soviet Military Trends* (Georgetown: Center for Strategic and International Studies, 1978), p. 113.

In 1983 the Reagan administration announced its "Strategic Defense Initiative" and declared that it hoped eventually to be able to provide U.S. citizens with some measure of direct protection against nuclear attack. The renewed interest in defense (which is, after all, intuitively appealing in a way that the notion of stability through vulnerability is not) has gained a certain degree of public support. It has also been roundly condemned by many scientists and some strategists who regard it at best as wasteful and at worst as dangerous. All that can be said with certainty at this point is that there is now simply no way in which societal vulnerability could be significantly reduced, reliably and at reasonable cost.

So we have moved in forty years from a situation in which the Soviet Union was open to attack but the United States was not to one in which the United States was theoretically exposed but had some plausible defense against assault to circumstances in which both sides are vulnerable and neither seems able to do much about it.

It may be that this condition of mutual vulnerability is inescapable. Perhaps it will even turn out to be stable over periods historically more significant than the mere forty-odd years that have passed since the end of the Second World War. Nevertheless, the unfolding of the strategic competition to this point has already begun to raise serious questions about the ability of the United States over the long term to continue to play the role it chose for itself at the close of World War II.

The problem has both political and military dimensions. In the aftermath of the war, U.S. statesmen were able to persuade the American public to overcome its residual preference for nonentanglement and to support an unprecedented policy of peacetime treaties, commitments, and overseas deployments of military forces. At the time, whatever their other risks, these steps did not carry with them the danger that they might lead to direct and devastating attacks on the continental United States. That fact has now quite obviously changed. Whether, under presently prevailing strategic conditions, the United States would today take on the responsibilities it assumed forty years ago is by no means obvious. Whether it will continue to be willing to bear such burdens indefinitely, in spite of the risks they now carry, remains to be seen.

For the moment, periodic bouts of diffuse public anxiety over the prospect of nuclear war have somehow been kept separate from an awareness that virtually the only way in which the United States could ever become involved in such a war would be by acting to support one of its overseas allies. Should these elements ever combine, they might well give rise to a form of nuclear isolationism that could hasten the collapse of existing arrangements.

On the military side the problems produced by the erosion in the strategic balance are more immediate and concrete. The secure second-strike capability that the United States now undoubtedly has, the capacity to respond massively even to a surprise first strike, may be enough to deter most large attacks directly on the United States. Since the late 1940s, however, the United States has also sought to "extend deterrence" by opening a protective umbrella over its friends and allies overseas. For the first twenty of the last forty years, the principal means of accomplishing this objective was the obvious American superiority in long-range offensive forces. The loss of that superiority has therefore had important implications for all aspects of U.S. military strategy and this is nowhere more apparent than in Europe.

The "Rimland"

As Melvyn Leffler indicated in the second chapter in this volume, most American strategists became convinced during the early 1940s that the conquest of western Eurasia by a single hostile power would be an unmitigated economic, military, and political disaster for the United States. This realization helped motivate U.S. intervention in the war against Hitler and it continued to influence American policy after 1945. At the close of hostilities the Soviet army had already succeeded in driving the Nazis hundreds of miles back into the center of Europe. As Soviet-American relations deteriorated in the wake of the war, fears of a possible final push from the Elbe to the Atlantic increased. Protecting Western Europe from Russian domination became the primary objective of American foreign policy and military strategy.

For the last forty years the specter of an invasion of Europe has continued to haunt western military planners and the question of how best to cope with the apparent superiority of eastern conventional forces has been at the center of every major strategic debate involving the United States and its NATO allies. The issue has come up repeatedly and it has been (depending on one's point of view) resolved or swept under the rug in a variety of different ways. As the overall military competition between the two superpowers has progressed, most of the solutions that would be cheap, easy, and acceptable to both the United States and its European partners have been tried and found wanting. Yet the problem of providing an adequate deterrent to eastern land power has not gone away, indeed it seems actually to have become more acute with the passage of time.

The first and most obvious way of dealing with Soviet and Warsaw Pact conventional forces would have been simply to match them in kind: to deploy land, air, and naval forces in the European theater of sufficient size and capability to deter any invader or to defeat him on the ground if he should decide to attack. This traditional approach was given serious consideration in the early 1950s when the United States decided to redeploy troops to Western Europe and the NATO nations agreed among themselves to more than triple the number of active divisions in their combined armies. The economic and political costs of such a buildup were soon judged to be so great, however, that the goal of conventional parity was given up in practice almost as soon as it had been formally adopted.

For most of the 1950s NATO relied instead on a policy of "massive retaliation" to deter Soviet aggression. If the Warsaw Pact invaded Western Europe, even if it used only conventional weapons to do so, the United States promised to respond with its nuclear forces, both the small, short-range, relatively low-yield, "tactical" or "battlefield" weapons, which could be dropped on advancing enemy armies, and the larger "strategic" weapons, intended for use against military and industrial targets inside the Soviet Union. The West might be relatively weak in ground forces, but its arsenal of high-technology nuclear weapons was still vastly superior. By exploiting this comparative advantage, it was assumed that the United States could at reasonable cost deter attacks and defeat them if they ever came.

Despite its rather barbaric character, the strategy of "massive retaliation" might have been acceptable indefinitely against a static opponent. But of course the Soviets did not stand still during the 1950s. They began during this period slowly to acquire a long-range capability for hitting directly at the United States and they made larger and more rapid strides in developing and deploying shorter-range forces for use in the European theater. By the late 1950s it had begun to seem likely that, if the United States used its "tactical" nuclear forces to support NATO, the Soviets would respond in kind. Heavy western reliance on such weapons seemed therefore to promise not defense but destruction. By the end of the decade, questions began to arise about whether the United States would be willing to use its longer-range strategic forces against the Soviet Union once the Soviets had acquired a capability to strike back in kind.

With these considerations in mind, in the early 1960s the Kennedy administration sought to reopen the question of a truly conventional response to Soviet ground forces. Administration officials argued not only that such a response was necessary because of the impending loss of American strategic and theater nuclear superiority, but that it was possible in light of a reexamination of the scale of the purported Warsaw Pact threat. With reasonable and affordable improvements, it was claimed, NATO could more than match its opponents, thereby reducing to a minimum any need to rely on nuclear weapons of whatever size or type.

As before and since, the European reaction to such proposals was at best lukewarm. A significant conventional buildup would still have been expensive and thus politically controversial. Moreover, many European experts had come to believe that the best way to deal with the possibility of ground attack was to deter it through the threat of prompt nuclear retaliation (however dangerous for all concerned), rather than by preparing to respond in kind. The awesome nature of this threat, it was reasoned, would make it extremely unlikely that it would ever have to be carried out. Emphasizing the need for conventional defenses, on the other hand, might encourage the Soviets to believe that they could fight and win a conventional war without running as great a risk of escalation. According to this logic, expanding ground forces might actually weaken deterrence rather than, as in the American view, strengthen it.

Out of this collision of strategic preferences there emerged a compromise. The United States and its allies agreed that if the Soviets initiated a war in Europe by using nuclear weapons, the alliance would make an equivalent response. But if the invasion was conventional, at least in its early stages, NATO would do its best to hold without resorting to nuclear weapons. If a conventional defense should be about to fail, however, the United States promised that it would still make first use of its nuclear weapons to prevent Europe's collapse and defeat.

This was the strategy of "flexible response," formally adopted by the alliance in

1967 and still in force today. The doctrine contained some inherent ambiguities: How strong in relation to their opponents would NATO ground forces have to be? How long would the conventional phase have to last before escalation was permissible, and exactly what form would it take if it did come? But then ambiguity is the glue that is sometimes required to hold alliances together.

Under the accumulated pressure of twenty years of change, that glue has become steadily weaker. In a sense, what had been feared in the fifties and early sixties finally came true in the early seventies. By that time, at the latest, the growth of Soviet intercontinental forces meant that the threat of a disarming American strategic attack had lost whatever credibility it might once have had. Meanwhile, at the theater nuclear level, the Soviets had succeeded in deploying forces larger and in some ways more capable than their western counterparts. Official doctrine still called for a U.S. first strike to rescue NATO if all else failed. But such an action, however big or small, now seemed likely to bring about an equally devastating reply. Under these conditions, the credibility of the American threat seemed to have diminished substantially. Having effectively cancelled out U.S. strategic and theater nuclear forces, the Soviets, some observers warned, might now be more likely at a moment of extreme crisis to risk a purely conventional attack on NATO.

Over the last fifteen years American strategists have tried to come up with various schemes for bolstering what they saw as an eroding deterrent. Under their prodding the NATO alliance has gone through in rapid succession a series of bitter but ultimately inconclusive debates about how to improve its position in response to Soviet advances. In the early seventies, United States officials alarmed their European counterparts by talking publicly about ongoing efforts to imagine plausible, limited, nonescalatory ways in which long-range strategic forces could once again be used, first if necessary to support NATO. For a brief interval in the mid-seventies, serious consideration was given to the possibility of deploying new, sophisticated tactical nuclear weapons to neutralize Soviet conventional forces. (These were the so-called enhanced radiation or neutron bombs, designed, as their opponents delighted in pointing out, to kill people but leave buildings standing.) The result was, predictably, unrest in the United States and Europe and a political fiasco on both sides of the Atlantic.

In the late seventies and early eighties the alliance proceeded, at the cost of considerable domestic political turmoil, to deploy intermediate-range nuclear forces to make the threat of nuclear use more credible again. Over the next few years those weapons are scheduled to be withdrawn under the terms of the Intermediate-Range Nuclear Forces Agreement, a treaty negotiated over the heads of the Europeans between the United States and the Soviet Union.

And so the circle has come around again to conventional defense. Since the late seventies a wide range of American observers have reached the conclusion that the United States ought, along with its allies, to deploy conventional forces strong enough to hold off a Warsaw Pact attack as long as necessary without having to resort to nuclear weapons. This recommendation is not so different from the one offered in the early sixties, and it has been received in Europe with only slightly more enthusiasm than were the urgings of the Kennedy administration. The problem is that since then, along with their other activities, the Soviets have been engaged in a major expansion of ground, air, and naval forces in the European theater. By any reasonable measurement the requirements of a sturdy conventional defense are higher now than they were in the early fifties or early sixties.

What are those requirements? Are they being met today? Can they be met in the future at reasonable political and economic cost? The present balance of conventional forces in Europe is not as good as some academic analysts have tried to make it out, although it may also not be as bad as some government officials have sometimes seemed to claim. Barring a far-reaching and highly favorable conventional arms control agreement, if NATO wishes to improve its defensive position and reduce its reliance on nuclear weapons, some nontrivial increases in conventional capabilities will be necessary. The costs of increases would be significant. In 1982 Bernard Rogers, then supreme allied commander in Europe, estimated that they might require as much as a 4 percent real increase in NATO spending over five years. For that very reason, the chances of achieving such increases in the next five to ten years are extremely small. Unless arms control saves the day, the failure to make the necessary increases will set the stage for

The neutron bomb, a would-be tactical nuclear weapon, was not well received on either side of the Atlantic. (Paul Szep, courtesy *Boston Globe*)

another, even more divisive cycle of debate, one that can only heighten animosities and further weaken the foundations of the alliance. The loss of nuclear superiority has had very real consequences in the European theater.

Asia

Since the end of the Second World War, American policy in Asia has been aimed above all else at preserving an independent and friendly Japan. As George Kennan pointed out in his earliest formulations, at the close of the war that country comprised one of only five areas where what he called "the sinews of modern military strength could be produced in quantity" (the others being the United States, the United Kingdom, the Rhine Valley, and the Soviet Union).[2] The objective of containment, in Kennan's view, was to see that no more than one of these key power centers fell under communist control.

By this calculus, the "loss" of mainland China was unfortunate but bearable in the coldest geopolitical terms, and in any case it was not something about which the United States could do very much with the military forces at hand. Korea, the other possible key country in the region, was of importance primarily as a potential staging area for attacks against Japan. Nevertheless, the Joint Chiefs of Staff concluded in 1947 that the forty-five thousand troops stationed in South Korea should be withdrawn for use elsewhere. With the outbreak of the Korean War in 1950, that decision was quickly reversed and U.S. forces have remained on the peninsula ever since.

From the early fifties the American military position in Asia has been anchored in Japan and Korea with a logistical tail trailing back through the Philippines, Hawaii, and connecting finally to the West Coast of the continental United States. That much has stayed constant, although with the recent domestic political upheavals in Korea and the Philippines it may not remain so forever. Let me note briefly four crucial regional developments or trends that seem likely to affect America's place as a Pacific power.

The first is of course the split between China and the Soviet Union. Kennan and a few others had foreseen this possibility and its benefits in the late forties and they tried to devise ways of promoting and exploiting it. The Korean War, domestic developments in China, and the undifferentiated intensity of American anticommunism in the fifties and sixties put such policies out of reach for almost twenty years.

The Sino-Soviet split is clearly the most significant political development of the postwar period. Over the long run it has denied the Soviet Union access to vast potential resources with which it might have been able to improve its position relative to the United States. More immediately it has also created pressing military requirements that the Soviets have had to pay a great deal to meet. This is a second important trend. Since the mid-sixties, when their differences with the Chinese began to deepen, the Soviets have engaged in a major military buildup in the Far East. By 1969 they had fifteen army divisions

2. George Kennan, *Memoirs, 1925–1950* (Boston: Little, Brown and Co., 1967), p. 359.

along the border with China.[3] Two years later that number had increased to thirty-three; today it stands at fifty-seven. Those ground forces are equipped with fifteen thousand tanks and accompanied by thirteen hundred tactical aircraft, about eight hundred nuclear armed short- and medium-range ballistic missiles, and by a Pacific Ocean fleet that includes two aircraft carriers, over two hundred surface combatants of various types, and almost one hundred submarines.[4]

Over the last two decades the Soviet Union has probably spent at least 15 percent of its annual defense budget on building and maintaining its Far Eastern forces.[5] In one sense, of course, all this has been an enormous boon to the United States and its NATO allies. It is interesting but also rather frightening to contemplate what Soviet strategic and European-based conventional forces might look like today if they had not had to share resources with a fast-growing Asian theater. As quickly as these other more directly threatening components of the Soviet armed forces have grown, they could have expanded even more rapidly and more fully if China and the Soviet Union had remained friends.

On the other hand, in responding to their concerns about China the Soviets have also increased the visibility and potency of their military presence throughout the Far East. Soviet forces now operate out of American-built facilities in Cam Ranh Bay, Vietnam. Soviet submarines and surface vessels patrol the sea lanes leading to Japan and their aircraft regularly overfly the northern portion of the Japanese home islands.

The Pacific and especially its northwestern reaches are no longer, as Douglas MacArthur described them in 1949, "an Anglo-Saxon lake."[6] The increasing Soviet presence there has diminished the relative advantage that U.S. forces once enjoyed in the region, but those forces have also tended to decrease in absolute terms. That is a third significant trend. In 1969 the Nixon administration revised downward the assumption that U.S. conventional forces had to be big enough to fight "two-and-a-half wars" simultaneously, one in Europe, one in Asia, and another "brushfire" conflict on the periphery. Given the continued focus of American policy on Europe and the increasing importance of the Persian Gulf, the regular peacetime American presence in Asia has dwindled since the end of the Vietnam War. Today there are only two ground force divisions in the

3. For a discussion see Aaron L. Friedberg, "The Collapsing Triangle: U.S. and Soviet Policies Towards China, 1969–1980," Comparative Strategy 4, 2 (1983): 113–46.
4. Department of Defense, Soviet Military Power, 1987 (Washington: GPO, 1987), pp. 18, 40–41.
5. In 1978 Secretary of Defense Harold Brown reported that: "Current intelligence estimates are that between 1964 and 1977, the Soviets spent an average of about 10–15 percent of their defense budget (measured in rubles) on forces oriented toward the People's Republic of China. At least 22 percent of the increase in the Soviet defense budget during these 13 years has been attributed to the buildup in the Far East." Harold Brown, Department of Defense Annual Report: Fiscal Year 1979 (Washington: GPO, 1978), p. 21. Given the harsh conditions of the Soviet Far East and the extra expenditure required to meet them, these estimates may actually be somewhat low.
6. John W. Spanier, The Truman-MacArthur Controversy and the Korean War (New York: W.W. Norton, 1965), p. 17.

region, one or two carrier battle groups, and a dozen tactical fighter squadrons.[7] This is a smaller contingent than at any time since 1950.

The shrinking American presence in Asia and the change in the regional balance of superpower forces have been noted with concern by some Asian observers. In 1976 the Japanese Defense Agency's Official White Paper contained a chart showing that since 1965 (before the beginning of the real Vietnam buildup), U.S. ground, naval, and air forces in the Far East had diminished substantially while those of the Soviet Union had grown.[8] The precise figures are probably less important than the document in which they appeared and the underlying uncertainty about the American commitment in Asia they seem to suggest. Over time there will undoubtedly be more explicit questions raised about the value of an American security guarantee. If American officials now express doubt about extending deterrence to Europe, why should their promises be taken any more seriously in Asia, where the U.S. presence is much smaller? What, precisely, could the United States do to defend Japan in the event of a global confrontation with the Soviet Union? And what, if anything, could it do to help deter or to influence a possible Sino-Soviet conflict, no matter how important to American interests the outcome of such a clash might be?

A fourth trend is now very familiar. That is the rapid advance of economic development throughout the Far East and its likely continuation. This process has already created new centers of industry and trade and it may one day produce major military powers as well. Japan's gross national product (GNP) could exceed that of the Soviet Union by the end of this decade and it may be significantly larger by the turn of the century. By that date China's GNP could conceivably begin to approach that of the Soviet Union. If the Chinese choose to increase their rate of military expenditure, by the year 2000 they could be spending a sizable fraction of what the Soviet Union does on defense.[9] Assuming that the Japanese defense budget remains at around 1 percent of GNP, in another ten or fifteen years Japan could be laying out almost as much each year as Germany, France, or Great Britain. If, on the other hand, the Japanese do what some commentators in this country have been urging and decide to spend, let us say, 3 or 4 percent of GNP on defense, they will be well on their way to achieving the status of an independent global military power. To expect that such a state would be content to act as nothing more than an offshore extension of American defense policy would be, to say the least, shortsighted.

To sum up: Asia is becoming more important to the United States than it has ever been before. But from a military standpoint at least the United States may be becoming less important to Asia.

7. Joint Chiefs of Staff, *Military Posture: FY 1988* (Washington: GPO, 1987), p. 14.

8. In 1965 the Soviets had 180,000 men, 700,000 tons of naval shipping, and 1,430 combat aircraft in the Far East. Ten years later those figures had increased to 300,000 men, 1,200,000 tons, and 2,000 aircraft. The American figures were 87,000 men, 900,000 tons, and 920 aircraft in 1965; 66,000 men, 600,000 tons, and 500 aircraft in 1975. Japanese Ministry of Defense, *Defense of Japan, 1976* (Tokyo: Ministry of Defense, 1976), p. 15.

9. For present GNP figures and historical growth rates see the CIA's *Handbook of Economic Statistics, 1985* (Springfield, Va.: National Technical Information Service, 1985).

The Periphery

Of all the theaters, U.S. strategy for the periphery has been the least clearly defined. This lack of clarity has its origins in the earliest debates over what ends the United States ought to seek in the less developed world and what means it should use to pursue them. Recall that George Kennan's formula for effective containment did not even include any country or region not already able to sustain large-scale industrial production. It is possible to argue that no other area ought to be of any real concern to the United States, regardless of what the Soviet Union or any other hostile power might do in them. Kennan did not claim this, although some who today fashion themselves as his disciples (I would call them the "hyperrealists") do reason in just this way. They urge a policy of detachment from countries, regions, even entire continents, based on a perusal of present GNP statistics. This seems imprudent, if for no other reason than that the distribution of production is already very much in flux.

In any case, there has always been an argument that from a purely power political standpoint, the United States ought not to be heavily (and in particular, militarily) involved on the periphery. The alternative to this is the view usually associated with NSC-68, the document accepted as the basis for national strategy in September 1950. Here the United States was portrayed as being locked in a worldwide duel to the death with the forces of international communism led by the Soviet Union. According to this interpretation, all developments on the periphery unfavorable to U.S. interests could be traced ultimately to Moscow, and no stake, however small, was too insignificant to be defended from communist encroachment. A failure to defend such places would display an absence of moral fiber but also and more dangerously a lack of will. In the words of NSC-68, "a defeat of free institutions anywhere is a defeat everywhere."[10]

The disagreement over ends is still very much alive and one has only to look at the debate over U.S. policy toward Nicaragua to see the form it has taken more recently. In the last forty years there have also been substantial variations in the means that the United States has chosen to pursue its objectives on the periphery, however these aims have been defined.

From the earliest stages of the Cold War, the United States has always displayed some interest in protecting existing friendly peripheral regimes, both from hostile neighbors (often backed by the Soviets) and from internal enemies. American support has manifested itself in a variety of forms, from the provision of military hardware to the design and implementation of counterinsurgency programs. The importance of this second instrument of policy increased steadily from the early fifties, when the United States tried to encourage fading colonial powers like France to do the job, to the early sixties, when increasing numbers of American counterinsurgency advisers were trained and dispatched to various

10. NSC-68, "United States Objectives and Programs for National Security," April 14, 1950. Reprinted in Thomas Etzold and John Lewis Gaddis, *Containment: Documents on American Policy and Strategy, 1945–1950* (Columbia University Press, 1978), p. 389.

parts of the world, to the middle and late sixties when substantial U.S. forces were committed to combat in Southeast Asia.

It is safe to say that the disastrous experience in Vietnam marked the high water mark of direct American military intervention on the periphery. With the exception of the Persian Gulf and perhaps the Middle East, it is extremely unlikely that the United States will fight a war anywhere in the less developed world between now and the end of this century and probably a good bit beyond. Limited displays of force are possible, but once-removed, relatively inexpensive assistance and training programs will be the norm.

In the last eight years the United States has also reversed roles and gotten into the insurgency business, supporting guerrilla movements of various ideological stripes against Soviet-backed regimes. If such effort cannot be undertaken more or less openly, with the approval of Congress, they probably cannot be sustained over the long run. Ironically, congressional approval may come easier in "distant places of which we know little" (like Afghanistan) than closer to home.

In the last forty years the Soviet Union has also gone through several stages in its development as a world power, able to throw its weight around on the periphery. From acting as an enthusiastic if quite circumspect supporter of national liberation movements, the Soviets have been drawn increasingly into propping up a few favored client regimes and in several recent cases protecting them from their American-backed internal oppositions. For a time in the mid-seventies it seemed that the Soviets might be on the verge of replacing a retiring, war-weary United States and developing the capacity for large-scale military interventions well away from their own borders. During this period they acquired and put to use in Africa and the Middle East a long-range air- and sea-lift capability unlike anything they had ever had before. That capability still exists. Global intervention is no longer the exclusive prerogative of the United States, but whatever enthusiasm there may have been in the Soviet Union for such adventures appears to have been cooled, for the time being at least, by the long and bloody aftermath of the invasion of Afghanistan.

The superpower competition on the periphery seems to have reached a plateau of sorts. Events in these areas have of course always had a logic of their own and they will go forward regardless of what either country does. The United States and the Soviet Union will continue to be willing to pay a modest price to protect their friends in distant places and to exploit each other's weaknesses and obsessions. That is nothing new. What may be changing is the ability of certain regional powers like Iran and Iraq to fight large and costly wars more or less on their own, without having to rely exclusively on the superpowers for support and, as a result, without having to submit directly to their control.

Conclusions

On balance American national strategy since 1947 appears to have been a considerable success, though not an effortless or inexpensive one. Although the potential vulnerability of the United States has increased enormously, there have been no direct attacks and, assuming the maintenance of an adequate deterrent, there is little reason to fear any in the immediate future. The independence of Western Europe and Japan has been preserved and their prosperity restored. With some notable and costly exceptions like Vietnam and Iran, the United States has also done reasonably well at preserving friendly regimes on the periphery.

That is a snapshot of how things appear today. Like all snapshots it captures some aspects of reality but not others. Imagine a picture of a man supporting a heavy weight above his head. All we know is that, at the moment the picture was taken, the man was able to hold the weight in place. We cannot be sure how heavy it is or whether more had been added to it over time. Even if we study the picture very carefully, we may also have no clue as to how hard the weightlifter is straining, how painful his exertion is becoming, how likely he is in the next instant to continue to support his burden or to drop it to the ground.

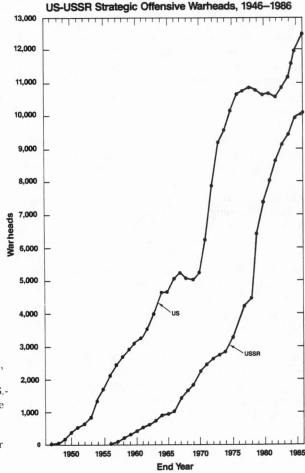

US-USSR Strategic Offensive Warheads, 1946–1986

Source: Robert S. Norris, William M. Arkin, and Thomas B. Cochran, "U.S.-USSR Strategic Offensive Nuclear Forces, 1946–1986" (Nuclear Weapon Databook Working Paper NWD 87-1, July 1987).

The situation I have been describing is one in which the United States has had to work harder over time to uphold its commitments or, to change the metaphor from a static to a dynamic one, it has been a time in which the United States has had to run faster just to stay in place. Over the last four decades (and especially during the last two) the Soviet Union has increased its military power fairly steadily. The capabilities of the United States have also undergone considerable absolute expansion (although with more fits and starts), but in relative terms they have quite clearly declined. Since 1947 the superpower military competition has proceeded at higher levels of effort. From the American side this means that the United States has had to do more to cancel out potential Soviet advantages, to preserve a rough balance of power, and to hold to a minimum the chances that deterrence will fail.

The question now being asked by a variety of observers is whether the United States can continue to keep up the pace. At this point it seems that the consensus answer, among academic specialists at least, is no. Some believe that Soviet capabilities have been exaggerated and that they can be met and existing commitments sustained at a considerably lower level of effort, albeit perhaps with a slightly greater risk of war. Others acknowledge the need for increasing western military capabilities in order to keep up, but want the allies to bear a much greater share of the overall burden. Many members of both groups believe that continued high levels of defense expenditure have already caused serious economic problems for the United States, problems that are only likely to get worse as this century draws to a close.

Out of this consensus there have emerged a variety of proposals, some of them quite radical, for trimming U.S. commitments in order to reduce peacetime military spending. One recent book, revealingly entitled *How NATO Weakens the West*, calls for a total withdrawal of American forces from Europe and Asia within the next five years.[11] Plans like this one have already begun to receive substantial attention among scholars and they are likely to gain more widespread support as current trade and budgetary problems are overlaid on existing alliance disagreements concerning military strategy and economic burden-sharing. Indeed, it seems likely that the 1990s will begin with a reexamination of the relationship between finance and strategy more searching than any that has been undertaken since the early 1950s.

It is important in all this to distinguish between the long and the short term and to be alert to the possibility that panic over immediate problems could produce sudden and imprudent changes in policy. That in a way is one of the lessons of the past eight years. In its eagerness to reverse what it saw as a deterioration in the nation's defense posture caused by the spending cutbacks of the 1970s, the Reagan administration undertook a vast and expensive military buildup. The economic problems that have followed were not caused by the buildup as such but rather by the fact that too much money was spent in too short a time, some of it was spent unwisely, and most of it was obtained through

11. Melvyn Krauss, *How NATO Weakens the West* (New York: Simon & Schuster, 1986).

foreign borrowing, not out of tax revenues or from some nationally agreed upon shift in government spending priorities.

Just as the defense feast of the eighties followed the famine of the seventies, the nineties are likely also to be a time of constraint. Defense spending will have to be slowed if budget deficits are to be reduced. In the short run the question is whether this can be done without a precipitous shedding of commitments or, if those are to remain constant, a dangerous weakening in the capabilities needed to support them.

Fortunately, the next few years seem to offer the possibility of a relaxation in tensions and a slackening of the superpower military competition, which may make it easier for the United States and its allies to put their respective and collective houses in order. There is certainly reason to hope that this period will last and that it will lead to some fundamental transformations in the superpower relationship. But the history of the last forty years does not offer much encouragement that this is likely to be the case.

Over the long run the problem remains the same as it was in the summer of 1948 when the State Department's Policy Planning Staff concluded that the United States needed to develop a level of military readiness that could be "maintained as long as necessary as a deterrent to Soviet aggression."[12] Can this country, if it needs to, sustain moderate and historically quite low levels of defense expenditure (say around 5 percent of GNP annually) consistently, over extended periods of time, without doing itself grievous economic harm? The answer is not at all obvious, although there has been some tendency recently to blame all the nation's many industrial problems on the alleged ills of defense spending. A fuller diagnosis will have to include some analysis of the impact of the entire range of government activities, including taxation and nondefense spending on patterns of consumption, savings, and productive investment.

Unless the Soviets begin to pursue far different policies than they have over most of the last forty years, it is already clear that moderate American exertions will not be enough, in and of themselves. The United States today relies on its allies to pick up a substantial portion of the costs of their own defense and it will undoubtedly be pressing them to do more in the years ahead. If they fail to do so, Americans may come to feel that continuing existing military arrangements involves running risks so large that they are simply no longer in the U.S. national interest. On the other hand, there is the possibility that endless haggling over burdens could cause the western alliance to fragment and collapse. Of course, even if it is able to coax greater contributions, the United States will have succeeded only in lessening the gap between its allies and itself, thereby diminishing its own predominant place in the coalition. That is both the irony of the present situation and a necessary objective of the next forty years of American national strategy.

---

12. NSC-20/2, "Factors Affecting the Nature of the U.S. Defense Arrangements in the Light of Soviet Policies," 25 August 1948. Reprinted in Etzold and Gaddis, *Containment*, p. 301.

PART II

ADJUSTING TO A WIDER DIPLOMATIC ARENA

5

The United States and the Postwar International Economy

ROBERT GILPIN

THE ERA from the end of the Second World War until the 1980s was one of the most remarkable in economic history. Following a period of reconstruction in the 1950s, there was an unprecedented rate of economic growth during the decade of the 1960s and the early years of the 1970s. By one reckoning, during these four decades the world gross national product tripled. International economic interdependence in trade, money, and investment advanced at an ever more rapid pace, leading to speculations and theories regarding the long-term consequences of these developments. Mankind, many Americans argued, was being integrated into a global market economy in which state and national boundaries were losing both economic and political significance.[1]

By the mid-1980s, however, this dream of an expanding world economy organized in terms of a self-regulating market had been shattered. In the 1970s, the novel phenomenon of "stagflation"—a combination of a low rate of economic growth, mass unemployment, and double-digit inflation—had replaced rapid and stable economic growth. This was followed by a greatly reduced rate of global economic growth in the 1980s. The achievements of successive rounds of trade liberalization were being eroded by the spread of nontariff barriers and various

1. This paper is adapted from the author's *The Political Economy of International Relations* (Princeton University Press, 1987) and "American Policy in the Post-Reagan Era," *Daedalus* Futures (Summer 1987): 33–67.

forms of economic protectionism, the international monetary system was in a state of considerable disarray, and the stability of the global financial structure was threatened by the mammoth debt problems of the less developed countries.

In order to appreciate the magnitude of the changes that have taken place in the world economy, especially during the Reagan tenure, and to see the challenges these changes posed for the United States, one must understand what I shall call the American system, i.e., the political, economic, and security ties between the United States and its major European and Japanese allies forged in the early postwar era. This system, which has provided a stable international political environment for the world economy, is in serious trouble. In the short term, decisive actions are required by the United States to shore up the system. In the long term, the United States and its allies undoubtedly must move beyond the system, at least in its present form, to more stable political and economic relations.

The American System

The United States emerged from the Second World War with a clear vision of the new international order that it wished to create: a universal economic and political system. The United Nations, and in particular the Security Council composed of the five permanent members, would be responsible for guaranteeing the peace. A constellation of novel economic institutions, including the International Monetary Fund (IMF) and the International Bank for Reconstruction and Development (World Bank) (i.e., the Bretton Woods system) would administer an open and multilateral world economy. The victors would build the peace that had eluded mankind after the First World War.

Within a brief period, the American conception of "one world" had been shattered. The American-Soviet confrontation over the territorial settlement in Eastern and Central Europe destroyed the wartime spirit of collaboration. The ideal of a reunited world economy collided with the realities of the economic devastation wrought by the war and what would become known as the Cold War. The United States set about the task of formulating a new foreign policy and of fashioning an economic and political bloc that would restore the economies of its allies, provide military security, and contain the expansionist Soviet Union. The American system emerged from this effort.

After four decades, the economic and political structure created by the United States and its allies between 1946 and 1950 still stands, but badly shaken following numerous severe crises and intense conflicts of national interest. The trauma of the Vietnam War, the dramatic reversal of American foreign economic policy by President Richard Nixon in 1971, and periodic clashes over nuclear strategy and arms control have strained allied unity. The foundations of the American system have been seriously eroded, although it still constitutes the dominant feature of world politics. It is a weakened structure, one that is unprepared to withstand the earthquake that is bound to come in the years ahead. If it is to survive or to be transformed in a way that conforms to American

Plenary Session of the 1944 Bretton Woods, N.H., conference which led to the creation of the World Bank, one of several new international institutions championed by the United States in order to achieve an open, multilateral world economy. (AP/Wide World Photos)

interests, the United States must construct a new and more secure foundation for its relations with other countries and especially with its allies.

Components of the System

The American system has had two basic components: the American relationship with Western Europe and American ties with Japan. Although these two quite separate alliances have certain common features, they also exhibit important differences, which have become more pronounced over time, have caused strains in the system, and have made it more difficult for the United States to reconcile tensions in the system.

The American–West European Component. As relations with the Soviet Union deteriorated after 1945, the United States realized that there were fundamental problems related to Western Europe that required solution. The most pressing need was to assist the revival of the West European economy while also finding a way to guarantee the military security of the West Europeans against the threat

Secretary of State Marshall with Harvard President James Bryant Conant and General Omar N. Bradley at the June 1947 Harvard Commencement exercise where he first proposed the "Marshall Plan" for European recovery. (AP/Wide World Photos)

from the Soviet Union. To achieve an American commitment to the pursuit of these goals, the American people had to be linked psychologically to Western Europe. A retreat into isolationism like that which followed the First World War and contributed to the outbreak of the Second World War had to be prevented.

The Marshall Plan, which encouraged intra-European cooperation, and the formation of the European Economic Community (EEC) or Common Market were regarded as the solutions to the economic problems of a devastated and fragmented Europe. The creation of a huge market in Western Europe would give the West Europeans the strength to resist native communist parties and the blandishments of the Soviet Union. Although the Common Market represented a violation of the American ideal of a multilateral world and entailed discrimination against American exports, American policymakers assumed that the Common Market with its external tariff and protective Common Agricultural Policy was a necessary stepping-stone to an eventual multilateral system rather than an end in itself. It was expected that once Western Europe had regained its economic strength and confidence, it would lower its external barriers and participate in the open world economy envisioned by the United States at Bretton Woods in 1944. Meanwhile, the United States required an economic *quid pro quo* in the form of access to the EEC for American multinational corporations. Thus, the United States tolerated what it assumed would be temporary discrimination against American exports in order to rebuild Western Europe and thwart Soviet expansionist designs.

The North Atlantic Treaty Organization (NATO) was formed in 1949 to link the two sides of the Atlantic and to bring Western Europe under the American nuclear umbrella. Through the strategy of extended deterrence, the United States communicated to the Soviet Union that an attack on Western Europe would be tantamount to an attack on the United States itself. The stationing of American troops on European soil has been a visible sign of this commitment. The NATO treaty identified and legitimated for Americans and West Europeans alike the linking of their security.

The American-Japanese Component. In Asia, the United States also found itself facing a political, economic, and strategic challenge because the Second World War and its aftermath had strengthened the position of the Soviet Union in East Asia. The Red Army had gained advanced positions in the region, the Japanese economy had been even more devastated than had initially been appreciated, and North Korea and China had become communist and part of the Soviet bloc. The traditional markets of Japan were now in hostile hands. There was thus an intense concern that the forces of economic gravity would pull Japan toward the Soviet Union and its Chinese ally. Today, it is difficult to understand that less than forty years ago American officials despaired over the problem of ensuring Japanese economic survival.

The United States wanted to integrate Japan into a larger framework of economic relationships and thereby to remove the attractiveness of the communist-dominated Asian market. There were, however, no large neighboring non-communist economies to which the Japanese economy could be attached. In order to overcome this problem of an isolated and vulnerable Japan, the United States took several initiatives. One was to expedite the decolonization of Southeast Asia. Had not one cause of the Pacific war been that European colonizers had closed these economies to the Japanese? The United States also sponsored Japanese membership in the "Western Club." Despite strong West European resistance based on intense fear of Japanese economic competition, the United States secured Japanese participation in the IMF, the World Bank, and other international economic organizations. In addition, the United States gave Japan relatively free access to the American market and American technology without an economic *quid pro quo*, although it did require strategic concessions, i.e., air and naval bases, from the Japanese.

In order to guarantee Japanese security, the United States also spread its nuclear umbrella over Japan. The American-Japanese Mutual Security Treaty (MST), however, differs fundamentally from the NATO alliance. Under the NATO treaty an external attack on any member obliges the others to consider measures of mutual defense. In the MST, the United States agrees to defend Japan if it is attacked but the Japanese are not obligated to defend the United States in like circumstances. Also, whereas the NATO agreement applies only to the territory of its members, the MST refers to the outbreak of hostilities in the entire Pacific region. Through this agreement the United States obtained the right to use air and naval bases in Japan to defend and secure its position in the western Pacific. The Japanese were given access to the American market in exchange for the right to anchor on Japan the American strategic position in East Asia.

The Foundation of the System

The United States is the fulcrum of the American system; the American–West European and the American-Japanese components of the system have little to do with one another. The lines of cooperation run through Washington. Although Japan and Western Europe are equal participants in the annual "western" summits, Japanese–West European diplomatic relations are primarily a function of both their ties to the United States. In the economic area, Japanese–West European commerce is relatively minor compared to the commerce of each with the United States. While the Japanese are attempting to expand these commercial relations, the Europeans prefer to keep the Japanese at bay. With respect to security, almost no military connections exist between Western Europe and Japan, despite Prime Minister Yasuhiro Nakasone's pronouncement at the Williamsburg Summit in 1983 that Japan is part of the western security system. An increasing deployment of the Soviet strategic missile force in and around the Sea of Okhotsk, however, could one day change this situation significantly. For the moment, in security as in diplomatic and economic relations, the American system rests squarely on American leadership or what many scholars call American hegemony. Common interests and understandings have enabled the structure to withstand innumerable attacks from without and serious differences within the alliances themselves, even though important differences between the United States and its allies have existed from the very beginning. International conditions have changed dramatically since the end of the war and the basic assumptions upon which the American system was founded have become less valid. What one might call the internal "contradictions" within the system have grown, and the foundations have eroded. The differences among the allies over the nature of the Soviet threat, over nuclear issues, and over economic problems have increased and threaten to cause a rupture of the system.

A shared perception of the Soviet threat has been central to the unity of the system. The western policy of containment was based on the assumption that the West faced an expansionistic and monolithic communist bloc. It was also generally believed that diplomatic resolution of East-West differences could not be achieved until the Soviet Union and international communism were transformed. The "negotiation from strength" position meant that serious negotiations must await Soviet recognition of western military superiority. The United States has simply assumed that there exists a global communist military threat; its allies have tended to see the problem more as a regional political challenge.

Differences in perception among the allies have grown over the years because of political and economic changes. A unified communist bloc no longer exists, West European communist parties have ceased to be a serious problem, and the

Soviet Union faces an independent and potentially dangerous China to the east. Despite its military might, the Soviet Union's serious economic problems and the economic strength of Western Europe have reduced the fear that the eastern market might ensnare the West Europeans. The Helsinki Agreements (1975) reduced the confrontation in Central Europe and commenced what many Europeans believe, or want to believe, is a gradual internal "liberalization" of the Soviet Union, a belief fostered by the diplomacy and reforms of Mikhail Gorbachev.

These and other changes have accentuated interallied political differences between the United States and Western Europe. In the words of Denis Healey, former British minister of defense, "it is difficult [for Europeans] to believe that the Soviet superiority is sufficient to tempt the Kremlin into a deliberate attack on Western Europe. . . ."[2] West Europeans have resisted the American desire to extend the scope of the NATO alliance and argue that NATO applies only to the security of its members and cannot be extended to the Middle East or other regions, despite U.S. pressures for strong actions against Soviet aggression in Afghanistan and Soviet support of Marxist regimes elsewhere. Powerful groups in Western Europe hope for an easing of the division of Europe as a result of Gorbachev's policies. Some consider Western Europe to be only a middleman needed to moderate the potentially dangerous clash between the two superpowers. Although the Western Europeans remain committed to the alliance, European and American interests have diverged considerably and the political tie has been attenuated.

Differences among the allies on the issue of defense have also grown. The American commitment to the defense of Western Europe, assumed when it began to be temporary, was never intended to result in the stationing of tens of thousands of American troops in Western Europe or to reach an annual cost of over $100 billion forty years after the founding of NATO. The Europeans were expected to be able to defend themselves, at least in the conventional sphere, and the United States was supposed to be able later to reduce its commitment. This crucial assumption was undermined by the unanticipated growth of Soviet power and European refusal to finance the necessary conventional buildup, both because of its costs and because of concern that a buildup might weaken the American nuclear guarantee. The Europeans alternate between worrying that the immature and pugnacious Americans will trigger a fight with the Soviets on European soil (as they did when the intermediate-range missiles were deployed in the early 1980s) and an equal fear that the United States will abandon them. This latter concern increased when the United States and the Soviet Union began negotiations over the removal of these same weapons. Meanwhile, American citizens are more frequently asking whether they are really willing to put their own society at risk in order to deter an attack on West Europeans who are unwilling to make the sacrifices necessary to defend themselves.

The Chinese conventional threat and the Soviet nuclear threat have been the

2. Denis Healey, "A Labour Britain, NATO and the Bomb," *Foreign Affairs* 65 (1987): 724.

"And to think I set him up in business!"

"Doc, my heart's fine, but I keep getting this pain in my wallet . . ."

Supported on security grounds, the European Economic Community came to be seen by many Americans as a threatening trade rival. (Top: Gib Crockett, *Washington Star,* August 1971; bottom: C. Sanford Huffaker, *The News and Observer,* Raleigh, N.C., 1971. Courtesy of Rothco Cartoons.)

foci of security concerns in East Asia. The American rapprochement with China and the Soviet nuclear, naval, and conventional buildup in that strategic theater have transformed that situation. American-Japanese political relations have greatly improved because the Japanese no longer fear that the United States will drag them into an American-Chinese conflict. With the growth of Soviet power in Asia, however, the United States has become increasingly impatient over the Japanese "free ride" with respect to their security and their resistance to extensive rearmament. American pressure on the Japanese to rearm more rapidly has caused great resentment in Japan. The Japanese vehemently resist a linkage of economics and security. The United States, on the other hand, links past economic concessions to Japan to increased Japanese cooperation in the security realm. Intensification of the defense versus economic conflict has stimulated nationalistic reactions in the Japanese and a tendency for Americans to feel that they have been "used."

Economic ties have complemented the political and security foundations of the American system. Even though the trading and monetary system established at the end of the Second World War facilitated an unprecedented period of economic growth and world commerce, differences among the allies over economic matters have always existed. Important changes in economic strengths and relationships during the past decade-and-a-half have accentuated interallied economic conflicts and today these conflicts seriously threaten the stability of the international economic system.

The United States and Western Europe have very different conceptions of the EEC. The United States tolerated EEC discrimination against American exports primarily for security reasons and assumed that the Europeans would soon reopen their markets to American exports, thus creating the multilateral trading system. For many Europeans, the EEC with its tariff barriers and its agricultural price supports constitutes an end in itself. This concept of Western Europe as a protected regional bloc has been strengthened as the number of nations in the community has grown. Although the United States initially gained politically and economically from the creation of the EEC, in recent years the economic costs of the community to American businesses and farmers have greatly escalated.

The other assumption on which the postwar world economy was established was that Japan was economically vulnerable. How could an overpopulated archipelago devoid of indigenous resources possibly survive? The American policy of supporting Japanese economic development has been so successful that Japan, after Canada, has become the primary economic partner of the United States. The American-Japanese economic nexus has become the central economic relationship for both countries. With the growth of the Japanese economy, the United States has demanded a more open Japan and the same access by American firms to the Japanese economy that Japanese firms have to the American economy. These pressures for greater liberalization, however, run directly counter to important aspects of Japanese society and have become a major source of conflict. Despite its competitive strengths and huge capital accumulation, Japan remains a highly vulnerable economy. It has no large, developed neighbors with which it can trade and it continues to be overly dependent upon the American market. It has yet to find a secure niche in the world economy. For the moment, the United States and Japan, for their own reasons, have formed a close but basically unstable symbiotic relationship.

Erosion of the economic foundations of these Atlantic and Pacific relationships is the most troublesome of the issues now affecting the American system. Because economic differences among the allies raise immediate and fundamental challenges for American domestic and foreign policy, the economic dimensions of this complex alliance structure should be stressed and the potential for serious conflict in this area among the allies should be examined and emphasized. Yet, all foundations of the system are in fact intimately joined and affect one another. For example, the continued stationing of large numbers of American troops in Western Europe and the building of a six-hundred-ship navy are contributing factors to the difficulties of the American economy. Let us begin this analysis by looking carefully at the economic crisis of the system.

The Relative Decline of American Power

The current economic crisis of the American system is in part a consequence of the long-term relative decline of the American economy and, more immediately, of the policies of the Reagan administration. Although the American economy is still the largest and most powerful in the world, it has declined relative to its competitors and, most importantly, it has declined with respect to what Americans and others expect from it. At the same time that the United States has assumed the largest portion of the burden of financing the American system and of confronting the growth of Soviet power, the American people have demanded an ever-rising standard of living and government services. Government expenditures have tended to rise faster than the gross national product (GNP); these expenditures have financed Social Security, including Medicare, congressional "pork barrels," and many weapons systems. American leaders have failed to confront the American people with the stark choices that they face. Instead, Americans have simultaneously had a massive defense buildup, expensive programs like Social Security, and rising domestic consumption. Few Democrats or Republicans have been willing to educate the American people to the trade-offs that they face.

In the early 1950s, the United States accounted for approximately 40 percent of the gross world product; by 1980, the American share had dropped by half to approximately 22 percent. Whereas the United States in the early postwar period produced 30 percent of world manufacturing exports, by 1986 its share had dropped to a mere 13 percent. American productivity growth, having outpaced the rest of the world for decades, declined dramatically from a growth rate of 3 percent annually in the early postwar years to an incredible low of 0.8 percent in the 1970s.[3] As American productivity growth has fallen behind that of

3. Isabel V. Sawhill and Charles F. Stone, "The Economy," chap. 3 in *The Reagan Record: An Assessment of America's Changing Domestic Priorities,* John L. Palmer and Isabel V. Sawhill, eds. (Cambridge, Mass.: Ballinger, 1984), p. 73.

other economies, particularly Japan, West Germany, and the newly industrializing economies (NICs), the economy has become less competitive and the relative American standard of living has been lowered. In terms of capital formation, technological leadership, and the quality of the labor force (human capital) the United States has not kept pace with other countries. Sadly, the United States is becoming an economy whose international competitiveness is increasingly based on "cheap labor." If this trend is to be reversed, the United States must increase its level of investment in plant and people in order to raise its rate of productivity growth.

In the closing decades of the twentieth century the United States faces an imbalance between its commitments and its decreased economic base. To keep pace with what it considers to be expanding Soviet military power, the United States has assumed increased costs to maintain its global political and military position; simultaneously, the rise of new industrial competitors and the loss of dominant positions in energy, technology, and agriculture have decreased the capacity of the United States to finance its many commitments. With a decreased rate of economic growth and a low rate of national savings, the United States lives far beyond its means and has also maintained domestic and international commitments that it can no longer afford.

The Reagan Legacy

Despite its superficial success, the Reagan administration has failed to reverse the relative decline of the American economy. On the contrary, the long-term problem of relative economic decline has been greatly compounded by its policies, policies that have largely been abetted by the Congress. The administration's theory of supply-side economics, the military buildup it financed, and the massive tax cut it engineered were geared to restore American power and prestige after the humiliations of the Carter years by rebuilding American military power and renovating the American economy, while simultaneously achieving domestic prosperity.

Despite its notable achievements in restoring self-confidence in the American population, reducing the rate of domestic inflation, and reviving economic growth, the Reagan administration did not solve the important problems of the relative decline of the American economy and of a nation living beyond its means. Instead, the policies of the administration have masked the underlying problem of the weakening economic foundations of American power. Indeed, its policies have further undermined the competitiveness of the American economy, transformed the United States into the greatest debtor nation in world history, and made the United States increasingly dependent upon foreign capital to maintain its domestic prosperity and global position. In the short term, this transformation of the American economic position has profound implications for America's relations with its allies, especially the Japanese. In the long term, it will force the United States to make drastic changes in both its economic and foreign policies.

The primary force behind these developments has been the massive tax cut and the resulting budget deficit. Anticipating the need to finance the deficit, American interest rates rose and led to a large capital flow into the American economy; this in turn raised the value of the dollar. With an overvalued dollar, American exports dropped and imports rose dramatically. The primary benefici- aries of this radical shift in macroeconomic policy were American consumers and foreign exporters, especially the West Germans, the Japanese, and the NICs of East Asia. These economies prospered because they shifted to an aggressive strategy of export-led growth, while American industry lost markets everywhere. The rapidly expanding American market in Latin America was destroyed because of the debt crisis, whose severity was accentuated by the rise of global interest rates. Latin American countries had to restrain their economies and cut back on American imports. The Reagan administration's economic policies have resulted in the loss of foreign markets for American exporters, the deindustrialization of the economy, and the decline of the United States to the status of a "net debtor" nation.

This shift of the United States from a creditor to a debtor nation is an event of immense historical significance, particularly in its effect on American trade, industry, and power. The budget deficit and the resulting greatly overvalued dollar reversed the favorable trends of the late 1970s. The American trade balance deteriorated and, by the mid 1980s, the annual trade deficit had reached the unbelievable figure of $170 billion. The huge net earnings on foreign investments ($34 billion in 1981) have been wiped out. Although foreign protec- tionism and the economic policies of other countries have been partially respon- sible for the deterioration of the American trading and payments situation, the basic explanation for this turnaround is to be found in simple economic rela- tionships telling us that the budget deficit *is* the trade deficit.

American macroeconomic policies resulting in a greatly overvalued dollar— and not the machinations of the Japanese—constitute the underlying cause of the trade deficit. The trade deficit is caused in Washington, D.C., and it is there that the problem must be solved. A distinguished economist of these macroeconomic relationships states:

> Macroeconomics impinges on the trade deficit through two laws of economic arith- metic. First, our net national dissaving—that is, the shortfall of savings in relation to the demand for them at home—must be financed by funds generated at home or abroad. Second, our account deficit equals the net capital inflow from abroad. This simply says that if the money foreigners get by selling us goods and services is not being spent to buy goods and services from us, then it must be spent in buying our assets [real estate, securities and Treasury bonds].
>
> If, at the prevailing exchange rates and interest rates, people's willingness to buy and sell, borrow and lend, is not compatible with these two equations, then the prices will change until the balances are restored.
>
> The U.S. has a large national dissaving because the public-sector dissaving (the Federal budget deficit) exceeds the net saving of the private sector. This raises our interest rates until foreign funds flow in to close the gap. That, in turn, raises the value of the dollar and increases our trade deficit by an equal amount.[4]

4. Avinash Dixit, *The New York Times*, 15 July 1985, p. A18.

In oversimplified terms, the causal relationship between the budget deficit and the trade deficit is as follows:

Budget deficit → Need to finance deficit → Rise in interest rate → Capital inflow → Overvalued dollar → Exports decrease and imports increase → Trade deficit

The macroeconomic policies of the administration not only had a devastating impact on American trade but also failed to raise the rate of national savings and domestic investment. Indeed, both declined dramatically, and the ratio of total debt to GNP has reached an unprecedented and disturbing level. Between 1980 and 1985, the necessity of financing the annual budget deficit of $200 billion or more caused the American savings rate to drop from approximately 17 to 12 percent; during this same period the personal savings rate plunged to a postwar low of 4 percent and even lower. (In contrast, the Japanese national savings rate has continued to be closer to 20 percent and, by some estimates, as high as 30 percent.) This $200 billion or so reduction of national savings per year has been balanced by reduced domestic investment and by foreign borrowing.

The budget deficit has also meant a relative decline in capital accumulation and domestic investment.[5] As the deficit has absorbed more than half of all national savings, it has raised interest rates and "crowded out" domestic investment; the rate of capital accumulation declined from about 17.5 percent of GNP in 1979 to 16.2 percent in 1985. The long-term effect of the $1.6 trillion decline in capital accumulation has meant "a loss of $160 billion a year in perpetuity."[6] The United States, it should be pointed out, throughout the postwar period has invested at home far less than its competitors. In contrast to a 17 percent or so investment rate for the United States, the West German rate is close to 25 percent and the Japanese rate is well over 30 percent.[7] Lowered capital accumulation means lower productivity growth, the acceleration of the deindustrialization of the American economy, and portends a significantly lower standard of living in the future. In effect, Americans have been able to consume more in the 1980s by paying lower taxes and by borrowing abroad, but they will one day have to pay the bill by means of exporting to repay their debt, higher taxes, or renewed inflation, or, more likely, through some combination of the three.

During the first five years of the Reagan administration, the national debt doubled and broke through the $2.0 trillion level.[8] By the year 1990, the debt could reach approximately $2.3 trillion or 40 percent of GNP; assuming 1986 interest rates, the interest payments will have increased by $200 billion and by 1990 would take 40 percent of all personal income taxes. At 1987 exchange rates the foreign debt or U.S. net obligations to foreigners was $200 billion and would

5. Martin Feldstein, "The Future of Economic Policy" (The Janeway Lectures, Princeton University, unpublished), pp. 2–3.
6. Ibid., p. 3.
7. Uwe E. Reinhardt, "Enjoy the Party—For Tomorrow Somebody Will Have to Pay," *Princeton Alumni Weekly*, 25 February 1987, pp. 13–19.
8. *The New York Times*, 22 September 1985, p. E5.

be approximately $800 billion by the beginning of the next decade.[9] The United States has in fact been mortgaging its future to a degree unprecedented in world history.

The level of private, public, and foreign debt of the American people and the costs of servicing this debt have become, in the words of the president of the Federal Reserve Bank of New York, threatening to the financial stability of the United States and the rest of the world.[10] Like other declining powers in the past, the United States has been indulging itself in overconsumption and underinvestment for too long. The result of this profligate behavior is the decline of the United States to the status of a "net debtor." It can not be emphasized enough that this shift of the United States from the world's foremost creditor to its largest debtor occurred in less than five years!

It should be noted that there is nothing wrong with foreign indebtedness as such. The United States was a net debtor internationally prior to the First World War. This foreign debt, however, was accumulated to create the productive assets with which the debt could eventually be repaid. The problem with the rapid descent of the United States into debtor status during the Reagan years is that the inflow of capital has been used primarily to finance private and public consumption, including the military buildup, rather than for domestic investment. What this means, therefore, is that the repayment of the debt will have to come out of future consumption, investment, or both. The result of this extravagance will obviously be a substantial lowering of the American living standard from what it would otherwise have been.

The experiment with Reaganomics has failed to address and has actually aggravated the fundamental difficulties of the United States. It did not substantially reduce governmental demands on the productive economy, but between 1980 and 1985, it "shifted about 1.5 percent of GNP from non-defense spending (excluding Social Security) over to defense with basically no net impact on the deficit."[11] Failing to adjust to changed economic circumstances, Reagonomics has made the long-term structural problems of the American economy still more difficult to solve and is leaving behind a burdensome legacy.[12]

Nevertheless, the Reagan administration has appeared successful because of an unusual alignment of its own interests with those of certain capital exporters. Japan has been the most important of those who have been willing to finance the budget deficit. The United States has been able to finance its defense buildup at the same time that it has reduced taxes because it has been in the interest of Japan to finance American power and domestic prosperity. Japanese capital flows to the United States have tripled from $20 billion in 1982 to $60 billion (annual

9. Martin Feldstein, "Correcting the Trade Deficit," *Foreign Affairs* 65 (1987): 801.
10. E. Gerald Corrigan, "Public and Private Debt Accumulation: A Perspective," Federal Reserve Bank of New York, *Quarterly Review* 10 (1985): 1–5.
11. Feldstein, "Future of Economic Policy," p. 7.
12. Robert O. Keohane, "The World Political Economy and the Crisis of Embedded Liberalism," chap. 1 in *Order and Conflict in Contemporary Capitalism: Studies in the Political Economy of Western European Nations*, ed. John H. Goldthorpe (Oxford: Clarendon Press, 1984), p. 37.

rate) in 1987.[13] The Japanese, having found a ready market for the output of their factories, have in effect loaned the United States the money to sustain their own strategy of export-led growth, to maintain a high level of domestic employment, and to help finance the American military buildup upon which the security of Japan rests.

As the economic and financial positions of the United States and Japan have been reversed, the political and economic relations of these countries have also been transformed. Each for its own reasons has entered into an intimate relationship in which the Japanese became the principal underwriters of President Reagan's policies. If Japanese capital flows were to stop, there would be a devastating impact on the American economy. In fact, it would be very difficult for the United States to fight another war on the same scale as the Korean or Vietnamese conflicts without Japanese permission and financial support of the dollar. Yet this crucial symbiotic relationship between the United States and Japan, which has developed during the Reagan years, is highly vulnerable. When it disappears or at least is attenuated, both the United States and Japan will be faced with difficult choices.

The global "good times" generated by the Reagan budget deficit appear to be over. American capacity and willingness to tolerate a massive trade deficit, to borrow the funds to pay for imports, and to plunge ever deeper into national debt have resulted in a potentially serious deindustrialization of the American economy and historically unprecedented national indebtedness. Now there is a threat of a congressional revolt through protectionist actions. As the United States retreats from the role it has played as the primary engine of growth for the world economy, unless growth rates increase elsewhere and the specter of a worldwide recession looms. The United States must quickly reverse its continuing economic and political decline.

The dollar has been the keystone of the American world position; as the dominant currency in the international monetary system, it has cemented the American system of global alliances and has been the foundation of American hegemony. With the dollar providing the base of the monetary system, the United States has been able to fight foreign wars, to maintain troops abroad, and to finance its hegemonic position without placing substantial economic costs on the American taxpayer. This crucial role of the dollar and the "exorbitant privileges," to use the term of Charles de Gaulle, that it has conferred on the United States have required a foreign partner to help support the dollar.

In the early postwar period, the American position in the world and the support of the dollar were based on American and British cooperation. This "special relationship," begun in the interwar years, was solidified by the wartime experience. Together, the Anglo-Saxon powers framed the Bretton Woods system and reestablished the liberal international economy. In 1967, the decline of the British economy forced the British to devalue their currency and pull away from the United States.

---

13. William H. Branson, "Capital Flows from Japan to the U.S.: Another False Alarm" (unpublished, 16 March 1987), p. 1.

West Germany replaced Great Britain in the late 1960s as the foremost economic partner of the United States and as the chief supporter of the dollar. Throughout the Vietnam War and into the 1970s, the Germans supported American hegemony by holding dollars and buying American government securities. The inflationary and other effects of this new special relationship led to a weakening of the relationship in the early 1970s and eventually to fracture in 1979, when the Germans refused to support the expansionary economic policy of President Carter.

During the Reagan administration, the Germans have been replaced by the Japanese, who have provided the financial backing of President Reagan's economic and military policies. Today, this American-Japanese special relationship is under severe strain due to American pressures on the Japanese to stimulate their economy, to the devaluation of the dollar, and to protectionist legislation in the Congress. A collapse of this fragile relationship would destroy a crucial underpinning of American power and domestic prosperity.

A Mixed System: Mercantilistic Competition, Economic Regionalism, and Sectoral Protectionism

By the mid-1980s, the liberal international economy established at the end of the Second World War had been significantly transformed. The trend toward liberalization of trade has been reversed and the Bretton Woods principles of multilateralism and unconditional Most Favored Nation status are being displaced by bilateralism and discrimination. With the collapse of the system of fixed exchange rates, conflicting interests gave rise to intense clashes over exchange values and other monetary issues among the advanced economies. The displacement of the United States by Japan as the dominant financial power and the global debt problem have raised troubling questions about the leadership and stability of the world financial system.

Although few doubt the reality of these changes, opinion differs greatly over their significance. Some believe that these developments reflect what John Ruggie has aptly called "norm-governed change" and a continuity of common purposes among the dominant economic powers.[14] Less sanguine observers, including the present writer, believe these changes are responses to hegemonic decline and are caused by diverging national interests among the advanced countries. As a consequence of profound structural changes in the international distribution of power, in supply conditions, and in the effectiveness of demand management, the liberal international economic order is rapidly receding.

Certain significant trends or developments can be observed. Growing mercantilistic competition threatens to increase economic nationalism, even though the vestiges of American leadership, the forces of historical inertia, and the common

14. John Gerard Ruggie, "Another Round, Another Requiem? Prospects for the Global Negotiations," chap. 3 in *Power, Passions, and Purpose: Prospects for North-South Negotiations*," Jagdish N. Bhagwati and John Gerard Ruggie, eds. (Cambridge, Mass.: MIT Press, 1984), pp. 412–13.

interest in avoiding conflict have thus far moderated the consequences of this situation. There is also a tendency toward the regionalization of the world economy. The closure of Western Europe, the economic consolidation of North America, and the rise of the Pacific basin point in that direction. Furthermore, sectoral protectionism has gained strength. The conflicting desires of nations both to protect particular sectors and to acquire foreign markets in these same industries strongly encourage this new protectionism. Although the relative importance of each cannot be determined, a mixed system of nationalism, regionalism, and sectoral protectionism is replacing the Bretton Woods system of multilateral liberalization.

The first factor suggesting an intensification of mercantilistic competition is the increasing role of the state and of economic power in international economic relations, e.g., growing protectionism. States (especially large states) have begun to use political and economic leverage extensively to increase their relative gains from international economic activities. The historic clash between economic interdependence and domestic autonomy is being more and more frequently resolved in favor of autonomy rather than interdependence, even though nations want the benefits of interdependence at the same time that they seek to limit its effects on their autonomy. They want the collective goods of liberalized trade and a stabilized monetary order without sacrificing their capacity to manage their own economies as they see fit. The result has been an expanding competition among states to maximize their own benefits from and to minimize the costs of global interdependence.

The second factor promoting mercantilistic conflict is the growing struggle for world markets. Because of such factors as domestic limits on economic growth in the form of high wages and inflationary pressures, the global debt problem, and the continuing need of most countries to import energy, almost every nation pursues export-led growth and aggressive export-expansion policies. These pressures on export markets will intensify because for the first time in the postwar era the United States must achieve an export surplus to repay its massive debt. This classical mercantilistic conflict over market shares is reflected in clashes over trade and macroeconomic policies.

Third, the challenge of Japan and the NICs also stimulates mercantilism. The structure of Japanese trade and the unprecedented rate of change of Japan's comparative advantage increase pressures on other economies. As Japan and the NICs move rapidly up the technological ladder, they impose heavy adjustment costs on other economies, thereby stimulating strong resistance and demands for protectionism. Japanese success reflects the activities of an adroit interventionist and mercantilist state, which has been able to manage social consensus, establish economic objectives, and increase the overall competitiveness of the economy. This success encourages other states to emulate the Japanese model and to develop interventionist policies of their own.

The mercantilism generated by these developments promises to be different in purpose and method from its eighteenth- and nineteenth-century predecessors. During the first mercantilist era, the objective was to acquire specie for military purposes, and the means employed was an export surplus. The purpose of nineteenth-century mercantilism was to speed industrialization, by means of protectionism and other policies. In the closing decades of the present century, the goal is at least survival in world markets and optimally the achievement of economic supremacy. Pursuing this goal, the Japanese and their imitators have implemented what the distinguished scholar Ronald Dore has aptly called a strategy of competitive development.

The success of the example of Japan and the NICs thus carries one step further and to its logical conclusion the twentieth-century transformation in the relationship of state and market. Through its control over economic levers, the modern state can direct and shape the economy to achieve its primary objective, whether it be the prosecution of war, the promotion of domestic welfare, or, as in the case of Japan, the industrial and technological superiority of the society. As a result of this change in the relationship of state and economy, a new form of mercantilistic competition, what the German economist Herbert Giersch has called "policy competition," has emerged.[15]

A powerful incentive exists for governments to manipulate economic policies in order to advance their economic, political, and related interests. The Japanese tactic of "preemptive investment," the American retreat to earlier ideas of "conditional reciprocity," and the temptation of all nations to move toward strategic trade policies are examples of such competitive policies. Developments in the 1980s such as the rise of the new protectionism, the spread of industrial policies, and governmental support of their own multinationals illustrate this predilection of individual states to adopt policies that benefit themselves at the expense of other economies.

How will "policy mercantilism" as a new form of interstate competition affect international economic and political relations? Will nations compete, for example, on an individual basis, or will what Giersch has called "policy cartels" arise?[16] If nations coordinate their economic policies and form economic alliances, who will participate and to what end? The rise of economic regionalism resulting from the erosion of a liberal international economic order may provide some answers to these questions.

The decline of American economic leadership and the difficulties of cooperation among the three centers of the world economy is causing the unity of the liberal international economic order to dissolve. Loose regional blocs are likely to result. In the 1980s, the world economy is coalescing along three axes. Debt, monetary, and trade matters, as well as changing security concerns, will surely pull the regions of the world economy further apart, but probably will not cause a complete break.

The European Economic Community constitutes one focus for regionalization of the world economy. A Europe-centered system would include the enlarged community, peripheral European states, and many of the former European colonies. It would no doubt form close ties to the eastern bloc and certain of the

---

15. Herbert Giersch, "The Age of Schumpeter," *American Economic Review* 74 (May 1984): 106.
16. Ibid.

Middle East oil exporters. As has been noted earlier, this region could be relatively self-sufficient except for energy and certain commodities. By the early 1980s, it had already achieved a high degree of monetary unity and policy coordination. In a world of increasing uncertainty and politicized economic relations, a more closely integrated Western Europe, as foreseen by the 1992 initiative, would be able to confront the United States, Japan, and the emergent centers of economic power more effectively.

The United States has begun to draw its northern and southern neighbors into closer interdependence, as both the Canadian and Mexican economies have become increasingly integrated with that of the United States. Although not enough attention is given to the fact, Canada is the largest trading partner of the United States, and these ties have increased with Canada's dramatic loss of its European markets over the postwar period. The United States is the largest importer of Mexican oil, and American multinationals have made the area along the southern Rio Grande one of the principal locales of "offshore" production. In 1984, approximately 80 percent of Mexico's exports went north of the border. Also, the Caribbean Basin Initiative was meant to bind that region, including parts of central and northern South America, more closely to the United States. The United States has established as well loose economic arrangements with its political and security dependencies: Israel, South Korea, Taiwan, and, for the moment, Saudi Arabia. In short, shifts in trading patterns, foreign investment, and financial flows have reinforced the regionalizing tendencies, and the debt problem has further strengthened these polarizing forces. For economic and security reasons, the United States is giving increased and special attention to its own hemisphere and to an as-yet-to-be-defined larger economic orbit.

The third and most amorphous emerging region is that of the Pacific basin or the Asian Pacific. Centered principally upon Japan and its East Asian economic partners, this region includes ASEAN (Indonesia, Philippines, Malaysia, Singapore, and Thailand), Australia, New Zealand, the Asian NICs (South Korea, Hong Kong, Taiwan, and Singapore) and parts of Latin America. The United States, especially the West Coast, has also become a major participant in this fastest-growing economic region. American trade with the nations of the Pacific overtook America's Atlantic trade in 1987 and subsequently has expanded much more rapidly than American trade with the rest of the world.

The Pacific basin in the 1980s became the fastest-growing and foremost trading region of the world.[17] Between 1960 and 1982, the ratio of its exports to world exports doubled; the expansionism has been even more remarkable in manufactured goods.[18] In just the two years from 1982 to 1984, American trade with the region expanded from $126.5 billion or 27.7 percent of total American trade to $169 billion or 31 percent, while two-thirds of Japan's exports go to the United States. But the most notable development of all has been that trade within the region has grown even faster than trade with the rest of the world. This region-

17. Staffan Burenstam Linder, *The Pacific Century: Economic and Political Consequences of Asian-Pacific Dynamism* (Stanford, Calif.: Stanford University Press, 1986).
    18. Ibid., p. 14.

alization has been a function of domestic economic growth, of complementarities of the economies involved, and of the relative openness of these economies.[19] Moreover, this intraregional trade has been shifting from a series of bilateral relationships to a more truly multilateral trading network.[20]

The size and dynamism of the Pacific region are indicative of its increased importance in shaping the future of the international political economy. The ratio of Pacific gross product to Atlantic gross product increased from 40 percent in 1960 to almost 60 percent in 1982. The region's share of global gross product rose in this same period from 16 to almost 25 percent and its ratio to American gross product shot up from 18 to more than 50 percent.[21] In the 1980s, Northeast Asia (Japan, Taiwan, and South Korea) became the electronics capital of the world. Partially reflecting this development, a substantial portion of both American and Japanese direct foreign investment has been in that region. As a distinguished European economist said, "the center of gravity of the world economy is indeed shifting from the Atlantic Basin to the Pacific Basin."[22] As with prior major shifts in the locus of global economic activities, the political consequences of this development will be profound.

The shape and internal relationships of the Pacific region, however, remain unclear, and several important questions have yet to be answered. The first and most critical is whether its two economic giants—the United States and Japan—can continue to be close partners or will become antagonistic rivals. The second concerns how the tension between the complementarity and the competitiveness of the East Asian economies will be resolved. While the complementary factor endowments of Japan, the Asian NICs, and ASEAN could lead to a relatively self-sufficient division of labor in the region, these economies are increasingly also competitive with one another in commodities and manufactured goods in the American and other markets. The third question is whether Japan will exercise economic leadership through such measures as opening its markets to the manufactured goods of its neighbors or exporting its huge capital surplus to China and other regional economies. The answers to these and similar questions will significantly affect the place of this region in the larger world economy.

The developing pattern of trading and investment relations is creating a regional division of labor with Japan and the United States as the two anchors. Whereas Japan is the foremost exporter of consumer goods and importer of raw materials, the American market is a vital element tying the region together. Moreover, American exports of capital and high-technology goods to the developing countries of the Pacific basin and to Latin America are becoming

19. Lawrence B. Krause, "The Structure of Trade in Manufactured Goods in the East and Southeast Asia Region," chap. 8 in *Trade and Structural Change in Pacific Asia*, Colin I. Bradford and William H. Branson, eds. (Chicago: University of Chicago Press, 1987).

20. Hugh Patrick, "The Asian Developing Market Economies—How They Have Affected and Been Affected by the United States-Japan Economic Relationship" (unpublished, 1983), p. 1.

21. Linder, *Pacific Century*, p. 10.

22. Ibid.

increasingly important. Between 1980 and 1985, LDC (less-developed country) exports to the United States increased from 40 to 60 percent of total U.S. imports, and in 1985, the LDCs took one-third of American exports.[23] American exports to the Pacific region rose from 13 percent in 1960 to 25 percent in 1985.[24] This trend will certainly continue.

The boundaries of these three partially coalesced regions are unclear and porous; the membership of the regions overlaps. The trading, financial, and other commercial relations among the regions and especially among the major powers remain strong, yet the lines of demarcation among the regions are discernible and becoming more pronounced with the spread of protectionism and other changes in the world economy. In the mid-1980s the pattern of international trade is strongly characterized by regional constellations.

This tendency toward greater regionalization means that large segments of the human race could be largely excluded from the world economy. The Soviet Union lies outside these regions, and a number of the Eastern European countries, with the failure of the debt-financed industrialization strategy of the 1970s and under the pressure of the Soviet Union, will be only partially integrated. The southern cone (Argentine, Chile, Peru, etc.), and other Latin American countries, which had become integrated into the world economy in the nineteenth century, appear to be falling out of the system.[25] Much of black Africa has become marginalized and is sinking into economic and political despair. Where China, India, and Brazil with their immense potentials will eventually fit is not yet determined. There is a great danger that a more regionalized world economy will be composed of a few islands of relative prosperity in a turbulent sea of global poverty and alienated societies.

A greater regionalization of the world economy also poses a threat to the economic health of the dominant economic powers themselves. If a market or capitalist system is to grow and be prosperous, it undoubtedly has to be outwardly expansive. Economic and technological stagnation result from the closure of an economic system. Considered from this perspective, the growth potential of the emergent high-technology industries of the future can probably be fully achieved only in a truly global economy. The cost of their development and the scale of these technologies necessitate the generation of a level of demand that can be achieved only in an integrated world market.[26]

The dynamic advantages to be gained from economies of scale, from corporate alliances across national boundaries, and from the sharing of technology suggested in the 1980s that sectoral protectionism, particularly in high technology and service industries, will also be a distinctive feature of the emergent international economy.[27] In place of multilateral tariff reductions, governments are

---

23. *The New York Times*, 4 October 1985, p. D1.
24. Linder, *Pacific Century*, p. 78.
25. Norman Gall, "The Four Horsemen Ride Again," *Forbes*, 28 July 1986, pp. 95–99.
26. Yasusuki Murakami and Kozo Yamamura, "Technology in Transition: Two Perspectives on Industrial Policy" (unpublished, 1984).
27. Hugh Patrick and Henry Rosovsky, "The End of Eras? Japan and the Western World in the 1970s–1980s" (unpublished, 1983), p. iv.

increasingly negotiating bilateral arrangements regarding market shares in specific economic sectors, arrangements that reflect the shift away from multilateralism and unconditional reciprocity to bilateralism and conditional
reciprocity.

Sectoral protectionism or what Vinod Aggrawal has called "liberal protectionism" is, of course, nothing new.[28] Nations have long protected particular
economic sectors, such as European and Japanese agriculture. The new element
is the increasing importance, as signified by the rise of the new protectionism, of
negotiating market shares on a sector-by-sector basis. In contrast, the various
rounds of the General Agreement on Tariffs and Trade (GATT) succeeded by
negotiating trade-offs across industrial sectors based on considerations of revealed comparative advantage. For example, concessions by a country in one
sector might be matched by concessions of another country in another sector.
The purpose of sectoral protectionism and "managed trade," on the other hand,
is to divide up individual sectors among various producers.

American and Japanese trade negotiations have become the foremost expression of this move toward sectoral protectionism. In the so-called MOSS
(market-oriented, sector-selective) discussions, the United States tried to decrease Japanese regulatory, tariff, and other import barriers in the sectors of
telecommunications, medical equipment and pharmaceuticals, electronics, and
forest products. Either because of the economic importance or political sensitivity of these sectors, it would have been difficult to take any other approach.

A central cause of the increasing importance of sectoral protectionism has been
that the new technologies associated with the contemporary technological revolution, such as the laser, the computer, and bioengineering, can never achieve
their potential in a fragmented world economy of restricted demand. Just as the
technologies of the second industrial revolution (steel, electricity, the automobile, other consumer durables, etc.) of the late nineteenth century could only
be fully developed in the continental mass market of the United States, the
exploitation of the technologies of the third industrial revolution will also require
the existence of a huge global market. A regionalized world economy composed
of relatively impervious national and regional markets could thwart the emergence of this full technology.

The nature of the contemporary technological revolution also suggests that
sectoral protectionism will be prevalent. The role of basic science has become
increasingly important to the generation and the diffusion of these technologies,
and these novel technologies are frequently neither sector-specific nor do they
provide merely a new product; instead they constitute novel processes, which
are ubiquitous in their effects and cut across the economy, affecting traditional as
well as modern industries. The computer, for example, is transforming all
aspects of economic life from agriculture to manufacturing to office management.

These newer technologies are also very costly to develop. They involve large
economies of scale and will require mass markets to amortize development costs.

---

28. Vinod K. Aggarwal, *Liberal Protectionism: The International Politics of Organized
Textile Trade* (Berkeley: University of California Press, 1985).

This means that there is unlikely to be any clear technological leader, as there has been in the past; instead there will be many centers of innovation and the technology will diffuse rapidly. The importance of these technologies to the wealth, power, and autonomy of national societies means that every state will want to maintain a presence in these technologies.

The rise of sectoral protectionism is associated with the tendency of multinational corporations to invade one another's home markets. A major reason for this cross or reciprocal foreign direct investment has been set forth by Kenichi Ohmae: "In such high-tech industries as computers, consumer electronics, and communications, the rapid pace of product innovation and development no longer allows firms the luxury of testing the home market before probing abroad. Moreover, because consumer preferences vary subtly by culture and are in constant flux, companies must intimately understand local tastes—and react instantly to changing market trends and prices."[29] Ohmae also points out that direct investment will continue to be necessary because insiders have greater immunity from protectionism; further, unless a corporation operates in all three of the regional centers of the world economy, it will not be able to achieve the economies of scale world-class automated plants demand in order to pay for themselves.[30] The new protectionism, the rise of joint ventures across national boundaries, and the like are reflections of the movement toward sectoral protectionism.

Under these conditions, sectoral protectionism has become attractive to governments. It enables them to keep foreign markets open while retaining some control over their own internal markets and establishing a national presence in the sector. Thus they could gain some of the benefits of economic interdependence without the attendant costs of a fully liberalized trading regime.

Although sectoral protectionism departs from the liberal emphasis on economic efficiency and nondiscrimination, it appears to be the only way to satisfy both the need for economies of scale and the desire of governments to possess what they consider to be high employment and strategic industries. Those economies with bargaining leverage, i.e., large internal markets, capital availability, or technological monopolies, would be the major winners through sectoral protectionism.

In the mid-1980s, it is not possible to determine the nature and extent of the industries that will propel economic growth in the advanced economies in the forthcoming era or to project which country or countries will be the winners or the losers in the competition. Would there be, as in the past, a clear technological leader such as Great Britain or the United States or would this leadership role be shared by two or more economies?[31]

Whatever the answer to this question, managed trade, along with mercantilism and regionalism, is a crucial feature of the transformed international

29. Kenichi Ohmae, *Triad Power: The Coming Shape of Global Competition* (New York: Free Press, 1985).
30. Ibid.
31. Angus Maddison, *Phases of Capitalist Development* (New York: Oxford University Press, 1982).

economic order. In a substantial number of economic sectors, world markets are characterized in the mid-1980s by voluntary export restraints, orderly marketing agreements, and reciprocal foreign direct investment. Bilateralism and conditional reciprocity are increasingly important determinants of economic relations.

An international economy based on sectoral protectionism might help to resolve the inherent tension between a liberal world economy and a decentralized state system.[32] By encouraging international joint ventures, establishing linkages among multinationals of different nationalities, and creating crosscutting interests among the three major centers of economic power, sectoral protectionism promises to counter the tendencies inherent in a regionalized system toward destabilizing conflict.

In the emergent configuration of the world economy, what portion of international economic transactions will be governed by mercantilistic competition, by economic regionalism, or by sectoral protectionism? It is too early to determine which tendency will predominate over the others. What can be said is that unless these three elements can be successfully balanced, the danger of severe mercantilistic conflict and destabilizing economic nationalism will surely increase, especially if American hegemony continues to decline and a new basis of international cooperation is not found. These tendencies toward mercantilistic competition, economic regionalism, and sectoral protectionism should not be minimized.

Liberalism and the principles embodied in it tend to depoliticize international economic relations and to protect the weak against the strong. The Most Favored Nation principle, nondiscrimination, and unconditional reciprocity provide as close to an objective basis for judging the legitimacy of economic behavior as may be possible. These principles place constraints on arbitrary actions. In a world of policy competition, regional alliances, and bilateralism, what will be the norms guiding and limiting more managed economic relations? For example, will there be more demands that economies must become more like those of other nations, demands that are similar to the American demands on the Japanese for reciprocity and for greater harmonization of domestic structures?

The attempts of the United States to open foreign markets, privatize other economies, and preserve a liberal economic order all in the name of liberal principles could prove to be counterproductive. The exertion of political pressures on the Japanese to harmonize their domestic structures with those of the West and the aggressive demand for reciprocity could inhibit the search for solutions more in keeping with the new economic and political realities. It would be far better for the United States to follow the European emphasis on sectoral protectionism than to attempt to force open the Japanese economy. As two leading American experts on the Japanese economy, Hugh Patrick and Henry Rosovsky, have pointed out, the Japanese could more easily learn to live with

32. Barry Buzan, *People, States, and Fear: The National Security Problem in International Relations* (Chapel Hill: University of North Carolina Press, 1983) p. 145.

sectoral protectionism.[33] If governments fail to heed this advice, then the present global movement toward benign mercantilism could degenerate into malevolent mercantilism. Uncompromising economic nationalism might become the new international norm, replacing state efforts to work out their economic differences with due regard both to market efficiency and national concerns.

Conclusion

The postwar era is over and the conditions underlying American policies for several decades have dramatically changed, partially as a result of American success. Although Western Europe remains militarily vulnerable and suffers from some real economic difficulties, the effort that began with the formation of NATO and the Marshall Plan has largely succeeded. Japan, despite its economic success, does continue to be vulnerable and overly dependent upon the United States, but it no longer faces a hostile China. In East Asia, the Soviet Union confronts strong powers, the United States, Japan, and China. What was once seen as a monolithic communist bloc has disintegrated and the economic failure of the Soviet system is forcing it, however slowly and reluctantly, to abandon many of its abhorrent features. Yet the United States continues to behave as if its power and wealth were inexhaustible. The fact of relative decline can no longer be denied and new policies must be shaped for a world in which neither the United States nor the Soviet Union is an unchallengeable superpower. The multipolar world foreseen by President Richard Nixon appears at long last to be coming into existence.[34] If the United States is to assume its rightful place in this multipolar system, it must act to stop the relative decline of its economy.

33. Patrick and Rosovsky, "End of Eras?"
34. *The New York Times*, 7 July 1971, p. 16.

6

The United States and the Third World: Decolonization and After

MILES KAHLER

OUR POSTWAR concentration on American rivalry with the Soviet Union has served to obscure the response of the United States to another historical change that accelerated after 1945: the collapse of the European colonial empires and the emergence of scores of independent countries as actors in the international arena. In the long view, that change may prove to be more profound than the Cold War in its effects on the international system.

It took some time for American elites to comprehend the scale and implications of this change, which they could only greet with mixed feelings. For decades, the United States, despite its anticolonial outbursts, could rely upon the exercise of European power in the empires to ensure political stability and the exclusion of unwanted radicalism (linked to Soviet expansion after 1945). The price was economic discrimination against the United States within most of the colonial spheres. After World War II, as its competition with the Soviet Union and China deepened and spread to these regions, the United States, without deep connections to many of the newly independent areas, faced the rapid crumbling of those imperial structures.

The challenge to the European empires from colonial nationalism often presented the United States with uncomfortable choices. The support of its European allies, essential assets in its rivalry with the Soviet Union, was balanced against the need to cultivate the new elites of the developing world. In similar fashion, on the plane of ideology, the professed anticolonialism of the United States had to be weighed quietly against the possibilities of radicalism and disorder that were perceived to benefit its strategic rivals.

In assessing the role of the United States in this international political transformation, observers of American foreign policy demonstrate a surprising divergence of views. One can discern three "lenses" on American policy—Left, Right, and Center—that reach different conclusions concerning the dominant motivations of American policy and the relative importance of the United States in the process of decolonization. In part, the variation among these lenses derives from their selection of cases, and the presentation of the assumptions and logic of each perspective which follows will examine the key cases that are advanced as evidence.

By offering an inclusive interpretation of United States relations with its allies and with the representatives of colonial nationalism, it will be possible to demonstrate that these competing logics still pervade debates over American policy toward the Third World. The lenses are not historical artifacts; each points to persistent patterns and contradictions in American foreign policy toward the developing world.

The Left: The United States as Counterrevolutionary Ally

Viewed through the lens of the Left, American anticolonialism was always more rhetorical than real, and its principal motivation was economic interest—wider access to colonial economies that were shielded from American penetration by mercantilist economic policies. As its conflict with the Soviet Union hardened, the United States stepped back from even its rhetorical endorsements of decolonization. The European economies were held to be the front line of defense against the Soviets; their reconstruction was dependent on rehabilitation of their prewar economies, including the ties between metropole and colonies. A reformed European colonialism seemed more likely to further American economic interests than radical colonial nationalism.

In those cases in which the anticolonial resistance was led by communists, the United States would offer military support to the European colonial powers. As Gabriel Kolko, an exemplar of this view, declares: "If the Left led the independence movement, then the Americans would sustain collaborationists, if possible, or colonialism if necessary."[1] The United States did not argue for the end of informal empires (such as its own sphere of influence in Latin America), particularly if the revised structures of influence provided equal treatment for American economic interests. In short, the Left lens does not take American anticolonialism very seriously. The United States was more interested in the form of imperial control than the fact of that control; it was willing to countenance a continuing role for the imperial powers in containing communist influence. The Left lens orders American preferences as: first, keeping out the

---

1. Gabriel Kolko, *The Politics of War* (New York: Vintage Books, 1986), p. 607.

communists (or the Left); second, opening up the European empires to American economic interests.

This lens, like the others, focuses on certain exemplary cases, and for the Left, Indochina is the prime exemplar. The contrast between American wartime rhetoric and later American behavior is more stark in this case than in any other. The outcome seems to reinforce the view that another path could have been chosen, one less blinkered by anticommunism and more accommodating to colonial nationalism, one that would have spared both the United States and the people of Indochina a disastrous engagement.

President Franklin D. Roosevelt's anticolonial diatribes were most harsh on the subject of French colonialism and the French role in Indochina. In the early years of American involvement in World War II, he declared that any peace settlement should replace the French with an international trusteeship.[2] This anticolonialism of 1942–44 faded even as American power vis-à-vis its European allies grew: the Joint Chiefs of Staff discovered that attacks on colonialism could endanger their plans for the Japanese-held Pacific islands; embarrassing implications could arise for Puerto Rico and the Virgin Islands; and the British (supported by Europeanists in the State Department) made clear that they would reject any concept of trusteeship applied to their own colonies and that they would support the French as a fellow colonial power.[3] Despite FDR's earlier fulminations, the United States did not oppose French reentry into Indochina. As the Cold War unfolded, American interests in Southeast Asia were redefined. By 1946, Ho Chi Minh had been identified by Dean Acheson as a communist linked to Moscow. American military support for the French grew and questioning of French colonialism subsided. The United States accepted the French definition of decolonization—the Bao Dai solution—even though it was a fig leaf for continued French domination.

Through the lens of the Left, the later years of the Cold War provide other examples of the same logic. William Minter has documented American policy toward Portuguese Africa, last of the European colonial empires. The American record displays the same biases: despite the weakness of Portugal and its relatively peripheral role in the NATO alliance, the Kennedy administration's policy of criticizing Portugal in the United Nations and placing restrictions on military assistance and arms sales to Portugal soon became a posture of "quiet diplomacy" that meant very little pressure.[4] During the Nixon administration, policy toward

2. On American wartime policy toward Indochina, see Walter Lafeber, "Roosevelt, Churchill, and Indochina: 1942–45," *American Historical Review* 80 (1975): 1277–95; D. Cameron Watt, *Succeeding John Bull: America in Britain's Place 1900–1975* (Cambridge University Press, 1984), chap. 10.

3. David Reynolds, "The Wartime Anglo-American Alliance," in *The "Special Relationship": Anglo-American Relations since 1945*, Wm. Roger Louis and Hedley Bull, eds. (Oxford University Press, 1986), pp. 27–29; Wm. Roger Louis and Ronald Robinson, "The United States and the Liquidation of British Empire in Tropical Africa, 1941–1951," in *The Transfer of Power in Africa: Decolonization, 1940–1960*, Prosser Gifford and Wm. Roger Louis, eds., pp. 32–40.

4. William Minter, *King Solomon's Mines Revisited: Western Interests and the Burdened History of South Africa* (New York: Basic Books, 1986), pp. 158–62; also John A.

southern Africa swung even more definitely in favor of reducing overt pressure on the Portuguese and the white-ruled regimes. Economic interests in the area played a role in this redefinition.[5]

The Right: The United States as Imperial Rival

The lens of the Right is worn largely by Europeans and is less familiar to most Americans. In this view the United States, mindlessly pursuing an anti-colonialism based on either misguided principles or calculated economic interest, set out to overturn the colonial empires without contemplating the political order that would replace them. In the version propounded by Lord Beloff, "The Pax Britannica had disappeared; the Pax Americana has yet to be made manifest." As a result, the world has "the catastrophe of decolonization," in which "the creation of a series of political voids has produced a time of troubles."[6] D. C. Watt, another British historian who endorses this view, traces American anticolonialism to "naïve populism" and awards it a prominent place in explaining not only outcomes in the Third World but also anti-Americanism in contemporary Europe, which he attributes to national humiliations suffered by the Europeans at the hands of their overbearing ally. The Right's lens refuses to accept the inevitable triumph of colonial nationalism, at least not the militant nationalism that was often awarded the seat of government in the postcolonial era. American anticolonialism was alleged to be founded on a distorted view of the colonial world: awarding the title of "people" to a congeries of conflicting ethnic groups, endorsing nationalist elites who sought only to replace colonialism with their own brand of authoritarianism.[7]

The Right lens focuses on the Middle East. Beloff largely restricts his thesis to that region; the *locus classicus* of the Right perspective is J. B. Kelly's vituperative critique of western policy in the Middle East, *Arabia, the Gulf and the West*, in which he claims that the United States was "so intent upon destroying these interests [those of Britain and France] for reasons of anticolonial sentiment and commercial advantage that she failed to realize the incongruity, let alone the injurious consequences of supporting the British and the French as allies in Europe and harrying them as rivals in Asia."[8]

The power of this point of view in postimperial European conservative circles is strengthened by the continuity of American policy in the region—the United

---

Marcum, *The Politics of Indifference: Portugal and Africa, a Case Study in American Foreign Policy* (Syracuse, N.Y.: Maxwell School and Program of Eastern African Studies, 1972), pp. 3–7.

5. See Anthony Lake, *The "Tar Baby" Option: American Policy Toward Southern Rhodesia* (Columbia University Press, 1976), pp. 123–34, and Mohamed A. El-Khawas and Barry Cohen, eds., *The Kissinger Study of Southern Africa: National Security Study Memorandum 39* (Westport, Conn.: Lawrence Hill and Company, 1976).

6. Lord Beloff, "The End of the British Empire and the Assumption of World-Wide Commitments by the U.S.," in Louis and Bull, *The "Special Relationship,"* p. 252.

7. D. Cameron Watt, *Succeeding John Bull*, chap. 11.

8. J.B. Kelly, *Arabia, the Gulf, and the West* (London: Weidenfeld and Nicolson, 1980), p. 477.

States had demonstrated its sharp elbows even before World War II—and by substantial American oil interests in Saudi Arabia, also in place before the war. After 1945 the United States cooperated with Britain when maintaining British influence served American interests; in other instances, such as American sponsorship of the House of Saud and its territorial claims, conflict between the two allies was apparent. Even in cases of close collaboration, such as the 1953 overthrow of Mosaddeq in Iran, the British complained of the pushy and overly energetic Americans. Anthony Eden knew that if the Americans masterminded the coup, they would exact a price (and did, in ending the British oil monopoly in Iran). He was irked that the Americans "had a desire to reach a quick solution at almost any cost" and "an apparent disinclination to take second place even in an area where primary responsibility was not theirs."[9]

Suez, perhaps the worst conflict to beset the NATO alliance, is the principal case for the Right's lens on American foreign policy. For European nationalists, the refusal of Eisenhower and Dulles to back Britain, France, and Israel in their military intervention against Egypt was a grave error, one whose consequences still plague western policy in the Middle East. Rather than assisting in the elimination of a major threat to western interests in the region (Nasser) and thereby setting back the forces of anti-Western Arab nationalism, the United States condemned the intervention in the United Nations and employed economic weapons (withholding oil and exerting financial pressure) to force the end of military operations. American interpretations, of course, generally reject the Right's lens on the Suez crisis, arguing that Britain and France were undertaking a badly planned expedition to overthrow a popular Arab leader with little thought of what would follow or what the costs to their international and domestic position would be.[10]

American opposition to colonialism of the Victorian variety (a phrase used by Eisenhower) did figure in American motivations. The Third World had become a major international audience, particularly in the United Nations, one that the United States could not leave to the Soviets. In the eyes of Dulles and Eisenhower, the developing countries were rapidly becoming the principal arena of competition in the Cold War. Deciding to turn to the United Nations for a cease-fire during the Suez crisis marshalled Third World support to the side of the United States and separated the Americans (at least temporarily) from the colonial powers. Henry Cabot Lodge, the American ambassador to the United Nations, told the president that there was "tremendous acclaim for the president's policy. Absolutely spectacular."[11]

Soon after the Suez crisis, the Eisenhower Doctrine proclaimed American

9. Cited in Stephen E. Ambrose, *Eisenhower*, vol. 2, *The President* (New York: Simon & Schuster, 1984), p. 110.
10. Compare, for example, the accounts of Watt, "Demythologizing the Eisenhower Era," and Louis, "American Anti-Colonialism and the Dissolution of the British Empire," both in Louis and Bull, eds., *The "Special Relationship*," chaps. 3, 16. On the use of economic instruments by the United States, see Diane B. Kunz, "The Importance of Having Money: The Economic Diplomacy of the Suez Crisis" (unpublished paper).
11. Ambrose, *Eisenhower*, vol. 2, p. 361.

concern over communist infiltration in the Middle East. As a corollary, American hostility toward more discreet European interventions, such as those that the British undertook in Jordan and later in Kuwait, declined. Nevertheless, for many European nationalists, Suez was a turning point, the moment at which Britain and France began their long eviction from the region at the hands of militant nationalism. And the United States, it appeared, had provided a crucial opening for the beginning of that eviction.

The Center: The United States as Anticolonial Spokesman

The lens of the Center is that of many American historians and policymakers: a view that attachment to the principle of anticolonialism was real and had an effect—if not always the dominant effect—on American foreign policy. In the words of William Roger Louis, a historian who exemplifies the Center lens, anticolonialism was not "merely a self-serving or shallow slogan."[12] Although principles were translated into policy, American influence on the course of decolonization itself was not great. The essential game in the transition to independence pitted each colonial power, with its own divided domestic politics, against the nationalists in each colonial possession. With or without American involvement, decolonization would have followed the same course, at the same pace.

The Center lens picks up its image of the American role in decolonization from many of the same cases used by the Left and the Right. One prominent early example of conflict with American allies on the question of decolonization was India. The Center lens, however, illuminates certain dimensions of the conflict between the colonial powers and the United States on the question of self-determination and progress toward independence. During the Congress Party's "Quit India" campaign in 1942, well before the military balance had swung in favor of the allies, the United States exerted considerable pressure on Britain to accelerate the end of colonial rule to the subcontinent, pressure that the British resisted. In Indochina, the Left points to American military assistance to the French; the Center emphasizes that the United States attempted to shift its aid to the associated states—the nominal representatives of the Indochinese peoples—and pressured the French to grant independence to moderate nationalists who could rally their populations against the communist Viet Minh.[13] During the Algerian War, Eisenhower refused to support the French, arguing at one point, "We cannot abandon our old principles of supporting national freedom and self-determination, and we cannot join the colonialists."[14] Although the West German chancellor, Konrad Adenauer, accepted the arguments of the French Right and saw dominoes ready to fall to the communists in North Africa, the American administration refused to accept that forecast. Even in the case of

12. Wm. Roger Louis, "American Anticolonialism," in Louis and Bull, eds., *The "Special Relationship,"* p. 273.
13. R.E.M. Irving, *The First Indochina War: French and American Policy 1945–54* (London: Croom Helm, 1975), pp. 101, 104.
14. Ambrose, *Eisenhower,* vol. 2, pp. 538–39.

Portuguese Africa, the Kennedy administration's mild criticism of Portuguese military action against the Angolan nationalists infuriated the Portuguese government. The United States, while continuing to supply arms to its NATO ally, also maintained discreet contact with and supplied very modest financial support to Holden Roberto, an Angolan nationalist whose ideological coloration found favor in Washington.

Lens and Blinkers: Illumination and Contradiction

Each of these images of American policy toward the Third World during the years of decolonization—the United States as counterrevolutionary ally, the United States as imperial rival, and the United States as anticolonial spokesman—contains a particular assessment of American influence over the process of decolonization. Left and Right agree on the importance of the United States and its ability to influence outcomes (though they disagree on which side the United States should have favored); the Center perceives the American role in more modest terms, not as wholly ineffectual, but apparent principally at the margins. Each of these lenses throws into relief important features of American policy toward the Third World, but each also includes difficult knots in the logic of its arguments.

The Left impresses us with the narrowness of American anticolonialism and underlines the limits that the United States placed on the principle of self-determination. American anticolonialism was always gradualist, even for Roosevelt in his most anticolonial moments. The concept of trusteeship was designed precisely to ensure a gradual transition to independence. Nor did the United States express opposition to informal empire—reliance on systems of influence rather than formal rule. After Suez, it did not oppose Britain's efforts to maintain a reduced sphere in the Middle East; by the mid-1960s, the United States pleaded with the Wilson government to retain British bases and influence east of Suez.

Its own experience and interests determined the American attachment to informal means of influence. Eisenhower and other members of the American elite held up the Philippines as a model for the European colonial powers. The Philippines had been granted formal independence shortly after World War II, but the United States had retained an array of powerful instruments that served to embed its influence in the new state, from the organization of trade relations to military bases.

Nor was there any hint of anticolonialism in our own informal sphere in Central America and the Caribbean. A telling exchange took place in 1954 when the United States orchestrated the overthrow of Guatemalan President Jacobo Arbenz. Britain and France announced that they would support Arbenz in the United Nations. Eisenhower was furious and told his aides that he would teach the Europeans a lesson and show them that "they have no right to stick their noses into matters which concern this hemisphere entirely." He later had UN Ambassador Henry Cabot Lodge inform the allies that "if Great Britain and France felt that they must take an independent line backing the present government in Guatemala, we would feel free to take an equally independent line concerning such matters as Egypt and North Africa."[15] With such a clear declaration of tit for tat, "our sphere for yours," Britain and France decided to abstain at the time of the crucial Security Council vote. One can well imagine their confusion at the time of Suez.

American anticolonialism was also very selective in its choice of nationalist clients in the Third World, and the United States seemed to become even more discriminating over time. Overt communist support for a noncommunist nationalist leader was fatal, as Mosaddeq was to learn in Iran; the Eisenhower administration turned against Sukarno of Indonesia for the same reason. Even in the absence of open communist support, radical nationalists were often suspected of communist leanings; they were perceived as "objectively" (to borrow a Marxist phrase) serving the interests of communism by creating instability and aligning themselves with the Soviet Union. One clear-cut example was Patrice Lumumba, a charismatic nationalist who convinced Eisenhower that he was a Soviet pawn. The United States administration decided to eliminate him, although it is still unclear whether Eisenhower personally ordered his assassination. Before the United States could act, soldiers under the command of General Mobutu murdered Lumumba. American policymakers often seemed to share the assessment given by a British official after World War II: "Clearly Communists always disguise themselves as Nationalists when they can, but this does not make it any easier to decide whether a Nationalist is also a Communist at heart— nor, in the last resort, does it really matter."[16]

Although the Left lens filters out much anticolonial verbiage and demonstrates the limitations of the American opposition to empire, it has a difficult task in assigning economic interest a major share of American motivation. Economic motivations should have produced a more consistent attack on the mercantilist elements of the colonial empires, a thrust that was clear in American postwar planning. Jeffrey Frieden has noted that the changing pattern of American economic interests in the developing world pointed clearly in the direction of support for less formal means of political influence. European capitalist interests on the periphery also shifted toward those less dependent on colonial rule.[17] The American tilt toward its European allies from the late 1940s becomes more difficult to explain. One possibility is to develop a Left lens in which counterrevolutionary ideology is not dependent on a particular definition of economic interests.[18]

The Right lens brings into focus a feature of the postwar international system that Americans often overlook—that superpower competition was not the only

15. Ibid., pp. 195–96.
16. Cited in Gary R. Hess, *The United States' Emergence as a Southeast Asian Power, 1940–1950* (Columbia University Press, 1987), p. 317.
17. Jeffrey Frieden, "The Economics of Intervention: American Overseas Investments and Relations with Underdeveloped Areas, 1890–1950," *Comparative Studies in Society and History* (forthcoming); Miles Kahler, *Decolonization in Britain and France* (Princeton University Press, 1984), chap. 4.
18. This is the approach taken by Michael H. Hunt in *Ideology and U.S. Foreign Policy* (Yale University Press, 1987).

competitive relationship in American foreign policy over the last four decades. The United States, as the new dominant power, was also competing with other capitalist and colonialist countries that were its allies in the Cold War. The Right also emphasizes that the European nations were still powers after World War II. Britain in particular commanded military forces that made it, in the words of John Gallagher, "much the strongest of the middle powers of the world . . . still the rich man in his palace, not the poor man at the gate."[19]

Like the Left, the Right perspective on American foreign policy has difficulty in explaining the wellsprings of an anticolonialism that was directed against its principal allies in an apparently foolhardy way, contrary to the long-run interests of the United States. Accounting for the behavior of an American elite set on a course contrary to the demands of international order and stability (in the eyes of Right critics) requires more than a reference to "populism." American politicians might have had a number of incentives to behave in this way, from the self-interest of segments of American business to electoral considerations that made support for European colonialism difficult or impossible. None of these models of American policy is elaborated in the Right critique. Nor does this perspective, which laments the absence of a Pax Americana to replace the European old order in the Third World, analyze why America failed in that apparently essential endeavor. Either the postcolonial order was not perceived as the disaster proclaimed by these critics or the United States was not so powerful as they allege.

Finally, the Center raises the important possibility that the American role in the drama of decolonization may well have been in fact marginal, that the newly hegemonic power did not control the deeper trends in Europe's relations with its dependent empires. As John Gallagher argues, the pressures that would bring about decolonization had been present in international and domestic political systems since at least the 1920s. Chief among them were changes in colonial politics that made it more and more difficult to find the collaborating elites necessary for imperial rule and rising demands for resources in metropolitan politics that competed with the needs of imperial maintenance. Imperial structures were subject to international pressures as well, among them the policies of the superpowers and the activities of newly independent nations in the United Nations, but it is difficult to establish the relative weight of the international factor in explaining the end of colonial rule after 1945.[20]

The awkward question for centrists in analyzing American policy toward the colonial empires is the significance of anticolonial ideology. While anticolonialism can be detected in many instances of American intervention in decolonization, overall it was remarkably ineffectual in determining the shape of American policy. The Center argues against viewing American attachment to self-determination and the end of colonial rule as mere ideological cosmetics (in contrast to the Left), yet it cannot produce a clear instance in which anticolonial ideology overrode perceptions of strategic necessity or economic interest.

19. John Gallagher, *The Decline, Revival and Fall of the British Empire*, p. 149.
20. Ibid., p. 74.

The Logic of American Foreign Policy in the Third World

Synthesizing a plausible explanation of American policy that spans cases can best be accomplished through three logics of American foreign policy toward the developing world, three decision rules that exercised different degrees of influence over time:

1. To block communism, support European allies.
2. To block communism, support moderate nationalist movements in the colonial empires.
3. To maximize American economic interests, increase American access to markets and raw materials in the colonial empires.

The two anticommunist logics were dominant throughout the postwar period; the weight of American economic interests is difficult to estimate over time because those interests could be maximized in some cases by supporting the European colonial powers against radical nationalists or communists and in other instances by supporting pliable moderate nationalists against mercantilist European colonialists.

The two anticommunist logics competed for influence over American policy, but their relative importance shifted over time, as the American interpretation of its competition with the Soviet Union changed. In the immediate postwar years, as the Cold War began, a central concern—perhaps *the* central concern—of American policymakers was the weakness of the European economies, a weakness that produced the Marshall Plan and the temporary shelving of postwar plans for economic organization (such as the International Monetary Fund) that demanded stronger partners for the American economy. European economic weakness required maintaining ties to the colonial economies as safe havens for European exports, assured sources of raw materials, and, perhaps most important, as earners of dollars for a dollar-scarce European economy.[21] These considerations influenced American policy toward both the Dutch colonial empire and the British position in the Middle East. Since the European theater was regarded as central in the early years of the Cold War, the first logic dominated American policy.

In the last years of the 1940s and particularly after the beginning of the Korean War, the second logic was given pointed expression in a State Department document, PPS 51: "Nineteenth-century imperialism is no antidote to communism in revolutionary colonial areas. It is rather an ideal culture for breeding of the communist virus. The satisfaction of militant nationalism is the first essential requirement for resistance to Stalinism."[22]

---

21. R. F. Holland describes the economic importance of the colonies in a dollar-scarce world in "The Imperial Factor in British Strategies from Attlee to Macmillan, 1945–63," *Journal of Imperial and Commonwealth History* 12 (May 1984): 166–68.
22. Cited in Robert J. McMahon, *Colonialism and Cold War: The United States and the Struggle for Indonesian Independence, 1945–49* (Cornell University Press, 1981), p. 290.

If one discounts the lurid medical imagery, this is a succinct statement of the logic that would drive American policy through much of the 1950s, until a reaction began at the end of the era of decolonization. The power of this second logic explains the turn of American policy toward Indonesia in 1949, when the United States intervened actively in the United Nations and threatened the Dutch with a cutoff of Marshall Plan aid.[23] Competition with the Soviet Union had shifted to Asia and the Third World. Moderate nationalists were seen as competitors with the communists who would overtake them if their demands were not granted; the growing band of independent states condemned the Netherlands and awaited a United States response. The anticommunist bona fides of some anticolonial nationalists were established by their own harsh treatment of local communists. (Repression of a communist-led rebellion at Madium was critical in shaping American perceptions of the Indonesian nationalists, for example.) In addition, by this time, and certainly by the 1950s, the European economies had been strengthened and their own perceptions of the need for colonial spheres, in a more secure multilateral system characterized by growing trade and investment among the industrialized economies, had diminished. (A subsidiary and countervailing consequence of Europe's economic strengthening was a decline in American economic leverage over its allies.)

These perceived changes in the international system and particularly in the arena of competition with the Soviet Union pointed to stronger rhetorical support for colonial nationalism. The United States rarely used direct economic pressure to force a change in its allies' colonial policies, however. (Exceptions include Indonesia, Suez, and possibly the latter stages of the French war in Indochina.) The first logic still set one absolute limit—no military assistance or even economic aid to anticolonial nationalists within a formal colonial empire. The United States continued to recognize the sovereignty of its allies over their empires and to act in accord with that recognition.

The three decision rules award primacy to American strategic goals (anticommunism) and economic interests. The place of ideology, prominent in both Right and Center perspectives, seems to disappear. Yet one can argue that anticolonial ideology did have two effects on American foreign policy. First, it created another set of limits on American action, parallel to the limits established by the first logic (support for European allies). If the American government respected European sovereignty in the colonial empires and rejected direct military or economic assistance to colonial nationalists, anticolonial ideology established a barrier to direct military support for the colonial cause as well. The American government implemented many policy twists and turns to avoid any appearance of contributing militarily to colonial wars in Indonesia, Indochina, or Portuguese Africa.

An even clearer test of this anticolonial limit came in 1954, on the famous "day we did not go to war" in Indochina. President Eisenhower had placed conditions on American military intervention in Indochina that were difficult or impossible

23. Ibid., chap. 8.

to fulfill. At the top of the list was a grant of full independence by the French. In an unpublished portion of his memoirs, Eisenhower declared:

> The strongest reason of all for the United States [to stay out] is the fact that among all the powerful nations of the world the United States is the only one with a tradition of anticolonialism. . . . The standing of the United States as the most powerful of the anticolonial powers is an asset of incalculable value to the Free World. . . . The moral position of the United States was more to be guarded than the Tonkin Delta, indeed than all of Indochina.[24]

Eisenhower's statement suggests that part of the power of anticolonial ideology for the American elite was its perceived utility on the international scene: anticolonialism was one issue on which the United States could comfortably align with the newly emerging nations. A second limit, however, was imposed by domestic politics. Although the American elite could fail to perceive interventions in Guatemala and elsewhere in the hemisphere as "colonial," a war or a deepening indirect intervention in support of a European colonial power would have entailed clear political risks. Following the second Netherlands police action against the Indonesian nationalists, for example, public opinion and congressional pressure would have made a policy of support for the Dutch very difficult to sustain.[25]

The limits set by anticolonial ideology among the foreign policy elite or the public were wide. If American presidents were reluctant to offer open military support to colonial powers, American politics also displayed little positive support for colonial nationalism, support of the kind that could be found in Britain and France on the political left. Two exceptions to this conclusion suggest domestic political reasons for the relative weakness of anticolonialism as a spur to American foreign policy. During World War II, when ideological appeals were necessary to mobilize the population for a costly total war, anticolonial ideology was deemed useful. Roosevelt, for example, alluded clearly to political pressures for extending the principles of the Atlantic Charter to the colonial empires; his contest with Wendell Willkie for the presidency influenced the tough line that was taken initially with Britain on the subject of Indian independence.

The second period of narrower limits began in the 1960s and has recently produced a sea change in the politics of American policy toward southern Africa. After World War II, only one domestic political group was likely to see a clear analogy between its own position and the position of colonial peoples and to act on that perception. Black Americans were most likely to resent and to resist a cardinal principle of formal colonial rule—domination based on race—but black Americans remained disenfranchised in most respects until the 1960s. Only then did the domestic politics of race become entwined with the foreign policy of decolonization in southern Africa, the remaining sphere of "colonial" relations. At first, the foreign implications of our own domestic policies of segregation

24. Ambrose, *Eisenhower*, vol. 2, p. 177.
25. Ibid., pp. 276–77.

Martin Luther King, Jr., in his celebrated 1963 address to thousands at the Lincoln Memorial. Black liberation had its impact on foreign policy, too. (AP/Wide World Photos)

seemed most significant, eroding the moral position claimed by Eisenhower and others, providing an easy mark for European colonialists and Third World radicals. The international implications of segregation could be direct and highly embarrassing for the American government: as a student growing up in Maryland during the early 1960s, I can recall the uproar created when the representatives of new African states were unable to rent a hotel room or enter a restaurant in much of the Washington area.

Although the international implications of racial discrimination worked at first to accelerate racial integration domestically, the enfranchising of black Americans eventually moved foreign policy, culminating in congressional support for broadened sanctions against South Africa in 1986. It was the first time that the second logic of anticommunism had clearly succeeded in influencing American policy toward South Africa—support for moderate nationalism was accepted as the best bulwark against increased communist influence. Black organizations and individuals played a major role in engineering that redefinition.

The United States and the Third World: Conflict in a Postcolonial World

With relatively orderly decolonization in sub-Saharan Africa and the French departure from Algeria, American relations with colonial nationalists, now often

Communist China's Chou En-lai *(left)* and Egypt's Nasser *(center, in military uniform)* at the 1955 Bandung Conference, a milestone in the creation of the "non-aligned" bloc of states. (UPI/Bettmann Newsphotos)

the leaders of new states, entered a brief era of good feelings. The Kennedy administration, despite its compromises with Portugal's imperial ambitions, was in many respects a honeymoon in American relations with much of the newly independent, postcolonial world. Kennedy himself seemed to identify with the aspirations of the new elites in Africa and Asia, and his administration set out to repair relations with regimes whose nonalignment had grated on John Foster Dulles.

The brief era of good feelings did not last. By the early 1970s, the United States had entered a period of estrangement from the developing countries that has persisted into the 1980s. Quite simply, American hopes for moderate postcolonial nationalism in the Third World—hopes derived from logics two and three—were disappointed in the years after decolonization, as they were bound to be.

Although most new nations embraced the principles of nonalignment, each American administration in its turn was to discover that nonalignment often failed to incorporate the aims of American foreign policy. John Lewis Gaddis has noted that "for the Eisenhower Administration the means of channeling nationalism into reliably anti-communist directions never quite seemed to be at hand."[26] Since the time of Arbenz and Nasser, it had been clear that developing nations would turn to the Soviet bloc for aid and support, including military support, to satisfy their own external goals or to meet a perceived American tilt

26. John Lewis Gaddis, *Strategies of Containment* (New York: Oxford University Press, 1982), p. 177.

toward their regional opponents. Thus, Syria, India, and other Third World states developed close military ties with the Soviet Union, to the irritation of American policymakers. No American administration has had any greater success than its predecessors in directing nationalism into channels congenial to the United States. American attitudes toward European involvement in the Third World changed dramatically as a result: any hint of rivalry disappeared as the United States nagged its allies for greater participation in areas outside central Europe and northeast Asia. France's role in sub-Saharan Africa was applauded; Britain's withdrawal from the east of Suez was resisted.

More significant in shaping the attitudes of a wider foreign policy audience in the United States were American attachments to a number of states that were viewed as pariahs in the postcolonial political universe. Increasingly, the United States faced hostile majorities and occasionally humiliating defeats in the United Nations over Taiwan (before Nixon's abrupt turn toward normalization with the People's Republic of China), South Africa, and most significantly, Israel. On the question of Israel, the rift between a broad consensus of the American elite and the majority of developing states became a chasm. Many developing countries chose to see Israel as a remaining colonial outpost in illegitimate occupation of the West Bank and Gaza; the United States esteemed Israel as an old and loyal ally, a lonely democracy in a chaotic and hostile region. Perhaps no other single issue has been as significant in alienating American policymakers and intellectuals from the aims of the developing nations.

Economic expectations were also disappointed. Instead of capitalist and open economies, the postcolonial elites often chose, as had nationalists in the past, a course of state-directed economic development and highly selective involvement with the international economy. By the 1970s, that inward-looking domestic program of industrialization was translated into a program for a new international economic order that would increase both the developing countries' influence over the international economic rules of the game and collective governmental intervention in economic transactions. Economic trends in the United States were running against this current, and the election of Ronald Reagan confirmed American opposition to any program in line with the developing countries' goals.

Finally, far harder to calculate or investigate has been a growing public disenchantment with postcolonial outcomes—political, economic, and social. Rather than the next cohort in liberalism's triumphant historical march, the developing countries by the 1970s presented at best a depressing and at worst an alarming spectacle to many American observers. Democratic regimes were on the retreat (at least until Latin America's democratization in the 1980s); human rights violations were widespread and shocking in their scale; the economic promise of the 1960s dissolved into inflation, debt, and decline in large expanses of the developing world. Viewed in this way, much of the Third World came to be seen by some as a likely ally of American adversaries and an unlikely partner in liberal political and economic projects.

That fatigue and the disappointment of American goals for the postcolonial world led directly to debates over American policy toward the developing countries in the 1980s, echoing arguments that had been made in evaluating American policy during the earlier period of decolonialization. The Right and the

Center/Left perspectives confronted one another in the altered and obscure terrain of an increasingly heterogeneous developing world.

The Center and Left have tended to portray international conflicts and internal turmoil in the Third World as resulting from superpower intervention or the lingering effects of colonialism. Conflict resolution in the Third World should be based on regional balances and regional security arrangements; the Center and Left implicitly assume that nationalist ambitions are satisfied and that excluding the superpowers will reduce or eliminate conflict. If domestic disorder and misery occur, it can be written off to the pains of state-building or to the consequences of inevitable revolutionary change.

Much of the American Right looks at the postcolonial world and sees the hand of Soviet intervention in political turmoil. That globalist argument is a less profound challenge to the opposing view than another, far more pessimistic, Right perspective that, like Lord Beloff, sees a string of catastrophes: international conflict, such as the bloodletting between Iran and Iraq (which has claimed half a million lives) or domestic horrors, a lengthening list that includes Cambodia, Lebanon, and Ethiopia. This image of Third World disorder refuses to accept the inevitability of such events and declines to attribute them to the aftereffects of colonialism or to the consequences of superpower competition. No, the Right argues, such disorder is the result of a loss of legitimate international order and a denial of necessary international hierarchy. The nationalism of developing countries may be as predatory as other nationalism and that nationalism has been permitted free sway by powers that should have taken on the responsibility for maintaining international order but have not done so.

The Blimpish recommendations of the Right, as exemplified by J.B. Kelly, need not be accepted to accept that at least part of the diagnosis is correct: much of the Third World does suffer from the destruction of an old international order that has not been replaced. In their pleas for understanding revolutionary nationalism, the Left and the Center have refused to address cases in which that nationalism has been as malign as any in the past. Nor have they dealt effectively with the issue of a legitimate international order and the possible need for hierarchy in an anarchic system. The questions of Hobbes have been neglected in the quest for liberation. Much misery has been excused in the name of an attachment to self-determination that often represents an irresponsible attitude of moral laissez-faire toward the developing countries.

The Left and the Center have their own challenge to fling at the Right, a Right that includes a segment of American conservatives with great faith in the possibility of halting almost any political change with the proper application of force. If the Left and Center have slighted the question of order, the Right has sidestepped the need for *legitimate* order. The key to the Right perspective is the notion that the colonial empires (and other international structures of the past) did not crumble inevitably but rather through a failure of will on the part of the colonial powers.[27] Their lens denies legitimacy to the colonial nationalists, whose political base is alleged to have been unrepresentative at best, a protection

27. "[T]he crucial fact that the collapse of the European empires in Asia and Africa was due less to the might of the anti-colonialist forces than it was to the sapping of the European powers' will to rule." (J.B. Kelly, *Arabia, the Gulf, and the West*, p. 502).

racket at worst. A few more gunboats, another whiff of grapeshot, and the facade of nationalist insurgency would have crumbled. This argument is parallel to conservative arguments in the United States regarding the utility of force in shoring up crumbling authoritarian regimes in Nicaragua, Iran, and elsewhere. There is little evidence that this scenario would have succeeded in most colonial situations (many colonial powers did not hesitate to use military force against their opponents) or would succeed in the contemporary Third World. Available collaborating elites are few and insubstantial politically; new nationalist elites could raise the costs of colonial rule beyond levels of the past.

In the postcolonial world, however, we have a harder and harder time identifying inevitable political change. Are secessionist movements inevitably successful? Are all self-identified revolutionary movements heralds of a future political order? Those of the Left and Center who espouse the good liberal principle of self-determination are a bit like Marxists confronting fascism in the 1930s: the available template does not equip one to interpret the new reality. Still, in grappling with that contemporary confusion and attempting to identify necessary and desirable change, those old templates are more likely to be of help than the Right's resolute insistence on forceful resistance to changes that appear threatening to American interests, whether those changes appeal to some widely shared notion of legitimacy or not.

In the efforts of the United States to meet both the need for a legitimate international order in a world of many states and the need to accommodate that order to inevitable political change, one can easily perceive the bridge between the era of decolonization and our own era. Perhaps no country or international order has ever effectively or for very long managed to avoid the oscillation between inflexible and brittle structures of domination and periods of wild and destructive disorder. And perhaps the United States could convince itself that the circle need not be squared by withdrawing from its involvement in the developing countries, by insisting that the glittering prizes of international competition lie, as many realists have claimed in the past, with Europe, Japan, and the other industrialized countries. It is difficult to imagine that the United States could live with those assumptions for very long, however. The fate of the developing countries, those diverse and unpredictable heirs to centuries of European domination, will necessarily concern any country that pretends to the status of Great Power. Whether it is an unfortunate and mistaken infatuation with empire, as some on the Left would allege, or a necessary and commendable search for a new order, as others in the Center and Right would maintain, America's often painful engagement with the developing countries is likely to continue. And the contours of our debate over that engagement are likely to remain those that emerged as the United States faced the demise of much older empires and the disorderly birth of new states.

PART III

FITTING THE MANY PARTS
INTO A WHOLE

7

The United States and
Western Europe

MARIO ZUCCONI

BITTER tensions juxtaposed against a preeminent interest in unity have characterized U.S.–Western European relations in recent times. Disagreement and
harsh competition between the two sides of the Atlantic have intensified and
spread to practically all dimensions of that relationship—economic, security,
policy toward Eastern Europe, crises in other regions. In each case, however, an
overriding need to stick together seems to compel the two sides to compromise
and to accommodate each other's positions and interests. In the early 1980s on a
hot issue such as the deployment of new intermediate-range forces (INF), the
Western Europeans accepted the more rigid U.S. position. Washington at the
same time receded from its attempt to impel the allies into a new Cold War
against the Soviet Union.

Adjusting to one another's position has been far from a painless process.
Bitterness and resentment directed at the other side accompanied such an
adjustment. In the early 1980s, West European resentment was intense for
having to yield to what was seen as Washington's exploitation of European
security to change the military and political balance with the Soviet Union—
resentment at being treated, in the words of the then chairman of the German
Social Democratic Party Willy Brandt, "like a colony." Charges of strategic
dilettantism and ineptitude, of ideologism, and of infatuation with military power
were directed at Washington. Those charges were mirrored by widespread anger
in the United States over what was termed European unreliability and in-

gratitude, and the inability of the allies to look beyond their narrow interests and acknowledge the threat of Soviet power on the global level. Although the overall relationship has smoothed out in the last two or three years, it is important to recall here those critical moments as reminders of the paramount interest of both sides in remaining united. Indeed, the relationship seems today as central to the policies of both sides of the Atlantic as it has been for the past forty years.

Disagreements bring American resentments to the surface and make threats of reprisal more explicit. In the midst of the transatlantic quarrel over European cooperation in the building of the Soviet pipeline, U.S. political scientist Robert W. Tucker pointed out the central feature of the "contract" originally established between the United States and its European allies. There had always been a "right," wrote Tucker, that followed from the U.S. "duty" of protecting the allies. "It was that Western Europe's human and political resources, on behalf of which we had extended our protective mantle, would not be placed at the disposal of the Soviet Union through the voluntary action of those to whom we had promised our protection." Disregard for that right, warned Tucker, could seriously weaken the United States' "principal incentive" for retaining the alliance.[1]

Like differences over relations with the East, the more recent European reluctance to help the United States patrol the Persian Gulf and what are seen as unfair trade practices have reawakened in Congress the question of allied "burden sharing"—the allegedly disproportionately large American contribution to the collective defense—with charges of European "free riding." (The same charges have been leveled at Japan and South Korea.) More than thirty measures to reduce the troop levels in Europe were introduced in Congress during 1987, a peak year.[2] Before withdrawing from the presidential race in the fall of 1987, Representative Pat Schroeder had picked that as a central issue for her campaign. In May 1987, when presenting a bill that linked import duties imposed on the allies to the difference between European and U.S. defense expenditures, she noted, "It is clear to me that if we want our allies to help more with the common defense we have to do more than plead and threaten. We have to force them to take over their own territorial defense."

Despite the growing support these positions have found in recent times, the United States appears to be far from folding its protective mantle. Even more than its predecessor, the Reagan administration took considerable pains to shield the allies from those charges. The 1987 *Department of Defense Report on Allied Contribution to the Common Defense* (a report prepared annually since 1981

1. Robert W. Tucker, "The Atlantic Alliance and Its Critics," in *The Atlantic Alliance and Its Critics*, eds. Robert W. Tucker and Linda Wrigley (New York: Prager, 1983), pp. 176–77. Given the character of this essay, references to documentary sources have been reduced to a minimum. Most of the documents of the late 1940s and early 1950s this essay refers to are reproduced in the series *Foreign Relations of the United States*, published by the Department of State, Washington D.C., in the volumes relevant to the given date. Other sources are mentioned in the footnotes.
2. See David C. Morrison, "Slashing Nato's Burden," *National Journal*, 30 May 1987. For more on the issue of allied burden sharing discussed in the last section of this essay, see Simon Lunn, *Burden-Sharing in NATO*, Chatham House paper No. 19, Royal Institute of International Affairs (London: Routledge and Kegan Paul, 1983).

" *1950, '51, '52, '53 ...... '68, '69, '70, '71 ...* "

The American feeling that Europeans are not contributing their fair share to NATO has been around for a long time. (John Fischetti, *Chicago Daily News*, 1971. With permission of the Chicago Sun-Times, Inc., 1988.)

under congressional mandate) tries to justify most of the quantitative disparities that exist between the U.S. share of the common defense and that of its European allies. For some important indicators, the report finds that "our NATO allies and Japan compare well with the United States." If in 1984 Senator Sam Nunn's troop reduction amendment came close to being approved on the Senate floor, most of the dozens of other similar legislative measures proposed in recent years were never discussed even at the committee level. Considering the 1987 defense authorization bill, the House of Representatives rejected three amendments that called for a reduction in U.S. military personnel stationed overseas. On that same occasion, it approved an amendment by Representative Bill Richardson barring any reduction of troops in Europe for 1988.

Indeed, the fear that tampering with existing arrangements within the alliance would make U.S. foreign policy move into the unknown has surfaced continuously in congressional debates. During the May 1987 floor debate on troop withdrawal and allied burden-sharing, Representative Beverly B. Byron observed, "National security is too important to hold hostage to trade concerns."

The same feeling also arises on the European side. With the exception of France in the 1960s, Western European bitterness and resentment has never come close to causing a break or even a substantial rearrangement of the Atlantic relationship. In fact, safeguarding the U.S. connection still appears to be a fundamental interest and a conditioning factor in European politics. At a critical moment Christian Democratic leader Helmut Kohl found support from a majority in West Germany in 1982 and 1983 over the issue of the deployment of the new INF. There was grave concern then in Germany that to resist such deployment would have put the vital American connection at risk.

The tensions and difficulties as well as many of the arguments presented by both sides of the transatlantic debate seem to reflect a divergence of interests and changes in the historical conditions that originally brought the United States and the Western Europeans together. In the context of a rapidly changing international system, of changes in the power, influence, and real roles of the countries of the Atlantic community, on the one hand, and of the immobility of the Atlantic institutional arrangement on the other, transatlantic discord and difficulties are unavoidable. Yet the basic understanding, the mutual expectations, and even the political culture associated with the relationship on both sides of the Atlantic have remained the same, and there is a great reluctance to introduce change. Indeed, international conditions and domestic factors in the Atlantic countries seem to combine in explaining both the institutional immobility and the growing Atlantic difficulties. This essay attempts to put those two issues into better focus by looking at the history of U.S.–Western European relations.

The Projection of U.S. Power toward Europe

From the moment U.S. leaders decided that a German victory over Britain (not a remote possibility at the end of 1940) would be intolerable for America, they started down the road that made Western Europe central to the strategy of global order that they were gradually to develop. Continued U.S. participation in the balance of power in Europe was to become, shortly after the war, the first condition for the establishment of that international stability that they deemed essential to the security and prosperity of America. Although different foreign policy perspectives would surface in the earlier postwar period, the preeminent interest of both the United States and Western Europe was the same.

The strategic importance of an independent Europe for American security and prosperity was frequently emphasized by U.S. officials in the early postwar years. In April 1947 the Joint Chiefs of Staff saw the countries of the "old world" as "potentially powerful and also potential allies of the United States." In September 1948 George Kennan defined the main strategic lines of an emerging global policy by identifying "five centers of industrial and military power which are important to us from the standpoint of national security." These five centers were the United States, Great Britain, Germany and Central Europe, Japan, and the Soviet Union, with only the latter then hostile to the United States.[3] And in 1951 Secretary of State Dean Acheson again emphasized the strategic importance of Europe before a Senate that was reluctant to accept a policy committing American troops to the defense of the continent. "Outside of our own country," Acheson testified during the hearings on troop deployment, "free Europe has the greatest number of scientists, the greatest industrial production and the largest pool of skilled manpower in the world. Its resources in coal, steel and

3. Quoted and discussed in John Lewis Gaddis, *Strategies of Containment: A Critical Appraisal of Postwar American National Security Policy* (New York: Oxford University Press, 1982), p. 30.

electric power are enormous. It has a tremendous ship-building capacity, essential to control of the seas. Through its overseas connections it has access to a vast supply of raw materials which are absolutely vital to American industry."[4]

Was the rationale presented by Kennan and Acheson sufficient to explain not only the original choice to project American power toward Europe, but also the permanence of that same projection and the continuous heavy investment of U.S. resources in the following decades? The importance of having major economic powers not weighing against the United States in the world balance was then and has remained an important factor in Washington's strategic calculation. But in the following decades, what would be considered a vital "power center" would greatly change, and that concept would be applied to more than the five centers mentioned by Kennan in 1948. Middle Eastern oil would supplant the importance of central European coal, and steel and ships would come to be produced and built more efficiently in the Pacific by newly industrialized countries.

In fact, a simple computation of geopolitically important areas falls short of explaining the centrality of the European relationship for postwar U.S. foreign policy and the extraordinary investment American leaders would make in order to build and maintain that relationship. Looking at the issue from the perspective of the four and a half decades since the Second World War, the European relationship assumes a broader significance in the context of America's developing global foreign policy.

Central to that policy was the ability to condition the postwar international order once the carving out of an exclusive area of interest in Eastern Europe on the part of the Soviet Union made the original plan for a "one world" system unworkable. The control of Western Europe was the most important road open to the United States, short of an all-out elimination of the Soviet problem. And the pursuit of such a goal led U.S. policy to meet the basic political interests that the Western European countries were beginning to identify in the new, postwar international arrangements.

That common interest with Western Europe was crucial to the development of a new policy of world order. It was to supply essential international support to the expanding international role of the United States in years when the United Nations was becoming a moribund institution. "Containment" of the Soviet Union—the central strategy of U.S. foreign policy—found its first and most important arena in Europe. And the application of that strategy to other regions could be based on the same assumptions as the defense of Europe.

Moreover, in 1945 Western Europe still controlled vast areas of the nonindustrialized world. And while renouncing the "one world" conception of the international system, American leaders began to have second thoughts about the desirability of quickly demolishing the residues of the European empires. "When the threat of Russia became ominous," concludes Wm. Roger Louis in a study of U.S. policy toward the British Empire, "the watchword 'security' began

4. See U.S. Senate, Committees on Armed Services and Foreign Relations, *Assignment of Ground Forces of the United States to Duty in the European Area*, Joint Hearings, Washington, D.C., 1951.

to eclipse 'independence.' In the colonial question this transformation [of the U.S. position] is especially noticeable in the spring of 1945."[5] At the United Nations San Francisco Conference, the fear of a Soviet intrusion into North Africa made the United States resuscitate Italy as the trustee for Libya. And in the early 1950s, French fighting in Indochina and the British military role in the Middle East would be aided and supported by Washington as a sort of burden sharing among the western allies.

It is in the context of historical factors like these that the centrality of Europe in U.S. foreign policy can be better understood. Of course, motivations for that relationship would in part change in the following decades. This historical background, however, helps to explain why that relationship remained central to the foreign policies of both the United States and the Western European countries. Among other reasons, that relationship would remain a function of the basic feature of the postwar international system—the division of the world into two rival blocs.

The Atlantic Community: The Permanent U.S. Entanglement in European Affairs

The paramount importance of the European question for evolving American foreign policy in the early postwar years is not sufficient to explain how the United States became permanently committed to supporting Western Europe militarily. Other options were open to the leaders of Western Europe to ensure the security of their countries. In fact, for a number of years American leaders viewed U.S. involvement in the affairs of the old continent as temporary—as a surrogate power offered to Europe while it recovered its strength and its ability to stand on its feet. It is rather in the context of the growing political interdependence between the two sides of the Atlantic that Western Europe became permanently dependent on the United States for its security and the United States became permanently entangled in European affairs.

The main steps that led to the formation of an Atlantic community are well known. The assistance extended to Greece and Turkey in early 1947 may be seen as a first move toward stabilizing the situation in Europe. Then came the European Recovery Program, linked to the need to unify the three western zones of Germany, followed by the creation of the NATO military alliance between the two sides of the Atlantic, the stationing of U.S. ground forces in Europe as a guarantee of the U.S. commitment to the defense of the continent, and the rearmament of West Germany and its integration into the North Atlantic Treaty Organization.

It should be stressed that these measures were not the implementation of a single, well-thought-out plan devised when containment became the central

5. Wm. Roger Louis, *Imperialism at Bay: The United States and the Decolonization of the British Empire, 1941–1945* (New York: Oxford University Press, 1978), p. 568. This work is an excellent analysis of the evolution of the U.S. position with regard to the colonial question.

strategy of U.S. foreign policy. They originated from the interacting of U.S. and Western European interests. Indeed some of these steps defeated the goals that one or the other party had originally attached to the development of the relationship. That was the case, for example, with regard to the recovery of Germany, which was intended at first as a way to permit the disengagement of the United States from Europe, but in fact contributed to the continuance of its presence there.

Already in 1946 the Truman administration saw that the United States could not guarantee the security of a divided Germany nor could it shoulder the related economic burdens for the indefinite future. Accordingly, the economic recovery of Germany became the cornerstone of a strategy that sought to strengthen Europe as the first bastion of containment.[6] The April 1947 Memorandum of the Joint Chiefs of Staff had stated the case clearly: "The economic revival of Germany is . . . of primary importance from the viewpoint of United States security."[7]

Such plans, however, touched the raw nerves of European preoccupations with German recovery. Many of the decisions of the United States that led to the creation of the Atlantic community may be traced back to the need to reconcile plans for Germany with the concerns and political vulnerabilities of the countries of Western Europe, and above all France. Thus, policymakers sought to embed Germany in the collective arrangements in which U.S. participation would allay other countries' fears. Such considerations led Secretary of State George Marshall to what became the European Recovery Program. It was after returning from the Moscow Conference of April 1947, where the stalemate on German reunification made him focus on a plan for merging the western zones, that Marshall instructed the Policy Planning Staff to prepare a report on European recovery.

The recovery and, after the summer of 1950, the rearmament of Germany also weighed heavily in the debate over U.S. adherence to the alliance and the need to contribute American ground forces in Europe. U.S. military presence there was important above all to the French, and on that issue the Truman administration had been ready to assure the French as far back as 28 February 1948 following the Prague coup. Marshall wrote then to his representative at the London Six-Power Conference on Germany: "The French are secure against Germany as long as occupation continues. . . . As long as European communism threatens U.S. vital interests and national security we can ill afford to abandon our military position in Germany. . . . The logical conclusion is that three power occupation may be of unforeseeable and indefinite duration, thus offering protracted security guarantees and establishing a firm community of interests."[8]

---

6. Timothy Ireland, among others, emphasizes the German question as a cause for the entanglement of the United States in European affairs. Timothy P. Ireland, *Creating the Entangling Alliance: The Origins of the North Atlantic Treaty Organization* (Westport, Conn.: Greenwood Press, 1981).

7. United States Department of State, *Foreign Relations of the United States*, 1947, vol. 1, p. 740.

8. *Foreign Relations of the United States*, 1948, vol. 1, p. 101.

Nobody Is Happy

What to do about Germany? A question shaping attitudes and actions in both East and West in the early postwar years. (Burt R. Thomas. Reprinted with permission from *The Detroit News,* a Gannett newspaper, 1949.)

Furthermore, by committing the United States to the principle of the peace-time alliance through the Vandenberg Resolution (11 June 1948), Washington gained French approval of a plan to merge the three western zones of Germany. In the debate over the North Atlantic Treaty the U.S. Senate recognized European fear of Germany as the justification for the exceptional commitment the United States was making. As John Foster Dulles put it before the Foreign Relations Committee, the alliance with the United States "will superimpose upon the Brussels Pact another western unity that is bigger and stronger, so that it does not have to fear the inclusion of Germany."[9] The need to reassure the French became even stronger when the North Korean invasion of South Korea put the question of German rearmament at the center of American European policy. In a 29 November 1950 letter, asking his French counterpart, Robert Schuman, to accept German cooperation in defense, Marshall's successor, Dean Acheson, noted that the United States had given "every evidence in statements, action and treaties, of the depth and permanence of its interest in Europe . . . of its willingness to cooperate with Europe."[10] Finally it is worth remembering that an important factor contributing to the defeat of the European Defense Community (EDC) plan by the French National Assembly in August 1954 was the

9. See U.S. Senate, Committee on Foreign Relations, *The North Atlantic Treaty,* Hearings, Washington, D.C., 1949, pt. 1.
10. *Foreign Relations of the United States,* 1950, vol. 3, p. 498.

French fear that Washington intended in this way to relieve itself of the burden of European security.

This is not to suggest that the emerging role of the United States in Europe depended solely on the need to accommodate French and other European interests. The arrangement that took shape between the two sides of the Atlantic derived from a complex interaction of the two sides, as well as from the evolution of international relations overall. In fact, the United States maintained most of the initiative while gradually centering its strategy on Europe.

Considering France's obsession with Germany even in 1948 as "outmoded and unrealistic," Washington looked to a larger European entity, including Germany and Great Britain, to form a western alignment against the Soviet Union. And things worked out that way. After the defeat of EDC, Paris had no choice but to accept the integration of Germany into NATO as the United States had demanded.

No less important was the influence that the U.S. intervention into European affairs and the global polarization of power exercised over the selection of domestic options in the European countries. The "special relationship" with the United States was unchallenged in British politics as being essential to Britain's economic viability. To many it was also the only means London had to maintain some measure of international influence. In countries such as Belgium or Norway, where wartime German occupation had discredited the neutralist option, participation in a western alliance gained acceptance as the crucial alternative.

Besides considering the United States essential for the balance of power in Europe, Paris badly needed American military aid if it was to keep control of important dependent areas such as Indochina. In France more decisively than in Italy, the benefits produced by the Atlantic connection rapidly reduced the influence of the Communists—the strongest party in the 1945 and 1946 national elections. And in Germany, while Schumacher's Social Democratic Party pursued the impossible goal of German unification through neutralization and thus offered only resentment toward the occupying powers, the Christian Democrats reaped the benefits of integration into the new geopolitical reality—fast economic recovery and a new legitimacy and respectability that came with being on the right side of a widening global struggle. Moreover, the Cold War context made it easier for German supporters of the American policy to blame the Soviets for the continued division of Germany.

Thus, the late 1940s and early 1950s brought about a gradual evolution of the policies of both the United States and the Western European countries around the need for a strong and cohesive western community. And that community in turn developed a "division of labor," an arrangement by which, first of all, the United States ensured the security of Europe. Thus European dependence and a permanent U.S. presence in Europe were institutionalized.

The Division of Labor within the Atlantic Community

If one were to cite a single factor that most contributed to making the U.S. commitment to the defense of Europe a fixed feature of U.S.–Western European relations, it would be the decision to entrust that defense to nuclear weapons. It was reliance on those weapons and the ensuing strategic arms race between the United States and the Soviet Union that brought about a division of labor in the security relation between the two sides of the Atlantic. The shape that Atlantic relations thus acquired would be very hard to change thereafter.

Heavy reliance on nuclear weapons came about as a substitute for conventional forces. Following the 1951 debate on the stationing of ground forces in Europe, the U.S. Senate had insisted that the American commitment be linked to evidence of a European "major contribution to allied ground forces," but this did not happen. At their February 1952 Lisbon meeting, the NATO defense, foreign, and finance ministers had decided upon the exact contribution (subdividing an established total of fifty divisions) each allied country was to make. The Lisbon goals, however, were never met—and that brought the alliance into a new phase. Abandoning the costly conventional option, the allies had accepted by 1954 the money-saving device of relying on U.S. strategic superiority, on the threat of "massive retaliation," as the basis for their deterrent posture. This had enormous consequences.

That choice constrained the alliance to mortgage its strategy to nuclear weapons. It created a new, inescapable, and potentially permanent dependence of Western Europe on the United States (the strategic arms race between the superpowers excluded the Europeans from that military competition), and consequently made the problem of a military balance in Europe a function of the military balance between the superpowers. Western European countries grew accustomed to living with a security deficit—to becoming, in a way, "semistates" that delegate their territorial defense to the United States.

That distinction of roles became difficult to change later on because it substantially conditioned the evolution of domestic policies in the Western European countries and of political expectations in the United States. It contributed also to shaping the patterns of resource allocation in the allied countries. And it created in the United States a conception of the alliance as a unilateral gift to the Europeans. There was thus a consequent expectation of gratitude, of solidarity, and even of political submissiveness. The reasons for which the United States had projected its power toward Europe and committed itself to the security of the continent in the first place became obscured in the American political consciousness.

Herein lay the roots of the gravest tensions that would beset the alliance in the early 1980s. The United States always considered Europe one of the theaters of global struggle with the Soviet Union. To the Western Europeans, however, their problem remains solely European, and subject to change with changing political relations in Europe. In such circumstances an incongruity could develop between the military order (which is dependent on the superpower competition) and the continental political order, and thus create serious difficulties in U.S.–Western European relations.

The nuclear solution chosen in response to the problem of European security does not give the whole picture of the transatlantic relationship that took shape in the first decade after the Second World War. A similar distinction of roles also grew up in relation to the problem of political control over the nonindustrialized world.

The United States had fought the war with the objective of establishing a different world order, one that would do away with the hierarchical system of prewar international relations. And U.S. leaders knew that they had the power to influence the evolution of that order. In a memorandum he wrote in early March 1947 (London had already asked Washington to take over in helping the conservative forces in Greece), Under Secretary of State for Economic Affairs William Clayton made three points: (1) Great Britain was fast losing the reins of world leadership; (2) either the United States or the Soviet Union would pick up those reins; (3) it was necessary for the United States to do so in order to avoid another war. Clayton had clearly seen the direction in which the situation would develop.

Although the United States was beginning to substitute for or supplement British and French power in a number of areas (Greece and Turkey and the Middle East are early cases), it would have been difficult for the United States to disregard European interests and implement a broad plan of international control. There were limits, moreover, to how far the United States could extend itself in policing the world, and, as we have seen, European control of the nonindustrialized world could be counted on as part of containment. A National Security Council report (of 13 February 1952) even speaks of the need "to oppose a French withdrawal" should the French no longer be willing "to carry the burden in Indochina."

The political effectiveness of the old European powers was declining when the demand for independence in the colonial areas was growing. Eisenhower recalled the problem in his memoirs: "Delay or equivocation in implementing complete independence could only serve to bolster the Communist claim that this was in reality a war to preserve colonialism. . . . It was almost impossible to make the average Vietnamese peasant realize that the French, under whose rule his people had lived for some eighty years, were really fighting in the cause of freedom."[11]

Decolonization, greatly spreading the influence of the Soviet Union, presented U.S. leaders with the problem of finding an appropriate strategy for maintaining western influence. Decolonization compelled the Atlantic community to adjust to the reality of a worldwide polarization of power. And it was the challenge of nationalism and of the Soviet Union in the Third World that again aroused the anticolonial impulse in U.S. leaders and made them take over from the Western Europeans the struggle for the control of the dependent areas. The Suez crisis in the fall of 1956 is the most dramatic moment of this clash between the United States and its allies.

When France and Great Britain joined Israel in the attack against Egypt with the aim of toppling Nasser, the Eisenhower administration did not hesitate to uphold international law and to challenge what it considered the obsolete

---

11. Dwight D. Eisenhower, *The White House Years*, 2 vols. (Garden City, N.Y.: Doubleday, 1963), p. 337.

policies of its best European friends. Secretary of State Dulles stated clearly the U.S. case at the National Security Council meeting that was to decide what stand to take at the United Nations:

> For many years [now] the United States has been walking a tightrope between the effort to maintain our old and valued relations with our British and French allies, on the one hand, and on the other, trying to assure ourselves of the friendship and understanding of the newly independent countries who have escaped from colonialism. Unless we now assert and maintain this leadership, all of those newly independent countries will turn from us to the USSR.[12]

Nor did the Eisenhower administration hesitate to push London into a dire financial situation in order to compel it to step back from Suez.

The problem foreseen in Clayton's 1947 memorandum was asserting itself: the Suez crisis gave a clear picture of the global power shift that the Second World War and subsequent developments had brought about. Having vetoed a resolution of censure in the Security Council, Britain and France—two of the five permanent members—were defeated in the UN General Assembly by the joint effort of the United States and the Soviet Union.

Suez demonstrated a number of things. First of all, it showed that a piecemeal defense of the old order by the European powers was not adequate to keep in check the new reality created by decolonization. And second, regional struggles tended to draw in the superpowers. The United States and the Soviet Union were the powers now facing each other in the global arena and in the Middle East. The threat of nuclear punishment that Moscow had cast over London and Paris, if hardly plausible, was a warning of the new scale of power regulating most regional issues. It was a reminder that global influence could no longer be wielded by those countries unable to discourage threats against their territory. Finally, Suez brought home to the Europeans the consequences of their security dependence. With its commitment to guarantee European security, the United States also had to decide how to manage the risk of a direct confrontation with the Soviet Union.

All this meant that henceforth it would be the role of the United States to ensure that as much as possible of the world remained aligned with the industrialized West. There was no lack of resentment in Europe over Suez, over the U.S. management of the decolonization of the Congo, and U.S. pressures over Algeria (the Suez crisis helped to build the European Economic Community). Some saw an incompatibility between NATO and the United Nations. "I am perfectly aware," former prime minister of Belgium Paul-Henri Spaak wrote to Kennedy on stepping down from the post of NATO secretary-general in February 1961, "that [European interests in Africa] will create problems and additional difficulties for a big country such as the United States which must defend its interests all over the world, but I remain convinced that an essential choice has

12. See Donald Neff, *Warriors at Suez: Eisenhower Takes America into the Middle East* (New York: Simon & Schuster, 1981), p. 390.

to be made. For the moment this choice can be summarized as follows: What is more important for the United States, the U.N. or NATO?"[13]

Dulles had given a provisional answer to that question in November 1956. Subsequent developments have shown that the Atlantic alliance was able to adapt to the centralization of western decision making and power in the United States. That, after all, was the only way in which the political control of vast regions of the world could remain a western affair. The division of labor within the Atlantic community was thus broadened to include world order. It left the United States the greatest role in managing international stability on behalf of its allies in the industrialized world. And it allowed the latter to devote themselves to strengthening their economies, also in line with the strategic interests of the United States.

Kennedy and de Gaulle

It is within this broad division of labor in the transatlantic compact that we find the roots of problems later bedeviling U.S.–Western European relations. While the division of labor remained basically the same, the premises on which it was based began to change. Change came in the international context and especially in the relative weights of the industrialized and the nonindustrialized worlds, as well as in those of the two sides of the Atlantic. The United States, now the center of most western international initiatives, would encounter both increasing difficulties in carrying out its foreign policy and diminishing support on the part of the allies. Such problems came to the fore as early as the 1960s. But the failure at that time to revise the old arrangement further solidified the structure of transatlantic relations that had taken shape in the 1950s.

The Kennedy administration saw a challenge and an opportunity in the movement toward European unification and it developed its policies accordingly. In 1961 and early 1962, while the countries of the European community were discussing further steps toward political unification, most major figures of the U.S. foreign policy elite (William Clayton, Christian Herter, Robert Bowie, John McCloy, William Fulbright, McGeorge Bundy, George Ball, and others) addressed the issue. Some saw a danger that "a Europe organized without the United States would be a Europe organized against the United States."[14] However, for an administration that was attempting to find a new basis for world stability, a stronger and more cohesive Europe offered above all a great opportunity.

Secretary of State Dean Rusk talked on 30 December 1961 of the "grand design" of a U.S. foreign policy that had moved from the original plan to assist in

13. As quoted and translated in Alfred Grosser, *The Western Alliance: European-American Relations since 1945* (New York: Vintage Books, 1982), p. 152. For the issue discussed in this section see chap. 5.
14. Press release of 27 December 1961 of the National Committee for an Effective Congress, quoted in Max Beloff, *The United States and the Unity of Europe* (Washington, D.C.: The Brookings Institution, 1963), p. 110.

the unification of Europe to a "pattern of constructive association among the whole of the northern half of the world, from Tokyo to Bonn, and with the new nations of the south." And President Kennedy himself dedicated a major speech to that issue. On 4 July 1962, he called for a "Declaration of Interdependence":

> We do not regard a strong and united Europe as a rival but as a partner. To aid its progress has been the basic object of our foreign policy for seventeen years. We believe that a united Europe will be capable of playing a greater role in the common defense, of responding more generously to the needs of poorer nations, of joining with the United States and others in lowering trade barriers, resolving problems of commerce, commodities, and currency, and developing coordinated policies in all economic, political and diplomatic areas. We see in such a Europe a partner with whom we can deal on a basis of full equality in all the great and burdensome tasks of building and defending a community of free nations.[15]

The centerpiece of Kennedy's plan was the building of a system based on a regime of low tariffs, freer trade, and economic aid. It would have left Western Europe to its unencumbered economic expansion, but it sought to channel Europe's surplus into aid to those parts of the world where the struggle against communism—economic and ideological—was being waged. The system itself would stand on the two Atlantic "pillars." It was an attempt to rearrange roles within the Atlantic community. But one of its basic premises, that a united Europe would include Great Britain, clashed with the plans French President Charles de Gaulle was trying to implement.

Frustrated in his attempt to create a western directorate with the United States and Great Britain, de Gaulle had focused on a European strategy that would reach its zenith with the Franco-German Treaty of Cooperation of January 1963. Opposed to the supernational institutions that some other European leaders were proposing, de Gaulle worried above all that an integrated Europe, having no policy of its own, "would follow the lead of some outsider who did have a policy."[16] And, above all, he did not trust Great Britain's European credentials.

What brought these different interests and plans into conflict was London's yielding to the United States on the issue of national nuclear forces in Europe. While de Gaulle had counted on Great Britain to help build a French national force and thus an instrument of European independence, many in Washington counted on British participation in the EEC as a way of keeping a united Europe within the Atlantic framework. "We need Britain as a broker and to insure an open door," stated a press release of the National Committee for an Effective Congress, in December 1961. With the Anglo-American Nassau Agreement of 21 December 1962, Prime Minister Harold Macmillan acknowledged that the Polaris missiles Britain was to buy would be used within the framework of the western alliance. Thus London proved to be an instrument of the American plan, not of de Gaulle's ambition. On 14 January 1963 the French president brought this affair to a conclusion by refusing to accept Great Britain in the EEC.

15. U.S. Department of State, *Department of State Bulletin*, 23 July 1962.
16. Press conference of May 15, as quoted and translated in Grosser, *Western Alliance*, p. 204.

European political integration was not the only issue separating Paris and Washington. France was also interested in regaining some freedom of maneuver internationally. And the French need to develop an independent nuclear force was linked to that interest. Paris was claiming, in other words, that it still had international interests and that such interests required military power, starting with nuclear weapons. A French strategic force, theorized General Ailleret, close adviser to President de Gaulle, "would be capable of intervening everywhere . . . at every point of the compass," and, "during future crises that may rock the world, would place France in a position where she could freely determine her own destiny."[17]

If access to American nuclear technology was the shortest road to achieving the goal of a national nuclear capability, that road was blocked by the strategic doctrine then being devised by U.S. Defense Secretary Robert MacNamara—a strategy that while deemphasizing reliance on nuclear weapons for the defense of Europe, postulated that for military and political reasons a dispersal of those weapons and of centers of decision was not desirable. Washington was willing to accede to French and British desires to acquire nuclear capabilities, but only, as with the Anglo-American Nassau agreement, in the context of the alliance. De Gaulle's decision in 1966 to take France out of the NATO integrated command should thus be regarded as the culmination of a long dispute with U.S. policymakers and with the Atlantic alliance.

If by vetoing British entry into the Common Market, de Gaulle wrecked Kennedy's "grand design," his own plans did not produce any important shift of power or rearrangement between the two sides of the Atlantic. De Gaulle's horizon always remained much narrower than that of the U.S.-led Atlantic community. The 1963 French rapprochement with Moscow came when the two superpowers were entering an era of political negotiations. His search for autonomy thus remained under the umbrella of the Atlantic security system; it was not an alternative to it.[18] Even within that horizon, de Gaulle's hegemonic aspirations worried the other Europeans. Thus, the Bundestag, while ratifying the Franco-German Treaty, added to it a preamble requiring that its implementation be pursued within the framework of the Atlantic relationship, of the NATO security system, of the EEC, and of a unifying Europe inclusive of Great Britain.

In short, nothing of the old division of labor changed—except for France. The old roles were confirmed and the rest of Europe, keeping clear of French hegemonic ambitions, found itself even more dependent on U.S. policy and leadership than before.

The 1960s might have been a turning point for U.S.–Western European relations. Both Kennedy and de Gaulle were moving in a context of international relations that were becoming more complex, a world system that was becoming much more difficult to manage. At the same time, the failure to rearrange roles further fixed Atlantic relations into an institutional arrangement that was in-

17. "Directed Defense," *Survival*, February 1968.
18. See Grosser, *Western Alliance*, chap. 7; and Anton W. De Porte, *Europe Between the Superpowers* (New Haven: Yale University Press, 1979), last chap.

creasingly incongruent with the real weight being acquired by the different
Atlantic partners, thus creating the conditions for discord and tension. In the
Vietnam War, the United States experienced the limits of its ability to impose its
own version of world order. Vietnam also caused the international consensus
regarding the American international role to fragment.

U.S.–Western European Relations in a Changing International Context

When the United States finally disengaged from Vietnam in early 1973, most
of the conditions that had created the Atlantic community had changed or were
rapidly changing. And change in the international system would continue to
shape the evolution of U.S.–Western European relations throughout the 1970s
and early 1980s. The incongruence between the roles and actual power of the
Atlantic partners erupted in a series of crises. Yet the old arrangement remained
in place, if somewhat reduced in its importance in a more complex world system.

The Atlantic division of labor had been built on the awesome power of the
United States following the Second World War and on the overwhelming American capacity to condition the international order, both in its East-West dimension and in managing relations with the nonindustrialized world. These were
basic assumptions. But their basis was changing. Speaking to a European audience in December 1973, Secretary of State Henry A. Kissinger summarized
the changes as follows:

- Europe's economic strength, political cohesion and a new confidence—the monumental achievements of Western unity—have radically altered a relationship that was
originally shaped in an era of European weakness and American predominance.
- American nuclear monopoly has given way to nuclear parity, raising wholly new
problems of defense and deterrence—problems which demand a broad reexamination
of the requirements of our security and the relative contribution to it of the United
States and its allies.
- The lessening of confrontation between East and West has offered new hope for a
relaxation of tensions and new opportunities for creative diplomacy.
- It has become starkly apparent that the great industrial democracies of Japan, Europe
and North America could pursue divergent paths only at the cost of their prosperity and
of their partnership. [19]

U.S.–Western European cooperation was entering a new phase of steady and
profound adjustment. As the military component was giving way to other components of international influence, the world system was moving toward fragmentation and relative dispersal of power. Heightened competition in the international
market and the abandonment of the gold standard and the fixed exchange rate
system had opened a period of currency turmoil among the western industrialized countries.

The foundations of the old transatlantic arrangement concerning European

19. *Department of State Bulletin*, 31 December 1973, pp. 777–78.

security had become unstable. The fact that the United States had lost its margin of strategic superiority made the security guarantee offered Western Europe stand solely on verbal assurances—and on European confidence in those assurances. A major problem was surfacing, rightly stressed by Kissinger, to which a satisfying solution may never again be found and with which the alliance continues to struggle even today.

In 1979, intervening in the debate over the new NATO nuclear forces, Kissinger, now out of office, bluntly stated the Western European quandary. His promise of "extended deterrence" at the NATO council meetings had amounted to:

> Magic words, which had a profoundly reassuring effect and which permitted the [allied] ministers to return with a rationale for not increasing defense expenditures. . . . [However] those words cannot be true. And we must face the fact that it is absurd to base the strategy of the West on the credibility of the threat of mutual suicide. Therefore, I would say—which I may not say in office—the European allies should not keep asking us to multiply strategic assurances that we cannot possibly mean or, if we do mean, we should not want to execute.[20]

Those foundations were seriously shaken, moreover, with regard to the second dimension of the old division of labor—the management of world order. The year 1973, which Kissinger had designated the "Year of Europe" (an occasion to revitalize Atlantic relations after the distraction of Vietnam), revealed—with the October Middle Eastern war and the onset of the oil crisis—that the internal contradictions of the Atlantic community were worsening in the context of rapidly changing international conditions.

The quadrupling of the price of oil led the Europeans to devise their own policies toward the Arab-Israeli conflict (essentially a new development, except for France). They distanced themselves from the United States—and later even managed to find some unity of action among themselves on the Middle East issue. This discrepancy between U.S. and European policy was not simply a difference of opinion over the October 1973 war. Western Europe actually refused to cooperate and hampered U.S. operations.

Great Britain denied the United States the use of its bases in Cyprus. Turkey allowed the overflying of Soviet aircraft that were resupplying the Arab countries. The Federal Republic, while permitting the use of U.S. bases in Germany, made it a condition that no publicity be given to such operations. The Europeans were reluctant even to follow Washington in forming an oil users' cartel and sought individual bilateral deals with the Arab producers. And in the years to come they would continue to be at odds with the United States and its stand on Israel, e.g., on the interpretation of Security Council Resolution 242, on the General Assembly resolution equating Zionism with racism (on which they abstained), and on the issue of the Palestine Liberation Organization.

What is the meaning for the evolution of Atlantic relations of the problems that emerged with the 1973 Middle Eastern war? Quite simply that U.S. Middle

20. Kissinger's speech is reproduced in *Survival*, December 1979.

Eastern policy became less relevant to Western Europe once the price of oil jumped from three to twelve dollars a barrel. Although the Europeans lacked a general approach to that region, Washington's policy no longer furthered their interests. Nor did the situation really change in the following years, despite the crucial role Washington played in the search for a solution to the Arab-Israeli conflict. The United States did not have the power to bring the oil users–producers relationship back to what it had been before the 1973 conflict. It was a shift of power in the direction of the Arab countries, and the Western Europeans were now simply dealing with that new center of power.

Finally, it is important to remember that the oil crisis only sharpened a serious, and at times bitter, competition among the western industrialized countries in the oil market. The Europeans were reluctant to form a user cartel, for they had already been struggling, before the oil crisis, to break free of the control the United States exercised over the oil market. And after the onset of that crisis, Washington was the first to reach for bilateral deals. Thus, the oil crisis gave the Western Europeans a chance to be on an equal standing with the United States in relation to the oil-producing countries.

The early 1970s brought dramatic changes in the conditions upon which the original transatlantic arrangement had been built. And yet even though Kissinger's call for unity went largely unheard, Atlantis was not lost.[21] It was not lost because of the oil crisis, nor was it lost because of the waning of strategic superiority, nor the Western economic and monetary turmoil, nor the isolationist backlash that emerged in the U.S. Congress after Vietnam which brought new attempts to withdraw U.S. troops from Europe. In fact, while requiring increasing compromise, Atlantic relations revealed an excellent resilience and confirmed their centrality for the policies of both the United States and the Western European countries.

This resilience means that the need to remain united—however different the reasons of the two sides—is such that it compels each side to compromise and adjust to the position of the other. That ability appeared clearly in those critical moments of the early 1970s and it would appear again in the crises that were to rock the Atlantic community in the early 1980s. Such an ability to adjust to the other's position and interests is a necessity, however, not a virtue. In fact, Atlantic relations are becoming increasingly difficult to manage.

American Unilateralism and the European Predicament

New problems came to the fore in the early 1980s as a consequence of the Afghan and Polish crises. At no other time did the old transatlantic arrangement's inability to reflect the evolving interests of the two sides appear more clearly than when those crises brought to the fore the profound gap existing between the United States and the Western European countries regarding their divergent

21. *Atlantis Lost: U.S.-European Relations after the Cold War* (New York University Press, 1975) is the title of a Council on Foreign Relations Book edited by James Chace and Earl C. Ravenal and reflective of the perception of the moment among U.S. experts.

policies toward the Soviet Union. In the end, once again, the two sides compromised and adjusted to one another's position, but at the cost of a serious erosion in public support for the relationship itself.

When the United States responded first to the Soviet intervention in Afghanistan and then to the December 1981 Polish crisis by adopting a wide range of political, economic, and military measures with the aim of punishing the Soviet Union, the European allies refused to follow suit, resisted heavy-handed U.S. pressures, and succeeded in insulating Europe from the crisis in U.S.-USSR relations. In this case the United States had to yield. In 1982 the firm resistance of the Europeans even compelled the Reagan administration to step back from measures it had taken to pressure them into action.

Such differentiation of western policies with regard to the Soviet Union was a new development—and a particularly worrisome one, since agreement on such issues constitutes the very reason for the Atlantic ties. This development stems largely from the fact that the Western European countries have ceased to challenge the Soviet Union politically in Europe. Western European—especially West German—policies had made a dramatic turn, starting from the late 1960s, substantially changing the basis of the old political and military postures in the continent. The center of the European question, the division of Germany, had been bypassed through agreements and negotiations relieving its harshest aspects—the absence of human contacts and exchanges between the two Germanies. A new political order, based on treaties and political agreements, had been established on the European continent.

For decades the Western European reasons for challenging the Soviet Union in the continent had coincided with the U.S. global strategy of containment. This was no longer the case. In contrast to the changes that had taken place in Europe's policies, detente with the Soviets did not eliminate the concerns that, for the United States, underlay the strategy of containment. Superpower competition had not subsided in the Third World. That meant that the confrontational component of the U.S.-Soviet relationship could always come back to the center of U.S. foreign policy.

Tensions in the Atlantic alliance in the early 1980s followed a similar course. Western European interest in a new structure of relations in Europe clashed with U.S. policy, especially when it reverted to a confrontational stand toward the Soviet Union. To the United States, the Russian bear it was now confronting in Southwest Asia (or elsewhere) was the same entity it had confronted in Europe for decades. To the Western Europeans, the Soviet presence in Afghanistan was, basically, the concern of the United States. The Soviet Union they were dealing with was only the one beyond the German border.

Different, although related, is the case of the tensions that grew out of the decision to deploy new nuclear forces in Europe. This brought home to the Western Europeans the consequence of having their security system coupled to the military balance between the superpowers. The potential contradiction inherent in the security arrangement devised in the early 1950s was now coming to the fore.

On this occasion the Western European leaders realized that the political

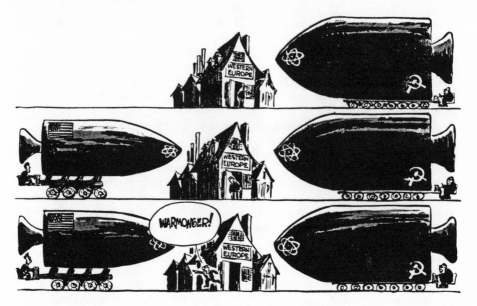

In Europe new credibility for neutralist positions, in the U.S. a sense of European ingratitude if not betrayal. (Gene Basset/United Features Syndicate)

order to which they aspired was limited by the fact that the military order on the continent of Europe could not be separated from the military order managed by the superpowers at the global level—especially in a context of heightened Soviet-American political confrontation such as that created by the Afghan crisis. The security guarantee offered Europe by the United States could not be curtailed by the special political interests of the allies.

Thus, in this case, it was Western Europe that had to adjust its aspirations to the reality imposed by its security dependence. A new problem seemed to confront the alliance. This may have been the first time that in Western Europe the mostly nonpartisan consensus on the alliance broke. On the issue of the deployment of the new INF weapons, two important parties, the British Labour party and the German Social Democrats, moved into opposition. Neutralist positions gained new credibility and there were signs of an important new problem emerging in the community.[22]

Atlantic relations were, if not trouble free, much calmer in the mid-1980s. Changes in Soviet leadership and the beginnings of a new dialogue between the two superpowers undoubtedly removed a major source of transatlantic tension. Similarly, the competition between Moscow and Washington in the nonindustrialized world has diminished, along with their capacity to control world affairs. But that does not mean that the problems that have come to the fore in

22. In general, on the transatlantic problems of the early 1980s, see *Western Europe and the Crisis of U.S.-Soviet Relations*, eds. Richard H. Ullman and Mario Zucconi (New York: Praeger, 1987).

U.S.–Western European relations, especially since the early 1970s, have disappeared. The separation of roles that characterizes those relations is still important. The United States continues to emphasize such factors as the superpower confrontation and the global military picture, but increasingly ineffective unilateral American actions cause the allies increasingly to distance themselves. This leaves the United States isolated and produces new tensions.

Yet, aside from the mutual accusations and recriminations that have accompanied the recent crises, there has been within the alliance no lack of awareness of the need to change the basic institutional arrangements between the two sides of the Atlantic. Among the NATO countries, the debate was particularly intense after the Afghan crisis.

In the early NATO meetings that followed, there was agreement on the seriousness of the situation (like possible threats to western interests in the Persian Gulf) and on the fact that the task of keeping the Gulf under control could not be left to the United States alone even if it was an "out of area"—out of the NATO jurisdiction—issue. What is important to notice here, however, is that the allies devised a division of roles that left it mainly to the United States to provide for the security of the Gulf and gave to the Europeans the task of assisting the United States indirectly, that is, by shouldering a greater burden in Europe. There was, however, limited direct French and British participation in patrolling the Gulf. The Europeans made clear that they did not intend to stretch their contributions much beyond what had already been established in the past. Above all, there was no real change in the special role assigned to the United States.

Among many responses given to these problems of the early 1980s, two are particularly interesting. Typifying the motivations that were to bring Ronald Reagan to the presidency, and himself to the Department of State, Alexander Haig in early 1980 pointed to the need to "restor[e] confidence in American leadership" as a way to stem "the centrifugal forces within the alliance." A quite different note was struck, however, in a pamphlet published in early 1981 by the directors of four authoritative foreign policy institutes in the United States, the Federal Republic, France, and Britain. They put forward the proposal for a directorate of the five major economic powers of the West to act as a collective decision center for the management of international crises.[23]

Haig's position was consistent with the traditional conception of the alliance and seemingly nobody felt uncomfortable with it. On the other hand, no debate at all grew along the lines of thinking contained in the proposal from the four institute directors. They, in fact, were proposing a fundamental rearrangement of the roles of the Atlantic (and Pacific) partners, an idea totally beyond the horizons of politicians on both sides of the ocean. Their proposal seems to have been unnoticed.

---

23. Alexander M. Haig Jr., "The Alliance in the 1980's," *Washington Quarterly* (Winter 1980): 139. Karl Kaiser, Winson Lord, Thierry de Montbrial, and David Watt, *Western Security: What Has Changed? What Should Be Done?* (New York: Council on Foreign Relations, 1981).

Thus the problem we find—which helps us understand the institutional immobility of Atlantic relations—is that politically it remains easier to rely on those relations the way they are than to try to rearrange them. Whatever their problems, Atlantic ties are too customary an element of the political life of the western countries for political leaders to take the risk of tampering with them. After all, much of the political life of the western industrialized countries grew while being conditioned by that vital, mutual connection. The rewards that come from it are still essential, and the risks of reforming it still seem unnecessary to most political leaders. The widespread, implicit acceptance of Haig's position is evidence of that fact. His words promised to restore the old division of labor.

Ultimately the problem is one of political leadership, not among but within the Atlantic countries. It is a question of change in the prevailing political culture and, for the European countries, of taking up more general international responsibilities. At stake is the very evolution of the international order. The Atlantic relationship remains one of the main structures of that order, and that relationship greatly influences the evolution of the international order as a whole.

8

In Our Own Neighborhood: The American Record in Central America

LARS SCHOULTZ

THE TITLE of this essay evokes the image of an accounting, of adding up the wins and losses of U.S. foreign policy toward the Central American region during a lengthy season of forty years. Under normal circumstances, that in itself would be a challenging exercise. But in recent years such an assessment has become even more difficult; unlike the early postwar period, today it is almost impossible to identify an acceptable unit of measurement, a yardstick by which to assess Washington's performance.

Take, for example, the disputes that arise if we employ the common yardstick of measuring performance against goals—of identifying our policy's goals in Central America and then examining the extent to which we have been able to reach them. Certainly this has never told us much about the wisdom of our goals, but it has had the benefit of not demanding that policymakers live up to standards they themselves have not selected. This has also been the simplest yardstick, for we have had only one overarching goal in our policy toward Central America since 1947—to contain the spread of communism. Indeed, most of our other postwar goals (economic development, for example) are not simply seen to be of lesser importance; they are, in the minds of most U.S. policymakers, more properly conceived as means to contain communism rather than as the objectives of U.S. policy.

Before turning to the disputes that surface over the use of this yardstick, it is important to note that there is nothing particularly innovative about the postwar policy of containment. It simply is our generation's name for the generic (and unchanging) U.S. goal of excluding rival powers from what policymakers once referred to as Washington's "soft underbelly." Beginning with the era of John Quincy Adams, secretary of state (1817–1825) during much of the struggle for independence in Spanish America, U.S. security has always been equated with the need to exclude rival powers from the Western Hemisphere—Soviet communists today, fascists yesterday, German imperialists at the turn of the century, European monarchies in 1823. Latin America *per se* has never posed a threat; the fear in Washington has always been that a major rival power would establish a political or military base in Latin America that could be used to threaten U.S. security. From the No-Transfer Resolution of 1811, to the Monroe Doctrine of 1823, to the Roosevelt Corollary of 1904, to the Magdalena Bay Resolution of 1912, and to the Reagan Doctrine of the 1980s, this exclusionary policy is one of the most basic themes that unites U.S. policymakers across the generations.

Given the goal of excluding other powers from the hemisphere—a goal we today call containment—how do U.S. policymakers today assess the record in Central America these past forty years?

Not surprisingly, the most optimistic assessment always comes from representatives of the incumbent administration. Times were tough in 1980, Secretary Shultz told the Senate Foreign Relations Committee on 10 September 1987, but the situation has improved after seven years of Reagan stewardship; not enough improvement, but enough to provide the basis for optimism. "In 1980–81, a lot of people thought it was too late to end the spreading turmoil and violence in El Salvador and Nicaragua and to stop the spread of communism in Central America," he said. But, he continued, "the President knew that the Soviets must not be permitted to add a strategic hold on the mainland to their position in Cuba. . . . So he decided to support Central Americans willing to work and, if necessary, fight for democracy and human dignity. . . . Today, with American support, the tide has turned in Central America." In his speech to the Organization of American States on 7 October 1987, President Reagan gave a similar assessment. He explicitly credited the pressure applied by U.S.-backed Contras for keeping Nicaragua from becoming a Soviet beachhead on the Latin American mainland.

Many of the Reagan administration's critics have responded that the tide never needed to be turned. They argued that U.S. policy was based upon an unrealistic perception of the Sandinista government as an expansionist, Soviet/Cuban-controlled regional troublemaker. But setting aside for a moment the question of Nicaragua, the administration could argue that there have been other successes in the region. On the eve of Mr. Reagan's inauguration, the rebel FMLN in El Salvador was engaged in its final offensive, while in Guatemala rebel groups with suspicious-sounding names like the Guerrilla Army of the Poor and the Organization of the People in Arms exerted effective control over significant portions of the heavily populated northwest highlands. By the end of his administration, President Reagan argued that the situation in both these countries was vastly improved.

In short, these administration officials asserted, as incumbent policymakers always do, that communism has been contained in Central America during the Reagan watch. Nicaragua remained a problem to the very end, but it has been neutralized. This was similar to the Kennedy administration's assertion that it had taken the offensive bite out of the Cuban revolution following the missile crisis of 1962. And certainly Nicaragua was no more of a problem by 1987 than Guatemala had been in 1947. The Central American part of Washington's southern flank was as secure in 1987 as it was four decades ago.

A much more pessimistic assessment of the U.S. record has come from the Reagan administration's moderate critics—senators like Florida's Bob Graham, North Carolina's Terry Sanford, and New Jersey's Bill Bradley. These moderates differ from conservatives in their belief that poverty rather than communist adventurism is the underlying cause of the turmoil that convulsed Central America during the 1980s. Thus they conclude that the U.S. record has been extremely poor, because the administration insisted upon treating the symptom (the turmoil) while ignoring the disease (poverty and injustice) that caused it. To these officials, it is only a question of time until a deteriorating domestic and international economic situation leads increasing numbers of Central Americans to rebel against a fundamentally unjust socioeconomic system. Then, when

In the Reagan years, just as earlier, policymakers disputed whether the root of Central America's problems was poverty and a rotten social system or Soviet-supported communism. (Dennis Renault, *Sacramento Bee*)

large-scale instability flares up once again, the United States will face the sad prospect of having to mount yet another major diplomatic, economic, and military effort in order to keep the countries of the region from slipping into the Soviet orbit. To these moderate policymakers, a policy based upon curing instability is ill-conceived. What is needed, they argue, is a policy based upon preventing instability by addressing the increasingly acute social problems confronting Central Americans.

There is also a third group of liberal policymakers—senators like Connecticut's Christopher Dodd, California's Alan Cranston, and Massachusetts' Edward Kennedy—who would refuse to answer directly the question of how well Washington has protected U.S. interests by containing communism in Central America. Instead, they would respond with two questions of their own. First, given the stark deprivation that characterizes human existence in most of Central America, and given the progressive role the United States conceives of itself as playing in the region, isn't a policy of containing communism in Central America somewhat unambitious? To measure up as "successful," must United States policy toward Central America do nothing more than stop communism? Second, given the clear evidence that Central Americans are, by themselves, not particularly attracted to the theory of communism or its practice in the Soviet Union or Cuba, is it really fair to measure the success of U.S. policy in terms of the absence of a phenomenon that in all likelihood would be absent without any effort from Washington?

These three different evaluations of recent policy underscore the profound differences that exist in Washington and among the informed public over the U.S. record in Central America since 1947. To focus upon an evaluation that measures performance against goals is to become deadlocked over both the selection of appropriate goals and the evaluation of recent performances.

Another approach to an assessment of the U.S. record in Central America is to focus upon adaptability. We all recognize that circumstances change with the passage of time, and therefore we can probably agree that the success of any policy will be determined at least in part by the ability of policymakers to adapt policy to changing circumstances. Setting aside many modest disagreements, most of us can probably agree that the U.S. record in Central America can be measured (and I would argue, measured best) by its ability to protect the nation's core interest in a peaceful, secure southern flank in an environment characterized by rapid change.

To make this assessment requires an initial focus upon the most significant changes that have occurred in world politics in the years since 1947. For an analysis of Washington's relations with Central America, six changes are of primary significance: two in Latin America, two in the global environment, and two in the United States.

The first change is a remarkable shift in Latin America's role in world politics. In the initial era of U.S.–Latin American relations, Washington's neighbors to the south were few in number and almost completely impotent. The basic geostrategic fact governing U.S. policy early in the nineteenth century was that Latin America was not much more than territory; sparsely populated and still largely disorganized, the region had no autonomous weight in international relations. What worried leaders like James Monroe and John Quincy Adams, therefore, was that the territory of Latin America might be used by European powers to threaten U.S. security. The result was the Monroe Doctrine.

For more than a century the United States was able to enforce its policy of excluding other powers from the hemisphere. At first the principal enforcement mechanism was not U.S. power but rather the rivalries of European powers, which served to reduce somewhat their incursions into Latin America. Later, as the United States developed its military capacities, Washington assumed responsibility for enforcing the Monroe Doctrine. For example, in an effort to keep European creditors (especially the Germans) from intervening militarily in the Caribbean region to collect debts, in 1904 President Roosevelt issued his corollary to the Monroe Doctrine:

> If a nation shows that it knows how to act with reasonable efficiency and decency in social and political matters; if it keeps order and pays its obligations, it need fear no interference from the United States. Chronic wrongdoing, or an impotence which results in a general loosening of the ties of civilized society, may in America, as elsewhere, ultimately require intervention by some civilized nation, and in the Western Hemisphere the adherence of the United States to the Monroe Doctrine may force the United States, however reluctantly, in flagrant cases of such wrongdoing or impotence, to the exercise of an international police power.[1]

Shortly thereafter, the United States invaded the Dominican Republic.

A few years later, in 1912, it appeared as if Japanese fishing interests, with linkages to the Japanese government, were about to purchase a large strip of land on Magdalena Bay, in Mexico's Baja California, from its U.S. owners. Henry Cabot Lodge, chairman of the Senate Committee on Foreign Relations, obtained the overwhelming endorsement (fifty-one to four) of his colleagues to a resolution proclaiming that:

> when any harbor or other place in the American continents is so situated that the occupation thereof for naval or military purposes might threaten the communications or the safety of the U.S., the government of the U.S. could not see without grave concern the possession of such harbor or other place by any corporation or association which has such relation to another government, not American, as to give that government practical power of control for naval or military purposes.[2]

This, the Lodge Corollary to the Monroe Doctrine, was a clear infringement upon the sovereignty of the Mexican government. But it also was an obvious extrapolation of the geostrategic tenet that prudent policymakers keep potential adversaries as distant as possible. Thus the father of modern U.S. naval strategy, Alfred Thayer Mahan, wrote in 1890 that "it should be an inviolable resolution of our national policy that no foreign state should henceforth acquire a coaling

1. Annual Message from President Theodore Roosevelt to the United States Congress, 6 December 1904.
2. *Congressional Record*, vol. 48, pt. 10, 1912, p. 10,045.

THE ORGANIZATION OF AMERICAN STATES (OAS)

United States

Mexico

The Bahamas

Jamaica

Haiti

Dominican Republic

Guatemala
El Salvador
Honduras
Nicaragua
Costa Rica
Panama

St. Kitts and Nevis
Antigua and Barbuda
Dominica
St. Lucia
St. Vincent and
  the Grenadines
Barbados
Grenada
Trinidad and Tobago

Venezuela

Guyana

Colombia

French Guiana

Ecuador

Suriname

Peru

Brazil

Bolivia

Paraguay

Chile

Uruguay

Argentina

position within three thousand miles of San Francisco—a distance which includes the Hawaiian and Galapagos Islands and the coast of Central America."[3]

But, as Bernard Brodie once observed, "in the field of modern strategy, time tends to deal severely with concepts as well as facts."[4] The lack of hemispheric solidarity during World War II (and especially Argentina's refusal to declare war on the Axis until about a month before Hitler's suicide) was a sobering experience for many in Washington. The basic lesson the United States learned about inter-American relations from World War II was that it could not deny an extra-hemispheric adversary access to the hemisphere without the active cooperation of Latin Americans. Unlike the hundred-year period from John Quincy Adams to Alfred Thayer Mahan, by the beginning of the Cold War, U.S. officials had come to recognize the existence of about one hundred million people in twenty neighboring republics. And so in 1947 U.S. leaders asked the leaders of Latin America's republics to meet with them in Rio de Janeiro, where they all signed the Inter-American Treaty of Reciprocal Assistance. The Rio Treaty was an attempt to formalize what everyone in Washington presumed: that in the rapidly

3. Alfred Thayer Mahan, *The Interest of America in Sea Power: Present and Future*, 12th ed. (Boston: Little, Brown, 1918), p. 26.
4. Bernard Brodie, *Strategy in the Missile Age* (Princeton University Press, 1965), p. v.

emerging rigid bipolar world, Latin America was going to be on the side of the United States.

The presumption was correct. After U.S. policymakers had straightened out a few kinks in the inter-American system—after they had persuaded Argentina's Peronist government to accept U.S. leadership and after they had helped to overthrow Guatemala's Arbenz government in 1954—Latin America played its proper role. The inspection of a number of indicators—perhaps voting patterns in the United Nations is the best—leads to the conclusion that for a number of years Latin Americans were Washington's toadies in international politics.

In this sense the Cuban revolution was a major watershed. It signaled the breakdown in hemispheric solidarity. Certain Latin American nations (Argentina and Mexico in particular) had never accepted their assigned role with any enthusiasm, and in the years since the Cuban revolution others have slowly broken away. Today, both the United States and the nations of Latin America are only nominally committed to the Rio Treaty.

There will probably never be a better example of this lack of commitment than the 1982 Falklands/Malvinas War between Argentina and Great Britain. Under the terms of the Rio Treaty, any signatory may request a Meeting of Consultation of the pact's foreign ministers in cases of armed attack or other threats to international peace and security. A request is sent to the Permanent Council of the Organization of American States (OAS), which decides by majority vote whether to call a Meeting of Consultation. Since 1947, the OAS has operated on the norm that any member's request for a meeting would be honored.

In the case at hand, Argentina called for a Meeting of Consultation in April 1982, to request assistance against Britain in the Falklands/Malvinas crisis. Recognizing that the OAS would side with Argentina in this dispute, the United States tried to convince the Permanent Council not to call a meeting. President Reagan commented that it would be "advantageous" if the OAS would delay acting upon the Argentine request, and the U.S. ambassador to the OAS told the Permanent Council that "at a time when Secretary Haig is engaged in efforts to promote a peaceful solution, it seems to my government particularly inappropriate to seek a resolution within the framework of the Rio Treaty." Despite this advice, the Permanent Council voted eighteen to zero to hold the meeting, with Colombia, Trinidad and Tobago, and the United States abstaining. By the time the meeting was held, however, the United States had made it clear that collective action in support of Argentina would have to be limited to verbal support for Argentine sovereignty over the islands. The Meeting of Consultation promptly passed a resolution to this effect, and then left the task of averting war to other international actors.

Regardless of who was "right" or "wrong" in this 1982 crisis, the obvious contrast between this institutional inaction, on the one hand, and the type of reaction that could be expected if a flotilla from any nation were sailing toward one of the United States' NATO allies, on the other, underscores the absence of a true inter-American security community. Public opinion polls indicate that those U.S. citizens who knew anything about the issue sided strongly with the British, and not a few U.S. Latin Americanists (especially, in my experience, U.S. human rights activists) were silently pleased by the humiliation of the Argentine military. What the Falklands fiasco demonstrated, then, is that the Rio Treaty is a thin reed. No one could possibly conceive of it as a viable mutual security commitment.

Stated differently, with the exception of Cuba and perhaps El Salvador and Honduras, the region is largely nonaligned in the true sense of the word. One of the best of our recent ambassadors, John Crimmins, captured this nonalignment well when he reported to Congress on his last assignment, Brazil:

> Brazil has shown, certainly publicly, no readiness to enlist in a significant way with us. The current formulators and directors of Brazilian foreign policy are as bent as ever on their standing guidelines that call for the primacy of economic interests, the retention of maximum freedom of action and the avoidance of obligations that are not clearly in Brazil's interests—as that interest is defined solely by Brazil.[5]

Similarly, Mark Falcoff writes that "Argentina has its own cultural traditions and history, its own sense of self, its own aspirations for the future, and it is extremely reluctant to allow others—especially Americans, whom Argentines of all political stripes do not particularly like or admire—to dictate, or appear to dictate, their course of action."[6]

In short, today only policymakers whose intellectual frame of reference remains locked upon the 1940s continue to conceive of Latin America as being on Washington's side of a rigid bipolar world. Certainly, in an abstract sense most of Latin America is on the side of "the West." But in a realistic political sense, today Latin America is on its own side, and where the countries of the region sit on any specific issue depends upon how they calculate their own interests, not on how Washington or Moscow calculates the global balance of power.

One major consequence of this "new independence" is that Latin American governments today seem comfortable with an assertive role that was simply unthinkable a short while ago; they no longer follow the leader. Two examples from 1987 underscore this change.

First, of course, is the Central American peace plan. Today, if peace comes to Central America it will come through Latin American diplomacy—through Contadora, the Support Group, and the Arias Plan. Today it is a Latin American president who lectures the U.S. Congress. On 22 September 1987, Costa Rica's President Oscar Arias Sanchez told Washington's legislators that they should "combat war with peace. Let us combat totalitarianism with the power of democracy. United in ideals and principles, joined by dialogue and democracy, we can and will bring hostilities to an end. We must give peace a chance." This is the kind of lecture that U.S. presidents and secretaries of state used to give to Latin American congresses.

It is not so much that Central Americans have developed their own peace plan,

5. U.S. Congress, House, Committee on Foreign Affairs, Subcommittee on Inter-American Affairs, *United States–Brazilian Relations*, 97th Cong., 2d Sess., 1982, p. 39.

6. U.S. Congress, House, Committee on Foreign Affairs, Subcommittee on Western Hemisphere Affairs, *U.S. Policy Toward Argentina*, 98th Cong., 1st Sess., 1983, p. 99.

but that the plan flies in the face of the explicitly stated policy of the United States. Latin Americans act as if they could not care less. One editorial captured the situation perfectly:

> Suddenly it is the United States, not Nicaragua, that is odd man out in Central America. Only a couple of years ago, Washington could count on a fair measure of support from Costa Rica, Guatemala, Honduras and El Salvador in its efforts to contain and eventually overthrow the Sandinista regime in Managua. No more. While these small nations still fear Nicaragua's outsized armed forces and its Marxist-Leninist system, they have evidently had their fill of the overbearing tactics of the Reagan Administration. . . .
>
> There is nothing new in these sentiments. What is new is that small, traditionally compliant nations are daring to defy Washington even in its own back yard. The perception of the United States as a mighty power resolute and strong enough to impose its will is fading.[7]

Guatemalan President Vinicio Cerezo best expressed his colleagues' sentiments: "We want to become the principal actor of our own history. We Central Americans understand the problems, and the answers to those problems, better than anyone else." In his December 1987 speech accepting the Nobel Peace Prize, Costa Rica's President Arias told both superpowers to "leave us in peace."

The second example of Latin America's emerging self-confidence is the eight-nation Latin American summit held in Acapulco, Mexico, in November 1987. "This is history," remarked Brazil's President José Sarney. "For the first time, we are meeting without having been convoked by a great power."[8] Not only was the conference actually held without Washington's blessing, but the principal discussions were threatening to positions advanced by the United States. First, the leaders proposed to invite Cuba to become once more an active participant in the Organization of American States. (Although Cuba has always remained a member of the OAS, at the 8th Meeting of Consultation at Punta del Este, Uruguay, in 1962, the present government of Cuba was excluded from participation in the inter-American system.) Proposals to reintegrate Cuba have been on the horizon since at least 1975, when at the 16th Meeting of Consultation in 1975 the OAS agreed to permit members to resume relations with Cuba "at the levels and in the form that each state deems advisable." The Acapulco proposal regarding Cuban participation was made by Uruguayan President Sanguinetti— no radical he—and strongly endorsed by Brazil and Peru; only Venezuela expressed reservations about the move. Second, the participants discussed (but reached no agreement on) ways to address the issue of Latin America's international debt, most of which is owed to U.S. banks. And, third, the presidents

---

7. *The Baltimore Sun*, 12 August 1987, p. 14A.
8. The Brazilian leader was exaggerating. Since 1826, when Simón Bolívar called the first Pan-American Conference in Panama (to which the United States was invited, but whose delegates arrived after the conference had ended), Latin American leaders have regularly met. The 1987 meeting was unique because it included so many Latin American leaders (including the leaders of all the major Latin American countries) and because it so pointedly excluded the United States.

discussed (but again reached no conclusion on) moving the headquarters of the OAS from Washington to a city in Latin America. Neither the summit meeting nor these specific proposals would have been conceivable a few short years ago.

The second major change is an end to Central America's subservient position in the hemisphere. Since shortly after declaring independence from Spain in the early 1820s, Central America has been dominated by the United States. Central America is where Washington wrote the book on hegemony. Take Nicaragua, for example. With the exception of the United States itself, no other country on earth has ever had a U.S. citizen (William Walker) as its president. No other country on earth has ever been invaded fourteen times by the United States (and this figure does not include the Contra war).[9] No other country has ever been obliged to negotiate an arrangement whereby its national bank was converted into a Connecticut corporation whose stock was largely held by New York bankers. No other country on earth has ever been occupied militarily by the United States for more than nineteen years out of a twenty-one-year period, in this case, from 1912 to 1933. No other country on earth in peacetime has ever had its harbors mined by the United States. And no other country on earth in peacetime has ever had a government that a U.S. president openly declared had to say "uncle" in order to restore its good standing in Washington.

By 1988 the Nicaraguan people had endured more than seven years of extreme pressure from the most powerful nation in the history of the human race. Yet what was the result? The economy had become an absolute shambles, with citizens asking their friends traveling from abroad to bring them not Scotch or some new electronic marvel, but toothpaste and toilet paper. Throughout the country, common citizens seemed exhausted by the daily pressures of a seven-year war, which came so quickly on the heels of the devastating civil war against the Somoza regime. And yet no Sandinistas were even thinking about saying "uncle." As historian Richard Millett once observed, "the utter bottom line of what it means to be a Sandinista is never to humble yourself in front of the United States. No matter what else it means, that is the bottom line. Any policy which thinks you can scare them, push them or get them to publicly do a mea culpa, is totally misinformed."[10] Jaime Wheelock, Nicaragua's minister of agriculture, captured this attitude best: "For Nicaragua, to be directed by the United States is now unacceptable. The people will fight against this to the end."[11]

At first, this type of talk may have seemed to be little more than revolutionary

9. The invasions occurred in 1853, 1854, 1857 (twice, in April and November), 1867, 1894, 1896, 1898, 1899 (twice, in February and March), 1910 (twice, in February and May), 1912, and 1926. Although some of these invasions were brief, none has been forgotten by the authors of the Nicaraguan textbooks, and some were either especially brutal (the 1854 destruction of San Juan del Norte to avenge an insult to the U.S. minister to Nicaragua, for example) and others (1912 and 1926, for examples) have had an indelible impact upon Nicaraguan history.

10. U.S. Congress, Committee on Foreign Affairs, Subcommittee on Inter-American Affairs, *Honduras and U.S. Policy: An Emerging Dilemma*, 97th Cong., 2d Sess., 1982, p. 86.

11. Interview, Managua, Nicaragua, 3 November 1984.

bravado, but after eight years of pressure from Washington the Sandinistas made believers out of a lot of skeptics. And if a tiny backwater of two-and-a-half million poverty-stricken Nicaraguans can challenge successfully the hegemonic designs of a neighboring superpower, imagine the new weight of comparative giants such as Brazil, Argentina, and Mexico.

The third change (and the first of two that focus upon the global environment) is an increase in Soviet power. Over the course of the past four decades, the Soviet Union has dramatically increased its ability to project power. By the early 1980s, this fact had come to dominate the thinking of many U.S. policymakers, including President Reagan. In his speech to the nation in March 1983, Mr. Reagan began by warning that "for twenty years, the Soviet Union has been accumulating enormous military might"; a year later, the president once more went before the television cameras to tell the public that "the growth of the Soviet military has meant a radical change in the nature of the world we live in."

Today, all well-informed U.S. citizens know that the Soviet Union of 1947 is not the Soviet Union of 1987, but aside from Soviet aid to Cuba and Nicaragua, few seem to recognize how the increase in Soviet power has shifted the geostrategic calculus in Latin America. Moscow is now an active participant in inter-American affairs.

The indicators of this participation are everywhere. Most obvious, of course, are Cuba and Nicaragua, but other indicators of Soviet activity in Latin America are probably more illustrative of the change that has occurred in recent decades. The Soviet Union's military presence, for example, has grown steadily. It is useful to remember that it was not until 1969 that the Soviet navy first ventured into the Caribbean; at that time, the very fact that they would sail into the region was remarkable. The fact that they have been doing so regularly for twenty years is no longer remarkable, nor are the Soviet air force flights along the U.S. East Coast to Cuba. What is remarkable is the reaction of the United States. One has only to consider what Theodore Roosevelt's reaction would have been if the German navy were prowling off the U.S. Gulf Coast, or what JFK would have done about a Soviet combat brigade in Cuba.

Today, the response from Washington is different, as illustrated by the combat brigade episode. In late August 1979, Democratic senators Frank Church of Idaho and Richard Stone of Florida were beginning what promised to be difficult reelection campaigns. In an apparent effort to bolster their images among conservative constituents, Church and Stone called separate news conferences to announce that the Senate Foreign Relations Committee had obtained secret documents revealing the existence of a Soviet combat brigade in Cuba. Both demanded the brigade's removal, arguing that its presence violated the 1962 Kennedy-Khrushchev agreement prohibiting any offensive Soviet military capability on the island. Church, chairman of the Committee on Foreign Relations, asserted that his support for ratification of the SALT II treaty was dependent upon the brigade's withdrawal.

After some days of intense media coverage, two facts became evident. First, Soviet troops had been stationed in Cuba since the early 1960s and, second, the Carter administration was having difficulty convincing the Soviets to withdraw the brigade. In a televised speech on 7 September, President Carter said that "we consider the presence of a Soviet combat brigade in Cuba to be a very serious matter and that this status quo is not acceptable." In his memoirs, however, the president wrote that three days earlier he had told Senate Majority Leader Robert Byrd that "there was no way to mandate that the Soviets withdraw those troops."[12]

Mr. Carter's apparent ambivalence no doubt stemmed in part from the ambiguity surrounding the brigade's mission. The Soviet position was (and is) that the brigade is a training unit, has no offensive capability, and therefore is not in violation of the 1962 agreement regarding offensive weapons. But U.S. intelligence sources have reported that the unit consists of twenty-six hundred soldiers divided into three infantry battalions and one tank battalion—not a normal training configuration. The brigade is equipped with forty tanks and sixty armored personnel carriers, which is not standard equipment for training units. Whatever the case, on 1 October President Carter accepted Moscow's assurances that the unit was a training brigade, and that was that. The troops remained in Cuba, Senators Stone and Church lost their bids for reelection, and Washington policymakers came to agree that some types of Soviet force deployments in Cuba will have to be overlooked, or, more accurately, defined as "nonoffensive" and therefore considered outside the confines of the 1962 accord.

For those who believe that the resolution of this problem primarily reflected the fact that Mr. Carter was simply not sufficiently assertive, it is instructive to observe that the most assertive president in recent memory, Ronald Reagan, has also been unable to remove the Soviet troops during his presidency. In fact, after some initial bombast about "going to the source" of hemispheric instability, he apparently never tried. The reason for this is extremely clear: the Soviets enjoy considerable strength that they lacked in 1962. There is no longer any assurance that, should we once again stand eyeball-to-eyeball, the Soviets will blink first, as they did during the Cuban missile crisis.

And the military dimension of this new power is not the only important aspect of the change that has occurred in the past generation. The trade-related position of power that the United States has long held in Latin America has also eroded. An excellent example is the U.S. sugar import program, under which the United States has for decades purchased sugar at prices substantially above the world market price. Because all foreign producers want to take advantage of this preferential pricing policy (which has its roots in the Cuban Reciprocal Treaty of 1902 and over time has been expanded to include most sugar producers), the United States assigns import quotas to individual countries. In many cases, these quotas spell the difference between prosperity and depression; they thereby provide Washington with considerable political leverage.

But the increase in Soviet power has meant a diminution of this leverage, as the case of Cuba demonstrates. In March 1960, as Cuban-U.S. relations were deteriorating rapidly, a bill was introduced in the House of Representatives to

12. Jimmy Carter, *Keeping Faith: Memoirs of a President* (New York: Bantam Books, 1982), p. 263.

authorize the president to reduce the Cuban sugar quota. Representative Harris McDowell, Jr. expressed the thinking of many of his colleagues when he remarked that "if Cuba's splendid people understand that they must sell their sugar or their economy will be destroyed, they will themselves find a way to deal with the present misleaders and fomenters of hatred." The bill passed the House by a vote of 396 to zero, and in July President Eisenhower slashed the Cuban quota from 779,000 tons to 40,000 tons for the second half of 1960. In December, the Cuban quota was eliminated entirely for the first quarter of 1961, and the United States has imported no Cuban sugar since that time. Since 1963, the Foreign Assistance Act has stipulated that Cuba shall not "be entitled to receive any quota authorizing the importation of Cuban sugar into the United States or to receive any other benefit under any law of the United States."

In response, Cuba arranged to sell its 1961 crop elsewhere: 2.7 million tons of sugar to the Soviet Union, 1.0 million tons to the People's Republic of China, and 300,000 tons to the Eastern Bloc countries of Europe. These purchases of four million tons exceeded both the U.S. quota and the amount of sugar Cuba had available for sale. Representative McDowell was both correct and naive. He was correct in noting that Cuba had to sell sugar in order to survive. He was naive in thinking that the United States was the only available purchaser.

And Cuba is no longer an isolated case. The Soviet Union now maintains an active presence throughout Latin America. In Nicaragua, of course, the Soviets have provided sufficient assistance to keep the Nicaraguan revolution from having to capitulate to the United States—they have done for Nicaragua exactly what they did for Cuba two decades earlier. In Peru, the Soviets are the principal suppliers of heavy weapons for the army. In Argentina, the Soviets have become the nation's principal trading partner. In 1960 there were three Soviet embassies in Latin America; today there are nineteen.

All this is not to argue that the Soviet Union has in any way challenged the United States as the overwhelming foreign presence in Latin America, let alone in Central America. Rather, the point to be made is that, unlike 1947, Washington's major rival is now prepared to play an active role in the region. If the United States refuses to purchase Cuban sugar, Moscow will buy it. If the United States refuses to sell arms to Nicaragua, Moscow will provide them. With limited resources, the Soviet Union cannot replace Washington, but it can (and does) take advantage of special opportunities in Latin America. And, as the cases of Cuba and now Nicaragua demonstrate, that is a major change.

The fourth change is a decline in U.S. resources. Perhaps the most intelligent single sentence written in recent years about U.S.–Latin American relations is by career ambassador and former assistant secretary of state Viron Vaky: "The problem which most Americans have in thinking about Latin America," he wrote, "is that they have come to consider the dominant position in the world and the overwhelming hegemony the United States exercised in the Hemisphere in the 20 years following World War II as the normal state of affairs."[13]

13. Viron P. Vaky, "Hemispheric Relations: 'Everything Is Part of Everything Else,'" *Foreign Affairs* 59 (1981): 639.

Of all the lessons that can be drawn from U.S.–Central American relations in the 1980s, the most important by far is that Washington's reach now exceeds its grasp in Central America. The United States now lacks the resources to realize its aspirations. Quite obviously, the United States retains all the power it will ever need to crush any opposition in Central America. But as policymakers discovered long ago in Vietnam, it is in large measure useless power.

Take, for example, the case of El Salvador, a tiny country the size of North Carolina, with a population of five million people. Following the 1979 Sandinista victory in nearby Nicaragua, the Carter administration began to pressure the Salvadoran government of General Romero to enact structural reforms, i.e., land redistribution, to defuse growing civil disaffection. When General Romero balked, in November 1979, a group of reformist civilians and a few reformist military officers, blessed if not encouraged by the United States, engineered a coup and announced plans for a series of sweeping reforms.

But despite strong backing from Washington, the reformists were stymied by their own conservative opposition. After three months of effort, they abandoned the government. The United States then searched frantically for an alternative to (a) the guerrilla Left, which by the end of the year would mount its "final offensive," (b) the reformist Left, which refused to participate in the government, and (c) the far Right, which the U.S. Congress would not support with aid. Washington settled on José Napoleón Duarte, a Christian Democrat who had been living in Venezuela since losing the presidential election (and suffering a vicious attack by the Salvadoran military police) in 1972. Having settled upon Mr. Duarte as its moderate representative, both the Carter and Reagan administrations proceeded to bolster his power with truly extraordinary amounts of military and economic assistance: an average of $438 million per year in the four-year period from 1983 to 1986. Never in the history of inter-American relations has the United States invested so heavily in the stabilization of a Latin American government.

And what are the results? As of 1988, virtually nothing has been resolved. The guerrillas are not as strong as they were in 1980, but they remain an active force capable of prolonging indefinitely their conflict with the Salvadoran military and disrupting indefinitely the Salvadoran economy—about $300 million in economic damage in 1986, which about equaled the U.S. economic aid program that year. Perhaps more important, the reforms promised in 1979 have been only partially implemented, and as a consequence the underlying causes of the civil war, which almost everyone agrees are poverty and injustice, have not been addressed.

Meanwhile, like a drug addict, in the 1980s the Salvadoran economy became hooked on U.S. aid, including the aid provided in the form of remittances from over 500,000 Salvadorans living illegally in the United States. As the U.S. Immigration and Naturalization Service began to implement the fairly stringent provisions of the 1986 Immigration Reform and Control (Simpson-Rodino) Act, President Duarte was forced to ask for an exemption. In a confidential letter to President Reagan written in April 1987, Mr. Duarte said that the return of these Salvadorans "would reduce drastically the amount of money received by poor

Salvadoran people in remittances from relatives now working in the United States. My government estimates that the total value of remittances is some place between $350 million to $600 million annually, and is thus larger than the United States government's assistance to El Salvador."

As for the direct provision of U.S. aid, most evaluations in the late 1980s were extremely pessimistic. One report issued in November 1987, by the Congressional Arms Control and Foreign Policy Caucus, was entitled "Bankrolling Failure." The report concluded that "despite seven years' involvement and $3 billion in aid from U.S. taxpayers, El Salvador remains a nation at war with itself, no closer to peace than when the U.S. began its massive infusions of dollars. Our vast investment in El Salvador has brought neither peace nor political stability nor a sound economy. Instead, we are witnessing a fragmentation—perhaps even a 'Lebanonization'—of Salvadoran society."

At the end of the Reagan administration, the one bright light on the Salvadoran horizon was the Arias peace plan, which pointedly excluded the United States as an active participant. In the forty years since 1947, the power of the United States to control events in El Salvador or elsewhere in Central America has all but disappeared. This is not to say that Washington is now impotent. As in the past, the United States can unseat any government in the region. But if today Washington policymakers want to determine who rules in Managua, they will first have to destroy Nicaragua.

That was not the case anywhere in Central America in 1947. In early 1953, the National Security Council produced a report, "U.S. Objectives and Courses of Action with Respect to Latin America" for the incoming Eisenhower administration. The report asserted that "our purpose should be to arrest the development of irresponsibility and extreme nationalism and their belief in their immunity from the exercise of U.S. power."[14] A year later a small group of Guatemalans—trained, financed, and supported by the CIA—overthrew the freely elected government of Jacobo Arbenz, demonstrating clearly that Central America was not immune to the exercise of U.S. power. It was that simple. It no longer is.

If today there is an imbalance between resources and aspirations, then U.S. policymakers can achieve a new balance in one of two ways. They can increase their resources or lower their aspirations. What more can be done, however, to increase Washington's ability to determine outcomes in Central America? In the 1980s, the United States devoted nearly every reasonably available resource to Central America. What more can be given? Surely future presidents will be unable to devote even more of their time and attention to Central America. Surely no future president, in the salad years of his tenure, will do what Mr. Reagan did in 1983 and devote two of his three speeches on prime-time television (one before a joint session of Congress) to talking about Central America. And surely no one can expect Congress to devote more of its energy and attention to Central America. Throughout the 1980s, this tiny region has been the single most important foreign policy issue to be addressed by Congress. The

---

14. National Security Council Report 144, 6 March 1953, p. 11.

U.S. political agenda is not so barren that future leaders can afford to spend even more of their scarce political currency on Central America.

Predictions are always dangerous, but here is one that is too safe to pass up: We have seen during the Reagan administration the largest expenditure of U.S. political and financial resources on Central America that we will see during the twentieth century. The administration tried hard, it did not succeed, and its successors will react to that failure in precisely the way Washington reacted to defeat in Vietnam: first by processing the refugees and then by withdrawing its attention.

And so the United States has to adjust its aspirations. This is, of course, a particularly difficult step for a people who have become accustomed to calling themselves the greatest power in the world. As a nation, the United States takes particular pride in its power. U.S. citizens do not like to cut back; instead, they meet challenges, they move ahead. A country involved in reducing its aspirations is antithetical to this image.

Nonetheless, it is instructive to note that the U.S. public and its policymakers are adjusting to the reduced level of U.S. influence elsewhere in the world. Everyone who follows international relations now realizes that the period of U.S. suzerainty in the years immediately following World War II was a transient phenomenon. The U.S. dollar has not been as good as gold for some time, and foreign producers have seized markets that U.S. entrepreneurs once thought were theirs by virtue of victory in World War II. The United States may still be the strongest nation on earth, but not by much. Its citizens are no longer the richest or the best fed. They no longer even pretend to have the best medical care or the longest life expectancy. They have learned to live with the relative diminution of their stature in the world.

(Oliphant Copyright 1983, Universal Press Syndicate. Reprinted with permission. All rights reserved.)

But not in Central America. To begin to discuss the difficulties involved in the adjustment of Washington's aspirations in this region of the world, we must first turn to the fifth change, the democratization of the U.S. policy-making process.

Citizens who became interested in U.S. policy toward Latin America in the late 1970s or 1980s often assume that the current high level of public involvement in policy debates is normal. In fact, it is absolutely unprecedented. In 1947, United States policy toward Latin America was made by a small handful of officials and influential outsiders. At the most, they numbered twenty-five. There was no public opinion regarding Latin America, for during the brief history of public-opinion polling in America, the small number of polling organizations had asked no more than a dozen questions about Latin America and all of them were related to World War II. In its first thirty-six years (1935–1971), for example, the Gallup Poll did not ask a single separate question about any Latin American nation, and during that same period the few existing inquiries by other polling organizations generally focused upon citizens' perceptions of major problems of U.S. foreign policy as opposed to Latin America *per se*, such as Axis activity in Latin America, communist involvement in the Cuban revolution, and U.S. intervention in the Dominican Republic. Moreover, in 1947 not a single interest group existed with a specific focus on Latin America—not a trade association, not a church group, not even the Latin American Studies Association. In 1947, few students studied Latin America in U.S. universities. Only one newspaper (*The New York Times*) had a full-time staff correspondent in Latin America, and as a result few citizens read anything about the region.

In Congress, there was no such thing as a "Latin Americanist." Public hearings on Latin America were unknown; instead, the State Department consulted privately with a few key members about U.S. policy. Disagreements between the two branches of government were almost nonexistent, because virtually everyone at both ends of Pennsylvania Avenue shared a common focus upon keeping the Soviet Union and communism out of the hemisphere. Policy disagreements were restricted to debates over important but secondary issues—the appropriate reaction to the expropriation of U.S. investments, for example—and to conflicts over tactics, timing, and budget priorities. Differences of opinion on these secondary issues were resolved in the atmosphere of civility that used to characterize the homogeneous U.S. foreign policy establishment. These white, upper-middle-class gentlemen from the Eastern establishment were pleased to listen with respect to the views of others, to offer alternative perspectives, and then to compromise quickly by splitting the difference, for the difference was always very small. No U.S. citizen with a Hispanic surname got within shouting distance of the policy-making process.

Look at the congressional votes on major administration foreign policy initiatives—from the Rio Treaty through the early resolutions on Cuba—and you will find consensus. United States participation in the United Nations was approved in 1945 by a 98 percent majority, the Truman Doctrine was accepted in 1947 by 86 percent, the U.S.-Korean Mutual Defense Treaty in 1954 by 93 percent, the Cuban trade embargo in 1961 by 100 percent, and, of course, the

Gulf of Tonkin resolution in 1964 by 98 percent in the Senate and 100 percent in the House of Representatives.

This consensus stemmed largely from the narrow spectrum of public opinion that participated in the policy-making process. Like all major conflicts, World War II had served to consolidate public opinion around the single objective of military victory. Then, after the war, when a normal fragmentation of opinion could be expected to reemerge, McCarthyism exerted a stultifying effect on political debates. It was only with the Vietnam War, which the Cold War internationalists could not resolve satisfactorily, that critics stepped out of the closet and the debates began to take place once again over the content and direction of United States foreign policy.

With the benefit of hindsight, it is now clear that the period since 1947 has been characterized by an absolute explosion of political participation in the creation of United States policy toward Latin America. The public's emergence from its postwar intellectual cocoon coincided with the explosive growth of colleges and universities across the country, with the Cuban revolution, with the Alliance for Progress, and with a general interest in the subject of Third World development. Thousands of citizens began to study Latin America and previously ignored subjects such as social change and instability. At the same time, large numbers of U.S. citizens went to live and work in Latin America, not as relatively wealthy businesspeople, but as Peace Corps volunteers and as church workers. They spent their time with the poor, and they developed new interpretations of Latin America's reality.

These citizens also developed an intense interest in United States policy toward Latin America. And their interest led them to take the quintessentially gringo step of forming interest groups, dozens and dozens of them, with representatives prowling the halls of power in Washington. In Congress itself, not only has there been a remarkable increase in the number of members with a major interest in Latin America—an interest that in many cases has been forced upon them by their constituents—but there has also been a stunning destruction of the cozy relationship that Congress once had with administration foreign policymakers. For better or for worse, broad currents of U.S. opinion now participate in the policy-influencing (and increasingly the policy-making) process.

The reason why this democratization of the policy process has led to conflict is—and here is the sixth and final change—that these new participants have startlingly different beliefs about what is actually happening in Latin America. This, of course, is not surprising, because the new participants come from startlingly different backgrounds. Senator Christopher Dodd, chairman of the Senate Foreign Relations Subcommittee on Western Hemisphere Affairs, spent two years of his life as a Peace Corps volunteer in a rural village in the Dominican Republic. The Rev. Joseph Eldridge, founder of the Washington Office on Latin America, was expelled from his post as a Methodist minister in Chile in 1973. Betsy Crites and Gail Phares, national directors of Witness for Peace, are former Catholic layworkers who spent years working with Christian base communities in Central America.

(Copyright 1962
by Bill Mauldin)

These people believe passionately that communism is not a problem to be addressed in Central America. The problem, in their view, is poverty and injustice. These people believe that instability in Latin America is the manifestation of a broadly human phenomenon: rebellion growing out of a "natural" opposition to a situation that is fundamentally unfair. These citizens agree with Barrington Moore: "There are indications of a widespread feeling that people, even the most humble members of society, ought to have enough resources or facilities to do their job in the social order, and that there is something morally wrong or even outrageous when these resources are unavailable." These citizens agree with Moore's conclusion: "personal and private retention *without use* of resources that are in short supply and needed by others is somehow immoral and a violation of the higher rights of the community."[15]

Ironically, Jeane Kirkpatrick has most effectively summarized the impact of this belief on U.S. citizens and their policymakers: "The extremes of wealth and poverty characteristic of traditional societies . . . offends us," she wrote in 1979.

15. Barrington Moore, Jr., *Injustice: The Social Bases of Obedience and Revolt* (White Plains, N.Y.: M.E. Sharpe, 1978), pp. 38, 47.

"Moreover, the relative lack of concern of rich, comfortable rulers for the poverty, ignorance, and disease of 'their' people is likely to be interpreted by Americans as moral dereliction pure and simple. The truth is that Americans can hardly bear such societies and such rulers."[16]

These perceptions of stark poverty and an uncaring selfish elite in Latin America are what most inflame many U.S. citizens. In some cases, it is the driving force in their lives. Crusaders for the poor of Latin America, they have chosen Washington as the field of battle. When these people heard President Reagan say that "the Soviet Union underlies all the trouble that is going on" in Central America, they became absolutely livid.

But when President Reagan, Ambassador Kirkpatrick, or Assistant Secretary Elliott Abrams hear these dewy-eyed liberals talking about poverty and injustice, they wonder about their common sense. Don't they know that often the only alternative to an admittedly unpleasant authoritarianism is communist totalitarianism? Don't they know that the United States can work to democratize authoritarian regimes, but that, once in power, totalitarian communists are all but impossible to unseat? In Kirkpatrick's view,

> traditional autocrats tolerate social inequities, brutality, and poverty while revolutionary autocracies create them. Traditional autocracies leave in place existing allocations of wealth, power, status, and other resources which in most traditional societies favor an affluent few and maintain masses in poverty. But they worship traditional gods and observe traditional taboos. They do not disturb the habitual rhythms of work and leisure, habitual places of residence, habitual patterns of family and personal relations. Because the miseries of traditional life are familiar, they are bearable to ordinary people who, growing up in the society, learn to cope, as children born to untouchables in India acquire the skills and attitudes necessary for survival in the miserable roles they are destined to fill. Such societies create no refugees. Precisely the opposite is true of revolutionary Communist regimes. They create refugees by the millions because they claim jurisdiction over the whole life of the society and make demands for change that so violate internalized values and habits that inhabitants flee by the tens of thousands in the remarkable expectation that their attitudes, values, and goals will "fit" better in a foreign country than in their native land.[17]

Kirkpatrick's point is that "a realistic policy" toward Latin America "will need to face the unpleasant fact that, if victorious, violent insurgency headed by Marxist revolutionaries is unlikely to lead to anything but totalitarian tyranny."

To these policymakers, communism is not only evil; it is expansionary. As Mr. Reagan told a campaign audience in 1980, "the Soviet Union underlies all the unrest that is going on. If they weren't engaged in this game of dominoes, there wouldn't be any hot spots in the world."[18] Don't liberal and moderate policymakers know, as Secretary of State Shultz remarked in 1984, that "the Soviet Union, most importantly and uniquely, is driven not only by Russian history and

---

16. Jeane J. Kirkpatrick, "Dictators and Double Standards," *Commentary* 68 (November 1979): 42.
17. Kirkpatrick, "Dictators and Double Standards," p. 44.
18. *Wall Street Journal*, 3 June 1980, p. 1.

Soviet state interest but also by what remains of its revolutionary ideology to spread its system by force"?[19] "Growth," wrote one of the administration's early advisers on Latin America, "is an organic psychological compulsion of the Soviet State."[20] Like an untreated cancer, the Soviet menace is compelled by its nature to attempt to spread until it destroys western civilization. That is why, as former representative John LeBoutillier told his colleagues in 1981, "there are black and white issues and the black and white in this case is that the Soviets and Cubans are wrong, and we are right. Castro and the Russians go around butchering people. We don't."[21]

It is difficult to overestimate the profound divisions that have come to characterize the contemporary policy-making process. This is the post-Vietnam loss of consensus, a much-discussed topic in the contemporary literature on United States foreign policy. By the late 1980s, Central America had become the principal example cited in this literature. The expanded policy-making process is dominated by equally matched groups of individuals who have fundamentally different beliefs about what is actually occurring in Central America. Unwilling to compromise over basic principles, these officials have checked one another.

This is where we are today. Six major changes have occurred in the years since 1947:

1. In Latin America's role in world politics.
2. In Central America's subservient position.
3. In the Soviet Union's ability to project power.
4. In the balance between our resources and our aspirations.
5. In the democratization of the U.S. policy-making process.
6. In the beliefs of U.S. policymakers.

These are profoundly important changes that will determine the trajectory of U.S.–Latin American relations well into the twenty-first century.

Given the recognition of these changes, we can now address the straightforward question: How well has Washington's recent policy served to protect U.S. interests in Central America? If we focus on United States policy toward Nicaragua in the 1980s, Washington's record is clearly less than satisfactory. First, U.S. policy has failed to recognize (and adapt to) Latin America's new role in world politics. There is no better example of this failure than the contemptuous U.S. treatment of Latin American diplomacy. Beginning in the mid-1980s, the Contadora initiative and later the Arias Plan became the mechanisms that Latin Americans created to serve as a bridge between the United States and the Sandinistas. Yet what was Washington's reaction? As the Latin Americans kept throwing U.S. policymakers life preservers, they, for reasons that will be incomprehensible to their grandchildren, promptly threw them back. Quite ob-

---

19. Address to the Creve Coeur Club of Illinois, Peoria, Ill., 22 February 1984.

20. Pedro A. Sanjuan, "Why We Don't Have a Latin America Policy," *Washington Quarterly* 3 (Autumn 1980): 32.

21. U.S. Congress, House, Committee on Foreign Affairs, *Foreign Assistance Legislation for Fiscal Year 1982*, 97th Cong., 1st Sess., 1981, pt. 1, p. 188.

viously, they prefer not to drown. The problem is that given Washington's two-century-old belief about Latin America's role in world politics, U.S. policymakers believe that Latinos are incapable of contributing to U.S. security—that their life preserver will not work. Fortunately, the slow acceptance of the Arias Plan suggests that many policymakers have begun to rethink this belief.

Second, the United States has continued to pursue an outmoded hegemonic relationship with Central America. U.S. policy toward Nicaragua in the 1980s resembles nothing so much as U.S. policy toward Guatemala forty years ago, and that is the same policy Henry Cabot Lodge suggested for Cuba in 1906—taking them by the scruff of the neck and shaking until they behave themselves.[22] We know what this type of policy eventually yielded in Cuba, yet eight decades later Washington is still pursuing it in Nicaragua.

Third, U.S. policy toward Nicaragua has facilitated the growth of Soviet power in Central America. By the mid-1980s, the very survival of the Nicaraguan revolution had come to depend upon support from the Soviet Union. It is not difficult to imagine the amount of leverage this provides Moscow.

Fourth, Washington's policy toward Nicaragua has been unable to accommodate the relative decline in U.S. resources, the democratization of the U.S. policy-making process, or the divergent beliefs of U.S. policymakers. As a result, the 1980s will enter history as the era of a stalemate. If by policy is meant a reasonably clear set of goals and a specified set of steps to attain them, then the United States has no policy toward Nicaragua.

For most of the 1980s, U.S. policy toward Nicaragua was being implemented by a group of fighters known as the Contras, whose motives were distrusted by a significant majority of informed public opinion in the United States. These Contras were supported by funds received from a variety of legal and illegal sources, none of which could be counted upon from one month to the next. By 1987, the prospects for continued U.S. aid were so dim that any Contra with an ounce of common sense was checking the airline schedule for Miami.

In short, if we evaluate U.S. policy in terms of the ability to adapt to changing circumstances, the unmistakable conclusion is that, in the two-century-old history of our foreign policy, it is difficult to identify a sorrier spectacle than United States policy toward Nicaragua.

But the picture is not unremittingly bleak. The four decades that have passed since 1947, and especially the decade of the 1980s, have been beneficial in the sense that they have demonstrated the consequences of continuing to act as if the changes we have discussed had not occurred. With some notable exceptions, nearly everyone in Washington now recognizes that the United States has wasted the past decade by attempting to solve problems with an outmoded, inappropriate policy. As the 1980s end, a new attitude is emerging among U.S. policymakers—a recognition that contemporary disputes in Washington and the vacillation they produce are luxuries the United States can no longer afford.

22. Henry Cabot Lodge, ed., *Selections from the Correspondence of Theodore Roosevelt and Henry Cabot Lodge, 1884–1918*, 2 vols. (New York: Charles Scribner's Sons, 1925), II: 233.

Today, most policymakers recognize that they have no alternative but to sit down and hammer out an agreement, first, on what constitutes the basic U.S. interests in Central America and, second, on how to protect U.S. interests in an increasingly complex hemisphere. The contours of this agreement will of necessity be quite different from the consensus that governed U.S. policy in 1947. It will be an agreement that the Cold War is not what needs to be fought today in Central America; that the struggle now is against the indigenous foes of poverty and injustice; and that the entire hemisphere will be a more pleasant and a more secure place to live only when all of us cease fighting the battles of the past and instead focus our energies upon the future.

NEW ARENAS

9

Still on Safari in Africa

HELEN KITCHEN

AFRICA is a large and distinct geographic entity entirely surrounded by water. The Organization of African Unity (OAU) since its founding meeting of heads of state at Addis Ababa in 1963 has embraced all of the nation-states of the continent and adjacent islands, while also holding the door open for a post-apartheid South Africa. In Articles 3 and 6 of the OAU Charter, moreover, the founding members took the pragmatic step of according permanent legitimacy to the geographically and ethnically bizarre borders imposed when the continent was divided up into more than fifty parcels at European bargaining tables in the 1880s.

To date, however, the U.S. policy community has never fully accepted either the cartographic guidelines or those of the OAU in defining Africa's identity. Nor is there anything approaching consensus on the extent, nature, and management of U.S. interests in Africa. Such a meeting of minds will remain blocked as long as there is no clear resolution of one basic set of questions that has divided both political parties, Congress, and the career bureaucracy since the Truman administration: Are the fifty-three political entities that Africa comprises primarily pieces on an East-West chessboard? Or are self-fulfilling prophecies cultivated when we box, label, and set aside as irretrievably "communist" any government or movement that uses quasi-Marxist terminology and/or turns to the Soviet Union for military assistance to deal with external or internal security crises?

The Bureaucratic Shuffle

Until World War II, all of the continent except Ethiopia (an independent polity since about 1040), Liberia (established as a republic by freed American slaves in 1847), and Egypt was a responsibility of the Department of State's Bureau of European Affairs (EUR). In 1943, the Bureau of Near Eastern and South Asian Affairs was renamed the Bureau of Near Eastern, South Asian, and African Affairs (NEA), with responsibility for all of North Africa (except Algeria, which remained with the Bureau of European Affairs) and a substantial part of the sub-Saharan region. The trend toward a more unified approach to Africa advanced another step in 1956 when responsibility for the Union of South Africa and Madagascar was transferred from EUR to NEA.

In July 1958, after a year and a half of negotiations with Congress, legislation was passed and signed into law by President Dwight Eisenhower authorizing the establishment of a separate Bureau of African Affairs headed by an assistant secretary. The new bureau included all of the African continent except Algeria (which remained in the Bureau of European Affairs) and Egypt and Sudan (which remained in NEA). Algeria became officially part of Africa upon achieving independence in 1962, and Sudan was eventually shifted there as well.

If this were the end of the story, it would not be worth telling. The next chapter opened in 1974, during Henry Kissinger's tenure as secretary of state, when Africa's identity was again redefined. Responsibility for Algeria, Libya, Tunisia, and Morocco was shifted, for reasons that apparently had more to do with personalities and departmental politics than policy considerations, from the Bureau of African Affairs to a new Office of North African Affairs within NEA.

The Kissinger reshuffle, which remains in force today, added several complexities to policymaking in relation to a segment of the continent that subsequently spawned two wars of more than passing interest to the United States. The assistant secretary of state for African affairs has responsibility for Chad, the Western (formerly Spanish) Sahara, Sudan, and an OAU that has been polarized since the early 1980s over Saharan issues. But responsibility for dealing with some of the principals in the still-unresolved wars in Chad and the Western Sahara—Morocco's King Hassan II, Libya's Muammar al-Qaddafi, and Algeria's Chadli Benjedid—rests with an NEA that is focused on critical matters east of Suez and has little time for the decidedly African complexities of Saharan politics.

When one moves across the Potomac to the Department of Defense, other definitional problems arise. Compilations of statistics on such matters as Soviet arms deliveries or commitments to Africa warrant careful study, for example, because in some instances figures for the Horn of Africa will be found in a Southwest Asia chart and information on the island nations of Madagascar, Mauritius, and the Seychelles will turn up in materials on the Far East. This makes sense only if one knows that there has been little change in the four decades since World War II in U.S. military strategists' view of Africa as an appendage of U.S. security interests in Europe, the Middle East, and Asia. The U.S. Central Command (CENTCOM) area of responsibility encompasses nineteen countries in Southwest Asia, the Middle East, and East Africa. The domain of the U.S. Pacific Command (PACCOM), the largest of the U.S. military's unified commands, stretches from the west coast of the Americas up to the east coast of Africa, from the Arctic to the Antarctic.

When one moves to Capitol Hill, the demarcations again shift. The Subcommittee on Africa of the House Foreign Affairs Committee deals with issues within its jurisdiction having to do with any and all countries in Africa except Egypt (which falls under the Subcommittee on Europe and the Middle East). The subcommittees of the Senate Foreign Relations Committee, on the other hand, follow the geographical breakdown of the Department of State's regional bureaus.

Presidential Politics, 1947–1987

Three bench marks of lasting significance in the limited interaction between the United States and Africa before the mid-twentieth century were the slave trade; the introduction of the principle of decolonization (i.e., Germany's) by means of the League of Nations mandate formula in President Woodrow Wilson's "Fourteen Points" at the end of World War I; and President Franklin Roosevelt's role in shaping the 1941 Atlantic Charter and the UN trusteeship formula that followed. It is noteworthy that Roosevelt made four visits to the African continent during his presidency (to Morocco, Gambia, and Liberia in January 1943; to Algeria, Tunisia, and Egypt in November 1943; to Egypt, Tunisia, and Senegal in December 1943; and to Egypt and Algeria in February 1945).

Although a prime mover in the establishment of the United Nations in 1945, the United States was not prepared for the full implications that began to take shape when the end of the colonial era in the 1960s and 1970s made Africa's fifty members the largest single regional bloc in the General Assembly. As Professor Rupert Emerson observed in 1967:

> To pick random examples, the opinion of Burundi on the limitation of armaments or of Upper Volta on Indonesia's "confrontation" of Malaysia would be of virtually no international consequence and probably would not even be formulated if each did not have a UN vote. Leaving aside the highly debatable question as to whether this is a sensible way to run an international system, it remains the fact that the African states as well as a number of other small UN members are endowed with a voting strength utterly out of keeping with any principle save the peculiar parody of democracy which calls for "one state, one vote." *This situation ensures that the African states will be wooed by all suitors who have an interest in the outcome of UN deliberations* (italics added).[1]

In 1983, Congress passed legislation (authored by Senator Robert Kasten [R-WI], chairman of the Foreign Operations Subcommittee of the Senate Appropriations Committee) requiring the Department of State to prepare an annual *Report to Congress on Voting Practices in the United Nations*. The 1985 report depicted the African group as having one of the "worst" voting records (i.e.,

---

1. Rupert Emerson, *Africa and United States Policy* (Englewood Cliffs, N.J.: Prentice-Hall, 1967), pp. 30, 31.

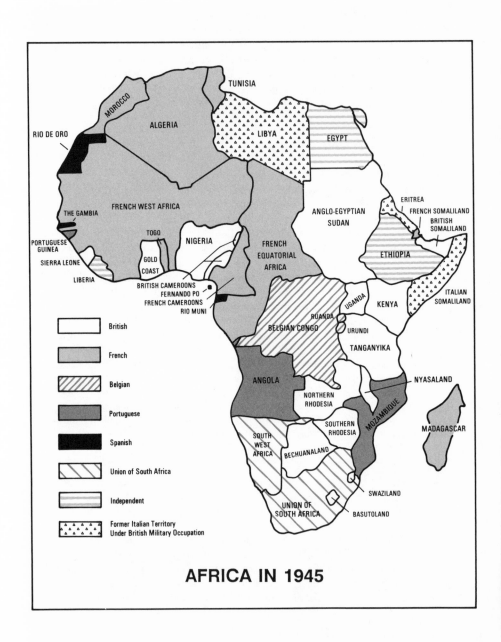

AFRICA IN 1945

174

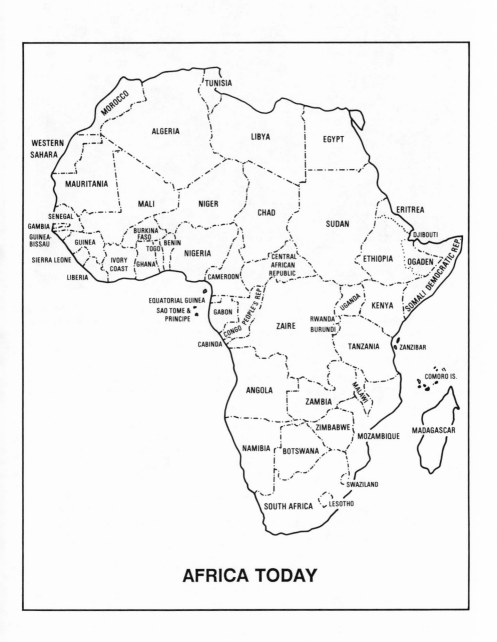

AFRICA TODAY

Little talk of Africa when Acheson was secretary of state. The core relationship was with
Europe. Anthony Eden of Britain, Robert Schuman of France, Dean Acheson and Konrad
Adenauer of West Germany in 1949. (National Archives)

voting records most at odds with that of the United States). Senator Kasten,
writing in *The New York Times*, called on his colleagues to keep this evidence of
"widespread lack of support for our positions at the United Nations in mind as we
review requests for foreign assistance."[2]

Surprisingly little attention has been given to evaluating how and how well the
State Department assesses the meaning of UN voting patterns. The two criteria
used (the overall percent coincidence of each country's votes with U.S. votes in
the General Assembly, and an evaluation of each country's behavior on ten
designated "key votes") have been criticized by objective analysts as seriously
flawed.[3] For example, the "percent coincidence" of recorded General Assembly
votes inevitably exaggerates the degree of disagreement between the United
States and other countries because many UN decisions are reached by consensus
with no vote recorded. Moreover, abstentions and absences are excluded from
the tally. The "key votes" criterion is subject to manipulation, since the ten votes
thus categorized are not selected until *after* the conclusion of each General

2. Robert W. Kasten Jr., "Our Alleged U.N. Friends," *The New York Times*, 17 June
1985.

3. See, for example, Michael Clough, "The UN: A Not So Dangerous Place?" in *CSIS
Africa Notes* No. 45, 24 July 1985. See also (Senator) Edward M. Kennedy, "Stop U.N.-
Bashing," *The New York Times*, 6 June 1988.

Assembly, and the official with major responsibility for compiling the list is the individual then serving as the U.S. permanent representative.

Whereas Daniel Moynihan viewed the UN as a "dangerous place" and Jeane Kirkpatrick compared her stint there to a "Turkish steam bath," both Andrew Young and Vernon Walters clearly enjoyed the assignment; indeed, Walters admits that he lobbied for the job. "Vote tallies alone," Walters observed in 1987, "are not sufficient to measure the results of the General Assembly. The increased cooperation, reduced rhetoric and behind-the-scenes help which characterized the 42nd General Assembly are difficult to capture in statistics."[4]

There were indications near the end of the Reagan administration that the Department of State tacitly shared this opinion; the introduction to its 1988 UN voting report was viewed by some observers as "a thinly disguised attack on the report's biased methodology . . . [which is] entrenched by Congress in the statute that requires the report."[5]

The Truman Years

In the years immediately following Franklin Roosevelt's death in 1945, the decolonization of Africa was a back-burner item on the Washington agenda.

Lucius Battle, who served as Secretary of State Dean Acheson's special assistant and close confidant for three key years of the Truman presidency, described to me recently the view of Africa from the State Department's seventh floor at the half century:

> When Dean Acheson was secretary of state, there was little talk of Africa. He considered the core relationship that the United States had in the world was with Europe. NATO was born and flourished under his leadership and he continued throughout his tenure to regard this as the cornerstone of American foreign policy. This point of view assumed the preservation, as much as possible, of the status quo of the various empires or near-empires that existed at the time. Little room was left for an emphasis on areas that have since attracted major attention. Not much attention was paid to the Middle East, almost none to Africa, and only symbolic lip service was given to Latin America, which we recognized as part of our own hemisphere and of importance to us. The relationships of the United States to Europe, and this included Canada as part of the British Empire, were paramount.[6]

This restrained approach to the issue of colonialism is illustrated in a May 1950 speech made by Assistant Secretary of State for Near Eastern, South Asian, and African Affairs George McGhee, in which Africa is referred to as a part of the world "where—in the broadest sense—no crisis exists" and, more specifically, where "no significant inroads have been made by Communism." McGhee's basic theme was that this crisis-free time should be used to deepen U.S. interest in, and study of, Africa.[7]

4. See David Brock, "Playing the U.N. Game with Gusto," *Insight* magazine, 30 May 1988, pp. 46–48, and Edward M. Kennedy, "Stop U.N.-Bashing."
5. Ibid.
6. Personal letter to the author, 19 January 1988.
7. *Department of State Bulletin*, XXII (19 June 1950): 999–1002.

From Truman to Eisenhower

The two-term Eisenhower administration (1953–1961) witnessed the first significant actions taken in relation to specific postcolonial African states. The initiatives that have received the most attention from historians were Eisenhower's personal involvement in intense cultivation of relationships with Tunisia's Habib Bourguiba and Morocco's King Mohammed V; the U.S. repudiation of British-French-Israeli actions during the Suez crisis of 1956; and the central role that Washington played in getting a United Nations peacekeeping force authorized and organized to deal with the chaos that erupted in the Congo (Zaire) immediately after independence in 1960. In all four cases, the U.S. initiatives were manifestations of a view of Third World nationalism as a pawn in the Cold War. Or, as Vice President Nixon phrased it in a report to Eisenhower after touring six African countries in 1957, postcolonial Africa was destined to become the new area of conflict "between the forces of freedom and international communism."

In an address to the UN General Assembly in the last year of his presidency (22 September 1960), Eisenhower outlined a five-point program for Africa that defined a broadened set of U.S. policy priorities. He called on the international community to "protect the newly emerging nations of Africa from outside pressures that threaten their independence and sovereign rights"; for help in ensuring the security of African states without wasteful and dangerous competition in arms; for emergency aid to the Congo (Zaire); for a marshaling of international assistance to shape long-term development programs; and for a major UN commitment in the educational sphere.

The Kennedy Epoch

John F. Kennedy inherited from the Eisenhower administration a U.S. commitment in the Congo (Zaire) that would be widely viewed as a test of his administration's will to deter a Soviet takeover of central Africa. Despite this legacy and the Cuban missile crisis of 1962, Kennedy's three brief years in the White House are best remembered by Africans and Africanists as the era of the American leader who succeeded (as Richard D. Mahoney phrased it in the concluding chapter of his 1983 book, *JFK: Ordeal in Africa*) in "identifying nationalism as the central reality of his age" and "establishing a common ground between African ideals and American self-interest."[8]

The specific achievements of the Kennedy years were less noteworthy than the human connections that were made between Americans and Africans—White House visits by twenty-eight African heads of state, follow-up personal correspondence with several of these leaders, and the care that went into choosing ambassadors and filling key positions in the management of U.S.-African relations. As illustrated by the following excerpts from an editorial published in the

8. Richard D. Mahoney, *JFK: Ordeal in Africa* (New York: Oxford University Press, 1983), p. 248.

venerable London-based (but now Nigerian-owned) magazine *West Africa* following the assassination, no U.S. president before or since has been able to deal so comfortably with Africans across a broad institutional and ideological spectrum:

> [Mr. Kennedy's interest in Africa] was shown long before he became President, notably when he was chairman of the Senate Foreign Relations Subcommittee on African Affairs. In 1957, he surprised many people, and upset the French leaders, by his Senate speech on Algeria. In this, he began by saying that "the single most important test of American foreign policy today is how we meet the challenge of imperialism, what we do to further man's desire to be free." Algeria, he maintained, was no longer just a French problem, and after severe criticism of the then American administration's policy, called for independence for Algeria.
>
> He finished this speech by saying: "If we are to secure the friendship of the Arab, the African, and the Asian, we cannot hope to accomplish it solely by means of billion-dollar foreign aid programs. We cannot win their hearts by making them dependent upon our handouts. Nor can we keep them free by selling them free enterprise, by describing the perils of Communism or the prosperity of the United States, or limiting our dealing to military pacts. No, the strength of our appeal to these key populations—and it is rightly our appeal, and not that of the Communists—lies in our traditional and deeply felt philosophy of freedom and independence for all peoples everywhere.". . .
>
> For West Africa, Mr. Kennedy's attitude toward Ghana, and his support for U.S. participation in the Volta Dam project, was particularly reassuring, in view of the influential voices calling Ghana "Red." The same is true of the late President's attitude to Guinea. The concept of the Peace Corps—about which many people who knew Africa had sincere misgivings, but which has been enormously successful—was the President's own. . . .
>
> The new President will follow Mr. Kennedy's policies, and he shares his attitudes. But no American can again win in Africa the status of the President who understood so well, and who shared, the African attitude to the world.[9]

Johnson's Priorities

Lyndon Johnson, who as vice president succeeded to the presidency following Kennedy's assassination, gave high and immediate priority to carrying forward the Kennedy domestic civil rights agenda. He could not have chosen a better way of introducing himself to Africans across the board. A combination of factors—the emotional impact on the nation of the Kennedy tragedy, Johnson's determination and his unique expertise in the art of congressional arm-twisting, and the thirty-seven additional House seats the Democratic Party gained in the 1964 electoral landslide—resulted in the enactment in 1965 and 1966 of more civil rights and other progressive legislation than seemed remotely possible at the beginning of the decade. Not since Franklin Roosevelt's presidency had so much happened so quickly in the realm of reformist domestic legislation.[10]

9. *West Africa* (London), 30 November 1963.
10. For further discussion of this sequence of events, see Arthur M. Schlesinger, Jr., *The Cycles of American History* (Boston: Houghton Mifflin Company, 1986), p. 411.

Lyndon Johnson's immediate priority to civil rights upon becoming president provided an excellent introduction to Africans, but as he became preoccupied with Vietnam "nonpriority initiatives in Africa and elsewhere were put on hold." (National Archives)

As Johnson became increasingly preoccupied with the war in Vietnam, nonpriority initiatives in Africa and elsewhere were put on hold. A case in point was the low-posture U.S. response to the unilateral declaration of independence (UDI) of the Ian Smith regime in Rhodesia in 1965. Throughout the remainder of the Johnson presidency (from 1965 to 1969), Washington followed London's lead on the UDI issue, observing sanctions invoked by Britain and the United Nations but taking no unilateral actions.

One high-profile gesture toward Africa made in this period was the goodwill trip made to nine countries (Ivory Coast, Liberia, Ghana, Zaire, Somalia, Zambia, Ethiopia, Kenya, and Tunisia) in late December 1967 and early January 1968 by Vice President Hubert Humphrey, Associate Justice Thurgood Marshall, and an unprecedented entourage of some forty staff and twenty journalists.

Nixon/Ford/Kissinger

Although the governing style of Gerald Ford, the vice president who succeeded to the presidency when Richard Nixon resigned in 1974, bore little resemblance to that of his predecessor, the "Kissinger factor" renders their Africa policies a continuum.

In the period he served as Nixon's (and, for a time, Ford's) national security adviser (from 1969 to 1975) and for three years after he became secretary of state in 1973, Henry Kissinger accorded African issues a very low priority. Actions taken and not taken reflected his (and Nixon's) assumption that no significant near-term political changes, violent or otherwise, would take place in the white-ruled countries of the southern part of the continent (Rhodesia, Angola, Mozambique, South Africa, Namibia).

President Nixon's first annual foreign affairs message to Congress in February 1970 described the policy deriving from these assumptions: "Though we abhor the racial policies of the white regimes, we cannot agree that progressive change in southern Africa is furthered by force. The history of the area shows all too starkly that violence and the counter-violence it inevitably provokes will only make more difficult the task of those on both sides working for progress on the racial question."[11] His third report to Congress in 1972 was even more explicit on the subject of violent change: "My Administration will not condone recourse to violence, either as a means of enforcing submission of the majority to a minority or as a formula for effecting needed social change."[12]

Events in the mid-1970s—notably the coup in Lisbon that abruptly ended five centuries of Portuguese colonialism, and the large-scale Soviet-Cuban intervention in the civil war that followed the precipitate Portuguese exodus from Angola—caused Kissinger to take an entirely new look at U.S. policy in Africa. Indeed, some Africanists refer to 1975 as the dividing line between Kissinger 1 and Kissinger 2.

In 1976, the last year of the Ford administration, Kissinger's high-profile shuttle diplomacy in southern Africa touched all bases. Presenting himself as an interlocutor rather than a negotiator, he focused on establishing amicable personal relationships with the leaders of the so-called Frontline States, beginning with the FLS chairman of that period, President Julius Nyerere of Tanzania, and he also held extended talks with South African Prime Minister B. J. Vorster, Rhodesia's Ian Smith, and other key players throughout the region.

It is generally agreed that Kissinger's speech in Lusaka, Zambia, on 27 April 1976 qualifies as a landmark event because it was the first comprehensive statement of U.S. policy regarding South Africa and its neighbors. The transitions from Ford-Kissinger to Carter's Africanists and from Carter to the Reagan-Crocker policy of "constructive engagement" involved changes of tactics, style, and priorities, but not of Kissinger's basic guidelines:

I have come to Africa because, in so many ways, the challenges of Africa are the challenges of the modern era. . . .More than any other region of the world, Africa symbolizes that the previous era of world affairs—the colonial era—is a thing of the past. . . .

There is nothing to be gained in a debate about whether in the past America has neglected Africa or been insufficiently committed to African goals. The United States has many responsibilities in the world. Given the burden it has carried in the postwar period, it could not do everything simultaneously. African nations too have their own priorities and concerns, which have not always accorded with our own. No good can come of mutual recrimination. Our differing perspectives converge in a common

11. *Congressional Quarterly* (May 1970): 134.
12. *Department of State Bulletin,* LXVI (13 March 1972): 366.

High profile shuttle diplomacy in Southern Africa. Above: Kissinger with President Kenneth Kaunda of Zambia. Left: Kissinger with President Nyerere of Tanzania. (Wide World Photos)

purpose to build a secure and just future for Africa. In active collaboration there is much we can do; in contention or apart we will miss great opportunities. . . .

Of all the challenges before us, of all the purposes we have in common, racial justice is one of the most basic. This is a dominant issue of our age, within nations and among nations. We know from our own experience that the goal of racial justice is both compelling and achievable. Our support for this principle in southern Africa is not simply a matter of foreign policy, but an imperative of our own moral heritage. . . .

Here in Lusaka, I reaffirm the unequivocal commitment of the United States to human rights, as expressed in the principles of the UN Charter and the Universal

Declaration of Human Rights. We support self-determination, majority rule, equal rights, and human dignity for all the peoples of southern Africa—in the name of moral principle, international law, and world peace. [13]

The Carter Administration's Approach

The Carter administration sought to differentiate itself from its predecessor on southern Africa policy by placing greater emphasis on the human rights dimension of the problems of the region and downplaying the strategic dimension, identifying the United States more publicly with the calls of Africa's black governments and leaders for change in South Africa, and creating the perception of a widened distance between Washington and Pretoria. [14]

The concrete manifestations of the Carter approach included: (1) a major U.S. role in helping Britain to orchestrate the unique multilateral effort that culminated in the Lancaster House accord negotiated in London in 1979, which set the stage for Zimbabwe's orderly transition to independence the following year; (2) the dogged pursuit by Deputy UN Ambassador Donald McHenry, chairman of the five-nation (United States, Britain, France, West Germany, Canada) "contact group," of an African and UN consensus on the formula for a peaceful transition to Namibian independence that was formalized on September 29, 1978, in UN Security Council Resolution 435;[15] (3) Vice President Walter Mondale's May 1977 meeting with South Africa's Prime Minister B. J. Vorster in Vienna, where the term "one-man one-vote" surfaced in a press conference; (4) a tightening up of restrictions on gray area exports to the South African police and military following the death of Black Consciousness leader Steve Biko while in police detention; and (5) expanding U.S. contacts inside South Africa with black activists.

There cannot be much argument with the judgment that U.S. relations with the South African government deteriorated during the Carter years and that U.S. credibility in the eyes of black South Africans improved substantially. The effect of these two developments on the pace of social and political change in

13. For full text, see Colin Legum, ed., *Africa Contemporary Record: Annual Survey and Documents, 1976–77* (New York: Africana Publishing Company, vol. 9, 1977), pp. C159–62.

14. The assessment of the lines of continuity and change in U.S. policy toward southern Africa under the Carter and first Reagan administrations expands on an analysis first published in Helen Kitchen and Michael Clough, *The United States and South Africa: Realities and Red Herrings* (Washington, D.C.: CSIS Significant Issues Series, vol. 6, No. 6, 1984).

15. UN Security Council Resolution 435 *inter alia* approved "the report of the Secretary-General . . . for the implementation of the proposal for a settlement of the Namibian situation" and announced the decision "to establish . . . a UN Transitional Assistance Group (UNTAG) . . . for a period of up to 12 months in order to assist [the Secretary-General's] Special Representative to . . . ensure the early independence of Namibia through free and fair elections under the supervision and control of the UN." For the full text of the resolution, see Colin Legum, ed., *Africa Contemporary Record: Annual Survey and Documents, 1978–1979* (New York: Africana Publishing Company, vol. 11, 1980), pp. C73–74.

South Africa is more problematical. Indeed, those primarily responsible for African affairs under President Carter had by their last year in office significantly lowered their expectations concerning U.S. leverage. Assistant Secretary of State for African Affairs Richard Moose acknowledged these limitations in testimony before a congressional committee in 1980:

> [Our] ability to influence events is limited. The future of South Africa will be determined by its own people, as it should be. We cannot afford to let our desire to help obscure other facts—that the South African economy is unusually self-sufficient; that dependencies between Western economies and South Africa's are mutual; and that no amount of political action from overseas can overshadow the solution to be worked out by South Africa's own people.[16]

Although Carter era veterans take special pride in the supportive role played in the Zimbabwe settlement and the lead role performed in achieving African and UN Security Council agreement on a formula for an eventual transition to majority rule in Namibia, there were other noteworthy developments in Africa policy in the 1977–1981 period.

The differing perspectives of Secretary of State Cyrus Vance and Carter's national security adviser, Zbigniew Brzezinski, came into play when the government of Somalia (with which the United States was negotiating military access and other agreements) moved troops into Ethiopia's Ogaden province in July 1977 in support of a secessionist uprising by the province's largely Somali population. The U.S. response to President Siad Barre's request for assistance was based on "regionalist" rather than "East-West chessboard" principles: (1) Although the inhabitants of the Ogaden are of Somali ethnicity and have an understandable preference for being part of Somalia, the option of redrawing colonial-era borders was ruled out in the OAU's 1963 Charter on the grounds that any exception would open up a Pandora's box of troubles. (2) While the United States was prepared to assist Somalia in case of Ethiopian aggression within Somali borders, it was not willing to provide either political or military support for Somali (or any other African nation's) irredentist ventures. (3) During a March 1978 visit to Mogadishu, Assistant Secretary Moose informed the Somali leadership that U.S. military aid to Somalia was contingent on that country's renunciation of aggressive designs against the territory of any of its neighbors. (4) In 1980 congressional testimony, Deputy Assistant Secretary of State for African Affairs William C. Harrop again underlined U.S. adherence to Article 6 of the OAU Charter: "Somalia must take no action against Djibouti, where ethnic Somalis are in a majority, or Kenya, where ethnic Somalis live in the northeast region adjoining Somalia and Ethiopia."[17]

Looking back at the Carter record in Africa in an article published in *Foreign Affairs* in 1981, Andrew Young, who had served as U.S. ambassador to the

16. From testimony by Assistant Secretary Moose before the Africa Subcommittee of the House Foreign Affairs Committee, 30 April 1980.

17. Deputy Assistant Secretary of State for African Affairs William C. Harrop, in testimony before the Subcommittee on Africa of the House Foreign Affairs Committee, 25 February 1980.

United Nations from 1977 to 1979, cited several factors that he believed had "radically altered the African-American equation" and would continue to influence both events and policy during the coming decade. At the top of his list was the emergence since 1975 of a new U.S. constituency for African affairs, consisting of civil rights organizations, young black professionals, church groups, some labor unions, college students, groups that had opposed U.S. involvement in the Vietnam War, and an increasingly significant corporate element. The corporate component grew out of the realization (initially by Gulf, Mobil, Boeing, and Lockheed) that it was possible to carry on business-as-usual in countries (such as Angola) where there was a significant Soviet presence. The major Africa policy blunder of the Carter administration, in Young's view, was its approval of military sales to Morocco. ("It is true that the United States needs a strong and stable ally at the mouth of the Mediterranean. . . . But instead of making every effort to extricate [King Hassan II] from his problems in the Western Sahara, U.S. policy now encourages [the war with the Polisario] at the expense of Moroccan domestic development priorities. Continued turmoil, regardless of the winner, is likely to lead to extended destabilization of Morocco. . . .")[18]

The Reagan Years

The two African missions that received priority attention (and aroused most controversy) in Ronald Reagan's two-term presidency were the effort to undermine Libya's Muammar al-Qaddafi and the search for a solution to the complex problems of southern Africa.

President Reagan's choice of Qaddafi as the West's archvillain in the Third World had mixed results. In the view of many European and African analysts, the inordinate attention focused on the Libyan leader accorded him a mask of power out of proportion to reality. Above all, U.S. policymakers (and Americans in general) tended to underrate the extent to which the fixation on Qaddafi aroused speculation that the United States had become a loose cannon on the deck. Virtually the entire Arab press condemned the U.S. role in the Gulf of Sidra incident of 1981, and the following excerpt from an editorial in *West Africa* is representative of the concerns one heard from many Africans after the April 1986 U.S. air raids on targets in the Libyan cities of Tripoli and Benghazi.

> The latest adventure in Libya makes comparison between President Reagan and Colonel Gaddafi inescapable. [The Reagan administration] accuses Gaddafi of sponsoring terrorists, by which [it] apparently means that the Libyan leader gives support to terrorists in the form of providing sanctuary, training, equipment and facilities. [The United States] sponsors persons [it] chooses to call freedom fighters, but who to most other people are terrorists. Those [the administration] feels no contradiction in sponsoring include the Contras in Nicaragua, the South African quisling in Angola, Jonas Savimbi. . . . [President Reagan] had no difficulty in defending the Israeli bombing of Tunis and the hijack of a Libyan civilian plane. . . . In Grenada, Nicaragua, Angola, and

18. Andrew Young, "The United States and Africa: Victory for Diplomacy," in the "America and the World 1980" issue of *Foreign Affairs* (February 1981).

now Libya, the U.S. administration in its easy disregard for international law when not convenient, seems determined to reestablish the principle of "might is right" in international relations, that philosophy of bygone days that launched gun-boats to impose solutions. Those who may wish to rejoice at Gaddafi's discomfiture must therefore ask themselves: Who next?[19]

In the case of southern Africa, the passing of the torch to the Reagan administration was unorthodox because one individual, Assistant Secretary of State for African Affairs Chester Crocker, was almost solely responsible for formulating, adapting, and implementing the policy, to which he gave the name "constructive engagement."[20] Crocker first spelled out the underlying assumptions of this approach in a series of articles and monographs written before he took office; these culminated in "South Africa: Strategy for Change," published in *Foreign Affairs* in the winter of 1980–81. Of his assumptions, the most critical was the acceptance of the reality of South Africa's overwhelming economic and military predominance in the southern region of the continent. It was *realpolitik* reasoning rather than ideological considerations that shaped Crocker's thinking on this question. Constructive engagement was a product of his assessment that the Botha regime's secure domestic and regional position, deriving from the nation's relative economic and military self-sufficiency, limits the effectiveness of such pressures as economic sanctions or arms embargoes.

Crocker's belief in the viability of constructive engagement as an alternative to the more confrontational strategy followed by the Carter administration also rested on a second, more arguable, assumption that Prime Minister P. W. Botha meant it when he said in 1979 that South African whites must "adapt or die," and that he could and would take the steps required for a sustained improvement in U.S.–South African relations—notably by initiating a clearly discernible process of internal reform, accepting Namibian independence, and developing mutually accommodating relations with South Africa's neighbors.

In his *Foreign Affairs* article, Crocker presented constructive engagement primarily as a means for reinforcing movement away from apartheid in South Africa. The Namibian issue and broader regional relations were only briefly mentioned. This emphasis changed quickly after he took up his portfolio in the State Department. By mid-1981, Namibia had become the main focus of attention and the tying of South African withdrawal from Namibia to a withdrawal of Cuban troops from Angola had become the linchpin of Reagan administration strategy.

This approach served two purposes. First, it provided Crocker with the argument he needed to enlist key administration officials on the right of the political spectrum who otherwise would have had little interest in the Namibian issue. By holding out the prospect of a rollback of Cuban and Soviet influence in southern Africa, he was able to get Secretary of State Alexander Haig and the

---

19. "The Bully Boy of the West," *West Africa*, 21 April 1986.
20. Kitchen and Clough, *The United States and South Africa*, pp. 3–5, 7–9.

Andrew Young, U.S.
ambassador to the United
Nations in the Carter
administration. (AP/Wide
World Photos)

White House committed to according Namibian independence a place on the administration's foreign policy agenda. Analysts who fail to give this domestic political aspect the attention it warrants do not have a full understanding of the linkage issue.

Second, Crocker believed that linkage of the Cuban and South African withdrawals was the most promising way of moving South Africa to agree to implementation of UN Resolution 435. His reasoning appears to have been that it would not be possible to coerce Pretoria into an agreement, but that the withdrawal of Cuban troops from the region would be an enticement, especially if it were coupled with the prospect of an improvement in bilateral relations between the United States and South Africa.

If this strategy had succeeded relatively quickly (i.e., by the end of 1982), as Crocker and his closest aides apparently envisaged, a self-reinforcing spiral of positive developments would have been set in motion in the region. A success would have boosted U.S. credibility throughout Africa. It also would have dealt a major diplomatic blow to Moscow, still regrouping from its failure to back Robert Mugabe, who won a decisive victory in Zimbabwe's first postindependence elections in 1980, defeating the Soviet-supported Zimbabwe African People's Union party led by Joshua Nkomo. A further hope was that a successful Namibian settlement would give the Botha government confidence to move faster with its internal reform program, which would in turn confirm the merits of constructive engagement. By late 1983, however, the Namibian negotiations had crawled toward a stalemate yet again.

Crocker's problems with the linkage knot made the broader regional dimension of constructive engagement progressively more significant. It was in a major policy speech in October 1981 that the assistant secretary first emphasized the importance of directing constructive engagement at the entire southern region of the continent: "Until there develops a structure of understanding—some reciprocally understood basis for coexistence—between South Africa and its neighbors, this situation will remain a major source of instability and could result in growing conflict across borders."

The most visible and positive result in 1983 of the Reagan administration's attention to the regional dimension of its strategy was the blossoming of a surprisingly warm relationship with Mozambique. This is an instance in which the United States was clearly sending a message to South Africa. The message was that Pretoria's quasi-covert support of the dissident Resistência Nacional Moçambicana (known as the MNR or Renamo) guerrillas in Mozambique could lead to something more than a local confrontation if Machel were left with no option but to invoke his Treaty of Friendship and Cooperation with the Soviet Union and seek military support in the face of a threatened takeover.

In the months following President Reagan's November 1984 election to a second term (by an astounding plurality of forty-nine of fifty states), the domestic debate over U.S. policy in southern Africa intensified. The prospect of four more years of constructive engagement aroused militants at both ends of the political spectrum. On the one hand, those who measured the policy against the single criterion of its effectiveness in moving South Africa toward majority rule joined forces to organize a campaign to step up the pressure for U.S. corporate withdrawal, to motivate universities and other institutions to "divest" stock held in companies failing to withdraw, and to lobby for major sanctions legislation in the halls of Congress. Meanwhile, movement conservatives within the Republican Party launched a media campaign for the replacement of both Crocker and Secretary of State George Shultz on grounds that constructive engagement was overly tolerant of Marxist regimes and not appropriately supportive of the region's "freedom fighters"—notably the MNR in Mozambique and Jonas Savimbi's União Nacional para a Independência Total de Angola (UNITA).

The confused state of play in Washington at the end of 1987 provided little guidance for crystal ball gazers. The Comprehensive Anti-Apartheid Act of 1986, enacted by Congress over a presidential veto, remained the harshest anti-Pretoria sanctions package yet imposed by any major western nation or association of nations. A total of 155 U.S. corporations had "disinvested" their South African operations, sometimes selling their interests at bargain prices. Legislation calling for new and harsher sanctions as well as penalties against U.S. oil companies still operating in the country was under consideration in the House of Representatives. South Africa was provisionally estimated to have recorded real economic growth of about 2.4 percent in 1987—less than the 3 percent projected, but much better than in 1986. The Reagan administration, having resumed military assistance to UNITA in 1986 (following congressional repeal in 1985 of the 1976 "Clark Amendment" banning aid for military or paramilitary operations in Angola), was reported to be considering doubling the previously approved $15 million per year figure.

Meanwhile, the State Department was still under attack from the Right for its continued dialogue with the government of Angola and for its refusal to receive the MNR's Washington representatives. A mailing from the Heritage Foundation, with a covering letter from Republican Congressman Jack Kemp, sought donations for a "State Department Assessment Project" that would focus *inter alia* on the department's opposition to U.S. assistance "to the freedom fighters in Angola," its "[support of] the communist regime in Mozambique," and its "[establishment of] relations with Oliver Tambo, boss of the South African terrorist group, the African National Congress."

Something approaching a consensus was developing among objective analysts that South Africa had entered what could be an extended period of stalemate—a government policy of limited socioeconomic reform at the local level combined with increased repression of political activism in the name of law and order. Conditions for negotiations did not appear to exist on either side of the racial divide, and the black majority lacked both the organizational cohesion and the military capability to launch a classic revolution.

Press reports were accumulating of "secret approaches" to South African diplomats by Soviet envoys proposing the opening of informal contacts on issues of mutual concern (rendered somewhat more credible by media quotes attributed to unnamed officials in Pretoria that "the time had come to ask who posed the greatest threat to South Africa—the United States or the Soviet Union").

One of the more positive developments seemed to be a growing consensus within the U.S. policy community that neither South Africa, Angola, Mozambique, Zimbabwe, Botswana, nor Namibia could henceforth be dealt with as separate issues. The futures of all the peoples of southern Africa were intertwined, for better or for worse, and the policies of outsiders who sought to remain "relevant" would henceforth have to reflect this reality.

Summing Up

Although the policy community's African safari has taken various twists and turns under the five Republican and four Democratic presidents who have occupied the White House since the end of World War II, several generalizations are warranted:

• As noted at the outset of this chapter, there has been no basic change over the last four decades in U.S. military strategists' view of Africa as an appendage of U.S. security interests in Europe, the Middle East, and Asia. Although the Department of Defense monitors developments throughout Africa, especially in countries with a significant Soviet or Cuban presence, major attention has remained focused on the states on the northern and eastern periphery of the continent because of their proximity to or location on access routes to areas of greater strategic priority.

In its 1987 report at the conclusion of year-long deliberations, the secretary of state's twelve-member bipartisan Advisory Committee on South Africa (appointed by Secretary Shultz as specified in President Reagan's Executive Order of September 1985) also downplayed strategic considerations in its findings on U.S. priorities in South and southern Africa:

> The United States has no specific stated military interests in South Africa. There is no U.S. military presence other than a small Defense Attaché Office and the Marine guards customarily attached to our embassies worldwide. South Africa's position astride the sea-lanes around the Cape of Good Hope is frequently used as an argument in favor of South Africa's military importance, but the apparent consensus among U.S. defense planners is that these sea-lanes are under minimal threat and that the active collaboration of the South African Government would not significantly increase our ability to protect them.[21]

• The addition of dozens of new fiefdoms, largely outside the Department of State, to the foreign affairs bureaucracy since World War II has militated against a conceptual approach to Africa in general or in fact to any region or specific country. The patchwork of incoherent policies is most evident in the area of aid. As of 1987, the United States had aid programs in over forty countries on the continent, involving small amounts of aid moneys per country but large amounts of overhead to finance AID (Agency for International Development) mission personnel. Over time, a mixture of uncoordinated aid channels evolved—security (military) assistance divided up into several separate programs, the Economic Support Fund (fast-dispersing, balance-of-payments support), development assistance (often project aid), food aid, the Peace Corps, U.S. contributions to multilateral organizations such as the World Bank, and aid through such institutions as the government-funded African Development Foundation.

• As the executive branch foreign policy conglomerate grew in complexity in the postwar years, Congress gradually created a foreign policy bureaucracy of its own to gather and filter information deemed necessary to assess judgments and requests coming from the executive branch, and also (increasingly) to make action recommendations that by the late 1980s amounted to micromanagement of some aspects of foreign policy.[22] In the FY 1988 omnibus continuing resolution enacted in the waning days of 1987, for example, Military Assistance Program (MAP) funding for sub-Saharan Africa was cut by 40 percent from FY 1987, Economic Support Funds (ESF) by 38 percent, and no funds whatsoever were

---

21. *A U.S. Policy Toward South Africa: The Report of the Secretary of State's Advisory Committee on South Africa* (Department of State, January 1987).

22. For an expanded discussion of congressional micromanagement, see Helen Kitchen, "The Making of U.S. Policy Toward Africa," in *Africa in the 1990s and Beyond: U.S. Policy Opportunities and Choices,* ed. Robert I. Rotberg (Algonac, Mich.: Reference Publications, 1988).

WE KNOW YOU'VE BEEN WAITING FOR A **Chad Quiz**

WHICH COUNTRY IS MOST
CLOSELY ASSOCIATED WITH CHAD?

A. LIBYA
B. FRANCE
C. JEREMY

MAP PART

1. LOCATE CHAD ON THIS MAP.
2. LOCATE ANYTHING ON THIS MAP.
3. LOCATE THIS MAP.

WHICH OF THE FOLLOWING
REPORTS IS TRUE?

A. "QADDAFI INVADES CHAD"
   - N.Y. TIMES
B. "KHADAFY INVADES CHAD"
   - ASSOCIATED PRESS
C. "GADDAFI INVADES CHAD"
   - TIME MAGAZINE
D. ALL OF THE ABOVE, WHICH IS
   WHY CHAD IS IN SUCH TROUBLE.

WHICH STATEMENT IS
MORE INTERESTING?

A. CHAD WAS A FRENCH COLONY, SO
THE U.S. NEEDN'T WORRY, SINCE
FRANCE WILL TAKE CARE OF IT.

B. VIETNAM WAS A FRENCH COLONY.

TOLES AND USPRA. WREN I. HERMAN
©1983 THE BUFFALO NEWS

MAP PART, PART II
1. HOW MANY OF THE FOLLOWING
CITIES CAN YOU LOCATE IN CHAD?

• FAYA·LARGEAU
• OUM CHALOUBA
• GOUKOUNI OUEDDEI
• HISSENE HABRE
• N'DJAMENA

2. HOW MANY OF YOU KNEW THAT
REBEL LEADER GOUKOUNI OUEDDEI
AND PRESIDENT HISSENE HABRE
WEREN'T CITIES?

IT'S BEEN SAID THAT KHADAFY
IS CRAZY.

A. HIS SUCCESS IN CHAD
   CONTRADICTS THIS.
B. HIS INTEREST IN CHAD
   CONFIRMS IT.

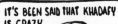

NEXT TROUBLE SPOT:
INNER MONGOLIA.
START STUDYING...

A 1983 cartoon originally published in the *Buffalo News* (N.Y.) deftly satirized the still limited and episodic nature of Americans' acquaintance with Africa's geography, history, and political relevance. (Toles Copyright 1983 United Press Syndicate. Reprinted with permission. All rights reserved.)

authorized for Foreign Military Sales (FMS) or for International Military Education and Training (IMET). In the same legislative package, the number of countries protected by congressional earmarks was increased from five to nine, which would cut back sharply on funds available for Kenya and Somalia, the two countries on Africa's eastern periphery with which the military has access agreements, and seemed likely to cut out Sudan completely. Military assistance to Mozambique, a country that had steadily increased its ties with the West in the 1980s, was explicitly prohibited unless "presidential certification" was provided.[23]

23. Helen Kitchen, *Some Guidelines on Africa for the Next President* (Washington, D.C.: CSIS Significant Issues Series, vol. 10, no. 4, 1988), p. 33.

• The episodic pattern of U.S. policy toward Africa cannot be understood, much less corrected, unless it is viewed as part of an American inclination to approach problems in the foreign policy realm as elsewhere with a task force mentality. Each of the major U.S. commitments of senior-level attention to Africa since World War II—Zaire in the 1960s, Angola and Rhodesia in the 1970s, the Carter and subsequent Reagan blueprints for resolving the Namibian independence issue, and the campaign against Libya's Qaddafi in the 1980s—has been perceived as a mission that would have a conclusive ending within a foreseeable time period.

• One reason that a clear set of guidelines on U.S. interests and objectives in Africa is still lacking as the 1980s draw to a close is that the executive branch lacks either a policy planning or intelligence component focused on integrating broad historical goals, realities, and options. Another reason is the low priority given to institutional memory in the "clean slate" approach that, more often than not, characterizes the changes that take place in key positions in the policymaking apparatus when presidential power is transferred from one party to another. And a third is the previously cited congressional inclination to micromanage more and more specific aspects of foreign policy substance and process.

10

The United States and South Asia

ROBERT F. GOHEEN, JOHN P. LEWIS, and WILLIAM H. WEATHERSBY

OFFICIAL relations between the United States and most of South Asia began just over forty years ago with the gaining of independence by India and Pakistan in 1947. Many years of trade and exchanges of religious workers, scholars, tourists, and others came before, and official influences between these two very different areas of the world also preceded Indian freedom from British rule.

Woodrow Wilson's Fourteen Points and his call for self-determination on 4 July 1918, for example, encouraged the independence movement. Similarly, the leadership of Mahatma Gandhi, as depicted by the press, scholars, and missionaries, had an impact on American opinion, and sympathy for the cause grew steadily between the two world wars. The Atlantic Charter of Franklin D. Roosevelt and Winston Churchill in 1941 advocated the right of all people to choose their own form of government. While Roosevelt by no means persuaded Churchill to preside over the liquidation of the British Empire, he did without much effect urge the prime minister to allow more Indian autonomy. Before Indian independence Roosevelt also sent to New Delhi two personal representatives, Louis Johnson as minister plenipotentiary and later William Phillips as ambassador to India.

In turn, Jawaharlal Nehru in 1946, leading an interim government, sent Asaf Ali as the first Indian ambassador to the United States. With partition and the simultaneous birth of independent India and Pakistan, their relations with the United States became extremely cordial. There was a high expectancy of mutual benefits between the United States and each of these two most influential of the countries of South Asia.

In the ensuing forty years of U.S. diplomacy, there have been ups and downs and considerable change in these relationships, and we shall undertake to examine some of the causes and consequences of them. For this discussion we are accepting the term South Asia to mean the area south of the Soviet Union and China that lies between Iran and Burma. Our principal focus will be on relations with India, by far the largest and now also the most economically and militarily powerful of the South Asian states. We shall, however, look also at least briefly at American diplomacy in relation to the other six South Asian states: Pakistan, Afghanistan, Nepal, Bangladesh, Bhutan, and Sri Lanka.

Endemic suspicion and recurrent friction and fighting between India and Pakistan, beginning with the short war over Kashmir during their first year of independence, have increased the difficulties of American diplomacy. Beneath the problem lies a conflict between the goals of the United States and those of India. Their purposes began to cross in the era of John Foster Dulles, when in the United States the geopolitical aim of containment of the Soviet Union encouraged military pacts, and neutrality was seen as an evil. In contrast, the early and persistent aims of India have been, through nonalignment, to avoid foreign entanglements and to concentrate its resources internally upon economic development.

Early in the 1950s Pakistan joined the SEATO and CENTO pacts, establishing a military relationship with the United States and receiving in consequence large quantities of American arms, while India declined pact invitations. President Eisenhower offered military assistance to India as well as assurances that he would undertake to halt any misuse of American arms by Pakistan. Having opposed a large military buildup from the start, Prime Minister Nehru declined the offer of arms and continued for some time to rely for them primarily upon India's traditional supplier, the United Kingdom. Later, in 1969, India also turned down a Soviet initiative for an Asian collective security system.

From the start, a number of disparities have underlain and complicated a record of recurring tension and misunderstanding between the United States and India. These include but are not limited to differences in cultural background, historical experience, and geographic position.[1]

Different cultural backgrounds inevitably affect our expectations and the ways in which we interpret experience. The favored mode of thought in the western tradition is empirical, rational, definitive, and it looks to the working of cause and effect in the here and now. Thought, in the indigenous India tradition, is more intuitive and fluid; the same thing may have many meanings; Karma, the law of

1. Elements of the discussion bearing on India reflect Robert Goheen's "Perceptions of Indo-U.S. Relations" in *Darshan* (April 1987) vol. 4, no. 4, a monthly publication of the Indian Consulate General in New York.

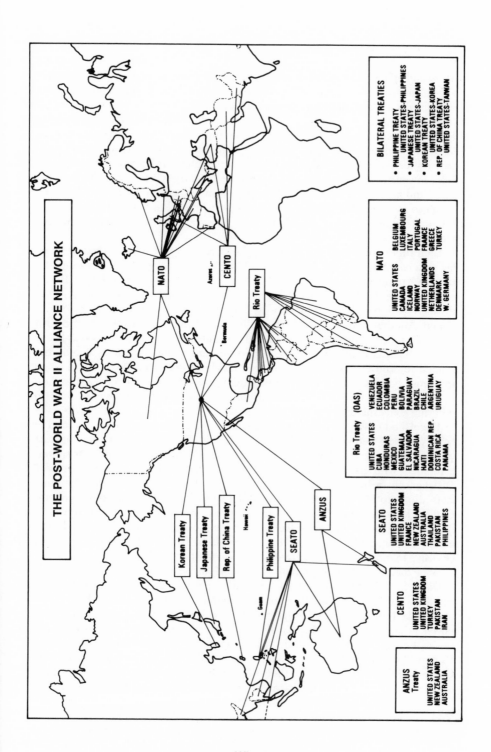

THE POST-WORLD WAR II ALLIANCE NETWORK

BILATERAL TREATIES
- Philippine Treaty
  UNITED STATES-PHILIPPINES
- Japanese Treaty
  UNITED STATES-JAPAN
- Korean Treaty
  UNITED STATES-KOREA
- Rep. of China Treaty
  UNITED STATES-TAIWAN

NATO
UNITED STATES	BELGIUM
CANADA	LUXEMBOURG
ICELAND	ITALY
NORWAY	PORTUGAL
UNITED KINGDOM	FRANCE
NETHERLANDS	GREECE
DENMARK	TURKEY
W. GERMANY	

Rio Treaty (OAS)
UNITED STATES	VENEZUELA
CUBA	ECUADOR
HONDURAS	COLOMBIA
MEXICO	PERU
GUATEMALA	BOLIVIA
EL SALVADOR	PARAGUAY
NICARAGUA	BRAZIL
HAITI	CHILE
DOMINICAN REP.	ARGENTINA
COSTA RICA	URUGUAY
PANAMA	

SEATO
UNITED STATES
UNITED KINGDOM
FRANCE
NEW ZEALAND
AUSTRALIA
THAILAND
PAKISTAN
PHILIPPINES

CENTO
UNITED STATES
UNITED KINGDOM
TURKEY
PAKISTAN
IRAN

ANZUS Treaty
UNITED STATES
NEW ZEALAND
AUSTRALIA

NATO

CENTO

Rio Treaty

Korean Treaty

Japanese Treaty

Rep. of China Treaty

Philippine Treaty

SEATO

ANZUS

Azores

Bermuda

Hawaii

Guam

cause and effect, has force over a sequence of lifetimes more than in the present. Or, again, the dominant western religious view is monotheistic, and so Americans find much bewilderment in the plethora of Hinduism's divinities—many of them able to take on a multitude of forms including the forms of each other. So, too, we are habituated in the West to seeing time as linear and history as moving forward—with periods of regression to be sure, but generally advancing from the past toward some higher future. In Indian thought that has not been westernized, in contrast, time is endlessly cyclical and history is repetitive. The fact that many Indians have had western-style education reduces these differences when it comes to diplomatic dealings, business transactions, and government-to-government relations; but it does not totally obliterate the differences in cultural viewpoint.

Then there are our different historical experiences that have worked to shape for each country different perceptions of important developments. For example, the absorption of Eastern Europe by the USSR following World War II is a remote matter for most Indians. For most Americans that was not the case. It has distinctly colored the way most of us and our government look on the Soviet Union. Another example may be found in the fact that America threw off British colonialism nearly two centuries before India did and never experienced as heavy a yoke. Consequently while we Americans are proud of our freedom, the immediacy and intensity of Indians' feelings about self-determination and being free from bondage are something we Americans often do not fully appreciate.

Differences in the geographic positions of the two countries also lead to differing concerns. For example, Americans are likely to feel bemused when the distinguished editor of *The Times of India* describes his country as an island of largely Hindu people living in jeopardy within a sea of Islam stretching east through Indonesia and west through Morocco. But that sort of perception, combined with its own large Muslim population, helps to account for why Pakistan causes India greater concern than most Americans recognize. The same facts also help explain India's dispatch of a special envoy to express support for Qaddafi following the U.S. bombing of Libya in April 1986. The gesture was in line with the long-standing Indian policy of supporting the Arab states and Arab causes in competition with Pakistani appeals to Islamic solidarity, but it was offensive to most Americans. Or at best it was felt to be unwarranted, even in the view of those who might deplore the American action.

Disparities in the weights of economic and military power that the two countries command are another potential source of friction between them. They mean that India's primary foreign policy concerns are regional. Though India's power is growing both economically and militarily, the Indian Ocean region is the extent of its effective reach. The primary foreign policy concerns of the United States in contrast are global, or have to be weighed in a global context. Consequently, for example, for the United States the People's Republic of China is a critical counter in its rivalry and conflict with the Soviet Union. For India, however, China has a different bearing: it is a powerful neighbor and regional rival that possibly has southerly expansionist ambitions. A frequent complaint is that the United States treats India merely as a pawn in its big-powers game.

Though influenced by the factors just mentioned, in our view the principal impediments in Indo-U.S. governmental relations are of a different, more political order, and they are twofold. First is the recurrent crossing of the bilateral relationship by the U.S.-Soviet and the Indo-Pakistan rivalries. The second deep-reaching set of complications lies in the strongly nationalistic character of Indian policy—its orientation toward independence and self-determination—where that policy confronts U.S. global concerns and the difficulty that the United States has so often shown in accepting nonalignment as Indians understand that concept.

There can be no doubt that containment of the Soviet Union since World War II has held—and still holds—a key, linchpin position in U.S. foreign policy. In our dealings with South Asia, this American orientation comes up hard against the solid support that India has received from the USSR since 1955. On Kashmir since the mid-1950s; on the absorption of Goa by India in 1961; when in the early 1960s India sought military aircraft following the Chinese invasion and when it looked for external assistance to build its fourth and largest public sector steel mill; again in the confrontations attending the establishment of Bangladesh in 1971—on all of these issues the USSR stood firmly with India, while the United States for its own reasons stood opposed. Geography aside, then, from India's point of view the maintenance of close, friendly relations with the USSR is a clear matter of self-interest, however Americans may feel about it.

That self-interest is reinforced because close ties with the Soviet Union also buttress India's position vis-à-vis the two neighbors with which it has had to fight wars—both powers the United States has been courting assiduously—namely, Pakistan and China. The first drafts of the Treaty of Peace, Friendship and Cooperation between India and the USSR predated 1971. India's decision to sign that treaty in that year however, coincided with the United States' patent tilt toward Pakistan during the Bangladesh crisis and U.S. moves to open relations with the People's Republic of China. Under the treaty, India and the USSR pledge to abstain from assisting any country engaged in conflict with either of the two and undertake to consult together in the event of a threat to the security of either.

The U.S. had in 1963 entered into a thirty-year contract to provide low enriched uranium to fuel two U.S.-origin nuclear power reactors at Tarapur in western India. In 1974 India exploded a nuclear device which it termed a peaceful nuclear explosion, and that PNE sent shock waves through Washington and other American nonproliferation circles. During the 1960s the U.S. was itself engaged in experimenting with PNEs in "Project Ploughshare" but by 1974 had concluded that they were indistinguishable from nuclear weapons and was strongly opposed to them. Consequently India's PNE provided strong impetus for a strict tightening of U.S. nuclear export policy, which occurred in the Nuclear Non-Proliferation Act of 1978. Under its restrictions the U.S. could no longer fulfill its supply commitment to the Tarapur reactors unless India could be persuaded to accept international safeguards on all its nuclear installations.

Sustained U.S. efforts to achieve that change in Indian policy, including the direct involvement of President Carter on more than one occasion, failed. The result in the late 1970s and up to 1982 was a serious strain in the broader Indo-U.S. relationship. That strain was finally, and skillfully, resolved by officers in the U.S. State Department who, with the agreement of the Indian Government, arranged for France to relieve the United States of its obligations toward Tarapur. Subsequently India has proceeded to enlarge its capabilities to produce nuclear weapons should its government at some point decide that developing them would be to its advantage.

From the start India has held the Non-Proliferation Treaty, now subscribed to by over 120 states, to be discriminatory against the nonnuclear-weapons states and an improper infringement on their sovereignty in the requirement imposed on them of full scope safeguards which is not shared by the nuclear weapons states. But while India has not proceeded since the 1974 explosion to develop a nuclear armory and has, indeed, shown commendable restraint in this respect, the government clearly remains intent on keeping the nuclear weapons option open against the possibility that its security environment may require India to move in that direction at some point.

A considerable incentive, resisted so far, is the knowledge since 1979 that Pakistan has been secretly developing its own nuclear weapons capabilities. A significant deterrent for India has been China's well-developed nuclear armaments and the close ties existing between China and Pakistan. U.S. diplomacy may have helped reinforce India's relative nuclear restraint to date, but it cannot be said to have altered or otherwise affected Indian nuclear policy.[2]

Since the early 1950s, the U.S. policy of containing the USSR has led to repeated U.S. efforts to build up Pakistan militarily as a forward-line anticommunist state sitting on the Soviet Union's southern flank. For a time during much of 1979 U.S.-Pakistan relations became strained and American military and economic aid to Pakistan had to be suspended under the terms of U.S. nonproliferation legislation when Pakistan's clandestine pursuit of nuclear weapons capabilities became unmistakable. The USSR's invasion of Afghanistan in December of that year, however, greatly magnified the importance to Washington of close relations with Pakistan, and in 1981 under the Reagan administration the country was granted a six-year exemption from the law which had barred U.S. assistance two years earlier. Pakistan gained a $3.2 billion package of arms and economic aid to be delivered over six years plus an agreement to be allowed to purchase the most advanced U.S. strike aircraft, F-16s. Needless to say, the Indians were less than pleased and promptly turned to France and the Soviet Union for countering advanced Mirage and MIG aircraft. The subcontinent's arms race was thus escalated one more costly spiral higher.

Despite continuing evidence that Pakistan was proceeding to develop a nuclear weapons capability—even while it denied the fact at the highest levels of government—in late 1987 Washington once again waived nonproliferation legislation that would have cut off further aid and granted Pakistan a new arms and economic assistance package of roughly $2 billion to cover the next two-and-a-

2. For a fuller account see Robert F. Goheen, "Problems of Proliferation: U.S. Policy and the Third World," *World Politics* (January 1988): 194–215.

half years. Considerable opposition by nonproliferation proponents in the Congress reduced this commitment to about one-half of what the administration sought. Here in striking fashion two U.S. foreign policy objectives came up hard against each other. Dominant proved the desire to secure the goodwill of the Pakistan government, ensure its readiness to permit a large continuing flow of arms to the Afghan *mujahidin*, and so maintain pressure on the Soviet Union for withdrawal from Afghanistan. Against these concerns, U.S. nonproliferation policy was judged to be expendable.

An earlier exception to the general pattern of U.S. arms supply to South Asia, in 1962, should not be overlooked. A long-smoldering border dispute resulted in that year in Chinese attacks on India in Ladakh and the northeast frontier area. Shortly before, the Soviet Union had agreed to supply MIGs to India and to help in aircraft manufacturing. Referring to the serious international crisis, the Soviet Union put off the deal following the Chinese incursions. Whether the crisis meant was the one on the Chinese-Indian border or the one simultaneously occurring in and around Cuba remains uncertain.

In some desperation India turned to Washington, and Defense Minister Krishna Menon, who had been an astringent critic of the United States, telephoned for an urgent meeting at the U.S. Embassy with Ambassador John Kenneth Galbraith. Knowing Menon wanted to ask for arms, Galbraith put him off by explaining he had an urgent letter from President Kennedy to deliver to the prime minister first, in order to obtain the arms request from Nehru rather from the longtime antagonist of the United States and many of its policymakers. Not long afterward Menon left the government. Nehru later remarked that Indian leaders had been "living in a world of our own illusions."[3]

American cargo planes flew some of the arms to Leh, in the highland center of Ladakh not far from the fighting, in an effort to halt Chinese incursions in that critical area. After the Chinese attacks ceased, India sought a much larger quantity of weapons, including fourteen squadrons of fighter planes and three squadrons of bombers. The request was favorably received by Galbraith and President Kennedy, but it was blocked by Congress. Some of the approximately $100 million in U.S. weapons previously committed remained in the pipeline, however, when the Indo-Pakistan war of 1965 began and American military aid to both India and Pakistan was halted.

Thereafter, Pakistan and India, under pressure from both the United States and the United Kingdom, which was also supplying weapons to India after the Chinese attack, held a series of discussions on the Kashmir dispute, but as each side seemed to have expected going in, nothing came of the talks.

Could there have been a major difference in the relations between India and the United States if, while the Soviet Union was withholding arms that had been promised to India, the Indian request for larger quantities of American weapons had been fulfilled? Opinions differ. However, it seems unlikely in view of the conflicts between these countries' perceived interests vis-à-vis the USSR, the

3. For a full account of the U.S. supply of arms to India see John Kenneth Galbraith, *Ambassador's Journal* (Boston: Houghton Mifflin Co., 1969), pp. 429–59.

intractability of the Kashmir issue, and the depth of the mutual suspicions that divide India and Pakistan.

The Reagan administration was somewhat ambiguous about restrictions on the use of arms supplied to Pakistan, and there appears no longer to be an explicit ban on their use against India. In addition, India continues to complain (as it has from the earliest) that the U.S. aid package for Pakistan includes types of artillery, tanks, and aircraft more suited to combat on the plains than in the mountains of the northwest frontier.

American policymakers have argued that India with its far greater economic and military power should no longer feel threatened by a Pakistan truncated by the breaking away of Bangladesh. That, however, is to overlook the emotional depths of the Indo-Pakistan antagonism, which has been at least as discordant as its American-Soviet counterpart, and to discount India's natural wariness concerning a Pakistan-China coalition.

To be sure, the U.S. government has largely moved away from the radical simplicities of its earlier view of nonalignment—that those who weren't for us were, *ipso facto*, against us. Despite occasional incantations to the contrary, the makers of American foreign policy seem now to be prepared by and large to accept nonalignment as a valid position for countries wishing not to be caught up in the power struggle between the superpowers. However, there are different ideas of what nonalignment means.

Because Americans commonly look at world affairs through anti-Soviet spectacles and so tend to see foreign events in East-West terms, acceptable nonalignment in their view is a position equidistant from each superpower—no tilt toward one or the other. Hence, when India votes with the socialist bloc in the UN, or continues to adhere to the Treaty of Peace, Friendship and Cooperation with the USSR, or supports pro-Soviet Vietnam against China as in 1979, Americans tend to find India's professed nonalignment a sham.

For Indian leaders, beginning with Nehru, who invented Third World nonalignment, the concept of nonalignment means something very different from equidistance. It represents instead a proud, nationalistic determination to remain free enough from entanglements with either superpower in order to make your own decisions according to your own perceptions of what is best for your nation in any particular circumstance. Thus, at a given time it may be best to incline more to the USSR, but at another time, or on another issue, it may be more advantageous to lean more toward the West. The important thing is maintaining the maximum degree of self-determination possible.

The further aim, of course, has been to concentrate attention and resources on internal development. Nonalignment viewed as nonentanglement aimed to permit both self-determination and internal socioeconomic progress is very close to the position advocated for the young United States by George Washington on leaving office. He urged the new nation to steer clear of involvements with the superpowers of the time, France and England, in order that the thirteen former colonies might enjoy peace and concentrate their energies and resources on domestic development.

If Indo-U.S. relations have been strained by the American tendency to look at the world through anti-Soviet lenses, they often also have been strained by India's tendency to look at the western world through anticolonial lenses. Perhaps the most salient example was the disparity between India's response in 1956 to the British-French-Israeli effort to seize the Suez Canal, and the Soviet Union's invasion of Hungary that same year. The first action drew immediate, blistering denunciation from Nehru. The second initially evoked no public reaction at all, and when disapproval finally was expressed, it was in rather mild and general terms.

An important difference in the way India perceived the two events was that the first was old-time colonialism asserting itself again. India was all too familiar with that and could react at once and with passion. The Soviet invasion of Hungary, on the other hand, was remote and unfamiliar, and so the freedom of the Hungarian nation and the rights of the Hungarian people could be discounted in the interest of improving India-Soviet relations. Moreover, support for Egypt was consistent with the general policy of supporting the Arabs, and the Middle East was a neighboring region of interest to India. Hungary and all of Eastern Europe, by contrast, were of no such direct concern.

Despite all the problems in the ways that the United States and India have viewed each other, there are several encouraging signs of prospects for improvement in their relations.

For one thing, a clear-eyed realism seems to prevail currently both in Washington and New Delhi. Washington now knows that the United States is not going to detach India from its friendship with the Soviet Union; most of our policymakers also know that India is in no way Moscow's minion. On its part, New Delhi recognizes that the United States had to support Pakistan militarily as long as it perceived the threat of a military takeover of Afghanistan by Soviet troops. What sorts of arms and to what degree can be highly debatable. But New Delhi seems to understand the nature of the United States–Soviet rivalry and how the American superpower could not but support Pakistan with substantial arms in the circumstances of the last few years.

At the same time, Washington now seems to understand the strategic importance of India as the most powerful nation, both economically and militarily, along the vast southern flank of Asia. India could, if it wished, play a very troublesome spoiler role for U.S. interests in that area. Consequently to be on good terms with India—or at least not deeply at odds with it—is recognized in Washington to be much in the interest of the United States.

There also seems to be in New Delhi a comparably heightened sense of Indian self-interest in good relations with the United States which springs from several causes. One cause has been the continued presence of Soviet forces at the historic gateway to the subcontinent, running counter to India's ambition to be chief overseer, if not hegemon, of subcontinental affairs. The situation has been of grave concern for many thoughtful Indians, and for the government it has increased the importance of good relations with the United States to serve as a counterpoise to possible adverse pressures from the Soviet Union.

This does not mean that India approves the prominent naval presence that the United States has now established in the Indian Ocean. What India wants as a counterpoise is something less menacing. The aim seems simply to be on sufficiently good terms with the United States to be able readily to rebuff any Soviet pressures that might run counter to Indian interests and to maintain or enhance India's access to American technology, investment, markets, and some, albeit diminished, economic assistance.

Changes in its economic needs and capabilities are drawing India closer to the United States and other free market economies that can provide the high-level technology and capital required for the sort of modernization India is trying to accomplish. Consequently, over the past five years India has taken significant steps to reduce protectionist barriers in order to gain both greater foreign investment and a higher degree of technological cooperation from the western nations and Japan.

The importance to India of its trade with the United States is another factor. In 1984, the two-way traffic amounted to more than $4 billion, with Indian exports to the United States accounting for about one-half the total. A rising tide of protectionism in the U.S. signals obstacles, but the Reagan administration, sensitive to the needs of developing countries, seemed determined to dampen domestic protectionist demands.

Another factor in the U.S. relationship with India and with all of South Asia has been the exchange of students and teachers, works of art, cultural perform-ances, books, and public information—some privately, but to a larger degree by governmental sponsorship, sometimes called "public diplomacy."

Within a few years after the first American embassies were opened in the area, information and cultural programs were undertaken. In one case, in Nepal, a resident cultural affairs officer and information officer preceded by several years the opening of an embassy. The wide variety of programs throughout the area included libraries, tours of art collections, musical performances and other cultural events, outstanding scholars and public figures for lectures, as well as book translations, periodic publications within the country, and the provision of regular information on U.S. cultural and political developments for the press. The Fulbright and other programs that have supported the exchange of literally thousands of South Asians and Americans for studying, teaching, researching, speaking, or otherwise performing probably have had a lasting impact in terms of greater understanding of the peoples and the goals of the countries visited.

The larger of the South Asian nations have somewhat similar programs in the United States. Pakistan is very active, particularly in Washington. India, also long active in Washington, recently made an enormous broader effort by spon-soring the "Festival of India," which featured major art exhibitions, cultural performances, lectures, conferences, and seminars across the United States during 1985 and 1986. While the measurement of positive effects from such undertakings is difficult or impossible, there is a widespread belief that in the long run they improve mutual understanding and advance relations.

Bilateral U.S. economic assistance to the countries of the Indian Subcontinent is now of relatively minor proportions, except with respect to Pakistan. Economic and development assistance has, however, been an important part of the Amer-ican initiative in South Asia during most of the forty years that the nations there have enjoyed political independence.[4] The beginning was an emergency wheat loan of $190 million to India in 1951. In 1952, that was followed by a technical assistance program instituted under President Truman's Point IV scheme. Over the next thirty-two years, measured in 1982 dollars, more than $30 billion in U.S. bilateral aid and U.S. contributions to multilateral assistance flowed to the subcontinent. This was perhaps one-eighth of the development assistance that the United States provided worldwide during that period.

Early economic assistance was mainly bilateral. In recent years more has been channeled through the World Bank (primarily the soft-loan window, IDA) and other international lending and development organizations. The story of U.S. economic assistance in Asia generally should prove to any purist that development assistance does not always have to be either bountiful or high-minded to be useful. Clearly the purposes of much of American official development assistance have been distinctly political. Yet there are many cases in the record—almost surely a predominant number—where the prodevelopment effectiveness of aid must be given high marks.

Like the early Point IV technical cooperation initiative, the Colombo Plan, which the United States joined in 1951, was largely aimed at development as an end in itself. By then there may have been little the United States did in the foreign policy realm that completely lacked a Cold War echo. For most Americans, however, Point IV represented a commitment to help without massive budget implications many of the world's poor and emerging nations. Point IV, however, was overtaken by the Korean War, whereupon U.S. foreign policy thinking seemed to snap back into a comparatively militant East-West idiom. The U.S. aid agency was transformed into the Mutual Security Agency (Point IV being folded in), and it became heavily preoccupied with matters of defense support in various countries, including Pakistan.

Yet there is a common perception that in a few countries—notably India—the American assistance effort mainly continued to be development driven. Probably this was also true in Sri Lanka and perhaps even in Nepal and Afghanistan.

In addition, a charismatic push had earlier been given economic assistance during the Truman administration by Chester Bowles, the only U.S. ambassador to serve two terms in India—in the Truman administration in 1951–53 and in the Kennedy and Johnson administrations in 1963–69. His kind of diplomacy proved unusually persuasive to Indian public opinion as well as to his own and the Indian government.

There are two overlapping explanations of why assistance continued for the sake of development in nonaligned countries at the same time that Americans were being taught by leading makers of policy that nonalignment in the East-West struggle was immoral. First, even with so dominant a figure as John Foster Dulles in charge of foreign policy, governments generally, and certainly the U.S. government, are never monoliths.

They pursue multiple objectives simultaneously. There was nothing unusual

4. In the following pages, material dealing with development assistance draws on John P. Lewis, *Asian Development: The Role of Development Assistance* (The Asia Society, University Press of America, 1987).

Chester Bowles and Prime Minister Jawaharlal Nehru in February 1962.
(AP/Wide World Photos)

about a mixture of goals being sought within the same administrative framework, or about different country programs being launched with different dominant purposes. And there also was a further aid-specific, bottom-up explanation, which some might say concerns the pathologies of bureaucracies. It is a fact that once a number of able, strong technical and other staff are recruited and placed in the field, they become a very considerable party-in-interest for the prosecution of their programs. They often succeed, whether going through or out of channels, in injecting their views into central decision making. Enough inertia exists in budgetary and other bureaucratic and legislative processes to let them often be effective.

Overall, South Asia is the scene of a success story in turning around what had been the prospect of massive starvation into the production of enough to feed the population, even though large fractions of the population continue to suffer malnutrition. Clearly, there have been instances in which food aid had disincentive effects on indigenous production. This was true, almost certainly, of the PL480 food that was supplied to India up to the mid-1960s. Without any of it, however, the political system might well not have survived the turmoil that urban food price inflation would have brought. But the increased supplies were overdone, as was also true at times in Bangladesh.

The lesson produced a formula in two parts for food donors: First, when food aid is provided, a desired balance should be maintained between internal supplies and demand. If there are macro shortages so that in the absence of food aid food prices would be rising unacceptably, one may want to raise the food supply relative to demand. Otherwise, to avoid an unwanted dampening of farmers' prices, demand should be raised as much as supply by giving the food to targeted groups or by employing the poor on labor-intensive activities, or by building reserve stocks. Second, the donor must make sure that the recipient government in no sense slacks off on its promotion of internal food production; the food aid must not become a psychological crutch for the regime. (This was one rationale for President Johnson's "short tethering" of PL480 aid in 1965–67. The procedure was ham-handed, but it strengthened those within the Indian government who were pursuing the new high priority for agriculture.)

India, Pakistan, and Bangladesh all settled on achieving self-sufficiency in food grain as a national goal. Pakistan became self-sufficient in the 1970s and began exporting a million tons a year by 1979. The world's second largest cereal importer in 1966 and 1967, India became basically self-sufficient before 1980 and has since become an exporter, although a severe drought in the summer of 1987 caused a major setback, at least in the short term. Bangladesh suffered great shortages after the revolution and has had a series of flood disasters, but it seems to be nearing self-sufficiency. An exception is Nepal, where high population density brought an increasing amount of marginal land under cultivation, while widespread deforestation produced erosion and agricultural production failed to keep up with population growth.

The most spectacular turnaround was in India, where the "green revolution" resulted from the government's decision to assign a higher priority to domestic agriculture, to have bold resort to the new agricultural technology becoming available, and to increase cultivators' incentives. The minister of agriculture, C. Subramanian, seizing on the advice of Norman Borlaug and his researchers in Mexico, authorized the importation of a massive amount of high-yielding wheat seed, which, together with intensive research activity and decisions stepping up the supply of such inputs as fertilizer, set the new strategy into effective motion. Years later Subramanian said, "These were major innovations; to be fully implemented, they needed a tremendous amount of assured resource flow." First the United States and other bilateral donors, then increasingly the World Bank via IDA kept such resources flowing.

From the beginning, the U.S. aid program in India grew incrementally on dedicated technocratic momentum. Food assistance, motivated initially by an American interest in surplus disposal, was then added. By 1958 the era of large, regularized capital transfers began in response to the foreign exchange crisis that befell India's second five-year plan. A U.S. Export-Import Bank $150 million line of credit was followed by the establishment of an Aid-to-India Consortium composed of Canada, Germany, Japan, the United Kingdom, the United States, and the World Bank. Washington committed itself to major bilateral concessional lending with the establishment of the Development Loan Fund, of which India was the first leading client.

It has been argued by some that in aid to Asian development, India has received too much attention because of its size and because it began ahead of others with formal, self-initiated planned development. The absolute amount of economic aid received by India since 1950 has been the largest in Asia and has played a significant role in that country. It should, however, be pointed out that if Official Development Aid to India is measured per capita, it has been lower than in any other continuing aid recipient in all of Asia (not counting China, which did not begin receiving western Official Development Assistance until recently).

Political static has accompanied U.S. aid to India concerning issues such as Vietnam, Indian votes in the United Nations, and particularly the Indo-Pakistan rivalry and wars. But the theme plainly was development *qua* development, until in 1971–72 at the time of the Bangladesh war the program virtually collapsed. Thereafter, the United States has expressed its interest more through its support for IDA's large flow of transfers to India than through the token bilateral program that remained.

In the case of Pakistan, U.S. assistance, which has fluctuated considerably, clearly has been driven more by global policies and regional considerations than by the case for development for its own sake. Strategic concerns, including reactions to the Indian-Pakistan rivalry and wars, have caused fluctuations in economic as well as military aid. Thus the U.S. security assistance to Pakistan that began in 1954 ended with Pakistan's 1965 war with India. The ups and downs have continued in reaction to the relations between Pakistan and India and other factors, such as the Soviet invasion of Afghanistan and nuclear issues, as discussed above.

Despite traumatic experiences since independence, however (including three coups d'état, three wars with India, the splitting off of East Pakistan to form Bangladesh, and the huge effort to care for some three million Afghan refugees), Pakistan has prospered economically more than the other countries of South Asia. Pakistan's growth rates in real gross domestic product—5.4 percent and 5.6 percent during 1965–73 and 1973–83, respectively—were the best for the region.

The economy had been fairly sluggish until Ayub Khan, upon the collapse of the first parliamentary government, seized power in 1959. Along with his encouragement of exports, liberalized imports, agriculture, and the private sector, he promoted foreign aid from international organizations, western nations, and particularly economic and military assistance from the United States. He once told members of the U.S. Congress that among the American allies Pakistan was the "most allied." For nearly ten years he also gave salience to economic policy and endeared himself to donor agencies and to many U.S. policymakers until he resigned and turned control over to General Yahya Khan.

Zulfikar Ali Bhutto's regime from 1971 to 1977 began by attracting considerable multilateral assistance and delighting the International Monetary Fund by devaluing the rupee and liberalizing imports, but some ill-considered heavy industry commitments and, most of all, a pattern of fiscal-monetary looseness alienated the World Bank. In the regime of General Zia-ul-Haq, however, after the brief setback over nuclear policy in 1979, U.S. aid picked up sharply.

Perhaps the severest test for American diplomacy in South Asia stems from the situation in Afghanistan. In some ways but not nearly to the extent of earlier British influence, the United States began in the 1950s to replace the British in the rivalry in Afghanistan with imperial Russia and later the Soviet Union, which had gone on for many years in the nineteenth and first part of the twentieth centuries.

Afghanistan, unlike most other South Asian states, never experienced direct colonial rule, but was long subjected to inducements and pressures from outside great powers, especially Britain and Russia. Afghanistan's modern diplomatic history is thus more nearly similar to that of Iran, its neighbor to the west. The United States got involved in this diplomatic contest—what Victorian Britons dubbed "the great game in Asia"—rather late and in limited measure. The first American resident diplomatic mission was established in Kabul in 1943. There followed a U.S. aid program in 1946, and for a time both American and Soviet economic and military assistance with advisory personnel flowed into Afghanistan. The Helmund Valley River Project, a massive undertaking financed by the United States and undertaken by the firm of Morrison and Knudsen, promised a great deal but failed to make the desert bloom. Invited to join CENTO, General Mohammad Daud Khan, who had assumed power in a 1953 palace revolt, declined, and later Afghan efforts to obtain U.S. weapons failed. Even so, further World Bank and U.S. AID economic help was received.

By the 1970s the Soviet Union had gained the upper hand in influence within Afghanistan. Sardar Daud, who had Marxist support within the country, and presumably Soviet sponsorship, in 1973 overthrew his brother-in-law, King Mohammed Zahir Shah. As he sought to improve relations with Pakistan, Daud in turn was overthrown. There followed a struggle among Afghan Marxist rivals until in December 1979 Hafizullah Amin, then holding power, was killed as Soviet troops pushed across the border bringing with them Babrak Karmal to head the Afghan government. His was clearly a puppet government and the *post facto* explanation that the Afghan government had invited the Soviet troops in to save the country from the rebel Muslim *mujahidin*, accused of plotting with the CIA, was widely disbelieved.

President Carter, addressing the nation on 4 January 1980, called the invasion a "callous violation of international law and the UN Charter." The United States would not do business as usual with the Soviet Union until the Soviet troops were withdrawn, he said. He stopped grain deliveries, froze talks on strategic arms, halted sales of high technology, and urged that the United States and other countries boycott the summer Olympics in Moscow.

As Afghan refugees poured across the border, President Zia of Pakistan charac-terized an American offer of $400 million in arms assistance as "peanuts." Subsequently, a much larger package of $3.2 billion in military and economic aid was put together by the Reagan administration and accepted by Pakistan. Support for Pakistan was accompanied by U.S. naval movements that increased the fleet from a few vessels in the Persian Gulf and the Arabian Sea to task forces ranging at times between thirty and forty ships. At the same time, base facilities at Diego Garcia were enlarged.

Those who had been on watch for decades believing that the Russian empire and later the Soviet Union would someday push toward warm water ports in the Indian Ocean (and in later days try to control the oil supply of the Persian Gulf) suddenly saw the severity of this danger increase. Had not the communists tried it in Iran once before in the days of President Truman?

With the shah removed and Iran no longer a bastion of strength capable of upholding western interests—however mistaken that notion may have been in the first place—with Soviet influence dominant in Afghanistan, and with U.S. aid frozen and relations at a low ebb with Pakistan, was the time not ripe for the Soviet move?

The Soviet occupation of Afghanistan brought forth U.S. military and humanitarian aid for the *mujahidin,* reversed the trend in American aid for Pakistan, and changed considerably the relations between the two countries. It also further complicated U.S. relations with India. When in June of 1980 the UN General Assembly by an overwhelming vote (104 to 18 with 18 abstentions) called for immediate withdrawal of foreign troops from Afghanistan, India abstained. American officials were not only disappointed by India's abstention but also by what seemed to be an equation drawn by Prime Minister Indira Gandhi (newly returned to office) between the Soviet occupation of Afghanistan and the building up of U.S. naval power in the Indian Ocean. Despite this position, which was seen in the United States as "soft" on the Soviet invasion, however, Mrs. Gandhi and other Indian leaders were understood quietly to have pressed the Soviet Union for withdrawal.

Certain strategists have seen the Soviet military involvement in Afghanistan as offering the United States a test of the long-standing containment policy comparable to that of Cuba. In any case by 1985 the U.S. supply of arms to the Afghan "freedom fighters" in and through Pakistan had become substantial, and by 1987 it had come to include some very advanced types of armament, including Stinger hand-carried ground-to-air missiles that greatly reduced the threat of Soviet airpower to the *mujahidin.*

At the same time indications began to appear that the Soviet leadership would like to extricate its forces from Afghanistan, and that was made virtually explicit in December 1987 when in an NBC interview prior to departure for that month's summit meeting, Secretary Gorbachev declared that the problem of Afghanistan could be swiftly solved by political means if the United States so desired.

For the Soviet Union to have secured a firm, untroubled hold on Afghanistan would have required destruction of the deeply rooted tribal structure of that society together with the independent spirit of its many tribal groups—a task of many years. The Soviet leadership apparently calculated in the end that such a result would also take many more Soviet casualties than the stake was worth. In consequence, with the United Nations as intermediary, an agreement was struck between Afghanistan, Pakistan, the USSR, and the United States that led to the pledged withdrawal of the Soviet forces on a nine-month timetable beginning in May 1988.

Tension persists as to whether or to what extent the United States and the Soviet Union will continue to funnel military assistance to their respective surrogates on the ground, namely the government of President Najibullah in Kabul and the various *mujahidin* groups in Pakistan and Afghanistan. The latter are by no means of one mind, which adds to the complexities. Whether some relatively peaceful means of accommodation can be worked out among the various parties, so that a mutually acceptable government can emerge, remains doubtful. More probably Afghanistan will remain an internally deeply divided and troubled country for quite some while. Its time as zone of confrontation between the superpowers appears, however, to be past for the foreseeable future.

During a visit to Washington 20 October 1987, India's Prime Minister Rajiv Gandhi received assurances from President Reagan that "our objective is stability and reduced tensions in South Asia and our assistance (to Pakistan) is not directed against India." Since the first U.S. gun sent to Pakistan, nearly every U.S. president has said about the same thing. One significant change, however, has been the concern felt within India about the Soviet role in Afghanistan and the presence of Soviet forces there at the historic northwestern gateway to the subcontinent. For this and the other reasons sketched earlier, slow growth seems to have been occurring in the understanding of the other's interests and motives by both India and the United States. After this second Reagan-Gandhi meeting, some initiatives for increased cooperation were announced, including decisions to proceed with joint construction of a new Indian light combat aircraft and with India's purchase of new supercomputers. Gandhi expressed hope for better relations, and press reports indicated he wanted the United States to become "more of a player" in relations with his country.

The birth of the newest nation in South Asia, Bangladesh, furnishes a clear example of how U.S. global policies have conflicted with regional interests in the area. After years of complaints of oppression by the more powerful West Pakistanis, the Bengali people of East Pakistan, who shared the Muslim faith but little else with the people of the west wing, revolted. In the course of a brief but bloody war, Indian troops joined the cause of their eastern neighbors and assured the victory and independence of the new nation, Bangladesh. The famous "tilt" of President Nixon and Secretary of State Kissinger toward West Pakistan during the latter stages of the conflict brought into the Bay of Bengal a U.S. naval task force complete with the aircraft carrier U.S.S. *Enterprise*. Some in India attribute Mrs. Gandhi's decision to allow her nuclear scientists to develop and explode a nuclear device to the perception of threat raised by the *Enterprise* task force. However that may be, the action did not affect the outcome of the war; it mainly engendered anger toward the United States in both India and East Pakistan on the eve of its rebirth as Bangladesh.

The reason for this U.S. behavior had very little to do with American interests in the area of war, and it departed, as happens more than rarely, from our traditional advocacy of freedom for seekers of self-government to replace rule from abroad (in this case rule by a different people on the opposite side of India). At that moment the great stakes of the Kissinger plan for a major move in the balance of world power depended upon Pakistan to make the secret arrangements for the negotiations with the People's Republic of China.

Later Kissinger referred to the new state of Bangladesh as an "international basket case." With well over one thousand people per square mile, it had a larger population on much less land than what was left of Pakistan.

The recipient of much private assistance from the United States and other countries immediately after its birth as a nation, Bangladesh has also been responsive to the heavy role that governmental and multilateral aid donors have played in its beleaguered economy. In one of the world's poorest countries, none of its regimes through a series of violent political changes could afford to be indifferent to the urgency of development. As has been the case with other South Asian countries, American assistance has increasingly been channeled through international organizations, although in Bangladesh as in Pakistan bilateral U.S. aid remains relatively as well as absolutely larger than in India.

The United States has looked with favor on the development of the South Asian Association for Regional Cooperation (SAARC), which grew out of a Bangladesh initiative. Regional stability and cooperation among the nations of South Asia are clearly in our general interest. Moreover, like the smaller states of South Asia, the United States sees the SAARC, a cooperative grouping of nominal equals, as a balancing weight working against what the smaller states see to be India's hegemonic tendencies.

Relations between the United States and the southernmost of the South Asian states, Sri Lanka, which became independent from British rule in 1948, have been generally tranquil, and the major U.S. initiative there has been through both bilateral and multilateral development assistance in fairly moderate amounts. For several years U.S. ambassadors in New Delhi were accredited to Sri Lanka (as well as to Nepal), making periodic visits to show the flag and conduct business. As the relationship developed, however, the United States assigned residential ambassadors to Kathmandu and Colombo. The latter in turn makes regular visits to represent American interests in the Maldives.

The primary external influence in Sri Lanka comes from its only near neighbor, India, although declared friendship between them at times has ranged between ambivalent and difficult. Indian naval vessels were sent around the island at the time of an uprising led by a Marxist group in 1971, but Sri Lanka managed to put down the revolt by itself. More recently Indian troops were requested, and they have engaged in a military effort to overcome resistance by radical Tamil groups to an accord negotiated between the governments of Sri Lanka and India wherein the latter sought to act on behalf of the Hindu Tamil minority concentrated in northern and northeastern Sri Lanka. The ethnic conflict between the Sinhalese (mainly Buddhists) and the Tamils in those parts of the country is of long standing. The armed strength and skill in guerrilla warfare of the Tamil resistance confronting the Indian army have proved so formidable that a long-festering struggle seems probable. It can only set further back the development activities that have been the principal focus of U.S. efforts in Sri Lanka.

There is also some ambivalence in the relations between Sri Lanka and the United States concerning superpower fleets in the Indian Ocean. In the early 1970s Sri Lanka put forward a Zone of Peace proposal before the United Nations to keep foreign warships out of the ocean. Subsequently, India has supported the proposal with more vigor than does its author, whose discomfort has increased as Indian naval power has grown. While not approving the U.S. naval base at Diego Garcia, Sri Lanka has made no great outcry about it and, until just recently, has welcomed shore visits by elements of the U.S. Navy. There is a widespread feeling in the country that there should be resources in the area to discourage any development of India's friendly and supportive role into an all-embracing one.

Even more limited than in Sri Lanka has been U.S. influence in Nepal, where the major American contribution may have been its share of the biggest Nepalese business—tourism. Its Himalayan remoteness helped Nepal maintain its independence for many years between China and British India. The United States opened its embassy in Kathmandu in the 1960s and has both supplied bilateral and helped with multilateral development assistance. On some occasions this effort has been coordinated with India. The Nepalese government perforce keeps a watchful eye toward not offending either of its powerful neighbors. Good relations with the United States help reinforce its measure of independence.

There are no diplomatic relations between the United States and another border state, Bhutan. A sovereign state, Bhutan nevertheless has agreed to be guided by Indian advice in foreign relations (as it earlier did with the British viceroy). Bhutan has been a member of the United Nations since 1971 and it receives economic aid from international agencies as well as from India. Since Ambassador Galbraith visited Bhutan in 1962, the Indian government has not looked with favor on visits there by U.S. officials. American tourists can, however, be accommodated.

During the last forty years, the American people and those of South Asia, particularly their leaders, have become much better acquainted with each other. There are estimates of over three-quarters of a million people of South Asian origin now living in the United States, and they, with the ties they keep with their homelands, will provide substance for the relationship that each side will be able to draw on.

A key to easing tensions between the United States and the area may be the resolution of the crisis in Afghanistan and resumption of its independent status. Such a happy outcome should further encourage improved U.S. relations with India, as it would permit lowering the level of American arms input into Pakistan over time. In brief, while the outcome in Afghanistan will depend heavily on internal factors, the apparent easing of the superpower competition there is encouraging and may permit steadier, more balanced U.S. attention to its interests in the subcontinent.

11

The United States
and the Middle East

L. CARL BROWN

IN THESE last years of the 1980s Americans take for granted an intensive involvement with affairs of the Middle East. Yet it was not always so. President Franklin D. Roosevelt in 1940 for example wrote on a policy paper, "Arabia is too far afield for us. Can't you get the British to do something?" In 1987 a major contingent of American naval forces was sent to the Persian Gulf to protect the flow of Arabia's oil.

During the Second World War Americans were so unfamiliar with Iran that "in the feverish planning of 1941, War Department intelligence had to turn for information on highways and transport routes in Iran to the Consultant in Islamic Archeology at the Library of Congress."[1] Today the U.S. government has de-tailed data on all aspects of Iran.

A social historian studying the daily press and radio dispatches of the 1940s would be hard put to find a single reference to "mullah" or "ayatollah," words that today's casual reader or television viewer immediately recognizes.

As late as the last years of the Truman administration, officials were insisting to the British that the United States planned "no military sacrifice to retain the

1. T.H. Vail Motter, *The Persian Corridor and Aid to Russia*, a volume in the series *United States Army in World War II* (Washington, D.C.: Department of the Army, 1952), p. 7.

countries of the Middle East." Instead, the United States role would be to bolster the "UK primary political and military responsibility in the area."[2]

In January 1980 President Carter unilaterally announced, "An attempt by any outside force to gain control of the Persian Gulf region will be regarded as an assault on the vital interests of the United States. It will be repelled by use of any means necessary, including force."[3] And seven years earlier during the time of the October 1973 Arab-Israeli War, the United States publicly placed American forces on nuclear alert—the only such commitment since the beginning of the nuclear age—when the Soviets talked of sending troops to support Egypt against Israel.

Before 1945 the American government smugly regarded Egypt and Palestine as areas being clumsily mishandled by Britain. In recent years Egypt and Israel (created in 1948 out of Palestine) have together received the lion's share of U.S. foreign aid. In 1979, admittedly a bumper year, Egypt and Israel together accounted for 82 percent of total U.S. military assistance and 42 percent of total bilateral economic aid.[4] The United States Embassy in Cairo with a huge Agency for International Development (AID) contingent is said to be the largest American diplomatic establishment in the world.

These few examples contrasting the 1940s with recent times demonstrate that in a tract of time amounting to roughly half the lifetime of today's average American the United States involvement in the Middle East has advanced from insignificant to insatiable. Only East Asia rivals the Middle East among Third World regions that have riveted American diplomatic attention since the Second World War. Moreover, while the Middle East has not lured American forces directly into protracted combat, as East Asia has done with both the Korean and Vietnam wars, the Middle East wins the dubious distinction of being the Third World region that has most uninterruptedly demanded American public attention over the past four decades.

The Middle East has provoked three American presidential "doctrines"— those of Truman, Eisenhower, and Carter, plus two military interventions in a country (Lebanon) roughly the size of Connecticut. The Middle East has been for several years the unrivaled major recipient of American military exports (amounting to $15.18 billion in the years 1981–1985 or more than half the amount to the entire developing world, to be compared to $13.79 billion sent to all NATO countries during the same period).[5] One country, Iran, has set in motion events that severely weakened the last two presidencies, those of Carter and Reagan.

---

2. Public records of 1950 and 1951 respectively as cited by William Stivers, *America's Confrontation with Revolutionary Change in the Middle East, 1948–83* (London: Macmillan, 1986), p. 5.

3. President Jimmy Carter's 23 January 1980 State of the Union address setting out what came to be called the "Carter Doctrine."

4. Charles William Maynes and Richard Ullman, "10 years of Foreign Policy," *Foreign Policy* 40 (Fall 1980): 6.

5. *World Military Expenditures and Arms Transfers, 1986* (Washington, D.C.: United States Arms Control and Disarmament Agency, April 1987), pp. 143ff.

The American embassy in Tehran besieged and held hostage (November 1979).
(AP/Wide World Photos)

Why this accelerated American involvement in the Middle East? The answer
is only partially that such a trend follows the global pattern. Yes, the tide of
American internationalism since 1945 has raised all regional boats, but it is worth
considering why and how the United States has become more heavily and more
consistently involved in the Middle East than in South Asia or Africa or even
Latin America.

• • •

As the Second World War was winding down, American official thinking
concerning the Middle East contained ideas and ideals which while potentially
contradictory were not necessarily so. It was thought that the major interest in
and responsibility for security in the Middle East would remain with Great
Britain. At the same time, the United States—consistent with its venerable
Open Door policy—would not let Britain or anyone else bar American economic
activity in the area.

Western imperialism was deemed at best an anachronism. The sooner it was
phased out, the better. American officialdom looked to an "orderly" decolonization, which was implicitly defined as one in which the emerging independent
states would be solidly prowestern.

The United States was thought to have a strong standing among Middle Eastern peoples as an antiimperialist power. As Cordell Hull observed, the American position in the Middle East rested on "a century of American missionary, educational and philanthropic efforts that have never been tarnished by any material motives or interests."[6] Other Americans felt much the same way. Sumner Welles in 1947 contrasted the potential "clash of empires" between Britain and the Soviet Union in the Middle East with the "one-world order" that Americans championed.[7] Even among presumably hard-boiled realists, the prevailing perception of America's Middle Eastern role was warmed-over Wilsonism.

That being the case, those few Americans concerned with affairs of the Middle East thought of facilitating decolonization while frustrating what might be dubbed "recolonization," with the Soviets seemingly the only threat on that score. With a mixture of mediating services openly accepted by the parties concerned plus judicious use of carrots or sticks as required, the United States would be able to guide the Middle East into a satisfactory postwar arrangement. It was to be a low-cost, minimal-commitment policy.

• • •

Three developments conspired to upset American planning: (1) In the Middle East the Soviets proved to be much more assertive than expected. (2) Britain was financially unable to play a leading role in the area. (3) Domestic pressures got the United States heavily involved in the Palestine problem and subsequent Arab-Israeli confrontations. All three developments got underway in the critical first few years following the Second World War. The first two remind us that the Cold War had Middle Eastern roots. Soviet pressures against Greece, Turkey, and Iran in the immediate postwar period seemed ominous. Then in early 1947 the Attlee government informed Washington that Britain's parlous economic situation ruled out further British action in this area, whose states share borders with the Soviet Union or with the Soviet bloc being established.

Suddenly, American officialdom discovered that they would not be able to implement a low-cost, minimal-commitment policy of balancing off the two imperialists in the Middle East, Britain and the Soviet Union. The response was the Truman Doctrine, announced by the president to Congress on 12 March 1947. An interesting footnote to Cold War history, this was some four months before the appearance in July of George Kennan's article in *Foreign Affairs*, "The Sources of Soviet Conduct," which provided the ideological underpinnings of containment.

This is not the place to review the debate sparked by revisionist historians who have argued for a less threatening interpretation of Soviet actions in the Middle

---

6. Cited in *Foreign Relations of the United States 1942*, p. 27.
7. This was in his introduction to E.A. Speiser, *The United States and the Near East* (1947), an early volume in the influential Harvard University Press "American Foreign Policy Library" series.

President Truman in March 1947 proposing what came to be called the Truman Doctrine. (National Archives)

East as elsewhere. This much, however, may be said. Americans saw the events of early 1947 in the light of Soviet pressures against Turkey and Iran beginning two years earlier, even before the end of the Second World War. Almost all American strategic thinkers of that day believed the American response to Soviet probings to be reasonable. Those "realists" who thought in balance-of-power terms could see the Soviet moves as consistent with Russia's historic drive for warm-weather ports and a dominant position in the Middle East, a diplomatic goal at least as old as the reign of Catherine the Great.

Those who regarded the Soviet Union as a revolutionary state bent on world domination could evoke the need to take a stand now rather than later. Even the world-order internationalists, brought up on the notion of collective security and "no more Munichs," could accept the need to bring counterpressure against a great power leaning heavily on vulnerable regional states. After all, Truman's speech had made an obeisance to the UN: "We have considered how the United Nations might assist in this crisis. But the situation is an urgent one requiring immediate action and the United Nations and its related organizations are not in a position to extend help of the kind that is required."

Moreover, in diplomacy just as in other activities, nothing succeeds like success. Seemingly, these American responses to Soviet initiatives in the Middle East from 1945 to the early fifties were solid victories at manageable cost. By 1951–52, for example, Greece and Turkey were members of NATO and Iran seemed firmly in the western camp.

Even decolonization in Libya had been achieved without permitting the Soviets a role in Mediterranean matters. As a wartime ally, the Soviet Union had a strong case for participating in the disposition of former Axis territories, such as Italy's African holdings. The Soviet bargaining advantage was, however, safely neutralized, and by 1951 Libya had emerged as an independent kingdom under the Sanusi leader, King Idris.

American intervention in the Palestine issue and the subsequent Arab-Israeli confrontation grew out of a different context, one virtually as old as American diplomacy itself. Even the venerable impulse of American isolationism has long had a contradictory element of interventionism—support for various nationalist movements. As long ago as the 1820s American public figures championed the Greek war of independence against the Ottoman Empire. In 1848 the different European revolutionary nationalists were acclaimed on this side of the Atlantic. And the long-festering Anglo-Irish problem reverberated powerfully in this country, with one Chicago mayor even threatening to "punch King George in the nose."

Zionism, as it impacted on American politics and diplomacy, fell within this tradition. As with earlier American support for nationalist movements in Europe and elsewhere, the hard core of support came from those Americans who identified, ethnically, linguistically, or religiously, with the alien nationalism. Such American supporters, whatever their earlier roots—Greek, Hungarian, Polish, Armenian, Jewish—have always been a tiny minority within the larger American political context, but they have always also represented a not inconsiderable group, well organized and fervently concerned about one issue and, what is equally important, not matched by an equally well-organized and fervently concerned group championing the other side of the issue.

Add to this the keen desire to "do something positive" that seized many Americans when the full horrors of Hitler's diabolical campaign to exterminate European Jewry became known in full detail, and the strong domestic pressure to support Zionism is easily understood.

The other, regional side of the Palestine issue was less well known to Americans. Palestine was not, as an early Zionist slogan had it, "a land without people for a people without land." Indeed, even in 1947, thirty years after Britain's Balfour Declaration and over sixty years after Zionist or proto-Zionist immigration to the Holy Land had begun, Jews constituted only about one-third of the population of mandate Palestine.

The other two-thirds were Arabs, overwhelmingly Muslim, but roughly 13 percent were Christians. All of which is to say that there were two emerging nationalisms in Palestine, Zionism and Palestinian Arabism. As wits at the time were wont to point out, this territory, the size of New Jersey, was "the twice-promised land."

Moreover, 1948, which brought the end of the British mandate, the creation of Israel, and the first Arab-Israeli war, was a time when Arabism was on the rise. Arabs everywhere from North Africa to the Persian Gulf had always championed the Palestinian Arabs and had opposed Zionism as either a new, devious form of European colonialism or as a cynical western decision to resolve a western problem—anti-Semitism—at the expense of the Arabs.

If the focus of attention here were either the Israelis or the Arabs, more would need to be said concerning why the issue was not resolved before 1948 or at some time in the subsequent forty years. Concentrating, however, on U.S. policy, the significant point is that strong American support for Israel changed Arab perceptions of the United States. Those Arabs seeking a scapegoat for Arab diplomatic and military reverses could single out the United States. Even those Arabs more resigned to the realities of international politics began to see the United States not as the friendly antiimperialist power that would counterbalance European imperialism, but rather as a new player in the old Middle Eastern balance-of-power game.

In the years immediately following 1948, the impact of America's tilt toward Israel was not all that evident to U.S. policymakers. Most Arab states in the late forties were either not yet independent or had only a shaky formal independence. The United States, championing decolonization, was still solicited as a useful counterweight to Britain. Moreover, after 1948 it was expected that a permanent settlement between Israel and the Arabs would be worked out. Then the regional tensions growing out of this issue would subside, and the United States could get back to a limited-commitment, low-cost posture in the Fertile Crescent. Since the Soviets were not yet actively engaged in this part of the Middle East, the United States apparently had time to work things out. (Soviet support for the creation of Israel—a clear thrust against what was perceived as Britain's strong position—was, however, an interesting harbinger of more assertive policies to come.)

It was not to be. The first peace treaty between Israel and an Arab state came thirty-one years after the 1948 war, with the 1979 Egyptian-Israeli treaty—brokered, it might be added, by the United States. Even this long-delayed breakthrough did not set in motion progress toward resolution of the original and continuing problem of the two nationalisms struggling over the same small territory. The continuing political difficulties dividing the Arab states (numbering nineteen today with a combined population of over 180 million inhabitants) guarantees that one political group or another will solicit U.S. backing, if only to counter pressures coming from within the region or from outside. This, however, is a far cry from the role Americans hoped for in the forties, that of monitoring from afar a regional state system favorably disposed toward the West.

•   •   •

Sadat, Carter, and Begin at the March 1979 White House signing of the Egyptian-Israeli peace treaty. (AP/Wide World Photos)

It is easy to see now, with the advantage of hindsight, that after Britain had backed out of Greece in 1947 and left the Palestine mandate in disarray the following year, the U.S. would quickly become the predominant western power in the Middle East. Indeed, given the global power balances for at least the first two decades after 1945, such predominance was well-nigh inescapable, in the Middle East as elsewhere. In time, however, a combination of factors eroded American political, economic, and military hegemony. (Among the most important factors were the Japanese economic "miracle," European revival, the Soviet push for military might, the consolidation of China, and the Sino-Soviet rift.)

America remained, and remains, a superpower but in a multipolar world. What needs to be traced here is the curious history of America's continued entanglement in Middle Eastern commitments, even while this country's relative global standing has been declining.

There is no better time or place to begin than in Iran in the spring of 1951 when the new government of Mohammed Mosaddeq nationalized the Anglo-Iranian Oil Company. Thus began a crisis that ended some thirty months later in August 1953 when a CIA-backed coup overthrew Mosaddeq and restored the

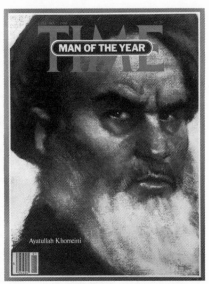

Two Iranian leaders were selected by *Time* Magazine as Man of the Year, Mosaddeq in 1952 and the Ayatollah Khomeini in 1980, a powerful indication of how the politics of a country most Americans ignored before the Second World War loomed large in post-war American diplomacy. (Reprinted by permission from *Time*.)

shah. Up to that time Britain had been the preeminent western power in Iran for well over a century. For equally as long, Britain's major rival for influence in Iran had been Russia. Iran was the epicenter of what Victorians dubbed "the great game in Asia," or the Anglo-Russian rivalry over that buffer zone stretching from the Bosphorus to the Afghan borders of British India. The great game continued after 1953, but with the United States taking Britain's place.

Both Mosaddeq and the British had attempted to gain American support from the beginnings of the confrontation. For a long time, the United States sought to play a mediating role. In the end, however, the United States not only sided with Britain but seized the initiative.

The post-1953 settlement readily revealed the new power alignment. Henceforth the shah and the United States were inextricably linked in regional eyes. Iranians, prone to weave complex theories concerning outside manipulators (for good reasons, as Iranian history since at least the 1870s attests) had a new devil. Uncle Sam had replaced John Bull. The American-Iranian collaboration lasted long—over a quarter century until January 1979 when the Islamic Revolution forced the shah from his throne and into exile. Also dethroned and exiled was Uncle Sam. The earlier patron of the Iranian regime thereafter became the "Great Satan."

Another aspect of the 1953 settlement was the creation of a new consortium of oil companies, with major American participation, to exploit Iranian oil resources. It is all very well to assert (and with some justice) that the stiff-necked leadership of the Anglo-Iranian Oil Company fully deserved this setback of being obliged to share the Iran concession with other, rival oil companies. Even so, the image in Britain was of America, an ally, using its diplomatic muscle for economic advantage. Nor did American self-righteousness (very much like that of earlier Victorians) help. Americans professed to be in the Middle East only to do good. Embittered Britons presiding over their declining empire saw that Americans managed to stay and do well.

During the same time the United States was attempting to mediate yet another thorny decolonization problem that pitted Britain against Egypt. The British wanted to maintain their military base at Suez, or failing that, to enroll Egypt in a western defense alliance. They also opposed Egyptian claims to sovereignty over the Anglo-Egyptian Sudan, which in spite of the name was under British control. The Egyptians were united in wishing to be free of any tie with Britain (which they could only view as subservience, however sugar-coated) and in seeking the "unity of the Nile valley."

When the corrupt regime of King Farouk was overthrown in July 1952 by Gamal Abdel Nasser's "Free Officers," the American government sensed that all the pieces were falling into place. Here to replace a despotic and inefficient system was a group of progressive young officers who, in addition, had good ties with American diplomats on the spot. (The Soviets were apparently convinced that the coup itself was "Made in America.") The earlier ideal of orderly decolonization leading to legally sovereign Middle Eastern states still safely within the western orbit appeared attainable. Nasser's Egypt, the most populous Arab state, would be the linchpin of the American-sponsored new Middle Eastern order.

To this end, the United States took a number of initiatives, such as quietly encouraging Britain and Egypt toward a settlement, sponsoring behind-the-scenes Egyptian-Israeli contacts intended to move them toward a peace treaty, and offering what was hoped would be attractive bait—a major Egyptian role in a western-sponsored Middle Eastern defense organization.

Except for the Anglo-Egyptian treaty, signed in October 1954, these interlocking initiatives came to nought. Neither Israeli nor Egyptian leaders showed the kind of diplomatic daring later exhibited by Nasser's successor, Anwar al-Sadat, and the Egyptian-Israeli contacts provided only bleak might-have-been footnotes to the ongoing Arab-Israeli confrontation.

More important, the American strategy was faulty in assuming that Nasser could accept being a junior partner in what all Egyptians saw as the very same western state system that had for so long oppressed them. When Nasser chose to take a leading role in the emerging nonaligned movement (symbolized by the March 1955 Bandung Conference) the American-Egyptian relationship began to go sour.

Then came the point of no return in September 1955, when Nasser announced a major arms deal with the Soviet bloc (formally a Czech-Egyptian arms deal but in fact the negotiations, and the ensuing commitments, linked Egypt and the

Soviet Union). The Russian bear had deftly leaped over the "northern tier" (e.g., Iran and Turkey) that Secretary of State John Foster Dulles had assumed would keep the Middle Eastern heartland secure from Soviet influence.

The Soviet-American competition in providing arms to the Middle East has since become so commonplace that it is difficult to evoke the sense of shock that this 1955 arms deal created in Washington. The illusion that the Middle East was a western preserve was shattered. At a time when American leadership considered nonalignment immoral, there suddenly loomed the even more serious threat that Middle Eastern states would choose to become, as Washington saw it, Soviet pawns.

American reactions to these events were confusing and contradictory. There was first an effort to ensure that the Egyptian-Soviet arms deal would be a one-shot affair. This led to an American-British World Bank offer to help finance the building of the Aswan High Dam, the keystone project in Nasser's developmental plans. Then in July 1956 Dulles peremptorily withdrew the American offer. Britain willingly joined in the withdrawal, and the World Bank had no choice but to follow.

Nasser, a consummate political counterpuncher, responded on 26 July 1956 by defiantly announcing the nationalization of the Suez Canal. This triggered an international crisis that ended in late October with an Israeli attack on Egypt followed by British and French landings in the canal zone (the whole operation growing out of earlier secret agreements among Britain, France, and Israel).

Kept in the dark by its two principal European allies, Britain and France, and equally so by Israel, the Eisenhower administration angrily insisted that the attackers withdraw. The Soviet Union, at that very time crushing liberation movements in Poland and Hungary, eagerly joined in condemning the attack on

A defiant Nasser announcing the nationalization of the Suez Canal, 26 July 1956. (AP/Wide World Photos)

Egypt. Thus, ironically, twice during the hottest periods of the Cold War—in 1947–1948 and again in 1956—the United States and the Soviet Union lined up together on disputes linked to the Arab-Israeli confrontation.

Thereafter, having astonished Nasser's Egypt and, generally, the more progressive (or radical or antiwestern—no neutral word is available) elements in the Middle East with this firm stand against America's closest allies, the Eisenhower administration veered sharply in the other direction with the Eisenhower Doctrine, announced in January 1957. The doctrine said in effect that Britain and France were too discredited to be able to play their accustomed roles in the Middle East. This created a political vacuum that the United States was obliged to fill. Otherwise, the vulnerable states of the area would surely fall victim to international communism. The unstated assumption was that the Middle East must remain a western preserve.

The immediate goal of the Eisenhower Doctrine was to prevent Nasser and Nasserism (seen as neutralism at best, as *de facto* alliance with the Soviet Union at worst) from gaining new strength in the Arab world. Just one decade after the Truman Doctrine had been articulated, the United States had assumed the role of primary, if not exclusive, guarantor of western interests in the Middle East.

Instead of letting the Middle East become a zone of great-power competition, of sublimated superpower conflict, even at worst of superpower proxy wars, Washington was trying to bring back western hegemony such as had existed in the period between the two world wars. At the same time, American policymakers sincerely saw themselves as championing Third World independence and seeking a new and more just international order transcending the older Eurocentric system. It was a classic case of cognitive dissonance. The American position was rather like that of Russian Tsar Alexander who, as Talleyrand maliciously noted, wanted everyone to be free provided everyone obeyed him absolutely.

• • •

The Eisenhower Doctrine was, however, the last significant step in a persistent effort to organize the Middle East under new management. Earlier, when Nasser had resisted offers to join a western security system equivalent to NATO in Europe and SEATO in Asia, Secretary Dulles pushed the idea of building an alliance with those states close enough to the Soviet Union to be prowestern for clear historical and geographical reasons. These states included Turkey, Iran, and Pakistan. Why not strengthen that alignment while also showing Nasser the limits of his control over the Arab world by bringing in Iraq? The result of this thinking was the Baghdad Pact, and Iraq led the way as the first Arab state to break away from Nasser-dominated neutralism. The plan got underway with an Iraqi-Turkish defense treaty signed in February 1955.

Iraq, however, was following outdated diplomatic assumptions. The ruling Hashemite family and their entourage had been linked to Britain ever since the British-backed "Arab revolt" against Ottoman rule during the First World War. They had remained in the Allied camp during the difficult days of World War II.

Since that time the regime had courted American support as British strength faded. Iraqi strongman and perennial Prime Minister Nuri al-Said personified the old approach to political success—find a strong outside patron, keep domestic opposition weak with a mix of occasional blandishments and no-nonsense repression, and then ignore ideologies or mutterings from "the street."

July 1958 proved just how out of date this conception was. A military coup overthrew the regime. Nuri himself was discovered by a frenzied mob and literally torn to pieces. King Faisal II also lost his life. This happened at the same time that Lebanon's openly anti-Nasser president, Camille Chamoun, facing a smoldering civil war, asked for American support. Eisenhower quickly responded and American troops soon poured onto the beaches of Beirut. Britain sent troops to Jordan where King Husayn, cousin of Faisal, was equally vulnerable to the rising tide of Nasserism.

At this point Washington initiated a major change of strategy, accepting what amounted to a truce with Nasser. No effort was made to reverse the loss in Iraq. U.S. troops were soon out of Lebanon, and the prowestern Chamoun was replaced as president by a man devoted to Lebanese neutrality, General Fuad Shihab. It was an arrangement that the United States could easily have reached with Nasser before the events of July. Even so, American actions after the coup in Iraq stand out as a solid achievement in damage control, because the temptation to waste additional diplomatic resources on unsound policies was resisted.

The United States at the same time implicitly accepted that the Soviets would be a major player in the Middle Eastern game. They would not be readily dislodged, perhaps not dislodged at all, short of an unthinkable major confrontation. Yet, by way of compensation for this seeming loss (actually more a loss of illusions than of reality), it became apparent that the Soviet Union, henceforth committed in the area, would not be able to gain cheap diplomatic victories there, as it had with the 1955 arms deals. Tensions and harsh words between Soviet Premier Nikita Khrushchev and Nasser in the late 1950s revealed the limits of Soviet influence. The Soviets were being taught the same lesson given the United States earlier—regional clients, readily forgetting past favors, will demand more. In any case the multiple regional problems neither stemmed from nor were controlled by the superpower rivalry.

The other side of the coin was this: A United States that seemed to have abandoned the dream of controlling the Middle East was often not only accepted regionally but its help was even solicited. The metaphor of Middle East politics was shown to be not falling dominoes but constant changes of position on the political seesaw to keep things in balance. There was even a certain flirtation between the United States and Nasser during the Kennedy presidency which, while it did not change the basic orientation of either side, did demonstrate the virtues of limited commitments by an outside superpower.

• • •

The year 1958 thus marks a watershed. Two developments had by this time reached a stable state. First, the process of shifting influence over Middle

Eastern affairs from Europe to America was virtually completed. Britain would remain as a guardian of the Persian Gulf area for another decade, but with the United States as the principal power in both Iran and Saudi Arabia, this British position was only an afterglow following the imperial sunset.

France, the other western imperialist power with deep roots in the Middle East, had never recouped following the Second World War. Even the French standing among the Christians of Lebanon (especially the Maronites), while certainly a passionate link, had limited political impact, especially after Suez. One need only recall that the outside power involved in modern Lebanon's first civil war in 1957–58 was not France but the United States. Moreover, by the late fifties France's North African empire was winding down. Morocco and Tunisia had received their independence in 1956. By 1958 the war in Algeria had caused the downfall of the Fourth Republic and brought Charles de Gaulle to power. Four years later Algeria too would be independent. Thereafter, de Gaulle did move France away from close cooperation with Israel (earlier Franco-Israeli discussions and arms transfers had laid the groundwork for the later Anglo-French-Israeli strike against Egypt in 1956) and France attempted to stake out a comprehensive pro-Arab policy during and after the June 1967 Arab-Israeli war. The scant diplomatic gains accruing to France revealed the limits of such initiatives.

No other power tried even this much. West Germany and Japan were content to engage in trade and to avoid politics. The European community as a body would not take stands on Middle Eastern issues until much later (e.g., the Venice Declaration of June 1980 did mark an EEC divergence from the American-sponsored Camp David formulas) and even then without significant impact. The outside world, including America's own allies, accepted a regional situation in which the only truly frightening scenario (the loss of western access to Middle Eastern oil) seemed unlikely given the inertia of regional political balances and the stalemated superpower confrontation.

The standing of the superpowers was the second development that matured in 1958. Politically, while the United States was accepted as the preemptive western power-wielder, in the Middle East it could not establish its dominance. American political clout was checked by that of the Soviet Union. The same held for the Soviets. Neither could oust the other and both implicitly accepted that truth. Indeed, in the Middle East from 1958 until the October 1973 Arab-Israeli War, the United States and the Soviet Union were like two cautious boxers, content to spar, neither dropping his guard to risk a knockout punch.

The lowering of superpower rivalry did not in any way becalm the Middle East, which indicates the extent to which regional and superpower diplomacy were loosely linked, at best. The period saw the Six Day War of June 1967 in which Israel's devastating defeat of Egypt, Syria, and Jordan confirmed Israel's status as a regional military power, severely damaged the already declining appeal of Nasserism, and produced an Israeli military occupation of the West Bank and Gaza that gave the Jewish state jurisdiction over the largest single gathering of Palestinians anywhere. It was also after the Arab defeat that the Palestine Liberation Organization (PLO), created earlier by Nasser and the Arab states with the intention of keeping Palestinian nationalism under the control of the Arab state system, began to emerge as a significant autonomous entity. The region and the world is still, one generation later, dealing with the many diverse forces set loose in June 1967.

As for the superpowers, it was clear that neither controlled its "client," either before that war or after. Indeed, the efficient use of the "hot line" of rapid communication between Washington and Moscow during the June War expressed political reality better than any public statements. The two superpower rivals immediately sensed that regional "clients" might drag them into direct confrontation, and they cooperated to avoid such an entanglement.

Thereafter, the Soviet-American rivalry in the Middle East waxed and waned, reaching one peak, for example, when Soviet pilots actually operated out of Egypt during the Egyptian-Israeli "War of Attrition" (1969–70), and grew more muted during such periods as that of superpower detente. The basic pattern, however, held. Both sides implicitly recognized the informal limits of acceptable probes and challenges. Both sides supported their respective regional clients verbally and with increasing amounts of military hardware while remaining on guard against letting those regional clients force their hands. Meanwhile, the rest of the world—including the industrial world of Western Europe and Japan dependent on the Middle Eastern oil—remained safely on the sidelines.

•   •   •

A renewed American effort to achieve clear superiority over the Soviet Union in the Middle East began with the October 1973 Arab-Israeli war. Egypt's Anwar al-Sadat, who had succeeded Nasser upon the latter's death in 1970, found the stalemated "no war–no peace" status with Israel unacceptable, especially since Israel occupied the entire Sinai peninsula right up to the eastern bank of the Suez Canal. The Egyptian leader also came to realize that the Soviet Union would protect his country against outright defeat at the hands of Israel. It would not, or it would not adequately, support Egypt in a daring effort to reverse the results of the June 1967 war.

Sadat, seeing that only the United States could influence Israel, took the first of his several bold steps by expelling the Soviet military mission to Egypt in July 1972. That measure evoked no major American response; Sadat then planned with Syria an attack on Israel designed—realistically—not to defeat Israel in the field but to demonstrate to Israel and the world that the prevailing situation was unacceptable to the Arabs. This, it was expected, would then provoke a super-power diplomatic intervention.

More particularly, Sadat and other Arab leaders were attempting their own variety of the carrot-and-stick policy toward the United States. Sadat signaled that he was prepared to carry out a veritable diplomatic revolution, moving Egypt from the Soviet to the American camp, provided that the United States put sufficient pressure on Israel to restore Egyptian territory and wind down the Arab-Israeli confrontation in a manner at least minimally acceptable to all parties. Saudi Arabia and the Gulf states cooperated in imposing an oil embargo following the outbreak of hostilities.

Secretary of State Henry Kissinger brilliantly perceived the strategy adopted by Sadat and those allied with him. On the tactical level, he adjusted American policy to take advantage of U.S. strengths and to minimize U.S. weaknesses, in the process giving international politics a new term—"shuttle diplomacy."

In the simplest (and necessarily overly simplified) terms, the Kissinger policy involved standing one aspect of traditional American diplomacy on its head. Instead of insisting that the United States was really "even-handed" as between Israel and the Arabs (which no Arab believed and the record did not support), Kissinger made a virtue of the strong link with Israel by arguing that the United States was the only significant outside power able to influence both Israel and the Arabs. It was an inspired way of hammering home a diplomatic truth: Whenever the parties in conflict wish to get beyond slogans and actually negotiate a settlement, the United States can be the most effective single mediator.

There were, however, two flaws in this tactic initiated by Kissinger but maintained in its essentials by his successors during the Carter administration. First, the American claim of being able to influence Israel looked increasingly dubious when, time after time in the years after 1973, Washington showed an incapacity to do other than accept this or that *fait accompli* imposed by Israel, such as the continued Israel settlement on the West Bank even after the Camp David accords and the peace treaty with Egypt or the 1982 Israeli invasion of Lebanon.

Second, in order for the strategy to work, the United States needed to keep the Soviet Union involved as a junior partner. Or, at the very least, the United States had to avoid throwing down the gauntlet, signaling an intent to "expel" the Soviets from the Middle East. This is for a simple reason. Although the Soviets lacked the regional resources to orchestrate an Arab-Israeli settlement, they clearly had the capacity to frustrate such a settlement if they chose to do so. The one-man show of Kissinger and then later of Carter at Camp David unmistakably showed that, unlike the earlier period from 1958 to 1973, we were now seeking to knock the Soviets right out of the Middle Eastern ring. As the record since 1973 demonstrates, the Soviet Union had no difficulty rallying Syria, the PLO, and other "rejectionist" states to its side. Or perhaps putting the matter the other way round is more accurate: Those in the Middle East opposing the policies championed by the United States in alliance with Sadat and others sought out a counterbalancing patron. The Soviets, frustrated by Sadat's diplomatic revolution and challenged by American regional assertiveness, readily obliged.

• • •

To many observers in the mid-seventies, the United States appeared to be going from success to success. The three most populous and powerful Middle Eastern centers—Egypt, Iran, and Turkey—were all seemingly in the American camp. Saudi Arabia and the Gulf states were equally so. And the persistent diplomacy begun by Kissinger and then continued by Carter promised an acceptable settlement of the Arab-Israeli confrontation.

That illusion was shattered in 1979. Yes, the year brought the major breakthrough of the Egyptian-Israeli peace treaty. It also brought the fall of Mohammed Reza Pahlavi, shah of Iran. Then on 4 November 1979 an Iranian mob seized the American Embassy in Tehran, beginning a 444-day hostage crisis that, more than any other event, crippled the Carter presidency.

Thereafter, it has been just one setback after another. Even earlier, the Lebanese civil war, beginning in 1975, had spilled over into the region, provoking the Israeli invasion of 1978. Active American mediation followed, with some positive results, but then Israel embarked on a major invasion of Lebanon in 1982. Stuck with its claim to be the outside power most able to influence all parties in the Arab-Israeli confrontation, and intent on holding together the very shaky if disparate cluster of presumed American assets in the region—especially Egypt, Israel, and Saudi Arabia—the Reagan administration sought a solution.

For the second time since the Second World War, American troops returned to Lebanon on a peacekeeping mission. But in contrast to the successful damage control accomplished in 1958, this time the American military presence ended in complete defeat. The October 1983 suicide-bomb attack on U.S. Marine headquarters in Beirut, leaving 241 Americans dead, poignantly exposed the futility of American diplomatic claims.

The reactive nature of America's Middle Eastern diplomacy throughout the eighties can be summed up in two words—hostages and terrorism. One need only list a few of the more dramatic incidents: the Palestinian hijacking of the Italian cruise liner Achille Lauro in October 1985 with an especially brutal murder of a disabled, elderly American, followed by the American interception of the Egyptian plane carrying those hijackers to Tunis (provoking a crisis both with Egypt and with Italy when the plane was forced down in Sicily); the off-and-on threats and then quiet bargaining with Syria concerning American hostages held in Lebanon; and finally the U.S. military strike against Libya in April 1986, in retaliation for alleged Libyan involvement in terrorist attacks against Americans in Europe.

Then in the fall of 1986 Americans learned of the Iran-Contra affair, the Middle Eastern part of which entailed secret arms deliveries to Iran as a possible opening to that avowed enemy in the hope that Iran, controlling Shi'ite radicals in Lebanon, would see that American hostages in Lebanon were released. This made a mockery of what had been constantly proclaimed as American policy: (1) no concessions to those holding U.S. citizens hostage; (2) support for Iraq in the Iraq-Iran war, both because Iraq, unlike Iran, has expressed a willingness to negotiate and, more important, to bolster Saudi Arabia and the Gulf states that greatly fear an Iranian victory.

In the wake of these revelations the Reagan administration then lurched sharply in the other direction, accepting a Kuwaiti request to reflag Kuwaiti tankers, and sending an American fleet to protect shipping in the war-ravaged Persian Gulf.

Meanwhile, since December 1987 Israel has confronted a serious and sus-

Tony Auth à la Goldberg.

tained Palestinian uprising in the occupied territories. Moreover, even after the November 1988 elections the Israeli public remains sharply divided on approaches to negotiations with the Palestinians and on whether to return the territories occupied in the June 1967 War (or any significant part of them). Although late in 1988 PLO leader Yasir Arafat decisively moved his organization toward recognition of Israel and acceptance of a "two state solution" (i.e. Israel and Palestine), hardliners in both Israel and the Arab world resist this diplomatic breakthrough. On another front an encouraging development has been the July 1988 cease-fire in the brutal Iraq-Iran war. In short, as happens so often in the confused, multipolar politics of the Middle East the occasional promising diplomatic gains seem offset by old problems that resist change or new ones that suddenly appear.

Having listed all the above, it seems almost excessive to mention that Greece and Turkey, NATO allies and presumably the two most outstanding examples of earlier American successes as long ago as 1947, are best described as belligerents in their own cold war over Cyprus. Again, it is the United States as the principal great power ally of each that must wrestle with the resulting problems.

• • •

As the decade of the 1980s winds down, it is clear that the United States is not in a position to manage matters in the Middle East. Neither is the Soviet Union.

No other outsiders are putting themselves forward as candidates to take on the job, although British and French ships in the Persian Gulf are perhaps an interesting harbinger of changes to come.

In certain respects the United States in the Middle East may be beginning another period not unlike that from 1958 to 1973. If so, then the lesson to be grasped would be that if we cannot control regional politics in the Middle East, then we should make a virtue of necessity and scale our commitments down to the point at which we get an acceptable return on the diplomatic resources we have invested.

A rough rule of thumb might well be that the United States and its allies, Europe and Japan, should work toward scaling back their commitment of diplomatic resources to the Middle East in proportion to the relative interest of each party in the area (meaning first and foremost access to Middle Eastern oil). To those who say that Europe and Japan will not, for one reason or another, accept to bear this burden, the best answer is that they have not yet been put to the test. America's preemptive policies beginning soon after the Second World War have made bearing it quite unnecessary. Indeed, it would have been folly for a European or Japanese statesman to insist on accepting risks and responsibilities in the Middle East as long as the United States was doing so unilaterally. America's allies may well not like the way the United States chooses to protect western interests in the area, but prudence would dictate a policy of quiet persuasion rather than active opposition. Such are the lessons of Suez and of de Gaulle's effort at an independent policy. It is no easy task to restrain America's Middle Eastern diplomacy when it is going full throttle.

Does such a restrained policy risk Soviet dominance of the Middle East? There are no sure bets in diplomacy, but a sound strategy should be based on a clear-eyed evaluation of the odds. That neither the United States nor the Soviet Union can oust the other from the Middle East is what the record since 1945 strongly suggests. Given this fact, it is even possible that the two rival super-powers can, at times, cooperate in the Middle East. The subtle diplomacy of what has been labeled building adversary alliances, or practical working arrangements among rivals on specific issues, needs to be used more often in this part of the world.

Finally, it might be asked if such a minimalist policy orientation reveals a distressing lack of concern for the security and well-being of the peoples of the Middle East. There are, indeed, awesome problems to be resolved as well as promising prospects to be explored in today's Middle East. The United States, however, has no magic formula for setting the Middle East right.

Moreover, the United States and the Middle East will never be able to recreate that innocence and idealism that permitted Cordell Hull to speak of an American position that has "never been tarnished by any material motives or interests." We are now as much a part of the Middle Eastern diplomatic scene as ever were imperial Britain or Russia or France. We are obliged to pay the price for having been heavily involved in the updated "great game in Asia," which is to say that peoples of the area are, at best, ambivalent toward us. They cannot leave us alone and they wish that we would leave them alone. We would be well advised not to misread today's ambivalent signals. Our policymakers today are seen in the Middle East much like yesterday's Lord Cromer or Lord Killearn, men representing governments to be feared, admired, loved, hated, accepted, and avoided. We should recognize the liabilities that come with great power and take as our guide the more modest principle of acting so as not to make matters worse.

12

Credibility and
the Trauma of Vietnam

YUEN FOONG KHONG

ANY EXPLANATION of why the United States went to war in Vietnam will have to take into account broad postwar U.S. concerns such as containment, the domino theory, and the lessons of Munich—as well as more immediate historical contingencies such as the fall of China, the Korean War, the Bay of Pigs, the Vienna summit, and the Great Society. The relative or contextual significance of these factors may be conveyed by an analysis that centers on the concept of "credibility." Of all the concerns that occupied America's Vietnam policymakers, none seems more central than the credibility of the United States. Thus the following account of U.S. intervention in Vietnam traces the origin, evolution, and demise of this concern with credibility (with respect to Southeast Asia); in so doing, the special chain of historical events extrinsic to Vietnam, events which have often been treated in a rather ad hoc manner, should emerge as explanatory factors in their own right.

Containment, Dominoes, and Credibility

The Second World War confirmed for many that the United States could no longer afford to remain aloof from the realities of "Old World" politics. America's late and reluctant entry into the Second (and for that matter the First) World War did save Western Europe but the delay was costly. Franklin Roosevelt had recognized the need for the four policemen in his postwar plans but with the abdication of Britain and Chiang Kai-shek's China, it became a one-cop and one-robber situation, at least from the perspective of the United States.

With the Greek crisis of 1947—the event that precipitated the Truman Doctrine and signalled the beginnings of the Cold War—U.S. policymakers came to terms with the new situation. Under Secretary of State Dean Acheson seized the opportunity to warn congressional leaders of the dangers confronting the United States in a bipolar world:

> In the past eighteen months . . . Soviet pressure on the Straits, on Iran, and on Northern Greece had brought the Balkans to the point where a highly possible Soviet breakthrough might open three continents to Soviet penetration. Like apples in a barrel infected by one rotten one, the corruption of Greece would infect Iran and all to the east. . . . The Soviet Union was playing one of the greatest gambles in history. . . . We and we alone were in a position to break up the play.[1]

Acheson's statement summarized three elements that were to characterize the early Cold War. First was the perception of ubiquitous Soviet (and soon Soviet *cum* Chinese communist) pressure against fragile noncommunist states. Second, the consequences of these pressures, if unchecked, were aptly conveyed by Acheson's "rotten apples" analogy. Third, the United States was the only power capable of containing the spread of this "rot." Having long vaunted its moral "exceptionalism" in rejecting "Old World" balance-of-power politics, the United States embarked on a new exceptionalism in which "we and we alone were in a position to break up the play" of the Soviet Union.

These premises were not restricted to the analysis of events unfolding in the eastern Mediterranean; they also informed the analysis of the problem in Southeast Asia. As a 1952 National Security Council (NSC) policy statement put it: "In the absence of effective and timely counteraction, the loss of any single country [in Southeast Asia] would probably lead to relatively swift submission to or an alignment with communism by the remaining countries of this group."[2] Or as President Eisenhower put it in 1954, substituting a more mechanical metaphor for Acheson's organic one: "You have a row of dominoes set up, you knock over the first one, and what will happen to the last one is the certainty that it will go over very quickly. . . ."[3]

The logical inevitability of the advance of communism, as expressed by rotting apples or falling dominoes, was taken by successive administrations as a given. Whether one uses Acheson's "breaking up the play" or NSC's "effective and timely counteraction," the prescription was also clear: the United States was to contain that spread. The point to note is how interdependent the ideas of "falling dominoes" and "containment" are; the former provided the diagnosis of the problem and the stakes in Southeast Asia; the latter, the prescription. This is the standard explanation for the United States decision to intervene in Vietnam in

1. Dean Acheson, *Present at the Creation* (New York, 1969), p. 219.
2. *The Pentagon Papers*, ed. Gravel (Boston, 1971), vol. 1, p. 385.
3. Ibid., p. 597.

the 1960s. While this explanation captures some broad essential truths, it is incomplete. It fails to account for the following puzzle: If the notion of falling dominoes and the policy of containment already had taken hold in the early days of the Cold War, why did it not prompt Eisenhower to intervene at Dien Bien Phu in 1954 to save the French and prevent Vietnam (the north at least) from becoming communist? If the consequences were bearable in 1954, why were they unbearable in 1965?

The issue of credibility, I suggest, attained a singular importance in the 1960s that it never had during the fifties. Credibility was not an issue with Eisenhower in 1954 because America had just demonstrated in Korea its willingness to commit its power and even bear heavy costs to help noncommunist nations defend themselves. With Kennedy, however, credibility became an issue because of a series of setbacks that his administration suffered in its first year. Johnson inherited a situation in which U.S. power had already been committed; it became important for him to see that commitment through. Otherwise, he and his advisers believed, the credibility of U.S. commitments would be undermined, and with it, the check against another major war. Nixon felt he could negotiate a gradual U.S. withdrawal from South Vietnam because by the early 1970s, U.S. credibility vis-à-vis the communist powers was no longer a major issue. This was not so much because of what the United States did in South Vietnam but because the Sino-Soviet split made China and the Soviet Union—the major targets of the U.S. "credibility campaign"—behave in ways which indicated that they would be among the last to question the credibility of American power.

The Credibility of U.S. Power and Commitments

"Credibility," "prestige," and "honor" are words that U.S. policymakers have used interchangeably, both in public and in private, during the postwar period. What do they mean? Why are they important? These questions can be answered by looking at the parties with whom U.S. policymakers felt they had to establish credibility. In general, there are three sets of audiences: one's adversaries, one's allies, and one's domestic population. Credibility entails maintaining the confidence of these parties about the willingness of the United States to use its power to confront them (as in adversaries) or to come to their help (as in allies) or to live up to their expectations (as in one's own citizens). There are two variants of this theme: the credibility of one's power and the credibility of one's commitments. The former focuses on convincing others of the palpability of one's power or showing that one is not a "paper tiger;" the latter deals with one's honor or keeping promises.

Credibility is important because U.S. policymakers believe that when the credibility of one's power or one's commitments is in doubt, one's allies are likely to capitulate instead of fight in a crisis and, perhaps more important, one's opponents are likely to embark on adventures that threaten one's vital interests and world peace.

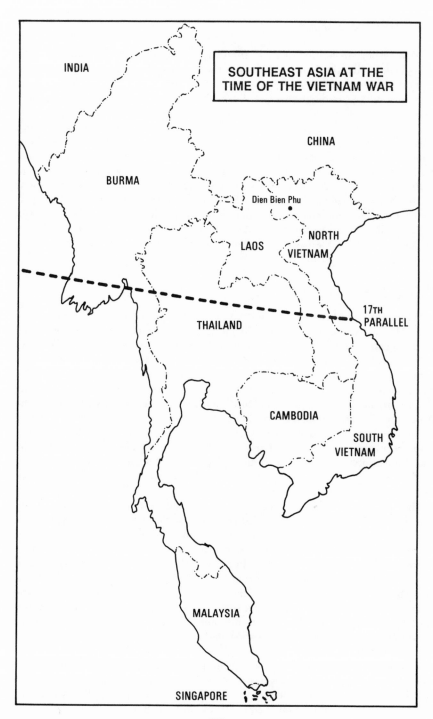

SOUTHEAST ASIA AT THE
TIME OF THE VIETNAM WAR

INDIA

CHINA

BURMA

Dien Bien Phu

LAOS

NORTH
VIETNAM

17TH
PARALLEL

THAILAND

CAMBODIA

SOUTH
VIETNAM

MALAYSIA

SINGAPORE

With respect to Southeast Asia, there was no question in the mind of U.S. policymakers that the United States was the only nation capable of checking the toppling of the dominoes. The question was whether the United States had a commitment to South Vietnam. Failure to come to the aid of South Vietnam would merely embolden the North Vietnamese and its supporters, the Soviet Union and China, and make all three more aggressive. Failure to help South Vietnam would also make our other allies question our reliability and make it difficult for them not to move toward accommodation of the communist bloc. Thailand, Malaya, Burma, the Philippines and even Japan would be subject to such pressures, and NATO countries would also question the U.S. commitment to the NATO alliance. There was, then, in the view of those American policymakers who were concerned about credibility, a direct relationship between U.S. credibility and world peace. An exploration of how and when credibility became an issue in Vietnam should shed some light on the rationale behind the American decision to intervene in South Vietnam.

Taking Sides, 1946–1954

When Ho Chi Minh proclaimed the independence of Vietnam on 2 September 1945, he was merely the latest in a long line of Vietnamese patriots who had fought against foreign domination of their land. There were two key differences between Ho and his predecessors: Ho was not merely a nationalist, he was also a communist; Ho's predecessors had fought against the Chinese and then the French colonialists while Ho had dislodged the Japanese in hopes of preempting the return of the French. Much has been made of Ho's borrowing from the American Declaration of Independence in his address to his audience of half a million Vietnamese; Ho also had reason to believe that the United States might actually practice what it (or rather Franklin Roosevelt) had preached during the war, the restoration of self-government to peoples who had been deprived of it. To this end, Ho wrote to Harry Truman, imploring him to support the independence of Vietnam from France.

The Truman administration, however, was less interested in self-determination than it was in ensuring Europe's recovery from the Second World War. European recovery was a goal in itself but it was also a necessary bulwark against Soviet expansionism in the West. Thus U.S. worries focused more on France than on Vietnam. The Western European bureau of the State Department prevailed upon Truman to refrain from resisting France's reimposition of colonial rule on Indochina. Truman thus rejected the Far Eastern bureau's position that the French be pressured into providing some sort of autonomy to the Indochinese. Pressuring the French on limited autonomy for Indochina, it was surmised, would destabilize the fragile domestic balance of forces in France and strengthen the position of the formidable French Communist party. The latter was clearly unacceptable for an administration solicitous of French participation in organizing Western Europe's defenses against the Soviet Union. The French exploited this U.S. fear of double communism and succeeded in making the Americans acquiesce in the reimposition of colonial rule in Indochina.

But Ho Chi Minh and the Vietminh that had come to power in the Tonkin area on the eve of Japan's defeat were reluctant to relinquish their rule and revert to the status of colonial subjects. Ho negotiated an agreement with the French in March 1946 which allowed the reintroduction of French troops in the north. Paris in return would recognize Ho's Democractic Republic of Vietnam as a free state with its own government and as part of the French Union. It soon became obvious that Paris was never interested in granting real independence to Vietnam—it would be too dangerous a precedent for its colonies elsewhere—and relations between the two sides deteriorated rapidly. A series of small incidents culminated in the French naval bombardment of Haiphong in November 1946. The Vietminh responded by attacking the French in Hanoi and thus began the first Indochina war.

Until 1950 the Truman administration gave only moral support to France in its fight against the Vietminh. Containment was still focused on Europe and the primary means was still economic. Two events changed all that. First the United States "lost" China in October 1949. Whatever the White Paper of August 1949 may have said about why the United States could not have prevented the fall of China, the triumph of communism there reinforced the notion that communism was expanding. The "incorporation" of China into the (Soviet) communist camp led U.S. policymakers to the view of a communist monolith, with the two giants united by an ideology which was not only hostile to democratic capitalism but also actively sought its overthrow.

In January 1950, barely four months after its inception, the People's Republic of China recognized Ho's Democratic Republic of Vietnam, and the Soviet Union followed shortly thereafter. For Secretary of State Dean Acheson these recognitions removed "any illusions as to the 'nationalist' nature of Ho Chi Minh's aims" and revealed Ho "in his true colors as the mortal enemy of native independence in Indochina."[4] The U.S. government responded by recognizing (soon to be South) Vietnam, Cambodia, and Laos as independent states within the French Union. In May 1950, the United States began to provide material aid to France to fight the Vietminh.

The second critical event was the Korean War. Coming as it did less than a year after China's turning communist and with some Soviet encouragement, it confirmed the worst fears of U.S. policymakers about the implacably hostile and expansionistic tendencies of communism. These perceptions were reinforced when Douglas MacArthur's attempt to roll back communism in North Korea brought China into the war. These events made it easy for U.S. policymakers to interpret the war between the French and the Vietminh in Vietnam as another battle against world communism. In 1951, U.S. aid to France amounted to $450 million or 40 percent of the cost of fighting the Vietminh that year; by 1954, the United States was underwriting 80 percent of the costs. The U.S. aim was to prevent the reinstatement of Vietminh rule in all of Vietnam, not just the south, where the communists' hold had been tenuous.

4. Cited in George Kahin, *Intervention: How America Became Involved in Vietnam* (New York, 1986), p. 35.

Korea, Eisenhower, and Credibility

Despite U.S. aid, France was losing the war to the Vietminh. By 1952, the French had lost so much territory to the Vietminh that only enclaves around Hanoi, Haiphong, strips along the Cambodian border, and Saigon remained under their control. The decisive battle was fought in the spring of 1954. The French chose Dien Bien Phu, a strategically worthless lowland where they had a fortress, to make their stand. Convinced that Vietnamese General Vo Nguyen Giap's forces would find it impossible to haul artillery up the surrounding hills, the French thought they could hold the fort as well as inflict devastating damage on the besieging Vietminh. The results were quite the opposite. The Vietminh disassembled their artillery, carried them piece by piece up the hills, reassembled them at the top, and delivered murderous volleys to the French garrison. Once the airstrip was destroyed, the fate of the French soldiers was sealed. It was at this point that the French requested U.S. intervention to save their beleaguered forces at Dien Bien Phu.

Despite the policy of containment and despite President Eisenhower's worries about falling dominoes, the United States failed to intervene to relieve the French garrison at Dien Bien Phu. Eisenhower did consider using U.S. ground troops and aerial bombardment to stop the Vietminh, but he rejected both options. The most common explanation for Eisenhower's behavior is that he was reluctant to intervene without congressional approval. When Secretary of State Dulles—who favored intervention—used the domino theory to alert congressional leaders to the stakes in Dien Bien Phu, their reply was quite different from the one that Acheson received during the Greek crisis in 1947. Instead of asking the administration to take the case to the public, they wanted "no more Koreas with the U.S. furnishing 90% of the manpower." But Congress would be willing to go along if the administration could get the allies of the United States, particularly the British, to join the military intervention. The British were reluctant to engage in any joint action and Eisenhower decided against unilateral intervention.

Historians disagree as to whether a wise Congress stayed Eisenhower's hand or a wise Eisenhower used Congress to ward off his prointervention advisers like Admiral Arthur Radford and Vice President Richard Nixon. The more interesting observation is perhaps that for Eisenhower, the credibility of American power or commitments was not an issue in 1954. This observation is especially interesting when contrasted with the premium placed on credibility in the 1960s. In 1954, however, the worries revolved around making issues out of prestige and credibility—by intervening. Thus the congressional leaders briefed by Dulles were worried that intervention might not stop with aerial bombing. "Once the flag was committed," they surmised, "the use of land forces would inevitably follow."[5]

Eisenhower himself carried the flag metaphor a step further when he speculated about the dangers of committing ground troops. The president reasoned that if he were to put a single combat soldier into Indochina, America's "entire prestige would be at stake, not only in that area but throughout the world."[6] The

5. Ibid., p. 48.
6. Ibid., p. 49.

implication here of course is that since there were no U.S. combat troops in Vietnam yet, U.S. credibility was not at stake. It was the French, after all, who were fighting (albeit with U.S. material help) and losing the war.

It is not surprising that Eisenhower saw no need to demonstrate the credibility of American power or the credibility of America's commitment. The former hardly needed demonstration. The United States had just recently used its military might to stop communist aggression in South Korea and did so at severe costs to itself even though the Korean peninsula had earlier been written off as not central to the defense perimeter of the United States. Equally important, Eisenhower wanted to know if U.S. power could succeed in stopping the Vietminh before committing American prestige to Vietnam—the containment policy and the domino effect notwithstanding. Dulles had posed the issue well to the president when he warned that if the United States intervened, its prestige would be "engaged to a point where we would want to have a success. We could not afford a defeat that would have worldwide repercussions."[7] In this regard, Army Chief of Staff Matthew Ridgway's advice that the United States would be bogged down in Dien Bien Phu at a scale comparable to that of Korea helped sow the seeds of doubt in Eisenhower. Ridgway had just returned from Korea after stabilizing the situation there and Eisenhower respected his opinion. As Ridgway would write later, he was "most humbly proud" of fighting against and perhaps contributing to the prevention of intervention in Indochina which he considered to be a "harebrained tactical scheme . . . which would have cost the lives of some thousands of men."[8]

Geneva and SEATO

Without American intervention, the French garrison at Dien Bien Phu was doomed. Dien Bien Phu fell on 7 May, one day before the Indochina phase of the Geneva Conference began. The latter resulted in the Geneva Accords of 1954 which divided Vietnam along the seventeenth parallel into two zones of regroupment. The seventeenth parallel was a provisional demarcation line, not a political boundary. Geneva created, in George Kahin's words, "two contesting parties within a single national state."[9] The final declaration also provided for national reunification elections to be held in 1956, an election in which Eisenhower himself thought that Ho Chi Minh would have received 80 percent of the vote.

The importance of this election to the victorious Vietminh cannot be overestimated. From August 1945 to December 1946, the Vietminh had actually ruled Vietnam as a united country. In the ensuing war against the French, the Vietminh lost portions of the south to the French but regained them toward the close of war. Yet at Geneva they settled for less than what they actually controlled in territory. They were willing to do this partly because of political pressures from China and the Soviet Union—which had their own agendas—and partly because they believed Vietnam would be unified after the elections of 1956. As

7. Dwight Eisenhower, *Mandate for Change, 1953–1956* (New York, 1963), p. 345.
8. Matthew Ridgway, *Soldier* (New York, 1956), p. 278.
9. George Kahin, *Intervention*, p. 63.

one of the cochairmen of the conference, Britain's Anthony Eden saw that Ho would never have agreed to the Geneva armistice had the reunification elections not been promised.

After Geneva the Eisenhower administration set up the Southeast Asian Treaty Organization (SEATO), comprising the United States, Britain, France, Australia, New Zealand, the Philippines, Thailand, and Pakistan. The proliferation of pacts or "pactomania" under Eisenhower and Dulles had come to Southeast Asia. It was almost as if the administration were seeking some commitment on which to stake U.S. prestige in Southeast Asia. Cambodia, Laos, and South Vietnam were not signatories to the treaty because the Geneva agreements had forbidden them to join any military alliance; but Dulles "circumvented" that by having a protocol which extended an "umbrella of protection" over these three areas. Although U.S. officials during the 1960s would refer publicly to the SEATO commitment as the reason for U.S. intervention in Vietnam, it will be seen that it was not the treaty as such—since the clause was sufficiently vague to suit any interpretation—but rather a broader sense of credibility and commitment which held sway with the policymakers.

From 1954 to 1960 the Eisenhower administration sought to create and build a noncommunist southern state under Ngo Dinh Diem. Although the United States had promised not to "disturb" the Geneva accords, it acquiesced in Diem's refusal to hold the reunification elections of 1956. Diem held his own elections in the south, and "won" 98 percent of the vote even though his American advisers suggested that 60 percent would have been adequate. From mid-1955 until 1960, Diem embarked on a systematic attempt to ferret out, incarcerate, and in many cases eliminate Vietminh members and their sympathizers who had remained in the south. By 1959, Diem's repression of ex-Vietminh supporters had reached such heights that Hanoi approved limited military action against the Diem regime. With the formation of the National Liberation Front in 1961, a full-scale insurrection to overthrow the Diem government was approved. From here on, the question of under whom a unified Vietnam would exist was to be decided by force. This was the situation inherited by Kennedy and his New Frontiersmen.

The Credibility of Power

For Eisenhower the recent U.S. involvement in Korea dispelled any doubts about the willingness of America to come to the aid of a friend. American power had been used firmly and successfully to prevent South Korea from going under. Moreover, with regard to Vietnam, Eisenhower was told that without a ground commitment on the scale of Korea, it was uncertain whether the United States could beat the Vietminh. For Kennedy, on the other hand, a peculiar series of events seemed to raise questions about the credibility of American power. With regard to Vietnam, Kennedy was told—and he also believed—the United States could probably defeat the Vietcong. Given the perceived need to demonstrate the palpability of American power, Vietnam seemed like the place to do it.

The years 1961 and 1962 would have taxed any administration; they were especially ominous, however, to an administration that had vowed to pay any price and bear any burden to ensure the survival of liberty. 1962 would be a critical year for analysts of U.S. nuclear policy, but for the purposes of this essay 1961 seems more pivotal. In that year a series of foreign policy challenges—Laos, Khrushchev's pledge to support wars of national liberation, the Bay of Pigs, the Vienna summit, the Berlin Wall—put the Kennedy administration on the defensive. The cumulative effect of these setbacks, as they were perceived, was that it led to the conclusion that it was necessary for the United States to demonstrate resolve elsewhere.

Laos was supposed to be the most urgent foreign policy problem that Eisenhower bequeathed to Kennedy. At the preinaugural briefing for the president-elect, Eisenhower stressed that if Laos went communist, the rest of Southeast Asia might follow suit. The stakes seemed sufficiently high to Eisenhower to recommend U.S. unilateral military intervention if that was necessary to prevent the communist Pathet Lao from taking power. Kennedy was clearly alarmed, but he chose to negotiate rather than fight, in part because the U.S.-backed Laotian government was politically and militarily inept and in part because the Bay of Pigs fiasco had made Kennedy suspicious of the military. The negotiations led to a neutralist coalition government in which the Pathet Lao was to play a major role.

At the same time, Khrushchev made his famous speech about Soviet support for wars of national liberation. Although analysts now agree that the speech was meant primarily for Chinese ears, the situations in Cuba, Laos, and Vietnam led Kennedy and his advisers to see it as a virtual declaration of war. Shortly thereafter, the Kennedy administration was saddled with the Bay of Pigs fiasco. Unlike Eisenhower's successes with Iran and Guatemala, the Cuban exiles covertly trained and backed by the United States were decimated or captured as they landed at the Bay of Pigs in an ill-planned and badly implemented attempt to overthrow Fidel Castro. Kennedy publicly took responsibility for the fiasco; it was hardly the kind of operation one associates with an administration that has vowed to pay any price and bear any burden.

Kennedy's June 1961 Vienna meeting with Khrushchev did not alleviate the President's siege mentality. The Soviet leader sought to browbeat the young American president into acquiescing on issues ranging from the right of the Soviets to support wars of national liberation to eliminating the Western presence in Berlin. Before the Vienna meeting Kennedy had told Arthur Krock of *The New York Times* that he wanted to make sure that Khrushchev did not misunderstand Cuba, Laos, and so on to indicate that the United States was about to yield on matters such as Berlin. When Kennedy returned from Vienna, he reportedly told James Reston that "now we have a problem in making our power credible, and Vietnam looks like the place."[10]

As indicated earlier, there were three constituencies with which the United States was interested in establishing or maintaining its credibility. First, America's adversaries—the Soviet Union and China—must not doubt its willingness to

10. Cited in William Westmoreland, *A Soldier Reports* (New York, 1976), p. 409.

protect its vital interests. The assumption was that if the communists questioned the credibility of American power, they would be prone to challenge America's interests all over the world. Thus Kennedy's fear that if Khrushchev misinterpreted the Bay of Pigs and Laos, he might mistakenly think that the United States would also yield in Berlin. The price of such a mistake might be a world war.

It was important to the Kennedy administration that credibility also be maintained with one's allies and one's domestic population. As Vice President Lyndon Johnson put it in his report about his Southeast Asian trip in 1961 to Kennedy: "The key to what is done by Asians in defense of Southeast Asian freedom is confidence in the United States. . . . There is no alternative to United States leadership in Southeast Asia."[11] Equally worrisome were the prognostications about the reaction of our European allies and domestic opponents if the administration did not show resolve in Southeast Asia. As the Rusk-McNamara report of November 1961 warned: "The loss of South Viet-Nam would . . . undermine the credibility of American commitments elsewhere. Further, loss of South Vietnam would stimulate bitter domestic controversies in the United States and would be seized upon by extreme elements to divide the country and harass the Administration."[12]

Why did Vietnam "look like the place" to do it? If one were to invoke treaty obligations to SEATO, the United States should have done in Laos what it did in South Vietnam, since both Laos and South Vietnam were "protected" under the umbrella clause. Vietnam looked like the place to demonstrate and stake one's credibility because Kennedy and his advisers thought that the United States had a good chance of succeeding. It was not so in Laos. Thus in late 1961 William Bundy wrote his boss, Secretary of Defense Robert McNamara, that America had a 70 percent chance of "arresting" the deteriorating situation in South Vietnam.[13] Similarly, most of the administration from Kennedy down saw Vietnam as a case of counterinsurgency and believed that the cases of Malaya and Philippines showed that it was possible to defeat the communist guerrillas. As Walt Rostow put it, by winning in Vietnam, "we shall have demonstrated that the Communist technique of guerrilla warfare can be dealt with."[14]

Thus the concern with credibility and a consensus that South Vietnam was the right place to do it because of the high probability of success were all-important when Kennedy made the decision to exceed the Geneva limit of 750 advisers. By the end of 1961, there were over two thousand of them, including helicopter crews participating in combat missions against the Vietcong, in South Vietnam. By the end of 1962 there would be nearly twelve thousand U.S. military personnel in Vietnam.

A brief comparison of Kennedy's 1961–62 decision to exceed the Geneva limits—"the most fateful" decision, according to former State Department official Paul Kattenburg—with Eisenhower's reasoning for not intervening at the far more epochal Dien Bien Phu is instructive.[15] The goal of containment was

11. *Pentagon Papers*, vol. 2, p. 57.
12. Ibid., p. 111.
13. Ibid., p. 79.
14. Cited in George Herring, *America's Longest War* (New York, 1979), p. 79.

important to both presidents, as was the concern about falling Southeast Asian dominoes if Vietnam went communist. The differences revolved around credibility, which was not an issue with Eisenhower in the mid-1950s as it was with Kennedy in the early 1960s; chances of victory were estimated to be much lower by Eisenhower than they were by Kennedy and his advisers. The improbability of success even with U.S. might influenced Eisenhower's decision not to stake U.S. credibility in Vietnam in 1954; the more optimistic assessments of what U.S. power could do in 1961–62 made it easier for Kennedy to see Vietnam as the place to make U.S. power credible.

Credibility of Commitments and the Decisions of 1965

His optimism notwithstanding, Kennedy seemed to be less aware than Eisenhower that demonstrating the credibility of one's power in Vietnam—by sending thousands of American personnel—meant committing American prestige in such a way that it fundamentally narrowed one's future options. This was the situation that President Lyndon Johnson faced in 1964–65. In that year there were seven coups in South Vietnam, a stark indication of the political instability that raged there. By 1965, with the situation deteriorating, Johnson faced a situation analogous to that confronting Eisenhower in 1954 and Kennedy in 1961: there was the distinct possibility that without further U.S. action, the south would be lost to the Vietnamese communists.

The credibility of U.S. commitments became a key issue throughout this period of deliberation. At this juncture, one is tempted to ask: What commitment? Although the administration would publicly refer to the SEATO commitment, SEATO figured in few of the discussions held privately. The issue was the more general notion of the credibility of commitments. Johnson was worried about the repercussions of not living up to one's commitments. Adversaries would be emboldened, allies would lose faith, and on the domestic front a backlash was possible. These were the recurring themes of the meetings called in July to decide on General Westmoreland's request for 100,000 combat troops in order to stave off a South Vietnamese defeat.

In the crucial 21 July meeting, Under Secretary of State George Ball was given the chance to make the case against intervention. Ball's main point was that the United States could not win. Sending in 100,000 troops, according to Ball, would be akin to "giving cobalt treatment to a terminal cancer case. I think a long, protracted war will disclose our weakness, not our strength." Ball suggested that the U.S. cut its losses in South Vietnam and he had "no illusions that . . . [South Vietnam] would soon come under Hanoi control." Johnson's retort is worth quoting in full because it illustrates his state of mind:

> But George, wouldn't all these countries say that Uncle Sam was a paper tiger, wouldn't we lose credibility breaking the word of three presidents, if we did as you have proposed? It would seem to be an irreparable blow. But I gather you don't think so.

15. Paul Kattenburg, *The Vietnam Trauma in American Foreign Policy, 1945–75* (New Jersey, 1980), p. 108.

Secretary of State Dean Rusk supported Johnson. According to the notes of NSC aide Chester Cooper, Rusk "emphasized that the nature and integrity of the U.S. commitment was fundamental. It makes the U.S. stance with the USSR creditable (sic). It would be dangerous if the Communist leadership became convinced that we will not see this through." Rusk had put this assessment in writing three weeks before that crucial meeting: "There can be no serious debate about the fact that we have a commitment to assist the South Vietnamese to resist aggression from the North. . . . The integrity of the U.S. commitment is the principal pillar of peace throughout the world. If that commitment becomes unreliable, the communist world would draw conclusions that would lead to our ruin and almost certainly to a catastrophic war."[16]

Johnson was worried that the United States would lose credibility with three constituencies: the communists (i.e., the Soviet Union and China), America's allies (in Europe and Asia), and domestic supporters and opponents. Since the Johnson administration's worries about the first two of the three constituencies closely paralleled those of Kennedy's, only the third needs additional comment. On the domestic front, Johnson perceived that he could not lose South Vietnam because that would undermine the credibility of his administration with Congress and the American people. As he later told Doris Kearns, "I knew that Harry Truman and Dean Acheson had lost their effectiveness from the day that the communists took over in China. I believed that the loss of China had played a large role in the rise of Joe McCarthy. And I knew that all these problems, taken together, were chickenshit compared with what might happen if we lost Vietnam."[17]

If the reason for maintaining credibility internationally was to ensure world peace, the reason for maintaining credibility domestically, for Johnson, was to build the Great Society. A country divided by an acrimonious debate over who lost Vietnam was unlikely to pass legislation ushering in the Great Society. As Larry Berman has emphasized, Vietnam was not the only item on the president's agenda, nor was it his favorite. By mid-1965, "thirty-six major pieces of legislation had been signed into law, twenty-six others [including Medicare and the Civil Rights Bill] were moving through the House and Senate, and eleven more awaiting scheduling."[18]

It is important, however, not to overemphasize the urgency of domestic credibility. The importance of not losing credibility in eyes of the communists and allies would have been sufficient for Johnson. For he shared the assessments—held by virtually all the senior decision makers of his administration—of the international consequences of losing one's credibility or prestige.

16. See Meeting on Vietnam, 21 July 1965, Notes (by Jack Valenti), Papers of Lyndon Johnson, Meeting Notes File; assembled from various sources, the most complete verbatim account of the 21 and 22 July 1965 meetings. See also Kahin, *Intervention,* pp. 366–78. For the Dean Rusk comment, see Note, Dean Rusk, 1 July 1965, Vietnam Memos, xxxvii, July 1965, Country File—Vietnam, National Security File, Lyndon Baines Johnson Library, Austin, Texas.

17. Doris Kearns, *Lyndon Johnson and the American Dream* (New York, 1976), pp. 252–53.

18. Larry Berman, *Planning a Tragedy* (New York, 1982), p. 142.

The discussion of U.S. credibility in 1965—like those of 1954 and 1961—was intertwined with discussions of two other calculations: an assessment of the costs of losing one's credibility and an assessment of the chances of the United States' achieving its objectives in Vietnam. These calculations are best seen in Rusk's discussion of how "fundamental" the integrity of U.S. commitments was. Unlike Eisenhower and Kennedy, and perhaps conditioned by remorse about his failure to predict the Chinese intervention during the Korean War, Rusk was also very cognizant of the dangers of maintaining one's credibility. All these calculations were part of Rusk's exposition—and his only extended discussion—of the importance of credibility in the July meeting. He said:

> If the Communist world finds out we will not pursue our commitments to the end, I don't know where they will stay their hand [the stakes]. I have to say I am more optimistic than some of my colleagues [the chances of winning]. I don't believe the VC have made large advances among the Vietnamese people. . . . I don't see large casualties unless the Chinese come in [the dangers].[19]

Where did this emphasis on the integrity of the U.S. commitment and the prediction of catastrophic consequences if it were questioned come from? A long answer would require a separate study. A short answer is that there is little doubt that Johnson and his advisers were very much influenced by the lessons of the 1930s and 1950s. Western indifference to the fate of victims of aggression in the 1930s—Czechoslovakia, Ethiopia, and Manchuria—emboldened the aggressors and helped bring about the Second World War. Especially disturbing was France's (and by extension Britain's) refusal to meet their commitments to Czechoslovakia when Hitler sought to annex parts of the Sudetenland. Instead of coming to the Czechs' help, Daladier and Chamberlain gave in to Hitler's demands at the Munich Conference of September 1938. Hitler was not appeased. He devoured the rest of Czechoslovakia and moved on to Poland, doubting the credibility of British and French commitments to the latter. By contrast, the experience of the 1950s—especially Korea—showed that when America stood firm, aggression could be and was halted, albeit at some cost.

These historical lessons informed the policymakers' assessments of cause-effect relationships in world politics and thus encouraged their preoccupation with maintaining credibility in Vietnam. President Johnson, Dean Rusk, and U.S. Ambassador to Vietnam Henry Cabot Lodge were among the strongest proponents of this reasoning: if the United States failed to live up to its commitments in South Vietnam, U.S. credibility would be undermined and that in turn would bring about catastrophic consequences. In Dean Rusk's words, "I don't know where they [the communist world] will stay their hands."

Strategic Innovation and the Decline of Credibility

If Kennedy's demonstration of the credibility of American power restricted Johnson's options, Johnson's way of preserving the credibility of America's com-

19. Cited in Kahin, *Intervention*, p. 377.

mitments tied the hands of the Nixon administration even more severely. "Our predecessors," wrote Henry Kissinger, "had done enough to produce a major commitment of American power and credibility but not enough to bring it to a conclusion." However much the Nixon administration wanted to end the U.S. involvement in Vietnam, it "could not simply walk away from an enterprise involving two administrations, five allied countries and thirty-one thousand dead as if we were switching a television channel." More important:

> As the leader of democratic alliances we had to remember that scores of countries and millions of people relied for their security on our willingness to stand by our allies, indeed on our confidence in ourselves. No serious policymaker could allow himself to succumb to the fashionable debunking of prestige or honor or credibility.[20]

Nixon and Kissinger chose to demonstrate U.S. self-confidence and credibility by expanding the conflict to Cambodia and Laos while simultaneously engaging in a phased, unilateral withdrawal of U.S. troops from South Vietnam. They ordered the secret bombing of Cambodia in 1969 and incursions into Cambodia and Laos in 1970 and 1971 respectively. The military purpose of these operations was to eliminate the headquarters and sanctuaries of the Vietcong; the political purpose was to remind friend and foe that the United States was still a force to reckon with. U.S. bombing and incursions drove the Vietcong further into Cambodia. It also led Hanoi to start large-scale support for the Khmer Rouge fighting Lon Nol in Cambodia. "The United States thus acquired," according to historian George Herring, "another fragile client government faced with determined internal opposition supported by Hanoi, and Cambodia became an active and particularly bloody theater of war."[21]

Between 1969 and 1973, the Vietnam War took the lives of another twenty thousand U.S. soldiers, not to mention hundreds of thousands of South and North Vietnamese. Against this background, Kissinger negotiated an agreement with Hanoi which called for the complete withdrawal of the United States from South Vietnam but which allowed the North Vietnamese to keep their forces in the south after the cease-fire. Apparently, four extra years of war under Nixon and Kissinger failed to extract any greater concessions from the North Vietnamese on this issue. To have their forces remain in the south was Hanoi's objective in 1969 and the Paris accords gave them just that. Vietnamization notwithstanding, it is hardly surprising that President Thieu resisted signing the agreement until the very last moment when Nixon threatened to sign it without the South Vietnamese.

Nixon and Kissinger saw their policy of escalation, withdrawal, and negotiation from 1969 to 1973 as actions that preserved U.S. credibility ; in their view these actions also brought "peace with honor." Those who saw the Paris Peace Agreements for what they were and those familiar with the fragility of the South Vietnamese government would certainly have found Nixon's and Kissinger's perspective incredible or self-serving or both. Oddly enough, whether the

20. Henry Kissinger, *White House Years* (Boston, 1979), pp. 226–28.
21. Herring, *America's Longest War*, p. 231.

settlement enhanced U.S. credibility might not be the most pertinent question. For in the early 1970s, American credibility became a less urgent issue. The Soviet Union and China, America's most formidable rivals, were the major targets of the credibility campaign. Their confidence in the United States had little to do with what the Americans had done in Vietnam in the previous decade. It had much to do with their complete lack of confidence in or rather overt hostility for one another. The Sino-Soviet split made each one of the two communist giants anxious for some kind of rapprochement with the United States against the other. The Soviets actually sounded Nixon out as to his likely response in the event of a Soviet nuclear attack against China. China was interested in a quasi-alliance with the United States to ward off the "social imperialists." Nixon and Kissinger played this triangular politics with consummate skill, achieving detente, the Anti-Ballistic Missile (ABM) Treaty and a Strategic Arms Limitation Treaty (SALT I) with the Soviets and rapprochement with China.

With both the Soviet Union and China seeking out the United States, the latter hardly needed to worry about its self-confidence or credibility. Indeed the lengths to which both the Soviets and the Chinese were willing to go to meet the United States did not bode well for the North Vietnamese. By their very willingness to receive Nixon in Beijing early in 1972, the Chinese indicated that they placed their strategic interests ahead of fraternal solidarity with Hanoi. The Soviets were even more disappointing. They failed to cancel a Brezhnev-Nixon summit in Moscow despite Nixon's decision to retaliate against the North Vietnamese spring offensive of 1972 by bombing Hanoi and mining Haiphong harbor. Those who Kennedy and Johnson feared would question America's credibility were acting as if that question were not a primary consideration. Under such conditions, it became easier for the Nixon administration to withdraw from Vietnam and to sign the Paris peace agreements.

The specter of a replay of Geneva 1954 must have occurred to Hanoi in 1972–73. Despite the material and personnel support that the Soviet Union and China were giving Hanoi, Hanoi must have seen the writing on the wall. In 1954, both the Soviet Union and China pressured Hanoi to settle for less than what they had won in the battlefield; in 1972, by their actions, the Soviets and the Chinese seemed to be distancing themselves from Hanoi again. In 1954, the French had held out rejection of the European Defense Community as an incentive for the Soviets to "encourage" Ho Chi Minh to settle; in 1972, Nixon and Kissinger capitalized on the Sino-Soviet split to drive a wedge between the Soviet Union and China from Hanoi. Through detente and rapprochement, Nixon and Kissinger managed to "coopt" the two communist giants to participate in the what Kissinger has termed the "stable structure of peace." At least for that brief period, the issue of credibility could not be more irrelevant.

National Will and Failure

The Vietnam war turned out to be a major debacle for the United States. Fifty-eight thousand deaths, over 300,000 wounded, and $150 billion dollars later, the

Two pictures that brought home the horrors of the Vietnam War to the American public: The National Police Chief of South Vietnam personally executing a Viet Cong officer in a Saigon street (February 1968) and terrified Vietnamese children fleeing an accidental aerial napalm strike (November 1972). The girl in the center has ripped off her burning clothes. (AP/Wide World Photos)

248

United States still failed to prevent the fall of South Vietnam to communism. Reunifying their country against the objection of the United States cost the Vietnamese communists 950,000 lives and countless wounded, not to mention the physical and environmental destruction that came with having more bombs dropped on their country than all the other countries combined in World War II. Why, despite the use of such massive force, did the United States fail to achieve its objective of preventing South Vietnam from falling under communism? What impact did the loss of South Vietnam have on the credibility of the United States?

The first question is easier to answer. The United States lost its will to fight somewhere along the way. By 1968, a majority of Americans felt that the war had been a mistake. Yet the Johnson administration continued to reassure Americans about the "light at the end of the tunnel." The Tet offensive of January 1968, brought vividly to the television screens of fifty million Americans, shattered any illusions about a quick victory. A military disaster for the Vietcong, the offensive proved to be a psychological watershed for the American public. Stalemate in Vietnam, and the increasingly bitter divisions it created within the United States made Johnson decide not to seek a second term and to deescalate the war.

The strategy of escalation-withdrawal-negotiation pursued by Nixon in Indochina from 1969 to 1973 failed to capture the public imagination. Nixon and Kissinger argued that their expansion of the war to Cambodia was necessary to strengthen the U.S. hand while it withdrew from South Vietnam, but the public responded with massive protests. In mid-1973 Congress was sufficiently incensed by Nixon's continued bombing of Cambodia that it voted to stop all bombing in Indochina. In November of the same year, Congress passed the War Powers Act, requiring the president to inform Congress within forty-eight hours if U.S. forces were engaged in any hostilities abroad and requiring them to be withdrawn within sixty days unless Congress approved of the president's action. The act might have made it more difficult for Gerald Ford to carry out Nixon's secret promise to Thieu that the United States would retaliate with "full force" if Hanoi violated the Paris peace accords. But Ford's reluctance to carry out Nixon's promise did not stem from the technicalities of the War Powers Act, for the act only required him to seek the consent of Congress within sixty days of the use of American force; it was what the act symbolized—the waning of the will to see Vietnam through—that proved critical.

To the waning of American will, it is necessary to add the determination of the North Vietnamese and the Vietcong. They saw themselves as fighting to rid their country of foreigners and to complete the unification which had been denied them in 1956. Their Marxist-Leninist ideology and impeccable organization, coupled with extensive Soviet and Chinese military aid (which however still amounted to less than what the United States provided to South Vietnam), made it possible for them to outlast the United States. Moreover, they seemed to have understood the American political system and the constraints of public opinion better than their adversaries in the south. What Ho Chi Minh told the French in the 1940s, "You can kill ten of my men for every one I kill of yours but even at those odds, you will lose and I will win," succinctly summarized the communists' fanatical devotion to their cause as well as their superb understanding of the domestic constraints on a democracy's war-making abilities.

Ultimately, however, the reasons the war was lost have to be found in South Vietnam itself. South Vietnam was much more divided along religious, rural-urban, and political lines than North Vietnam ever was. Any leader would have found it difficult to satisfy the conflicting political demands of the Buddhist majority, the Catholic minority, and members of sects like the Cao Dai and Hoa Hao, not to mention the expectations of the military, the intellectuals, and other noncommunist groups. Within such a demographic and political context, the leaders of South Vietnam, from Ngo Dinh Diem to Nguyen Van Thieu were of no special help. If Diem had had the pragmatism and vision of a Magsaysay, the Filipino leader whom Americans hoped Diem would emulate, he could have built a viable society and South Vietnam might have gone the way of South Korea. But he used his time unwisely and instead of building support, he embarked on a ruthless extermination of former Vietminh sympathizers—forbidden by the Geneva accords—and succeeded only in driving large numbers of them underground as well as alienating a segment of the liberal intelligentsia.

By 1963, Diem was considered such a liability to the American effort to contain the communists that the United States supported a coup to depose him. The coup ended with the gratuitous killing of Diem and his brother, Nhu, but it did not improve the ability of the south to fight the communists. Instead it ushered in years of political instability characterized by an incessant jockeying for power by Generals Duong Van Minh, Nguyen Khanh, Nguyen Van Thieu, and Nguyen Cao Ky. Early in 1965, Lyndon Johnson had to hold off bombing the north for two weeks because the south was so politically unstable that he was doubtful about its ability to withstand a North Vietnamese retaliation on the ground. "Governmental chaos" was the term George Ball used to describe the situation in South Vietnam and to argue why it was not in America's interest to make a stand in that part of Southeast Asia.

The incompetence of the southern leadership is vividly illustrated in the last days of Saigon when Thieu's own indecisiveness hastened the fall of key cities in Military Regions I and II. None of Thieu's military or civilian advisers, chosen primarily for their loyalty instead of competence, could provide the leadership demanded by the moment. Especially unhelpful was Thieu's commander of Region II, General Pham Van Phu, who evacuated himself from Pleiku by helicopter first instead of staying to lead the evacuation of his troops. A rout ensued when some of the troops who were to be left behind turned their guns on others who were leaving.[22] The rapidity with which the South Vietnamese army and positions collapsed took the advancing North Vietnamese troops by surprise. When the North Vietnamese launched the final offensive in early 1975, they expected to take two years to capture Saigon. They did it in four months.

The most important liability of the successive South Vietnamese regimes, however, was not incompetence, corruption, or repressiveness. It was the degree to which they were beholden to the United States. It made it impossible for them to steal the mantle of nationalism away from the communists. As the

22. Nguyen Tien Hung and Jerrold Schecter, *The Palace File* (New York, 1986), pp. 266–69.

Vietnamese historian William Turley put it, a key element of Vietnamese identity was the "image of heroic resistance to foreign rule." Furthermore, "leaders who fulfilled this image could extract intense loyalty and enormous sacrifice from a broad spectrum of the population" while those who were perceived to have "succumbed to foreign pressure . . . or accommodated foreigners . . . suffered self-doubt and weak support."[23]

In spite or perhaps because of their dependence on the United States, Thieu and his advisers had difficulty understanding the domestic constraints on American policy from 1973 to 1975. They did not understand Watergate and how it could sap the power and prestige of the presidency, not to mention drive Nixon out of office. They could not have failed to see that the majority of Americans had turned against the war by 1968 and that by the early 1970s most Americans opposed any involvement whatsoever in Indochina, as they still do. Perhaps it is unfair to expect the South Vietnam leaders, fighting for their country's existence, to absorb the implications of such popular constraints on U.S. policy.

Still, a particularly poignant incident in the last days of the Thieu regime, an incident indicative of South Vietnam's psychological and material dependence on the United States as well as its leaders' complete misunderstanding of the American political process, was Thieu's response to the advancing North Vietnamese troops in Military Regions I and II. Thieu proposed an enclave defense that focused on defending key coastal towns. He ordered that even if all the other enclaves were abandoned, Danang was to be held at all costs. Danang was to be held at all costs because until the final moments, Thieu harbored hopes that the Americans would return—just as they first splashed ashore in Danang in March 1965—to save South Vietnam.

Many South Vietnamese argue that the way the United States negotiated itself out of the morass of Vietnam and its refusal to intervene in the wake of North Vietnam's attack in 1975 indicate that the credibility of America's power and commitments have been irreparably damaged. The reaction of the rest of the world is probably more difficult to gauge. Some may trace Soviet adventures in Angola and Nicaragua plus the invasion of Afghanistan to the loss of American credibility in the post-Vietnam era. That is plausible but not probable. The Soviets, moreover, have not been able to impress most of the noncommunist nations in the Middle East, Western Europe, and the Asia Pacific region. Few nations in these regions have turned to the Soviet communist bloc since Vietnam; neither have they distanced themselves from the United States. Quite the opposite. Virtually all of them have continued to demand an American presence in their region. The irony is that today it is the United States which is turning a deaf ear to the cries of the noncommunist Southeast Asian countries for a stronger presence in the region.

It would be foolish to deny that U.S. prestige took a beating in Vietnam. The question is whether that happened because the United States was unwise to get involved in an unwinnable war in a strategically unimportant place to begin with or that the United States failed to live up to its commitments by not fighting to

23. William Turley, *The Second Indochina War* (Boulder, Colo., 1986), p. 2.

(Copyright 1975 by Jules Feiffer)

the end. There are also many other possibilities in between about which one could argue. What seems less arguable is that the prognostications of the policymakers of the 1960s have not materialized. The damage done to U.S. credibility in Vietnam did not embolden America's adversaries or force America's allies and friends to "submit swiftly" to communism. Neither did it lead to the general war that policymakers, influenced by the lessons of the 1930s, saw as probable. If only Kennedy and Johnson had been less self-conscious about the credibility of the nation they led and if only they had been more aware of how much credibility and goodwill the United States enjoyed to begin with, the saga of Vietnam might have been less tragic.

NEW ALIGNMENTS

13

Diplomatic Revolution: The Changing China Policy

DAVID BACHMAN

IN THE YEARS since 1945 the United States has gone from threatening China with nuclear attack to offering to sell nuclear technology to China; from denouncing Mao Zedong to sending a condolence telegram to his successors at the time of his death in 1976; from fighting battles with Chinese forces to selling lethal munitions to China; and from embargoing trade with China to becoming China's second or third largest trading partner. These dramatic contrasts, and others that could be mentioned, suggest that since 1945, U.S.-China relations have undergone a degree of evolution perhaps unmatched in postwar American foreign policy.

Apart from the unusual magnitude of these postwar changes in policy, several other factors establish the inherent importance of Sino-American relations: China's geographic and demographic size; its nuclear arsenal; the frequency of Sino-American confrontations; and China's large, but technically backward economy. In addition to these obvious reasons for studying American policy toward China, two other less obvious reasons also exist.

First, many of the problems the United States has encountered in its relations with the Third World initially emerged with regard to China. How was the United States to respond to revolutionary nationalism? What was America to do about new regimes not committed to maintaining the international status quo? What was to be done about nuclear proliferation? How was Washington to respond to a state that denied the utility of fundamental strategic doctrines, which argued that nuclear weapons are "paper tigers"? All these questions were central to American foreign policy in general, and they first appeared in the specific context of U.S.-China relations. Moreover, it was often relations with China that revealed to architects of American foreign policy the flaws in their conceptual foundations.

Second, U.S.-China relations are important in a symbolic sense. Many myths have sprung up in the United States about the nature of U.S.-China relations or about China more generally. These myths all have a grain of truth and have often in mysterious ways energized or hindered the development of bilateral relations. But more important, these myths, from the myth of the China market to the myth of a State Department conspiracy to deliver China to the communists to the myth that contemporary Chinese reforms will make China similar to the United States (among others), are deeply revealing of the American psyche and the American view of international affairs.

This essay will concentrate on the inherent importance of postwar Sino-American relations, especially on U.S.-China relations as representative of a broad class of problems facing American policymakers. Less attention will be given to myths concerning China as a useful way of understanding American ideas about the way the world works.

Since the Second World War, American policies toward China have been overwhelmingly the result of two kinds of processes: (1) the pursuit of American geostrategic interests and (2) U.S. domestic politics. Indeed, with the exception of American-Israeli relations, no other American bilateral relationship has been as colored by domestic politics. The interplay of four groups was largely responsible for the formulation of American China policy: the foreign affairs bureaucracy, especially the Foreign Service; the leaders of the executive branch of government (the president, the secretaries of state and defense, the national security adviser, and the director of central intelligence); the leaders of the Congress; and the public, or more broadly, public opinion.

This overview will focus on the interplay of these processes and the interactions of these four groups. The discussion will be divided into the following periods: (1) what to do about China, from 1945 to June 1950; (2) the Korean War, June 1950–July 1953; (3) pressuring China, 1953–1961; (4) continued isolation, slightly improved atmospherics, 1961–1969; (5) rapprochement and normalization, 1969–1981; and (6) toward realistic relations, 1981–1987.

What to Do about China? 1945–June 1950

By January 1947, U.S. policymakers knew they had a severe problem on their hands with respect to American policies toward China. George Marshall, President Truman's personal representative to China, had been attempting to mediate between the two rival Chinese factions for national power, the Kuomintang (KMT) or Chinese Nationalist party led by Chiang Kai-shek, and the Chinese Communist party (CCP) headed by Mao Zedong. Marshall left China in frustration. The fact that the United States was providing the KMT with significant amounts of logistical assistance and economic and military aid during Marshall's year in China all but foredoomed to failure the central task of the Marshall mission: the formation of a coalition government. But even without U.S. intervention on behalf of the KMT, the antagonisms between the KMT and the CCP were so deeply rooted that real compromise by either side was extremely unlikely. Marshall could not contain the drift toward civil war, and with his departure no pretense was made that anything other than all out victory was the goal of each side.

American policymakers knew that the KMT was extremely corrupt and incompetent. While Chiang's forces were numerically and technologically superior to the CCP's, few knowledgeable Americans were confident that the generalissimo would win. Indeed, after a series of minor victories in early 1947, the KMT lost the initiative in late 1947. By late 1948, they had lost Manchuria, and by October 1949 they had been all but run off mainland China and were preparing to make a last stand on Taiwan.

What was the United States to do about the fall of its wartime ally and the establishment of the communist-controlled People's Republic of China (PRC)? Different segments of American political society had different answers to this question, but the overall trend in policy evolution from early 1947 to 25 June 1950 was one that seemed to have reasonable amounts of support. To be sure, there were very vocal critics of the Truman administration's China policy, but their influence was not strongly felt until the start of the Korean War.

For the administration, China simply did not matter very much, and even if it had, there were almost no resources available to carry out policies in relation to China. The focus of attention was on Europe, where containment of the Soviet Union and economic recovery were America's twin goals. China ranked thirteenth on the list of Defense Department priorities. With rapid demobilization and fears of economic recession affecting President Truman's calculations, there was simply no reason and no way for the United States to do much, even had it wanted to.

Yet the policy of the administration was not to do nothing. In fact, three parallel lines of action emerged over the course of this period. The first was to end U.S. support for the KMT. While the Congress prevented the administration from terminating aid to the KMT, President Truman and Secretaries of State Marshall and Acheson clearly intended that such aid be ended. Even after the Korean War broke out, Truman argued that aid should not go to the KMT because it all ended up in U.S. real estate anyway.

The second track of U.S. diplomacy toward China was to encourage the emergence of nationalism within the CCP. After the Stalin-Tito split in 1948, American policymakers were quick to observe that many of the conditions in China paralleled the situation in Yugoslavia. Thus it was thought that a communist China need not necessarily be a Soviet puppet. Accordingly the administration, in its public statements and by planting stories with friendly journalists (among other things), emphasized the Soviet threat to Chinese sovereignty, and held out the prospect of reasonable relations with the United States if China would maintain its independence. In other words, the United States wanted to drive a wedge between China and Russia and held out the hope that the United States and the PRC could work together.

The third element of U.S. policy was to prepare the way for eventual diplomatic recognition of the new PRC government. In Acheson's pregnant phrase, the United States had to "wait for the dust to settle" before U.S. policy was definitively announced, but from all appearances, diplomatic recognition was a foregone conclusion after the communist forces invaded Taiwan (preparations for which were well underway by mid-1950) and probably after the 1950 midterm elections. Indeed, the defeat of the KMT on Taiwan would remove any good reason not to recognize the PRC.

The administration had devised a reasonable strategy for responding to the China question. This strategy did not hold out the prospect for an immediate breakthrough in U.S.-China relations, but doors would have been kept open, as trade and other forms of contact continued. The Truman-Acheson policy served the limited nature of U.S. interests in China and reflected the lack of resources available to implement any other policy in China.

Top executive officials were strongly supported by the professional foreign affairs bureaucracy, particularly the "China hands" in the Foreign Service. With long experience dealing with the problems of the KMT, they were the first to realize that the KMT was doomed to lose control of China. They realistically called for an end to American support for the KMT, for early contact with the CCP, and for rapid recognition for the PRC. They were also outspoken in their view that China under the CCP would not be a satellite of the Soviet Union.

The "China hands" were perhaps the most extraordinarily talented group ever to work in the State Department. Objective to a fault, their honest reporting of events in China during World War II and their recommendation that the United States not equate its interests in China with Chiang Kai-shek earned them a number of significant enemies, most notably the erratic U.S. Ambassador to China in 1944–1945, Patrick Hurley. At the time of his resignation, Hurley accused the China hands of disloyalty and procommunist sympathies. In addition, John Service, the American who had had the most contact with Mao Zedong, was arrested and charged with espionage for having passed on classified documents. A grand jury unanimously voted not to recommend Service's prosecution, but the Hurley accusations and Service's arrest became weapons repeatedly hurled against the China hands to impugn their loyalty. Even before the Korean War broke out, the hostility of the China bloc in the Congress to the China hands had made their positions within the State Department very difficult.

The Congress was divided on the issue of what to do about China. To be sure, there was a very active and outspoken China bloc, but despite their lobbying for the KMT, they did not command much attention from non–China bloc legislators. Some of the administration's critics in the Congress were longtime supporters of Chiang Kai-shek; others were hard-core anticommunists. Not a few saw the China issue as one to exploit for partisan advantage. Republicans joined Democrats in supporting American foreign policy in Europe, but the administration's failure to consult Congress on Asian policy and the fact that many Republicans were Asia-firsters (meaning they were more interested in developments in Asia than in Europe) meant that China policy was explicitly exempt from bipartisanship agreement. Yet even though the China bloc was virulent in its criticisms of the administration, a majority of the Congress was prepared to support the administration on its China policy. Until the Korean War, Congress might have been obstructionist, but it had little leverage to employ against the Truman-Acheson position.

Public opinion was also generally supportive of the State Department's views. Overall, businessmen, missionaries, journalists, and other elements of the concerned public were interested in maintaining a *modus vivendi* with the new regime in Peking. Again, there was a vocal minority opposed to contacts with the PRC at all costs, but public attitudes ranged from widespread indifference and ignorance to agreement with the administration's policies.

Thus on the eve of the Korean War, the United States was continuing its policy of disengaging from the KMT, encouraging the expression of Chinese nationalism vis-à-vis the Soviet Union, and preparing the groundwork for diplomatic recognition of the PRC. These policies served the limited U.S. geopolitical interests in China, which were to try to sow hostility between China and the Soviet Union and to establish contact with the PRC so that the United States could capitalize on Sino-Soviet tension. The view of Truman and Acheson had strong support within the State Department bureaucracy; they had general but not strongly felt approval from the public; and they had perhaps somewhat more grudging backing from the Congress. There was opposition to the administration's views, but that opposition had not seized control of the agenda, and it was having a hard time gaining additional support. Domestic politics was an intrusive force in China policy making, but it was not yet an impossible constraint on the president's freedom of action in regard to China policy questions.

One final point should be made in relation to this historical period. It has been argued by a number of scholars and journalists that if the United States had granted diplomatic recognition to the PRC in late 1949 or early 1950, two decades of Sino-American hostility would have been avoided. This view is flawed for at least two reasons. First, it ignores Chinese nationalism. Many Chinese were extremely angry with the United States, and this feeling would not have been dissipated by diplomatic recognition. Second, and more important, for this "lost chance" argument to hold true, one would have to believe that the Korean War would not have broken out and that the United States would not have fought the war the way it did (and without Douglas MacArthur commanding). But the best evidence suggests that the Chinese were not informed of the North Korean plans to invade the south; U.S. recognition of China would have had no effect on the outbreak of fighting. Truman's order to the Seventh Fleet to prevent attacks in either direction across the Taiwan Straits appears to have been almost a knee-jerk response. His use of the Munich analogy to guide his actions would not have been altered by formal relations with China.

Moreover, Truman and Acheson did not consult with the Soviet ambassador about the North Korean attack; it is unlikely they would have consulted with a Chinese official if one had been in Washington. The interposition of the Seventh

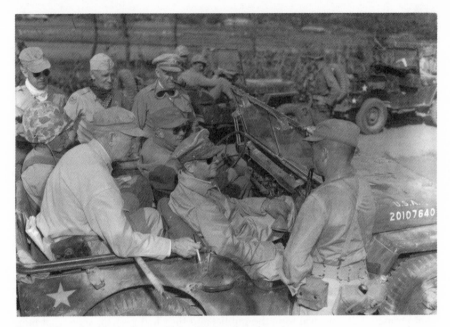

General Douglas MacArthur in Korea (National Archives)

Fleet, the event that guaranteed very hostile Chinese views of the United States, would not have been prevented by U.S.-China diplomatic relations. Finally, with MacArthur in command it is doubtful that the march to the Yalu could have been prevented. Zhou Enlai might have had the chance to try to warn the United States off directly, rather than through the auspices of the Indian ambassador, but at least one China hand in the State Department expressed the seriousness of Zhou's comments to higher levels. But State simply had no control over Mac-Arthur (indeed no one did). Thus, it is hard to believe that the Chinese would not have intervened, which of course guaranteed a Chinese-American war and very hostile attitudes toward the PRC in the United States. In short, U.S. recognition of the PRC would not have prevented the extreme Sino-American hostility caused by the Korean War.

The Korean War, 1950–1953

It is hard to overestimate the effect the Korean War had on Sino-American relations. All flexibility on both sides was lost after the Chinese intervened in large numbers in late November 1950. On the Chinese side, the positioning of the Seventh Fleet between the mainland and Taiwan meant that the United States was once again supporting the CCP's mortal enemy, the KMT. The Chinese civil war remained unresolved, and as the leaders of the new communist government saw it, the true attitudes of the United States were revealed by this act. To Chinese leaders, it could only appear that the United States was unreconciled to revolutionary China. The creation of the Taiwan issue by Truman's order to the Seventh Fleet on 27 June 1950 fully confirmed all hostile ideological views of the United States within China. Indeed, the Taiwan issue continues to color Sino-American relations to this day.

On the American side, the Korean War rearranged the power and ranking of the four principal groups involved in making China policy. The China hands were purged from the State Department. The public, reacting to the shedding of the blood of American soldiers by Chinese troops, not surprisingly took a very negative view of the PRC. The China bloc in Congress told the executive branch "I told you so," and would not allow the executive branch any freedom of action on China questions for two decades. Finally, Truman and Acheson lost all initiative on China questions (not that they were not equally outraged by the Chinese intervention). They had no alternative to pursuing a militantly anti-PRC policy. Domestic politics had become more important than the pursuit of geostrategic influence, and from 1950 to 1969, China policy was captured by domestic political calculations.

Other than the loss of lives caused by the Korean War, the most tragic outcome of that conflict was the purge of the China hands from the State Department. They were hounded from their jobs by countless investigations within the State Department, the executive branch, and on Capitol Hill. All personnel with sources of independent expertise on China were removed from any Asia assignments. The lesson to all members of the foreign affairs bureaucracy was clear: Tell your bosses what they want to hear, do not stick your neck out. One organizational result of the purge of the China hands and the very hard line taken with regard to the PRC was that "mainland China affairs" were placed under the control of the Republic of China [Taiwan] desk within the State Department. This meant that U.S. interests regarding the then five hundred million people on the Chinese mainland were managed by people whose primary task was to pursue U.S. interests vis-à-vis the seven million people on Taiwan led by the KMT. Needless to say, U.S. interests in these two areas were not compatible. Only in 1962 would a separate desk for the mainland be created in the State Department.

The fall of the China hands is inextricably linked with the rise of the junior Senator from Wisconsin, Joseph McCarthy. The McCarthyite campaign of slander and vilification began prior to the Korean War, but only after the fighting began did he mobilize a mass following. Other legislators joined McCarthy in his hunts for supposed communists in the State Department and in the executive branch generally.

By the actions of these predators, a myth emerged that Chiang Kai-shek and the KMT had not lost the civil war, but rather that the United States, manipulated by communists in the government, had denied Chiang the victory he could have won. Anyone who questioned this interpretation became a likely subject for investigation by various congressional committees. This myth grew out of the frustration of many Americans who could not understand why the world's most powerful country in 1945 was incapable of making things go right. It seemed much easier to believe in some hideous conspiracy than to face the fact that there were even then severe limits to American power.

McCarthy and those who pursued a similar agenda effectively prevented alternative points of view from being heard and alternative courses of actions from being pursued. The domestic political consequences of being "soft on communism" in general and on communism in China in particular were not lost on candidates for office. The emotive and symbolic power of this issue would long outlive the influence of McCarthy. Congress would remain hostile to China until the Nixon visit of 1972.

As a result of the Korean War, Congress came to hold a veto power over the administration on China policy questions. The nearly unanimous congressional view meant that any president or secretary of state who tried to change China policy would face severe retribution. The costs of any such congressional action were greater than leaders of the executive branch were willing to bear. Consequently, Congress became, arguably, the dominant institution shaping U.S. policies toward China.

If the Congress had gained power on China questions as a result of the war, the president and the secretary of state had lost it; indeed, the Korean War would ultimately cost these particular men their offices. The stalemate in the fighting after April 1951 angered the populace, which saw American lives being lost without any progress being made toward ending the war. Chinese human-wave attacks raised the specter of a war of attrition that would bleed the United States white.

Yet despite their domestic unpopularity and the pressure they were under from the political opposition, Truman and Acheson did what they could to achieve long-term U.S. interests in China. They continued to emphasize the threat the Soviet Union posed to Chinese sovereignty, hoping to keep the wedge strategy going. (Given that China was actively engaged in a war with the United States at the time, this U.S. message was unlikely to be heeded in China.) State Department officials even met with Chinese emissaries in Hong Kong in 1951 in an effort to find an end to the war. These meetings led to nothing, but they do suggest that Truman and Acheson saw some utility in keeping channels of direct communication with the PRC open. However, circumstances and congressional pressures led to the naming of a new ambassador to the Republic of China on Taiwan and to new military and economic aid programs for the KMT.

Little needs to be said about public opinion. Those elements of the public that had previously supported U.S. recognition of the PRC quickly changed their minds when China embargoed American trade, expropriated foreign-owned enterprises, froze foreign assets, and seized mission property. The onset of direct Chinese-American hostilities unified the public's views. China under the communists was perceived by the American populace as the enemy of the United States. But a great emotional tinge was imparted to this view: China was not just the enemy, China itself was somehow inhuman. Years of supposed American beneficence in China (highlighted by America not setting up its own concession areas, the Open Door notes, U.S. economic assistance, and so forth) was now being returned by hostile actions. China was seen as deeply ungrateful. Moreover, the human-wave attacks of the Chinese troops reinforced the old stereo-typed view that Asians do not hold human life sacred. The United States was seen as facing a profoundly alien threat from communism in China. Finally, the Chinese intervention convinced everyone that the Chinese communist leaders were indeed Stalin's henchmen.

The Korean War made it impossible for one of the four key actors—the professional foreign affairs bureaucracy—to play any independent role for more than a decade. It hardened the attitudes of the public and Congress and made creative approaches to China questions impossible. Presidential prerogatives in foreign policy, at least in respect to China, were severely circumscribed. The disasters of the Korean War for both the United States and the PRC might have been avoided had MacArthur been stopped at the thirty-eighth parallel. But even if MacArthur had been halted, the PRC was deeply aggrieved by U.S. actions in the Taiwan Straits. Hostility would still have been the result.

Pressuring China, 1953–1961

The Eisenhower administration came to office determined to end the Korean War and carry out a strong foreign policy (in contrast to the vacillation of the Democrats, or so the Republican campaign trumpeted in the 1952 election). But Eisenhower was also a fiscal conservative who wanted balanced budgets and limited defense spending. While the American public (and the leaders of the new administration) were hostile to China, Eisenhower's priorities did not imply the need or the likelihood of new confrontations with the PRC. Yet this admin-istration was marked by more confrontations with China than any other admin-istration in the 1945–1987 period, and the question of the use of nuclear weapons alone was broached at least four times between 1953 and 1958 in relation to American policy toward China. Arguably, China was a bigger foreign policy problem for the United States during this period than was the Soviet Union, which was largely focused inward after Stalin's death.

The United States and China were involved in wars, battles, and/or confronta-tions in Korea in 1953, Indochina in 1954, on the offshore islands (of China) in 1954–55, and on Quemoy in 1958. Conversely, however, the PRC and the United States also began to reestablish diplomatic contacts in multilateral and bilateral contexts. Unfortunately, it was usually only after the onset of one of the crises mentioned above that Sino-American contacts were resumed.

At the end of the Korean War, Chinese leaders were most concerned with domestic development, but in a policy area that spanned both domestic and international politics, the PRC was still vitally interested in terminating the Chinese civil war by extending its control over Taiwan. With the United States supporting Taiwan, the key intermediary step in regaining Taiwan was to sever the links between the Republic of China and the United States. The Chinese attempted to do this by launching a series of attacks on islands off the coast of China that were under KMT control. These islands had no strategic significance, but the KMT used them to harass coastal shipping and to launch commando raids on the mainland. The PRC appeared to be saying to the United States that

American support for the KMT would draw the United States into stupid and pointless confrontations on small pieces of land that were essentially valueless. Nonetheless, the United States did support KMT forces on most of the offshore islands, cementing rather than weakening U.S.-ROC ties, and the Chinese use of force further reinforced the American image of China as aggressive. But the Chinese were able to force the United States to agree to formal bilateral discussions, which largely focused on the Taiwan issue. This was a small gain for the Chinese.

The views of the administration were more complex and sophisticated than the rhetoric of Secretary of State John Foster Dulles would have people believe. Eisenhower and Dulles faced the same constraints of public opinion and a Congress hostile to any dealings with the PRC as had the Truman administration. In addition, Dulles made it clear that he had no use for foreign service officers who did not loyally support U.S. government positions. Professional bureaucrats would have no role in provoking reconsiderations of administration policy.

In public, the administration took the view that it would have nothing to do with the PRC. In perhaps its most extreme statement, Dulles averred that "communism . . . is a passing and not a perpetual phase. We owe it to ourselves . . . to do all that we can to contribute to that passing." The rhetoric was of restoring the KMT to the mainland, of employing massive retaliation for any acts of Chinese aggression, and of denying the PRC any but outlaw status in the international system.

But under the surface there were signs of some greater appreciation of China issues, and of the potential for somewhat greater flexibility in dealing with China. This is seen perhaps most clearly in the continuation of the wedge strategy by Eisenhower and Dulles. But rather than posing the issue in carrot-and-stick terms, as Truman and Acheson had, the new administration would drive a wedge between the Russians and the Chinese by applying heavy pressure against the Chinese (refusing to trade and talk to the PRC and resisting what was perceived to be Chinese expansionism with military force, including the use of nuclear weapons if need be). The underlying rationale was that such pressure would force the Chinese to make greater demands on their Russian allies, until at some point the Soviet leadership would either say enough is enough and terminate the alliance or the Chinese would be so dissatisfied by niggardly Soviet responses to their requests that they would terminate their alliance with the Soviets.

Thus, while nuclear threats were intended to serve a number of goals, including to force China to end the fighting in the Korean War, to terminate its aid to the Vietminh in Indochina, and to end its activities in the Taiwan Straits, one of the most important goals was to raise the cost of the Sino-Soviet alliance to each of the members of that alliance. And in fact, U.S. pressure on China during the 1954–1955 and 1958 offshore islands crises significantly contributed to the Sino-Soviet split, even though differing ideological visions were its primary cause.

The logical consequences of a hard wedge strategy were not thought through. If the strategy was successful, what was the United States prepared to do? Off the record, Eisenhower felt that trade with China was a possibility, but no real

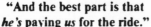

"And the best part is that *he's* paying *us* for the ride."

While an important "China Lobby" supported Chiang Kai-shek, a less influential minority insisted that the U.S. was being exploited. (Copyright 1958 Bill Mauldin)

contingency planning was done on what to do about China if the wedge strategy worked. Moreover, policymakers in Washington failed to calculate how the Chinese might view a United States that continually pressured them. Certainly, China would hardly be reconciled to American power. Finally, the hard wedge strategy also failed in relation to the logic of the balance of power. As implemented, the strategy reinforced Chinese hostility, but it contributed to the Sino-Soviet split. The wedge strategy did nothing about the Soviet Union, which remained the principal U.S. adversary. A balance-of-power strategy would have argued that after fracturing the Sino-Soviet alliance, the United States should try to entice the Chinese to embrace a more pro-American position in order to further strengthen its anti-Soviet position. Presumably, American domestic politics made the pursuit of the balance-of-power logic impossible. One other negative consequence of the hard wedge strategy and of Dulles's unwillingness to have anything to do with the PRC should be mentioned. CCP leaders quickly realized that the only way they could compel the United States to pay China any heed at all was to use force. Face-to-face diplomatic interactions came about only after warfare or a crisis. In a perverse way, the hard wedge strategy encouraged the Chinese to use military power; it did not deter them from using it.

After the Quemoy crisis of 1958 and Dulles's resignation, modest signs of flexibility began to appear in U.S. policy. Two years after the Chinese first suggested it, the State Department finally authorized the issuance of visas to U.S. journalists to visit and report on conditions in China. The new secretary of state, Christian Herter, employed less virulent rhetoric than Dulles's when discussing China questions, but there was no real change in policy. By late 1958, however, all signs of flexibility on the part of the Chinese, quite apparent in 1956–57, had disappeared. The failure of the United States to respond to the earlier Chinese overtures to increase contacts, such as people-to-people exchanges and perhaps to negotiate a cease-fire in the Taiwan Strait, growing Sino-Soviet tensions, and the advent of the Great Leap Forward symbolizing the ascendancy of radicalism in China, all meant that China was not interested in improved atmospherics with the United States.

Given the constraints it operated under, the Eisenhower administration's China policy was reasonably effective. The hard wedge strategy did contribute to the Sino-Soviet split. But the administration was unable to pursue the fracturing of Sino-Soviet relations to full advantage because of fear of how Congress and the public might react to attempts to recruit China into an anti-Soviet coalition. Thus, the pursuit of U.S. global strategic advantage was hampered by the operation of domestic politics. If the Eisenhower-Dulles policy was more supple than is usually supposed, it was still unable to move the United States and China beyond mutual hostility and suspicion.

Continued Isolation, Slightly Improved Atmospherics, 1961–1969

The Kennedy administration came to office prepared to reconsider all aspects of American foreign policy, blaming the Republicans for a perceived weakness in the U.S. position in the world. While China was not central to this review of policy, Kennedy was prepared to acknowledge that the CCP was likely to remain in power in China and that some acceptance of this fact should be a part of Sino-American relations. But even the modest initiatives of the Kennedy administration met with no success, and the Johnson administration was even less committed to improving relations with China than Kennedy had been. Yet, while the Kennedy administration was frustrated by Congress and public opinion, subtle processes of change were underway during this period that slowly eroded the constraints that Congress, the public, and the bureaucracy posed against new China initiatives.

According to his biographers, Kennedy was prepared to adopt a "two Chinas" policy formally in his second term. This meant that the United States would recognize the existence of both the PRC and the ROC (a position that both Chinese states regarded as totally unacceptable). In an effort to move in this direction, the administration floated a trial balloon, suggesting that the United States establish diplomatic ties with Outer Mongolia. The ensuing howls of outrage from Congress and the China lobby quickly forced Kennedy to back off, but his intentions were revealed by this action.

Other Kennedy initiatives fared hardly any better. He offered the Chinese emergency food aid to relieve the famine caused by the Great Leap Forward. The Chinese rejected this, knowing full well that to accept the aid would be to admit that the CCP had grossly mismanaged the Chinese economy. More successfully perhaps, Kennedy made it clear to the KMT that the United States would not support a KMT invasion of the mainland in 1962. Chiang Kai-shek had concluded that in the wake of Great Leap famine, the time to return to the mainland had arrived. This, too, suggested that Kennedy saw CCP rule as a permanent feature on the mainland. There were moves toward easing travel restrictions as well.

Perhaps the most lasting legacy of the Kennedy administration was not in particular policies pursued, but in changing official attitudes. De facto recognition of the CCP as the ruling government of the Chinese mainland was implicit in Kennedy administration actions. Moreover, about the time of Kennedy's assassination, top Asian policymakers began to put forward the "second generation" argument. This view held that the older generation of Chinese revolutionaries headed by Mao were so ideologically hostile to the United States that progress in U.S.-China relations would be impossible until this group passed from the scene. But the second, more technocratic generation of leaders would be more receptive to U.S.-China ties. In short, the administration was pointing to a future when the United States and China might have reasonable relations.

Lyndon Johnson was less interested than Kennedy in China questions, and his administration saw a retreat from the very modest steps forward taken by the Kennedy administration. In particular, Johnson and his aides often justified U.S. intervention in Vietnam as an effort to contain Chinese expansionism. The building of an antiballistic missile system was needed to counter the emerging Chinese nuclear threat, the Johnson administration argued. When it became clear that China would detonate a nuclear device in 1964, the Defense Department gave serious thought to launching a preemptive strike (either nuclear or conventional) against Chinese nuclear facilities. In the period of detente with the Soviet Union that emerged after the Cuban missile crisis, the Kennedy and Johnson administrations and the general public came to see China as a bigger threat to world peace (and to American interests) than the Soviet Union.

Not all of the Johnson administration's actions toward China were negative, however. Through either tacit bargaining or an explicit, though still secret agreement, the United States and China were able to avoid a serious confrontation over Vietnam. Questions of issuing travel visas for several American doctors to visit China worked their way through the bureaucracy. In 1968, Johnson invited Chinese correspondents to come to the United States to cover the 1968 elections and the Republican and Democratic National Conventions. But all in all, the Johnson administration did not go beyond the limited steps taken by the Kennedy administration, and in many ways, Johnson retreated from a number of Kennedy's initiatives.

In contrast, real change was taking place within the three other groups involved in China policy. Some of this change was barely visible, but the consequences of alterations in the composition of interests of these groups would have a powerful cumulative effect.

In the foreign affairs bureaucracy, personnel and structural changes were underway that would increase the capability of the bureaucracy to think creatively about China questions. In 1962 a separate mainland China affairs desk was created, liberating thinking about China from the control of the ROC desk. New specialists began to be trained and placed in positions relating to China. People with strong academic backgrounds in Chinese studies, such as Allen Whiting and James C. Thompson, worked in the bureaucracies, helping to promote the airing of independent and original views about China. The net effect of these developments during the Kennedy-Johnson years was perhaps not great, but the State Department and other foreign affairs bureaucracies emerged less deficient in knowledge about China.

Public attitudes toward China continued to be hostile; China was seen as the greatest threat to world peace in the 1960s. But this overall view did not translate into the view that the United States and China should not talk to each other. Indeed, after the Chinese detonated their first nuclear weapon in October 1964, a majority of the populace favored direct U.S.-China contacts. In particular segments of the population, fresh attitudes toward China began to emerge. The influential Council on Foreign Relations sponsored a series of works on China and on Sino-American relations in the mid-1960s, designed, at least in part, to stimulate new thinking on China. Concurrently, new academic specialists concentrating on the PRC began to receive their Ph.D.s. Many would go on to serve as consultants for government agencies. Finally, as the Vietnam War grew increasingly unpopular, general skepticism about all U.S. government policies and views about Asia emerged. This did not translate into a necessarily favorable attitude toward the PRC, but it did mean that the old refrains about CCP expansionism and hostility were met with increasing doubt.

Congressional attitudes also began to change as a result of the Vietnam War. This is evidenced most clearly in a series of hearings convened by the Senate Foreign Relations Committee in 1966 and 1967. During the hearings, China specialist A. Doak Barnett urged the United States to end its policy of trying to isolate China, and to shift to a strategy of containing China in a way that held the door open to improved U.S.-China relations in the future. Many members of the Foreign Relations Committee strongly agreed with Professor Barnett. Growing dissatisfaction with the war in Vietnam led increasing numbers of legislators to advocate a new U.S. policy for Asia, one that included a new attitude toward China. Still, by the time Johnson left office, congressional support for the KMT remained strong.

While developments on the U.S. side in the mid-1960s laid the groundwork for better Sino-American relations (even if few recognized that this was so at the time), developments in China seemed to indicate that any progress on the U.S. side was all for naught. Chinese foreign policy rhetoric was extremely radical and anti-American (and anti-Soviet) in the early 1960s. The brief Chinese border war with India in 1962, the testing of an atomic bomb in 1964, and support for Vietnamese and Indonesian communists all seemed to portend a lack of Chinese interest in dealing with the United States on anything other than adversarial terms. An American image of China as a nation ruled by madmen was only reinforced by the onset of the Cultural Revolution in 1966. This period of mass demonstrations, chaos, and near civil war left all foreign observers with the impression that China was not governed by leaders who thought in terms of rational interests. This made it extremely difficult to find any common ground with the PRC.

Thus, the very limited steps the United States made to inaugurate a dialogue with the PRC in the 1960s fell on increasingly deaf ears in China. The actions of the executive branch were still sharply constrained by the Congress, the bureaucracy, and public opinion. But the strength of the opposition to change in each of these groups in relation to U.S.-China policy began to ebb. A major change in Sino-American relations did not seem imminent, but increasing flexibility on some China issues appeared to be in the offing. These changes of attitude within the Congress, the bureaucracy, and the public were important, but how far these changes would allow the next administration to go were unclear. Ultimately, Richard Nixon would show that the constraints imposed by the bureaucracy, the Congress, and the public could all be at least partially circumvented in ways that no one except the new president could imagine.

Rapprochement and Normalization, 1969–1981

Richard Nixon redefined the terms of the debate about American China policy, and in the process, greatly expanded the president's freedom of action in the making of China policy. His secretive foreign policy effectively prevented the bureaucracy and Congress from interfering with his grand initiative, and the images of the president in China electrified public opinion. In a sense, Nixon's trip represented the triumph of geopolitical interest over domestic politics (like the crafty politician he was, Nixon parlayed geopolitical interests to his domestic political advantage). Nixon, Gerald Ford, and Jimmy Carter were still subject to the exigencies of domestic politics, but by the time formal diplomatic relations between the United States and the People's Republic were established on 1 January 1979, the role of American domestic politics in the shaping of China policy had greatly diminished, and geopolitical concerns largely shaped the development of U.S.-China ties in the late 1970s.

Of course, the China breakthrough could not have occurred without considerably increased Chinese interest in positive ties with the United States. Geopolitics, economic concerns, and Chinese domestic politics all contributed to Chinese desires for a rapprochement with the United States.

Chinese strategic concerns in the late 1960s and early 1970s are well known. In August 1968, the Soviet Union invaded Czechoslovakia in order, in Russian words, to save socialism. The Brezhnev Doctrine, which postulated that the Soviet Union had the right to intervene to restore socialism in countries where socialism was in danger, was announced shortly thereafter. Given the chaos of the Cultural Revolution in China, a plausible case could be made that China was the next target for the application of this doctrine. Soviet propaganda certainly raised this possibility. In March 1969, a series of border clashes were fought in northeast China. China appears to have initiated the first of these battles in an apparent effort to deter a much larger conflict. More battles were fought along the northwest border in the summer of 1969. The Soviet leadership gave serious thought to launching a major attack (either nuclear or conventional) through

1969–70. Here was a pressing threat to Chinese national security that the Chinese might not have been able to cope with by themselves. United States support for China would make the Soviets more hesitant in considering an attack on the PRC.

Second, as the most chaotic period of the Cultural Revolution drew to a close, there was a growing recognition by the Chinese leadership that China's national security could never be ensured without a modernized economy. Since China's colleges and universities were still closed, external sources of technology and equipment were seen by some as an important way to speed up China's modernization. The flow of technology would be accelerated if there were detente in Sino-American relations.

Finally, throughout 1969–71 a power struggle was occurring in the highest reaches of the Chinese government between Mao's designated successor, Lin Biao (the minister of national defense), and Zhou Enlai (and later Mao Zedong himself). One of the issues in this struggle was the definition of the international situation. Lin argued that the Soviet Union and the United States were equally hostile to China, while Zhou argued that the Soviets were the greater threat, and that approaches to the United States could be made that likely would enhance China's ability to deter a Soviet attack. Moreover, U.S. support would make the military, headed by Lin, a less important factor in the Chinese political system. Zhou persuaded Mao of his view by October 1970, and ultimately Lin Biao died trying to flee the country in September 1971. Thus, an opening to the United States had domestic Chinese political implications as well.

From Richard Nixon's perspective, an opening to China was part of a complex strategy for achieving peace and guaranteeing his reelection in 1972. He saw China as a card to play against both the North Vietnamese and the Soviets. He hoped to extract concessions from the Vietnamese at the Paris peace talks and from the Soviets on strategic arms limitation. He correctly saw peace with Vietnam, an arms treaty with the Soviets, and a trip to China as invaluable in seeking reelection.

Nixon persuaded his national security adviser, Henry Kissinger, of the desirability and utility of an opening to China, and together they managed the U.S. side of the rapprochement. To improve the general atmosphere, Nixon announced a series of unilateral measures that conveyed to the Chinese a willingness to consider new options for U.S.-China relations. Thus, shifting from a "two-and-a-half war" to a "one-and-a-half war" military capability indicated that the United States would be reluctant to intervene in Asia. In November 1969, the president terminated patrols by the Seventh Fleet in the Taiwan Straits. Travel and trade restrictions were eased.

Through the leaders of France, Pakistan, and Rumania, Nixon and Kissinger covertly informed the Chinese that they were interested in talks at the highest levels. In July 1971, Kissinger secretly went to China, and Nixon announced that he would go there in the early part of 1972. As a result, China was finally admitted to the United Nations, and a wave of China fever hit the United States. Trade expanded from nothing to several hundred million dollars over the next three years.

**"I'm not sure of the rules,
but it looks like an interesting game."**

(Copyright 1971, *The
Courier-Journal* and
Louisville Times Co.
Reprinted by permission of
Hugh Haynie.)

The Nixon visit and the Shanghai communiqué issued at the end of it affirmed that the United States and China had both complementary and competing interests. The chief common interest was preventing further Soviet advances in Asia. Their principal difference was on the question of Taiwan, which was left unresolved.

Relations advanced smoothly until late 1973, when domestic politics stymied further progress on both sides. Liaison offices were established in both capitals, which were embassies in all but name. But as the Watergate scandal eroded the president's power and threatened his position, Nixon was forced to back away from formal recognition of China (which he apparently had promised would occur during his second term). He feared that he would lose the support of conservative senators, which might be vital to prevent his conviction on impeachable offenses, if he moved forward with normalization. In China, Zhou Enlai's cancer was diagnosed in 1972, and Mao was suffering from Parkinson's disease. The struggle for succession began in earnest in 1973, and the moderate faction led by Deng Xiaoping could not afford to compromise with the United States on the Taiwan issue for fear that it would lose support.

It was not until 1977 that both sides were in a position to resume serious discussions on the normalization of relations. President Gerald Ford did go to China in December 1975, but he found Deng had no room to maneuver. In addition, the more moderate Ford faced a challenge in the upcoming Republican primaries from the right in the form of Ronald Reagan. Ford needed to hold on to his own conservative supporters, and recognizing China (and derecognizing the ROC) was not the way to do it. Jimmy Carter came to office in 1977 without having to worry very much about right-wing concerns. Similarly, the arrest of the radical faction after Mao's death in September 1976 gave Chinese leaders more freedom of maneuver.

To the Carter administration, China was not originally a high priority. But Soviet activities in Angola, Ethiopia, and Afghanistan all suggested to U.S. policymakers that the Soviet Union had embarked on an aggressively expansionist foreign policy. After the fall of Vietnam in 1975, the public was not inclined to support a major U.S. defense buildup or an interventionist U.S. foreign policy. China was seen, particularly by National Security Adviser Zbigniew Brzezinski, as a valuable geopolitical card that could be played against the Soviets. Brzezinski was able to persuade Carter of the wisdom of normalized relations with China, which were finally announced on 15 December 1978. The United States recognized the PRC, announced its intention to terminate the mutual defense treaty with Taiwan, and agreed to close down all U.S. military bases on Taiwan. The United States did insist that it had the right to continue to sell arms to the ROC on Taiwan, however. The agreement on normalization was followed by a visit of China's paramount leader, Deng Xiaoping, to the United States in January and February 1979.

Further impetus to better U.S.-China relations was imparted by the Soviet invasion of Afghanistan in December 1979. In very short order, a quasi-alliance developed between the United States and China. The export of nonlethal

Nixon's celebrated visit to China (February 1972). From left: Chou En-lai, an interpreter, Mao Zedong, and President Nixon. (AP/Wide World Photos)

military equipment began, as did planning work on the sale of weapons to China. The United States established a secret monitoring station in China's Xinjiang Autonomous Region to replace some of the facilities lost as a result of the Iranian revolution. Military, intelligence, trade, and other forms of cooperation developed very rapidly after the normalization of relations.

Yet the basis of relations was not really consolidated. Each side seemed to be trying to "free-ride," or to impose more of the burdens of Soviet containment on the other. What exactly were U.S. interests in China? (And Chinese interests in the United States?) Basic questions about what the emerging military security relationship was supposed to achieve were not addressed. The failure to consider the full implications of a United States almost desperate to prove its toughness toward the Soviet Union allied with a militarily and technologically backward China meant that the relationship could deteriorate if an administration less wedded to U.S.-China cooperation in stopping the Soviets came to office. This is precisely what happened.

Before going on to the Reagan administration, the views and activities of the other three domestic American groups must be discussed. Nixon was able to avoid the constraints of public opinion, Congress, and the foreign affairs bureaucracy by not informing them of his actions until he could present them with a *fait accompli*. Public opinion responded very favorably to the opening to China, but throughout the 1970s the public remained opposed to normalization at the expense of U.S. relations with the ROC. Nonetheless, when Carter presented the public with his *fait accompli*, there was no public outpouring of dissatisfaction. The drama of various presidential initiatives and the long-term changing of perception and knowledge about the China issue significantly eased public constraints on China policy.

The bureaucracy also responded quickly to the China opening. While the State Department had been excluded from the decision-making process behind the Nixon trip, it reacted positively to subsequent developments throughout the decade, and real expertise reappeared within State. Perhaps symbolically, the "China hands" were officially rehabilitated and honored in early 1973. Of more significance, however, was growing interest within the Pentagon in a strategic relationship with China. Such thinking was underway by the mid-1970s, and the military seems to have been extremely interested in developing close ties with China. While the full details of such planning remain secret, the U.S. military has become a major bureaucratic force favoring the development of good U.S.-China ties.

Congress remained ambivalent about U.S.-China policies in the 1970s. It generally supported the Nixon visit of 1972, and somewhat more grudgingly supported Carter. But some conservatives, most notably Barry Goldwater, opposed all U.S. initiatives with regard to the PRC. Moreover, the Congress as a whole was angry at the repeated failures of both Nixon and Carter to consult with it on China policy. Prior to normalization, the Congress had repeatedly gone on record as favoring relations with the PRC but not at the expense of the mutual defense treaty and relations with Taiwan. Reacting in part to this failure to consult it (and in fact, to the failure of two administrations to listen to the views of

Congress) and in part to what was seen as the Carter administration's extremely weak draft legislation governing U.S.-Taiwan relations, the Congress wrote a tough Taiwan Relations Act that guides the conduct of U.S.-Taiwan contacts to this day. The act displeased the PRC, but Congress overwhelmingly supported it, giving Carter no choice but to sign it.

A complete transformation in U.S.-China relations occurred between 1969 and 1981. Bold presidential initiatives finally brought about the normalization of U.S.-China relations, and various forms of cooperation developed very quickly. The public and the bureaucracy rallied to suppport these actions, with Congress responding more coolly. Yet U.S.-China ties were not institutionalized, and the election of Ronald Reagan threw the new relationship into question.

Toward Realistic Relations, 1981–1987

The position Ronald Reagan espoused during the 1980 election campaign—that he would grant formal diplomatic status to the representatives of Taiwan in the United States—threatened to lead to a deterioration of U.S.-China ties. Similarly, disputes in the first two years of the new administration about weapons sales to Taiwan in general and an advanced fighter plane in particular continually raised the specter of retrogression in the U.S.-China relationship. Yet, nearing the completion of Reagan's second term, Sino-American relations seem to be firmly rooted in the interests of both sides, and reasonably friendly relations, without excessive expectations, have been consolidated.

The trials and tribulations of the Chinese and Ronald Reagan have had the ironic effect of strengthening ties between the two countries. Reagan's conservatism, his outspoken support for Taiwan, the rhetoric he employed against the Soviets, and the defense buildup—which seemed predicated on the belief that the United States must be prepared to go it alone—all threatened to undermine U.S.-PRC relations, many Chinese leaders felt. Moreover, occupied with modernizing and reforming their country, Chinese leaders increasingly saw a quasi-alliance with the United States aimed at the Soviets as counterproductive. It prevented any improvement in Sino-Soviet ties, and perhaps more important, it forced the Chinese to spend too much to buy weapons of doubtful utility against possible Soviet attacks. The Chinese were now sufficiently confident that their nuclear deterrent would suffice to make any Soviet attack unlikely. The Soviets had also repeatedly tried to improve relations with the Chinese, and it became clear to Chinese leaders that there were good economic reasons for expanded contacts with the Soviets. Finally, the Chinese shrewdly perceived that Reagan would scare the Soviets, forcing them to devote all their attention to Washington. It was therefore appropriate for the PRC largely to drop out of the strategic triangle. Consequently, in 1982, the Chinese began to enunciate what they called their "independent policy of peace." This did not mean Chinese equidistance between the United States and USSR, but it did mean that China approached the United States critically.

On the American side, China policy was not central to Reagan. After severe fights between his advisers, the president backed away from his campaign rhetoric, and he did not in the end upgrade the status of U.S.-Taiwan relations. In 1982, he supported an agreement that promised to phase out U.S. arms sales to Taiwan gradually. He also decided not to sell the advanced fighter to Taiwan. This was undoubtedly more than Chinese leaders had dared hoped for, but all the wrangling over these issues and a number of smaller, more transient incidents led to a certain distancing in contacts in 1982–83. By 1984, however, these problems had been overcome sufficiently to allow Chinese Premier Zhao Ziyang to visit the United States and for Reagan to visit China. It seems clear that the progress of China's economic reforms had something to do with the more favorable view Reagan took of ties with China. In his public addresses in China, he spoke of "so-called communist China."

Military, technical, and trade cooperation have expanded significantly since the early 1980s. The United States now sells munitions to China. A nuclear cooperation agreement was signed by both sides. Trade has grown to about $8 billion per year and the United States is the second largest investor in China. Hundreds of thousands of Americans have traveled to China for various purposes, and thousands of Chinese have come to the United States to study or for other reasons.

Sino-American ties are not without problems. Taiwan, trade issues (the rapid increase of Chinese textile exports to the United States and China's own version of neomercantilism are cause for American concern), technology transfer questions (what technologies the United States should make available to China, and the impact of such technology transfers on U.S. relations with other countries and regions) have caused disagreements for a number of years. Recently, concerns about human rights in China and Tibet, Chinese arms sales to Iran and elsewhere, and other Chinese actions have provoked criticisms in the United States, and as increasing numbers of Chinese students in the United States try to stay here, more rows are likely to develop. But shared geopolitical interests in Afghanistan, Korea, and to a lesser extent in Southeast Asia and South Asia, and the advantages of trade and technology transfer outweigh the problems.

Relations with China are now largely so mundane that public opinion is not very concerned with China issues. Dramatic events in China are reflected in public opinion polls, but the China issue has all but disappeared in electoral politics, and it is hard to imagine that the public really constrains U.S. policies toward China. The public did seem concerned however when Reagan's rhetoric on Taiwan threatened to disrupt U.S.-China relations, and Democrats savored the irony of using the "who lost China" question against the Republicans. Fortunately, the reinjection of partisan calculations into China policy was avoided by the evolution of the administration's views.

The professional foreign affairs bureaucracy was active in promoting the development of better relations, and in resolving some of the problems in Sino-American contacts. The staff at the State Department was well aware of what an upgrading of ties with Taiwan would do to U.S.-PRC relations. The military was also anxious to keep lines of communication and exchange with China open. But probably the most active of the bureaucracies was the Department of Commerce. Under the leadership of Malcolm Baldridge, Commerce energetically pursued the goal of furthering U.S.-China trade. The efforts of the Commerce Department no doubt contributed to increases in trade levels, and Commerce clearly wants to go further in developing trade and technology transactions. All of these bureaucracies played a role in checking a more pro-Taiwan policy by the administration.

Members of Congress manifested mixed feelings about China. They pressured Reagan to avoid a breach of relations with the PRC, and hoped that U.S.-China relations would move forward. But the Congress has also placed obstacles in the path of developing China ties. Conservatives led by Jesse Helms believe that a Sino-Soviet rapprochement is imminent, and that the United States should therefore have only limited contact with the PRC. Helms and others remain strong supporters of the ROC. Liberal members of Congress have also criticized China for putatively passing on the technology to build nuclear weapons to Pakistan. They had also criticized China on human rights grounds. While protectionist pressures in Congress have been aimed at Japan, textile interests have not ignored the PRC, and the rapid increase of Chinese textile imports, China's high rate of economic growth, and the experience of other East Asian economies has led to the argument that China should be constrained now, rather than after domestic producers have been disrupted by China's penetration of the American market.

By the end of 1987, and despite a shaky start, Ronald Reagan and the Chinese had come to an understanding, and U.S.-China relations were reasonably friendly and consolidated on the basis of realistic appreciations of each side's interests in the other. The foreign affairs bureaucracy saw the need for developing ties with China, and it has helped to keep relations on track. China is not an issue that concerns large numbers of the public; except for extreme developments, China policy has been largely depoliticized at the mass level. Congress, which remains more skeptical of relations with China, is the most likely articulator of tensions in the relationship at this time. Even so, Congress is more flexible on China issues now than it has ever been in the last forty years.

Conclusion

Some brief comments about the interactions of the four major American groups in the making of China policy since 1945 are in order here. These conclusions may not be very surprising or very different from conclusions about American foreign-policy interactions with other countries. Arguably, what has been most atypical about U.S.-China relations has been the impact of domestic American politics in limiting the pursuit of U.S. geopolitical interests in China.

The leadership of the executive branch has been the most active element in the making of China policy. Presidents have proven capable of bold initiatives that have succeeded in reshaping the attitudes of the other groups involved in China policy making. Although the executive branch has been the major source of policy changes in China relations, presidential leadership on China issues has never gone unchallenged or uncontested. Congress and the public have at times discouraged the president and his advisers from doing anything new about

China. Throughout the 1950s, in fact, the president lost the ability to initiate new policies, and his influence on China questions increased only marginally in the 1960s. With the dramatic departures of 1971–72 and 1978, the president has been able to tranform public attitudes about the PRC, but Congress remains not fully reconciled to administration dominance in the realm of China policy making.

The Congress has been the most conservative of the major groups involved with U.S.-China policy. In the early 1980s, this conservatism (in the sense of opposition to change) was perhaps useful in discouraging President Reagan from upgrading ties with Taiwan, which was sure to lead to a retrogression in U.S.-PRC relations. But at most other times, congressional conservatism has been a real impediment to a realistic American policy toward China. Fear of alienating or provoking Congress has often affected the timing of developments in U.S.-China policy, and it has often constrained the airing of new policy proposals. This drives the administration to resort to end runs around Congress, which in turn may only further heighten congressional concerns about the administration's handling of China questions, and so on. Finally, Congress's assault on State Department officials during the McCarthy era was one of the most sordid developments in the history of the Congress, and ultimately it deprived the government of the abilities of a uniquely qualified group of China experts. Indeed, this had a profoundly demoralizing effect on the foreign service, one from which it might never have fully recovered.

The influence of the foreign-affairs bureaucracy reached a pinnacle in the late 1940s, and it declined precipitously with the onset of the Korean War. Only in the 1970s and 1980s has the bureaucracy begun to recover from the trauma of McCarthyism and the congressional witch-hunts of the early 1950s. The bureaucracy's lack of expertise and its unwillingness to look at U.S. foreign policy in new ways only encouraged Nixon and Kissinger to ignore it. This in turn only further exacerbated the decline in influence of and morale within the foreign-affairs bureaucracy. While the situation has improved over the last fifteen years or so, the capabilities of the bureaucracy will likely never equal the experience of the "China hands" of the late 1940s.

Finally, the public's view of relations with China has come full circle. From apathy about China issues in the late 1940s to vehement hatred in the 1950s, to fear in the 1960s, to friendship, even euphoria in the 1970s, to apathy again in the 1980s, the American general public has exhibited the greatest degree of changeability on China. Attitudes were most often shaped by dramatic events, but once shaped, popular views seemed to last a relatively long time. The record of public opinion on China questions suggests that if the president and his top advisers choose to make the effort to try to inform the public about American policy in regard to China, the public will react positively to the administration's actions. But when no such effort is made, the public and the electoral connection sharply constrain the range of presidential action.

Of course, American policy making on China must not be viewed in a vacuum. The overall context within which the United States operated, and even more important, Chinese views of the United States, shaped, constrained, and channeled American policies toward China. It is extremely unlikely that hostile Sino-American relations could have been avoided after the Korean War broke out. Indeed, it could be argued that given China's experiment with radicalism in the late 1950s and 1960s, it would have been hard to advance the dates of U.S.-China rapprochement and normalization. But this does not excuse the leaders of either side from their duty of trying to understand the actions and aims of the other. American attitudes and policies toward China contributed to U.S. involvement in Vietnam. This was the ultimate consequence of American ignorance, and of attempts to isolate the PRC. The consequences of PRC attitudes and policies toward the United States are more difficult to assess. How different the grim history of the PRC might have been from 1958 to 1976 if it too had pursued different policies toward the United States is impossible to say. Clearly, the United States was not alone in its misperceptions and wrongheaded policies.

This legacy of mutual misunderstanding and often willful ignorance on the part of each society toward the other should induce a proper feeling of caution in forecasting the future of U.S.-China relations. Today, each side is much more open to the other than ever before. Mutual understanding is growing. But the influence of harmful stereotypes, cultural biases, different ideologies and political systems, and the rise of new, complex issues all mean that a satisfactory future for Sino-American relations requires careful nurturing and management by each side.

14

The United States and Japan: From Occupation to Global Partnership

KENT E. CALDER

HISTORY, as the increasingly important institutionalist school of political analysis ever more insistently reminds us,[1] provides crucially important insights into why public policies take the forms they do. However insistently leaders may proclaim their ability to make the world anew, they are constrained by institutions and long-standing *modi operandi*—pressures lightened only intermittently by recurring periods of institutional flux, normally amid political or economic crisis.[2] In the absence of pressures so powerful as to induce total collapse of existing institutions or to call them sharply into question, policies will typically continue in their previous courses, even when they demonstrably continue to address long-passed crises rather than current reality. Nowhere in today's international

1. See, for example, Peter Gourevitch, *Politics in Hard Times* (Cornell University Press, 1986); Peter Evans, Dietrich Rueschemeyer, and Theda Skocpol, eds., *Bringing the State Back In* (Cambridge University Press, 1985); Chalmers Johnson, *MITI and the Japanese Miracle* (Stanford University Press, 1982); and Stephen Skowronek, *Building a New American State* (Cambridge University Press, 1981).
2. On the details of such a dynamic applied to Japanese Public Policy, see Kent E. Calder, *Crisis and Compensation: Public Policy and Political Stability in Japan, 1949–1986* (Princeton University Press, 1988).

political economy are the tensions between long-established institutions and current realities deeper than in U.S.-Japan economic and security relations. For nearly the entire two decades since the OECD first suggested the emergence of a structural Japanese trade surplus in 1969,[3] Japan's global trade surpluses have continued to grow, with a deepening concentration of those surpluses in the American market. The American trade position has continued to worsen. Yet considering the protectionist steps of other major powers, and the magnitude of the trade deficits this country has sustained, the United States has responded with remarkably little protectionism.

American and Japanese security policies likewise present an apparent paradox. Despite a steadily eroding economic base, the United States has continued to sustain far-flung global commitments, including many in areas of the world of primary strategic and economic interest to Japan. Conversely, Japan, despite rising stakes in the international economy, flowing from its explosively growing trade and foreign investment, has persistently refused to rearm or to assert itself on multilateral economic and security questions.

Historical analysis goes far toward explaining the apparent contradictions and paradoxes of the current U.S.-Japan economic and security relationships. It reveals the circumstances of the early Cold War period—particularly deepening American fears of communism in East Asia and U.S. pessimism regarding future prospects of the Japanese economy—which inspired the United States to offer Japan broad access to the American market. These realities also spurred the United States to sponsor Japan's integration into broader multilateral trade and investment regimes, even as important barriers to foreign access in Japan remained. History also helps to explain why the United States accepted Japan's reluctance to rearm after 1950, despite escalating Cold War tensions, and why U.S.-Japan relations have remained cordial, despite Japan's persistent subsequent failure to assume a more substantial defense burden. History, finally, helps us to account for the uneven profile of tensions and cooperation in the U.S.-Japan relationship, including the mutual bitterness of the early 1970s and the subsequent improvement in ties, even as U.S. trade deficits worsened and pressures for a more substantial Japanese security role began to mount.

The Prewar and Wartime Heritage

To understand the past four decades of U.S.-Japan relations and their implications for the current trade and security dilemmas confronting both nations, it is important to recall the historical context in late August 1945, as Douglas MacArthur landed at Atsugi to inaugurate the Allied occupation. There was inevitably a deep residue of bitterness stemming from nearly four years of Pacific war in which 350,000 Americans and over three million Japanese (60 percent civilian) had been killed, many at each other's hands.

These memories transcended Pearl Harbor, Bataan, Hiroshima, and Nagasaki,

3. Organization for Economic Cooperation and Development, *Japan* (Paris: OECD Economic Surveys, 1969), pp. 39–41.

to include the struggles for Saipan, Iwo Jima, and Okinawa, as well as incessant air raids like the 10 March 1945 incendiary strike on Tokyo, in which forty-eight thousand bombs were dropped in only four hours, leaving 124,000 Japanese dead or maimed, and an estimated one million homeless.[4]

Memories were further complicated by the racial dimension of twentieth-century U.S.-Japan conflicts.[5] Racial tensions in U.S.-Japan relations predated World War II, reaching back to the 1924 Exclusion Act, which barred all Japanese immigration to America, and to earlier measures depriving Japanese-Americans of the right to naturalization and the right to own land in the United States.

Yet despite some bitter, complex memories with which both Japanese and Americans have confronted the postwar era, there was also a long-standing tradition of economic interdependence, and broader personal and intellectual ties than Japan had shared with perhaps any other western nation. Japan's diplomats, to be sure, had persistently paid greater attention to Europe; no America bureau existed in the Japanese Foreign Ministry as late as 1934. But intellectual interchanges with America had begun with Perry's initial missions to Japan during 1853–54; Americans such as Horace Capron, William Clark, James Curties Hepburn, Henry Willard Denison, and a host of others, many of them missionaries, had been influential educators and technical advisers in Japan from the early Meiji Period.

Japanese economic ties with the United States have also been persistently strong, and they have given rise to a human network and common corporate interests that transcended World War II to help provide a basis for postwar cooperation.[6] From the mid-Meiji Period on, Japan quite consistently sent about one-third of its exports to the United States; by the mid-1920s, this ratio had risen to 45 percent, due to U.S. absorption of 90 percent of all the raw silk that Japan sent abroad. While Japan was not nearly as important economically for the United States as vice versa, Japan was clearly more important to the United States than was China; over the period from 1861 to 1938, U.S. exports to China never reached even 3 percent of total U.S. exports, while those to Japan rose above 5 percent of the U.S. total. Joint ventures such as those that gave birth to NEC (1899) and Toshiba (1905 and 1909), both electronics giants of the postwar period, also helped bind U.S. and Japanese firms across the Pacific.

Military rule in Japan from 1931 until the war's end in 1945 severed or complicated a wide range of transpacific human and economic ties. But as Akira Iriye, Edwin O. Reischauer, and others have shown, the prewar residue of

4. Asahi Shimbun, *The Pacific Rivals* (Tokyo: Weatherhill-Asahi, 1972), pp. 106–7. For a detailed chronicle of wartime casualties and property loss from Allied bombing of Japan, see Naikaku Sori Daijin Kanbo Kanri Shitsu, *Zenkoku Sensai Shi Jitsu Chosa Hokokusho* (A Survey of the History of Actual Wartime Casualties). (Tokyo: Naikaku Sori Daijin Kanbo Kanri Shitsu, March 1979).

5. See John W. Dower, *War Without Mercy: Race and Power in the Pacific War* (New York: Pantheon Books, 1986).

6. On these transwar personal networks linking Japan and the United States, see, for example, John Roberts, *Mitsui* (Tokyo: John Weatherhill, 1974).

continuing relationships established before World War II was a crucial basis upon which proponents of stronger ties could later build.[7] Americans were disposed to aid the recovery of Japan and to assist in fostering democratic tendencies there, although the precise mechanisms through which they proposed to do this remained somewhat unclear as they approached the formidable tasks of the postwar occupation.

The Occupation: Reform and Retrenchment (1945–1952)

As in the case of West Germany and to a lesser degree that of Italy, the Allied occupation of Japan had a profound impact on the Japanese national role in the international economic and security systems by significantly restructuring a wide range of domestic institutions during the early postwar years (1945–1948). Most important, the occupation dismantled the Japanese military, and it imposed the so-called "no-war clause," Article 9 of Japan's 1947 constitution, by which Japan "forever renounced war as an instrument of national policy," and asserted that "offensive military forces will never be maintained." Japan was, in Douglas MacArthur's early postwar phraseology, to become "the Switzerland of the Orient."

As in West Germany, the occupation radically decentralized the Japanese police forces and local administrative apparatus, abolishing the Home Ministry at the end of 1947 and purging fourteen hundred of that proud ministry's officials. But in contrast to the German case where administrative decentralization occurred in the chaos of war's end, in Japan the domestic nonindustrial policy bureaucracy was thrown abruptly into disarray more than two years after the war ended, after local political parties had already begun to gain some cohesion. The result was strong political party influence over the Construction Ministry and Local Autonomy Agency, the successors to the dismantled Home Ministry. These developments encouraged government public works spending and intensified domestic counterpressures against a resurgence of military spending. This public works bias toward spending for roads, bridges, and port facilities, rather than alternatives such as armaments or public-service employment, became much stronger in Japan than in the other nations that the Allies occupied. Extensive land-reform proposals by SCAP (Supreme Commander Allied Powers),[8] and the simultaneous dismantling of the conservative agricultural associations *(nokai)* in the spring of 1947 also intensified pluralism and political uncertainty in the countryside by simultaneously undermining the prevailing conservative power structure and strengthening the position of small freeholders as an alternative. SCAP's initially strong support for unionization had parallel implications in the cities. With SCAP encouragement, the number of unions in

7. Akira Iriye, *Power and Culture: The Japanese-American War, 1941–1945* (Cambridge: Harvard University Press, 1981).

8. This acronym is commonly used to collectively denote the command headquarters staff of the Allied occupation forces which ruled Japan from August 1945 until 29 April 1952.

Japan increased from one in August 1945 to twelve thousand—with 3.7 million members—by late 1946.

To further assist democratic tendencies in Japan, the occupation also initially moved to break up the *zaibatsu*, or large industrial groups which had dominated the pre-1945 Japanese economy. Less than a month after Japan's formal surrender, the initial postsurrender policy for Japan (22 September 1945) stressed American support for *zaibatsu* dissolution. Under this directive the *zaibatsu* holding companies and the major trading companies were dissolved. Mitsui and Company, the largest general trading firm, was split into 170 separate successor companies, and Mitsubishi into 139 companies.

SCAP's initial objective, in short, was to dismantle the Japanese war machine and to democratize Japan. Achieving economic stability was at first distinctly secondary. But by 1948 the economic costs of the occupation to American taxpayers had begun to rise sharply. The geostrategic objectives of the United States with respect to Japan had also begun to shift, with the intensification of the Cold War and the increasing strategic importance of Japan for the United States that accompanied Chiang Kai-shek's impending defeat on the Chinese mainland. As George Kennan pointed out, "Japan . . . was the sole great potential military-industrial arsenal of the Far East",[9] one whose prospective capabilities loomed increasingly large as the likelihood of China's becoming an adversary of the United States grew ever stronger.

The shift in American priorities—the so-called Reverse Course—can be seen graphically in U.S. reparation proposals to Japan and in projected American foreign aid. Initial U.S. demands were for $670 million in reparations, subsequently reduced to $450 million, then $180 million, and then cancelled altogether. Projected U.S. economic aid conversely was projected at $350 million, and then rose to $470 million, $550 million, and finally reached a total of $2.1 billion over the seven-year life of the occupation.

After the decision was conclusively made in Washington around mid-1948 to place the priority on stability rather than democratization, occupation policies abruptly began to change across a wide range of policy sectors. The *zaibatsu*-dissolution campaign ground to a halt; the thorough dismantling of holding and trading companies that had occurred did not proceed to the banks. Political support shifted away from socialists and middle-of-the-road liberals such as Katayama, Ashida, and Miki toward more conservative politicians like Yoshida Shigeru, bent on the consolidation of right-wing preeminence. At SCAP insistence, a "red purge" during 1949–1950 ousted fourteen thousand communists and other left-oriented activists from government offices, key industries, and the press.

The most important element of the so-called Reverse Course was the appointment of Bank of Detroit President Joseph Dodge, an avowed fiscal conservative, as senior economic adviser to SCAP, effective 1 February 1949. Dodge insisted strongly on a balanced budget and the dismantling of the Reconstruction Fi-

9. George F. Kennan, *Memoirs, 1925–1950* (Boston: Little Brown and Co., 1967), p. 374.

nance Bank, which had been financing economic recovery in manifestly inflationary fashion. Although offset to some extent by off-budget government spending through the Trust Funds Bureau (Yokin Bu), the deflationary policies mandated by Dodge pushed the Japanese economy into a deep recession by early 1950 from which it was rescued only by the Korean War.

Fashioning the Postwar Economics and Security Framework (1946–1953)

Seen in comparison with other American bilateral relationships of the past forty years, the most distinctive aspects of the U.S.-Japan relationship are twofold. First of all, military security has been provided overwhelmingly by the United States, with Japanese military capacities developing much less fully than those of U.S. allies in Europe. Secondly, the bilateral U.S.-Japan economic relationship, together with the broader multilateral framework within which it came to be embedded during the 1950s and 1960s, has offered broad economic opportunities to Japan that have not been paralleled by equivalent opportunities provided by Japan to the United States. These dual characteristics of the U.S.-Japan relationship emerged during the seven years after initial drafting of Japan's "no-war" constitution in 1946, and they have persisted in basic outline ever since.

The security side of the equation was initially shaped by Wilsonian impulses within the Truman administration and SCAP-Tokyo to make Japan the "Switzerland of the Orient." These were embodied in Article 9 of the new constitution, first published in draft form during April 1946 and formally promulgated in May 1947. Even before the outbreak of the Korean War, the U.S. position began to change, with John Foster Dulles reportedly pressing Yoshida Shigeru for defense commitments at their first meeting in mid-June 1950.[10] In July 1950, following the outbreak of the Korean War, MacArthur ordered the creation of the Japanese Police Reserve Force; both he and Dulles again stressed in January 1951 to Yoshida the necessity of Japan's rearming. During the fall of 1952, State Department Assistant Secretary of State for Far Eastern Affairs Walter S. Robertson, together with Joseph Dodge, tried to commit Japan to significantly expanding its defense force over the succeeding few years.[11] Dulles reiterated these demands in congressional testimony during July 1953, proposing that Japan should increase its troop strength from 120,000 to 350,000 men. Four months later, before the Japan America Society in Tokyo, Vice President Richard Nixon called Japan's "no-war" Article 9 a mistake and urged a Japanese military force of at least 320,000.

The Japanese response to American pressure was uneven, and often contradictory, in its early stages. There was a period during and even after the Korean War when the acceleration of Japanese defense spending and the emergence of

10. John W. Dower, "The Eye of the Beholder," Bulletin of Concerned Asian Scholars 2, 1 (October 1969): 22.

11. See John W. Dower, Empire and Aftermath (Cambridge, Mass.: Harvard University Council on East Asian Studies, 1979), pp. 449–63.

substantial Japanese defense capability appeared to be quite possible. Several major Japanese business groups, especially the defense committee within *Keidanren*, principal representative of the big-business community, sensed that arms production and exports could help sustain the economic momentum of the Korean War special procurements boom. In the economic downturn at the end of the Korean War, alternate civilian prospects looked bleak. In addition, many conservative politicians favored a military buildup; during the 1952 general election campaign, for example, the Reform Party *(Kaishinto)* set 3.5 percent of GNP (gross national product) as an appropriate level for Japanese defense spending, only to see Hatoyama Ichiro call for an even higher level of 4 percent.[12]

In the face of combined U.S. and right-wing conservative pressure within Japan (from both Hatoyama and the Progressives), the Yoshida cabinet was forced to propose some major rearmament. In September 1953 the Safety Agency released a draft of its own tentative five-year defense plan. This plan proposed 210,000 men for the ground forces, a navy of 170 ships, and 1,400 aircraft—all to be achieved by 1958. In 1954 Japan signed a mutual defense assistance agreement with the United States that provided for some strengthening of Japanese forces; it also formally upgraded the Safety Agency into a Defense Agency *(Boeicho)*. After Yoshida left office, defense spending continued at levels close to 2 percent of GNP through fiscal 1956, a share of the Japanese national budget comparable to defense levels in West Germany.[13]

Despite some gestures under U.S. pressure toward expanded Japanese military commitments, however, the continual effort of the Yoshida administration was to limit expansion of the Japanese military. Such increases in military spending as actually occurred were always substantially less than the U.S. demanded, and they came more frequently in the form of symbolic and future plans for change than actual institutional transformation. Yoshida succeeded by and large in deflecting U.S. pressures for two basic reasons: because the United States strongly desired Japanese cooperation in its containment of mainland China, and because the United States remained uncertain of the underlying economic and political stability of Japan. It was hence reluctant to press the fundamentally friendly Japanese conservative government too strongly to take controversial steps that might threaten that government's domestic political viability.

On the China question, Japan had considerable leverage against the United States from the fall of China in 1949 throughout the 1950s and 1960s. Postrevolutionary China was generally eager for better relations with Japan. And the major Japanese opposition parties were happy to oblige, together with a significant portion of the big business community, particularly in the Kansai area of western Japan, which had traded heavily with China before World War II. Britain's 1949

12. American Embassy-Tokyo to Department of State, "Weekly Political Notes from Japan," September 11–18, 1952.

13. In 1956, defense spending was 9.7 percent of total government expenditures in Japan compared to only 9.3 percent in West Germany. See G. Warren Nutter, *Growth of Government in the West* (Washington, D.C.: American Enterprise Institute, 1978), pp. 64, 66.

recognition of the People's Republic, and its objections to Dulles's proposal that Taiwan be invited to the San Francisco Peace Conference, gave Yoshida additional room and incentive to maneuver. A longtime Anglophile who had served as Japanese ambassador to the Court of St. James's during the late 1930s, Yoshida clearly preferred the British position on China to the "containment" strategy of Dulles. In the face of British opposition to sole Taiwanese participation, Dulles arranged that neither Taiwan nor mainland China would be invited to the peace conference, and that Japan would later conclude a formal peace with the party of its choosing.

In the face of persistent opposition questioning, Yoshida on 29 October 1951 announced to the Upper House Special Committee on the Peace Treaty that he was thinking of opening trade relations with China and of establishing a commercial office in Shanghai.[14] Dulles and Senate Foreign Relations Committee Chairman John Sparkman warned Yoshida that recognition of Peking would prevent U.S. ratification of the peace treaty, and thus postpone Japan's recovery of its independence. Dulles ultimately forced Yoshida to commit Japan in writing to establishing normal relations with Taipeh; on 28 April 1952—the very day it resumed its independence at occupation's end—Japan formally signed a peace treaty with nationalist China. But there remained a host of nuances in Japan's relations with mainland China—particularly the volume and character of Sino-Japanese trade and later Japan's diplomatic stance in the United Nations. These provided Japan with continuing leverage against the United States.

With the fall of China and the onset of the Korean War during 1949–50, there was a quantum jump in Japan's geostrategic importance to the United States as Dulles, John Allison, and other American policymakers responsible for Pacific affairs acutely sensed. "Japan," Assistant Under Secretary of State John M. Allison argued in 1952, "holds the key to victory or defeat in the fight against Communism in the Far East." Yet there were fundamental economic and political uncertainties in Japan's underlying circumstances that deeply concerned the United States. Japan's per capita GNP in 1950 was below that of Brazil, Malaysia, and Chile; its weakest sector was international trade.[15] Shorn of its colonies, Japan was heavily dependent on imported raw materials, while most industrial nations, except for the United States, had closed their markets to Japanese industrial goods. Japan had twelve times as many people to feed per square mile of farmland as did the United States, and more than twice as many as even overcrowded China.

The geostrategic importance of helping Japan to overcome its economic difficulties was enhanced in American eyes by the fragility of Prime Minister Yoshida's domestic political circumstances. To be sure, Yoshida had won a resounding victory in the January 1949 general elections. But communist strength had risen to thirty-nine seats and 9.7 percent of the popular vote, the highest shares held by the Japan Communist party until the early 1970s. Factionalism

---

14. Asahi Shimbun, *The Pacific Rivals*, p. 207.

15. Hugh Patrick and Henry Rosovsky, eds., *Asia's New Giant: How the Japanese Economy Works* (Washington, D.C.: The Brookings Institution, 1986), p. 11.

Dulles, Prime Minister Yoshida, and Acheson at the September 1951 signing of the peace treaty with Japan in San Francisco. (National Archives)

was also deeply rooted within Yoshida's ruling Democratic Liberal party. Most worrisome in American eyes was a steady resurgence of the militarist right, given momentum by the gradual return of many initially purged by the occupation for complicity with the Axis war effort to active political life during 1950–51. Although the Japanese economy was given a temporary stimulus by wartime procurements in Korea—which provided 40 percent of Japan's total exports in 1950—there was the continuing danger of stagnation, rising unemployment, and possible political unrest in Japan once again when that economy decelerated at war's end.

The combined economic and political vulnerabilities facing the Japanese conservatives created a clear imperative for the United States: to provide Japan with the wherewithal to sustain itself through international trade, so that it would not become a ward of American taxpayers. Such a strategy implied support for an efficient competitive economic structure within Japan, through measures such as the Dodge Line,[16] antiinflationary measures (1949–1950), sharp cutbacks in overstaffing at public corporations (1949), and curbs on militant labor (1949–50).

16. Named after SCAP economic adviser and former Bank of Detroit president Joseph Dodge, the Dodge Line was a program of fiscal austerity and related retrenchment in Japanese public employment undertaken during 1949–50 to cut inflation and improve economic efficiency in Japan.

But it also meant integrating Japan into the broader world political economy on terms that would allow that vulnerable nation to prosper through trade. The key steps taken in this regard were the establishment of the fixed Y360 = $1.00 exchange rate of April 1949, together with U.S. sponsorship of Japanese membership in the International Monetary Fund (IMF) and the World Bank (29 May 1952); the Economic Commission for Asia and the Far East, or ECAFE (June 1954); GATT (September 1955); and the United Nations (December 1956). The conclusion of a bilateral U.S.-Japan treaty of friendship, commerce, and navigation (April 1953) also helped to stabilize Japan's economic situation by allowing it broad, albeit reciprocal, access to the American market.

Japanese Growth amid Lingering Vulnerability (1954-1969)

Despite the initial Korean War boom, the Japanese economy continued to be feeble and plagued by persistent balance-of-payment deficits throughout the 1950s and the 1960s. If special military procurements are excluded, Japan's imports exceeded exports every year from 1946 to 1964, and the economy alternated between deficits and minor surpluses for the following five years as well.[17] In 1955 Japanese raw material, mineral, fuel, and food imports together came to $2.17 billion, or $160 million more than the country's entire export income in that year. In 1960 such imports still consumed 86 percent of export income.[18] On five occasions, three during 1953–54 and twice again during 1957, Japan was forced to draw major loans from the IMF to finance its basic imports.[19] Even as late as 1960 Prime Minister Ikeda Hayato could raise the specter of unemployment—the problem of finding work for over 1.7 million new workers expected to join the labor force by 1962–63—in support of his income doubling plan.[20]

For two decades from 1955 onward Japan grew persistently at a double-digit pace, its national GNP doubling every five to seven years. Meanwhile its military capabilities largely stagnated, even as American forces in Japan steadily declined.[21] But Japan remained at once militarily strategic to the United States and economically vulnerable, eliciting continuing American support for its desires to avoid military outlays, while simultaneously being integrated more and more fully into the U.S.-dominated political economy of the advanced industrial nations. Intermittent signs of political volatility in Japan, such as the dramatic

17. Toyo Keizai Shinpo Sha, *Showa Kokusei Soran*, vol. I, pp. 613, 649, 652. Figures are drawn from Ministry of Finance customs clearance data.
18. Bank of Japan Research and Statistics Department, *Keizai Tokei Nenpo* (Economic Statistics Annual), 1985 ed., p. 281.
19. Uchino Tatsuro, *Japan's Postwar Economy*, pp. 77–78, 99–100.
20. *Asahi Shimbun*, 6 September 1960.
21. In 1955 there were 150,000 U.S. troops stationed in Japan; by 1967 there were only 36,400. See Asahi Shimbun Sha, *Jieitai* (Self-Defense Forces) (Tokyo: Asahi Shimbun Sha, 1968), p. 266. On the broader U.S.-Japan security relationship of this period, see Martin E. Weinstein, *Japan's Postwar Defense Policy, 1947–1968* (Columbia University Press, 1971), pp. 43–103.

U.S.-Japan security treaty crisis of 1960, which forced cancellation of Dwight D. Eisenhower's scheduled Tokyo visit,[22] also encouraged the United States to actively promote Japanese economic growth. In April 1964, with U.S. support, Japan became the first nonwestern nation to join the OECD. In October it staged the Tokyo Olympics, the first Olympics ever held in Asia. In June 1965, Japan at last concluded with strong U.S. backing a peace treaty with South Korea, opening the way to expansion of Japanese exports to and foreign investment in that neighboring country.

The deepening U.S. military involvement in Vietnam after 1965 had profound indirect effects on the U.S.-Japan relationship that have yet to be fully explored.[23] The two nations entered their involvement with that conflict in a relatively harmonious hierarchical relationship, symbolized by the "Reischauer diplomacy" of the Kennedy administration. They emerged in the early 1970s with their economic relationship fundamentally redefined, Japan having become a serious competitor of American industry in automobiles, electronics, and machine tools, as well as steel, shipbuilding, and other lower-technology sectors. Security relations and interpersonal ties also underwent strain, as the United States persisted in an Asian land war that filled Japanese pocketbooks, but also offended Japanese sensibilities, particularly because the victims of American attacks were also Asians.

Years of Redefinition (1968–1973)

Of all major periods in the history of post–World War II U.S.-Japan relations, this was with little doubt the most tortured and difficult. Both the United States and Japan were in the midst of fundamental internal redefinition, both structural and spiritual. In the United States, frustration with the dual traumas of the Vietnam War and economic decline made Americans increasingly truculent; an economic structure still biased toward industry rather than distribution, in which multinational corporations and pro–free trade lobbies lacked the influence they were later to gain, responded more violently against relatively modest import penetration than was later to be the case. In Japan, a sense of pervasive vulnerability flowing from a lack of food and raw materials made trade concessions—and especially market access for foreign manufactures in Japan— appear dangerous. This sense of vulnerability likewise prevented Japanese negotiators from responding easily to demands from abroad. The stage was set for deepening transpacific confrontation.

Some aspects of U.S.-Japan relations went remarkably smoothly during these years of redefinition. The United States sensitively accommodated Japan's nascent nationalist aspirations by returning first the Bonin Islands (including Iwo

22. On the Security Treaty crisis see George Packard, *Protest in Tokyo* (Princeton University Press, 1966).

23. For a useful initial effort that concentrates most heavily on following the details of antiwar protest movements in Japan, see Thomas Havens, *Fire Across the Sea: The Vietnam War and Japan, 1965–1975* (Princeton University Press, 1987).

Jima) in June 1968, and then agreeing in November 1969 to an Okinawa reversion three years thereafter. As Destler, Fukui, and Sato have pointed out, the Okinawa negotiations were one of the smoothest and most successful in the history of postwar U.S.-Japan relations, in part because of sensitive political orchestration and long-term planning.[24] Fears of violence within Japan in connection with the 1970 renewal of the U.S.-Japan security treaty seem to have encouraged a deft handling of inherently complex and delicate issues.

The major frictions of the 1968–73 period occurred in the area of trade. Bitterest, perhaps, was the three-year wrangle over Japanese textile exports to the United States, which led the Nixon administration to threaten first import quotas and then broader sanctions under the Trading with the Enemy Act, passed to deal with Imperial Germany during World War I.[25] Failures of communication in both the United States and Japan, centering particularly around what the Nixon administration perceived as a *de facto* American agreement to Okinawa reversion in return for Japanese imposition of controls on textile exports, were a major factor behind the trade friction. But more fundamental were the underlying interest group politics. Textiles remained among the largest employers in the United States, with factories stretched across a broad range of electoral districts, and the industry had struck a political deal in 1968 with then presidential candidate Richard Nixon, to provide political support in return for trade protection. The Japanese textile industry was incapable of sensitively appreciating Nixon's political circumstances, and Prime Minister Sato did not fully communicate within the networks of Japanese domestic politics the nature of the pressures he was receiving from Nixon on the textile issue. The textile wrangle was the product of a particular epoch in U.S.-Japan relations, and it might well not have been as intractable either before or after as it was during the 1969–71 period.

There were several other sharp conflicts around the time of the textile controversy, involving a broad range of individuals and sectors, which suggest that the unusually intense conflict of this period flowed from more than just personalities. In December 1970, for example, the Treasury charged Japanese television manufacturers with dumping, in the same month that the United States rejected Japan's final proposal on textiles. In July 1971, President Nixon abruptly announced a visit to Peking, in a sharp reversal of long-standing U.S. China policies; Nixon's move suddenly upstaged a Japanese government, which since 1949 had wanted to forge stronger bilateral ties with Peking itself, only to be continually dissuaded by Washington. Exactly a month later, Nixon once again shocked Tokyo by imposing a 10 percent surcharge on all imports, and suspending the convertibility of dollars into gold.

In December 1971, Secretary of the Treasury John Connally forced a 16.8 percent revaluation of the yen on Japan at the G-10 Smithsonian financial

24. I.M. Destler, Haruhiro Fukui, and Hideo Sato, *Managing an Alliance: The Politics of U.S.-Japanese Relations* (Washington, D.C.: The Brookings Institution, 1976).
25. See I.M. Destler and Hideo Sato, *The Textile Wrangle* (Cornell University Press, 1979).

conference which brought ten influential industrial nations together in Washington to realign major global exchange rates on a multilateral basis. Also a stormy year was 1972, with a proliferation of dumping petitions lodged in the U.S. against Japan, and in February 1973 the United States summarily called an end to the fixed exchange rate system upon which Japan had come to rely for a quarter of a century. In the five years after 1968, the year in which the United States had returned the Bonin Islands and met with Japan for the first time to discuss dollar defense, the two nations struggled to redefine themselves and their relationship against the backdrop of a rapidly changing world. The process was not an easy one, particularly given the tensions between prevailing interest group structures and changing economic realities.

Emergence of the Transpacific Political Economy (1973–1985)

The U.S.-Japan trade deficit in 1970, as the bitter transpacific conflicts of the early 1970s began to escalate, was $1.2 billion, and it never rose above $3 billion at any point during that stormy period. By 1987 the U.S. bilateral deficit with Japan had reached forty times the 1970 amount; it was complemented by large-scale deficits with Taiwan, South Korea, Hong Kong, and even Singapore, of which few observers in the early 1970s would have dreamed. The only remaining major U.S. trade surplus in the Pacific was with Australia. Eighty-six and a half percent of the expansion in U.S.-Japan trade between 1980 and 1986 had consisted of Japanese exports to the United States, and patterns with nations elsewhere in the region were generally similar.

Yet transpacific tensions in the 1980s remained remarkably muted, considering the magnitude of the economic imbalances. Congress in 1982 defeated local content legislation for automobiles, which proposed practices long prevailing in much of Western Europe, and it failed in 1986 to override presidential vetoes of protectionist textile-trade legislation. In the late 1980s the executive branch abandoned its insistence on voluntary Japanese restraints on exports of autos to the United States which it had demanded in 1981. Following the decisive defeat of Richard Gephardt in the strategic Super Tuesday regional presidential primary of 1988, Congress passed an omnibus trade bill conspicuous for its lack of strong protectionist trade provisions.

As import penetration rose in the United States during the 1980s, interest groups and even U.S. commerce and trade authorities launched a rash of antidumping and unfair trading practice investigations in specific, narrow product lines, moving to impose an unprecedented retaliatory tariff on Japanese electronic products in early 1987. But while the emergence of this so-called Section 301 regime, named after the relevant unfair trading practices clause of the U.S. Trade Act of 1974, has attracted considerable media attention, and conveys the impression of bitter U.S.-Japan conflict emerging, the commercial stakes in the specific cases litigated are relatively small. Furthermore the acceptance rate of domestic industry claims has remained low, and the remedies provided by the federal government modest, even as trade litigation has steadily

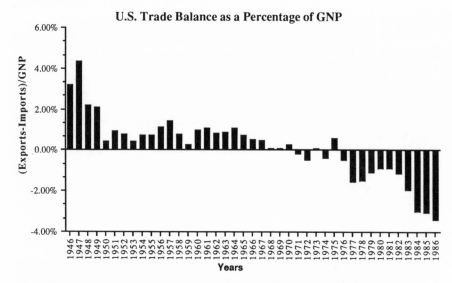

U.S. Trade Balance as a Percentage of GNP

Years

The unfavorable balance of trade with Japan and other Pacific rim states was a major factor in the dramatic change of America's international commercial relations. Source: *Economic Report of the President 1988* (Washington, D.C., 1988), pp. 248, 364.

increased, together with the U.S. trade deficit.[26] The broader framework of trade and financial relations thus remains fundamentally stable. The White House itself continues to stand forthrightly for an open trade and financial system and for close diplomatic ties with Japan and other nations of East Asia; increasingly influential state and local authorities are also forging active links throughout the Pacific, links that in many cases did not even exist at the beginning of the decade. The United States in the 1980s did *not*, in short, appear to be on a clear "slippery slope" toward protectionism, despite periodic abridgment—less than most other major nations—of liberal economic principles.

At the root of the remarkably mild American national response to sharply larger U.S. trade deficits and the rapid buildup in U.S. foreign debt during the 1980s have been fundamental changes since the early 1970s in the structure of the American domestic political economy. One development has been its sharpening segmentation. Sharply contrasting Americas of abundance and decline have emerged—their differences accentuated by the effects of two oil shocks since 1973, the vast acceleration of defense procurements, and the rapid pace of technological change over the past decade. As a consequence, opinion and interests on global trade issues have differed more and more along sectoral and regional lines.

Throughout most of the past twenty years, the South and the West of the

26. Judith Goldstein, "The Political Economy of Trade: Institutions of Protection," *American Political Science Review* 80, 1 (March 1986): 161–84.

United States, broadly speaking, have steadily gained relative to the rest of the country in both population and share of aggregate national wealth. By 1990 the combined populations of these areas are expected to account for about 54 percent of the U.S. total. Despite deep recession in Texas and neighboring parts of the Southwest during the mid-1980s due to the sharp fall in oil prices, inflation-adjusted incomes have grown twice as fast in the South and West as in the Northeast and Midwest over the past two decades.

During the 1980s new growth points have also emerged, tied to defense and service industry development in such states as New York, Connecticut, and Massachusetts. These developments, like the depression in the Southwestern oil industry, have narrowed some of the broad, regionally specific contrasts between growth and prosperity that were implicit in the "Sunbelt shift" pattern of the 1970s to create a more nuanced picture. But the complex interweaving of prosperity and depression in Snowbelt states has complicated protectionist efforts there, as is clear, for example, in the state of Ohio. While the heavy industry around Cleveland and Youngstown has been badly depressed, central Ohio has been more buoyant, stimulated by projects such as the new Honda auto plant in Marysville.

The continuing shifts in the locus of economic power in the United States have encouraged parallel shifts in patterns of political influence, which have in turn reinforced the ongoing economic shifts. Every president elected to office since Lyndon B. Johnson has had substantial southern or western political back-ground. Gerald Ford, who does not fit that qualification, was not elected, but succeeded to office following the Nixon resignation. For a century before that, southern or western background was a rarity among chief executives. In addi-tion, for the past two generations the chairmen of major congressional commit-tees have tended to be westerners and especially southerners. In the Super Tuesday regional presidential primary of March 1988, the South once again showed its strategic political influence, assuring the Republican nomination of transplanted Texan George Bush, and grievously wounding protectionist Demo-crat Richard Gephardt.

The increasingly salient regional and sectoral divisions in the American politi-cal economy have since the late 1960s coincided ever more closely with attitudes concerning trade policy toward Japan. Generally speaking, protectionist senti-ments have been concentrated in the relatively stagnant, heavily unionized, industrialized centers of the Northeast and Midwest, which have borne the brunt of competition with Japan. Unemployment rates during the first half of the 1980s across this so-called Rustbelt have been frequently double the national average, and anti-Japanese protectionist feeling, as expressed in state-enacted "Buy America" legislation and strong support for federal domestic content legislation, has been high.

Yet despite the rising vehemence of anti-Japanese sentiment in these areas, there have been important regional countertrends that have prevented a protec-tionist common front from emerging, even in relatively depressed Rustbelt areas. Several industrial states, including Ohio, New Jersey, and recently even Michigan, have both sought and successfully attracted Japanese investment. And the service industries rising throughout the country, especially banks, law firms, and consulting companies, have often had a major stake in transactions with Japan and other nations of the Pacific basin.

The South and West together with the financial centers of the United States have generally favored free trade more strongly than other parts of the United States. Underlying this relatively liberal orientation have been strong complementarities of economic interest with Japan and other manufacturers of the Pacific rim. There is, for example, not a single integrated steel mill on the entire American West Coast. The only auto plant there is the recently opened General Motors–Toyota joint venture plant at Fremont, California. Even in the semiconductor industry, Silicon Valley's relatively hard attitude toward Japan has been moderated by a broad market segmentation: California producers specialize in microprocessors and customized chips, while Japanese producers specialize in commodity RAM chips.

Roughly one-third of the entire U.S. trade deficit with Japan is accounted for by the trade that passes through California ports. Yet this has stirred remarkably little antagonism in California, due to the transpacific economic complementarity and the state's relatively rapid growth. Indeed, San Francisco, San Diego, and Long Beach, like Seattle and Portland, profit substantially from shipping to and from East Asia, regardless of in which direction trade predominantly flows. In addition, the auto and electronics dealer networks, which have a substantial stake in a smooth flow of imports, are large and vocal. And across the West, union membership as a proportion of total employment (excluding agriculture) ranges from a low of under 18 percent in right-to-work states like Utah to around 27 percent in California. This is substantially lower than the 30 to 40 percent union membership ratios common in the Midwest and Northeast.

Like the West, the South tends, broadly speaking, to be economically complementary with Japan, and it has been relatively quiescent on trade issues, aside from textiles. Its lukewarm response in early 1988 to Democratic presidential hopeful Richard Gephardt's protection-oriented trade policy appeals flowed in part from this underlying economic structure. The major southern exports are agricultural—soybeans, corn, cotton, sorghum, and tobacco. The beef and orange trade questions that have caused so much U.S.-Japanese political friction are not major issues in the South, except in Florida. And Japan imports over $5 billion annually in agricultural products from the United States, mostly from the South.

Historically, the South has had a pronounced free trade orientation. In addition, a great deal of Japan's rising investment in the United States—projects such as Nissan's truck plant at Smyrna, Tennessee—has been concentrated there, with most of the rest in other Sunbelt states such as California. Overall, well over half of Japanese manufacturing investment in the United States during the mid-1980s has been concentrated in sixteen Sunbelt states; the top three were California, Texas, and Georgia. Yet enough investment is distributed elsewhere to undercut protectionist activity even in the Rustbelt states most adversely affected by economic competition with Japan, such as Michigan and Ohio. Japanese direct investment in the United States, totaling more than $35 billion in 1987, already provides over 250,000 jobs, with this number expected to quadruple to over one million jobs within fifteen years.

Like the economically healthy regions, the sectors of the U.S. economy that have grown vigorously over the past decade have found themselves in a broadly symbiotic relationship with Japan and other major East Asian industrial exporters. For the construction industry, Japan and South Korea have often meant cheaper steel or better delivery times—and hence increased profits on bids. In finance, Japan has meant increased market opportunities: A wide range of American banks with fund surpluses, many of them regional and local, have benefited by financing much of Japan's rapidly growing dollar-based trade and investment. Since the mid-1980s a growing number of U.S. state and local governments have also been raising funds in Japan for a broad range of public purposes, and their activities may be widened to include other nations of the Pacific with major capital surpluses.

Reinforcing these regional and sectoral complementarities with Japan and its neighbors are the growing stakes that many U.S. multinationals have in maintaining smooth transpacific relations. These stakes are especially high in the electronics, banking, energy, and automotive sectors so central to the U.S. political economy. By the end of 1986, direct U.S. investment in Japan was $11.3 billion and rising, particularly in high-technology sectors. Texas Instruments produced all the 64K RAM computer chips for its global operations in Japan, and IBM sourced over half of its IBM PC components there. General Motors, Ford, and Chrysler have all made heavy captive exports to the United States from Japan of both components and finished automobiles.

To a much greater extent than most Americans realize, Japan's transpacific trade surplus stems from the sourcing decisions of such multinationals, together with those of major U.S. distributors, rather than from autonomous export drives by Japanese firms. Over 10 percent of Japan's exports to the United States in the mid-1980s consisted of parts exports, largely to U.S. firms. Big Three sourcing in Japan of auto parts alone came to over $1 billion in 1986. Roughly 7 percent of Japan's U.S.-bound exports are items like video tape recorders and 35-millimeter cameras that are virtually not produced in the United States, yet are marketed by U.S. retailers under Japanese brand names. A further 2 to 3 percent of Japan's exports to the United States are sold under the private brand names of U.S. distributors—Japanese-made Sears home appliances, for example. Finally, about 5 percent represent exports of finished products from Japan to the United States by foreign firms, largely American, that manufacture in Japan. In short, over a quarter of Japan's current exports to the United States appears to be structurally linked to the production and marketing activities of U.S. firms on their home territory. Thus U.S. firms have a massive economic interest in imports from Japan; in practice this inevitably limits the options of U.S. policymakers. A predictably strong exchange value for the yen, continuing over a period of some years, may be required to change this; even then change will probably occur only slowly.

The explosive growth of Japanese capital markets during the mid-1980s has inspired additional interest among multinationals in assuring smooth dealings with Japan, for they see potentially enormous opportunities in funding, underwriting, and brokerage activities. The Tokyo bond market, well over five times the scale of 1980, passed London to become the second largest in the world during 1984; the Tokyo Stock Exchange passed even New York to become the largest in the world, in terms of market capitalization, during mid-1987. Between 1984 and 1987, virtually all the major American multinational financial firms sharply increased their securities and merchant banking staffs in Tokyo, sensing an expanded global role for the yen as well as rapidly growing offshore dealings there in western currencies. By 1988 U.S. banks were handling the bulk of the 45 percent foreign share of foreign-exchange trading in Tokyo, a highly lucrative business.

Traditionally, much of Japan's attractiveness for U.S. multinationals has been rooted in profitability. Although U.S. companies employed only 1 percent of the Japanese work force during 1982, they registered 3.3 percent of the corporate profits in Japan. Over the past fifteen years, the return on investment of U.S. manufacturing firms in Japan has averaged roughly twice the return realized by U.S. affiliates in Canada, the United Kingdom, or France.

In addition to Japan's profitable domestic markets, made ever more lucrative by a strengthening yen, U.S. multinationals often find in Japan an excellent production base for sourcing operations worldwide. Both the quality of the work force and the favorable regulatory climate seem to have encouraged this development, which persisted despite the yen's post-Plaza strength. Since June 1982, U.S. firms in Japan have been eligible for Japan Development Bank loans on a case-by-case basis, and have received low-interest government small-business financing as well. Favorable regional development incentives are being given to U.S. high-tech firms willing to start up operations in Japan, and export financing is reportedly available for global sales from Japanese production bases. Opportunities for American financiers are also expanding in such areas as trust and investment banking.

American multinationals have grown increasingly active in U.S. trade policy formation since 1970, as they have come to perceive their interests threatened by protectionist sentiment both in Congress and abroad. Generally, this rising activism on the part of multinationals, through such groups as the Emergency Committee for American Trade (ECAT), has helped keep U.S. markets open to Japanese imports—a substantial and rising share of which, as noted above, has been captive imports by U.S. multinationals from Japan to the United States. Since 1981, the AT&T consent degree, the end of the Justice Department suit against IBM, and the Reagan administration's generally supportive attitude toward multinationals have significantly increased the leverage such firms can exert on behalf of free trade policies.

A parallel development has been the rising activism and influence in Congress of major distributors—a result of their growing stakes in an open trade regime. Companies like Sears Roebuck and K-Mart, together with the smaller-scale automobile and appliance distributors, have massively increased their foreign sourcing over the past decade—to their considerable profit. The strength of the dollar between 1981 and 1985 increased this profitability, insofar as an oligopolistic market structure prevented exchange rate windfalls from being passed on to the consumer. But even the sharp revaluation of the yen during 1985–87 did not extinguish foreign sourcing, both because Japanese exporters absorbed much of the exchange rate shift, and also because many of the imported goods handled by distributors came from newly industrializing countries (NICs) like South Korea and Taiwan, whose currencies did not rapidly appreciate. The business contacts of U.S. distributors simply broadened to new areas of the Pacific basin. The distributors are said to be highly active on Capitol Hill; the fact that their outlets are scattered across a broad geographic area and the often intimate involvement of local distributors in grass-roots politics serve to enhance these firms' political influence. Because distributors can benefit from any sort of merchandise transaction, and because Japanese manufacturers have placed a high priority on establishing and rewarding a distribution network, these distribution firms have become powerful open trade advocates.

A little noticed but increasingly active and potent political ally in the United States of an open trade and financial regime is state and local government. With the gradual retrenchment in nondefense federal government spending over the past fifteen years, and with the active devolution of governmental functions to the states which the Nixon, Ford, and Reagan administrations have encouraged, local government's role in the overall federal system has expanded.[27] Promotion of new investment was a traditional function of local governments long before the recent expansion of their responsibilities; they have seized on the expansion of foreign investment as a major new opportunity with particular fervor in view of the new policy demands and long-run need for revenue expansion placed on them by recent federal budget cutbacks.

State and local governments have taken generally moderate policy stands on international trade and financial policy questions, to the extent they have addressed them; Indiana Governor Robert Orr's 1987 opposition to congressional sanctions against Toshiba in the wake of the Toshiba Machine Tools technology-diffusion scandal, with a major Toshiba plant investment decision in the United States pending, is a typical case in point. Thirty American states had representatives in Tokyo at the end of 1987, most of them oriented toward investment and export promotion. With Japanese investment alone in the United States expected to rise tenfold over the next fifteen years, creating a fourfold increase in jobs and possibly an even greater rise in local tax revenues, the nonfederal elements of government in the United States cannot easily be anything but a force for moderation and for deepening transpacific integration, possible tensions due to cultural differences notwithstanding.

In addition to this support from multinationals, from distributors, and from local governments, foreign firms striving to preserve an open trade regime have had potent help from Washington's largest corps of professional lobbyists. In the mid-1980s, lobbyists for the Japanese government and private sector, working both to catalyze the diverse supporters of an open trade system in the United

27. On this development see Richard P. Nathan, Fred C. Doolittle, and associates, *Reagan and the States* (Princeton University Press, 1987).

States and to explain U.S. realities in Japan, reported fees double those received by representatives of any other nation. Knowledgeable Washington analysts estimate total Japanese lobbying expenditures at over $60 million annually, including outlays for which formal reports are not required. One out of every five registered Washington lobbyists in 1987 worked for Japanese firms, Japanese industry associations, or the Japanese government, with these lobbyists garnering 30 percent of the fees paid to all registered lobbyists combined. Since congressional decision-making processes have gotten much more complicated over the past fifteen years as the subcommittee system has expanded, there are now many more access points at which outside groups can exert their influence. Japan's representatives and those of other foreign economic partners of the United States clearly benefit from this situation.

Just as the political and economic strength of U.S. groups with interests complementary to those of other Pacific economies has risen since 1970, the position of antagonistic groups has declined. Most notably, the political clout of organized labor has fallen off sharply, as a result of high manufacturing sector unemployment, declining union membership, and the antilabor sentiment of much of the conservative Sunbelt coalition. According to AFL-CIO estimates, union membership declined from 35 percent of the work force in 1955 to less than 19 percent in 1985. This drop has been especially steep since the 1979 oil shock. Between 1981 and 1983, for example, union membership declined by 800,000. The membership of the United Steelworkers Union has fallen by half— from 1.4 million to 700,000—between 1981 and 1985, with most of the decline since 1980. Other indications of the erosion of labor's position include the union concessions and givebacks that have been common in recent labor agreements, the 1982 failure of domestic content legislation and other protectionist efforts, and the fortunes in 1984 of the AFL-CIO's endorsed candidate Walter Mondale—both his difficulties against Gary Hart in the primaries and his subsequent sweeping defeat by Ronald Reagan. The difficulties of Richard Gephardt in 1988 point in the same direction.

Structural transformation within the American political economy will never be complete, as the process of change is a continuing one. The effects of that transformation are mediated through two major political parties, which in the American context stand to some degree on contrasting social bases. The Democratic Party has had more sympathy for and stronger ties to Snowbelt and organized labor groups adversely affected by the emergence of the transpacific economy than has the Republican Party, and tends to be more solicitous of these disadvantaged groups.

But as noted above, the role of organized labor in the American work force is in a process of long-term decline. The locus of influence in both the Democratic Party and the nation as a whole has shifted elsewhere, as the travails of Walter Mondale in the 1984 campaign and Richard Gephardt in 1988 would seem to indicate. Suburban and minority inner-city electorates appear to have gained relative salience for Democrats. More generally, the decline of organization in American politics, a continuing phenomenon since at least the 1950s, has made it more difficult for groups affected adversely by economic change to express their opposition effectively through the political process.

Confronting the Consequences: 1985 and After

Transformation in the structure of the American domestic political economy during the 1970s and early 1980s helped to sustain a remarkably open orientation in U.S. trade and investment policy through a period of depression in American industry and in agriculture in the Midwest and Northeast during the early 1980s. This openness toward imports and foreign investment accompanied the strong dollar and the huge current-account deficits generated by the Reagan administration's simultaneous defense buildup and tax cut. But the obverse side of this openness and the resulting economic efficiencies has been an erosion of the American industrial base, a structural dependence on imports, and political obliviousness to the rapid escalation of U.S. foreign debt at a pace that in the long run is not sustainable. At the end of 1987, net U.S. external liabilities were around $400 billion and increasing at the rate of $150 billion annually. By the early 1990s, if recent trends continue, the annual U.S. foreign debt service burden will be as large as the current yearly U.S.-Japan trade deficit.

The emergence of the transpacific economy, in short, has meant a surge of imports, stimulating competition, and an escalation of debt. These are mere abstractions until they must be paid back through a real decline in living standards vis-à-vis more productive parts of the Pacific basin. But that reckoning day must inevitably come.

Throughout the early 1980s, the United States was insulated from the long-run consequences of its declining productivity and rising debt by the anomalous strength of the dollar and the consequent eagerness of foreigners to invest in the United States. But following the Plaza international monetary accords of September 1985 and the steady subsequent revaluation of the yen and the Deutschmark, those inevitable long-run consequences have become increasing clear. Within little more than two years, the purchasing power of the yen in the United States doubled, while the value of dollars in Tokyo conversely fell to half of pre-Plaza levels. Although American exports to Japan have been frustratingly slow in rising, in part due to the complexity of the Japanese distribution system and the large share of the exchange rate profits to the Japanese nation as a whole that it absorbed, Japanese investment in the United States surged rapidly. In 1987 Japanese direct foreign investments in the United States rose to over $35 billion—nearly 50 percent higher than the previous year. This new surge of Japanese direct investment in the United States generated a range of new transpacific economic policy issues, such as the propriety of government restrictions on joint ventures and acquisitions, like the abortive Fujitsu effort to acquire Fairchild Semiconductors in 1981.

Among the perverse long-run consequences of the overvalued dollar of the early 1980s in the context of an emerging transpacific economy was the heavy and rapid erosion of the U.S. industrial base in semiconductors, particularly in advanced memory components. To offset some of the losses it suffered, the semiconductor industry went to government. What followed during 1986–87 was a clumsy intrusion of government into U.S.-Japan high-technology trade, which from the beginning had dubious objectives, limited prospects of success, and which ultimately aggravated U.S.-Japan relations without achieving substantial new market opportunities for American firms in Japan. MITI and the U.S. Department of Commerce negotiated an agreement to set guidelines for semiconductor prices and U.S. market shares in Japan. That agreement rapidly proved unenforceable, leading in the spring of 1987 to recriminations and the first U.S. retaliatory tariffs on Japanese exports to the United States since World War II.

At a bilateral level, the emergence of the transpacific economy during the 1970s and the early 1980s stimulated deepening economic and political interdependence between the United States and Japan, and frictions inevitably arose. Increasing American and Japanese intimacy had even more important implications for both nations in relation to the global political economy as a whole. As the world's largest creditor and debtor, with credits and debits of over $200 billion and $400 billion respectively at the end of 1987, Japan and the United States find themselves as the central actors in the international financial system. They are jointly responsible, to an unprecedented degree for two nations, for the stability of global exchange rates and capital markets.[28] Consuming together nearly 40 percent of world oil imports, the two nations also have a fundamental stake in the stability of world energy markets, and powerful incentives to cooperate to ensure that stability.[29]

Perhaps the most important consequences of the emerging transpacific economy are its profound implications for the national security of the United States and its allies, including Japan. As Robert Gilpin has pointed out, Japan since the late 1970s has become the most powerful and strategic supporter of American global hegemony, assuming a role played in the early postwar period by Great Britain, and subsequently by West Germany.[30] The principal mechanism of Japanese financial support until mid-1987 was Japanese private sector portfolio investment in the United States, which reached roughly $100 billion in 1986. During 1987–88 capital flows from Japan continued, although increasingly in the form of official flows; Bank of Japan holdings of dollar assets, for example, increased more than $30 billion for the second half of 1987. Thanks to these huge capital inflows from Japan, which began just as the Reagan administration began

28. Analysts on both sides of the Pacific are speaking of a "G-2" condominium dominating the international monetary system. See C. Fred Bergsten, "Economic Imbalances and World Politics," *Foreign Affairs* (Spring 1987): 789–93; and Funabashi Yoichi, *Nichibei Keizai Masatsu* (Japan-U.S. Economic Friction) (Tokyo: Iwanami Shinsho, 1987), pp. 194–230.

29. On the U.S. and Japanese roles in global energy markets, see Raymond Vernon, *Two Hungry Giants: The United States and Japan in the Quest for Oil and Ores* (Harvard University Press, 1983).

30. See Robert Gilpin, *The Political Economy of International Relations* (Princeton University Press, 1987), pp,. 134–51.

its major defense buildup, the United States was able to sustain both its huge defense buildup of the early 1980s and one of the most rapid rates of overall growth and employment creation among the major industrialized nations, without suffering a debilitating and politically disastrous credit crunch.

For the 1990s, American global defense commitments continue to loom large. But the intractable U.S. fiscal deficit and the increasing reluctance of foreign investors to fund it has cast into increasing doubt the United States' economic ability to sustain existing global commitments. Exchange-rate realignments set in motion by the Plaza Accords give Japan, together with West Germany, increasing economic capacity to share the American security burden. This ability has been enhanced still further in the Japanese case by the administrative reforms and domestic subsidy cutbacks of the early 1980s, coupled with important changes in tax structure introduced during 1988 by the Takeshita administration. Japan is increasingly capable of shouldering the cost of U.S. defense burdens, if it can be persuaded politically to do so.

During the early 1980s Japan steadily increased its so-called strategic foreign aid to nations like Pakistan, Oman, and Mexico, which were of demonstrable military and political importance to the United States. Following the fall of the Marcos regime, Japan also became the largest source of foreign aid to the Philippines. American assistance to nations hosting American bases was $1.47 billion in fiscal 1988, up from $941 million in 1980, although still $700 million less than the Reagan administration requested in 1988 from Congress.[31] Japan could expect to pick up an increasing share of such costs in the future while also assuming some share of the $6 billion expended annually by the United States for the actual operation of its foreign military bases under an indirect offset arrangement.

As the United States and Japan look to the future of a relationship that has come to have fundamental importance on the global scene, the underlying structure of their bilateral ties remains remarkably similar to the pattern with which they began their independent relationship together at the end of Allied occupation nearly forty years ago. The United States supplies the military security, while serving also as defender of open global markets for trade and finance that strongly benefit Japan, together with other U.S. allies. The rapid accumulation of American foreign debt, and the increasing reluctance of foreign investors to fund it, suggest with increasing urgency that the status quo is not indefinitely viable. The pressing challenge to both the United States and Japan is to find a means of smoothly sharing the economic burdens of global leadership so as to preserve an economic and security regime that has brought unprecedented prosperity to both countries and to the world as a whole since its inception four decades ago.

31. *Wall Street Journal*, 28 December 1987. The five nations in question were Turkey, Greece, Spain, Portugal, and the Philippines. Figures for 1988 represented subcommittee recommendations, with supplemental funding expected for the Philippines.

PART IV

THEORY AND PRACTICE OF DIPLOMACY

15

The Practitioner/Theorist in American Foreign Policy: George Kennan

DAVID MAYERS

BY PRACTICALLY any standard of evaluation, the diplomatic and intellectual career of George Frost Kennan has been as important as it has been fascinating. Virtually every student of twentieth-century U.S. foreign policy tries to come to grips with Kennan's position and role in policymaking, especially during the early Cold War, and with his scholarly evaluation of contemporary and historical American diplomacy. During the late 1920s and 1930s, he was one of a select group of Foreign Service officers who received specialized training about the Soviet Union, and was called upon in World War II and soon thereafter to provide the American government with advice and guidance as it sought to order its relations with the USSR. Throughout the critical years from 1946 to 1950, when the Soviet Union and the United States moved from being uneasy allies to major rivals, Kennan helped to define the problems and direction of U.S. foreign policy. Henry Kissinger has recorded appreciatively that "George Kennan came as close to authoring the diplomatic doctrine of his era as any diplomat in our history."[1] He also served in 1952 as ambassador to Stalin's Russia and during John Kennedy's administration was accredited as American envoy to Belgrade. As a critic of U.S. foreign policy, Kennan has always been lucid, often incisive,

---

1. Henry Kisssinger, *White House Years* (Boston: Little, Brown and Company, 1979), p. 135.

and widely followed, even though his views have never met with anything approaching universal agreement.

Indeed, since Walter Lippmann blasted the policy of containment as a "strategic monstrosity" in 1947, Kennan has been a controversial public figure, alternately heralded and damned by numerous critics, including liberals and conservatives, diplomats, journalists, and scholars. To the historian Louis Halle, Kennan's service during the Cold War was characterized by "Shakespearian insight and vision." John Paton Davies, a career diplomat and one of the original members of the State Department's Policy Planning Staff, has been especially impressed by Kennan's "intuitive and creative mind, richly stored with knowledge, eloquent in expression, and disciplined by a scholarly respect for precision." Though disappointed with some of his views, principally those regarding the Third World, the Harvard political scientist Stanley Hoffmann has likened Kennan's mind to the exact mechanism of a fine watch. The trustees of the Albert Einstein Peace Prize and the German Booksellers Association accorded him special recognition in the early 1980s as an outspoken, articulate opponent of the nuclear arms race. Yet, in the pages of *The New Republic* in 1977, Henry Fairlie attributed Kennan's advocacy of improved Soviet-U.S. relations to advancing senility. And William Buckley and the social scientists Paul Hollander and Paul Seabury have all expressed dismay at one time or another for what they regard as Kennan's transformation from an unabashed opponent of the USSR and supporter of firm policies against it to a promoter of a rather abject species of appeasement.[2]

The reason why Kennan has been the object of such intense conflicting feelings is that throughout his many years in government and later political counsel, he has written or recommended strongly about practically every important foreign policy dilemma that has confronted the United States from the period of Franklin Roosevelt to that of Ronald Reagan. These include not only the proper ordering of U.S. relations with Soviet Russia and the avoidance of another, even more catastrophic world war, but also America's relations with Europe, the Far East, and the Third World.

In a short essay, one cannot possibly touch on all of these policy issues; the topic of Kennan as a practitioner and theorist is immense and forces one to choose. Instead of discussing his role as a diplomat and policymaker, this essay will concentrate on Kennan the theorist. It should be stressed from the outset that this venture is somewhat risky, for the following reason. Kennan has never deliberately attempted to create a theory of international relations or of U.S. foreign policy. He has not produced any corpus of philosophical writings; rather,

---

2. Louis Halle, *The Cold War as History* (New York: Harper & Row, 1967), p. 116; John Paton Davies, *Dragon by the Tail* (New York: W. W. Norton & Co., 1972), p. 390; Stanley Hoffmann, "After the Creation or the Watch and the Arrow," *International Journal* (Spring 1973); Stanley Hoffman, *Duties Beyond Borders* (Syracuse University Press, 1981), pp. 102–3; Henry Fairlie, "The Special Senility of the Diplomat: Mr. X[2]," *The New Republic*, 24 December 1977; William Buckley, "George Kennan's Bomb," *National Review*, 4 April 1980; Paul Hollander, "The Two Faces of George Kennan," *Policy Review* (Summer 1985); Paul Seabury, "George Kennan vs. Mr. X," *The New Republic*, 16 December 1981.

he is a diplomat-turned-historian, who most of his life has eschewed theorizing as too constricting or simply irrelevant to the affairs of state. In other words, in referring to Kennan's theory, one should do so advisedly and probably place quotation marks around the term.

Nevertheless, this project of attributing a type of theory to Kennan—and trying to reconstruct and assess it—is worthwhile for a couple of reasons. First, it is simply the case that over the course of his long career, he has evolved a set of underlying concepts and assumptions that in their totality suggest a theory of politics and international relations—his impatience with academic social science and his skepticism about most formal philosophy notwithstanding.[3] In evaluating what might be construed as Kennan's theory, or what we can at least label as his philosophical precepts, we can also draw some broad conclusions about his overall contribution to U.S. foreign policy.

Albeit not deliberately created by him, Kennan's "theory" has informed his recommendations about every political and diplomatic dilemma that he has confronted, be it nuclear weaponry or the USSR or his thinking about America's social and domestic political problems. In turn, his personal experience with these matters has, quite naturally, further influenced his general views. Too scholarly to be a bland functionary, Kennan's advice as a government official was suffused with historical interpretations and ethical judgments. Too worldly to be only donnish or abstract, Kennan's notions about international policy are strikingly devoid of the misleading scientism and abstruseness that have spoiled so much of international relations theory in recent decades. His own contributions to theory are not without flaw, but on the whole they are instructive about the nature of world politics and helpful as a guide to U.S. action abroad.

In a certain sense, Kennan's ideas about politics and external affairs have the effect—despite his stated preference for other, particularly European, intellectual milieus—of placing him in a recognizable American tradition. His pronouncements about politics reverberate with echoes of American strains stretching from John Winthrop to Reinhold Niebuhr and Walter Lippmann and including Roger Williams, Alexander Hamilton, John Quincy Adams, and some of the more notable mugwumps.

As in Winthrop's instruction to the New England Calvinists that, to build a "Citty vpon a Hill," they must labor and suffer together as one body, so Kennan has enjoined his countrymen to greater discipline, collective effort, and purposefulness. In keeping with Roger Williams, who bore witness to the failure of Massachusetts as a model of Christian community and a willing victim of the "common Trinity" (profit, preferment, pleasure), Kennan has condemned America's straying from the gold of Puritan ascetic idealism and pursuing the dross of modern comforts. Like Hamilton, Kennan is by instinct and intellect a Federalist and has attributed many modern evils to the alleged excesses of democracy. Indeed, if any one person out of the American tradition can be singled out for his

3. Kennan to Professor Mead, 1950, File "2-A-1950" in Box 29, Kennan Papers; Kennan to Robert Lovett, 22 August 1947, Policy Planning Staff Papers, RG 59, NA; George Kennan, et al., *Encounters with Kennan: The Great Debate* (London: Frank Cass and Company, 1979), p. 82.

political commonality with Kennan, it must be Hamilton. They have both recommended national salvation in the form of increased governmental centralization and *dirigisme* to prevent the "raucous egalitarian republic" (Kennan's words) from spinning apart. Together they would insist on the executive branch as the sole legitimate center of gravity in handling all exceptional matters— foreign policy, as well as war. Although sharing with Thomas Jefferson a distrust of urban commercial culture and a predilection to wax eloquent on the virtues of nature and rural life, Kennan has been as likely as not to dismiss as "Jeffersonian heresy" any proposal that would further advance the influence of public opinion beyond presently established institutional arrangements.

In addition to invoking John Quincy Adams as an authority during testimony (about Vietnam) before the Senate, Kennan has regularly affirmed with him that the United States must set a modest international agenda for itself and resist the temptation of intervening on behalf of various putatively humane causes abroad, as recklessness in this regard leads to ruinous wars and the corruption of political life at home. In company with the mugwumps, Kennan has not been drawn to any party or partisans operating in American politics and has yearned for the day when the United States might cultivate a deeper tone and greater seriousness in its cultural and civic life. His displeasure, in fact his resentment, at the influx to American shores of millions of immigrants representing civilizations that share no affinity with his own recalls some of the typical mugwump ferocity on the subject (for example, that of E. L. Godkin). Similar to Lippmann, Kennan has exhibited the paradox of many modern pedagogues in combining a disdain for the popular mind and pessimism about its potential for growth with a vestigial Enlightenment optimism about education. Hence Lippmann's and Kennan's voluminous writings and lectures intended to tutor the public about political affairs. Finally, as to Niebuhr, whom Kennan has credited with exercising a greater intellectual influence on him than anyone else, the two of them—while differing in important ways, especially in their assessments of American democracy—have held out for an intellectual elite that would take upon itself the political and spiritual improvement of their nation. Whereas Niebuhr looked to what he termed a "prophetic minority," Kennan, at least once explicitly and many times implicitly, has called for a "protest minority" that would solemnly promote a level of aesthetics and ethics more attuned to life's verities than that produced by an overindustrialized, overarmed, overpolluting American society.[4]

Probably there is no adequate single label under which could be grouped those Americans with whom Kennan might be usefully compared. Still, the line of thought that combines these seventeenth-century New Englanders and later

4. Kennan, "Statement for National Book Awards," 6 March 1968, File "1-C-161" in Box 22, Kennan Papers; Raymond Aron, ed., *World Technology and Human Destiny* (University of Michigan Press, 1963), pp. 191–95; Kennan, "Sermon," 17 March 1963, File "1-C-120" in Box 20, Kennan papers; Kennan, *American Diplomacy* (University of Chicago Press, expanded ed. 1984), pp. 3–20. Also see Richard Fox, *Reinhold Niebuhr* (New York: Pantheon Books, 1985), p. 238. Fox reports that while Kennan did not recall (1980) describing Niebuhr as "the father of us all," he had an abiding appreciation for the theologian's "philosophical perspective."

mandarins is decidedly conservative in the conventional European, if not mainstream American, sense. At its most politically influential, this tradition—really a merging of Calvin and Burke—thrived in the 1790s under the guidance of Hamilton, but since his era it has become increasingly weak and diluted until in late twentieth-century America it has nearly completely disappeared. As there is no European-style social democratic party or conscience in the United States, neither is there a genuinely conservative one along (pre-Thatcher) British Tory or continental lines. Rather, as Kennan has ruefully noted, there is in a doctrinal sense only one sect of consensus—the two so-called parties being "ideologically undistinguishable, their pronouncements form[ing] one integral body of banality and platitude." In such a political setting, a conservative of Kennan's taste is fated for political isolation and continuous frustration; thus his repeated remarks that he is not a citizen of this epoch.[5]

Despite Kennan's feelings of political marginality, he has had some reason to feel, intermittently at least, at home in post-1945 America. As one who has been closely identified with the realist tradition in international relations, Kennan has been part of that school of thought that has dominated political science circles— through the person of Hans Morgenthau and his disciples—and has played a role in practical affairs, exemplified by the career of Henry Kissinger.

Within the framework of both those who have practiced and interpreted U.S. foreign policy, the realist school represents a basically centrist position. On the one hand, it is at odds with a host of apologists for America's alleged international exceptionalism. Historians such as Dexter Perkins and Samuel Bemis and practitioners like Woodrow Wilson and Cordell Hull have maintained that the United States is unique among nations because it has pursued policies of humane inventiveness (e.g., the United Nations) and liberality (e.g., the Marshall Plan and aid to poor countries), and affirms in its diplomacy the virtues of democracy and fairness. In Wilson's words, the United States is "the most unselfish nation in history."[6] On the other hand, the realist school has had to grapple with an economic interpretation of U.S. foreign policy represented by William Appleman Williams, Gabriel Kolko, and David Horowitz, among others, who claim that the mainspring of America's international behavior is the multiple requirements of domestic capital. According to these scholars, in the service of capital the United States government has followed an increasingly aggressive imperial policy that mocks professed American idealism and over the decades has forced Washington, on more occasions than a democratic polity can afford, to align itself with reaction and repression around the globe. To the realist, the United States has been neither singularly triumphant as a light to the nations and morally uplifting in its foreign policy, nor unusually venal. The actual lineage of the realist tradition in the United States originates in Alexander Hamilton, who in surveying the cause of international disputes and wars concluded, "To presume a

5. Aron, *World Technology*, p. 123: Terry Deibel and John Gaddis, eds., *Containment: Concept and Policy* (Washington, D.C.: National Defense University Press, 1986), p. 31.
6. Reinhold Niebuhr, "The Social Myths in the Cold War," in *Image and Reality in World Politics*, John Farrell and Asa Smith, eds. (Columbia University Press, 1967), p. 55.

want of motives for such contests would be to forget that men are ambitious, vindictive and rapacious."[7] And, alas, Americans are no exception, but they, like the rest of humanity arbitrarily divided into states, must scrap for survival and take those measures necessary to safeguard security and prosperity. In the twentieth century, Reinhold Niebuhr, Hans Morgenthau, and Henry Kissinger have in their distinctive ways each shared with Kennan this orientation toward foreign politics that emphasizes a pessimistic notion of human nature, is deeply suspicious of utopian schemes, and relies on prudence and a strict respect for the shifting dictates of the balance of power. Kennan himself expressed what might pass for the realist credo, as well as anyone else could have, when he impressed upon students at the National War College in 1950:

> the necessity of distinguishing constantly between that which is really important to us in this world in terms of potential power and that which is not. In doing that, I hope you will put aside such things as emotional judgment and moral indignation and require yourselves to look at our world environment absolutely coldly and realistically, with the clinical detachment of the surgeon or the research scholar, making a particular effort to understand precisely those things which are annoying and displeasing and irritating because they are the ones which are the most important to understand rather than to get mad about.[8]

As with any broad category of thinkers, there is among the American realists a wide spectrum stretching from orthodoxy to liberal to admixtures with other traditions; and it would be rash to minimize the differences, say, between Morgenthau, the political scientist, with his gothic conception of power and continuous struggle, and Niebuhr, the Christian theologian. So, too, Kennan can be distinguished from Kissinger, Morgenthau, and Niebuhr. Far more than any of them, he is a conservative in the late eighteenth-century meaning of that word and sees in modern nationalism and mass democracy the sources of the twentieth century's political instability and its unprecedented, disastrous wars. Indeed, what is most striking about Kennan's version of realism is that it blends principles of power politics with elements of conservatism (sometimes romantic) and an ethic of duty based on orthodox moral and religious precepts.

A Realist Perspective

The core of Kennan's realism and conservatism is rooted, like that of his Scottish Calvinist ancestors, in a view of human life and human nature that stresses tragedy and fallenness. Of the former and in reference to the individual self, Kennan has never lost sight of the ephemeralness of human experience, the chance phenomenon of injustice, the liabilities of the physical body, the loneliness of bereavement, and—taken from Freud—the endless conflict that arises

7. Clinton Rossiter, ed., *The Federalist Papers* (New York: New American Library, 1961), Hamilton No. 6, p. 54.

8. Kennan, "International Political Relations—Where We Are Going," 29 August 1950, Larry Bland Papers, Lexington, Va.

in civilization between the emotional needs and physical instincts of the individual and society's requirements of order and restraint. These phenomena are built into every human life and impart to it, in Kennan's vivid phrase, an "ineradicable tragic dimension that nothing can change." Nor has Kennan doubted the partiality of human knowledge and understanding or the essential corruption embedded in human personality. Having witnessed at close quarters the ill effects produced in individuals by poverty, war, and purges, he has come to gloomy conclusions about people's capacity for weakness and cruelty: "Panicky, violent, chaotic behavior is always closer to the surface of man's nature than many of us suppose."[9]

Like Niebuhr, Kennan holds that man's self-will and vanity limit all human enterprises without exception—no matter how selflessly phrased or altruistically conceived they might appear to their authors. The sad fact is that human vision and judgment are circumscribed from the outset by the overwhelming power of self-love. And it takes multiple perverse forms in political life, often in ways more subtle than just the familiar shapes of self-glory and self-vindication. In a 1969 article for the *Princeton Seminary Bulletin,* Kennan wrote with the experience of himself and former colleagues no doubt in mind: "The mere experience of participation in government is an unsettling thing. . . . It arouses and stimulates a whole series of human qualities that have nothing to do with Christian purposes: ambition . . . greed, envy, competitiveness, the love of public attention, the appetite for flattery. These motivations enter at a thousand points into the final product of any political effort."[10] In view of this consideration and in view of the imperfections of human life, Kennan has repeatedly suggested that governments and citizens would be well served by being self-consciously skeptical, even humble, about their most morally ambitious projects. Certainly, he believes that no scientific breakthrough—such as a Strategic Defense Initiative (SDI)—or application of a clever philosophical-political formula—such as Marxism—will ensure security or happiness or eliminate the tragic element from life.

For Kennan, as for virtually all traditional conservatives, civilization is fragile, and it cannot sustain violent shocks as caused by modern war or swift change. Vigorous diplomacy must preempt large-scale international violence; social and technological changes must come gradually. Like Burke, Kennan has consistently warned that abruptness and a supervelocity of change can shatter the vital fabric of society and of people's lives and cause vastly more harm than anyone ever intended. All utopian projects—the history of Russian Marxism being, for Kennan, a powerful example—provide persuasive evidence that not only are people unable to create paradise on earth, but their energetic and enthusiastic efforts to do so invariably cause boundless mischief. (Similarly in Kennan's mind,

9. Aron, *World Technology,* p. 191; Kennan's "talk" for Mount Kisco Conference, Summer 1963, File "1-C-129" in Box 21, Kennan Papers; Kennan, "Princeton Alumni Day Speech," 21 February 1953, File "1-B-22" in Box 2, Kennan Papers; Martin Hertz, ed., *Decline of the West? George Kennan and His Critics* (Washington, D.C.: Ethics and Public Policy Center, Georgetown University, 1978), p. 36.
10. Kennan, "The Relation of Religion to Government," *Princeton Seminary Bulletin* (Winter 1969): 43.

the accomplishments of American science and technology and the conveniences they have produced cannot compensate for the myriad difficulties they have inflicted on the environment or on human understanding about man's relationship with the natural order.) He connects the failure of political utopian schemes not only to the fact that they are impossible of achievement, but to the blindness of their sponsors to recognize that methods—witness the Bolsheviks' war communism or Stalin's later brutalities—will determine the practical outcome. Worthy results cannot follow from unworthy means; rather, the means determine, and often become, the end. The politically responsible person for Kennan, as for Morgenthau, therefore recognizes that all choice exists along a spectrum of evil; one must distinguish gradations and choose the least imperfect policy from various unhappy possibilities. Kennan has given this rationale for his reliance on an ethics of the lesser evil:

> In a less than perfect world, where the ideal so obviously lies beyond human reach, it is natural that the avoidance of the worst should be a more practical undertaking than the achievement of the best, and that some of the strongest imperatives of moral conduct should be ones of a negative rather than a positive nature. The strictures of the Ten Commandments are perhaps the best illustration of this state of affairs.[11]

Ever since his Walgreen lectures at the University of Chicago in 1951, Kennan has also taught that utopianism in international life will lead to confusion and often disaster. As with most realists, his portrayal of international relations is basically Thomas Hobbes's state of nature writ large: a conflict of all against all. In such a severe situation, in which the conventions of diplomacy and an etiolated species of law and international organization do not substitute for the continuing absence of a universally accepted moral or political authority, Americans cannot expect that a regime of order, justice, and peace will be allowed by sovereign, competitive states to prevail. And, alas, the record of American participation in attempts to outlaw war (the Kellogg-Briand Pact), to establish an embryonic world government, or to rescue foreigners from themselves (Vietnam) is a discouraging one. Kennan has expressed the hope that one day his countrymen will, as a mark of their own political maturity, come to accept the inherent limits of foreign policy:

> We are *not* going to change the nature of man, nor to solve the dilemmas of political society. We are not going to find means to overcome the great irrational, emotional currents that sweep through nations and races and entire world areas. . . . We are *not* going to be understood, as a nation. In many instances, we are *not* going to understand.

---

11. Kennan, et al., *Encounters with Kennan: The Great Debate*, p. 9; Kennan, "Sermon," 17 March 1963; Kennan, "Sermon," 15 April 1962, File "1-C-115" in Box 20, Kennan Papers; Kennan, "Christianity Reexamined," 6 December 1953, File "1-B-31" in Box 3, Kennan Papers; Kennan to Arnold Toynbee, 7 April 1952, File "1952" in Box 29, Kennan Papers; Michael Smith, *Realist Thought from Weber to Kissinger* (Louisiana State University Press, 1986), p. 139; Kennan, "Morality and Foreign Policy," *Foreign Affairs* 64, 2 (Winter 1985/1986): 212.

George Kennan, author of
the containment doctrine,
testifying before Congress on
Vietnam in 1966. "In a less
than perfect world . . . the
avoidance of the worst."
(AP/Wide World Photos)

All that Americans should do, apart from trying to make their own country a
more satisfying place in which to live, is to follow the precepts of moderation and
tolerance in foreign policy.[12]

Kennan's understanding of these principles has led him to object to the
fighting of total wars and the aim of unconditional surrender, to protest the
demonization of U.S. adversaries and the idealization of its associates, and to
urge the primacy of diplomacy over force. And his interpretation of these
principles accounts for his long-sustained campaign against American political-
moral evangelism. Since the early 1950s, when Father Edmund Walsh took
Kennan to task for his statement at Chicago that the United States ought not to
make itself into a slave of international law and morality, various critics have
charged him with believing that there is no place for concepts of right and wrong
in judging the actions of independent states—except in making Machiavellian
determinations about expediency. Walsh warned that such an ethic was appropriate only for the jungle and inadvertently helped lead to the exoneration of
totalitarian aggression and inhumanity. Was Stalin not subject to the moral laws
of the human race?[13] In recent years, critics have faulted Kennan for not more
forcefully condemning South African apartheid or Soviet persecution of Jews and

12. Kennan, *American Diplomacy*, pp. 95–103; Kennan, "Princeton Alumni Speech,"
21 February 1953; Kennan, "American Capitalist Democracy in a Collectivist Environment," 2 May 1947, p. 6, Policy Planning Staff Papers, RG 59, NA.
13. Kennan to *The New York Times*, 11 August 1952, File "1-E-3" in Box 26, Kennan
Papers; Barry Rubin, *Secrets of State* (New York: Oxford University Press, 1987), p. 42.

dissidents. His response, really a discourse conducted for over three-and-a-half decades about the role of morality in foreign affairs, has been coherent and reflects a Niebuhrian anxiety about the willfulness of national pride, oblivious to the dangers of hegemonial purpose and conceit.

In keeping with Niebuhr, Morgenthau, and other realists, Kennan has been eager to maintain the distinction between the moral obligations and ethical code of the individual person living in organized society and that of states existing in an anarchical system. Individuals in civil society can rightly be held to a fairly rigorous standard of personal ethical conduct, which in the case of martyrs, or saints, might even entail self-sacrifice. A government, however, operating in the foreign field, is charged with protecting its subjects' lives and property and beyond that is not properly concerned with anything else. Arthur Schlesinger, Jr., has described this position succinctly: "Saints can be pure, but statesmen must be responsible. As trustees for others, they must defend interests and compromise principles. In consequence politics is a field where practical and prudential judgment must have priority over simple moral verdicts."[14] Still, as Kennan once tried to assure James Shotwell (a proponent of the League of Nations and other forms of internationalism during the interwar period), an ethic of responsibility should be no more confused with an effort to promote cynicism in foreign policy than an ethic of ultimate ends. Kennan also told Shotwell that he had long despised the hypocrisy and the exploitation of moral sentiment by diverse American political leaders to gain domestic political advantage or to curry favor with one ethnic group or another. Besides, as he once wrote for another audience: "Morality is such a thing which, like dignity of character generally, loses its meaning and ceases to exist the moment one claims it or refers to it one's self."[15] True as this observation is in application to the individual, it is even more so in Kennan's view (taken from Niebuhr) in the case of nations: a people's self-perception is primitive, usually complacent and overdrawn, and the demon of collective self is almost impossible to subdue. Finally, as Kennan has often observed, the moral issue in any given international conflict is not always plain to see—even for a community based on shared values—and ascriptions of blame or praise are frequently meaningless. He would have us consider, for example, the Arab-Israeli dispute, in which neither side is wholly pure nor evil. This being so, the United States should seek solutions in a dispassionate manner and with the aim of containing the worst types of violence. In other words, nothing like a perfect solution is likely to exist for any international situation and Americans hamper their cause and that of others by incessantly invoking allegedly universalistic principles.[16]

14. Arthur Schlesinger, Jr., *The Cycles of American History* (Boston: Houghton Mifflin Company, 1986), p. 72.

15. Kennan to James Shotwell, 11 January 1957, File "2-B 1957" in Box 28, Kennan Papers; Kennan to George Kateb, 15 December 1967, File "2-B 1967" in Box 28, Kennan Papers.

16. Kennan to Senator Ralph Flanders, 30 November 1956, File "2-B 1956" in Box 28, Kennan Papers; Kennan, "Morality and Foreign Policy," 1957, File "1-E-14" in Box 26, Kennan Papers.

Too often, then, the American propensity to moralize has appeared to Kennan as a substitute for real decency and intelligence in diplomacy; only constant reference to its own national interest can safely guide the United States as it tries to steer through the maze of conflicts between itself and others and between third parties.

In contrast to Morgenthau, the national interest for Kennan does not possess anything so majestic as its own "moral dignity"; neither can it be defined concisely "in terms of power." Rather, he is relaxed about precise definitions of national interest. (Eugene Rostow was thus inspired to remark that his mind does not move along mathematical lines, but is like that of an impressionist painter or a poet.[17]) To Kennan, the U.S. government, like that of every country, must use foreign policy to foster conditions conducive to national security and prosperity. Americans might enjoy talking about a high-sounding national purpose that manifests itself in foreign policy, but this is a delusion. Like people everywhere, they are mainly involved in the struggle for economic well-being and living without undue hindrance from the outside. These purposes are not reprehensible in themselves, but neither do they constitute an elevated morality. They are fundamentally neutral from a moral standpoint and represent a necessity handed down by an inexorable historical process that has culminated in an international system still dominated by rival nation-states. Kennan has agreed that Americans naturally do and should let their moral values play a dominant role in domestic matters, and it would be folly for the United States to adopt internal policies that represent a degradation of national tradition—for example the 1947 Loyalty Order and boards of interrogation. Regarding other nations, however, Americans should judge not lest they themselves be judged. In 1957, he wrote:

> I do not profess to know—I prefer, in fact, to ignore—what is moral and virtuous for the sovereign state of Libya or Viet Nam. And while I should always be interested, as a matter of practical politics, to learn their views on the actions and diplomatic methods of my own country, I should be reluctant to accept instruction from the inhabitants of these states on what is right or what is wrong in the conduct of foreign policy. I should resent, in fact, the suggestion that their traditional concepts ought to be relevant to our problems.[18]

So, too, the United States should exercise a comparable measure of restraint and admit that it has not been appointed guardian of the world's virtue: let Americans practice their version of morality at home and by their adherence to it impress the world with their steadfastness and seriousness of purpose. At the same time, Americans must be made to understand that nothing is more dangerous than moral feeling divorced from responsibility. Kennan has recorded: "In the eyes of many Americans it is enough for us to indicate the changes that ought, as we see it, to be made. We assume, of course, that the consequences

17. Herz, *Decline of the West?*, p. 114.
18. Kennan to *The New York Times*, 11 August 1952; Kennan, "Morality and Foreign Policy," 1957.

will be benign and happy ones. But this is not always assured." The offending government and peoples must live with the consequences, not those Americans who enjoy measuring the moral deficiencies of others against the presumed superiority of their own qualities.[19]

The fact that Kennan has not discerned any unique genius or special excellence in the U.S. political system reinforces his objection to the impulse of American moral universalism. It is obvious to him that a country that is wasteful of its natural resources, is spiritually and physically weakened by bad living habits, and confuses the incidental longevity of its constitution and governmental institutions with wisdom has little, except by negative example, to teach others. And yet, at exactly this point, Kennan the *American* diplomat would interpose: regardless of the injuries it inflicts upon itself, regardless of its political defects, the United States can without apology expect that other states will, on the basis of reciprocity, respect U.S. interests abroad. According to Kennan, whatever failings they embody, Americans are not a warlike or aggressive people, and there is no reason that other countries cannot gracefully accommodate the United States on the basis of mutually tolerable arrangements.[20] To obtain these ends, the United States must unsparingly encourage its professional diplomacy.

Kennan has periodically likened the conduct of a state's diplomacy to that of good manners in personal life. In each case, the principal obligation is to one's self. And as dignity of behavior has its origins in the needs of the person who practices it—rather than in "external compulsion"—so do such qualities as integrity and courtesy in international life stem from the inner dynamics of a country. Not only do these qualities enable a state to coexist with others, more important, they allow a nation to live with itself. The United States, for example, must preserve and nourish a certain image on which is dependent self-respect and ultimately the continuation of successful national life. Therefore, Kennan has reminded audiences over the years, the United States has always been well served in practicing honesty, decency, and helpfulness in small things. On the other hand, pettiness and a gross insensitivity to others have hindered the advancement of U.S. foreign interests.[21] As for the actual vocation of diplomacy, it demands in Kennan's opinion persistence, composure, and personal equanimity. To be effective, the diplomat and negotiator must also renounce self-righteousness and realize that, as the best solution is unobtainable, one must concentrate on the acceptable. This implies that mechanical devices of multilateral treaties, international law, and so forth are inferior in ensuring peace to diplomatically inclined governments. Certainly, Kennan's preference has always been for the traditional flexibility and freedom to act unimpeded by mass domestic constituencies that characterized eighteenth- and nineteenth-century European diplomacy. Although he has readily acknowledged that such techniques and arts as practiced in previous centuries cannot be resurrected, he has urged his government not to move too rapidly away from them.[22]

19. Kennan, "Morality and Foreign Policy," Winter 1985/1986, p. 210.
20. Kennan, "Morality and Foreign Policy," 1957; Kennan, *Realities of American Foreign Policy* (Princeton University Press, 1954), pp. 47–50.
21. Kennan to Louis Halle, 3 January 1956, File "2-B 1956" in Box 28, Kennan Papers.
22. Kennan, "Morality and Foreign Policy," 1957.

Two of the important implications of Kennan's views on diplomacy are that the United States is not obliged to restrain violence between third parties or to practice charity on a large scale (for example, in trying to "develop" the Third World). Though it might sometimes be in the U.S. interest to perform one or both of these tasks, neither should be automatic. Just as the United States cannot serve as the international conscience, so, too, it should reject the Rooseveltian urge to police the world. Except in those instances that infringe upon the security or economic interests of the United States and its major allies, the undertakings or predicaments of great masses of people abroad should not be a cause to American diplomacy for moral or military excitement. The serious task of U.S. diplomacy is to find modalities and strike compromises with other states that will allow them all to continue as national entities and to develop, however they can, their particular talents.

To ensure their international success, Americans must not only deploy a skillful diplomacy, but they must attend to the power of example and the conditions of social health in their own polity. On this subject, perhaps on more than any other, Kennan has been adamant for decades. Sensitive to the point of personal anguish about his country's real (and imagined) shortcomings, Kennan has periodically pummeled it for lacking a sense of history, high culture, and refinement. The automobile has invaded and destroyed neighborhoods; rootlessness and an ethos of the peripatetic have killed any sense of community. These problems, combined with the country's low intellectual level of politics, have meant for Kennan, at times, that the United States is fundamentally lacking in texture, that it is boring. While he has discovered solace in a sort of personal antiquarianism, his Norwegian summer home, sailing, and other private pursuits, he has periodically recommended a "dramatic stiffening of public authority" for the United States. On the eve of the two-hundredth anniversary of the American Constitution, he suggested that it should be examined by a body of distinguished people to determine its suitability as a basis for government in the late twentieth century. As he has admitted on other occasions, his desire for a more disciplinary regime cannot be realized until a new philosophy (Kennan is vague here) has gained popular approval. In any case, however idiosyncratic he sometimes is on the subject, Kennan clearly belongs to that American political tradition that defines national greatness largely in terms of domestic behavior and cohesion. In 1985, at the National War College, he told an audience that the primary task of the United States for the foreseeable future was one of *self-containment:* it must master its fantastically high budgetary and trade deficits, cure its addiction to exorbitant defense spending, cease further violations against the environment, and carefully regulate the immigration of masses of people from alien political traditions. If the United States continues to live beyond its means and ignores its formidable domestic problems, it should not hope to play a constructive future role in world affairs.[23]

23. Kennan, "International Exchange in the Arts," *Congressional Record,* 27 January 1956; Kennan, "Commencement, 1955," *Social Research* 22, 2 (Summer 1955), pp. 127–37; Kennan to Dean Frank, 23 March 1964, File "2-B 1964" in Box 31, Kennan Papers; "unused material for memoirs," 1970, File "1-E-28:1970" in Box 27, Kennan Papers;

Nostalgia and Custodianship

As the above suggests, Kennan partakes deeply of the realist canon. Like Morgenthau, he has crusaded against the crusading and moralistic spirit of American foreign policy, has insisted on some version of the national interest as primary, and has uncompromisingly affirmed the superiority of diplomacy over the rigidity of military thinking on the one hand and naive internationalism on the other. With Niebuhr, Kennan has warned against national self-righteousness and has shared with him and Kissinger the conviction that the United States has been handicapped in its understanding of politics because, unlike the Europeans and their searing experience, the ebullient Americans are essentially nescient of life's darker side. And, like the British realist E. H. Carr (also a diplomat-turned-scholar), Kennan has repeatedly asserted that the ultimate success of the West in the Cold War—and by extension America's own international standing—ultimately depends on the resolution of issues related to internal resilience and on coping with the dilemmas of mass civilization.[24]

At the same time, Kennan's general thinking about international relations, foreign policy, and the United States has been permeated with some qualities that seem more distinctively his own or are, minimally, less germane to political realism as conventionally understood. For one thing, his version of conservatism—quite apart from its classically Burkean pessimism about human progress—has been anchored in an incurably romantic attachment for the past. In this respect, his realism suffers as it is oddly balanced by a kind of conservative utopianism in which the past possessed all manner of superior habits and institutions. By this standard of judgment, the United States reached its apogee in the age before televisions, automobiles, and great industrial conglomerations. In Kennan's imagination the "America of the barefoot boy and the whitewashed board fence, the America of the Webster cartoon . . . was a wonderful old America." In a similar nostalgic vein, he has expressed regret for the passing away of a quainter Department of State as it existed around 1900, when it was furnished with black leather rocking chairs and brass cuspidors, exuded quiet dignity and old-fashioned simplicity, and was peopled by truly cosmopolitan gentlemen. As for Europe, he has found particular merit in the multinational, Christian empires, exemplified by the Holy Roman Empire, and has expressed a marked preference for the world of pre-1789.[25]

Kennan, "The U.S., Its Problems, Impact and Image in the World," 2 December 1968, File "1-B-169" in Box 15, Kennan Papers; Kennan, "In the American Mirror," *The New York Review of Books,* November 1986, p. 6; Kennan's "talk" for Mount Kisco Conference, Summer 1963; Stanley Hoffmann, *Gulliver's Troubles or the Setting of American Foreign Policy* (New York: McGraw-Hill Company, 1968), p. 479; Kennan, "Morality and Foreign Policy," Winter 1985/1986; Kennan, "The Origins of Containment," in Deibel and Gaddis, *Contentment: Concept and Policy,* p. 30.

24. Representative works by realists other than Kennan include: E. H. Carr, *The Twenty Years' Crisis, 1919–1939: An Introduction to the Study of International Relations* (London: Macmillan Company, 1946); Reinhold Niebuhr, *Moral Man and Immoral Society: A Study in Ethics and Politics* (New York: Charles Scribner's Sons, 1932), *The Nature and Destiny of Man,* 2 vols. (New York: Scribner's, 1943, 1964), *The Irony of American History* (New York: Scribner's, 1952), *The Structure of Nations and Empires* (New York:

The consequences of this romantic idealization of the past are attractive in Kennan himself. It is related to his appreciation for traditions ceremonious, his personal courtliness, and his love and practice of a high literary style. This last trait, incidentally, apparently worried Dean Acheson as he feared he might become beguiled by Kennan's use of language into adopting ill-considered policies.[26] On the more serious side, Kennan's dreamy view of the past has caused him to exaggerate the defects of the modern world and to trivialize some of the past's more unpleasant aspects. His indulgent view of European imperialism in Asia and Africa, for example, has helped blunt his sensibility to Third World dilemmas and grievances and has caused him to adopt a defensive tone about them. Combined with the fact that he has not enjoyed good physical health while in tropical climes and has been given to some racial and ethnic stereotyping, Kennan's reservations about western collaboration with and assistance to Third World states are imbued with more than a standard realist's concern about national interest, technical feasibility, and overinvolvement.[27] Moreover, Kennan's preference for a mythical golden age of diplomacy when an aristocratic few masterfully sorted through international conflicts of power has misled him to the point where he finds almost nothing of value in modern summitry and not much more in international law, international public organizations, and multilateral negotiations. Now this is *not* to say that Kennan has been wrong in attacking the "stubborn illusion" of much American statesmanship that has regarded legal arrangements alone as adequate to absorb the strains and changes in strength of various countries. Indeed, à la Kennan, there is no substitute for sustained diplomacy in the nuclear age and for steady statesmanship. But, as he was forced to admit in 1950 when the United States government debated whether to build the hydrogen bomb and as he has recognized throughout the 1980s, unless clear-eyed diplomacy receives some additional boost in the form of new concepts and creativity, then the perils of the nuclear era will linger indefinitely.[28] In addition, contrary to Kennan, Americans

---

Scribner's, 1958), *The Children of Light and the Children of Darkness* (New York: Scribner's, 1945); Hans Morgenthau, *Scientific Man vs. Power Politics* (University of Chicago Press, 1946), *Politics Among Nations* (New York: Alfred A. Knopf, latest ed. with Kenneth Thompson, 1985). Recent critical books about realism include: John Vasquez, *The Power of Power Politics: A Critique* (Rutgers University Press, 1983); J.E. Hare and Carey Joynt, *Ethics and International Affairs* (New York: St. Martin's Press, 1982); Michael Smith, *Realist Thought from Weber to Kissinger* (Louisiana State University Press, 1986); Robert Keohane, ed., *Neorealism and Its Critics* (New York: Columbia University Press, 1986).

25. Kennan, *Realities of American Foreign Policy*, p. 109; Kennan, *American Diplomacy*, pp. 91–92; Kennan to R.E. Ward, 26 November 1952, File "2-A-1952" in Box 29, Kennan Papers. Also see my "Nazi Germany and the Future of Europe: George Kennan's Views, 1939–1945," *International History Review* viii, 4 (November 1986): 550–72.

26. Kennan, "Commencement Speech at Dartmouth College," 11 June 1950, File "1-C-8" in Box 18, Kennan Papers; Loy Henderson interview, 3 October 1970, File "14" in Box 8, C. Ben Wright papers, Lexington, Va.

27. Kennan to Bernard Gufler, 12 April 1952, File "2-A-1952" in Box 29, Kennan Papers.

28. Kennan to Erich Hula, 13 February 1957, File "2-A-1952" in Box 29, Kennan Papers; Kennan, *The Nuclear Delusion* (New York: Pantheon Books, 1983), pp. ix–xxx.

need not be wary of conferences between their leaders and those of the Soviet Union. They can be useful so long as both sides meet in good faith, do not posture or raise unrealistically grand expectations, and view such exercises as the symbolic ratification of negotiations successfully completed. As for multilateral meetings, they are indeed cumbersome and prone to propagandistic abuse, but it is also certain, as never before in history, that some international problems— including those important to Kennan: nuclear proliferation, global pollution, population explosion—canot be managed on bilateral or ad hoc bases.

Kennan's fancy that the pre-1789 world enjoyed a social coherence, intellectual balance, and basic reasonableness all notably absent in contemporary life has inclined him to embrace a dubious, antidemocratic viewpoint in politics and diplomacy. Staunchly opposed to egalitarianism in political and other walks of life, he has never doubted that sophisticated foreign policy can only be conducted by trained, dedicated individuals not forced to consult constantly with an emotional Congress and uninformed public.[29] As illustrated by his 1942 plans for a foreign service academy, he has even thought it possible to produce a quality of statesmanship from which venality, indiscipline, and other forms of human frailty have been bred out.[30] Kennan's problem here, however, again derives from his version of conservative utopianism as it fails to deal adequately with the potential abuse of power or failure of leadership by political and diplomatic officers not subject to public accountability. Even the "best" people, irrespective of their background and capacity, are subject to misjudgments, temptations, and all the other failings of mortal men and women—as Kennan the Calvinist and student of Niebuhr should more readily have acknowledged. As Niebuhr might have protested, it was, for example, a combination of unbridled pride of power and pride of knowledge that led the "best and brightest" of one generation to commit the United States to a hopeless war in Southeast Asia. In other words, given the absence of angels and philosopher-kings in government, and given the contingent character of all human purposes—including the formulation and execution of U.S. foreign policy—democratic constraints have a useful role to play in diplomacy. From a purely theoretical standpoint, as per Plato's Republic, this is not a perfect situation. But, in view of the actual condition of human material, it is not so bad as the worst case: policy by autocrats. Finally, contrary to Kennan's presumption, the broad citizenry in a representative democracy is not necessarily more intemperate or unreasonable than its government. From his perspective, it must have struck Kennan as ironic when a December 1981 Gallup poll indicated that 75 percent of American adults supported his proposal for a one-half reduction of all Soviet and U.S. nuclear weapons, while the government and

---

29. Barton Gellman, *Contending with Kennan* (New York: Praeger, 1984), p. 100; Kennan, "Seminar Essay," File "1-E-19" in Box 26, Kennan Papers; Kennan, "Philosophy and Strategy in America's Postwar Policy," 11 May 1965, File "1-C-141-IV" in Box 21, Kennan Papers.

30. For an assessment of Kennan's ideas for an improved foreign service and a foreign service academy, see my "Young Kennan's Criticisms and Recommendations," *Biography* 8, 3 (Summer 1985): 227–47.

its battery of experts on diplomacy and armaments either ignored or denounced the idea.[31]

While Kennan's conservative disposition and interpretation of history are the source of his complaint against various expressions of modernity, they have also served positive ends; in particular, they have been a source of insight and have helped sustain his eloquent pleas, both in government and since, for diplomacy and the avoidance of large-scale interstate violence. Central to Kennan's thinking, especially in recent decades, has been the concept of custodianship. Constant in expressing appreciation for natural beauty, the sturdiness of Christian faith, and the aesthetic and intellectual achievements of great civilizations, Kennan has derived from these a sense of the obligation to be discharged by the present generation: to pass the planet on to succeeding generations in a condition no poorer or less able to support "the wonder of life" than that in which they received it. This duty also stretches backward in time and entails a responsibility to history and its progression through the ages of man and nature. In the words of Kennan the Christian moralist:

> We of this generation are only the custodians, not the owners, of the earth on which we live. There were others who lived here before, and we hope there will be others who are going to live here afterward. . . . We have an obligation to both of them, to past generations and to future ones, no less than our obligations to ourselves. I fail to see that we are in any way justified in making, for the safety or convenience of our own generation, alterations in our natural environment which may importantly change the conditions of life for those who come afterward. The moral laws which we acknowledge predicated the existence of a certain sort of world—a certain sort of natural environment—in which the human predicament had its setting. This presumably reflected God's purpose. We didn't create it; we do not have the right to destroy it. . . . When we permit this environment to be altered quite basically by things we do today, and altered in ways the effects of which we cannot even predict, we are taking upon ourselves a responsibility for which I find no authority in Christian faith.[32]

From these considerations have sprung Kennan's refrains against further testing of nuclear weapons and nuclear stockpiling and his insistence on serious diplomacy as a means of averting catastrophic Soviet-U.S. war. He has also advised Americans to tailor their general foreign policy so that it does not run against the complex, organic processes of international life: the great forces of nationalism, rapid social change, technological progress, and the rest cannot be decisively affected by American will or power. Rather, for Kennan the United States must approach international issues with the patience of the gardener and work to influence the world environment in a direction that will contain or prevent fatal explosions.[33] This sensibility in turn requires Americans to under-

31. J.A. Nathan and J.K. Oliver, *Foreign Policy Making and the American Political System* (Boston: Little, Brown and Company, 1986), pp. 221, 227.

32. Kennan, "Certain World Problems in Christian Perspective," 27 January 1959, File "1-B-78" in Box 7, Kennan Papers.

33. Ibid.; Kennan, "Why Do I Hope?" 13 February 1966, File "1-B-143" in Box 12,

stand that one's adversaries do not have a monopoly on evil, but have an ordained role to play within a vast scheme of history and purpose that surpasses human understanding.[34]

Conclusions

In its essence, Kennan's intellectual career represents the submerged European conservative tradition in American political thought. Its strengths and its penetration, its weaknesses and its embarrassments, are equally Kennan's. This strain of thinking has never really commended itself to the jaunty American outlook, based on optimism, materialistic success, and the legend of the rugged individual who triumphs over all odds. And certainly the familiar themes of Kennan's and earlier conservatism are not in keeping with the irrepressible temper of twentieth-century (pre-Vietnam) Americans, be they conventional liberals or Republican conservatives.[35]

To begin with, Kennan's religiosity, his occasional tart remarks about "sickly secularism," and his unabashed conviction that all reliable ethics reside in religious beliefs run counter to the prevailing liberal consensus, which rests on a wide tolerance of competing viewpoints and ways of living. And to those Republicans of the Reagan stripe who still dominate their party, Kennan must be a source of incomprehension when he says that evil is not an external problem located in America's adversaries—be they global communism, the Soviet Union, or Iran. Against this simplemindedness, he has brought to bear the devastating insight of those seventeenth-century New England divines who were not deceived about the pervasiveness and ingeniousness of evil; its stain attaches equally to American and non-American alike. Speaking of anticommunism in 1964, Kennan declared:

> I must reject it . . . and not just as a matter of critical logic, but rather out of a sense of Christian duty, because it implies a certain externalization of evil—a tendency to look for evil only outside ourselves—which is wholly incompatible with Christian teaching. Evil is an omnipresent substance of human life: around us and within us as well as without us. . . . When we struggle against it we must always regard that struggle as in part an overcoming of self. We cannot, for this reason, identify ourselves self-righteously with all that is good and clothe whatever opposes us in the colors of unmitigated evil.[36]

Kennan Papers; Kennan's "talk" for Mount Kisco Conference, Summer 1963; Kennan, "Education for What?," 30 March 1960, File "1-C-95" in Box 20, Kennan Papers; Kennan, "Remarks at Stevenson-for-President Committee," 30 April 1956, File "1-C-56" in Box 19, Kennan Papers; Kennan, *Realities of American Foreign Policy*, pp. 93–94; Aron, *World Technology and Human Destiny*, p. 183.

34. Kennan, "The Relation of Religion to Government," p. 47; Kennan, "Sermon," 18 October 1963, File "1-B-27" in Box 3, Kennan Papers; Kennan, "The Ethics of Anti-Communism," 28 October 1964, File "1-B-128" in Box 10, Kennan Papers.

35. See Clinton Rossiter's still timely and very good *Conservatism in America: The Thankless Persuasion* (New York: Vintage Books, 1962). Chapter 7 contains a useful comparison between European and U.S. versions of conservative principles.

36. Kennan, *Democracy and the Student Left* (Boston: Little, Brown and Company,

Kennan also recognized in assuming the roles of a diplomat and policymaker that he (as Max Weber taught) had of necessity to contract with "diabolical forces." This realization could account for his willingness to live only on the "fringes of power." Except for one inhibition or another, Kennan might have pursued personal power beyond the rank of counselor of state or ambassador. Elements within the Democratic Party were prepared to support his running for Congress or the Senate, but he declined. Greater taciturnity and a willingness to go along with the prevailing line might have won him a more secure position within Acheson's State Department, or saved his career under Dulles's regime, preserved his standing with Adlai Stevenson, and won him some position more significant than envoy to Belgrade during Kennedy's administration. But he was clearly ambivalent about governmental work and often on the verge of official resignation from it. The administration of executive power even within so limited a setting as an embassy or the Policy Planning Staff did not come naturally to him, and he was an ineffective bureaucratic operator. Did the prospect of exercising greater power in a larger arena so unsettle him that he *chose* not to seek it? From a purely philosophical standpoint, he certainly did not fully share Niebuhr's hope (and expectation) that justice could really be implicated in the manipulation of U.S. power abroad.

And yet any case to be made about Kennan's reluctance to accept increased political responsibilities must take into account his earlier personal ambitions and vanity. As a young diplomat posted in Moscow, he could be snobbish toward fellow Foreign Service officers who lacked his training in and understanding of Russian history, language, and politics. As an instructor at the National War College, he was proud that his lectures were often attended by cabinet officers, generals, and senators. And he was careful at that delicate time in his career (1946–47), when he was acquiring both reputation and position, not to let his interpretations alienate the affections of people who could advance his career. This concern was evident when he trimmed his memorandum—later the "X article"—for Secretary James Forrestal. Similarly, when George Elsey sent to Kennan in 1946 a draft of the Clifford-Elsey report, which went further in recommending military measures against the Soviets than he thought advisable, he muted his stronger objections and offered only minor suggestions for improvement.[37] He might also have pushed harder than he did in 1947–48 to let Lippmann know that the two men were in substantial agreement about Soviet aims and U.S. policy despite misimpressions caused by the "X article." But then, would such clarification by the Director of Policy Planning have complicated his

---

1968), p. 189; Kennan, "Morality and Foreign Policy," *Foreign Affairs* 64, 2 (1985/1986): 217; Kennan, "The Ethics of Anti-Communism," 1964.

37. The phrase "the fringes of power" is from the title of John Colville's published diaries, *The Fringes of Power: 10 Downing Street Diaries, 1939–1955* (New York: W. W. Norton and Company, 1985); Kennan, *Memoirs: 1925–1950* (Boston: Little, Brown and Company, 1967), p. 306; Walter Isaacson and Evan Thomas, *The Wise Men* (New York: Simon & Schuster, 1986), p. 376; Hugh De Santis, *The Diplomacy of Silence* (University of Chicago Press, 1980), pp. 15–16. For more about Kennan's relations with Acheson, Dulles, and Stevenson see my *George Kennan and the Dilemmas of U.S. Foreign Policy* (New York: Oxford University Press, 1988), chaps. 7–10.

Returning to diplomatic service, Kennan presents his credentials as U.S. ambassador to Yugoslavia's Tito, May 1961. (Wide World Photos)

relations with Forrestal and further irritated George Marshall, at the time already miffed by what he considered to be Kennan's indiscretion in *Foreign Affairs*?[38] None of this speculation is meant to suggest that Kennan was a dissembler, but like most people he was trying to get by without giving undue offense to individuals who could be professionally helpful. Still, the ambivalence remained strong in Kennan. While he wanted to be appreciated in the late 1940s by the government as a resident intellectual and to be deferred to in matters of large interpretation, he hesitated or became annoyed when powerful people invoked his concepts (e.g., containment), but put them into practice in ways that made him uneasy.

Irrespective of the complications that surrounded Kennan's attitude about exercising power and increased responsibility, his career possibilities in government were doubtless restricted by his aversion to both practical politics and America's mass democracy. While PPS director, he was too impatient and otherwise engaged to bother much with rallying support—either in the government apparatus or in the larger public—for policies that he thought were obviously worthwhile. Very likely, had he ever come to occupy a major political position, say, secretary of state, he would have failed even more than Acheson to retain public support for foreign policy. Later, as a private citizen, had he been able to overlook some of the less appealing aspects of the anti-Vietnam pro-

38. For more about the circumstances surrounding Kennan's writing of the "X article" and his reaction to Lippmann's criticisms, see my "Containment and the Primacy of Diplomacy: George Kennan's Views, 1947–1948," *International Security* II, 2 (Summer 1986): 124–62.

testors, he could have helped improve their diplomatic-political education. And their popular movement might have served him well as a vehicle by which to spread his thoughtful objections against the war to the nation at large. Only recently and in a qualified way has Kennan permitted his name to be associated with a mass movement—that against nuclear testing and arms buildup.

It is really as a diagnostician of American and international problems and as a prescriber of remedies, rather than as an implementer, that Kennan must finally be evaluated. And here, on balance, the record is very strong. However near he might have come to it, Kennan in the end has not completely despaired of the United States. As a consequence, he once entertained hopes for a third political party (oriented toward environmental issues); he has tried teaching his compatriots to distinguish between the appearance of morality and its real substance in foreign policy; and he has reminded them that ultimate international success for a wealthy, diverse, continental-sized state will be decided in the domestic sphere. This last point is especially important for Americans at large, whose understanding—witness the Reagan government—of national power and prestige tends to be depressingly narrow. Military might, after all, is only one feature of a country's strength; by emphasizing it and neglecting other aspects of power, the United States threatens to damage its overall security and world standing. Although Kennan might not phrase it this way, it is consistent with his viewpoint that continued neglect of social programs will eventually leave the United States less well nourished, less well tutored, and more divided than it can afford. Unless a comprehensive campaign against poverty, urban blight, and environmental destruction is aggressively fought, the United States as a power in the conventional sense and an exemplar of enlightened wealth and orderly liberty will fade, just as Kennan has warned. As for the weaknesses in his assessment of the United States, the chief one—apart from a stunning myopia about immigrants and related ethnic issues—has been his inability to grant that representative democracy and its institutions have virtues that should recommend them to a conservative mind. Admittedly, American political institutions are not especially efficient and are often not run by high-minded people. But they are more responsive and appropriate as a corrective to a national leadership's misjudgment or moral waywardness than any realistic application of Kennan's elite principle.

Respecting foreign policy, Kennan's brand of conservatism holds little that can be very helpful in the management of relations between the Third World and the West. The existing structural problems of the international economic order are lost on him, as is a strong sense of the need to alleviate harsh conditions in the Third World in order to promote stability in a global system that, for good or ill, is increasingly interdependent. Yet Kennan's other contributions to an understanding of U.S. foreign policy have been astute. In the past, he has wisely counseled that to be effective the United States must recognize the limits of its power, acknowledge some hierarchy of interests abroad, play national differences in the communist world against each other, and pursue moderate balance of power policies in Europe and the Far East. As for the promotion of human rights, Kennan has recognized that the U.S. government is more often effective when it uses discreet and diplomatic means than when it publicly bludgeons another regime—for example, the USSR and the Jackson-Vanik legislation. Kennan's most significant lesson for Americans is to be patient with history and historical processes. This is particularly important advice for a nation that traditionally has assigned a positive value to historical forgetfulness. While it might make sense—for purposes of integrating and forming a society from people of diverse cultural and racial backgrounds—that Americans not dwell on their respective heritages, their eagerness to assimilate has come at psychological cost to the American collectivity as well as to the individual. One of these costs is to place a low premium on history. Kennan has insisted that international problems can be understood only when viewed in their historical context and that successful diplomacy requires taking the long view of both problems and solutions. Certainly, his emphasis on patience and on allowing the forces of reform adequate time to begin operating in Soviet internal and foreign policies seems vindicated as Gorbachev's innovations—even more than Khrushchev's before him—represent that very mellowing of Soviet paranoia and police power for which Kennan (in the 1947 "X article") hoped.

To study Kennan is far more than an examination of American foreign affairs; it is to study diplomacy as an art and international relations in a universal context. He himself would undoubtedly agree that the character of world politics is incompatible with "progressivist theory" and that international history is foremost a story of evanescent success and of tragedy. In certain measure, Kennan would also accept the severe truth of Thucydides' Athenian at Melos that in international affairs, "they that have odds of power exact as much as they can, and the weak yield to such conditions as they can get."[39] And yet, while Kennan has warned against extravagant forms of internationalism that promise more than they can deliver, he has not given up on a world in which diplomacy and national self-restraint still exist. The following statement of Kennan's is really a testament of faith in diplomacy and the politics of amelioration:

> The best humanity can hope for . . . is an even and undramatic muddling along on its mysterious and unknowable paths, avoiding all that is abrupt, avoiding the great orgies of violence that acquire their own momentum and get out of hand—continuing, to be sure, to live by competition between political entities, but being sophisticated and wise about the relationships of power: recognizing and discounting superiority of strength . . . rather than putting it suicidally to the test of the sword—imagining the great battles rather than fighting them; seeing to it that armies, if they must be employed at all, are exercised . . . "by temperate and indecisive contests"; remembering at all times that civilization has become a fragile thing that must be kept right-side up and will not stand too much jolting and abuse. In this sort of world, there is no margin for that form of self-indulgence which is called moral indignation, unless it be indignation with ourselves for failing to be what we know we could and should have been.[40]

39. Alastair Buchan, *Can International Relations Be Professed?* (Oxford: Clarendon Press, 1973), p. 12; Richard Schlatter, ed., *Hobbes's Thucydides* (Rutgers University Press, 1975), p. 379.
40. Kennan to Arnold Toynbee, 7 April 1952, File "1952" in Box 29, Kennan Papers.

At the core of Kennan's conception of diplomacy is a preoccupation with the continuity and intrinsic value of human cultures and history. As the West's supreme object must be the preservation of its civilization, and as the overriding challenge to Soviet and U.S. leaders is to avoid nuclear war, this understanding of Kennan's will have to prevail.

16

John Foster Dulles: Theorist/Practitioner

RICHARD D. CHALLENER

THROUGHOUT his career as secretary of state and for nearly two decades afterward John Foster Dulles was regarded as the chief architect of American foreign policy from 1953 until his death in 1959. His president, Dwight David Eisenhower, so ran the conventional wisdom, was the man of garbled syntax who delegated responsibility for American diplomacy to his subordinate and cared less about burning issues than about sinking his putts at Burning Tree.

But in the last decade, that interpretation has changed—and changed dramatically. With the opening of the Eisenhower papers and publication of new volumes in the *Foreign Relations* series, historians have recognized—some, to be sure, grudgingly—that Dwight Eisenhower was fully involved in every aspect of his administration, and in every major policy decision. He was never the chief executive who reigned but did not govern. Foreign policy decisions were not just handed over to Foster Dulles; rather they were shared decisions to which both men contributed equally. Some political scientists, most notably Fred Greenstein, have praised Eisenhower's "hidden hand" leadership as particularly effective, while an increasing number of political economists, whether they are concerned that America is a "declining hegemon" or simply appalled by present-day budget deficits and trade imbalances, show more than a little sympathy for Eisenhower's insistence that excessive military expenditures threatened the economic health of the nation. John Gaddis, in sharp criticism of Presidents Kennedy and Johnson, has recently concluded that their departure from the

Eisenhower tradition in foreign policy produced a devastating gap between intentions and results. "The Kennedy and Johnson administrations," he maintains, "would have done better to stress . . . those aspects of their strategy that reflected the Eisenhower legacy and to steer clear of those that did not."[1] Clearly, in the historical profession Eisenhower revisionism has moved from being a cottage to a big industry.

Similarly, no contemporary historian would continue to portray Dulles as simply the Presbyterian moralist who thundered about atheist communism, preached massive retaliation, and regarded the Sino-Soviet bloc as monolithic and unbreakable. The latest writings of John Gaddis, for example, stress that Dulles's ideas about the actual use of atomic weapons were measured, balanced, and judicious and that he was among the first to practice "self-deterrence" with respect to the use of atomic weapons. Additionally, it is argued that he developed a sophisticated strategy of pressure to separate Beijing from Moscow.[2] At a recent conference on John Foster Dulles held at Princeton in February 1988, several speakers insisted that Dulles did not regard all forms of neutralism as immoral and was far more open than previously imagined to the possibility of significant negotiations with the Soviets.[3] Clearly, it is no longer, as Townsend Hoopes once wrote, the Devil and John Foster Dulles.

Although Eisenhower stock is up in the current historical market, it is still appropriate to consider Dulles as both a theorist and a practitioner. In the 1950s, after all, both the press and the public did regard him as the man who made American foreign policy. It was Dulles who on a day-to-day basis most frequently articulated the administration's position on Cold War issues; and in the cabinet and National Security Council, he was—with the possible exception of Treasury Secretary George Humphrey—the most influential member. Moreover, the Eisenhower style of leadership was to put men like Dulles in the highly visible forefront and let them take the criticism and the flak—a tactic he employed to keep his options open. It was the way Ike had run World War II, when General Bedell Smith served as the point man in the controversies with such military prima donnas as Patton and Montgomery, thereby enabling Eisenhower to remain above the immediate battle. But one of the most compelling reasons for continuing to study Dulles is that he himself consciously sought the limelight.

Like his later successor, Al Haig, he wanted to give the impression that he was in charge. "I think that Foster," his immediate successor Christian Herter once wryly commented, "always liked it being a Dulles policy."[4]

There are three interrelated keys to the understanding of John Foster Dulles.

1. John Lewis Gaddis, "The Eisenhower Legacy and American Grand Strategy, 1960–1968," preliminary paper prepared for U.S. Military Academy Symposium "The Theory and Practice of American National Security, 1960–1968," 15–18 April 1988.

2. John Lewis Gaddis, *The Long Peace: Inquiries into the History of the Cold War* (New York, 1987), pp. 123–46, 174–94.

3. John Foster Dulles Centennial Conference, "The Challenge of Leadership in Foreign Affairs," held at the Woodrow Wilson School of Public and International Affairs, Princeton University, 25–27 February 1988. The papers are currently being edited for eventual publication.

4. Interview with Christian Herter, Dulles Oral History Project, Mudd Library, Princeton University (hereafter cited as DOH).

President Eisenhower and Secretary Dulles. (Courtesy Dwight D. Eisenhower Library)

There is, first of all, his long career as one of the most successful corporate lawyers on Wall Street in the 1920s and '30s, a man deeply involved in the legal side of American private foreign investment in Europe—most notably in Weimar Germany. The second key is his role in the late thirties and throughout World War II as churchman and prominent lay leader of American Protestantism in its crusade to give America its "second chance" to fulfill the internationalist vision of Woodrow Wilson. The third key is his own personal—and his family's—direct involvement in the making of American foreign policy. His maternal grandfather, John Foster, had been Benjamin Harrison's secretary of state, and his uncle, Robert Lansing, had served Woodrow Wilson in the same capacity. Foster Dulles himself had played a not insignificant role in the development of reparations policy at the Paris Peace Conference in 1919; by 1940 he had emerged as Governor Thomas Dewey's foremost adviser in foreign policy; he was an adviser at the San Francisco conference that established the United Nations and later served on American delegations to the General Assembly; and, as one of the architects of postwar bipartisan foreign policy, he had served as Republican adviser and consultant to the Truman administration, most prominently in negotiating the Japanese Peace Treaty.[5]

This background helps to explain many of Dulles's decisions and much of his behavior after he became secretary of state in 1953. His legal background often led him to produce documents that, to his critics, seemed to be legal briefs

5. For more detailed information about Dulles's career before 1953, see Ronald W. Preussen, *John Foster Dulles: The Road to Power* (New York, 1982), especially pp. 276–87; and Mark Toulouse, *The Transformation of John Foster Dulles: From Prophet of Realism to Priest of Nationalism* (Macon, Ga., 1985).

designed to defend and protect his client, the government of the United States. Anthony Eden believed that the Suez Canal User's Association—the device that Dulles put forth in the early months of the Suez crisis in 1956—was simply a document deliberately filled with legal loopholes through which the United States could escape, leaving Great Britain holding an empty Egyptian bag.[6] SEATO was primarily a lawyer's document, a treaty whose primary purpose was to secure the written commitment of both Congress and America's European allies to possible future intervention in the Far East in the aftermath of Dien Bien Phu, the Geneva Conference, and the failure of "United Action." Even Dulles's strongest advocate, Dwight Eisenhower, once suggested that his secretary of state sometimes came across as an international prosecuting attorney, and he once asked him to tone down a speech that sounded too much like an indictment of the Soviet Union.[7]

On the other hand, while John Foster Dulles was not a man for all seasons, his religious upbringing and his close associations with the church made him particularly effective in using the traditional language of American Protestantism to sustain and encourage the American people in the great crusade against communism. The bitter family memory of how Robert Lansing had been excluded from the policymaking process at the time of Wilson's illness in 1919 informed the advice he gave Richard Nixon and Sherman Adams to hold cabinet meetings at the time of Eisenhower's heart attack.

Two items from his own immediate political and diplomatic experience are of special relevance. Dulles had closely observed the way in which his predecessor, Dean Acheson, had become the prisoner of his critics—most notably his congressional critics—in the bitter, partisan debates that followed the "loss" of China, the furor over domestic subversives, and the frustrations of the stalemated war in Korea. Thus from the onset he made a conscious, deliberate attempt to build a domestic base of support in the United States Senate, especially with those conservative Republicans who were not only zealous supporters of Chiang Kai-shek but who also believed that most American diplomatic troubles arose from the presence of alleged subversives in the Department of State. Moreover, Foster Dulles, in his capacity as chairman of the board of the Carnegie Endowment for International Peace, had been the employer of Alger Hiss and had gone to unusual lengths to try to dissociate himself from Hiss both before and during the latter's famous perjury trial. Consequently, Dulles, determined that there would be "no Alger Hisses" aboard during his watch and equally determined to win the support of the Republican Right, brought the objectives, if not the tactics, of McCarthyism into the Department of State. An early speech to the department demanded "positive loyalty," while he himself personally examined every case of suspected loyalty brought before him by his

6. For Eden's reaction to the User's Association, see *Full Circle: The Memoirs of Anthony Eden* (Boston, 1960), pp. 529–44.
7. Eisenhower to Dulles, 8 September 1953, Memorandum for the Secretary of State, papers of John Foster Dulles, Mudd Library, Princeton University (hereafter cited as DP). See also John Lewis Gaddis, "The Unexpected John Foster Dulles: Nuclear Weapons, Communism and the Russians," unpublished paper read at Dulles Centennial Conference, Princeton University, 26 February 1988.

review boards. The result, not surprisingly, was the separation from the department of any one against whom even the smallest shadow of doubt could be cast.[8] And as part of the same support-winning tactic, he stoutly defended the cause of Chiang. Results were mixed. On the one hand, the Republican Right was not simply appeased but in the long run coopted, and it had disappeared as an effective force by the end of Eisenhower's first term. On the other hand, morale in the Foreign Service was severely damaged: former diplomats of the stature of George Kennan advised college graduates not to enter the Foreign Service; and Dulles himself became suspect to the liberal community.

More important, Foster Dulles was—and would have regarded himself as—a theorist of international affairs. By the time he became secretary of state he had published two books, one in the late thirties, the other in 1950, both sweeping, highly generalized analyses of the problems of war and peace. Neither, to be sure, had gained great recognition; nor did either book possess the intellectual force or compelling logic of the writings of George Kennan and Henry Kissinger. But Dulles had been writing about world affairs for three decades. As early as 1921–22, for example, he contributed articles to *Foreign Affairs*, *The New Republic*, the Foreign Policy Association *Bulletin*, and *Britannica* on the subject of war debts and reparations, a topic which was then at the very heart of American foreign policy and on which Dulles, from his Versailles experience, was a recognized expert. And he could be original. In 1925, well before professional historians like Elie Halévy had begun to theorize about the domestic, internal causes of war, Dulles gave a speech in which he argued that international wars most frequently occurred when governing elites felt that their domestic interests were threatened. On that basis he maintained that Austria-Hungary and imperial Russia were the powers most responsible for the outbreak of war in 1914.[9]

In the 1930s Dulles developed a sophisticated and complicated argument to support his deep conviction that the United States should remain isolationist in the face of the coming threat of another war in Europe. A frustrated Wilsonian, Dulles always believed that Woodrow Wilson had stood for the right principles and pursued the right policies at the Paris Peace Conference. The fault, he charged, lay not with the text of the Versailles Treaty but with the statesmen who had failed to live up to its provisions. Wilsonianism, he told a Princeton audience in 1936, had not failed; it had never been tried.[10]

A new European war now loomed on the horizon, Dulles argued, because the status quo powers—England and France, and, it should be added, the United States—had refused to pay attention to Article 19 of the treaty, the article that called for the peaceful revision of treaties once the objective conditions of world affairs had changed. Instead, they were jealously holding on to what they had

8. For a lengthier discussion of Dulles's role in the Hiss affair, see Richard D. Challener, "New Light on the Dulles-Hiss Relationship," *University* 73 (Spring 1973): 1–3, 28–33.

9. "On Economic Influences and How They Lead to War," DP, Speeches and Articles file.

10. "Peaceful Change Within the Society of Nations," Stafford Little Lecture, 19 March 1936, DP, Speeches and Articles file.

gained and steadfastly refusing to recognize the needs of the "dynamic" powers—Germany, Italy, and Japan—which were threatening to burst out of the "envelopes" in which they were constrained. He became an advocate of peaceful change. According to Dulles, the only way to avoid another war was for the status quo powers to break down the artificial barriers—particularly the economic barriers—between nations and promote peaceful change by allowing for the freer exchange of peoples, goods, and capital. Moreover, once he cast his lot with the peace movement of the churches in 1937, Dulles became increasingly critical of the principle of national sovereignty. The concept that every nation should think only of pursuing its own rigidly defined national interest, Dulles argued, was one of the root causes of international conflict. As war came ever closer, Dulles consistently demanded that the United States should not become involved. If the western allies won, they would only reimpose the same kind of conservative status quo that had existed after 1919, thereby guaranteeing yet another cycle of repression, reaction, and eventual conflict.[11]

One obvious trouble with Dulles's arguments was that they often sounded like apologies for the policies of the Germans and Italians. One of his major articles calling for peaceful change and the need to accommodate the "dynamic" nations appeared in the *Atlantic Monthly* in November 1935, an untimely date, since Italy had recently invaded Ethiopia and been called before the Council of the League of Nations for its actions. The Italian ambassador in Washington, to whom Dulles had sent an offprint of his article, promptly responded that he "had gone to the heart of the problem." Moreover, he added, "it would have been an excellent thing if you had been sitting at the Council table at Geneva and had made a speech along the lines of your article."[12]

During World War II Foster Dulles had worked long and arduously for the cause of the United Nations. The principal publication of the Commission on a Just and Durable Peace—a blue-ribbon commission of the Federal Council of Churches that Dulles had chaired—was its 1943 pamphlet, the "Six Pillars of Peace." This widely circulated pamphlet was a clarion call for the creation of a new international organization to fulfill the Wilsonian dream. It contained many concepts with which Dulles himself had long been associated—for example, the idea that the next peace must be flexible and not repressive, creative and curative, not vindictive. Proposition III was the concept of "peaceful change" arrayed in new clothing: "The peace must make provision for an organization to adapt the treaty structure of the world to changing underlying conditions."[13] Moreover, the Dulles of the war years had seriously believed in the prospect of

---

11. In addition to the "Peaceful Change" article, see "The Road to Peace," *Atlantic Monthly* (October 1935); "As Seen by a Layman," *Religion and Life* (Winter 1939); and such speeches as "America's Foreign Policy," 18 March 1939, before the Foreign Policy Association, and "America's Role in World Affairs," 28 October 1939, before the YMCA in Detroit, DP, Speeches and Articles file.

12. Ambassador Rosso to John Foster Dulles, 28 September 1935, DP Correspondence files.

13. "A Just and Durable Peace: Discussion of Political Propositions," pamphlet published by the Commission to Study the Bases of a Just and Durable Peace of the Federal Council of Churches of Christ in America, DP, Speeches and Articles file.

accommodation with the Soviet Union. Somewhat ironically, he had also been one of the first Americans to raise moral and ethical questions about the use of the atomic bomb at Hiroshima. As late as the early months of 1946, he was still more worried about American attitudes toward the United Nations than about Soviet behavior at the first meeting of the General Assembly. As he wrote Senator H. Alexander Smith in March of that year, "It was inevitable that the first session of the UN would reflect past discords and old habits and cannot yet reflect the new program of common effort for common good. However, I am far from satisfied with the spiritual and intellectual contribution being made by the United States."[14]

The Dulles who became secretary of state in 1953 had long since changed his mind, had become someone whose interpretation of Soviet behavior rested upon an ideological base. That change undoubtedly resulted from a combination of many factors: his firsthand experiences in dealing with the Russians at the UN after 1945; his own growing political ambitions as he became ever closer to the Republican presidential aspirant, Thomas Dewey; and, perhaps most important of all, his conviction, growing out of his religious heritage, that the Soviet denial of individual liberty violated one of the fundamental moral laws of God. By 1952 Dulles had become not only the very model of the modern cold warrior but also an acerbic critic of the containment policy of George Kennan and the Truman administration. His views were most stridently proclaimed in an article that appeared in *Life* magazine in the late spring of 1952. That article roundly condemned containment as a negative, sterile doctrine that compelled the United States to remain on the defensive and gave it no alternative except to respond to the initiatives of the Soviet Union. Dulles called for a new American policy of boldness that would regain the initiative for the United States.[15] He had also become a critic of the Truman administration's Far Eastern policy, fully subscribing to the belief that support for Chiang and his exiled regime on Taiwan was vital to American national security. Small wonder that in the course of the Eisenhower campaign he would be associated with the concepts of "rollback" and the "liberation" of Soviet satellites in Eastern Europe and with the fatuous "unleashing" of Chiang Kai-shek. Small wonder, also, that when the new administration came into office in January, Dulles could find no role for George Kennan.

Much of this, to be sure, was campaign rhetoric, part of the normal electoral process whereby challengers feel compelled to stake out new positions from those of the incumbents. It should be added, however, that both the Dulles article and Eisenhower campaign did capture the sense of frustration felt by millions of Americans over the downfall of Nationalist China and, above all, by the continuing stalemate of Korea.

But with Dulles it was more than rhetoric or politics. Aboard the cruiser *Helena*, when Eisenhower was returning from his postelection trip to Korea, the incoming secretary of state sketched out his theory of how America should respond to Soviet aggression. His basic premise was that the Russian strategy

14. Dulles to Senator H. Alexander Smith, 4 March 1946, DP, Correspondence file.
15. "A Policy of Boldness," *Life*, May 19, 1952, pp. 146–60.

was to exhaust the United States internally by mounting a series of actions around the world, at times and places of their own choosing, and especially at locations like Korea and Indochina where any American response would be one of high cost. So far, Dulles complained, America had been a country that fought by the Queensberry rules, even when its opponent struck below the belt. This must end. America must be prepared to match the Soviets at their own game, use the same tactics, foment unrest and discord, and above all assume the initiative in areas where the United States was strong. Moreover, Dulles continued, the Russians expected a Republican administration to be tougher than the Democrats. If it was not, then the Soviets would undoubtedly expand the limits of what they thought they could get away with. Dulles anticipated Russian responses to any new American initiatives, acknowledged possible dangers, but concluded that the risks were less than those of perpetuating the present situation, "which means certain disaster."[16]

A year and a half later, in the late spring of 1954, the secretary of state produced another paper that summarized his ideas on the kind of "counter policies" required to meet "the aggressive strategy and techniques of Soviet communism." First, the well-known policy of deterring "open armed aggression by the capacity and willingness to retaliate at places and means of our own choosing so that the aggressor would be hurt more than he could gain"—what became, in shorthand, "massive retaliation." Second, the restoration of western strength by "closing the Franco-German breach which has for a century caused the West to war with itself and expend its vigor in internecine strife." Third, and no less important, "the distraction of the Soviet Communist rulers from indirect aggression by our compounding their internal difficulties." Here the goal should be to find resourceful ways to exploit internal differences within the Communist parties and try to promote the spirit of nationalism in Eastern Europe. Fourth, and finally, "vitalizing liberty and freedom within the free world so that it becomes a dynamic force countering the revolutionary spirit with which Communism imbues its followers."[17]

These two documents, especially the 1954 memorandum, provide a concise overview of the way that Dulles conceptualized the Soviet problem and the appropriate American grand strategy to meet it. Moreover, many of these ideas are constants in his thought—some, indeed, had roots in ideas to which he had adhered long before he became secretary of state. Unquestionably he did view the Soviets as ideologically motivated. And he just as consistently bewailed the unwillingness of America's allies to stand firm. He long continued to express apocalyptic views—worst possible scenarios—of the disasters that irresolution would produce. To name but a few of his dire prophecies: the possible loss of all of Africa and Asia at the time of Dien Bien Phu; the toppling of all the Asian dominoes during the second Quemoy-Matsu crisis; the loss of all the Arab countries to Nasser at the time of the Lebanese crisis.

16. *Helena* notes, 11 December 1952, DP, Subject Series, Alphabetical Subseries, Box 6, Pre-Inauguration Materials.
17. "United States Foreign Policy," 16 May 1954, DP, White House Memoranda Series, Box 8, General Foreign Policy matters (2).

The concept of disrupting and distracting the communist world by creating internal strains was also a constant in his thought. Dulles never subscribed to the belief that the Sino-Soviet bloc was such an iron monolith that American action could not weaken it. He viewed the death of Stalin, for example, as providing the West with an opportunity to exploit potential internal problems in the Soviet sphere rather than a chance to discover if Stalin's successor was more amenable to negotiation. At the Bermuda conference, he advised Churchill that it was possible to split Communist China from Moscow. The best way to do so was by putting relentless pressure upon the Chinese and not offering them inducements to defect, as the Truman administration had allegedly done. It was, to adopt John Gaddis's terminology, the "wedge strategy," the tactic of driving the Communist Chinese closer to Moscow in the expectation that the Russians could or would not assist them, thereby creating fissures and strains within the "monolith."[18]

The concept of applying pressure rather than offering inducements was one that Dulles did not limit simply to communists. When the French appeared to be backing off from their commitment to the EDC, pressure on Paris took the form of statements about how the United States might have to rethink its commitments—the so-called agonizing reappraisal. In the spring of 1956 he outlined a hard-line policy toward Nasser based on the idea of demonstrating to the Egyptian leader that he could not expect "most-favored nation" treatment from the United States as long as he sought arms and assistance from the Soviets. The demonstration would involve denying licenses for arms shipments, delaying Egyptian requests for oil and grain, and, above all, delaying negotiations on the financing of the Aswan Dam. The hoped-for result: to drive Nasser closer to the Russians only to find that they could not fulfill their promises and commitments.[19]

Some of Dulles's ideas had strong roots in his earlier beliefs, for example, his idea that some nations are more dynamic, have a stronger sense of purpose, than others. It was a concept, some have speculated, which owed much to his study of Bergson when he had a fellowship to the Sorbonne in the year after he graduated from Princeton in 1908. In the thirties, dynamism was of course associated with the fascist powers, but by the forties the Soviet Union—propelled "by the revolutionary spirit with which communism imbues its followers"—had become the dynamic nation. In the thirties his response had been appeasement in the guise of peaceful change, but in the forties and even before Dulles had become a committed cold warrior, the essential task was to restore the faith and moral vigor of the West. Consequently, his public discourse involved a steady drumbeat upon Americans to rally round the flag of liberty, freedom, and individualism and thereby regain their dynamic faith. In the process, it might be added, he helped to turn the Cold War into a crusade.

18. For an extended discussion of the policy of "dividing adversaries" and the "wedge theory" in both the Truman and Eisenhower administrations, see Gaddis, *Long Peace*, pp. 147–94.

19. Memorandum for the President: Subject: Near Eastern Policies, 26 March 1956, DP, Subject Series, Box 5.

Foster Dulles had long believed that the American federal union was a model that in many ways should be put before the nations. Before World War II he had seriously flirted with Clarence Streit's "Union Now," and he loved to quote the Federalist papers about how individual states standing alone could accomplish little but, united in a federal union, they could bring about peace and prosperity. In the immediate postwar era, Dulles was particularly proud of a speech he had given in support of the Marshall Plan at the American Club in Paris in which he had called upon the Europeans to move closer to the American federal system. It was his solution to the age-old problem of Franco-German enmity, the problem that he believed was at the root of Europe's historic conflicts. [20]

But there was another constant in his theories of international relations: the conviction that war is most likely to occur not as a result of premeditation or intent but from miscalculation. It is doubtful if the secretary of state ever really believed that the Soviet Union intended to make war on the United States. Far more likely was the danger that the Soviets, or the Chinese, would misjudge the American response to one of their aggressive acts of expansion. He often argued, for example, that there would have been no war in 1914 if Lord Grey had made it clear that Britain would fight in defense of Belgium; no war in 1939 if the United States had made Hitler understand that this country would provide material assistance to the Allies (which, of course, was not what he had advocated in 1939); and, above all, no war in Korea if Dean Acheson had not gone before the National Press Club in 1950 and indicated that South Korea lay outside the American defense perimeter in Asia.

Thus, the essence of his strategy of deterrence was an attempt to articulate certain positions and to establish certain lines that, if the communists overstepped them, would trigger an American response—lines and positions that would be made clear to the Soviets and the Chinese. In discussions with his advisers in the State Department during the Dien Bien Phu crisis in 1954, Dulles declared that there was much value in drawing a line and saying no further. Such an approach, he argued, gave an opponent an opportunity to back off, to stay his hand; conversely, it maximized the opportunity to rally allies to your own position. (But not everyone in his audience, it might be noted, was intellectually convinced. The next line of the transcript reads: "Admiral Radford did not give the impression of being impressed by this line of thought.")[21] This logic informed his two famous and successful attempts—the congressional resolutions on the offshore islands of Quemoy and Matsu and on the Middle East—to bind the Congress in advance to support whatever policies the administration might choose to pursue in the future if there was further communist aggression. Both resolutions were intended to make it clear that any advance beyond certain lines would result in an American reaction and thereby avoid a war by Soviet or Chinese miscalculation. Both resolutions, it should be added, were also designed

20. "European Unity," speech to the American Club of Paris, 19 November 1948, DP, Speeches and Articles file. See also interview with Jacques Reinstein, DOH.
21. Memorandum of Conversation on Indochina at the Secretary's Residence, 9 May 1954, Subject Series, DP Box 9.

to demonstrate to the communists that Congress backed the president and secretary of state—that America transmitted a clear signal with one united voice. The situation would not be confused, as it presumably had been during the Truman years, when Congress and the chief executive were so often at odds, especially on Far Eastern matters.

What emerged might best be termed the "certainty/uncertainty principle." Certainty as to the fact that the United States would react, but uncertainty as to the means that would be employed, the time to be chosen, or the place to be selected. Or, as a transcript from the second Quemoy-Matsu crisis reads: "Secretary Dulles outlined his theory of X and 2X—that any time the enemy wished to attain X, we would exact a cost of 2X from them."[22] In the aftermath of the Geneva Conference of 1954, Ambassador John Allison wrote from Tokyo for clarification of American policy. In response Dulles emphasized that although the United States did not intend to employ major military forces in Indochina and was redeploying troops from Korea, the communists clearly understood that certain American military actions—he cited authorizing the navy to patrol the offshore islands and sending patrol planes over the China coast—demonstrated to the Chinese that the United States had not only the capacity to retaliate but also the will to do so. We have set out, he argued, to impress Communist China, "the source of the past and future aggressions in Korea and Indochina that we are 'willing and able' to make the aggressor suffer at places and by means of our own choosing, i.e., where our sea and air power are preponderant." With, of course, the corollary that the Chinese will "suffer damage outweighing any possible gains from aggression." Moreover, Dulles emphasized, "the prevention of miscalculation by what is going on off the China coast will, I feel, give the best chance of deterring further aggression in Korea and Indochina." He was convinced, as he put it, that "those in Moscow and Peiking who see the picture as a whole and who read our policy speeches carefully, do not suffer from confusion"—with the result that "I do not believe that the Chinese Communists are in fact now prepared to challenge us in any major or sustained way and provoke further our sea and air power along their coast."[23]

Foster Dulles is best remembered for the numerous public speeches in which he outlined the national security policy that came to bear the label "massive retaliation." Massive retaliation was more than simply the theory of deterrence that accompanied and gave meaning to the "New Look" military posture adopted in the first year of the Eisenhower administration—a policy that involved a reduction in the size of American ground forces and increasing reliance upon the Strategic Air Command and the nuclear deterrent. Massive retaliation was designed to accomplish many goals. First, by holding down military costs, it would help the administration to attain its holiest of all holy grails: the balanced budget. It perfectly matched Eisenhower's conviction that excessive military

22. Memorandum of Meeting Held in the Secretary's Office, 28 March 1955, DP, White House Memoranda Series.
23. JFD to Ambassador John Allison, 20 August 1954, DP, Chronological Series, Box 9.

spending carried with it a threat to basic American institutions and might create the preconditions for his much feared "garrison state." Massive retaliation also appeared to offer a technological solution to the problem of avoiding a war of attrition, like Korea. America could rely on its still-clear superiority in both nuclear weapons and delivery systems and not have to confront either the Chinese or the Soviets in land warfare where demography gave them tremendous advantages in manpower. No longer would there be the fear of being "nibbled to death" in future Koreas. Additionally, of course, massive retaliation—retaliation at times and places of our own choosing—was presumed to restore the initiative to the United States. And finally, it was part of the broader concept of avoiding war by miscalculation; an off-balance enemy would be convinced that America could and would retaliate.[24]

Furthermore, the intent of the strategy was to minimize both the costs and the risks (though later critics, to be sure, would question whether the policy, by reducing conventional forces, did not maximize the latter). As the response to Allison indicated, Dulles emphasized that even if we were redeploying troops from Korea and had no intention of committing ground forces to Indochina, the risk of war was minimized because the United States was relying on resources, its air and sea power, in which it was clearly superior, and since the communists understood the firmness of our purpose.

But the test of the theorist is not in the theories themselves but in their implementation and how well they work in practice. The newly available official records of the Eisenhower years make it abundantly clear that both the secretary of state and the president understood many of the inherent difficulties and practical dilemmas posed by their stated policy of massive retaliation. The records of the Dien Bien Phu crises—along with those pertaining to the two offshore island crises—reveal many discussions about the dearth of appropriate targets for atomic weapons as well as the realization that the dropping of an atomic bomb might well create more problems of fallout for the Chinese Nationalists than for their adversaries. Both men realized that nuclear weapons were inappropriate for many potential situations. "We cannot," Dulles once confessed, "splurge our limited supply of nuclear weapons without serious danger to the balance of power"—which meant, in effect, they could only be used in cases of major aggression. Both men were also sensitive to possible political repercussions—that, in view of Hiroshima and Nagasaki, Asians would interpret the use of nuclear weapons in the Far East as a racist act. Dulles once ruefully commented that it would be politically counterproductive if a Nationalist attempt to regain the mainland was preceded by American use of an atomic bomb. And the secretary of state deliberately requested curtailment of talk about the use of atomic weapons during the spring of 1954. Because of European

---

24. For a more detailed discussion of massive retaliation, see my chapter, "The National Security Policy from Truman to Eisenhower: Did the 'Hidden Hand' Leadership Make any Difference?", in Norman Graebner, ed., *The National Security: Its Theory and Practice, 1945–1960* (New York: Oxford University Press, 1986), pp. 37–75.

concerns about nuclear weapons, such discussion might prevent European ratification of the much-desired European Defense Community.[25]

Thus it is far more accurate to describe massive retaliation as the "declared" rather than the "actual" policy. Both Eisenhower and Dulles always sought to give the impression that the United States would use nuclear weapons; but in the various crises that occurred, there is little evidence that they actually intended to do so. Indeed, on some occasions it almost seems as if Dulles and Eisenhower were looking for reasons to avoid their use. This is not to say that there were not veiled threats—over Korea, Indochina, and the offshore islands. Nor is it to deny that Dulles later boasted that these threats had accomplished their deterrent purpose—driven the North Koreans, for example, to agree to a truce in 1953. But in retrospect, even these veiled threats now appear more "declaratory" than "actual."

Dulles always insisted that the United States must possess sufficient conventional weapons and nonnuclear forces to be able to implement his certainty/uncertainty principle. In general, he was satisfied that the United States did possess the necessary range and resented the charges of those who maintained that the New Look, by reducing conventional forces, was gradually putting the country in a situation where the only option in any crisis was to go nuclear. But at the same time, the secretary of state generally deferred to what he regarded as the superior knowledge of President Eisenhower. When, for example, Robert Bowie attempted to get him to take a more active part in the discussions over force levels in order to make sure that he had the instruments necessary to implement his policies, Dulles tended to resist playing that role.[26]

More important, as early as 1954 Dulles realized that the era of America's near-monopoly on atomic power would be short-lived and that, as the Soviets developed their own weapons and delivery systems, the nuclear threat would lose its credibility. Europeans, for example, would begin to wonder if the United States would actually drop the bomb for something less than an all-out threat if use of the weapon threatened the destruction of American cities. Indeed, in Eisenhower's second term, in 1957 and 1958, Dulles was in the forefront of those, especially after Sputnik, who believed it necessary to begin a fundamental reexamination of the entire national security concept. Still, he never fully abandoned the faith. On his deathbed in Walter Reed Hospital in the spring of 1959, Foster Dulles told his successor, Christian Herter, then wrestling with the Berlin crisis, that "there is a total failure to grasp or accept the whole concept of our deterrent strategy. We can't rely on, whenever there is a threat, having to buy our way out by making concessions rather than standing firm and relying on our deterrent power to keep the peace."[27]

In the overall context, it makes little sense to try to resolve the question of whether Eisenhower or Dulles was more understanding about the dilemmas

25. Memorandum of Meeting Held in the Secretary's Office, 28 March 1955, DP. See also the extended discussion of the Eisenhower administration's perception of the nuclear dilemma in Gaddis, *Long Peace*, pp. 123–46.

26. Interview with Robert Bowie, DOH.

27. JFD to Christian Herter, 10 April 1959, DP, Telephone Conversation Series.

inherent in using nuclear weapons in times of crisis, or to determine which man was more prone to talk about their possible employment. To be sure, it still appears that the secretary of state—especially when he was discussing nuclear issues with his close associates in the department—was more inclined to take the hard line, more inclined, too, at the outset of a crisis to think in terms of resolution by force. President Eisenhower often appears as a moderating presence. Once, during the second confrontation over Quemoy and Matsu, when Ike opted for caution, Dulles complained, "But I thought we had acknowledged the risk of the political and psychological dangers of the use of these weapons when we included them in our arsenal."[28] And, it must be emphasized, both men did believe and believe firmly that there might be serious threats such that some form of atomic response, most likely at the so-called tactical level, would be required. And they frequently worried that the American public needed to be educated on this crucial matter. A memorandum that Dulles prepared after a meeting in the Oval Office during the first Quemoy-Matsu crisis reads:

> This talk was a renewal of the conversation I had with the President the day before. We reviewed the importance of education with reference to the distinction between atomic missiles for tactical purposes and the big bomb with huge radio-active fall outs. The President mentioned that our own troops were maneuvering very close to areas where atomic missiles were used. We went over the draft of my proposed talk and we discussed whether or not to make in it reference to atomic missiles. The President thought it might usefully be done in an incidental way.[29]

Reading through such documents reminds one of the absentminded Oxford don who, so the story goes, concluded a lecture series by saying that he had made a mistake—that students should correct their notes and substitute the word "Greeks" wherever he had said "Romans." In this case, when one has said "Dulles" one can just as often substitute "Eisenhower."

The real problem with Foster Dulles was not so much with his theories of deterrence but with his continuing problem of communication. There was often a gap between what he said and wrote in private and what he communicated to the leaders of other nations and to the American public. In private he wrote brilliant, incisive memoranda, with no moralizing, no reliance upon Presbyterian rhetoric, and he used the value-free language of the social scientist. One memorandum, for example, written in the early fall of 1956, was a clairvoyant, dispassionate analysis of the international disaster that would fall upon Great Britain if it attempted to overthrow Nasser on the issue of the Suez Canal. But he could never communicate with Anthony Eden. Eisenhower once went out of his way to inform his secretary of state that the British leader complained that he often could not comprehend what Dulles was driving at and was left with the impres-

28. Memorandum of Meeting Held in the Secretary's Office, 28 March 1955, DP. See also the extended discussion of the Eisenhower administration's perception of the nuclear dilemma in Gaddis, *Long Peace*, pp. 123–46.
29. Memorandum of Conversation with the President, 7 March 1955, DP, White House Memoranda Series, Meetings with the President.

sion that the secretary thought he was "dumb." And just a few days before the British did launch their ill-fated invasion, one of Dulles's close friends, General Alfred Gruenther, sent a blunt letter that pointed out that Dulles had failed to make the British and French understand what he really wanted. "If I were one of your staff officers," Gruenther concluded, "I would probably say something like this to you. 'Mr. Secretary, I don't know what it is that causes your approach to misfire on occasion, but certainly it does. I strongly recommend that at the earliest possible moment we have a private meeting of the three foreign ministers, or, better yet, the three heads of government to resolve what I think is a deteriorating situation.'"[30]

Foster Dulles wanted—indeed, assiduously sought—the support of the American public. But he tended to believe that the average American couldn't fully comprehend complicated issues of foreign policy and that it was necessary to phrase your ideas in dramatic, capsule phrases that would capture the headlines and seize the attention of the TV audiences. As a result he often came across as just the opposite of what he intended, appearing as a reductionist who oversimplified and overdramatized. His name is still most frequently associated with such simplistic phrases as "agonizing reappraisal," "rollback and liberation," "brink of war," and "massive retaliation." The public in short never saw the man who wrote the logical and comprehensive memoranda that now appear in the *Foreign Relations* series.

The classic example was the famous "brinkmanship" article that appeared in *Life* magazine early in 1956 and that gave Dulles the image, which has lasted to this day, of a secretary of state who reveled in bringing the United States and the Soviet Union to the very brink of Armageddon.[31] The article described how on three separate occasions the United States had gone to the brink of war and had preserved the peace only by its willingness to face the brink. It grew out of a free-wheeling interview that Dulles had held with three journalists. What he wanted to explain were his underlying assumptions about the essence of great power confrontations: his belief that, during an international crisis, the leaders of a nation cannot afford to indicate in advance that they will give in or surrender. To do so, Dulles maintained, would only tempt the opponent to raise the ante, to press his advantage too far—and, in the process, to create an even more dangerous situation. It was in this context—and this context only—that the secretary spoke of the possible need to be prepared to go to the brink of war. But the more he talked, the more Dulles began to resort to dramatic phrases. At one point he described how, when he had made a particular point to Eisenhower, the president "came up taut." The editors of *Life* compounded the problem. They shortened and tightened the script; they added their own dramatic subheads within the piece; and they put a huge blurb on the cover: "Three Times to the Brink of War." Poor staff work in Dulles's office kept anyone from realizing what had happened until the issue was in print, the damage done. Later, to be sure,

30. General Alfred Gruenther to JFD, 29 October 1956, DP, General Correspondence Series, Box 2.
31. James Shepley, "How Dulles Averted War," *Life*, January 16, 1956, pp. 70–80.

Henry Luce sent Dulles a personal apology for what his editors had done, but even Dulles recognized that the article had made him appear as an intemperate man who dashed around the world threatening nuclear destruction.[32]

There were other problems of implementation. While the "wedge theory" may in the long run have had an effect on Sino-Soviet relations, it ran into difficulties in Eastern Europe at the very outset, as indicated by the inability of the Eisenhower administration to exploit the East German uprisings in the spring of 1953 and later those in Hungary in 1956. The European allies, as Dulles himself realized, were unenthusiastic: "Our allies think it too dangerous 'to prod the bear' by exploiting internal weakness as the Communist exploit them within the free world," he wrote somewhat testily in the spring of 1954.[33] There is evidence too that Eisenhower had his own reservations about bear-baiting. Similarly, the attempt to draw clear lines, particularly with respect to Taiwan and the offshore islands, produced confusion in the minds of both the European and American publics. Both the secretary of state and the president, believing Quemoy and Matsu indefensible and hoping to convince Chiang to change his troop dispositions, had deliberately "fuzzed up" the question of whether or not the United States would fight for these islands, unless a communist attack appeared to be a clear prelude to an assault upon Taiwan. Here the "certainty/uncertainty principle" became problematic. It was intended to make the Chinese uncertain about how and where America would respond, but the "fuzzing up" only transferred the uncertainty to the minds of Americans—many of whom, as time would demonstrate, could approve of the defense of Taiwan but had genuine doubts about the wisdom of getting into war over the offshore islands.

But forty years after the Truman Doctrine and the Marshall Plan had revolutionized American foreign policy and almost thirty years after Dulles's death, we can ask whether the Dulles-Eisenhower years should be regarded as a sort of "golden age" in the Cold War, indeed a measuring rod against which to criticize the excesses of both predecessors and successors. Dulles was unquestionably more flexible and his views more balanced than the public ever realized. He could approve of neutralism, as in the case of Austria when it was a part of his policy and was not forced upon the Austrians. He was more open on the prospects for negotiation than once imagined, and he did begin the practice of self-deterrence with nuclear weapons. But problems still remain. There is, for example, his (and equally Eisenhower's) much-expressed concern about avoiding American identification with European colonialism. Running through all the documentation on the French disaster at Dien Bien Phu in 1954 are statements about the danger of getting too close to French imperialism and, no less important, the necessity for recognizing the force of nationalism in the Third World. But in the last analysis, these concerns were always overridden by what

32. See interviews with Henry R. Luce, James Shepley, and Charles J.V. Murphy, DOH.
33. "United States Foreign Policy," 16 May 1954, DP, White House Memoranda Series.

appeared to be the greater threat: communist expansion that must be checked lest the dominoes topple. Moreover, given his views about the contradictions within the communist system and his understanding of the force of nationalism, it is surprising that Dulles did not attempt to exploit the historic differences between the Vietnamese and the Chinese.

And there remain further questions about the "wedge theory." On several occasions in 1957 Eisenhower passed on to Dulles suggestions that Nasser might be interested in reopening negotiations with the West and that his cooperation with Moscow was the result of the lack of an alternative. But the secretary of state returned hard-nosed replies which in effect rejected these suggestions—all of which, along with Dulles's response to the death of Stalin, suggest possible missed opportunities.[34] And while the pressure on China might indeed have driven some wedges between Mao and the Soviets, it is also possible that it might have increased Chinese fears of American intentions.

Moreover, implementation of the wedge strategy and Dulles's hard-line public speeches about Chinese communism may well have prevented any positive American response to political and diplomatic changes in the Far East. The secretary's tough stance on China, to be sure, did neutralize and eventually marginalize the Republican Right and the China lobby. But there was a price to pay. That price was the freezing of public attitudes toward the People's Republic of China to such an extent that it was not politically possible to achieve any breakthrough until the presidency of Richard Nixon more than a decade later. Finally, Dulles's ideological approach—as evidenced by his speeches and not by what he actually said within the Oval Office or the department itself—helped to fasten Cold War values on America and made the Cold War itself even more ideological than it had been in the days of Truman and NSC-68.

Also running through the newly available official documentation is Dulles's continuing skepticism about summit conferences. Whether they are useful or not, whether they enable a national leader to "measure" and better understand his opponent, whether they foster disillusion, is not the question. The point is that Dulles always resisted summit conferences not only on the grounds that they raised public expectations to excess but also because they might lead to a letdown in the public's willingness to maintain a firm, unyielding posture against the Soviets. Thus, even when he was agreeing to take the first steps toward suspension of nuclear tests, he went on to say that this was a "good thing," since it warded off pressure for a summit. At the end of his life, when he was in Walter Reed Hospital and when the Eisenhower-Khrushchev summit was about to occur, he expressed his skepticism to Richard Nixon. He had spent the last year and a half of his life, he told the vice president, trying to keep a summit from occurring. "Why go at all?" he asked.[35]

It is also worth noting that it was Foster Dulles who made the basic American

---

34. Eisenhower to JFD, 13 November 1957, and JFD Memorandum for the Record, 15 November 1957, DP, Correspondence Series.

35. JFD to Mr. Greene, 24 March 1959, DP, Telephone Conversation Series.

"Yes, We'll Be There, Rain And Shine"

(From Herblock, *Here and Now*, New York: Simon & Schuster, 1955.)

commitment in Vietnam, the decision that the protection of the South Vietnamese government of Diem was vital to the national security of the United States. On this, to be sure, he was never really tested. The gamble on Diem appeared to be working—indeed, to be working so well that both Washington and Saigon could ignore the national elections called for in the Geneva Accords. Political, economic, but not military aid seemed sufficient. It was not until the last months of Dulles's life that the National Liberation Front became a serious threat to American policy in Vietnam. Thus in his lifetime he never had to confront the quite different dilemma that faced Kennedy and Johnson: how to support a collapsing regime that, it seemed all too clear, would topple without direct American military involvement. Then too the official record reveals the many telephone calls between the two brothers—Foster Dulles at State, Allen Dulles at the CIA—which relate to covert operations, part and parcel of the objective of fomenting discord within the communist sphere. These graphically

"Don't Be Afraid—I Can Always Pull You Back"

(From Herblock, *Here and Now,* New York: Simon & Schuster, 1955.)

demonstrate the way in which the Eisenhower administration often chose the covert route to achieve its objectives, most notably the overthrow of unwanted leftist regimes in Iran and Guatemala. Covert activities with John Foster Dulles became, for better or worse, a recognized instrument of national policy. The short-term, easy successes of Guatemala and Iran led directly to the long-run price paid at the Bay of Pigs.

It can certainly be argued that many of the policies that John Foster Dulles implemented did contribute, albeit inadvertently, to creating the conditions of stability that now exist in Soviet-American relations. The newly released documents on the Solarium project in the spring and summer of 1953 clearly delineate how the Eisenhower administration eventually accepted the containment doctrine which it had originally rejected almost with contempt.[36] Though it was to be sure a greatly expanded containment that came to include treaties covering Dulles's famous ten-thousand-mile "frontier of freedom" that stretched from the Taiwan Straits via the Near East to Europe. The administration backed off from "rollback and liberation" in Eastern Europe even before the dust had settled in East Germany, leading to the eventual tacit recognition by each superpower of the other's sphere of influence. And with massive help from Eden and other Europeans, Dulles did surmount the impasse over EDC and eventually succeeded in bringing West Germany into NATO. This was a genuine accomplishment that is frequently overlooked but was an integral part of his deep conviction that the age-old Franco-German rivalry must be ended if peace was to have any prospect. Chiang Kai-shek was in fact put back on the leash; he probably enjoyed less freedom to manipulate the United States under Dulles and Eisenhower than he had enjoyed under Truman and Acheson. There was, additionally, the avoidance of direct confrontation with the Soviets and the Chinese as well as a clear recognition that massive retaliation was not appropriate for anything less than a massive challenge. All of these policies, when examined from the perspective of the 1980s, did help to create stability. But the achievement, as measured against Dulles's statements on the *Helena* before he assumed office, is ironic. It was not what he had intended.

Perhaps the best way to evaluate John Foster Dulles is to observe that he turned out to have, in conjunction with President Eisenhower, real skills in crisis management. His name will never be associated with a long-term strategy like that of George Kennan. Nor did he produce a theory of international relations like that of Henry Kissinger, which rested on an appreciation of the balance of power and a sense of limits. But he showed real ability as a crisis manager. The administration survived Dien Bien Phu and the offshore islands; it ended the war in Korea; it got through Suez and Lebanon without conflict.

There was, however, always the ironic dimension. The "certainty/uncertainty principle" was meant to ensure deterrence. It was supposed to minimize risks since, assuming American superiority in air and naval power, the enemy would be deterred from pushing too far. But particularly after Sputnik, the administration's many critics could make the plausible argument that on the cost/risk scale, Dulles and Eisenhower had put their country at peril—had maximized risks—because they did not possess the instruments for their policy. And the admin-

36. The "Solarium" study was the fundamental reexamination of national security policy conducted by the Eisenhower administration in the spring and summer of 1953. Three separate task forces examined the containment policy and possible alternatives. Robert J. Watson, *History of the Joint Chiefs of Staff*, vol. 5, *The Joint Chiefs of Staff and National Policy, 1953–1954* (Washington: U.S. Government Printing Office, 1986), pp. 11–14.

John Foster Dulles
at a January 1956
press conference.
(UPI/Bettmann
Newsphotos)

istration, particularly in the months after Dulles had died, was never able to convince its critics or the public that their grand strategy had been and remained effective. John Kennedy would ride into power in considerable part on the argument that massive retaliation had been a failure and that the only viable grand strategy was one that would be based upon "balanced forces."

17

Theorist and Practitioner: Henry Kissinger

MICHAEL JOSEPH SMITH

AT LEAST since the late eighteenth century, when Immanuel Kant wrote his essay "On the Old Saw: That May Be True in Theory, but It Won't Work in Practice," the relationship between theory and practice has fascinated us. We assume the dichotomy defines an opposition, or at least a tension. Recognizing this, Kant—about whom Henry Kissinger has written at length—tried to disprove the notion of inevitable opposition, concluding that "whatever reason shows to be valid in theory, is also valid in practice."[1] But however one resolves the issue in the abstract, the theorist-practitioner dichotomy provides an especially useful framework for assessing the contributions of Henry Kissinger to postwar American foreign policy.

Indeed for Henry Kissinger the dichotomy is doubly appropriate. First, more than the other figures considered in this book, Kissinger came to office with a worked-out set of ideas that can legitimately be called a "theory." As an academic, Kissinger sought to become a "conceptualizer" (his term) about the issues facing the United States in the world. Second, as a thinker Kissinger demonstrated a fondness for setting out dichotomies and oppositions, such as freedom versus necessity, creativity versus bureaucracy, idealism versus realism, conservative versus revolutionary statesmen. Thus the tension or opposition be-

1. Hans Reiss, ed., *Kant's Political Writings* (Cambridge University Press, 1970), p. 92.

tween theory and practice not only fits Kissinger's career, it characterizes his mode of thought.

My goal here is to trace these oppositions in both the theory and the practice of Henry Kissinger. Perhaps uniquely among postwar American statesmen, Kissinger's actions in power reflected his ideas in theory—even when the practice seemed to diverge from the theory. Kissinger's goals for American foreign policy were broadly ambitious. He and Richard Nixon tried to move American foreign policy beyond containment, beyond the sterile debates between idealists and realists, toward what they called a new geopolitical equilibrium. This attempt, I shall argue, did not succeed; and the failure can be traced both to aspects of theory and practice. This essay will explore the tension between theory and practice in two sets of issues vital to Kissinger's approach: the first concerns the tasks and nature of leadership; the second, the actual substance of the Nixon-Kissinger foreign policy, together with the standards we can define and apply for judging it.

Kissinger and Leadership

Kissinger's preoccupation with leadership in all its aspects has been a constant throughout his career. In his unpublished (but much analyzed) Harvard undergraduate thesis, in his academic work, in office, in his memoirs, and now in his current newspaper columns, Kissinger has worried over the essence of leadership. What distinguishes creative and memorable leaders from those who are merely ordinary? What obstacles face the aspiring leader? How can a creative vision hold its own against the inevitable tendencies to pragmatic compromise? Kissinger has never been self-conscious about treating these large questions in or out of office, and one can distinguish three sets of contrasts identified by him as illuminating the general problem.

The first of these dichotomies restates the hoary philosophical issue of freedom versus necessity. As a twenty-six-year-old senior at Harvard College, Kissinger treated this issue at length in his Government Department thesis modestly entitled "The Meaning of History: Reflections on Spengler, Toynbee and Kant." In this work Kissinger attempts to solve the dilemma of necessity, at least for himself, with an extraordinarily personal conception of freedom. His conclusion bears quotation: "Freedom . . . must result from an inward state which imposes its patterns on phenomena. . . . The experience of freedom in a determined world implies that we can transcend necessity only by imparting our individuality to the inexorable unfolding of events." Thus, for Kissinger freedom is an intensely personal experience which allows one "to impart meaning to history."[2]

Of course one might dismiss these sentiments as youthful romanticism. But in a 1968 essay on Bismarck—an essay recently cited by William Hyland as a key to

2. Kissinger, "The Meaning of History: Reflections on Spengler, Toynbee and Kant," A.B. thesis, Harvard University College, 1951, pp. 259, 235. I have analyzed this work more fully in my *Realist Thought from Weber to Kissinger* (Baton Rouge: Louisiana State University Press, 1987), chap. 8; also see Peter Dickson, *Kissinger and the Meaning of History* (New York: Cambridge University Press, 1978).

understanding Kissinger's approach to leadership and foreign policy—he echoes the terms of his undergraduate essay. A "revolutionary" leader, Kissinger wrote, "must possess at least two qualities: a conception incompatible with the existing order and a will to impose his vision." Bismarck possessed both the vision and the will; he had truly experienced freedom. "The insistence on identifying his will with the meaning of events would forever mark Bismarck's revolutionary quality." Thus for Kissinger, genuine leadership results from an intense "inner experience of freedom in a determined world." This experience not only imparts creative vision but also the will required to impose it on external events. Kissinger's vision of freedom is intensely personal. Even ethical judgment seems to derive from the same kind of "inward" experience. Or, as he put it in *A World Restored*, "Men become myths not by what they know, nor even by what they achieve, but by the tasks they set themselves."[3]

What tasks did Kissinger set himself on coming to office, and what obstacles did he believe he faced? Here we come to the second of Kissinger's contrasts about leadership, and to an area where his academic theory had enormous influence on his practice. In and out of office, Kissinger has consistently noted the opposition of creativity to bureaucracy, of leadership to administration, of the rule of "experts" to the insight of creative leaders. Before coming to power, Kissinger routinely decried the baleful influence of bureaucracy on American foreign policy. In office he battled against it, describing these battles with relish in his memoirs, and even now he uses his newspaper column to point to the capacity of the American bureaucratic process to "generate spontaneous inconsistencies."

Why is Kissinger so hostile to bureaucracy? His indictment recalls the sociology of Max Weber. Bureaucracy, to Kissinger, is the enemy of true innovation, of long-range planning, of genuine vision in foreign policy. A bureaucracy, by definition, has no sense of purpose other than to prolong its own life, to develop standard operating procedures and pseudo-objective standards of performance. In a bureaucracy, Kissinger has written, "substantive problems are turned into administrative ones." "Serving the machine becomes a more absorbing occupation than defining its purpose"; "the need to provide a memorandum outweighs the imperatives of creative thought."[4]

The pervasiveness of modern bureaucracy, together with an inherent preference among Americans for pragmatic adjustment, combined in the postwar period to cripple American foreign policy in what Kissinger has persistently called a "revolutionary period." It led to an excessive emphasis on "problem solving" instead of a clear definition of long-range goals and interests. Policy "stagnated" for a lack of creative planning; American policy suffered from a "paralysis of imagination." It had got to the point, Kissinger wrote in 1968, that

3. William G. Hyland, *Mortal Rivals: Superpower Relations from Nixon to Reagan* (New York: Random House, 1987), p. 194; Kissinger, "The White Revolutionary: Reflections on Bismarck," *Daedalus* (Summer 1968): 889, 894; Kissinger, *A World Restored* (Boston: Houghton Mifflin, 1957), p. 322.

4. Kissinger, *The Necessity for Choice*, (New York: Harper & Row, 1961), p. 344; Kissinger, *American Foreign Policy* (New York: W. W. Norton, 1969), pp. 18, 19.

"the chief significance of a foreign policy speech by the President may be that it settles an internal debate in Washington." The "central task" facing a new administration in 1969 was to "analyze anew the current international environment and to develop some concepts which will enable us to contribute to the emergence of a stable order." That task would require a new "burst of creativity" in American policy.[5]

With his appointment to direct the National Security Council (NSC) under Richard Nixon, Kissinger found himself in the position to provide that creative burst. He came into office determined not to allow a pervasive and unsympathetic bureaucracy to block his path. Together with President Nixon, who shared his dim view of the foreign policy establishment in the government, Kissinger proceeded to restructure the foreign policy process within the executive with the goal of unleashing creativity as never before. Kissinger's method for doing so can perhaps be set out as an antibureaucratic set of guidelines:

1. For the National Security Council, assemble a small, loyal staff of people known to be brilliant, but preferably without existing ties to the other parts of the bureaucracy. Tolerate, even encourage, the politically unorthodox: but make it clear that the price of such toleration is absolute devotion to oneself. Keep this staff on a short lead, drive it hard, and encourage an atmosphere of embattled brilliance. Employ at least one unimaginative "straight arrow" to serve as your enforcer.

Kissinger's early staff reflected these guidelines. Men like Roger Morris, Anthony Lake, Helmut Sonnenfeldt, C. Fred Bergsten, and Morton Halperin (among many others) brought to the otherwise politically monochrome Nixon administration both personal and political diversity; only in Kissinger's NSC could one find liberals like Lake or Halperin. But most did not last, and many left with considerable bitterness, as is amply, even excessively, documented by Seymour Hersh in his indictment of Kissinger. Particularly corrosive was Kissinger's willingness to tolerate, if not order, wiretaps on his closest aides to search out potential "leakers."[6]

2. To the extent possible, monopolize the flow of information, and jealously guard all access to the president.

Kissinger's skill at this—particularly at the expense of Secretary of State William Rogers—is well documented. The arrangement also suited Nixon's management style of relying on only a few aides whose loyalty was absolute, and it soon became clear that Nixon felt comfortable with the former Harvard

---

5. Ibid.
6. Seymour M. Hersh, *The Price of Power: Kissinger in the Nixon White House* (New York: Summit Books, 1983), chap. 7; for Kissinger's own account of the wiretapping, see Kissinger, *Years of Upheaval*, pp. 115–22. The "enforcer" on Kissinger's staff was, of course, Alexander Haig.

professor. Hersh explains this in rather nasty terms: "Nixon had a consuming need for flattery, and Kissinger a consuming need to provide it." But surely more than this was involved, for a president never lacks flatterers. Nixon and Kissinger shared both a strategic vision and a tactical sense of how to achieve it. More than the inevitable palace intrigue, this shared view accounts for Kissinger's success at controlling the information reaching the president. As Kissinger himself puts it, "a Presidential Assistant soon learns that his only strength is the President's confidence; without it, his position will rapidly erode."[7]

3. Open "back channels" of communication and negotiation, both with adversaries and within the government.

In his memoirs, Kissinger cites the advantages of his "back channel" with Soviet Ambassador Anatoly Dobrynin: "We would, informally, clarify the basic purposes of our governments and when our talks gave hope of specific agreements, the subject was moved to conventional diplomatic channels. If formal negotiations there reached a deadlock, the Channel would open up again. We developed some procedures to avoid the sort of deadlock that can only be resolved by a test of strength." Similar channels were opened between Kissinger and several of our ambassadors abroad. Here, too, Nixon's cooperation was essential. Distrustful of the wider bureaucracy, he and Kissinger tried to guarantee that their initiatives could not be frustrated by "standard operating procedures."[8]

4. To win bureaucratic battles within the government, cultivate good relations with the press by conducting extensive "deep background" briefings with prominent reporters. Deploy all the charm at your disposal. But be certain that you are the only one doing this; this option should definitely be closed to your staff.

5. If you wish to see your policy properly executed—and to prevent it from being "ground down by the bureaucratic steamroller"—adopt a direct, active, and above all, secret role as negotiator.

The record of Kissinger's secret negotiations need not be rehearsed: its eventual disclosure brought him not only wide public adulation as "Super K", but also the Nobel Peace Prize for his part in the Vietnam negotiations. But as I shall suggest presently, omnipresence has its limits, even when accompanied by apparent omniscience. It is also worth remembering that Robert MacFarlane's first line of defense when the Iran-Contra scandal began to unfold was that he was following the precedent of Kissinger's secret negotiations with China.

This set of "anti-guidelines" clearly served Kissinger well during his tenure as NSC adviser. By any measure, he gathered an unusually talented and dedicated staff and he managed to gain some control over the elephantine executive. But as

7. Hersh, *Price of Power*, pp. 39–40; Kissinger, *White House Years*, p. 1455.
8. Kissinger, *White House Years*, p. 139.

By mid-1974 Kissinger's popularity and political stature had reached such heights that the *Newsweek* cover depicted him as Super K. (Courtesy *Newsweek*)

Kissinger himself admitted when he became secretary of state, there were serious costs attached to his methods. Some were human. William Watts, who came to the NSC via Nelson Rockefeller's presidential campaign, described his experience thus: "I came down really full of idealism. It was an exciting thing; an extraordinary chance. Starting on day two, it was a process of steady disillusionment and enormous unhappiness." Morton Halperin, the aide who later sued Kissinger for his role in ordering wiretaps, reflected that "people didn't like to conduct foreign policy as if it was a conspiracy."[9]

Other costs were substantive. Perhaps the most celebrated (and best documented) specific incident with important policy implications concerned the preparations for the signing of the SALT I treaty at the Moscow summit of May 1972. Kissinger's extensive use of his back channel with Dobrynin had kept the American negotiating team in Geneva completely uninformed of many new decisions about the complex issues in the treaty. Chief negotiator Gerard Smith, who arrived in Moscow late and hungry (the victim of what Kissinger politely calls "honest bungling"), was constrained to tell reporters at a briefing that he was not aware of many of the treaty's exact provisions. The whole summit was

9. Quoted by Hersh, *The Price of Power,* pp. 117, 113.

characterized by an extraordinary degree of last-minute improvisations and ill feeling among the American participants. It was by no means the well-oiled machine that Kissinger tends to evoke in his recent critiques of summitry during the Reagan administration. The entire negotiating team led by Smith was reassigned in the aftermath of the Senate ratification hearings, replaced, ironically enough, by a team far less sympathetic to Kissinger's overall approach.

Some critics have suggested that the concentration on bureaucratic infighting and on monopolizing the policy process—not on a long-term creative vision—led to the exclusion of multiple warheads (MIRVs) from the SALT treaty, an omission later regarded by Kissinger himself as unfortunate. Scientists like George Rathjens, Paul Doty, Carl Kaysen, and Richard Garwin urged Kissinger to abandon antimissile defenses and the offensively potent MIRVs at the same time; Kissinger demurred, apparently because he believed this approach to be unachievable. But as Garwin recounts, Kissinger's methods may have defeated this goal from the start: "I told him he was doing a terrible thing by working outside the State Department and Pentagon bureaucracy on SALT because they would go along working on their own plans and he would have no support for his proposals when he needed it. . . . It was a high-risk policy to leave the bureaucracy in the dark. Kissinger misunderstood the democratic process: He thought he could do things better than anybody else."[10]

Garwin evokes a larger point suggested by Kissinger's antibureaucratic *modus operandi*—the problem of building a consensus around one's policy. Certainly Kissinger's worry about the bureaucracy's grinding down any genuinely creative policy is understandable. And clearly coherence in policy is gained when only a few key players are involved in its formulation; no one can deny the difficulty of moving the complex executive bureaucracy in a single, let alone innovative, direction. And yet, if one fails to make the effort to carry one's policy in the major executive departments, the task of building support in Congress and in the country beyond becomes even harder. The departments must learn sooner or later about the substance of the policy. If they have been effectively frozen out of the process, they will mobilize their own ties to Congress, to affected interest groups, and engage in selective leaking of their own. All this will work to the detriment of the "creative" policy. Kissinger admits as much in his discussion of SALT II negotiations, when he was secretary of state; he ascribes the resistance he encountered to any flexibility in the American position to the "the bureaucracy's revenge for my freewheeling diplomacy in Nixon's first term." One might also recall Kissinger's verdict on the statecraft of Bismarck: "Statesmen who build lastingly," he wrote, "transform the personal act of creation into institutions that can be maintained by an average standard of performance. This Bismarck proved incapable of doing."[11]

The last of Kissinger's contrasts concerning the tasks and nature of leadership sets the conceptualizer or strategist against the improviser or tactician. Not surprisingly, as a theorist Kissinger preferred the long-term thinker to the

10. Quoted in Hersh, *The Price of Power,* p. 154.
11. Kissinger, *Years of Upheaval,* p. 1017; Kissinger, "Bismarck," p. 890.

" THERE GOES THE 8:05 "

Kissinger's Middle East mediations after the October 1973 Arab-Israeli war produced a
new term in international politics—"shuttle diplomacy." (Don Wright, *The Miami News*)

negotiator whose horizon was limited by his current task. The roles clearly are
distinct, and Kissinger's preference for the longer view remains intact. His
newspaper columns have called on President Reagan to "leave a historical legacy
by raising the [foreign policy] debate to a conceptual level," and he has raised
objections about the INF treaty because it seemed to be devoid of a long-term
strategy for dealing with the Soviets.[12]

Yet while he was in office, as the previous contrast suggests, Kissinger almost
inevitably emphasized his role as negotiator. The reasons for this grew out of his
distrust for bureaucracy as well as his confidence in his own capacity for creative
leadership. But here there is a curious double gap between Kissinger's theory
and practice. First, and quite obvious, is the gap between the academician who
valued the deep concepts and the statesman who originated "shuttle diplomacy"
and hammered out a disengagement agreement by haggling kilometer for kilometer—perhaps losing sight of the larger picture of lasting peace in the Middle
East. And although Kissinger continues to evoke the underlying concepts,
consciously or not he confirms the primacy of his role as negotiator by devoting
so great a portion of his voluminous memoirs (2,690 pages covering five-and-a-
half years) to his negotiations within and between governments. Sprinkled
among these often excruciatingly detailed accounts, one does find fascinating
passages on negotiating styles, the idiosyncrasies of particular figures, and the

12. Kissinger, *Washington Post*, 24 November 1987.

rhythms of an extended negotiation. The "conceptual" passages of the two volumes are not only thinner, but also considerably less rewarding than the sections on day-to-day policymaking.

Second, and less clear, is the gap between his writings and the extraordinary diplomatic skill, psychological insight, and the feeling for nuance that Kissinger displayed in office. Little in his academic corpus would have led one to conclude that Kissinger would himself prove to possess the skills of which he wrote so admiringly in his appreciations of Metternich or Bismarck. After all, writing about such skill hardly guarantees that the author will demonstrate it. Yet Kissinger's accomplishments as a negotiator remain impressive. The opening to China, the achievement of the SALT I treaty, and, perhaps less heralded, the change of course in American policy toward southern Africa marked by the Lusaka statement of May 1976 all demonstrate Kissinger's adeptness as a negotiator. This last example also shows the importance of on-site experience to Kissinger. As the "conceptual" NSC adviser, Kissinger showed little interest in Africa, and he even commissioned a study premised on the notion that the white regimes in South Africa and Rhodesia (as Zimbabwe was then known) were "here to stay." And before he undertook his trip to southern Africa as Ford's secretary of state, the official American attitude had been to remain aloof from any attempt to end white minority rule in Rhodesia. Once on the scene, however, Kissinger realized that American interests would not be served by continuing to recognize the Smith regime. The change of course (described by William Hyland as "an international bombshell") represented a strategic change of course largely suggested by tactical experience in the field.[13]

Kissinger's other famous negotiations, on Vietnam and the Middle East, had more mixed results and cannot be treated in any depth here. As I have already suggested, some critics have argued that Kissinger's decision not to try for more than a disengagement agreement after the October 1973 war reflected a short-term tactical choice. With his prestige on the line, Kissinger did not wish to risk attempting a more comprehensive agreement. Defenders, of course, reply that this is easy to say in hindsight and that even the disengagement agreement did not come easily. The least one can say is that Kissinger's decision to concentrate on what he regarded as achievable was not exactly Napoleonic in the scope of its vision; rather it seemed to reflect a negotiator's keen sense of the possible. This does contrast sharply with the Kissinger who pronounced that "men become myths not by what they know, nor even by what they achieve, but by the tasks they set themselves."[14]

Concerning Vietnam, it seems fair to suggest that Kissinger's long and intimate

13. See M.A. El-Khawas and B. Cohen, eds., *The Kissinger Study of Southern Africa* (Westport, Conn.: Lawrence Hill & Co., 1976) for an analysis of National Security Study Memorandum 39; Hyland, *Mortal Rivals*, p. 166.

14. For representative critiques, see Edward Sheehan, *The Arabs, Israelis, and Kissinger* (New York: Reader's Digest Press, 1976); Stanley Hoffman, *Dead Ends: American Foreign Policy in the New Cold War* (Cambridge, Mass.: Ballinger, 1983), chaps. 2–3; William Quandt, *Decade of Decisions: American Policy Toward the Arab-Israeli Conflict, 1967–1976* (University of California Press, 1977); Kissinger, *A World Restored*, p. 322.

"Conceptualizer" by preference, Kissinger in office acted more as the negotiator and tactician. (National Archives)

involvement in the intricate details of a negotiation that often seemed fruitless may have blinded him to the overall strategic costs to the United States in continuing to pursue the war. In one of his final meetings with South Vietnamese President Nguyen Van Thieu, Kissinger quotes himself as telling Thieu in considerable frustration that "for four years we have mortgaged our entire foreign policy to the defense of one country." The remark may be truer than he realizes. It is not only hindsight to conclude with Elliot Richardson that "surely we could have achieved the same result sooner and at less cost both to ourselves and to the South Vietnamese." Here Kissinger the theoretician would criticize Kissinger the practitioner. An excessive concentration on the details surrounding the extended negotiation caused us to lose sight of the high price—both at home and abroad—of "mortgaging" our foreign policy to South Vietnam. Thus by concentrating on his role as negotiator, Kissinger neglected his responsibility as conceptualizer. To take a single concrete example: surely a Kissinger sitting in Washington in October 1972, less elated about his personal breakthrough with Hanoi, would have anticipated the hostile reaction to the settlement from Thieu. Yet Kissinger presents himself as surprised and dismayed by this reaction. Negotiators do get caught up in the details of their current task, and Kissinger proved no exception.[15]

The broader point to make about Kissinger's contrast between the strategist and the tactician is this: Despite his theoretical and oft-expressed preference for

15. Kissinger, *White House Years*, p. 1386; Richardson quoted by Stanley Hoffmann, "The Sulking Giant," *The New Republic*, 3 May 1975, p. 16.

the "conceptualizer," Kissinger proved in office to act far more often as the negotiator and tactician. Given his aptitude for this role, the achievements were very real. But many of the criticisms made by Kissinger the theorist of an overemphasis on the limits of the tactically possible could be applied with justice to Kissinger's own performance in office, most significantly in the area of arms control, in the Middle East, and in the drawn-out agony of Vietnam.

The Tasks of American Foreign Policy

The next set of contrasts involves Kissinger's view of the substance of American foreign policy and also presents the opportunity to compare his writings as a theoretician with his actions as a statesman. The three dichotomies in this area include Kissinger's conception of "geopolitics" versus what he regarded as the dead end of containment; the contrast between the needs of national security, as he conceived it, and the dictates of domestic politics; and finally, the contrast between scholar and statesman, which Kissinger has both written about and, obviously, exemplified. Hans Morgenthau liked to characterize this last contrast as the dilemma of truth and power, suggesting that there was a kind of inevitable tension, if not contradiction, between the two. We shall see that sensitivity to this contrast provides no guarantee that one will overcome it.

As an academic specialist in American foreign policy, Kissinger had in the 1950s and 1960s developed a standard critique centering on the central concept of containment. What, in his view, was wrong with it? In late 1968, as Kissinger was preparing to enter office, the question seemed almost absurd. The Vietnam War had driven Lyndon Johnson from office and had elected Richard Nixon, at least partly because of his secret plan to end it. Containment had ceased to provide any positive rationale for dealing with the Soviet Union and it was being roundly blamed by scholars and activists alike for having landed the United States in the Indochina morass. The consensus around the concept of containment, a mainstay of American policy since 1947, had shattered. Riots in the streets of Chicago during the Democratic convention seemed to symbolize its demise.

Kissinger's critique of containment recognized these manifest failures, but his notion ran along very different lines; it had more in common with "realists" like Hans Morgenthau or George Kennan than with the disillusioned critics of the Vietnam War. Like other realists, Kissinger argued that containment failed to integrate power and diplomacy. Rather than providing the United States with a rationale for using its power for worthwhile political ends, it encouraged us to stand pat. It encouraged Americans to believe that there was somehow an end point to the international struggle; it pandered to uninformed American idealism and to the naive belief that power need not be used. Strategically, containment placed too great an emphasis on military technology and on the vertical dimension of the international struggle. It failed to recognize the political and ideological aspects of our competition with the Soviets. Above all, Kissinger argued, containment failed to define a positive strategy for coping with a sophisticated Soviet threat in an increasingly hostile world.

Kissinger developed a concept of "geopolitical equilibrium" to correct all these failures. The United States had to learn to calibrate power by replacing the exclusively vertical East-West division of the world with the horizontal triangle of Washington/Moscow/Peking, giving American policy new flexibility not only for coping with the Soviets, but also for dealing with a range of political and ideological threats throughout the world. Kissinger used an elevated language to convey his ideas. Terms like "linkage," "emerging multipolarity," and "geopolitics" began to appear in presidential addresses. Kissinger and Nixon even introduced an annual speech on foreign policy matters modestly entitled the "State of the World" address. In essence Kissinger envisioned the United States as the self-conscious manager of a new balance of power, an undertaking that required "perseverance, subtlety, not a little courage and above all under-standing of its requirements."[16]

Despite the high language, the basic ideas were not that difficult and critics have had a good deal of fun "deconstructing" them. The *Washington Post,* for example, offered this summary: "With the European intellectual's bent for conceptualization and the European survivor's knack for maneuver, Henry Kissinger was precisely the man to elaborate and execute the Nixon design. It consisted, quite simply, of playing China against Russia." Theodore Draper wrote that "Dr. Kissinger's prescription for handling the Soviets was right out of Dr. Spock's immortal opus on child care," while Stanley Hoffmann preferred the image of B. F. Skinner's box for training pigeons. The underlying message was the same: the United States would deploy the Chinese at our will to balance the Soviets, and we would learn to manipulate rewards and punishments to induce the Soviets to behave as we wished.[17]

In fairness one should quote Kissinger's own characterization of his vision. In March 1976 he described his goals in these terms:

> It is our responsibility to contain Soviet power without global war, to avoid abdication as well as unnecessary confrontation. This can be done, but it requires a delicate and complex policy. We must strive for equilibrium of power, but we must move beyond it to promote the habits of mutual restraint, coexistence, and, ultimately, cooperation. We must stabilize a new international order in a vastly dangerous environment, but our ultimate goal must be to transform ideological conflict into constructive participation in building a better world. This is what is meant by the process called "detente"—not the striving for agreements at any price, not the mindless search for friendly atmosphere which some critics use as naive and dangerous caricatures.[18]

There was—and remains—much in this vision to recommend it, and yet it is clear that it failed to recast American policy. As many have recognized, Kissinger overestimated the willingness of the Soviet Union to be induced or "trained" to accept our management of the balance, as well as our capacity to undertake the necessary management and training. The scheme relied too heavily on the

16. Kissinger, *White House Years,* p. 115.

17. Quoted by Hyland, *Mortal Rivals,* p. 193; Theodore Draper, "Kissinger Re-divivus," *The New Republic,* 31 January 1981, p. 30; Stanley Hoffmann, *Primacy or World Order* (New York: McGraw-Hill, 1978), p. 46.

18. Quoted in Hyland, *Mortal Rivals,* p. 198.

supposedly determining impact of the central triangle on the rest of the world. Countries in Asia, Latin America, and Africa (to say nothing of the Middle East), with conflicts and agendas of their own, defied centralized control. And Kissinger's insistence on viewing those conflicts through the lens of the central balance seemed to rob the United States of the flexibility needed to make distinctions between vital and peripheral interests. In a world of inexorable linkages, any event anywhere could upset our management of the balance. A change to a left-leaning regime anywhere in the Third World would harm American prestige and the perception of its power. Thus Kissinger was willing to "destabilize" regimes like Allende's Chile and to insist on becoming involved in Angola despite determined congressional resistance.

In short, Kissinger tried to implement a policy that was positively Bismarckian in its vision of interlocking strings all converging in Washington—with Kissinger as the chief puppeteer. Unfortunately for Kissinger, the would-be marionettes proved to be irritatingly independent and recalcitrant, and the master himself increasingly had to ward off competitors for control of the strings. The policy required an implicit trust in the goals and tactics of the policymakers. Difficult in the best of times, this trust became a virtual impossibility after Vietnam and Watergate.

Kissinger, of course, has repeatedly blamed Watergate for the failure of his vision, but he seems to have remained blind to the connection between his Vietnam policy and the destruction of trust between government and people that Watergate symbolized. A fundamental prerequisite for the success of Kissinger's policy was an early and minimally divisive end to the Vietnam War. Had they been willing at once to make the concessions they eventually agreed to make by 1972, Nixon and Kissinger could have managed this. Instead, we had the invasions of Laos and Cambodia, unprecedented domestic unrest, and finally the pattern of governmental abuses summarized by Watergate. The climate of paranoia within the administration was nurtured by the notion that all opponents of the war were traitorous. The wiretaps, the spying within and by the administration (for about a year the Joint Chiefs of Staff assigned a navy yeoman to provide copies of all NSC secret documents to them; he even rifled through Kissinger's personal luggage during the trip to China) all combined to defeat any possibility of genuine trust. It is far too easy for Kissinger to blame Watergate.

This leads to the second substantive contrast I shall consider here—the opposition between foreign policy and domestic politics. Although Kissinger had written in *A World Restored* that "the acid test of policy is its ability to gain domestic support,"[19] his academic work fit more comfortably with a typical realist attitude toward American domestic politics, which ranged from being uncomprehending to being unsympathetic to being positively disdainful. Here there is a consistent gap in Kissinger's approach. He demonstrated little grasp of the intricacies of congressional relations or interest-group politics as a professor and he showed no great aptitude for them in office. To be sure, he was skilled at handling the press, and many have agreed that when he was in top form he could be a matchless performer at congressional briefings.

19. Kissinger, *A World Restored*, p. 326.

Serving a president who was not exactly a bridge-builder, Kissinger proved considerably less adept at negotiating with Congress than he was with the Russians or Chinese. He acknowledges in his memoirs that Senator Henry Jackson (and his *éminence grise*, Richard Perle) outflanked him on the issues of arms control and detente. More generally he confesses his utter lack of sympathy for the "nightmarish" influence of interest groups, where "each issue seemed to produce its own constituency." Lacking any experience with the Congress, Kissinger tended to deplore its influence and to lament the passing of leaders who could be counted on to deliver the necessary votes and to keep unruly troops in line. And concerning his relations with Nixon's political operatives in the White House, he cultivates in the memoirs the idea that he tried to remain as aloof as possible from their machinations.

The problem of how to build domestic support for a complex foreign policy in our messy democracy is genuine. In office Kissinger did not ignore the problem, but instead he ran through a number of tactics designed at least partly to address it. In his first two years as NSC adviser—when he was banned from television and his voice was deemed nonrecordable because of his accent—he charmed the press by giving extensive "deep background" briefings. Later, he and Nixon relied on stage-managed spectacle, the high point of which was the trip to China. On that trip, it may be recalled, NBC journalist John Chancellor complained that the Chinese press was more free to cover events there than he and his fellow Americans. As Watergate increasingly enveloped the administration, Kissinger became a talisman of virtue amid all the tawdriness; the "stable structure of peace" and the "achievements of our foreign policy" were recited rather like a mantra by Nixon and his increasingly besieged defenders.

After Nixon's resignation and in response to the challenges to his foreign policy from the Republican Right and the Democratic Left, Kissinger as secretary of state launched into a series of speeches across the nation on the virtues of detente and geopolitical equilibrium. Many of these speeches were lucid and quite persuasive (an excerpt on detente was quoted above), warning against a self-righteous moralism from either side of the political spectrum. In fact, if one changed the references to contemporary events, many of these speeches bear a striking resemblance to those of George Kennan in the early 1950s. Kennan, too, had warned against moralism and the illusion that there could be an end point to the Soviet-American rivalry and he had urged that the United States devote itself to the prudent management of the balance of power. But even as Kissinger sounded these realist themes, it was clear that his efforts came too late. Discourses on the rationale for a foreign policy in the final year of an administration cannot avoid the whiff of irrelevance; the failure to build consensus on the new policy had already become apparent.

This failure to build support for policy goes beyond the usual charges of "overselling" detente; it speaks, I think, to a fundamental lack of understanding of the substantive and institutional requirements of the American constitutional system. Of course it is far easier to invoke the need for this understanding than it is to achieve it. But Kissinger's response, quite typical of realists, is to denounce the system, to decry our "wallowing in national self-absorption," as he put it in a recent newspaper column. Broad support for a complex foreign policy would have required a concerted and continuing effort to educate the public, to bring in the Congress, to build consensus within the executive branch itself. An approach that assumes the primacy of foreign policy and treats domestic concerns as somehow parochial and illegitimate simply cannot work.[20]

Finally, what of the final contrast between the scholar and the statesman, the intellectual and the policymaker, often raised by Kissinger himself? Kissinger is that rare person who has lived and served in both worlds with distinction, though it is perhaps fair to note that the emergence of the statesman did revitalize interest in the work of the scholar. He came into power with a considered body of thought about how to wield it and quite conscious of the tension between the two worlds. His rocky relations with his former colleagues in the academy, detailed both in his memoirs and in critical books about him, speaks to this tension.

Certainly his experience in office demonstrates that power does exact a real price. As Max Weber wrote in his classic "Politics as a Vocation" essay, "he who lets himself in for politics—in other words for power and force as means— concludes a pact with diabolical powers."[21] Kissinger's "pact" led him to order secret bombings, to agree to wiretap close aides, and to acquiesce or cultivate ignorance about the activities surrounding Watergate and its cover-up. And yet from the safety of our own enclaves, we must judge circumspectly. Kissinger served with dedication in a frankly unethical environment and survived with his personal integrity more or less intact. The line dividing loyalty and malfeasance in the Nixon White House must have been very hard to observe. One might wish that Kissinger in his memoirs were more frank about those difficulties and more forthcoming in accepting responsibility for his own decisions; but as Stanley Hoffmann has observed, people rarely write memoirs to advertise their mistakes.

Two concluding points remain to be made. First, Kissinger as a statesman proved increasingly deaf to the genuine arguments of his former academic colleagues. He quotes his own impatience with his academic critics' "overweening self-righteousness" and "headlong retreat from responsibility." But as an academic himself, Kissinger had written that "the intellectual must guard his distinctive and . . . most crucial qualities: the pursuit of knowledge rather than administrative ends and the perspective supplied by a non-bureaucratic vantage point." In office he proved resistant to that outside perspective, and in his memoirs he virtually refuses to engage seriously the arguments of his academic critics. Only criticisms from the Right are taken seriously enough to refute.[22]

Finally, there is Kissinger's behavior since he left office in 1976 and even more since he published *Years of Upheaval* in 1982. He has acted more like an underappreciated statesman-in-exile than as a scholar who might reflect on his unique experience and knowledge of American foreign policy in a detached,

---

20. Kissinger, *Washington Post*, 24 November 1987.

21. H.H. Gerth & C.W. Mills, eds., *From Max Weber* (New York: Oxford University Press, 1946), pp. 125–26.

22. Kissinger, *The Necessity for Choice*, p. 353; Compare his discussion of right-wing critics of detente in *Years of Upheaval*, pp. 235–62, with his angry treatment of academics in *White House Years*, pp. 514–16.

sustained, and thoughtful way. Of course he has written two mammoth volumes of memoirs and published several collections of speeches; one could never accuse him of idleness. But the memoirs are a conscious effort to assure his place in history. The books lack a synthetic distillation of his ideas and experiences as they might influence the contemporary debate. Rather than a third volume of blow-by-blow description, a work of detached scholarship could achieve what Kissinger has been urging in his news commentary. Henry Kissinger could inspire a conceptual debate on the deep and enduring issues facing America in a dangerous, complex, and confusing world. One would welcome, for example, his sustained thoughts on Paul Kennedy's recent treatise *The Rise and Fall of the Great Powers* or on the future direction of Soviet-American relations. Kissinger's arguments, as opposed to his pronouncements on these subjects, could make a lasting contribution to our understanding. Perhaps the experience of the practitioner cannot easily be brought to bear on the tasks of the theorist. Is it too much to hope that the scholar turned statesman will turn once again into a penetrating scholar?

18

The Realist School and Its Critics

RICHARD FALK

THE WAY we remember the past shapes the way we understand the present and prepare for the future. How are we to interpret the American response to the world that unfolded after 1945? It was a remarkable period of intense encounters between opposing forces and of fundamental changes in the character of international relations. The role of the United States in these years was one of unquestioned leadership. What ideas, precepts, and interpretations guided the exercise of American leadership in the postwar world? And, finally, is the postwar world itself being superseded by a new set of conditions that makes the old ways of thinking more or less obsolete? This chapter responds to these questions by examining the general orientation toward the world of politics as it is conceived by the realist school.

Even if the Soviet-American rivalry persists, it makes sense to talk of the ending of the postwar world, because of at least three factors: the active entry onto the world scene of Japan and Germany, the defeated powers in World War II; an essential resolution of the most controversial issues in Europe by an acceptance of post-1945 territorial boundaries in the Helsinki Accords; and, finally, the decentering of the world system as a result of the completion of the decolonization process and the loss of U.S. primacy in the economic, diplomatic, and cultural domains.

What does realism have to do with our understanding of these developments? It is connected with a debate between realists and others as to the political significance of these forty momentous years of international history. Reviewing that debate can clarify immediate issues about whether the Cold War can and should be ended and how to go about restoring confidence in the American capacity to hold its own in the world economy. Beyond this, it enables us to uphold and strengthen our vision of what is desirable and possible on the global level of politics during the period ahead.

Realism and Alternatives

The post-1945 rise of the realist perspective was a natural consequence of a widely shared learning process that interpreted the meaning of World War II and generated a critique of American diplomacy during the 1930s. This realist understanding of the world was crystallized by some powerful intellectual figures who were closely associated with the policy-forming process in the early postwar years, especially Dean Acheson and George Kennan. These prominent public figures found their outlook influentially reinforced, in the academic world by Hans Morgenthau and in religious circles by Reinhold Niebuhr.

Several historical circumstances shaped postwar realism in the United States. There was, above all, a conviction held by each of these individuals that American participation in world affairs had been deflected by a past infatuation with idealistic strains of thought, especially as associated with the thought and presidential diplomacy of Woodrow Wilson. Wilson, it should be recalled, insisted in the aftermath of World War I that balance-of-power approaches to international order were incapable of sustaining peace in Europe and that the machinations of statesmen needed to be replaced by the procedures of international institutions and by a gradual enlargement of the rule of law at the expense of the rule of force. Realists, in contrast, agreed that legalism and moralism were poor guides to policy in a world of sovereign states. The realist reconstruction of the past emphasized the failure of appeasement to contain Hitler and argued that only capabilities for defense and deterrence, not a sentimental attachment to a world beyond power politics, can sustain peace by dissuading would-be aggressors.

Another strong implication of realism was its internationalist conception of U.S. national interests. This conception necessarily included a repudiation of America's traditional stance of peacetime isolationism, a position initially articulated mainly to keep the United States from getting drawn into recurrent European wars. The realists strongly believed that American security required an intimate involvement in European affairs for the foreseeable future, leading to the image of Euro-American solidarity in the form of an Atlantic alliance. Such an embrace of Atlanticism, formalized by the formation of NATO in 1949, was undoubtedly accelerated by the perception of the Soviet Union as an expansive adversary with the capacity and inclination to encroach upon the sovereign realities of Western Europe. In the background also was the realization that United States interventions in World Wars I and II had shaped the outcome of both struggles, but that in the future a reactive entry into warfare in Europe was hardly feasible. This realist assessment meant that to succeed, diplomacy in the future must be both preventive in style and effective, avoiding war rather than hoping to win on the battlefield. Realists saw the liberal constitutional identity of the Western European countries as once more threatened, this time from the East (rather than by Germany), and as lacking the internal cohesion and resolve to act successfully on their own in the years after 1945.

The realist grasp of this historical situation seemed powerfully persuasive both in terms of overcoming the errors of the past and as a guide to the future, and it generally controlled the behavior and outlook of the postwar generation of leaders in the United States. During these decades realists successfully domi-nated the political imagination of both policymakers and their counterparts in the academic world. A realist orthodoxy has emerged in this period that has both sharpened and constrained discussions about foreign policy. Having said this, it is only proper to point out that realists span a broad ideological and meth-odological spectrum that has quite diverse policy consequences, ranging from those who are freewheeling "cowboys," seemingly always eager for a good fight in international relations, to those who diligently build upon realist premises to bolster support for moderation.[1] Zbigniew Brzezinski and Cyrus Vance during the Carter years provide a vivid example of the gap that separates the tough-minded realist who relishes the prospect of military encounters from the more judicious realist who relies on negotiations and diplomacy as the main vehicles for the pursuit of American national interests.

What, then, do the various realist perspectives have in common and what alternatives to "realism" are worth considering when interpreting the recent international history of U.S. foreign policy? Realists, regardless of divergencies, share at least these several features:

1. A focus on sovereign states as the basic unit in international relations, and especially on the leading state (or states) as the provider of international order at a given period. Such a focus remains "realist" even if the emphasis is explicitly shifted to the perception of those who act on behalf of the state, or if it takes into account economic and domestic dimensions of statecraft. The crucial distinguish-ing mark of realist thought is its state-centric character.[2]

2. An acceptance of the states system—of interacting states—as the only feasible framework for international order, implying a rejection of alternative forms of world order as utopian or chaotic.

3. An acceptance of conflict as the essential but not the exclusive wellspring of

1. These issues of the conceptual identity are discussed from various angles in Robert O. Keohane, ed., *Neorealism and Its Critics* (New York: Columbia University Press, 1986).

2. In this respect, I take a more inclusive view of realism than that of Joseph S. Nye, Jr., "Neorealism and Neoliberalism," *World Politics* XL (1988): 235–51. Whereas Nye treats Robert Gilpin's *War and Change in World Politics* (New York and Cambridge: Cambridge University Press, 1981) as an instance of updated realism and Richard Rosecrance's *The Rise of the Trading State* (New York: Basic Books, 1986) as an expression of liberalism, I regard both as being within the realist tradition. Both are state-centric, influenced by the shifting structure of international relations and by the impact of technology on the viability of the military instrument. Both offer adjustment strategies in light of their interpretation of the current phase of geopolitics.

political relationships among states that possess mainly antagonistic interests and beliefs, and the application of such presuppositions to East-West, Soviet-American relations in the post-1945 period.

4. An unspoken ethical assumption (or the suppression of the ethical inquiry) that any side in an international conflict can be legitimately expected to threaten unlimited destruction to the extent that this effectively discourages attacks and provocative challenges by its enemies; in other words, an acceptance of the security role of violence, maximized as nuclear deterrence—even in the form of mutual assured destruction. Reliance on deterrence is treated as an acceptable if unfortunate basis for stabilizing security in the nuclear age.

5. An acknowledgement that the character of conflict is influenced by international economic policy, by the degree to which war is perceived as a rational instrument of statecraft, and by domestic political cultures and the prevailing ideological outlook of the principal international rivals.

Existing as alternatives to realism have been at least three traditions of thought, each with a following in intellectual circles, but none consistently influential in Washington or capable of loosening the grip on the mainstream by which realism has controlled the political imagination relevant to United States foreign policy during these years. These nonrealist traditions can be identified as follows.

First, there are several varieties of Marxist and post-Marxist interpretations of international relations; these interpretations highlight the economic motivations for and class basis of political conflict, and they often tend to view the Cold War mainly as a pretext for capitalist and imperialist expansion as facilitated by United States militarism, a pattern that gave rise to President Eisenhower's celebrated warning about the growing influence in the governing process of "a military-industrial complex" in his farewell address. In international relations this line of interpretation underlines many of the contentions of the Nonaligned Movement, centering on the contention that the world economy is structured so that the North reaps disproportionate benefit. It should also be noted that many Marxist scholars have mounted devastating critiques of state socialism and Soviet bloc relations over the years, emphasizing the betrayal of socialism and the rise of a new, exploitative bureaucratic class.

The second alternative to realism involves various deterministic extensions of the belief that conflict between forces of good and evil is at the center of human experience. One contemporary expression of this fatalism, generally associated with apocalyptic variants of religious fundamentalism, even tends to regard the prospect of nuclear annihilation as a kind of blessed assurance that divine providence is helping history along toward its preordained end point.[3] This kind of fatalism, often embraced by the extreme Right in America, tends to regard the Cold War as inevitably leading to an outcome of victory or defeat for our side or theirs. For these geopolitical fatalists, peaceful coexistence is an illusion and

3. A.G. Mojtabai, *Blessed Assurance* (New York: Houghton Mifflin, 1986)—on living with the bomb in Amarillo, Texas.

detente a snare. There are many types of fatalism alive and active in the political domain around the world. A formidable expression of fatalism has surfaced in the form of Islamic fundamentalism. The Islamic Republic in Iran in its war with Iraq lured military recruits with the assurance that battlefield casualties would gain them immediate ascent to heaven, asserting that a martyr's death is an automatic consequence of dying in the course of a sacred struggle.

A third alternative to realism is a continuation of idealism by other normative concepts, especially by reference to the comprehensive reform of the current state-centric system of international relations. There are almost as many world-order approaches as there are variations on the realist theme, but a unifying thread of world-order approaches is their common conviction that the reality of the realists is something to be overcome, something to be superseded by safer, more equitable, more durable political arrangements than can be provided over the long haul by the states system. World-orderism has sometimes in the past put its bets on some plan for world government, or at least on a strengthened United Nations. More recently, world-order thinking has emphasized liberation from below by way of grass-roots democracy and new social movements that erode the cultural and societal foundations of statism. Yet these concepts deliberately avoid offering any advance blueprint for a preferred world-order structure. Just as realism is distinguished by its statist orientation, world-orderism is identifiable through its stress on "the whole," normally "the world," but in some variations "the region" or "the civilization," as the appropriate unit of analysis.

Each of these alternatives to realism has had some adherents in the United States in the period since 1945, but save for brief exceptions that will be noted later on, none has seriously threatened the realist consensus in either academic or policy circles. The realist triumph over each of these alternatives has proceeded along distinct lines. Accompanying the rise of the Cold War, especially up through the 1950s, was a generalized stigma attached to Marxist orientations, a hostility that swept through the society as a tidal wave of intellectual suppression during the late 1940s and early 1950s in the form of McCarthyism, which even when it receded as an overt attack upon Left dissent cast a dark shadow over radical thinking. The severe corrosion of the Soviet reputation during the 1950s and 1960s in light of exposures of its internal repression and harsh occupation of Eastern Europe added to the pressure to avoid any taint of communist sympathy. Under these conditions few academics and no policymakers in the United States were willing to endorse explicitly Marxist readings of international relations. Indeed, a process of informal institutional self-censorship contributed to the virtual disappearance of Marxist influence in elite educational settings as well as in governmental arenas of influence. Despite the stature and influence of Marxist thinking elsewhere in the world, it absented itself from the American scene almost completely until the aftermath of the Vietnam War, when some greater tolerance for radical thought became evident within university settings, although at no time within or close to the policymaking realms of government.

Realist master thinkers including Morgenthau, E.H. Carr, and Reinhold Niebuhr generally met the idealist/world-orderist challenge by showing that the power dynamics at the crux of international relations cannot be tamed by normative approaches based on the promotion of international law and morality. Arguments that contend that the state system is heading for a crash landing or that conceive of the normative potential of international relations as including the abolition of war as a social institution are derided by these thinkers either as wallowing in doomsday or as exercises in utopianism. Realists on the liberal, Democratic Party side of the mainstream political scale often reinforce their realist credentials by world-order bashing. Some influential social scientists with moral concerns locate their thought on one side of the realist camp by claiming liberal credentials, striking a balance by combining sharp criticism of tough-minded realists with even harsher attacks on their supposedly utopian colleagues. The realist school fights off both the Right and Left by seeking to occupy the moderate Center, claiming for itself the high ground of reason and the golden mean between the unhealthy and unworkable extremes. This is expressed especially through contrasting attitudes toward the role of force in international relations.

Oddly enough, it is only geopolitical fatalists who have managed to challenge the realists in the councils of government, and even they have done so only briefly, ineptly, partially, and in the end ineffectually during the Reagan years. Earlier attempts by fatalists to advocate preventive-war strategies, especially during the first phases of the Cold War when the United States enjoyed an initial monopoly over nuclear weaponry and then a definite superiority, came to virtually nothing. The realist emphasis on deterrence and on making adequate preparations for war consistently rejected scenarios of victory through recourse to "preventive war." One major element of the realist consensus was the claim that being ready for war contributed to the maintenance of peace. The realist consensus, thus, corrected the belief of the interwar years that demobilization and appeasement were the most appropriate war-avoiding postures for the United States to adopt. Thus, in an important sense, realists have been peace oriented, and no more amenable to war-waging approaches than to the advocacy of disarmament and isolationism.

These fatalists have been an important societal presence throughout these years. They are powerfully represented in the bureaucracy, and are especially prevalent among military and business elites that often have close links with the organized political and religious Right. They have the resources at their disposal to make their voices heard and, occasionally, even the political clout to threaten realist control over policy making. The private network of foreign policy operatives revealed by the Iran-Contra disclosures established that geopolitical fatalists had temporarily gained a foothold in the inner circles of the Reagan administration. Their basic outlook is locked into the view that the Soviet Union and communism are irremediably evil and that a struggle to the bitter end between the superpowers is both inevitable and uplifting. Fatalists with such attitudes are never far from the levers of power, even if they do not exert much visible influence in academic life or in the national media, except in the setting of evangelical pedagogy. They can also lay claim, quite credibly, to the mantle of patriotism and to that of societal virtue and tradition, maintaining purist loyalty

Such normative passion often puts the realist con-
way that leftist attacks never do.

alist Consensus

pecifically restricted to the period following upon
₃ qualification the extent of this triumph remains
some forty years later. It is characteristic of almost all dimensions of
societal life that "a prevailing view" dominates research, discussion, and leadership attitudes at a given time. Realism definitely became the conventional
wisdom of the postwar world, providing a convincing "fit" with global circumstances and American political culture that seemed attractive, even "correct," to
a wide spectrum of societal opinion. This realist consensus occupied the entire
middle of the political spectrum, providing a context for purposeful debate
within an agreed bipartisan framework. Only the extremes of radical Right and
radical Left felt excluded.

The absence of ideologically oriented political parties and corresponding
media outlets as compared with the Western European democracies perhaps
further narrowed the range of responsible debate in the United States during
most of the postwar period. Furthermore, within the realist camp there have
been ebbs and flows of influence among subgroups, as policies have oscillated
between reliance on force and on negotiations. In these contests for influence,
especially within the councils of government, hard-line realists have generally
prevailed. The more moderate realists, such as Kennan, Vance, and George Ball,
have not fared nearly so well in Washington as have militant realists such as
Henry Kissinger, Brzezinski, and Paul Nitze. These generalizations are confused
by the importance of public mood. It is a paradox of the postwar world that
militant realists have often taken the initiative in realizing moderate foreign
policy goals, and vice versa. It was Nixon and Kissinger who normalized relations
with China, initiated detente, and proclaimed the replacement of "confrontation" by "negotiation." More recently, it has been Reagan who has fashioned the
first arms treaty ever that calls for the destruction of a class of nuclear weapons.
Contrariwise, liberal presidents such as Kennedy and Johnson engaged in provocative statecraft as at the Bay of Pigs, the Dominican intervention, and taking
the decisive escalating steps during the course of the Vietnam War. These
observations suggest that the policy-making situation often takes precedence
over adherence in the abstract to a particular style of realist discourse.

Before 1945, idealists and even Marxists exerted influence and had some
access to power in the United States. Only the fatalists were then excluded as
foolish extremists, and were at the time everywhere marginalized by a consensus
among those with influence as to the character of responsible politics in the
nuclear age. The sudden political relevance to the foreign policy debate that was
achieved by the Moral Majority and kindred outlooks seems now to have been a
1980s phenomenon that is unlikely to persist into the nineties, especially in the
aftermath of a series of scandals implicating several leading TV evangelicals. How

then can we explain this ascendancy of realism in the more than four de[cades?] have transpired since 1945? Let me offer a brief account that convey[s] highlights.

Above all, we need to look at the widely shared reading of interwar (19[18–] 1939) history as having been beset by the normative illusion that power politic[s] could be superseded and by the related refusal of leaders in the main constitu- tional democracies to take account of the role of force and counterforce, includ- ing the positive function of a balance of power, in the adjustment of conflict among states. The realist approach crystallized in reaction to earlier American tendencies to exaggerate the role of law and morality in the relations among sovereign states. Carr, Morgenthau, Niebuhr, Walter Lippmann, Kennan, and Acheson spearheaded the use of realist thought and influence in the early postwar period.[4] Much of their criticism of idealist tendencies focused on the wrongheaded diplomatic hopes of Woodrow Wilson after 1918 that international relations could transcend the messy domain of power politics and alliances. In the end, then, the realists insisted that America's approach to relations with the outside world must take account of power dynamics if it was to succeed in the future. The European democracies acknowledged that their attempts at appease- ment as an alternative to military resolve prior to World War II had made matters far worse. In retrospect, it became obvious that the aggressiveness of Hitler's Germany, Mussolini's Italy, and imperial Japan could only have been met by superior military force or not at all. The lessons of Munich and Pearl Harbor were construed to mean that national interests could only be defended by military strength, constant vigilance, and commitments to protect victims of aggression in distant places. There was also appreciation that meeting aggression at an early stage achieved an economy of means as measured both by costs of warfare and human casualties. Standing up to Hitler in the Rhineland and elsewhere in the 1930s would have been far more "economical" than the ordeal of World War II. As Lyndon Johnson liked to say, it was better for Americans to fight in the jungles of Vietnam than on the beaches of California. To secure peace required the country to be prepared for war in a manner that would confront any likely adversary with the unmistakable prospect of defeat.

This general disposition was reinforced by a postwar consensus as to the character of the Soviet challenge, seen as immediately testing the will and capacities of the industrial democracies. The Soviet pressure for hegemony in East Europe, well-organized and large communist parties in several key war-torn Western European countries, and the Soviet bid for an extension of its influence to Greece and Turkey clinched the realist contention that the East-West rivalry wa the central issue of postwar foreign policy. Realists were encouraged to provide authoritative guidance for policymakers, including the warning that a repetition of earlier patterns of sterile legalism and isolationist withdrawal from contested geopolitical zones would likely bring about an intolerable third world war in this century.

---

4. For a useful survey see Michael Joseph Smith, *Realist Thought from Weber to Kissinger* (Louisiana State University Press, 1986).

Furthermore, the realists presented themselves in a nonaggressive idiom, as a new variety of peacemaker, and hence with a policy outlook that did not overtly threaten the still strong American image of innocence and virtue. To the realists, even those who favored intervention in the Third World, it was a matter of adopting the posture suitable for a Hobbesian setting in which the most destructive forces at large in international life will push outward as far as they can until they are deterred by credible prospects of resistance and pain. The realists were never adventurers or "crazies." They were mainly as worried about "macho" warriors as they were by what they conceived to be the naiveté of nuclear pacifists and the outmoded romanticism of isolationists. The realist approach—on the terrain of policy—was to confront a potential aggressor with the prospect of pain greater than any anticipated gain, and to believe that an adversary was rationally receptive and was likely to be under such circumstances contained, or in nuclear settings, deterred.[5] Extending this approach to the Soviet challenge required a western appreciation of the deeper rhythms of revolutionary nationalism, including the realization that aggression could proceed indirectly by way of Moscow-controlled communist parties or by movements situated as Trojan horses in targeted foreign societies. The containment effort necessarily disposed realists to engage in overseas interventionary diplomacy. Such a marriage of academic sophistication and power politics peaked during the Kennedy-Johnson years when "the best and the brightest" championed the Vietnam War as the epitome of realist wisdom. For the sake of fairness let me note that there were realist defectors, like Ball, Morgenthau, and John Herz, who all along as realists in good standing questioned the viability of the Vietnam undertaking and were generally opposed on grounds of national interests to U.S. interventionary diplomacy elsewhere.

Shared insight into the relevance of power and the dynamics of the war system in world politics was not always accompanied by a policy consensus. Those moderate realists who exerted the most constructive influence in the postwar period were consistently alive to the special risks of war in the nuclear age, to the dangers of taking on a range of foreign policy commitments that exceeded national capabilities, and to the constraints of public opinion and constitutionalism in a political democracy. The more militant realists were more disposed to ideological interpretations of conflict that made it difficult to shift away from failed policies. They tended to reduce diplomacy to military prowess and were uncomfortable about subordinating their overseas goals to the requirements at home of democratic support and constitutional procedures. Throughout the postwar world there has been a consistent tug-of-war between moderate and militant realists, a rhythm of to-and-fro that seemed to be guided by whether a given stance was regarded as successful or disappointing in relation to the overall protection of national interests.

What is more, the realist mind-set seemed to be responsive to the complex demands of security in the nuclear age. Considerations of survival put a premium on war-avoidance (as distinct from war-fighting) and yet the requirements

5. See T.C. Schelling, *Arms and Influence* (Harvard University Press, 1966).

of the post-Munich international order made it essential to discourage geopolitical expansion. Thus containment plus deterrence evolved naturally and coherently as central elements of United States foreign policy.

Realists were also conscious of the importance of centralized international economic management and Keynesian fiscal strategies if a recurrence of worldwide depression was to be avoided. The 1930s fixed the image of a challenge to capitalism as strongly on the postwar leadership in the United States as fascism had challenged the stability of political democracy. Global planning for trade, currency exchange, and capital flows was deemed integral to the overall notion of security in the postwar world.

And finally, the realist interpretation opened the way after 1945 for Americans to take advantage of opportunities for U.S. economic and diplomatic expansion. The collapse of the colonial order and the depletion of the economies of Western Europe and Japan gave the United States an extraordinary opportunity to fill a geoeconomic vacuum. The Marshall Plan, foreign aid programs, and multinational financial institutions were creative instruments of expansion that were inherently beneficial in their effects. Incidentally, they bolstered containment and were consistent with the geopolitical master plan of meeting the Soviet challenge at an early enough stage so as to avoid the need to fight a third world war.

Explaining the ascendancy of realists is distinct from telling us how realists interpreted these four critical decades. Because realists dominated the political landscape, most of the debates that are given currency are *among* realists, not between realists and their critics. There were two exceptions. One was the brief period during the Vietnam War from shortly after the Tet Offensive in February 1968 to the signing of the Paris Peace Accords in early 1973. The discrediting of the American claims in Vietnam created a temporary opening for a wider debate and discussion about militarism and the loss of democracy. This opening scared a portion of the realist establishment—Henry Kissinger remembers the period as one in which the country was on the brink of civil war—and it provoked a realist backlash that complained about a decline in respect for authority, as in Samuel Huntington's contribution to the Trilateral Commission volume on *The Crisis of Democracy*.[6] Thereafter, containment realists recovered control over the policy process, ending the Vietnam War, defeating George McGovern, and bringing a temporary lull in international relations during Nixon's first presidential term.

The second exception to realist consensus has been associated with the early years of the Reagan presidency when fatalist rhetoric and policies gave realists (and others) several jolts. Careless nuclearist posturing, the appearance of moving from deterring nuclear war to prevailing in a nuclear war and from containment to rollback as a basis for Third World diplomacy, and proposing the Strategic Defense Initiative (SDI), and, then in a dizzying reversal, endorsing a proposal to abolish all nuclear weapons at the 1986 Iceland summit—all these were unexpected. The Reagan presidency with its odd mixture of ideological

6. (New York: New York University Press, 1975).

geopolitics and utopianism has challenged the realist domination of debate and policy, both by placing ideologues in positions of influence and by seeming to have a penchant for its own special variant of utopianism, a belief in technocratic panaceas, of which SDI is certainly the most notable expression. The Iran-Contra breakdown of constitutional process amounts to an assault upon realist ideas of governance. The public revelation of this breakdown fostered the resumption of a foreign policy posture of prudence and flexibility. The realist recovery of dominance became manifest in the presidential appointments of Frank Carlucci at Defense, William Webster at the CIA, and Howard Baker as White House chief of staff; by a renewed emphasis on the positive side of arms control negotiations and of prospects for moderating East-West relations; but even more by the successful repudiation of Reagan's flirtation with nuclear abolitionism at Iceland.

Having depicted the realist ways of seeing the world, it is now possible to describe briefly how realists (and their critics) have interpreted the last forty years, emphasizing the way they construe the past as a foundation for present questioning and reflection, and how they would adjust U.S. foreign policy in the decades ahead to what most experts regard as a global situation with important new elements.

The claims made on behalf of the realist control over American foreign policy in the last four decades or so are substantial:

1. The avoidance of World War III in the face of high geopolitical tensions.
2. The containment of Soviet expansion by way of military conquest, either directly undertaken or carried out by proxies. Responding in 1950 to the North Korean attack on South Korea illustrates the extent of the American military commitment to containment.
3. The postwar reconstruction of a world trading and monetary system that helped all sectors of international society achieve robust and sustained economic growth.
4. The stabilization of Europe as a conflict zone, including an apparently enduring "solution" for the German problem.
5. The overall accommodation of many changes in the international order, including the acceptance of decolonization, the growth of nonwestern participation in the international system, and the normalization of relations with such revolutionary political actors as the People's Republic of China.
6. An acceptance of the Soviet presence in the world as a legitimate actor, provided its activities are confined within its own sphere of interests.

Realism as an orientation avoided the poles of appeasement and interventionary rollback. Between these poles considerable controversy has occurred as to what sort of foreign policy is appropriate. As I have argued, there are several strands of realism that have produced disagreement, especially on issues of nuclear weapons policy and on the appropriateness of intervention in the Third World.

But realists have not recovered the sort of assured control over foreign policy they possessed in the early Cold War years. Reagan's continued efforts to support the Contras in Central America, to sustain "constructive engagement" in southern Africa, and to push ahead with the militarization of space under the rubric of SDI are divisive commitments that stretch realism beyond its natural limits.

Realists have also been criticized by those who take idealist and progressive positions. These criticisms have focused on the need to take dramatic steps to end the nuclear arms race and to renounce the reliance on nuclear weaponry, as well as to declare an end to all efforts to intervene against revolutionary nationalist movements in the Third World. On more constructive lines, the Left antirealists have wanted to rely more heavily on law and institutions, especially the United Nations, to displace a foreign policy calculus based on power and national interests. These normative perspectives have been more confident about the emergence of an organized global community to replace the dominance over international relations associated with the sovereign state and the state system. Criticisms along these lines briefly assumed prominence in the last years of the Vietnam War (1968–72), but never threatened to take over the control or direction of governmental policy.

These elements of failure, when taken together with the opportunities for international cooperation afforded by the Gorbachev leadership and the altered setting of a relative decline in United States power, have induced some realists to begin asking harder questions of the present as a basis for going forward.

There is, first of all, a common feeling that the past forty plus years have generally witnessed a success story that should be altered only gradually, if at all. Looming in the background is an anxiety that the postwar order could unravel dangerously, especially in Europe, if the arrangements in place are dismantled. It is widely believed that any rapid dissolution of NATO or withdrawal of U.S. troops could lead to a new version of "the German problem," even to a German drive to acquire nuclear weaponry. Yet at the same time, realists acknowledge that cumulative pressures make it desirable to make some adjustment, however cautiously, in U.S. foreign policy at this time, with at least two objectives—to cut the financial cost of foreign policy in light of the deficit and the falling dollar and to diminish still further the risk of general warfare, especially as connected with nuclear weaponry. Others contend that the weight of Europe in world affairs is such that it deserves more influence within the framework of the alliance and that some sort of restructuring by way of "devolution" or "dealignment" is needed.[7]

Realists also generally agree that the Gorbachev leadership offers possible opportunities for improving East-West relations that should be explored, but they are not prepared to regard the superpower rivalry as over, or even as entering a phase that makes intra-allied economic rivalry of greater consequence. Other realists, however, are beginning to argue that political economy issues have become a greater challenge to U.S. national interests in the 1980s than the East-West rivalry, and that a redirection of energies is required to meet

7. See Mary Kaldor and Richard Falk, eds., *Dealignment: A New Foreign Policy Perspective* (Oxford: Basil Blackwell, 1987).

the challenges of the relative U.S. economic decline. Such a reorientation of effort is required if American political leaders are to stop further deterioration of the U.S. position or to manage international indebtedness and volatile financial markets in order to avoid a breakdown in the world economy. On these matters realists seem to be in agreement on the broad nature of the new challenge.

Beyond this generalized view, there are several interesting, more distinct realist variations on these themes that lead to quite divergent policy outcomes:

1. The Cold War has mutated from a corrosive confrontation to a kind of constructive framework for problem-solving and for tacit cooperation. Underneath this view, most ably argued by John Lewis Gaddis, is the sense that nuclear deterrence has provided a bedrock of stability that should not be scrapped too readily.[8] In the background of such thinking lies the belief that bipolar forms of stability tend to work better than multipolar forms. This kind of understanding sees in the Cold War a source of benefits as well as detriments. In particular, the Soviet-American rivalry as played out in Europe contributed to a solution of the German problem by instituting a permanent, now legitimized division into two countries. In addition, the Cold War has facilitated tacit cooperative arrangements between the blocs in Europe that have helped to reduce the risk of inadvertent nuclear war.

2. The success of postwar arrangements was linked to U.S. hegemony. These arrangements cannot be adapted to increasingly multipolar circumstances. As a result, some realists argue that it is necessary to reduce some U.S. commitments and shift a greater portion of the burdens of alliance security to the Europeans and the Japanese. This line of interpretation advocates adjustment via devolution.

3. Some realists now argue that the persistence of Cold War fixations have distracted policymakers from the need for politically unpopular adjustments at home—especially higher taxes and smaller deficits. Similarly, some realists argue that an overemphasis on military research and development has undermined the relative U.S. competitive position, as expressed by declining increments in productivity increase for the United States resulting in an unfavorable competitive position compared to its main industrial rivals. Proponents of this realist thesis contend that the next real war is with Japan.

4. Some realists contend that the United States has consistently misunderstood the Soviet challenge by construing it as primarily military in character. Such a misunderstanding has itself generated dynamics that are dangerous, especially with regard to the nuclear arms race. Denuclearization becomes a higher priority than maneuvering for tactical advantage on Cold War issues. This view has been put forth vigorously in recent years by such influential realists as George Kennan and Robert McNamara, among others, who were in the Cold War mainstream earlier.

5. And there are among realists those who consider the Soviet Union as an

---

8. Gaddis, "How the Cold War Might End," *Atlantic Monthly*, November 1987, pp. 88–100.

implacable foe that has become either more vulnerable or more dangerous, depending on whether the weakness of its economy or the vigor of its new leadership is emphasized. They argue that now is the time to push against this weakness or at least not to drop the western guard. These militant realists (and, of course, their more risk-prone fatalist collaborators) have argued for such a view, even attacking Ronald Reagan from time to time for succumbing to alleged tender-mindedness, as evidenced by summitry, arms control, and most of all, by his encouragement of a vision of a world without nuclear weapons. The *Wall Street Journal*, Henry Kissinger, Richard Nixon, and Zbigniew Brzezinski, among others, argue in different ways that now is the time to wage the Cold War (or its geopolitical equivalent) with renewed resolve, and above all else to avoid the delusion that a period of international serenity lies ahead.[9]

The realist sense, then, of these past forty years is currently in a state of creative flux, accounting for emergence of a wide range of interpretations. Realist thought has recently been displaying a capacity for conceptual and policy innovation. Yet at the same time, there are those who believe that the limitations of the realist approach are more damaging now than earlier. I will leave aside the fatalists who are merely more extreme and dogmatic versions of tough-minded realists and who believe that the struggle against communism must be waged unconditionally and inevitably, that there is no way out other than the victory of one side and the defeat of the other, and that realists who shrink from this apocalyptic assessment are not worthy to lead or to influence leaders. Of greater relevance are criticisms of realism associated with world-order perspectives, noting again that here also there exist several crucial variations in the basic position. Nevertheless, the realist approach has generally been charged with several weaknesses by world-order critics.

Perhaps the most basic charge is what might be called "the Melian syndrome," the tendency of realists to reduce international relations to actual or potential tests of force, as measured mainly by military capabilities, a view reinforced in realist theorizing by selective readings of key texts and historic events from Thucydides onward.[10] One doesn't have to be a devotee of Jacques Derrida and deconstructionism to take issue with the extreme selectivity with which realists

9. These militant realists are also concerned that the U.S. government will retreat from its global role in response to criticisms about over-extension. See Samuel P. Huntington, "Coping with the Lippmann Gap," *Foreign Affairs* 66 (1988): 453–77; Zbigniew Brzezinski, "America's New Geostrategy," *Foreign Affairs* 66 (1988): 680–99. An important expression of this new brand of militant realism is the Pentagon-sponsored study of the Commission on Integrated Long-Range Strategy entitled *Discriminate Deterrence* (Washington: Government Printing Office, January 1988). Perhaps the most articulate popular statement of this general outlook is Richard Nixon, *1999* (New York: Simon & Schuster, 1988).

10. "The Melian syndrome" refers to the famous discussion in Thucydides, *History of the Peloponnesian War*, trans. Rex Warner (New York: Penguin Books, 1954; rev. ed. 1972), bk. V, pp. 400–408. The Athenians, with their superior military power, warned the Melians to submit or be destroyed. Thucydides conveys the basic message that in relations among sovereign entities, relations of power are decisive and matters of rights and equity, almost irrelevant.

have often read the past in order to validate their imagery of the present and future. In effect, the world-orderist critique of realism contends that policymakers have been overly preoccupied with tests of force in their interpretation of conflict and security, thereby missing both the opportunities and the dangers associated with a wider and continually expanding agenda of international concerns.

A closely related criticism is directed against what is seen as a realist tendency to discount both the normative aspirations of society and the normative potential of institutional arrangements that challenge the states system. Especially prominent in realist writing is a tendency to denigrate the United Nations as well as international law, and their frequent contention that international legal approaches were tried in the immediate postwar period and failed as foreign policy instruments. Also, realists are charged by world-orderists with neglecting the contributions and potential future development of law and institutions in international life.[11]

A further charge is that realists have a disappointing record when it comes to the new agenda of problems associated with the global commons. Matters pertaining to the oceans, space, and the environment are either ignored altogether or treated as technical details. In their accounts of international relations, realists rarely pose or confront the challenge of how to evolve a long-range unified approach to this new international environmental agenda, one that can be effectively enforced in a world as politically fragmented and anarchic as the states system. Their failure to address these issues effectively, world-orderists insist, will do serious harm to human health and well-being of present and future generations in a variety of respects.

World-orderists also charge that realists by excluding long-term effects of political fragmentation in an interdependent world from their assessment of national interests are able to keep challenges to their interpretations of the world at a safe distance from the main policy-making and opinion-producing arenas. In effect, at a time when new approaches are most needed, the political imagination is kept preoccupied with the traditional agenda of conflict among states, inducing a sense of entrapment within society in relation to such fundamental challenges as nuclearism and interdependence. The realist position makes one believe that the framework is fixed for the indefinite future.

In the end, world-order critics contend that realism is a source of misleading reassurance and undue caution, fostering the illusion that traditional concerns about power and wealth are all that matter in international relations, as if no conditions of urgency or relevance arise from normative issues of nuclearism, mass poverty, and environmental decay.[12]

The growing conviction of experts and among the public that the challenges of international life cannot be met successfully over time by existing problem-solving approaches engenders an overarching cultural atmosphere of both com-

11. See Richard Falk, "Normative International Relations: A General Introduction," in *The End of World Order* (New York: Holmes & Meier, 1983).
12. For elaboration see Richard Falk, *The Promise of World Order* (Philadelphia and Brighton, Temple University Press and Wheatsheaf, 1987) especially pp. 1–33.

placency and despair. By restricting the foreign policy debate to its main postwar points of geopolitical reference, a basic impression is created that changes of tempo and modality in relations among rival states and groups of states is about all that can be expected, that is, the achievement of a transitory sense of stability and moderation. These criticisms, however, are overstated. Realism as an orientation toward international life has displayed considerable openness and resilience. The moderate realists of the Kennan/Herz/Ball persuasion in particular have consistently sought to adapt their realist prescriptions to continually changing international circumstances. Keeping realism flexible assures at least in the short run that institutions and leaders will incorporate the new agenda of interdependence and environmentalism into their working definition of "national interest."

Marxists and world-orderists offer ways of understanding the international scene that may add to our capacity to interpret the world. There are many variations of perspective beneath the rubrics of Marxism and world-orderism, but they cumulatively serve as signposts to identify useful directions of thought not adequately treated by the realist school. Most Marxists have argued that the pretext of the Cold War was the mask behind which militarism, neocolonialism, and interventionary diplomacy has often hidden and that realism by itself often lends the mask a credibility that sustains public support. Beyond this, recent Left objections to the policies of the past forty years have called attention to the cultural consequences of preparing for nuclear war—what E.P. Thompson has identified as a commitment to exterminism—and to the rending effects on the fabric of political democracy arising from making national security the permanent centerpiece of peacetime concerns.[13]

World-orderists, in contrast to the Marxist Left, emphasize the global structural dangers of present trends and the importance of building a capacity at the global level both to realize human values and to meet the functional challenges of interdependence and the abused global commons.[14] World-orderists want to encourage a belief that the world can be unified around a sense of human identity and global interests. They rely upon supportive cultural developments and social movements to build the societal basis for developing a foreign policy that is both more hopeful and more responsive to the particular challenges of this era.

In the end, most world-orderists are ready to acknowledge that the realist school presided successfully over the complex dynamics of economic and political reconstruction in the years following World War II. And, further, that realism has managed to keep post-1945 tensions from degenerating into open warfare

13. E.P. Thompson, "Notes on Exterminism, the Last Stage of Civilisation," *New Left Review* 121 (May–June 1980): 3–31; see also R.J. Lifton and Richard Falk, *Indefensible Weapons: The Political and Psychological Case Against Nuclearism* (New York: Basic Books, 1983).

14. For the range of thinking see Saul H. Mendlovitz, ed., *On the Creation of a Just World Order* (New York: Free Press, 1975); Mendlovitz and R.B.J. Walker, eds., *Towards a Just World Peace* (London: Butterworths, 1987); and R.B.J. Walker, *One World/Many Worlds* (Boulder, Colo.: Lynne Rienner, 1988).

without a repetition of the appeasement diplomacy of the 1930s. In this regard, realism has provided a robust ideology for the political democracies of the liberal West in the specific setting of this stage of international history.

This stage now seems to be drawing to a close, being superseded by the new complexities of global interdependence and by the decentering of political and economic control in international relations, as well as by the waning of Soviet expansionary zeal. In this altered setting of the late 1980s, realism seems less satisfactory as a comprehensive account of international relations, although it retains a critical utility because of its focus on relations of power and wealth and its refusal to be blinded by sentimental considerations in analyzing the play of forces that constitute international relations. This utility has been confirmed once more by the realist debate that has sprung up around Paul Kennedy's *The Rise and Fall of the Great Powers,* which poses the crucial question about whether America faces incipient imperial decline and can adapt to such a prospect by a prudent reassessment of the relation between capabilities and commitments—adapting by cutting down commitments rather than by stretching capabilities beyond their true limits. Once more the moderate realists, of whom Kennedy is an outstanding example, are seeking to direct American policy on a positive course. And once more the militant realists insist that the country's capabilities can be enhanced and shaped so as to sustain imperial ascendancy for the United States. Realists alone possess the stature and access to leadership that lets this discussion continue.

Realism is also needed in the period ahead to ensure that the instructive lessons of the postwar world are not forgotten. The vitality of realism offers some protection against those who would reassert American exceptionalism as a basis for an aggressive overseas promotion of our way of life or who are prone toward new expressions of fatalism, perhaps this time in the form of a cataclysmic struggle to control space militarily. The realist understanding of international politics does continue to contribute to a positive sense of America's place in the world. The contrary claim argued here is a limited one—namely, that some variants of Marxism and world-orderism offer additional insights that are more needed than they were earlier when the realist understanding encompassed virtually the full range of constructive policy debate. Nothing is more uncertain than the future, but the complexity and fragility of international life makes it seem unlikely that the next several decades will be as dominated by the narrative of superpower rivalry and geopolitics as have the last several decades. Realism should not be relegated to the historical past, especially if its central interpretations of statecraft can be complemented by the less statist forms of political understanding advocated by some world-order theorists who start with the world and its common problems as their basic units of analysis.

19

Covert Action and American Democracy

GREGORY F. TREVERTON

DURING THE investigations in 1975 of the first Senate Select Committee on Intelligence, often called the "Church Committee," Committee Chairman Frank Church likened the Central Intelligence Agency to "a rogue elephant on the rampage."[1] A decade later in the Iran-Contra misadventure, rogues again appeared to be on the loose. Both times the same question was at issue: Are intelligence activities, and especially secret operations, compatible with an open, democratic society?

This nagging question has attached to all of foreign policy in postwar America, but it has special force for secret operations. What is different about those operations is that policymakers usually assume that the action, not just the decision, will remain secret, or at least that the hand of the United States will be hidden. All governments plan in secret. The decisions, for example, to prepare and then to authorize the raid to free the American hostages in Iran in 1980 were taken in the strictest secrecy. The secrecy held; word of the preparations did not leak. Yet those decision makers all knew that the action itself would be public. They presumed they would be held publicly accountable for the operation's success or failure and thus for the decision's wisdom or folly.

Secret operations in which the American role is intended to remain secret, or

1. This chapter is drawn from the author's *Covert Action: The Limits of Intervention in the Postwar World* (New York: Basic Books, 1987).

382

"covert actions," to use the technical term of the intelligence profession, are different. And such actions raise different questions. In addition to the question of whether such practices are compatible with democratic procedures other questions might be added: Are they effective? Do they remain secret?

The history of America's ventures into covert actions thus offers a picture in sharp relief of the presumptions and expectations of this country's political leaders in their postwar encounters with the rest of the world.

Intelligence and Covert Action

Surprisingly, perhaps, from the perspective of the 1980s, the covert operations that are the subject of this chapter did not at first figure prominently in the postwar American national security debate. The first priority was improving the often sorry war record of cooperation among the military services. The second priority was related to the first, how to avert another "Pearl Harbor"—a problem defined as fragmented military intelligence that could neither sort out warning indicators from surrounding "noise" nor make its assessments compelling to officials at the top of government.

Indeed, "covert action" does not appear in the National Security Act of 1947 that established the Central Intelligence Agency. Nor do "covert operations," "clandestine warfare," or "paramilitary operations." Nor, for that matter, do "espionage" or "clandestine intelligence collection." Rather the act authorized the CIA to "perform such other functions and duties related to intelligence affecting the national security as the National Security Council may from time to time direct."[2]

It was the perception of an imminent Soviet threat that moved official Washington to covert action. In February 1948 a communist coup succeeded in Czechoslovakia, while communist agitation grew in France and Italy. By March the government had whipped itself into near hysteria when the American High Commissioner in Germany, General Lucius Clay, cabled his warning that war with the Soviet Union "may come with dramatic suddenness."[3] The first line of American response to the onset of the Cold War was overt, the surge of assistance to Europe through the Truman Doctrine and the Marshall Plan. But the second line was renewed interest in what was then called covert "psychological warfare"—what would now be called propaganda, a way to respond to the Soviet Union that was less than war but more than nothing.

This "extra dimension" of foreign policy quickly came to comprise not just secret propaganda but also other forms of secret action, all intended to influence the politics of foreign countries. Political actions did so indirectly, through covert support to friendly political parties, media, or labor unions, while paramilitary operations sought effect more directly, through providing arms and training for opponents of governments the United States deemed hostile. Between 1951 and

2. *Foreign and Military Intelligence*, Book 1 of the *Final Report of the Senate Select Committee to Study . . . Intelligence Activities*, 94th Cong., 2nd Sess., 26 April 1976, p. 477 (hereafter cited as *Final Report*).

3. Quoted in Walter Millis, ed., *The Forrestal Diaries* (New York: Viking Press, 1951), p. 387.

1975 the U.S. Central Intelligence Agency mounted some nine hundred major or sensitive covert actions, plus several thousand smaller ones.[4]

Yet covert action has always been, and remains, only a part of the world of intelligence—accounting for 3 percent of CIA officers in 1988—although a part that is sensitive far out of proportion to its size.[5] The classic task of intelligence comprises two parts: collecting information and putting it together to see what it means, usually referred to respectively as "collection" and "analysis" or "assessment." These tasks together now consume some 95 percent of the total budget of the U.S. intelligence agencies, collectively referred to by custom as the "intelligence community." Collection, especially by satellites and other so-called national technical means, is the most expensive, consuming the bulk of the community's $20 billion plus annual budget.

By comparison to technical collection, analysis and even secret operations abroad are cheap. The collecting is done by a variety of institutions of the American government: the State Department, the CIA, military attachés, the National Reconnaissance Office, the National Security Agency, and the Foreign Broadcast Information Service, to name the most prominent. The task of assessment is largely the province of one half of the CIA, the Directorate of Intelligence, though the Defense Intelligence Agency (DIA) provides analysis of military issues; the State Department has its own small Bureau of Intelligence and Research (INR); and there are still smaller groups of more specialized analysts scattered throughout the government. These analysts work in Washington, not abroad. Their job is to sift through the piles of information from all sources, secret and not, that can be made available to them. They get much of their information about foreign governments and their actions in the same way we learn about our own government: they read foreign newspapers and magazines. By temperament they are more professorial than conspiratorial.

The other half of the CIA, the Directorate of Operations (which used to be called, in bureaucratic euphemism, the Directorate of Plans)—America's secret intelligence service usually called the Clandestine Service—is responsible for both secret information-gathering, that is, espionage, and covert action (as well as for counterintelligence). The two involve relationships between American CIA officers and foreigners that are clandestine, but the purposes of the contacts are different. The purpose of espionage is information, not action. For covert action, by contrast, action is the point, though the relationship is secret.

Espionage and covert action are kin—networks of agents for one can be used for the other, and sometimes are—but some tension between the two is inherent. Espionage is a patient craft; agents recruited today may not be in a position to provide valuable information for years. By contrast, covert action seeks quick results, and so may distract effort from—and worse, even reveal, or "blow" in the language of the trade—relationships patiently tended for espionage purposes.

4. *Final Report*, p. 445.

5. This percentage and the next were cited by Robert Gates, deputy director of central intelligence, in his "The CIA and American Foreign Policy," *Foreign Affairs* (Winter 1987–88): 216. The dollar estimate is mine, compiled from interviews and press accounts. Needless to say, it is rough, since intelligence budgets remain official secrets.

"Plausible Denial" and the "Buddy System"

When the Church Committee, which I served, surveyed American covert action in the postwar period, it did not find many rogue elephants in the CIA; indeed, those we found were more likely to be wearing FBI crew cuts. What we did find were "plausible denial" and the "buddy system." In the words of Richard Helms, the CIA's deputy director for plans and later director of central intelligence (DCI):

> It was made abundantly clear . . . to everybody involved in the operation that the desire was to get rid of the Castro regime and to get rid of Castro . . . the point is that no limitations were put on this injunction . . . [but] one . . . grows up in [the] tradition of the times and I think that any of us would have found it very difficult to discuss assassinations with a President of the U.S. I just think we all had the feeling that we're hired out to keep those things out of the Oval Office.[6]

Helms's subject was the CIA plots of the 1960s to kill Cuba's Fidel Castro. If he had ever thought he would later have to testify before Congress about what he had done, Helms reflected, he would have made sure that his orders were clear, and in writing.

What Helms described was the concept of "plausible denial," or the ability to protect the American government in general and its president in particular from being linked to any covert operation that might later be exposed. The first important authorizing document for covert action, National Security Council directive NSC 10/2 in 1948, directed that secret operations were to be "so planned and executed that any U.S. Government responsibility for them is not evident to unauthorized persons and that if uncovered the U.S. Government can plausibly disclaim any responsibility for them."[7]

As a result, CIA officials spoke with each other only in riddles about these operations. And if they spoke of them at all with those outside the CIA charged with approving covert operations, they did so "indirectly" or in "circumlocutions." Thus, the Church Committee spent hours trying to unravel whether terse references in documents to "disappear" or "direct positive action" or "neutralize" referred to assassination. We could not be sure. And that was precisely the point of plausible denial. Those CIA officials who spoke in circumlocutions could feel they had done their duty as they understood it. Their political superiors could understand what they would, ask for more information if they desired, but also forbear from asking. If things went awry, they could if they chose disclaim knowledge and do so more-or-less honestly.

These effects of plausible denial are extreme in the case of the Cuban assassination plots, but similar effects ran through covert actions of the 1950s and 1960s. Dean Rusk, who served Presidents Kennedy and Johnson as secretary of

---

6. *Alleged Assassination Plots Involving Foreign Leaders*, Interim Report of the Senate Select Committee to Study . . . Intelligence Activities, 94th Cong.; 1st Sess. 20 November 1975 p. 149 (hereafter cited as *Assassination Report*).

7. Reprinted in William M. Leary, ed., *The Central Intelligence Agency: History and Documents* (University of Alabama Press, 1984), pp. 131–33.

state, observed that he routinely knew little of CIA operations: "I never saw a CIA budget, for example . . ."[8] Of some thousands of covert action projects between 1949 and 1968, only some six hundred received consideration outside the CIA by the National Security Council body then charged with reviewing covert operations.

For its part, in these first postwar decades the American Congress was more interested in making sure the CIA had what it needed in the fight against communism than in overseeing its operations. That several congressional initiatives for improving oversight came to naught in these early years is eloquent testimony to the mood of the times and the temper of the Congress. In early 1955 Senator Mike Mansfield, later chairman of the Foreign Relations Committee, introduced a resolution calling for a Joint Oversight Committee; the resolution had thirty-five cosponsors. It also had the strong opposition not only of the executive branch but also of the "club" of senior members of Congress. In hearings on the resolution, Mansfield elicited the following comment from Senator Leverett Saltonstall, the ranking Republican on the Armed Services Committee and its Defense Subcommittee, then the CIA overseers:

> It is not a question of reluctance on the part of the CIA officials to speak to us. Instead, it is a question of our reluctance, if you will, to seek information and knowledge on subjects which I personally, as a Member of Congress and as a citizen, would rather not have, unless I believed it to be my responsibility to have it because it might involve the lives of American citizens.[9]

In April 1956 the resolution was voted down, 59 to 27, with a half dozen cosponsors voting against it.

The debate, however, did result in the creation of formal CIA subcommittees in both Armed Services Committees. Yet what we on the Church Committee came to call the "buddy system" remained largely unchanged. Allen Dulles, the DCI, was a near-legend: his CIA was credited with a major, if covert, role in helping the Italian Christian Democrats fend off a challenge from the Communists in the 1947 Italian elections. More recently, with a few men and a lot of derring-do, it seemed, CIA covert operators had rid the United States of two troublesome Third World leaders—Mosaddeq in Iran and Arbenz in Guatemala. These early "successes" consolidated the ascendancy of operations over assessment in the CIA, and within the Clandestine Service, of covert action over espionage. Running big covert actions became the way to make a career.

Relaxed and candid with senior members of Congress, Allen Dulles had their absolute trust. In the Senate Armed Services Committee, Senator Richard

8. Richard B. Russell Library, Oral History No. 86, taped by Hughes Cates, 22 February 1977, University of Georgia, Athens, cited in Loch Johnson, "Covert Action and American Foreign Policy: Decision Paths for the 'Quiet Option,'" paper presented to the American Political Science Association Annual Meeting, Washington, D.C., 1986, p. 4.

9. Quoted in Anne Karalekas, "History of the Central Intelligence Agency," in *Supplementary Detailed Staff Reports on Foreign and Military Intelligence*, Book 4 of *Final Report of the Senate Select Committee to Study . . . Intelligence Activities*, 94th Cong., 2nd Sess. 23 April 1976, p. 54 (hereafter cited as "CIA History").

Russell appointed to the formal subcommittee those senators with whom he had been meeting informally on CIA matters—Saltonstall and Harry Byrd. Later he added Lyndon Johnson and Styles Bridges. When in 1957 the Appropriations Committee formed a subcommittee for the CIA, its members were Russell, Byrd, and Bridges. They did both "authorization" and "appropriation," often at the same meeting. Most CIA business continued to be conducted as before—by Dulles and Russell, meeting informally.

Plausible denial and the buddy system did not emerge because the CIA had broken free of its political masters. They emerged because that was how both administrations and Congress wanted it at the time. The executive and the CIA did not want to tell Congress much; Congress also accepted the primacy of secrecy and did not want to know that much. With the Cold War at its height, members of Congress shared the feeling that the United States had to act. They were prepared to give the president considerable discretion in conducting clandestine operations, including covert action. In the instance of Guatemala in 1954, Congress as a whole showed little public interest in finding out what American actions were afoot until very late. And even then the names of the committees that planned to hold hearings suggest the tenor of congressional concern: they were the House Select Committee on Communist Aggression and the Senate Subcommittee on Internal Security.

Allen Dulles, Director of Central Intelligence from 1953 to 1961, a "near legend" who had the "absolute trust" of Congress. (National Archives)

President Kennedy consulting with former President Eisenhower at Camp David after the abortive Bay of Pigs operation. (AP/Wide World Photos)

Moreover, such of the public as was attentive to foreign affairs shared views similar to those of their elected officials. In 1954 when news of the covert attempt to unseat President Arbenz of Guatemala leaked out, the leaks were discredited, not the operation. The vivid prose of *Time* magazine reflected the temper of the times in Washington: the revelations were ". . . masterminded in Moscow and designed to divert the attention from Guatemala as the Western Hemisphere's Red problem child."[10]

10. 8 February 1954.

"JUST BETWEEN US, FELLOWS, WHO WAS AT THE CONTROLS?"

(Copyright 1960 Bill Mauldin)

The Climate Changes

The Bay of Pigs invasion of Cuba in 1961 was a stunning defeat for an agency that had been known publicly only for its successes. President Kennedy took responsibility for the debacle, but Allen Dulles and his deputy for covert operations, Richard Bissell, were eased out of their jobs, to be replaced by John McCone and Richard Helms respectively. The Dulles era was over.

Yet neither executive procedures for nor congressional oversight of covert action changed all that much. Plausible denial seemed threadbare after the Bay of Pigs: Kennedy did not feel he could make use of it; nor had his predecessor, President Eisenhower, when the Soviet Union shot down a CIA U-2 reconnaissance aircraft over Russia in May 1960—an intelligence-collecting operation, not a covert action.

Within the executive branch, procedures for reviewing covert actions became more formal, and the criteria for which proposals needed to be reviewed outside the CIA were made more explicit. Each administration created a cabinet group to review major proposals; successive NSC directives changed the names of the groups more than their composition—the Special Group later became the 303 Committee and then in the Nixon administration the 40 Committee—with 303 and 40 both derived from the number of the authorizing NSC directive. Still, most covert action projects proceeded without having been approved by anyone outside the CIA; most of these were small operations, often propaganda, deemed not risky by the rough guidelines in effect. By the early 1970s only about a fourth of all covert actions came before the NSC review body. [11]

More committees of Congress received more information from the CIA than in the early days. In 1967, thirteen committees in addition to the four with oversight responsibilities were briefed by the CIA. [12] Most of those briefings, however, concerned intelligence products, not clandestine operations. About those operations, the CIA did not often volunteer information and Congress did not frequently ask. The role of Congress had not changed from receiving information to overseeing operations. In 1961 after the Bay of Pigs and again in 1966, Senator Eugene McCarthy attempted to revive the idea of a CIA oversight committee, but it still was an idea whose time had not yet come.

If Congress did not much want to ask about covert action and the CIA did not much want to tell, all of that changed with Watergate, on the heels of the Vietnam War, and with revelations about the CIA's role in Chile before and during the tenure of Salvador Allende, a self-proclaimed Marxist who was elected president in 1970 and killed in a coup in 1973. Congress's disinclination to ask was the first to change. It created special committees to investigate intelligence—the Church Committee in the Senate and a parallel one in the House chaired by Representative Otis Pike. It also in 1974 passed the Hughes-Ryan Act, the operative paragraph of which reads:

> No funds appropriated under the authority of this or any other Act may be expended by or on behalf of the [CIA] for operations in foreign countries, other than activities intended solely for obtaining necessary intelligence, unless and until the President finds that each such operation is important to the national security of the United States and reports, in a timely fashion, a description and scope of such operation to the appropriate committees of Congress. [13]

"Finds" was turned into the noun "finding," a written document bearing the president's signature. As at other times in other areas of policy, Congress sought

11. *Covert Action in Chile,* Hearings before the Senate Select Committee to Study . . . Intelligence Activities, 94th Cong., 1st Sess. 4 and 5 December 1975, p. 41.
12. "CIA History," p. 72.
13. Officially, section 622 of the Foreign Assistance Act of 1974.

to influence the executive not by determining specific decisions but rather by changing the process by which decisions were made. Hughes-Ryan largely undermined plausible denial, which seemed in the mid-1970s to have confused procedures within the executive, and deluded Congress, more than it protected anyone. Needless to say, the many congressional efforts to address the problems of relations between the legislative and executive branches in the matter of covert actions were not intended to destroy the capacity of the government to carry out activities secretly. Congress did not want covert actions to be exposed or traced to official United States sources. Nevertheless, by expanding the circle of those who "need to know" about covert action and by creating a clear "paper trail" right up to the president (the written "finding" signed by the president), this legislation clearly destroyed plausible denial once the official American connection was exposed.

Hughes-Ryan required the president to put his name and his reputation on the line. It was meant to ensure that there would be no future wrangles such as those over assassinations: covert actions, wise or stupid, would reflect presidential decisions; there would be no doubt that someone was in charge. It also tied the hands of members of Congress: they would find it harder to assert that they had been kept in the dark. Less often could they speechify in professed ignorance of covert action.

Reshaping the Constitutional Bargain

Whatever their results, the special committees and the Church Committee in particular were an innovation in constitutional relations between the executive and Congress.[14] Our own language mirrors ambiguity about what constitutes "the government," particularly in foreign affairs. High school civics textbooks show the Congress as a coequal branch of "the government," yet often we use "government" more narrowly to refer to a particular administration in power. In the autumn of 1975 the administration and the congressional investigations were engaged in a guerrilla war over access to secret documents. For those of us on the Church Committee staff, the war accentuated the hurry-up-and-wait that is characteristic of Congress even in "normal" times. We would work long days gearing up for hearings that then would be cancelled at the last moment because the administration had held back documents. Then the wrangling over which secret documents we would get access to and under what terms would begin again. At the heart of all our wranglings with the Ford administration over access to classified documents lay the constitutional issue: Were those secret documents, written and classified by the CIA or the State Department, the property of the executive only? Or were they the "government's" documents, to which Congress should have access on terms decided by it and which could be declassified by its decision as well as that of the executive?

14. For an intriguing account of the Senate Select Committee, see Loch Johnson, *A Season of Inquiry: The Senate Intelligence Investigation* (University Press of Kentucky, 1985).

We did not, in 1975–76, reach a clean resolution of this fundamental question. In the nature of our system, we could not have. But we did move a long way toward the view that even in matters of clandestine operations, Congress has its own right to the "government's" secret documents—and bears the responsibility that goes with that right. In seeking to establish that position, the Church Committee was meticulous about leaks. So far as I am aware, not a single secret worth mention seeped out through the committee and its staff.[15] For similar reasons, successor oversight committees have been nearly as meticulous.

The Ford administration was a grudging partner in reshaping the bargain between the executive and Congress. A few in the administration, William Colby, the DCI, foremost among them, believed the reshaping was fundamentally correct; others, no doubt, simply felt the administration had no choice. The administration thus wound up with a kind of dual approach to the Church Committee. At one level, as a matter of principle, it was opposed to the investigation and its results. At another level, however, it was prepared to work with the committee, particularly to protect intelligence sources and methods.

As the committee groped toward a changed constitutional bargain, my immediate concern was Chile. From the outset, the general sense of the committee had been that we ought to lay one covert action out in public. That seemed essential to this once-in-a-generation clearing of the air. As it was, the swirl of charges, many of them excessive, some of them untrue, did the CIA itself no good. If we were to make one covert action public, Chile was the logical candidate. Newspaper revelations about covert action in Chile were part of the reason the committee had been created in the first place. President Ford himself had stripped what remained of the fig leaf of plausible denial from the operation in September 1974 when he confirmed it at a press conference. By the middle of 1975, not much was secret about the operation except some particulars of truth.

The committee argued with the administration about Chile throughout 1975, an argument interrupted by our inquiry into assassination attempts, like those against Castro. Against the administration's strong view that a public hearing on Chile would damage the national security of the United States, the committee reconsidered, eventually deciding to go ahead. Again, the administration's approach was dual: in principle, it remained opposed to any hearing, and it refused to permit any sitting officials or retired CIA officers to testify in public; yet if we went ahead, it was prepared to work with us, again ostensibly to protect "sources and methods."

Given the administration's unwillingness to let those officials who had been closest to the Chile operations testify in public, the committee decided to issue a staff report to lay out that story. We did a draft based on CIA and State Department documents and supplemented by numbers of interviews with participants. The hearing was scheduled for 4 and 5 December 1975. The days just

---

15. The same could not be said of the Pike Committee, whose report found its way to the journalist Daniel Schorr after release had been voted down by the House. The Church Committee, however, was more often the victim of leaks than the perpetrator. See Johnson, *Season of Inquiry*, pp. 206–7.

before it began I spent with the draft in a secured room at CIA headquarters in Langley with a shifting set of CIA officials, by then colleagues. Our topic of discussion was meant to be sources and methods. In fact, we argued through every line of the report. Was a particular conclusion, even if tentatively drawn, fair in light of the evidence? Did a particular verb overstate the point?

The argument went on and on. It was exhausting but also exhilarating. It seemed to me, then and now, to represent the American system working well. The executive had its position, the committee had its own. Neither changed its mind. But we worked together to avoid needless damage to interests we both held dear. The process forced me and my Senate colleagues to think again about the evidence and to sharpen our prose. And in the end it was the committee itself that would decide whether it published the report or not, and with what included and what excluded.

As with our report on assassinations, the final issue of contention was names. On most of those we relented, yet a few seemed to us either appropriate to publish or were so well known already that their exclusion would only convey the impression that we were trying to hide something. For instance, for *"El Mercurio,"* our friends at the CIA wanted us to substitute "major Santiago daily." Their phrase was tantamount to naming the paper, given all the press play Chile had received. It seemed to us more likely to spread confusion or to suggest deception than to protect anything. The committee accepted our advice on all the contended names, and the final report, *Covert Action in Chile,* contained them all.

At the end of its investigation, the Church Committee's principal recommendation was that it be made permanent. We hoped it would in time absorb all the existing oversight functions and so provide a single focal point for the Senate's consideration of the intelligence community. That hope was in fact realized, as it was in the House, an institutional legacy that has turned out to be important. The committees include members who sit simultaneously on the Armed Services, Foreign Affairs, Judiciary, and Appropriations Committees, giving those committees the opportunity to relinquish their oversight function without feeling that they have been entirely cut out. Moreover, the committees established the principle of rotating memberships to broaden their representation within the Congress, thus guarding against a recurrence of the buddy system in image or in fact. An earlier innovation in congressional oversight, the Joint Atomic Energy Committee, was widely regarded as having become the captive of those agencies that it oversaw.

The procedural legacy, that messy constitutional bargain between executive and Congress, was at least as important as the institutional one. Congress secured its access to information about intelligence activities, including covert action, as a matter of right, not of executive courtesy. (Whether Congress always likes knowing about covert action is another matter.) Secret documents became the property of "the government," not just the executive branch.

Making the president sign on the dotted line for major covert actions and reinforcing that with congressional access to secret documents would, we hoped, induce administrations to think and think again before resorting to covert intervention. Prudent presidents, we thought, might come to use the overseers as a source of seasoned counsel about the political risks of an operation, and so as a check on the CIA's can-do mentality or the temptations of White House staffers. The process would also make Congress share the responsibility at both "takeoff and landing," in one staffer's phrase, even if the operation failed and the landing was a hard one.

The Inherent Tension

The Carter administration in its first years in particular was disinclined to resort to covert action. Its internal review committee, labeled the Special Coordination Committee (SCC), included the attorney general. And in other ways as well the administration tightened its review of covert action. For instance, formalizing a practice begun during Colby's tenure, proposals were passed to the CIA's Directorate of Intelligence, then called the National Foreign Assessment Center. The agency's analysts would have some chance of knowing what its covert operators were up to.

With few covert actions, the administration's dealings with Congress over covert actions were easy. Its continuation of the Ford practice of submitting blanket findings—covering, for instance, a range of covert actions against terrorist targets in a single finding—was not much of an issue. Nor was the fact that Carter's DCI, Stansfield Turner, rejected the notion of "prior notification"—that is, notifying the Congress before operations were underway.[16] The administration and Congress cooperated in passing the Intelligence Oversight Act of 1980, the most important law passed by Congress in the realm of covert action.[17] The law made clear that Congress wanted to be notified of all covert actions, not just those carried out by the CIA. Secret executive recourse to other agencies, in particular the military, was ruled out.

Congress did tiptoe toward prior notification: the "timely fashion" of Hughes-Ryan (within twenty-four hours of an action's beginning came to be the understanding) became "fully and currently informed," including "any significant anticipated intelligence activity," in the 1980 act. Yet notifying Congress still was not a "condition precedent to the initiation" of covert action. And the act gave the president another escape hatch, because in emergencies he was permitted to limit prior notice to eight members—the chairmen and ranking minority members of the intelligence committees, the speaker and minority leader of the House, and the majority and minority leaders of the Senate—the "gang of eight."

Enter the Reagan administration, determined to make covert assistance to "freedom fighters" around the world a key element of its global pressure on the Soviet Union. In setting out what came to be called the "Reagan doctrine," the president said Third World trouble spots "are the consequence of an ideology

16. See Stansfield Turner, *Secrecy and Democracy: The CIA in Transition* (Boston: Houghton Mifflin, 1985), p. 170.
17. Officially, Section 413 of the Intelligence Oversight Act of 1980.

imposed from without, dividing nations and creating regimes that are . . . at war with their own people. . . . And in each case, Marxism-Leninism's war becomes war with their neighbors."[18] Mr. Reagan's Executive Order No. 12333 slightly expanded the definition of covert action, termed "special activities," over the Carter order. And, strikingly in light of what came later, it gave the CIA full responsibility for those activities, except in time of war or by specific presidential instruction.[19]

The administration reshaped its internal review processes to manage the increase in covert actions. In place of the SCC, it created the National Security Planning Group (NSPG). That group included the vice president, the secretaries of state and defense, the DCI and the national security adviser, but, for reasons of secrecy, the other SCC members were dropped. In their place, three presidential advisers were added—the White House chief of staff, his deputy, and the president's counselor. The president himself was a member of the group. The intent was to make the process more responsive to the president's desire for more frequent resort to covert action. The risk was that sources of expert advice, the attorney general or the Joint Chiefs of Staff, for instance—especially advice that might be cautionary—were lost.

By 1985 the administration had created a group to backstop the NSPG, somewhat in parallel to an SCC working group in the Carter administration. Like its predecessor, it was composed of the deputies of the NSPG members. Formally nameless, it was dubbed the "208 Committee" after the room where it met in the Old Executive Office Building in the White House complex.

With the new administration, however, attitudes had changed more than procedures. One congressional staffer disapprovingly identified men like Lt. Col. Oliver North as eager for action, long on energy, but short on political savvy. Even more colorfully, another staffer described the attitude of one CIA director of congressional affairs, a career clandestine service officer: he behaved as if "Washington was a foreign country and he was the station chief in hostile terrain, mounting operations against the Congress."

William Miller, the staff director of both the Church Committee and the first permanent Senate Intelligence Committee, observed that the CIA and its sister agencies were led in the late 1970s by people who had been through the experience of investigation and reform. They were "so immersed in the constitutional questions that they could recite chapter and verse. Questions of law and balance occurred naturally to them." By contrast, the Reagan leadership was dominated by "advocates, people who were always trying to get around the roadblocks, who were looking for a way to get it done."[20]

Nicaragua, and aid to the Contras in particular, became the focal point of tension between administration and Congress. McGeorge Bundy, who had run the 303 Committee for the Kennedy and Johnson administrations, reflected on

18. Speech to the United Nations, 25 October 1985, as quoted in the *Washington Post*.
19. The order was printed in *The New York Times*, 5 December 1981.
20. Interview, 16 January 1986.

(Copyright 1985, John Trever, *Albuquerque Journal*. Reprinted by permission.)

the difficulty reviewers outside the CIA confront in a way that congressional overseers of the Contra operation would appreciate: "I think it has happened that an operation is presented in one way to a committee and executed in a way that is different from what the committee thought it had considered."[21]

The administration justified covert support to the Contras in terms other than overthrowing the Sandinistas; that was the purpose that, as Robert R. Simmons, then the staff director of the Senate Intelligence Committee, put it, "everyone discussed but few admitted."[22] The aid would slow the infiltration of arms from Nicaragua to the rebels fighting the American-backed government of El Salvador, or it would focus the Sandinistas inward, away from the export of their revolution, or it would pressure the regime into serious negotiations with its neighbors and the United States. Yet the Contras did not have limited purposes, much less ones that suited American convenience. They wanted not to constrain the Sandinista government but to replace it.

When in November 1981 the president signed a finding for the Contra operation, the program seemed very broad—leading to the first of a number of disputes between the administration and the intelligence committees of Congress over exactly what the purpose of the Nicaraguan project was. The Novem-

21. Quoted in the *Washington Star,* 12 November 1975.
22. Interview, 18 January 1986.

ber language—"engage in paramilitary . . . operations in Nicaragua and elsewhere"—seemed to permit almost anything.

The series of congressional responses suggests that the committees, particularly the House Committee where Democrats held a majority, did not believe that the administration was sincere in professing limited objectives, that the committees and the administration did not agree on what the objectives were, or both in some combination. The congressional committees first made clear in their classified reports on the CIA budget that they opposed covert efforts to overthrow the Sandinistas; then, at the end of 1982, they put that language as the Boland Amendment publicly into the appropriations bill.[23] Named for Representative Edward P. Boland, the chairman of the House Intelligence Committee, it stipulated that no money could be used "for the purpose of overthrowing the Government of Nicaragua or provoking a military exchange between Nicaragua and Honduras."[24]

Assessing purposes required congressional overseers to get deeply into the details of ongoing operations, hard for them and uncomfortable for covert operators in the executive branch. They were, and are, hard-pressed to keep up with the details of forty-odd covert actions. As one staffer close to the process put it: "How can you know which detail will jump up and bite you? Things move fast. Entire operations may take only a few weeks." Critical details could fall between the cracks even with the best of wills on both sides.

And suffice it to say that wills were not always the best. The direct CIA role in mining Nicaraguan harbors is a case in point. The operation plainly was risky because it threatened not only Nicaraguan vessels but also international shipping, including that of American allies. It also represented a new phase in the covert war, albeit a phase suggested by the original CIA proposal. The president approved the recommendation in the winter, probably in December 1983.[25] On 31 January 1984, the DCI, William Casey, met with the House committee, whose members had been persistent critics of covert action in Nicaragua, and he mentioned the mining, even though the meeting was primarily about releasing further funds for the overall Contra project. Several members of the Senate committee and its staff may also have been briefed. The Senate, however, was pushing toward its February recess, and the administration twice asked for a delay so that Secretary of State Shultz could attend. As a result, a full briefing of the Senate committee was delayed, and many, perhaps most members remained unaware of the operation, and especially of the direct CIA role in it. So did the staff director.

Casey first met with the full committee on 8 March for over an hour, but this meeting, too, dealt primarily with authorizing the release of funds, over which the Intelligence Committee was fighting a jurisdictional battle with Appropria-

23. See the Senate Select Committee on Intelligence, *Report*, 1 January 1983 to 31 December 1984, 98th Cong., 2nd Sess. (1985), pp. 4–5.

24. Officially the bans were attached to the fiscal 1983 appropriations bill (Public Law 97-377, Section 793) and the fiscal 1985 defense budget (Public Law 98-473, Section 8066).

25. See reports in *The New York Times*, 13, 16, and 17 April 1984. See also the account in Senate Select Committee on Intelligence, *Report*, cited above, pp. 4ff.

Bill Graham, *Arkansas Gazette*. (Reprinted with permission of the *Arkansas Gazette*.)

tions. Only one sentence dealt with the mining, and it, like the rest of the briefing, was delivered in Casey's inimitable mumble.[26] Many on the committee did not learn of the mining until a month later, almost by accident on the floor of the Senate.

Casey honored the letter of the law with his brief reference, but the episode angered even Senator Barry Goldwater, the committee chairman and a man not known for his opposition to covert action. He had not understood the reference. When he learned about the operation, once the committee staff received a full briefing on 2 April, he was furious. His letter to Casey, which leaked into the press, was notable for its unsenatorial prose as well as for its displeasure: "It gets down to one, little, simple phrase: I am pissed off!"[27]

It may be that committee members, like Goldwater, were not paying attention. The episode also demonstrates another peril of oversight, for if the two houses share a distrust of the executive, no matter which party is in power, they are jealous of each other as well, and so the two committees do not automatically share information. However, as Turner concluded, Casey's performance, if it squared with the letter of the law, was "hardly the intent. . . . The CIA did go through the motions of informing, but it wasn't speaking very loudly."[28]

An Unnatural Act

Even if it knows of them, overseeing secret operations remains, for Congress, something of an unnatural act. Members of Congress, like other people, are

26. Interviews with intelligence committee staff members, January 1987.
27. The letter was dated 9 April; see the *Washington Post*, 11 April 1984.
28. Turner, *Secrecy and Democracy*, p. 168.

fascinated by secret operations—at the beginning of the 100th Congress in 1987, sixty members of the House applied for four openings on the Intelligence Committee—but they still have little political reason to become involved in oversight, and many reasons not to. Sometimes they feel they know more than they want to know. Senator Daniel Inouye, the first chairman once the permanent Senate Intelligence Committee was created, used language not much different from Saltonstall's thirty years earlier: "How would you like to know a very, very high official of a certain government was on our payroll?"[29]

More than a decade ago, in designing new oversight arrangements for intelligence, it was apparent that covert action would be the most sensitive task. We tried to strike a delicate balance: Congress would have the power to persuade by having the ability to know; single points of oversight, constructed to be representative of the entire house, would enhance accountability by permitting a real sharing of information even about these most secret of governmental operations. At the same time, Congress would not have the right of prior approval; it would not have to vote up or down on every significant covert action. That did not then seem either wise or necessary, nor did it seem what either the executive or Congress desired.

Most of the time the process seems to have worked as it was intended. The congressional overseers have been informed of covert actions and have recorded their views; sometimes those views have prevailed. In other cases, they have said, in the words of one staff member, "Hey, do you know how risky that is?" Hearing an affirmative response, they have let the program go ahead despite their doubts. Most of the time, in either case, the process has remained secret. The Reagan administration wanted to make use of covert action much more frequently than its predecessor, and the oversight committees, reflecting the mood of Congress and probably of the American people as well, assented to that expansion of covert action.

Indeed, there is the risk that the committees will become as much protectors of the intelligence community as overseers—the risk that runs through all relations between Congress and executive agencies from Agriculture to Defense. It was a risk we sought to minimize through rotating memberships. So far the risk seems small with regard to covert action, although it is true that the committees have been instrumental in tripling the total budget of the intelligence community in a decade to some $20 billion per year, most of that for large new technical collection systems.

However, in first limiting, then cutting off, then resuming aid to the Contras, the Congress confronted an administration determined to continue to find ways to help them, an administration arguing that the United States had a commitment to the Contras. Under these circumstances, Congress was bound to pay attention to the spirit of the law, the administration to the letter. With passions running high on both sides and the sense of frustration in Congress deep, Congress was driven toward broad bans, just as it was a decade earlier in passing the Clark-Tunney Amendment on Angola. In both cases, Congress said in effect

29. As quoted in *The New York Times*, 7 July 1986.

that it did not trust the administration or its designated overseers of covert action or both.

There can be no full resolutions to these dilemmas, because they are rooted in the paradox of secret operations in a democracy. It still does not seem appropriate to make Congress approve of every covert action in advance. Getting the intelligence committees to authorize and the Congress to appropriate specific budgets could take months. Instead, the intelligence committees might be required to approve any withdrawal from the CIA Contingency Reserve, expressly intended to enable the CIA to react quickly to changing circumstances. That would be uncomfortable for the committees in that it would put them more directly on the line in the eyes of their congressional colleagues, but it would at least spare them the discomfort of having to choose between silent opposition to an operation and public exposure of it.

So far, also, administrations have very seldom resorted to informing only the "gang of eight" when they feel secrecy is at a premium.[30] If relations between Casey and the committees had been better, perhaps the Reagan administration would have consulted the gang of eight before selling arms to Iran. The consultation would not necessarily have resulted in a wiser policy, because it is conceivable that the gang of eight would have been seduced down the path from geostrategic interests to releasing hostages just as the president had been. But the subsequent debate would then have been about the wisdom of the policy, not about whether Congress was deceived.

The fundamental conclusion to be drawn about the overt "covert" actions like the ones related to Nicaragua is the straightforward one: when covert operations are large and when both they and the larger foreign policies of which they are a part are fiercely contended by American political leaders, those covert operations cannot remain secret. In those cases, it is not that oversight has broken down, but rather that in our democratic society no tidy, secret process can be sustained.

Looking Backward . . . and Forward

In looking at American foreign policy through the lens of covert action, I am struck by how much we as a people have changed. In the atmosphere of the 1950s, several major covert actions of the 1950s remained secret for a long time: the CIA's assistance to Tibetans resisting the domination of their land by China, regarded in intelligence lore as a successful holding action, is still little discussed, all the less so because it is an embarassment now that Sino-American relations have thawed. The effort to unseat President Sukarno of Indonesia, who had earned Washington's opposition for his espousal of nonalignment, ranged from covert political actions to a paramilitary operation. It is not much better known than the Tibetan operation.[31] Americans are now more skeptical of their

---

30. Interviews with CIA officials, January 1987.
31. For accounts of both, see chaps. 8 and 9 of John Prados, *Presidents' Secret Wars: CIA and Pentagon Covert Operations Since World War II* (New York: Morrow, 1986).

government, of its information and its capacity, a skepticism that is a legacy of recent history labeled "Watergate." When Ronald Reagan, the most popular president in generations, first denied in 1986 that his administration had traded arms sales to Iran for the release of American hostages in Lebanon, most Americans did not believe him. The skepticism has been reinforced by other developments. One is investigative journalism, which now is everywhere; every cub reporter aspires to be Woodward or Bernstein of Watergate fame. The media now contain more people asking hard questions, even of secret operations, and probing for leaks, and fewer people who are prepared to take the government at its word.

Moreover, if the leak does not initially come from Washington, the scent will be picked up by the American press from overseas—even if, as in 1986, the first article is published in Beirut in Arabic. Despite heavy-handed attempts by many Third World governments to control information, their nations' media are more active, and more sophisticated, than they were three decades ago. And leaders and media in the Third World may have a powerful incentive to reveal a U.S. covert operation, especially if their nation is its target.

Now, moreover, more covert operations are controversial inside the governing establishment—and outside when leaks occur. The series of events captured by the label "Vietnam," with "covert intervention" perhaps as a subtitle, has made Americans more skeptical that every upheaval in the poor countries of the world threatens U.S. interests enough to warrant intervention, covert or open. The public ambivalence in the United States about Nicaragua reflected that skepticism. On the one hand, the drift of the Sandinista government was worrisome, still more so if it took Managua closer to Havana or Moscow. Yet on the other hand there was no conviction that the threat justified spilling American blood. CIA intervention was preferable to a military commitment, but even that was controversial.

Certainly, there will be cycles in American attitudes, as there have been before. Concerns over Soviet power coexist with worries about nuclear war and peace; one predominates, then the other. In the early 1980s, most Americans evidently shared their president's concern with the Soviet threat, and their congressional representatives went along with huge increases in defense spending—and in spending for covert action. So, too, Ronald Reagan was able to rebuild considerable authority and discretion in the American presidency, thus ending a cycle begun by Vietnam and Watergate. Indeed, the saddest consequence of the Iran-Contra debacle may be that it will undermine that rebuilding.

Even now, not every covert action is controversial. Of the forty or so covert actions underway in the mid-1980s, at least half had been the subject of some press accounts. Yet only several were controversial enough so that the first leaks became continuing stories. Most of the rest were open secrets, more unacknowledged than unknown; they were so because most members of Congress thought they made sense, as did most Americans who knew or thought about them—and, no doubt, most of the journalists who reported them. William Colby characterized the reaction to revelations of American assistance to the resistance in Afghanistan: "Afghanistan was a two-column headline in the *Washington Post* for one day, then almost nothing."[32]

Lessons, Not Processes

At first blush, the Iran-Contra affair seems to reflect no delicate dilemma in relations between the executive branch and Congress. When the president finally approved a finding for the arms sales to Iran in January 1986, that finding was explicit: do not tell Congress. The congressional overseers did not find out about the Iran operation until the following autumn—not "fully and currently informed" by anyone's definition. Later on, it was the president himself who apparently was not told, when the Iran and Contra operations crossed, that the proceeds from the former were being secretly channeled for the benefit of the latter.

Yet the affair ran parallel to previous episodes in some respects and reinforced lessons of the history of covert action in others. This time, if there were rogue elephants, most of them were in the White House, not the CIA. Indeed, the January finding ensued because the institutional CIA insisted that if CIA officers were to participate in the arms sales, a finding was required. Those CIA officers who crossed the line by participating in resupplying the Contras during the period when such support was banned were led across the line by some combination of their own zeal, their sense of commitment to the Contras, and, most crucially, their feeling that the visible White House lead, personified by North, constituted authorization of a kind.

The arms sales reflected the primacy of action over intelligence. Intelligence on Iran was weak, the specific legacy of the shah's fall. Yet that weakness was also part of a more general legacy: the priority accorded to operations over intelligence and to technical collection over espionage. What intelligence there was offered precious little support for the premises of the arms sales, especially for the notion that there were Iranian "moderates" who might be detached from their more extreme colleagues.

Moreover, in deciding to sell arms to Iran, the president pursued a line of policy opposed by both his secretaries of state and defense, about which he was afraid to inform the congressional intelligence committees, and which was liable to be revealed by Iranian factions as and when it suited them. It is hard to imagine any system providing more warning signals. When the opposition of most of the government's senior foreign policy officials means they have to be cut out of the policy, it is likely that the policy, and not they, are wrong. The president thus proceeded at his own peril.

With regard to the diversion of money for the Contras, the lesson is not that the NSC staff should be eliminated or the national security adviser made subject to Senate confirmation. Presidents will always have need of a source of private advice and a means of brokering the actions of the many foreign policy agencies of government. Moreover, if presidents are determined to get something done,

32. Interview, 9 January 1986.

Lt. Col. Oliver North at the Iran/Contras hearings, July 1987. (Wide World Photos)

they will be able to find someone, somewhere in the White House, to do it. So, too, if the United States continues to have a foreign intelligence service, presidents will be tempted to resort to covert action.

Rather, the lesson is a caution for presidents and those who advise them: don't do it. And, especially, don't do it from the White House. Two decades ago, it would have been unthinkable for an administration to run a covert operation from the White House. Then, the reason was that presidents wanted to stay at arm's length from such things, even if they could not in a pinch plausibly deny them. Now, if covert actions are to be undertaken, they should be done by the agency of government constructed to do them—the Central Intelligence Agency. It has the expertise. Whatever else can be said about the arms sales to Iran, the operation was amateurish in the extreme.

Moreover, if the president's closest advisers become the operators, the president loses them as sources of detached judgment on the operations. The president's own circle become advocates, not protectors of the president's stakes (even if he does not quite realize his need for protection). So it was with Robert McFarlane and John Poindexter, President Reagan's national security advisers. Once committed, they had reason to overlook the warning signals thrown up by the process. And the chances increased that someone like North, misguided, would interpret the president's interest after his own fashion.

To exclude Congress was to elude one more "political scrub," one more source of advice about what the range of the American people would find acceptable. Perhaps we were optimistic a dozen years ago in hoping that presidents might come to see the oversight committees of Congress as colleagues, as counselors, in decisions about covert action. The American Constitution does not quite preclude such a relationship, but it does not make it easy: witness how rare it has been in postwar foreign policy more generally—President Truman and Senator Vandenberg, or President Johnson and Senator Dirksen. Still, though, simple prudence argues against excluding Congress.

In William Miller's reflections on the process from the Church Committee to the Iran-Contra misadventure he says: "If clear lines hadn't been drawn a decade ago, there would have been no hue and cry now."[33] The result of this crisis, I hope, will be to draw those lines again, more sharply, as lessons for future administrations. At least they will be on notice; that, plus the processes already in place, is about as good as we can do in managing the paradox of secret operations in a democratic society.

33. Interview, 16 January 1987.

20

Conclusion

L. CARL BROWN

THE DIFFERENT subjects addressed in the preceding chapters all serve to emphasize two important points: First, the labels "international relations" and "world politics" have become in recent decades increasingly accurate descriptions. The world has become a single arena.

It is true, of course, that the world has been evolving into a single economic unit ever since the Industrial Revolution, if not indeed since the even earlier Age of Discovery, beginning in the late fifteenth century. Nor should it be overlooked that by the First World War European colonialism had managed to bring virtually all of the rest of the world under a formal or informal pattern of domination. The point, however, is that up to roughly the 1940s the peoples in what we now call the Third World were not active participants in the ongoing diplomatic game. Not so since the 1940s. The world has become increasingly one big diplomatic playing field.

Second, in the decades since 1945 one sovereign political community from among the roughly 170 existing today has played a prominent role unmatched in previous history. That political community, the United States of America, is admittedly one of the globe's larger and more populous states. Still, its citizens account for less than 5 percent of the world's population. That the United States would have had an important role to play in world politics needs no special explanation. The dominant role that the United States actually did assume in the world's political, economic, and even cultural life in the years following 1945 does cry out for study. This striking conjuncture of America's moving so decisively to

405

the center of a stage that was at the same time expanding to girdle the globe will provide scholars for generations to come with one of history's most clearly marked milestones.

The closest parallel to this age of American hegemony is that of Great Britain in the nineteenth century. Many significant similarities mark the striking British rise to power in the previous century and the American dominance following 1945. Both states enjoyed a geographical isolation from potential and actual enemies. Both relied on economic and maritime strength in order to bring increasingly large portions of the world within their network. It might even be argued that each developed an imperial system "in a fit of absence of mind" (with the contrast, of course, that Britain managed to create a formal empire on which the sun never set while the United States after 1945 constructed an empire of alliances and informal controls).

Even so, a significant difference in intensity distinguishes the two examples. Britain never controlled the European state system, not politically, not economically, and certainly not militarily. Even in the periods of greatest British power the United Kingdom was never regarded as the dominant military force. Britain remained one of several great powers in the multipolar European state system. And that European state system remained the main arena of world diplomacy until the Second World War. By contrast, the United States after 1945 exercised a political, economic, and military dominance on the world stage rivaled politically and militarily, but certainly not economically, by only one power, the Soviet Union.

This emphasis on America's unique standing after 1945 is not an outburst of vainglorious patriotism. It is rather an effort to underscore the significant and multifaceted role the United States has played in world politics since the end of the Second World War. The often harsh and certainly never muted criticism of American diplomacy since 1945 found in the chapters of this book makes quite clear that the authors are not confounding power with principled behavior.

At the same time, the message of this book is not to bemoan a lost age of presumed American innocence and isolation. The United States has never been an introverted society. The covered wagons and the clipper ships of the previous century remind us that this country has always sought to extend its frontiers in one way or another. Earlier American expansionism, however, was regional in its politics (largely confined to the Western Hemisphere with later thrusts into the Pacific) and commercial in its wider orientation. The Monroe Doctrine and the Open Door policy were the two fundamental pillars of American diplomacy on which that the ideology of isolationism rested.

If there was a continuity of lusty American activism toward the outside world both before and after 1945, the change in the American self-image could hardly have been more striking. Let President Truman's words, announcing in 1947 what came to be called the Truman Doctrine, epitomize the new ideology:

I believe that it must be the policy of the United States to support free peoples who are resisting subjection by armed minorities or by outside pressures.

This rallying cry of the new age of American diplomacy can then be set alongside the words of John Quincy Adams speaking in 1821:

> Wherever the standard of freedom and independence has been or shall be unfurled, there will be America's heart, her benedictions, and her prayers. But she goes not abroad in search of monsters to destroy. She is the well wisher to the freedom and independence of all. She is the champion and vindicator only of her own.

Along with the changing ideology went an increased commitment to world politics that can be measured in material terms. In the 1930s, for example, the number of American military personnel averaged about three hundred thousand. A generation later that figure had increased tenfold to average about three million. In 1938 the U.S. Department of State did not have even one thousand employees. After 1946 there were never fewer than five thousand.[1] Early American activism went hand in hand with the classical liberal notion of both limited government and limited governmental activity abroad. It has been completely different since 1945, for the United States has brought into existence the institutional underpinnings of what has been dubbed "the national security state."[2]

The position taken in this book has been neither to praise the United States for having explicitly assumed global responsibilities rejected in the past nor to blame this country for a policy of meddlesome interventionism. Rather, each contributor has sought, first of all, to place in its appropriate context the major change in America's impact on the world—and the world's impact on America—since 1945.

• • •

Still, this group effort by twenty different authors, bringing to their tasks almost as many different specializations, has sought to achieve something more. That is to study the experiences of the past in order to better plan the future.

A seemingly laudable and appropriate task, but as every historian knows, the matter can easily get out of hand. Historians attempting to extract "lessons" from the past may all too readily let their own values and preferences shape their findings. Henry Steele Commager forcefully sounded the warning:

> The historian is not God. He is not called upon to judge the quick and the dead. If he sets himself up as a judge he changes the whole pattern of his intellectual and professional role from one dedicated to objective inquiry to one devoted to prosecution or defense.[3]

1. Ernest R. May, "Writing Contemporary International History," *Diplomatic History* 8, 2 (Spring 1984): 103.
2. This phrase figures in the title of the influential book by Daniel Yergin, *Shattered Peace: The Origins of the Cold War and the National Security State* (Boston, 1977).
3. Henry Steele Commager, "Should the Historian Make Moral Judgments?" *American Heritage* 17 (February 1966): 92–93.

Moreover, it is presumably easier to attain greater detachment in surveying events long past. The historian of earlier times often contends only with other students of the period, to the complete indifference of politicians, bureaucrats, and journalists. The dust of controversy has settled, the archives are open, and the subjects of the historian's inquiry are no longer around to dispute the fine points. Contemporary historical studies offer just the opposite. Indeed, certain traditionalist historians draw a strict conclusion from all this, insisting that the study of any period not at least a century removed from the present age is not history but politics itself.

Nor is history simply philosophy teaching by example. The now hackneyed phrase of George Santayana—"Those who cannot remember the past are condemned to repeat it"—has been blisteringly dismissed by Wilfred Sheed as follows:

> Two things can confidently be said about history. One is that anyone who has ever heard Santayana's famous statement about the past is destined to repeat it; the second is that if you DO remember the past . . . you are, according to W. Churchill, in for an endless series of dismal shocks.[4]

These many cautions about "learning from history" have been carefully noted. Even so, a certain degree of demonstrable "lesson learning" can be extracted from the study of the past, if it is approached in the right way. Perhaps a sports metaphor best explains how this can be done. Historians in performing their tasks must see themselves not as players on any specific team, not as members of the coaching staff, not certainly as cheerleaders, and not even as observers in the stands. They are not referees or umpires. Historians should be like sportswriters sitting up in the press box with an especially good view of the playing field, understanding the rules of the game, and armed with research notes of past games and strategies used, plus the strengths and weaknesses of the individual players.

Under such circumstances, is it fanciful to claim that these sportswriters can with a very high degree of accuracy predict how the game will be played and who will win? Yes, there will be unanticipated "upsets" and routs. Games will turn on fortuitous happenings or in layman's language, luck. Uncharacteristic enthusiasm or negligence on the part of the players can produce the unexpected. Even so, the careful sportswriter can provide informed insights concerning what will or will not likely prove to be effective in a specific contest. Historians reviewing the game of international politics can do as much, provided they do their homework and abide by the rules of the profession.

Is it proper, however, to compare world politics to a series of games? In matters involving the very life and death of peoples and of states, it could be argued that this is to make light of a subject deserving greater concern. Yet this potential weakness (appearing to trivialize issues of war and peace) can become a

---

4. Wilfred Sheed, "The Summer of 1960," *New York Times Book Review*, Sunday, 6 July 1980, p. 2.

source of strength. Games themselves are sublimated conflict, and the connection between the two has long been accepted. Didn't the Duke of Wellington maintain that "the battle of Waterloo was won on the playing fields of Eton"?

Accordingly, if peoples on this planet can manage to reduce world politics to the sublimated orderliness of games with their rules, that will surely be a step forward.

Even more important for the role of the historian, keeping in mind the sports parallel can serve as a healthy check against the tendency to write the story in favor of "our side" or even to take too seriously the often pompous posturing of those involved in the international relations game, on all sides.

In this spirit, a review of the American diplomatic record since 1945 suggests that a game plan for future American diplomacy should include the following:

1. Policy should be formulated on the basis of present realities, not past practice. This is the simplest, and best, answer to the question of whether the United States must continue to bear the many global burdens that came to be assumed following the Second World War.[5] Remaining faithful to past practice even in the face of changed circumstances diverts attention from the present alignment of forces. Insisting that imperial systems almost necessarily overextend and then decline is equally to be faulted. It substitutes deterministic judgment for hard-headed analysis of existing realities.

2. Magnanimity is an excellent tool when properly used by a great power, even more by a superpower. A minor concession, even turning the other cheek in the face of abrasive action by a lesser power, can hardly be misinterpreted as weakness. On the other hand, an overly zealous defense of a country's rights when carried out by the strong in facing the weak can be unproductive. Everyone longs to see the bully get his comeuppance. The superpower must work overtime to avoid appearing to be a bully, for that appearance—even if incorrect—becomes an obstacle to effective diplomacy.

3. Studying the special hopes and fears of the different peoples and states with which this country must deal can provide handsome dividends. It has been rightly said that individuals are often as concerned to have their case carefully appreciated as to gain a favorable outcome. The same holds true for individuals governing states and for the public they represent.

---

5. Moving words, those of Pericles, about shouldering "the burdens of empire":

> It is right and proper for you to support the imperial dignity of Athens. This is something in which you all take pride, and you cannot continue to enjoy the privileges unless you also shoulder the burdens of empire. . . . Nor is it any longer possible for you to give up this empire, though there may be some people who in a mood of sudden panic and in a spirit of political apathy actually think that this would be a fine and noble thing to do. Your empire is now like a tyranny: it may have been wrong to take it; it is certainly dangerous to let it go. [Thucydides, *History of the Peloponnesian War*, trans. Rex Warner (New York: Penguin Books, 1954), bk. 2, p. 63].

Beautiful but wrongheaded. A state must constantly adjust ends to available means. The policymaker is better advised to follow the actual fate of Athens in the Peloponnesian War than the brilliant rhetoric of Pericles.

4. In facing potential threats and likely enemies, the United States should keep in mind the worst-case scenario but allocate defensive resources consistent instead with the most likely cases. Otherwise, the United States ultimately becomes overextended and thus defeated by a self-created enemy—bankruptcy at worst or the relative decline of this nation's world economic standing at best.

5. Better a national defense buildup that is relatively steady and consistent rather than successive policies of deep cuts followed by regardless-of-cost rapid military expansion.

6. The country's defense policies, like a family's insurance plans, should be geared to avoid ruinous catastrophe, not to meet any and all possible setbacks. To be "overinsured" militarily is to weaken national security with constant fiscal excess. Moreover, "overinsurance" in relatively calm times leaves no margin of available increase for emergencies.[6]

7. Unilateral statements of position (such as presidential "doctrines") should be avoided, because they are crude policy tools. Allies or neutrals who might find it in their interest to join in support of the American position have less motivation to do so after the United States has preempted with a unilateral commitment. Adversaries are less awed, seeing that those other states that might have had good reason to support the American initiative have not done so.

8. Credibility is a contingent, not an absolute, value. To the extent that the United States follows foolish policies, it becomes a credible fool. The only credibility worth preserving is that of being expected to consistently follow policies demonstrably in the national interest, adjusting these policies as necessary to evolving circumstances.

9. The United States as a "have" power has a clear interest in maintaining whatever exists of international order and in working with others to achieve a more coherent international order. "A decent respect for the opinion of mankind" as announced in the Declaration of Independence is more than an ideal firmly embedded in the American heritage, although it is surely that. The United States serves its own long-term interests to the extent that it supports the United Nations and the observance and extension of orderly procedures in the field of international law.

10. The United States is an open society ill-disposed to the keeping of secrets. It will be wise to make the best of that fact. This means that covert operations undertaken by this country will not likely remain covert. Accordingly, such operations in addition to being deplored by some Americans as unethical (and in violation of the need to foster a more effective international order) are also impractical.

11. International relations involve too many critical issues to be "above pol-

6. Note Sir Robert Peel's response to those always demanding higher naval expenditures:

> I believe that, in times of peace, we must, by our retrenchment, *Consent to incur some risk.* I venture to say that, if you choose to have all the garrisons of all your colonial possessions in a complete state, and to have all your fortifications secure against attack, no amount of annual expenditure will be sufficient to accomplish your object [cited in John Garnett, ed., *Theories of Peace and Security* (London, 1970), p. 32].

At different times both superpowers have been skeptical about the United Nations. (*Above:* Auth copyright 1971, 1988, *Philadelphia Inquirer.* Reprinted with permission. All rights reserved. *Below:* The Soviet humor magazine *Krokodil* cartoon.)

THE TOO EAGER MAJORITY
(Scene in the UN Assembly)

"Gentlemen, what's the matter with you? Put your hands down!
Mr. Austin is smoothing his hair!"

itics." The ideal of a bipartisan foreign policy is illusory. Citizens should debate and vote on such fundamental matters as defense, international trade, the pattern of American alliances, and the like. American foreign policy, rather than being placed above politics, needs to be even more closely tied to politics. Foreign policy, however, must take priority over the demands of narrow domestic interest groups. This will not be easy to achieve, since the compromising of different narrow interests is the essence of the American political process. Foreign policies resulting from diverse domestic pressures instead of in response to international circumstances constitute one of the major weaknesses of democratic governments. It has often been noted that the Department of State has no natural domestic constituency as do other departments, such as Defense or Agriculture or Commerce. The best political spokesman for the entire nation is necessarily the president, elected by all the people from all the states. Following thereafter in sharply descending order come the members of the Senate and then those of the House of Representatives. Citizens knowledgeable in world affairs can best provide the "effective diplomacy" lobby that can hold the president and the Congress accountable for furthering the national interest and not becoming hostage to a variety of single-issue pressure groups.

12. American policymakers and the American public need to guard against our marked tendency to depict international issues in Manichean terms of good and evil. Both good and evil forces do exist in the world, of course. They can sometimes even be clearly identified, but usually this is not possible. In any case, identifying good and evil with "us" and "them" is readily seen by adversaries and friends alike as simpleminded. A nation that places its routine foreign policy in a highly charged moralistic context falls into the trap of crying wolf too often. We risk not being believed even when addressing truly evil (or good) forces.

13. Because the United States is a superpower of continental proportions with either oceans or friendly powers on our borders, never having faced a formidable enemy as an immediate neighbor, Americans find it difficult to understand the traditions of states living in a more threatening environment which must be attentive to the balance of power among the states in their immediate region. Our seeking to classify such states according to our bilateral standard of pro- or anti-American is woefully inept.

14. Americans would rightly find unacceptable the Palmerstonian maxim of having no permanent friends, only permanent interests. Even so, permanent interests, if carefully defined in terms of realistic and sensible long-term goals, can provide a good gauge for measuring friendship in the international community. Nations change. Despots overthrow democrats. Militarists replace peacemakers. Or things can go from bad to better. Gorbachev is not Stalin. The Germany and Japan of the 1980s are not to be compared with these two countries in the time of Hitler and Tojo. Even states that have not experienced such extreme changes have their ups and downs. This country opposed the Anglo-French-Israeli invasion of Egypt in 1956. America's allies took strong positions against the U.S. intervention in Vietnam. Both friends and enemies should be

appraised according to their current policies. We must also expect that treatment from others, friend and foe.

15. In deciding when to use force in international politics, Americans could hardly find better guidelines than those worked out by Augustine and Thomas Aquinas in the traditional theory of the just war. As summarized in modern times by Coral Bell, they are:

> Firstly, for a just cause, secondly with a right intention, thirdly with a reasonable chance of success, fourthly if successful, it must offer a better situation than would prevail in the absence of action, fifthly force used (or threatened) should be proportional to the objective sought (or the evil repressed). And sixthly, it must be used with the intention of sparing non-combatants, and a reasonable prospect of doing so.[7]

16. Americans might well be advised to adapt the pragmatic tradition that usually characterizes America's domestic political life to world politics. Of course, in the process it would be necessary to remove the outer shell of flamboyant rhetoric that often covers domestic politics and get to the solid substance inside. In domestic politics we Americans have a commendable record for being flexible problem solvers, not rigid ideologues. Our diplomacy, however, is all too often based on crusades that then burn out or degenerate into quixotic incoherence. A touch of cynicism and a well-developed sense of limits to what is possible are necessary to all politics, domestic and international. That masterful if unscrupulous diplomat, Talleyrand, offered as a guideline for diplomacy a maxim still cited with approval: "Above all, not too much enthusiasm." Alben Barkley's tongue-in-cheek anecdote expresses the same idea in a very American idiom: A constituent when asked whom he supported for sheriff replied, "I haven't made up my mind yet; but when I do, I'll be bitter as hell."[8]

17. Finally, the sports metaphor can take us only so far. Games come to an end. Not so the great game of international politics. It just goes on and on, ever changing but ever present. We must accept the challenge well posed by Dean Acheson when he asserted that involvement in foreign affairs:

> is a long and tough job and one for which we as a people are not particularly suited. We believe that any problem can be solved with a little ingenuity and without inconvenience to the folks at large. We have trouble-shooters to do this. And our name for problems is significant. We call them headaches. You take a powder and they are gone. Those pains . . . are not like that. They are like the pain of earning a living. They will stay with us until death.[9]

• • •

The United States and the world may be coming to the end of the era that began in 1945. Certainly the relative power and influence of the United States, of

7. Coral Bell, *The Conventions of Crisis* (1971), p. 101.

8. As reported by Dean Acheson in his *Present at the Creation* (Signet), p. 815.

9. Dean Acheson, "Random Harvest," *Department of State Bulletin* 16, June 1946, p. 1047, as cited by David S. McLellan, *Dean Acheson: The State Department Years* (New York, 1976), p. 51.

unprecedented proportions in the immediate post-World War II period, has already declined and may decline even more. This is not in itself a cause for concern. Some part of this relative decline stems from the successes of earlier American policies in facing the challenge of postwar reconstruction. In any case, the United States can better achieve its potential in the global arena if it is simply a major player—for now and the foreseeable future still *the* major player—in an increasingly multipolar world.

The world is too intractable, too cumbersome, to be monitored by one single power. Over four decades ago Henry Luce could announce the advent of "the American century." Today we know better and can take solace in the realization that America's international chores, while heavy, are somewhat more realistically proportioned.

Americans may now take the initiative in cutting back this country's international role. They may choose to "stay the course" and let the changing international power alignments determine the American position in the world arena. Or they might even consider a greater American commitment in the international arena, although no significant voices are now making this appeal. Whatever the next phase of America's foreign policy is to be—reintrenchment, essentially more of the same, or increased activism—Americans should find a useful cluster of "lessons" in the history of international relations since 1945.

Chronology

Aug. 14, 1941	Atlantic Charter, laying out principles for peace in postwar world and asserting right to national self-determination, issued by U.S. and Britain.
Dec. 7, 1941	Japanese planes attack U.S. naval base at Pearl Harbor, killing scores of enlisted men and destroying several naval vessels; U.S. declares war on Japan next day, marking entry into World War II; war declared on Germany and Italy Dec. 11.
Nov. 22–26, 1943	Franklin D. Roosevelt, Winston Churchill, and Chiang Kai-shek discuss war aims in Far East and surrender terms for Japan at Cairo Conference.
Nov. 28– *Dec. 1, 1943*	Roosevelt, Churchill, and Joseph Stalin meet in Tehran to discuss allied invasion of France and possible entry of USSR into war against Japan.
July 1–22, 1944	Representatives of 44 nations gather at Bretton Woods, N.H., to design trade regime and institutional structure of postwar world

This Chronology through July 1985 first appeared in *Estrangement: America and the World*, ed. Sanford J. Ungar (Oxford University Press, 1985). It is reprinted, and updated, with the permission of the Carnegie Endowment for International Peace. In addition, some portions of this chronology are drawn from the annual America and the World issue of *Foreign Affairs* 64, 3; 65, 3; 66, 3; 68, 1. Such entries are reprinted by permission of *Foreign Affairs*. Copyright 1986, 1987, 1988, 1989 by the Council on Foreign Relations, Inc.

economy; International Monetary Fund and World Bank established.

Feb. 4–11, 1945   Yalta Conference lays out terms for allied occupation of Germany and Stalin's entry into war against Japan; national boundaries and governmental structures for some East European countries determined.

April 12, 1945   Roosevelt dies; Harry S Truman becomes president.

April 21, 1945   Stalin concludes mutual-assistance pact with communist-led Lublin government of Poland.

April 30, 1945   Adolf Hitler commits suicide.

May 7, 1945   Germany surrenders unconditionally to Gen. Dwight D. Eisenhower at allied headquarters in Reims, France.

June 26, 1945   United Nations Charter signed by delegates from 50 countries gathered in San Francisco.

July 16, 1945   First atomic device successfully detonated in New Mexico test.

July 17–
Aug. 2, 1945   Potsdam Conference, last of wartime summits, finalizes and implements terms of previous agreements on postwar Europe and termination of war in Pacific.

Aug. 6, 1945   First atomic bomb dropped on Hiroshima, Japan.

Aug. 9, 1945   Second atomic bomb dropped on Nagasaki, Japan.

Sept. 2, 1945   Japan formally surrenders to Gen. Douglas A. MacArthur aboard U.S.S. *Missouri* in Tokyo Bay.

Sept. 8, 1945   U.S. troops move into southern Korea as part of postwar occupation of territories formerly held by Japan.

Nov. 29, 1945   Assembly elected Nov. 11 proclaims Federal People's Republic of Yugoslavia with Marshall Tito as president.

March 5, 1946   In speech at Westminster College in Fulton, Mo., Churchill declares that "an iron curtain has descended across the continent" of Europe.

June 14, 1946   At first session of UN Commission on Atomic Energy. Bernard Baruch presents American proposal for international control of fissionable material and destruction of all stockpiles of atomic weapons.

July 4, 1946   Philippines gains independence from U.S. in accordance with timetable set earlier by Roosevelt and Congress.

Sept. 30, 1946	Guilty verdicts handed down for 22 former Nazi officials by international war crimes tribunal at Nuremberg.
Nov. 23, 1946	France launches military effort to retain Indochina colonies with bombing of Haiphong, Vietnam.
March 12, 1947	In major speech before joint session of Congress, Truman outlines ambitious new U.S. foreign commitment to counter spread of communism throughout the world, known as the "Truman Doctrine"; Truman calls upon Congress to appropriate $400 million in economic and military assistance to combat communist insurgency in Greece and political instability in Turkey.
June 5, 1947	In Harvard commencement address, Secretary of State George C. Marshall outlines program of financial aid for postwar European recovery, known as the Marshall Plan; Soviets reject Eastern bloc participation in the plan during July.
July 1947	Diplomat George F. Kennan advocates U.S. policy of "containment" toward USSR in anonymous article in *Foreign Affairs*.
Aug. 15, 1947	India gains independence from Britain; Muslim areas remain dominions of British Crown, becoming Republic of Pakistan in March 1956.
Dec. 30, 1947	King Michael of Rumania forced to abdicate by communist-dominated government.
Jan. 1, 1948	General Agreement on Tariffs and Trade (GATT), negotiated during 1947, comes into force, significantly lowering trade barriers among its 23 signatories.
Jan. 30, 1948	Indian independence movement leader Mahatma Gandhi assassinated by Hindu extremists.
Feb. 25, 1948	In bloodless coup in Czechoslovakia, President Eduard Benes forced to accept communist government under Klement Gottwald.
May 14, 1948	State of Israel proclaimed as British mandate in Palestine expires; neighboring Arab nations invade the new country the next day, commencing the "War of Independence" in which Israel significantly enlarges its land area and takes control of part of Jerusalem.
May 26, 1948	National Party prevails in parliamentary elections in South Africa, bringing the Afrikaner ethnic minority to political power; in coming years, National Party governments will construct body of laws and political and social institutions, known as apartheid, which enforce strict segregation of races.
June 28, 1948	Yugoslavia expelled from Cominform following series of disagreements with USSR.

July 25, 1948   U.S.-sponsored Berlin Airlift begins, delivering food and supplies to West Berlin, severed from greater West Germany by Soviet blockade.

Aug. 15, 1948   Republic of Korea (South) established.

Sept. 9, 1948   Democratic People's Republic of Korea (North) established.

Oct. 27, 1948   Voice of America, worldwide U.S. government radio broadcasting network, established by Congress.

Nov. 2, 1948   Truman defeats Republican Thomas E. Dewey in presidential election.

Dec. 27, 1948   Hungarian Cardinal Mindszenty arrested for outspoken criticism of communist government; death sentence later commuted to life imprisonment; in 1956, he will seek asylum in American Embassy.

Jan. 18, 1949   Council for Mutual Economic Assistance (COMECON) established by Moscow, tightening economic links among Soviet bloc countries.

April 4, 1949   North Atlantic Treaty signed, establishing North Atlantic Treaty Organization (NATO), the western military alliance.

April 18, 1949   Republic of Ireland established; Northern Ireland region remains part of United Kingdom.

May 12, 1949   Berlin blockade lifted by Soviets; U.S. airlift continues until Sept. 30.

May 21, 1949   Federal Republic of Germany (West) established.

June 29, 1949   U.S. occupying forces withdrawn from South Korea.

Oct. 1, 1949   People's Republic of China proclaimed by victorious communist forces led by Mao Zedong after protracted civil war with Nationalists under Chiang Kai-shek.

Oct. 7, 1949   German Democratic Republic (East) established.

Dec. 14, 1949   Israel transfers capital to Jerusalem.

Feb. 9, 1950   In speech before Ohio County Women's Republican Club in Wheeling, W. Va., Sen. Joseph McCarthy sparks major "red scare" in U.S., claiming to have list of known Communists in State Department.

March 1, 1950   Chiang Kai-shek becomes president of Republic of China, based on Taiwan, where Nationalist Chinese establish government after losing mainland China to Communists.

March 8, 1950	Soviets announce successful development of atomic bomb.
May 8, 1950	Truman sends economic aid and establishes military mission in Vietnam, marking first step toward direct U.S. involvement.
June 25, 1950	North Korea invades South Korea, beginning Korean War.
June 27, 1950	UN Security Council approves military aid for South Korea; 15 nations will send troops as part of UN force.
June 30, 1950	U.S. troops under command of MacArthur enter Korean War.
Sept. 15, 1950	U.S. troops land at Inchon, South Korea; driving north, they reach the Yalu River on the Chinese border on Oct. 24, provoking Chinese counterattack which forces MacArthur to retreat into the south.
Sept. 30, 1950	Truman approves NSC 68, recommending an unprecedented, ambitious peacetime program to expand U.S. conventional and nuclear forces and to rearm American allies.
April 11, 1951	MacArthur, accused of insubordination, is relieved of command in Korea by Truman.
June 14, 1951	At U.S. Census Bureau, Univac I becomes first commercially manufactured computer operated in U.S.
Sept. 8, 1951	Peace treaty signed with Japan by 49 nations in San Francisco; U.S. and Japan agree to mutual security pact.
March 10, 1952	Cuban presidential candidate Fulgencio Batista seizes power and maintains authoritarian rule until 1959.
July 25, 1952	Adopting new constitution, Puerto Rico becomes self-governing commonwealth of U.S.
Oct. 2, 1952	Britain tests its first atomic device.
Oct. 31, 1952	First hydrogen bomb detonated by U.S. in the Marshall Islands.
Nov. 4, 1952	Republican Dwight D. Eisenhower defeats Adlai E. Stevenson in presidential election.
March 5, 1953	Stalin dies and is succeeded as Soviet premier by Georgi M. Malenkov.
June 17, 1953	Anticommunist riots in East Berlin lead to general strike; Soviet troops used to quell disturbances.
June 19, 1953	Ethel and Julius Rosenberg electrocuted for espionage, the first such peacetime execution in U.S. history.

July 27, 1953	After more than two years of negotiation, armistice ending Korean War signed at Panmunjom between UN forces and North Korea; border secured at 38th parallel with demilitarized buffer zone dividing North and South Korea; under terms of separate mutual aid pact, U.S. will provide South Korea with protective military presence and economic assistance for decades to come.
Aug. 12, 1953	Soviets explode hydrogen device.
Aug. 19, 1953	CIA sponsors coup overthrowing leftist Iranian Prime Minister Mohammed Mossadeq in response to Eisenhower administration concerns about rising Soviet influence in Persian Gulf; Mohammed Reza Shah Pahlavi reinstated on Peacock Throne, ruling until 1978 Islamic fundamentalist revolution.
Sept. 13, 1953	Nikita Khrushchev becomes first secretary of Soviet Communist Party; becomes premier in 1958, achieving preeminence in Soviet leadership.
Jan. 21, 1954	First nuclear-powered submarine, U.S.S. *Nautilus*, launched.
April 7, 1954	"Domino theory" first propounded by Eisenhower.
April 22, 1954	McCarthy accuses Secretary of the Army Robert Stevens of communist sympathies; Army counteraccusations lead to televised Army/McCarthy hearings.
May 7, 1954	At Dien Bien Phu, Vietnam, French forces suffer devastating defeat by communist nationalist forces under Ho Chi Minh.
May 17, 1954	Supreme Court decision in *Brown* v. *Board of Education* outlaws school segregation in U.S.
June 27, 1954	CIA-backed military revolt deposes leftist Guatemalan president Jacobo Arbenz.
June 27, 1954	First nuclear power station begins operation near Moscow.
July 20, 1954	After several years of fighting between French and Vietnamese anticolonial forces, Geneva Accords divide Vietnam at 17th parallel, establishing communist regime in north and noncommunist nationalist regime in south and providing for elections and reunification in two years; French withdraw from Indochina.
Oct. 22, 1954	Eisenhower authorizes training program for South Vietnamese army.
Oct. 23, 1954	Western alliance governments sign Paris Agreements, permitting West Germany to rearm and enter NATO.
Dec. 2, 1954	Senate votes to censure McCarthy.

Jan. 12, 1955	Secretary of State John Foster Dulles propounds nuclear strategy of massive retaliation.
April 17–24, 1955	At conference in Bandung, Indonesia, representatives of 29 less-developed nations launch nonaligned movement, dedicating themselves to conducting their affairs independently of superpowers.
April 29, 1955	Armed conflict breaks out between communist forces from North Vietnam and noncommunist forces from the south.
May 5, 1955	With end of U.S. occupation, West Germany becomes sovereign state.
May 14, 1955	Warsaw Pact alliance, Soviet bloc counterpart to NATO, formed ostensibly to offset West German remilitarization.
Oct. 26, 1955	South Vietnamese proclaim republic, rejecting elections stipulated in Geneva Accords.
Feb. 14, 1956	Khrushchev's denunciation of Stalin at opening of 20th Soviet Communist Party Congress marks beginning of period of political liberalization in USSR and Eastern Europe.
April 23, 1956	Supreme Court outlaws racial segregation on all public transportation in U.S.
June 28, 1956	More than 100 people killed in anticommunist demonstrations in Poznan, Poland.
Oct. 29, 1956	Israel invades Sinai following Egypt's blockade of the Gulf of Aqaba; Britain and France intervene militarily on Israel's side on Oct. 31 after Egypt rejects cease-fire. On Nov. 5, British paratroopers recover Suez Canal, seized by Egyptian leader Gamal Abdel Nasser in July; Anglo-French action condemned by UN and U.S.; cease-fire takes effect Nov. 7, and UN peacekeeping force arrives Nov. 15.
Nov. 4, 1956	Soviet troops crush Hungarian uprising led by Imre Nagy, who had sought to create a Hungarian national communism distinct from Soviet model.
Nov. 6, 1956	Eisenhower reelected, defeating Stevenson again.
March 25, 1957	European Economic Community (Common Market) established.
Sept. 24, 1957	Eisenhower dispatches federal troops to Little Rock, Ark., to enforce desegregation of Central High School.
Oct. 4, 1957	Sputnik I, first man-made satellite, launched into earth orbit by USSR.

July 15, 1958	U.S. marines land in Lebanon to restore order amid sectarian strife.
Jan. 1, 1959	Cuban dictator Batista flees as rebel forces under Fidel Castro sweep into nation's cities, establishing the first communist regime in Western Hemisphere.
Feb. 1, 1960	Black students denied service at a Greensboro, N.C., lunch counter begin sit-in protests.
Feb. 13, 1960	France becomes world's fourth nuclear power.
March 21, 1960	South African police open fire on unarmed black demonstrators in township of Sharpeville, killing 69 and wounding more than 200.
April 27, 1960	South Korean president Syngman Rhee resigns following massive anticorruption demonstrations in Seoul and U.S. rebuke for political repression; Park Chung Hee eventually succeeds to presidency.
May 1, 1960	American U-2 spy plane shot down over USSR.
Aug. 12, 1960	U.S. launches world's first communications satellite.
Nov. 8, 1960	John F. Kennedy defeats Richard Nixon in presidential election.
Jan. 3, 1961	U.S. severs diplomatic relations with Cuba.
March 1, 1961	Peace Corps founded.
March 13, 1961	Kennedy proposes Alliance for Progress, ambitious program for economic and social development in Latin America.
April 17–20, 1961	CIA-sponsored invasion of Cuba by anti-Castro exiles, staged at the Bay of Pigs, collapses in disarray.
May 4, 1961	"Freedom Riders," civil rights protesters, begin peaceful demonstrations in Birmingham, Ala.
May 31, 1961	South Africa breaks all ties with British commonwealth, becoming fully independent republic.
Aug. 15–17, 1961	Berlin Wall constructed, permanently closing off eastern sector of Berlin from traffic and visitors from the west.
Nov. 14, 1961	Kennedy sends first U.S. helicopter companies to Vietnam.
June 25, 1962	Supreme Court declares mandatory prayer in public schools unconstitutional.
Sept. 30, 1962	U.S. marshals escort James Meredith to University of Mississippi, which previously excluded him on racial grounds.

Oct. 22, 1962	Kennedy announces U.S. naval blockade of Cuba after installation of Soviet missiles is discovered; on Oct. 28, at brink of war, Khrushchev agrees to remove missiles; U.S. blockade ends Nov. 20.
Aug. 5, 1963	Limited Nuclear Test Ban Treaty signed in Moscow by foreign ministers of Britain, USSR, and U.S.
Aug. 30, 1963	"Hot line," direct crisis communications link between Washington and Moscow, goes into service.
Nov. 22, 1963	Kennedy assassinated in Dallas; Vice President Lyndon B. Johnson becomes president.
May 28, 1964	Palestine Liberation Organization (PLO) founded.
July 2, 1964	Civil Rights Act of 1964 signed into law by Johnson; prohibits discrimination on basis of race, religion, or national origin in all forms of public accommodation.
July 18, 1964	Race riots erupt in Harlem and spread to other northern cities.
Aug. 7, 1964	Responding to allegedly unprovoked North Vietnamese attack on U.S. vessels on Aug. 2, Congress passes Gulf of Tonkin Resolution granting Johnson broad powers to defend U.S. forces; resolution later used to justify vast buildup of U.S. combat forces in Vietnam.
Oct. 15, 1964	Khrushchev ousted as Soviet leader; Leonid Brezhnev assumes party leadership, and Alexei Kosygin becomes premier.
Oct. 16, 1964	China announces successful nuclear test, becoming world's fifth nuclear power.
Nov. 3, 1964	Johnson elected to full term as president, defeating conservative Republican candidate Barry Goldwater.
Dec. 3, 1964	Free Speech Movement at University of California in Berkeley holds sit-in demonstration in which 814 people are arrested, the largest mass arrest in U.S. to date; Berkeley protests spark campus unrest across the country.
Feb. 1, 1965	Rev. Martin Luther King, Jr., and 770 other civil rights demonstrators arrested in Selma, Ala., while protesting racial discrimination in voter registration.
Feb. 7, 1965	Johnson initiates bombing of selected targets in North Vietnam.
March 7, 1965	While marching to state capital in Montgomery, Ala., black protesters led by King are attacked in Selma by more than 200 state police; with protection of 3,000 U.S. national guardsmen, marchers successfully reach Montgomery on March 25.

March 8, 1965	First U.S. combat troops land in Vietnam.
April 28, 1965	U.S. marines intervene in civil unrest in Dominican Republic.
Aug. 10, 1965	U.S. Voting Rights Act goes into effect; federal officials begin registering black voters in Alabama, Louisiana, and Mississippi.
Oct. 15, 1965	Protest march from Berkeley to Oakland army base in California, nation's first major antiwar demonstration.
Nov. 25, 1965	Bloodless coup establishes Gen. Joseph Mobutu as president of the Congo after five years of civil war; in expression of cultural nationalism, Mobutu later changes country's name to Zaire and his own name to Mobutu Sese Seko.
Dec. 17, 1965	Ferdinand Marcos elected president of Philippines; by early 1970s, after declaring martial law, he will exert dictatorial control over national life.
Feb. 3, 1966	Soviet craft achieves first soft landing on moon.
March 12, 1966	Indonesian nationalist leader and president, Sukarno, overthrown by Lieutenant-General Suharto, who establishes military dictatorship.
July 1, 1966	Citing American threat to country's independence of action and its need to develop own nuclear deterrent force, Charles de Gaulle withdraws France from NATO.
Jan. 27, 1967	Treaty prohibiting use of space for military purposes signed by 62 nations in ceremonies in London, Moscow, and Washington.
June 5, 1967	"Six-Day War" breaks out in Middle East; Israel captures and occupies Sinai, West Bank, and Golan Heights territories.
Aug. 8, 1967	Indonesia, Malaysia, Thailand, Philippines, and Singapore launch Association of Southeast Asian Nations (ASEAN) to promote regional economic and political cooperation.
Dec. 2, 1967	First human heart transplant performed in Cape Town, South Africa, by Dr. Christiaan Barnard.
Jan. 23, 1968	U.S.S. *Pueblo,* naval intelligence ship, seized off coast of North Korea by that country's armed forces; 83-man crew held until Dec. 22, 1968.
Jan. 30, 1968	Tet offensive by North Vietnamese and Viet Cong forces begins; although unsuccessful militarily, Tet has significant impact in turning Americans against Vietnam War.

March 16, 1968	U.S. army unit under Lt. William Calley massacres approximately 200 Vietnamese civilians in village of My Lai; revelation of massacre in fall of 1969 catalyzes public opposition to American involvement in war; Calley, who claims to have been following orders, given life sentence for murders in March 1971; sentence later reduced to ten years.
April 4, 1968	King assassinated in Memphis.
April 23, 1968	Columbia University shut down by massive student demonstrations and sit-ins.
May 10, 1968	First peace talks between U.S. and North Vietnam begin in Paris.
May 22, 1968	Major wave of worker-student unrest begins in France, nearly toppling government of Charles de Gaulle.
June 5, 1968	Sen. Robert F. Kennedy assassinated in Los Angeles while campaigning in California Democratic presidential primary.
Aug. 20, 1968	Soviet forces invade Czechoslovakia, suppressing reformist regime of Alexander Dubcek.
Nov. 5, 1968	Nixon defeats Hubert H. Humphrey in presidential election.
Nov. 12, 1968	Brezhnev enunciates the "Brezhnev doctrine," asserting Soviets' right forcefully to intervene in affairs of sovereign nations when an established communist regime is in danger of collapse or subversion.
March 2, 1969	Soviet and Chinese troops clash for first time on mutual border; hostilities mark beginning of significant Sino-Soviet tension.
March 18, 1969	U.S. commences secret bombing of Cambodia.
April 21, 1969	British troops stationed in Northern Ireland called in to enforce order in wake of violent rioting between Catholics and Protestants.
June 8, 1969	After conferring with South Vietnamese President Nguyen Van Thieu, Nixon announces beginning of phased withdrawal of U.S. troops from Vietnam; "Vietnamization" of war underway.
July 21, 1969	Neil Armstrong is first man to walk on moon.
Sept. 1, 1969	Capt. Muammar al-Qaddafi stages military coup in Libya and proclaims socialist Libyan Arab Republic.
Nov. 3, 1969	"Nixon Doctrine," calling on U.S. allies to bear increased military burdens for their own defense and protection of American foreign interests, publicly enunciated for first time in televised address;

doctrine had initially emerged in press briefings during Nixon's trip to the Pacific the previous spring.

Nov. 24, 1969   U.S. and USSR sign UN-sponsored Treaty on the Non-Proliferation of Nuclear Weapons.

Jan. 12, 1970   Leaders of Biafran independence movement surrender to Nigerian government, ending catastrophic 31-month civil war.

May 4, 1970   Four Kent State University students killed by Ohio national guardsmen during campus protest against American armed incursion into Cambodia.

Sept. 28, 1970   Nasser dies of heart attack and is succeeded by Egyptian Vice President Anwar Sadat.

Nov. 3, 1970   Salvador Allende, first Marxist to be democratically elected head of government in the West, sworn in as president of Chile.

Jan. 25, 1971   Ugandan president Milton Obote deposed in bloody military coup led by Maj. Gen. Idi Amin.

June 13, 1971   *New York Times* begins publication of "Pentagon Papers," Defense Department's classified internal account of Vietnam decision-making process. Nixon's Justice Department obtains federal court order interrupting publication on June 15; other newspapers begin to publish documents and are also hit by court rulings; Supreme Court rules against government on June 30, and publication resumes; Daniel Ellsberg, source of the documents, charged with espionage and theft of government property, but case is later dismissed.

Aug. 15, 1971   As part of package of emergency reform measures, Nixon announces end of convertibility of U.S. currency into gold in effort to free dollar for devaluation relative to other currencies, to slow speculation against dollar, and to close balance of foreign payments deficit.

Oct. 25, 1971   UN General Assembly votes to seat Communist People's Republic of China, replacing Taiwan.

Dec. 16, 1971   With Indian assistance, nationalist rebels in East Pakistan succeed in breaking away from Pakistan, establishing independent nation of Bangladesh.

Feb. 20, 1972   Nixon arrives in Beijing, becoming first American president to visit People's Republic of China.

May 22, 1972   Nixon is first American president to visit Moscow.

June 17, 1972   Five employees of Nixon reelection committee arrested while breaking into Democratic National Committee headquarters in Watergate office complex in Washington.

Sept. 5, 1972	Members of Black September Arab terrorist group seize Israeli athletes at Munich Olympics; 11 hostages killed during day-long standoff and subsequent gunfight at Munich airport.
Oct. 3, 1972	SALT I and Anti-Ballistic Missile (ABM) arms limitation treaties signed by U.S. and USSR in Washington.
Nov. 7, 1972	Nixon wins presidential reelection, defeating liberal Democrat George McGovern.
Jan. 27, 1973	North Vietnam, South Vietnam, Viet Cong, and U.S. sign Agreement on Ending the War and Restoring Peace in Vietnam, the Paris Peace Agreement.
March 29, 1973	Last U.S. troops withdrawn from Vietnam.
July 23, 1973	Asserting constitutional right to executive privilege, Nixon defies federal court order to hand over tape recordings of White House conversations to Justice Department officials investigating Watergate scandal.
Aug. 15, 1973	U.S. bombing of North Vietnamese logistical targets in Cambodia terminated against president's wishes after Congress halts funding in effort to bar further U.S. military action in Indochina.
Sept. 11, 1973	Chilean military overthrows Allende.
Oct. 6, 1973	Egypt and Syria attack Israel, beginning Yom Kippur War.
Oct. 10, 1973	Vice President Spiro T. Agnew resigns under pressure, pleading no contest to charges of tax evasion; Nixon selects House minority leader, Gerald R. Ford, to replace him.
Oct. 19, 1973	First oil embargo by member nations of the Organization of Petroleum Exporting Countries (OPEC) leads to debilitating oil shortages and economic disruption in nations dependent on imported oil.
Oct. 20, 1973	In "Saturday Night Massacre," Attorney General Elliot Richardson and Deputy Attorney General William Ruckelshaus resign and Special Prosecutor Archibald Cox is fired following disagreements with Nixon over Justice Department's role in Watergate investigation.
April 25, 1974	Portuguese premier Marcello Caetano ousted; revolutionary turmoil continues for two years, contributing to dissolution of Portugal's African colonial empire. Government signs agreement freeing Portuguese Guinea on Aug. 26.

May 9, 1974	U.S. House Judiciary Committee votes to impeach Nixon.
May 18, 1974	India explodes nuclear device, becoming world's sixth nuclear power.
July 15, 1974	Coup d'état by Greek officers in Cypriot National Guard ousts government of Archbishop Makarios in Cyprus, prompting July 20 invasion by Turkey to protect Turkish Cypriot minority; fighting continues through end of summer, when UN-sponsored cease-fire holds.
Aug. 9, 1974	Nixon resigns under threat of impeachment; Ford sworn in as first nonelected president in U.S. history.
Sept. 4, 1974	U.S. establishes diplomatic relations with East Germany.
Sept. 8, 1974	Ford grants Nixon full pardon for any wrongdoing in Watergate affair.
Sept. 12, 1974	Radical military leaders depose Ethiopian emperor Haile Selassie after 58-year reign; socialist state declared on Dec. 20.
April 16, 1975	U.S.-backed Cambodian government of Lon Nol falls to communist Khmer Rouge, ending five-year civil war; under ultraradical new regime led by Pol Pot, 1 to 2 million people will die by execution, starvation, and disease over next four years.
April 30, 1975	Saigon captured by North Vietnamese after surprise offensive overwhelms South Vietnamese army; South Vietnamese president Duong Van Minh surrenders unconditionally as Americans remaining in Saigon are evacuated by helicopter.
May 12, 1975	Cambodian forces seize U.S. cargo ship *Mayaguez* along with 40-man crew; rescue mission on May 14 frees crew, but gunfight and helicopter crash result in deaths of 41 U.S. marines.
Aug. 1, 1975	At conclusion of Conference on Security and Cooperation in Europe, 33 European nations, Canada, and U.S. sign nonbinding pact freezing postwar borders, broadening detente, and pledging respect for human rights.
Aug. 23, 1975	After 20 years of war and two of coalition government, Vietnamese-backed communist Pathet Lao establish exclusive control over Laos.
Nov. 10, 1975	Portugal's African empire fully dissolved as Angola gains independence after 15 years of civil war; within three months, Soviet-backed Popular Movement for Liberation of Angola emerges victorious from power struggle among guerrilla factions.

Dec. 15, 1975	UN General Assembly passes resolution proclaiming 1976–85 period the "U.N. Decade for Women: Equality, Development, and Peace"; economic, social, and political objectives of U.N. Decade previously set forth in "World Plan of Action" approved at July 1975 Mexico City conference on women.
May 28, 1976	Treaty prohibiting underground nuclear explosions signed by Ford and Brezhnev.
June 16, 1976	Protest by more than 10,000 black students in South African township of Soweto begins.
July 2, 1976	Vietnam formally reunited as one nation, under communist rule.
Sept. 9, 1976	Mao Zedong dies, sparking succession struggle eventually won by Hua Kuofeng.
Nov. 2, 1976	Democratic candidate Jimmy Carter defeats Ford in presidential election.
Jan. 21, 1977	Carter grants full pardon to Vietnam War era draft resisters.
Sept. 7, 1977	Panama Canal treaties signed, establishing timetable for turning over eventual control of canal to Panama and guaranteeing its perpetual neutrality.
Nov. 9, 1977	Egyptian president Sadat travels to Jerusalem to meet with Israeli prime minister Menachem Begin; two weeks later Sadat breaks diplomatic relations with several hard-line Arab nations that denounced meeting with Begin.
April 27, 1978	Afghan president Mohammed Daud Khan ousted by military; Communist party leader Noor Mohammed Taraki assumes power.
Sept. 17, 1978	With Carter mediating, Sadat and Begin reach Egyptian-Israeli peace agreement at American presidential retreat in Camp David, Md. Camp David Accords signed on March 26, 1979.
Oct. 16, 1978	Polish Cardinal Karol Wojtyla becomes Pope John Paul II.
Jan. 1, 1979	U.S. and China establish diplomatic relations.
Jan. 7, 1979	Vietnamese invasion forces bring down Cambodian government of Pol Pot and occupy country, putting in place pro-Hanoi Cambodian communist regime under Heng Samrin.
Jan. 16, 1979	Shah and family leave Iran as regime collapses under pressure of Islamic fundamentalist revolution; Ayatollah Ruhollah Khomeini, fundamentalist spiritual leader, returns to Iran at the end of the month, taking control of government and imposing strict Islamic code upon nation's social and political life.

Feb. 17, 1979   Approximately 250,000 Chinese troops invade Vietnam in response to border clashes and aggression in Cambodia; both sides suffer massive casualties before Chinese troops withdraw on March 15.

March 28, 1979   First major U.S. nuclear power plant accident occurs at Three Mile Island reactor near Harrisburg, Pa.

April 11, 1979   Force of Ugandan exiles and Tanzanian troops occupies Ugandan capital of Kampala, ending brutal eight-year regime of Amin, who flees to Libya.

May 3, 1979   In landslide victory for Conservative party, Margaret Thatcher becomes Britain's first woman prime minister.

June 18, 1979   Carter and Brezhnev sign SALT II Treaty in Vienna.

July 17, 1979   Insurrectionary forces led by Sandinista National Liberation Front (FSLN) take over Nicaraguan capital of Managua, ending 50-year dictatorial rule of Somoza family; President Anastasio Somoza flees.

Oct. 1, 1979   U.S. Canal Zone formally dissolved as Panama takes control of territory in accord with 1977 treaties; canal itself scheduled to be turned over to Panama on Dec. 31, 1999.

Nov. 4, 1979   U.S. embassy in Tehran stormed by Iranian militants who seize 66 American hostages; 52 ultimately held for almost 15 months; among other demands, militants call for shah to be returned to Iran to stand trial; after leaving U.S., shah dies in Egypt in July 1980.

Nov. 21, 1979   Islamic fundamentalists burn U.S. embassy in Pakistan.

Dec. 12, 1979   Under so-called two-track decision, NATO governments, excluding France and Greece, agree to deploy 572 new intermediate-range nuclear missiles in Europe by end of 1983 while simultaneously pursuing agreement with USSR on controlling all intermediate-range weapons based in Eastern and Western Europe; projected deployment of new missiles, first such weapons capable of reaching targets inside USSR from European soil, prompts massive anti-nuclear demonstrations in Europe during early 1980s.

Dec. 25, 1979   Following Moscow-engineered coup by Babrak Karmal, Soviet forces invade Afghanistan and shore up new Marxist government; Carter administration recalls U.S. ambassador to Moscow, imposes embargo on grain and technology exports to Soviets, and asks Senate to delay ratification of SALT II treaty; U.S. Olympic Committee, under pressure from White House, later votes to boycott 1980 Olympic Games in Moscow.

April 6, 1980   After thousands of Cubans storm Peruvian embassy seeking asylum, Castro opens port of Mariel in Cuba, allowing thousands of small boats to leave for U.S.; before port is closed at the end of September, approximately 125,000 Cubans, many convicted criminals and mental patients, will have emigrated.

April 17, 1980   Ending 90 years of white rule and 8 years of interracial civil war, independent, majority-ruled nation of Zimbabwe created from white-ruled Rhodesia; nationalist leader Robert Mugabe, whose party had won landslide parliamentary electoral victory in March, sworn in as prime minister.

April 24, 1980   Eight U.S. commandos die in aborted attempt to rescue American hostages in Iran.

May 21–27, 1980   An estimated 1,000 people killed by South Korean military forces during uprisings in Kwangju spurred by detention of opposition leader Kim Dae Jung.

July 19, 1980   Summer Olympic Games open in Moscow without participation of U.S. and other boycotting western nations.

Aug. 30, 1980   Eastern Europe's first independent postwar trade union, Solidarity, formed in Poland.

Nov. 4, 1980   Republican Ronald Reagan defeats Carter in presidential election.

Jan. 20, 1981   Remaining 52 hostages released in Iran moments after Reagan is sworn in as president.

March 30, 1981   Reagan shot in Washington by John W. Hinckley, Jr., but recovers quickly.

May 10, 1981   François Mitterrand becomes first Socialist Party candidate elected president of France.

May 13, 1981   Pope John Paul II shot in Rome by Mehmet Ali Agca, a Turk; Italian investigators later charge three Bulgarians with plotting the attempt.

Oct. 6, 1981   Sadat assassinated in Cairo by members of radical Muslim sect; Vice President Hosni Mubarak succeeds to presidency.

Oct. 22, 1981   Leaders of 22 nations meet in Cancun, Mexico, to discuss ambitious agenda of issues concerning economic cooperation between industrial countries of the north and developing countries of the south.

Dec. 13, 1981   Declaration of martial law in Poland results in banning of Solidarity trade union.

Jan. 8, 1982   Justice Department and AT&T reach settlement in which latter agrees to divest itself of 22 regional Bell System companies, breaking its monopoly over nation's phone services.

April 2, 1982   Suspending negotiations, Argentina invades contested Falkland (Malvinas) Islands in South Atlantic, provoking British Prime Minister Thatcher to dispatch naval task force which retakes islands on June 14; Argentine defeat hastens fall of military junta, leading eventually to return of civilian democratic rule.

June 6, 1982   Israel invades Lebanon in effort to secure its northern border region from terrorist and artillery attacks and to crush PLO's military apparatus.

June 30, 1982   Legal deadline passes for ratification of Equal Rights Amendment to U.S. Constitution; only 35 of required 38 states have ratified ERA, which would prohibit discrimination on basis of sex.

Aug. 25, 1982   U.S. marines land in Lebanon as part of multinational peacekeeping force; leaving after two weeks, they return for extended stay on September 29, along with French and Italian contingents, after massacre of more than 800 Palestinian men, women, and children by Lebanese Christian militiamen at Sabra and Shatila refugee camps in Beirut.

Sept. 12–13, 1982   Major shake-up of Chinese leadership results in election of Deng Xiaoping as chairman of newly formed Central Advisory Committee to the Communist Party, consolidating his power in both party and government.

Nov. 10, 1982   Brezhnev dies; Yuri Andropov, former KGB chief, succeeds him as general secretary of Soviet Communist Party on Nov. 12.

March 23, 1983   In nationally televised speech, Reagan outlines plans for funding research on Strategic Defense Initiative, a space-based missile defense system familiarly known as "Star Wars."

April 18, 1983   U.S. embassy in Beirut bombed, killing more than 50.

May 20, 1983   Car bomb detonated outside South African air force headquarters in Pretoria kills 18 in most serious single terrorist attack to date by black resistance forces.

July 21, 1983   Martial law repealed in Poland.

Sept. 1, 1983   Korean airliner with more than 300 passengers aboard shot down over Sea of Japan by Soviet fighter plane after entering Soviet airspace.

Oct. 3, 1983   Barracks of U.S. marines participating in Lebanon peacekeeping force destroyed by car bomb, killing 241 servicemen; 58 die in similar attack on French headquarters on same day.

Oct. 25, 1983   Citing threat to U.S. security interests and to lives of American medical students, U.S. forces invade Caribbean island of Grenada, deposing extreme left-wing faction that had ousted and killed Prime Minister Maurice Bishop one week before; hundreds of Cuban construction workers and soldiers are routed and captured during subsequent days; new elections held under U.S. sponsorship in 1984.

Oct. 30, 1983   Radical Party leader Raul Alfonsin elected president of Argentina, defeating a candidate of the influential Peronist movement and ending eight years of repressive military rule.

Nov. 2, 1983   White voters approve new South African constitution providing representation in separate chambers of parliament for Indians and mixed-race "Coloureds," but not for black majority.

Nov. 23, 1983   Soviet delegation walks out of Intermediate Nuclear Force reduction talks in Geneva; one month later, Soviets refuse to set date for resumption of Strategic Arms Reduction Talks (START).

Dec. 30, 1983   Despite substantial popular opposition and protest, first nine Pershing II missiles called for in NATO's 1979 nuclear modernization scheme become operational in West Germany.

Feb. 9, 1984   Andropov dies and is succeeded by Konstantin Chernenko.

April 6, 1984   Reports disclose CIA role in directing mining of Nicaraguan ports; Sandinista government appeals to World Court, but Reagan administration announces in advance that it will not recognize court's jurisdiction in this case.

May 6, 1984   José Napoleon Duarte, moderate candidate favored by U.S. government, elected president of El Salvador, defeating right-wing candidate Roberto d'Aubuisson.

July 19, 1984   Democratic National Convention in San Francisco nominates Geraldine Ferraro as first woman vice presidential candidate for major party in U.S.

July 28, 1984   Summer Olympics open in Los Angeles, with USSR leading boycott of communist nations.

Sept. 20, 1984   New U.S. embassy in West Beirut bombed.

Sept. 25, 1984   Resolution banning visits by nuclear-armed warships introduced in New Zealand parliament, sparking controversy with U.S. and threatening future of 1951 tripartite Australia-New Zealand-U.S. security agreement commonly known as ANZUS.

Oct. 20, 1984   Chinese Communist Party issues major document approving Deng's program for liberalization and decentralization of Chinese economy.

Oct. 31, 1984   Following series of protracted, violent clashes between Sikh militants and Indian police and military in Punjab state, Indian Prime Minister Indira Gandhi assassinated by Sikh members of her own personal guard; her son Rajiv succeeds her in office.

Nov. 6, 1984   Defeating former Vice President Walter F. Mondale, Reagan re-elected president.

Nov. 20, 1984   Red Cross representatives from North and South Korea meet to discuss reunification of families separated by Korean War.

Dec. 9, 1984   With passing of deadline for signatures of UN Treaty on the Law of the Sea, U.S. fails to join 138 countries and 21 international organizations which have put their names to the document.

March 10, 1985   Chernenko dies; Mikhail Gorbachev, first member of successor generation of Soviet leadership, ascends to power.

March 12, 1985   Comprehensive U.S.-Soviet arms control negotiations involving linked talks on strategic, intermediate-range, and space-based weapons systems resume in Geneva after more than one-year hiatus.

June 14, 1985   TWA flight hijacked and American passengers taken hostage by Lebanese Shi'ite Muslims demanding release of Shi'ite prisoners held by Israel; negotiations lead to freeing of hostages 17 days later after personal intervention by Syrian president Hafez al-Assad.

July 2, 1985   Andrei Gromyko, a major architect of postwar Soviet foreign policy, named to ceremonial office of president of USSR after 28 years as foreign minister; Eduard Shevardnadze becomes foreign minister; Reagan and Gorbachev agree to November 1985 summit meeting in Geneva, first such encounter for both leaders.

July 10, 1985   Greenpeace ship monitoring French nuclear testing in Pacific sunk. Action revealed as taken by French intelligence service.

July 20, 1985   In face of escalating unrest in black townships, white government declares state of emergency in certain regions of South Africa; violence intensifies as police arrest more than 1,500 opposition figures under new law-enforcement guidelines.

July 23, 1985   North and South Korean officials meet to plan reunification talks.

Sept. 12–13, 1985	New Contadora peace plan for Central America. Nicaragua later rejects it (Nov. 11) as not banning U.S. military activity in the area.
Oct. 1–10, 1985	Israelis bomb PLO headquarters in Tunis; Palestinian terrorists hijack Italian cruise ship *Achille Lauro* and kill American; later surrender to Egyptians; U.S. downs in Sicily the Egyptian aircraft carrying the terrorists to Tunis.
Oct. 7, 1985	U.S. announces it will no longer automatically comply with International Court of Justice decisions, claiming court decisions "abused for political ends."
Nov. 19, 1985	Geneva Reagan-Gorbachev summit meeting.
Dec. 2, 1985	Liberal Party defeats separatist Parti Québécois in Quebec National Assembly elections.
Dec. 4, 1985	National Security Adviser Robert McFarlane resigns, replaced by Vice Admiral John M. Poindexter.
Dec. 8, 1985	OPEC states abandon official oil pricing structure.
Dec. 27, 1985	Abu Nidal groups mount terrorist attacks against Rome and Vienna airports.
Jan. 1, 1986	Spain and Portual become eleventh and twelfth members of European Community.
Feb. 7, 1986	President for Life Jean-Claude Duvalier, forced from office by revolutionary violence, leaves Haiti.
Feb. 11, 1986	Iran captures Fao peninsula, the high point of Iranian success in its war with Iraq.
Feb. 25, 1986	At the Twenty-Seventh Congress of the Soviet Communist Party Gorbachev calls for major economic reforms.
Feb. 25, 1986	Following earlier elections widely regarded as fraudulent and resulting pressure from Filipinos and from the Reagan administration Philippine president Ferdinard Marcos leaves country. Corazon Aquino assumes office.
March 14, 1986	UN report charges Iraq with use of chemical weapons.
April 15, 1986	U.S. air raid in Libyan military and political targets.
April 26, 1986	Explosion of nuclear reactor at Chernobyl in Soviet Union. World's worst nuclear accident.
April 28, 1986	U.S. announces it will not be bound by military commitment of the

ANZUS treaty (signed 1951) if New Zealand bars nuclear-powered or nuclear-armed U.S. ships.

April 29, 1986   Extremist Sikhs who had seized Amritsar Golden Temple on January 26 declare creation of independent Sikh state, Khalistan. April 30, Indian paramilitary police capture the temple.

June 4, 1986   Former U.S. intelligence official Jonathan Pollard pleads guilty to charge of spying for Israel.

June 12, 1986   *New York Times* reports Panamanian army commander Manuel Noriega involved in drug traffic. Later (June 21) reports he overturned results of 1984 Panamanian presidential election to get his candidate into office.

June 28, 1986   International Court of Justice rules that U.S. violated international law by aiding Nicaraguan Contras.

Aug. 18, 1986   First (but limited) diplomatic contacts between USSR and Israel since USSR broke relations at time of June 1967 Arab-Israeli war.

Aug. 23, 1986   Soviet physicist and UN scientific officer arrested in New York on spying charge. Aug. 30, Nicholas Daniloff, *U.S. News & World Report* journalist arrested in Moscow. Both freed and returned to their countries, end of Sept.

Sept. 9–15, 1986   Meeting of seventy-four member states of the General Agreement on Tariffs & Trade (GATT) meet at Punta del Este, Uruguay.

Oct. 5, 1986   Capture of U.S. citizen Eugene Hasenfus after U.S. plane carrying supplies to Contras downed in Nicaragua exposes pattern of U.S. covert aid to Contras.

Oct. 11–12, 1986   Reagan-Gorbachev summit meeting in Reykjavik, Iceland. Apparent major agreement on reduction of nuclear arms negated by disagreement on U.S. Strategic Defense Initiative ("Star Wars").

Nov. 13, 1986   Following Beirut newspaper exposure Reagan in television speech admits small quantity of U.S. arms sent to Iran but denies any arms-for-hostage intention.

Nov. 20, 1986   Babrak Karmal resigns as president of Afghanistan.

Nov. 26, 1986   Reagan names former Senator John Tower, former NSC Adviser Brent Scowcroft, and former Secretary of State Edmund Muskie to special panel examining the National Security Council activities in the "Iran-Contra" affair.

Jan. 27–29, 1987   Abortive coup by approximately 500 Filipino soldiers supporting former President Marcos.

Jan. 28, 1987	Oliver Tambo of African National Congress meets in Washington with Secretary of State Shultz.
Feb. 6, 1987	Sen. Sam Nunn warns of "constitutional crisis" if administration adopts broad interpretation of 1972 Anti-Ballistic Missile treaty without consulting Congress.
Feb. 26, 1987	Tower Commission investigating Iran-Contra affair criticizes Reagan's "personal management style."
Feb. 26, 1987	USSR conducts underground nuclear tests, ending eighteen-month unilateral moratorium.
Feb. 28, 1987	Gorbachev offers to sign agreement eliminating intermediate nuclear weapons in Europe.
March 4, 1987	Reagan in televised speech concedes his Iran policy "deteriorated" into arms-for-hostage trade.
March 4, 1987	Jonathan Pollard, former intelligence officer who pleaded guilty of spying for Israel, sentenced to life in prison.
March 23, 1987	U.S. offers military protection to Kuwait vessels in Persian Gulf.
April 14, 1987	USSR announces plan to lease Kuwait three tankers, hints Soviet naval escort in Gulf as well.
April 27, 1987	U.S. bars Austrian President Kurt Waldheim from entering U.S., citing his wartime Nazi connections.
May 5, 1987	Joint House-Senate hearings on Iran-Contra affair begin.
May 17, 1987	Iraqi plane attacks U.S. frigate *Stark*, killing 37.
May 19, 1987	U.S. agrees to reflag Kuwaiti oil tankers and provide naval escort in Gulf.
May 29, 1987	Warsaw Pact nations end summit meeting calling for talks with NATO to reduce conventional forces and tactical nuclear weapons.
June 4, 1987	New Zealand Parliament passes legislation banning nuclear-armed or nuclear-powered ships from its ports, putting into law government policy adopted three years earlier.
June 9, 1987	Beginning of serious demonstrations in South Korea against government of President Chun. Demonstrations continue throughout the year.
June 11, 1987	British Conservative Party wins election. Prime Minister Thatcher continues in power.

July 26, 1987	President Jayewardene of Sri Lanka and Indian Prime Minister Gandhi sign agreement designed to end rebellion of Tamil minority in Sri Lanka.
July 31, 1987	Iranian pilgrims clash with Saudi police during Hajj, leave 402 killed.
Aug. 4, 1987	Reagan Administration and House Speaker Jim Wright agree on proposed peace plan for Nicaragua.
Aug. 7, 1987	Presidents of Guatemala, El Salvador, Honduras, Nicaragua, and Costa Rica agree to peace plan proposed by Costa Rican President Arias.
Aug. 11, 1987	U.S. and USSR in Geneva talks agree on compulsory "challenge" inspections of chemical weapons facilities.
Aug. 28–29, 1987	Abortive army coup against Aquino government in Philippines.
Oct. 16–19, 1987	U.S. stock market crash sends shock waves throughout the world economy.
Nov. 2, 1987	Gorbachev at seventieth-anniversary celebration of Bolshevik Revolution attacks Stalinism and defends perestroika (restructuring).
Nov. 2–17, 1987	Nicaraguan President Ortega offers cease-fire proposal based on plan worked out with House Speaker Jim Wright. Reagan administration denounces Wright's involvement. Wright and Secretary of State Shultz agree (Nov. 17) to work together on Central American peace efforts.
Nov. 8, 1987	Arab summit meeting in Amman supports Iraq in war with Iran, allows Arab League members to restore diplomatic relations with Egypt.
Nov. 18, 1987	Joint House-Senate committee report on Iran-Contra affair. Criticizes NSC advisers, the late CIA director William Casey, and Attorney-General Edward Meese. Unable to discern precise role of Reagan.
Nov. 25, 1987	UN Security Council unanimously condemns South African "illegal entry" into Angola.
Dec. 8, 1987	Reagan and Gorbachev sign treaty providing for destruction of 2,611 INF missiles and verification inspections.
Dec. 9, 1987	Incident in Gaza strip sparks demonstrations throughout Gaza and West Bank. Beginning of the Palestinian *intifada* against Israeli occupation.

Dec. 16, 1987	Roh Tae Woo, Chun's designated successor, wins South Korean presidential election against divided opposition.
Jan. 22, 1988	French President Mitterrand and West German Chancellor Kohl sign agreement establishing Franco-German councils on defense and economic issues.
Feb. 4, 1988	U.S. federal grand jury indicts Panamanian strongman Manuel Noriega on charges of racketeering and drug trafficking.
Feb. 25, 1988	Panamanian President Del Valle named replacement for General Noriega. Following day National Assembly votes unanimously to oust Del Valle.
Feb. 25–March 4, 1988	Shultz meetings in Israel, Jordan, Syria and Egypt in unsuccessful effort to advance "Shultz initiative" for Arab-Israeli peace.
March 19, 1988	Saudi Arabia confirms purchase of 1,600-mile range missiles from China.
April 3, 1988	Ethiopia and Somalia sign peace agreement.
April 14, 1988	Agreement for Soviet withdrawal of troops from Afghanistan by Feb. 15, 1989 signed in Geneva under UN auspices by Afghanistan, Pakistan, U.S., and USSR.
April 16, 1988	Israeli assassination team kills PLO Military Chief Khalid Wazir (Abu Jihad) in Tunis.
May 16, 1988	Algeria and Morocco resume diplomatic relations broken twelve years earlier.
May 18, 1988	Indian troops and police successfully end siege of Golden Temple occupied by Sikh extremists.
May 22, 1988	Janos Kádár removed as Hungarian Communist Party general secretary and many Kádár loyalists ousted from Central Committee.
May 25, 1988	Panamanian General Noriega rejects U.S. proposal he leave Panama in return for U.S. dismissal of drug trafficking charges.
May 25, 1988	Col. Qaddafi recognizes government of Chad and announces all problems solved between Libya and Chad.
May 27, 1988	Senate approves, 95–5, INF treaty with Soviet Union eliminating U.S. and Soviet missiles in 300–3,400 mile range.
May 29–June 2, 1988	Reagan summit meeting in Moscow with Gorbachev. Ratify U.S.-USSR INF Treaty, June 1.

June 15, 1988   Supreme Soviet of Armenian Republic votes that portion of neighbor Soviet Republic of Azerbaijan be reunified with Armenia, exacerbating the ethnic rivalries between the two USSR republics.

June 19, 1988   Haitian Chief of Staff Gen. Henri Namphy seizes power after civilian President Manigat attempts to oust him. Manigat flees Haiti June 20.

June 28, 1988   Gorbachev at Soviet Communist Party Conference calls for major governmental changes including strong presidency and more representative legislature. Approved July 1.

July 23, 1988   U.S. cruiser *Vincennes* downs Iranian commercial jet in Persian Gulf. All 290 aboard killed.

July 31, 1988   King Husayn abandons Jordan's claim to West Bank in favor of PLO.

Aug. 17, 1988   President Zia of Pakistan and U.S. Ambassador Arnold Raphel killed in aircraft explosion.

Aug. 20, 1988   Cease-fire in eight year old Iraq-Iran war.

Aug. 30, 1988   Morocco and Polisario accept joint UN–Organization of African Unity plan for cease-fire and referendum in Western Sahara.

Sept. 17, 1988   Haitian President Namphy ousted in coup. General Prosper Avril assumes power, Sept. 18.

Sept. 29, 1988   Nobel Peace Prize awarded to UN peacekeeping forces.

Oct. 4, 1988   House fails to override Reagan veto of bill restricting imports of textiles, clothing, and shoes.

Oct. 4–11, 1988   Serious riots throughout Algeria.

Oct. 5, 1988   Chilean referendum votes against new term for President Pinochet.

Nov. 8, 1988   Republican George Bush defeats Democrat Michael Dukakis in presidential elections.

Nov. 14, 1988   Palestine National Council (PNC), parliament in exile of PLO, meeting in Algiers accepts UN Security Council Resolution 242.

Nov. 23, 1988   Former South Korean President Chun Doo Hwan publicly apologizes for abuses during his administration and enters Buddhist monastery.

Dec. 1, 1988   Benazir Bhutto appointed Pakistan prime minister after her People's Party wins plurality of seats in November general elections.

Dec. 6, 1988	Gorbachev at UN General Assembly announces plan to reduce Soviet military by 500,000.
Dec. 7, 1988	Major earthquake in Soviet Armenia.
Dec. 14, 1988	U.S. opens talks with the PLO.
Dec. 21, 1988	Terrorist bomb destroys Pan American airliner over Scotland, killing all 259 people on board.
Dec. 22, 1988	U.S.-brokered agreement signed by Angola, Cuba, and South Africa for transition to independence in Namibia.
Dec. 24, 1988	Canadian House of Commons approves trade accord with U.S. Previously approved by U.S. Congress, accord goes into effect Jan. 1, 1989.
Jan. 19, 1989	Conference on Security and Cooperation (all European states except Albania plus Canada and the U.S.) concludes 26-month review of 1975 Helsinki Accord.
Jan. 23, 1989	Guerrilla opposition Farabundo Marti National Liberation (FMNL) agrees to participate in El Salvador elections and abide by results if elections are postponed for six months. President José Napoleón Duarte rejects offer, January 25.
Feb. 15, 1989	Last Soviet troops leave Afghanistan.

America and the World since 1945:
The History and the Historians
A Bibliographical Essay

L. CARL BROWN and
RICHARD D. CHALLENER

> Of our conceptions of the past, we make a future.
> Thomas Hobbes

Book titles can epitomize an age. Consider the following titles that treat essentially the period of history being covered in this work:

Rise to Globalism
The Age of Global Power
The United States in the World Arena
The Imperial Years
Nation or Empire?
Pax Americana
Power and Impotence: The Failure of American Foreign Policy
The Arrogance of Power
The Retreat of American Power

The same theme can be seen in works by foreign authors, as the following general study by a French author well illustrates:

La Fin de l'Innocence: Les Etats-Unis de Wilson à Reagan[1]

The twin ideas of power and global reach are strikingly present in all these works. Some authors come to praise, others to condemn the new American role in world affairs. Still others view with alarm the apparent decline so soon after the United States had reached the pinnacle of world power. In all cases the basic assumption shared by all these books is that the United States has become ineluctably involved in world affairs. We are a far cry from earlier assumptions of isolationism, of Fortress America.

The period in American diplomatic history since World War II can thus be divided from earlier times, or at least this is the case as regards American self-perceptions. This postwar period, in turn, can be divided into two parts. In roughly the last half of the era since 1945 (that is, since the mid-sixties), the weight of historical writing has moved away from an earlier self-confidence and optimism and has taken a negative, critical turn. Again, book titles well illustrate the point:

Shattered Peace: The Origins of the Cold War and the National Security State
Our Own Worst Enemy: The Unmaking of American Foreign Policy
Endless Enemies: The Making of an Unfriendly World
Estrangement: America and the World[2]

This change from upbeat optimism to a decided pessimism coming roughly at the end of the first postwar generation can be readily explained. Americans, first of all, ignored the advice of the famous baseball pitcher, Satchel Paige, who insisted "Never look back. Somebody may be gaining on you." Americans began both to look back in time and also to look all around them. They discovered that not just our adversaries but also our allies were gaining in relation to the United States. This was not really surprising, since the United States was the only major power to emerge from the carnage of World War II undevastated. That American power would decline relatively thereafter was normal and, indeed, healthy. It was evidence that the world was recovering. Even so, discernible power shifts usually trigger strong reactions on the part of the people affected, reactions that can readily become exaggerated or irrational.

Second, and of more immediate importance in changing the mood about

1. Authors and date of publication of these books are, in the order listed: Stephen E. Ambrose (first published 1971, 2nd edition 1980), Norman A. Graebner (1979), W. W. Rostow (1969), Alonzo Hambry (1976), Robert W. Tucker (1968), Ronald Steele (1967), William Pfaff (1966), J. William Fulbright (1966), Henry Brandon (1974) and Denise Artaud (1985). Several cover the period since 1939 or, in one case, since Wilson, but the thrust of all—and the inspiration of the titles—derives from the post–World War II period.

2. Again, authors and date of publication are in the order listed: Daniel Yergin (1977), I. M. Destler, Leslie H. Gelb, and Anthony Lake (1984), Jonathan Kwitny (1984), and Sanford J. Ungar, ed. (1985).

America's world role, was the national trauma of involvement in Vietnam. Some drew the practical conclusion from this bitter experience that containment and collective security had their limits. America could not police the world. Others drew the moral conclusion that Americans should not police the world. Still others insisted that American hesitations about and then withdrawal from Vietnam reflected a dismal lack of will to be a world leader. In the clash of these differing ideas the establishment thinking that had emerged triumphant by the late forties was challenged.

The move toward a new national consensus concerning America's role in world affairs is still underway. Signs at this time of what that consensus might become are confusing and contradictory. On the one hand, a Yale historian highly regarded by his peers but hitherto scarcely a household name to the American public wrote a book that remained on the best seller list throughout much of 1988. Paul Kennedy's book had the rather intimidating title of *The Rise and Fall of the Great Powers: Economic Change and Military Conflict from 1500 to 2000*. With over six hundred pages of text and notes, the work might have seemed destined for a limited if honorable niche among the assigned readings of graduate students in history. Instead, the book was reviewed by the mass media and read, or at least purchased, by American opinion molders.

Kennedy argued that imperial or hegemonic powers have a tendency to overexpand militarily beyond what their economic resource base permits. They thus set in motion the process of their own decline, to be replaced by some other, rising power. Most of Kennedy's readers, it can be assumed, moved quickly to his final chapter, "The United States: The Problem of Number One in Relative Decline," for his book was interpreted as claiming that the United States, just like past imperial powers, had become vulnerably overextended.

Kennedy's thesis did not go unchallenged. For example, the Winter 1988/1989 issue of *Foreign Affairs*, the journal of the influential Council on Foreign Relations, had an article entitled "The U.S.—Decline or Renewal." Its author, Harvard political scientist Samuel P. Huntington, challenged Paul Kennedy's idea of "imperial overstretch." Indeed, Huntington introduced the neologism "declinists" in disputing the argument of Kennedy and his ilk.

A no-holds-barred attack was penned by W. W. Rostow, appearing in the Spring 1988 issue of the same *Foreign Affairs*. Lest anyone might misunderstand his position, Rostow entitled his review of Paul Kennedy's book "Beware of Historians Bearing False Analogies." Here the battle of generations—both individuals and eras—was truly joined. Rostow himself, while serving in the Johnson administration came to be identified as one of the most assertive spokesmen of worldwide containment policies in Vietnam and wherever else the need might arise.

Perhaps more to the point, during the 1988 presidential campaign neither George Bush nor Michael Dukakis sought to stake out a position that America must be more modest in its global commitments. In large measure each was cautious not to appear "weak" on matters of national defense, whatever the cost. There was no echo, however faint, of the cry "Come Home, America" that George McGovern raised in his ill-fated 1972 campaign. In short, the kinds of arguments that McGovern, the politician, raised earlier and Kennedy, the scholar, has presented recently do not appear to have significantly modified mainstream American foreign policy assumptions.

And yet, can we be so sure? The 1988 presidential debates as regards foreign policy as well as the writings of those who would dismiss the "declinists" may well be the dying battle cries of an earlier received wisdom. Or they may be rallying Americans to an updated version of the post-1945 notion that the United States must take the role of world leader in a global policy of containment and collective security. History is not prophecy. The collective wisdom of historians can, at best, do no more than suggest likely outcomes of future events based on the identification of apparent behavior patterns of those involved. History is an inexact science.

What is the relevance of all this to the task of these pages, which is to review writings on American diplomacy since 1945? The answer, surely, is that Thomas Hobbes was right in asserting that "of our conceptions of the past we make a future." The writing of history is an enterprise closely connected to the ongoing public debate over present and future policy, and there will accordingly be a wide range of interpretations of the same historical past. This is always openly the case with partisans and polemicists whom scholarly purists would prefer not to call historians at all. It is necessarily true, as well, for even the most dispassionate and fair-minded professional historian.

Good history writing is more than just the careful accumulation and classification of facts, although it certainly must be that to be worthy of the name. Making sense out of those available facts is subject to different and ever-changing interpretations. What becomes accepted as accurate history involves an ongoing dynamic tension between, on the one hand, the discovery of new facts as well as the reordering of already known historical facts and, on the other hand, the varying interpretive vessels into which those facts, new or old, are placed.

This is not to say that changing styles in history writing are as arbitrary as the length of women's skirts or the width of men's ties. There are rules. This can be illustrated with reference to the simple (if not completely accurate) distinction between "facts" and "interpretations."

The uncovering of more facts about America's diplomatic history since 1945 constantly changes our understanding of events. Two examples may be cited: The availability of public documents for the years of the Eisenhower presidency have modified our veiw of Eisenhower's relationship with his secretary of state. Eisenhower is no longer seen as passively guided in foreign policy by Dulles. It is clear that he was very much a "hands-on" president.

Newly revealed facts have also changed our understanding of the 1962 Cuban missile crisis. These take the form of recent revelations by Americans serving in high official positions at the time of that tense Soviet-American confrontation.[3] Other such facts concerning past foreign policy issues are always being uncovered, either routinely as public archives are opened to scholars, or by

3. See J. Anthony Lukas, "Class Reunion: Kennedy's Men Relive the Cuba Missile Crisis," *New York Times Sunday Magazine*, 30 August 1987.

unexpected disclosures as was the case with the recent new light shed on the Cuban missile crisis.

Equally important is the reordering of known facts, but both newly discovered facts and facts long a part of the known public record becoming meaningful only by being interpreted—that is, by being explained in a way that the public finds plausible. This is a process of continual change, sometimes in rather sharp breaks with earlier received wisdom (as from the operative ideal of isolationism before the Second World War to that of internationalism after), but often in imperceptibly slow stages. Jacob Burckhardt suggested as the rock-bottom, minimal definition of history: "What one age finds worthy of note in another."

Burckhardt's maxim, however, needs to be expanded. Variations in historical orientation occur not just from one age to another but in the same age among different nations, different classes, different ethnic groups and the like.

In the same way, it is often said that history is written by, and for, the winners. This is never quite true, but even accepting that the assertion has some measure of validity, what if yesterday's losers achieve power and standing today? The way in which Americans have changed their views of their own domestic history in response to, for example, black and women's liberation movements has its parallels in American perceptions of the rest of the world. One need only note how present-day American views of Japan or South Africa have changed from what they were a half century ago. Many other such examples could be added— Germany or China or the entire Third World, the latter being a designation that did not even exist earlier.

Historians, accordingly, need to study both the facts and the varying interpretations of those facts. This, moreover, must be done in a spirit of accepting that both the facts and the interpretations will always be in a fluid state. Such is even more the case in the history of international relations, for it treats history on a global scale and deals with issues about which people rightly feel strongly, issues that involve security, prosperity, war and peace.

This bibliographical essay seeks to offer a representative sampling of what we know (or better, what we think we know) about American diplomacy since 1945—in short, a presentation of the available "facts." It seeks as well to survey with representative examples the many different interpretations of American diplomatic history since 1945.

Soviet American Relations and the Cold War

The one issue that more than any other has provided the context for post-American diplomacy is that of the adversarial relations with the Soviet Union. Indeed, it can be argued that this one continuing issue has often tended to overshadow badly needed American foreign policy (and American historical) writing on other issues in postwar international politics. One of the goals of *Centerstage* is to provide a more balanced survey of American relations with the entire world without falling into the trap of linking these relations to American-Soviet bipolar confrontation. Even with a more truly global approach to American diplomacy, however, the history of American-Soviet relations properly remains the principal organizing framework for this bibliographical study.

How did the Cold War begin? That, in all its simplicity, has been a major question. In the early years from soon after World War II until roughly the end of the 1950s, most historians of the Cold War as well as those individuals who made American foreign policy tended to see the answer as obvious. The expansionist policies of the Soviet Union, seeking to exploit weakness anywhere it was to be found, brought on the Cold War. American policy was seen as defensive, as responsive to Soviet imperialist ambitions. Most American diplomatic historians, in fact, were more concerned to trace the dramatic American move from isolationism to internationalism, and the generally accepted interpretation (with only a very few lonely voices registering their disagreement) was that this move represented a laudable, indeed long overdue, acceptance by the U.S. of its international responsibilities.

By the 1960s, however, with the doubts and disillusionment that set in with America's involvement in the Vietnam War, this sanguine interpretation of American diplomacy seemed less and less adequate. Revisionist historians began to get a hearing largely denied them in the earlier period of confidence regarding America's role in the world. A seminal work challenging the establishment view was that of William A. Williams, *The Tragedy of American Foreign Policy*. He asserted that American foreign policy had always been expansionist. Since its origins the United States had consistently pursued an economic "Open Door" policy in order to advance its own economic interests.

Several significant works followed this line of argument set by Williams. These include Walter LaFeber, *America, Russia and the Cold War, 1945–1980;* Lloyd Gardner, *Architects of Illusion: Men and Ideas in American Foreign Policy, 1941–1949;* and Thomas G. Paterson, *Soviet-American Confrontation: Post-War Reconstruction and the Origins of the Cold War.*

Many revisionists have argued that the United States was largely responsible for starting the Cold War. Gar Alperowitz in *Atomic Diplomacy* has contended that the United States dropped the first atomic bomb to coerce the Soviet Union rather than to defeat Japan, while Richard M. Freeland in *The Truman Doctrine and the Origins of McCarthyism: Foreign Policy, Domestic Politics and Internal Security* contends that the 1947 Truman Doctrine was the product of the administration's domestic needs. The most sharply revisionist, and Marxist, interpretation is that of Gabriel and Joyce Kolko, *The Limits of Power: The World and United States Foreign Policy* which insists that American postwar expansionism was necessitated by the very structure of the American capitalist economy.

An interesting and influential example of what might be dubbed "moderate revisionism" was Daniel Yergin's *Shattered Peace: The Origins of the Cold War and the National Security State.*

More recently, a group labelled the "corporatist" school has argued for a continuity in American foreign policy growing out of the continuing relationship between business and government in this century. Illustrative of this school are Michael Hogan, "Revival and Reform: America's Twentieth Century Search for a

New Economic Order," *Diplomatic History,* no. 8 (Fall 1984); and Thomas J. McCormick, "Drift or Mastery: A Corporatist Synthesis," *Reviews in American History* (December 1982).

As often happens when a well-established "orthodox" view of history is challenged, the challengers in turn are called to task for overstating their case. The result of this dialectical process seems to have been a synthesizing reinterpretation. Many new historical accounts tend to move away from apportioning blame and toward approaches that emphasize foreign policy as an untidy resultant of unconsciously embraced ideologies, imperfect knowledge of the presumed adversaries, domestic constraints, and other such contingencies. In the process, the sharply etched interpretations in black and white give way to various shadings of gray. Among the best of this genre are Adam Ulam, *The Rivals: America and Russia since World War II;* Louis J. Halle, *The Cold War as History,* and Joseph Nye, *The Making of America's Soviet Policy.*

The literature on the Cold War and American-Soviet relations is enormous. Even specialists despair of being able to keep up with all the detailed monographs or even the many different general works of interpretation. A useful way to get more quickly a certain sense of the context within which the historical arguments are set is to read the chapter-length collected essays of historians who have devoted their scholarly careers to this large subject. Three such collections can be recommended. They are Norman Graebner, *America as a World Power: A Realist Appraisal from Wilson to Reagan;* John Lewis Gaddis, *The Long Peace: Inquiries into the History of the Cold War;* and Thomas G. Paterson, *Meeting the Communist Threat: Truman to Reagan.*

Recent books which break out of the standard Cold War historiography and pay more attention to what might be called the study of available policy options are Alexander George, ed., *Managing U.S.-Soviet Relations: Problems of Crisis Prevention;* and Alexander L. George, Philip J. Farley and Alexander Dallin, eds., *U.S.–Soviet Security Cooperation: Achievements, Failures, Lessons.*

National and Nuclear Strategy

There can be little doubt that the advent of the nuclear age has changed both the reality of, as well as thinking about, international relations. On the role of the atomic bomb in American national security policy in the immediate postwar period see Paul Boyer, *By the Bomb's Early Light: American Thought and Culture at the Dawn of the Atomic Era;* and Gregg Herken, *The Winning Weapon: The Atomic Bomb and the Cold War, 1945–1949,* a book which shows how poorly prepared the United States was to develop a coherent policy with respect to nuclear weapons. On the evolution of deterrence theory works are legion. Among the most influential are Bernard Brodie, *The Absolute Weapon;* Thomas Schelling, *The Strategy of Conflict* and *Arms and Conflict;* Henry Kissinger, *Nuclear Weapons and Foreign Policy* and his *Strategy in the Nuclear Age;* Alexander L. George and Richard Smoke, *Deterrence in American Foreign Policy: Theory and Practice;* and Robert Jervis, *The Illogic of Nuclear Weapons* as well as his *Perception and Misperception in International Politics.*

For a quick but solid introduction to the main lines of America's nuclear strategy the following two chapters in collected works are recommended: Lawrence Freedman, "The First Two Generations of Nuclear Strategists," in Peter Paret, ed., *Makers of Modern Strategy from Machiavelli to the Nuclear Age;* and David Alan Rosenberg, "The Origins of Overkill: Nuclear Weapons and American Strategy," in Norman A. Graebner, ed., *The National Security: Its Theory and Practice, 1945–1960.* The recent general study by McGeorge Bundy, former National Security Adviser in the Kennedy and Johnson administrations (until February 1966), *Danger and Survival,* is also recommended.

The best single overview that also links the two subjects of American-Soviet relations and America's national security policy is John Lewis Gaddis, *Strategies of Containment: A Critical Appraisal of Postwar American National Security Policy.*

Chronological Approach by Presidential Administration

From Truman to Bush there have been nine different presidential administrations, only two of which lasted for a full two terms. Given the importance of America's presidential form of government, an especially useful way to study American foreign policy is to compare and contrast the history of each presidential administration. Moreover, doing this in conventional chronological order from Truman to the present has the advantage not only of following developments in their proper sequence but of highlighting the effort of each administration to distinguish itself from its immediate predecessor. This occurs in the American system even when the successor president is from the same political party as his predecessor.

Most of the standard surveys of American foreign policy since 1945 adopt a mix of chronological and thematic approaches. While this has its advantages, it does perhaps tend to obscure the clear milestones of presidential administrations. One general survey that does stick closely to a president-by-president treatment is *American Foreign Policy: FDR to Reagan,* by James E. Dougherty and Robert L. Pfaltzgraff, Jr.

As mentioned, Gaddis's *Strategies of Containment* does trace a major theme—containment and national security policy—essentially by presidential administration from Truman to Nixon. An interesting treatment of a single foreign policy issue as it changed from administration to administration is Steven L. Spiegel, *The Other Arab-Israeli Conflict: Making America's Middle East Policy, From Truman to Reagan.*

Worthy of note is the encyclopaedic (over 1100 pages) study by Raymond L. Garthoff, *Detente and Confrontation: American-Soviet Relations from Nixon to Reagan.*

The literature on each of the American presidencies from Truman to the present would fill pages. It would be going too far afield to list even the best of the general studies and memoirs of each presidential administration, but one must not forget that such works often contain very penetrating insights on American foreign policy. They also have the advantage of situating foreign policy in its very real, if elusive and untidy, framework of tensions between the legislative and executive branches, party politics, personality conflicts, the management of a large and necessarily cumbersome bureaucracy, and the whole spectrum of changing domestic concerns and needs.

Instead, only a few works devoted to certain of the presidential administrations will be quickly passed in review. For the Truman administration many of the books already cited in tracing the historiography of Cold War origins are directly relevant. To this should be added the two-volume study of the Truman years by Robert J. Donovan, *Conflict and Crisis: The Presidency of Harry S. Truman, 1945–1948* and *The Tumultuous Years, 1949–1953*. Two especially useful memoirs are, first, Dean Acheson's *Present at the Creation: My Years in the State Department*. Read now almost two generations after the period covered (after an interesting Part One tracing his early life and career, Acheson devotes the remainder of this substantial book to the period 1945–1953), *Present at the Creation* offers a participant's interpretation of developments and, in the process, helps the reader recreate the ideology of that period of emerging internationalism and Cold War containment. It is especially useful to set the Acheson account alongside coverage of the same years in George Kennan's memoirs (*Memoirs, 1925–1950*). Both were key players in the newly emerging internationalist role of the United States and both can now be situated within the frame of what might be called, in retrospect, first-generation establishment internationalism. Acheson personified the more assertive, Kennan the more modest, orientation within America's newly emerging internationalist orthodoxy.

As for Eisenhower the book by Fred I. Greenstein, *The Hidden Hand Presidency: Eisenhower as Leader,* makes it clear that the general who became president proved to be a very active commander in chief. Good studies that take into account this revised view of Eisenhower's presidential activism are the series of essays in *Reevaluating Eisenhower: American Foreign Policy in the Fifties,* edited by David Melanson and David Mayers. Also useful is the little book by Robert A. Divine, *Eisenhower and the Cold War.*

A well regarded general study of the Eisenhower administration is Charles C. Alexander, *Holding the Line: The Eisenhower Era, 1952–1961*. In addition, volume 2 of Stephen E. Ambrose's biography *Eisenhower* covers major foreign policy issues of these years with a sure hand.

The earlier very favorable picture of the Kennedy administration depicted by those from within the Kennedy circle (e.g. Arthur M. Schlesinger, Jr., *A Thousand Days: John F. Kennedy in the White House* and Theodore C. Sorensen, *Kennedy*) has been modified by later, more critical appraisals. These include Henry Fairlie, *The Kennedy Promise: The Politics of Expectation* and Richard Walton's New Left revisionist *Cold War and Counterrevolution: The Foreign Policy of John F. Kennedy.* Even Arthur Schlesinger's later *Robert Kennedy and His Times* offers a more nuanced account of these years. Also to be noted is Herbert S. Parmet, *JFK: The Presidency of John F. Kennedy.*

General studies of the Johnson administration include Philip V. Geyelin, *Lyndon B. Johnson and the World;* Eric Goldman, *The Tragedy of Lyndon Johnson,* and the controversial psychobiography by Doris Kearns, *Lyndon*

Johnson and the American Dream. Two books by individuals who were in the inner circle of power wielders during these years of Democratic administrations in the sixties (but with quite different foreign policy perspectives) are *Diplomacy for a Crowded World* by George W. Ball and Walt Whitman Rostow's *Diffusion of Power.*

For the Nixon and Ford years one can consult Robert E. Osgood et al., *Retreat from Empire? The First Nixon Administration;* Tad Szulc, *The Illusion of Peace: Foreign Policy in the Nixon-Kissinger Years,* and Garry Wills, *Nixon Agonistes.* In a class by themselves are the huge two-volume memoirs of Henry A. Kissinger, *White House Years* and *Years of Upheaval.* As with any former public official, Kissinger seeks to explain (and justify) his actions. Even so, for sheer breadth of coverage of his years in power plus the many thoughtful insights on the nature of diplomacy the Kissinger volumes are extraordinary. Harshly critical appraisals of Kissinger's policies are Seymour M. Hersh, *The Price of Power: Kissinger in the White House* and William Shawcross, *Sideshow.*

The two principal foreign policy advisers during the Carter years, Secretary of State Cyrus Vance and National Security Adviser Zbigniew K. Brzezinski, wrote interesting accounts of their years in office. *Hard Choices: Critical Years in American Foreign Policy* by Vance and Brzezinski's *Power and Principle: Memoirs of the National Security Adviser, 1977–1981* also help to make understandable the differences, and at times the foreign policy disorder, during the Carter years, for Vance and Brzezinski espoused two sharply conflicting approaches to diplomacy. A very good, sympathetic view of these years is to be found in *Reason, Morality and Power: The Foreign Policy of Jimmy Carter* by Gaddis Smith.

On the Reagan administration there is Fred K. Greenstein, ed., *The Reagan Administration: An Early Assessment;* and Kenneth A. Oye, Robert J. Lieber, and Donald Rothchild, *Eagle Defiant: United States Foreign Policy in the 1980s.* Reagan's first secretary of state, Alexander Haig, has written his memoirs, *Caveat: Realism, Reagan and Foreign Policy.*

This brief survey of works on the diplomacy of each of the presidents from Truman to Bush has not listed the many memoirs of the presidents themselves. Needless to say, however, these more nearly official statements of presidential administrations are essential. The memoirs of Truman, Eisenhower, Johnson, Nixon and Carter are to be found in the alphabetical listing that follows this bibliographical essay.

American Relations with Selected World Areas

The Far East

Although the American-Soviet Cold War relationship may claim precedence over any other single diplomatic issue in the post World War II period it should be remembered that America's two wars since 1945 have been fought in Asia— Korea and Vietnam. The Far East also contains the world's most populous nation, China, and the state, Japan, that has outstripped all others in economic recovery since World War II. Moreover, Japan's neighbors South Korea and Taiwan and other East Asian states such as tiny Singapore have developed such economic muscle that those tracking diplomatic trends are inclined to predict major power shifts toward what have come to be called the nations of the "Pacific Rim". For all of these reasons, many scholars have studied the complex and often stormy patterns of America's relations with the Far East since 1945.

General studies of America's relations with China include Warren I. Cohen, *America's Response to China;* and Arnold Xiangze Jiang, *The United States and China.* For the early postwar period one can consult Tang Tsou, *America's Failure in China, 1941–1950;* Akira Iriye, *The Cold War in Asia;* and William Whitney Steuck, Jr., *The Road to Confrontation: American Policy toward China and Korea, 1947–1950.*

This, in turn, leads to consideration of the Korean War. Among the more recent books on this subject are Max Hastings, *The Korean War;* and Rosemary Foot, *The Wrong War: American Policy and the Dimensions of the Korean Conflict, 1950–1953.* Books showing the impact of American domestic politics on the Korean War include an earlier work by John Spanier, *The Truman-Mac-Arthur Controversy and the Korean War;* and Ronald J. Caridi, *The Korean War and American Politics: The Republican Party as a Case Study.* An innovative study on the period leading up to the war is Bruce Cumings's *The Origins of the Korean War: Liberation and the Emergence of Separate Regions, 1945–1947* which argues that the U.S. badly mishandled the post-1945 situation in Korea.

On American-Japanese relations the influential work by Edwin Reischauer, *The United States and Japan* can be noted. This book is one in the Harvard University Press "American Foreign Policy Library" series which offers a reliable summary of the history and politics of the country or area considered and then provides a concluding chapter on the history of American relations with that country. (For a selection of other books in this useful series see the following authors in the bibliographical list which follows this essay: W. Norman Brown, John K. Fairbank, Charles F. Gallagher, and William R. Polk.) A more recent study is Charles E. Neu, *The Troubled Encounter.*

Much can be said for tracing the history of American diplomacy with the larger region of East Asia instead of studying bilateral American relations with any one East Asian state. Good surveys include Ernest R. May and James C. Thomson, Jr., eds., *American–East Asian Relations: A Survey;* Warren I. Cohen, ed., *New Frontiers in American–East Asian Relations;* and Akira Iriye, *Across the Pacific: An Inner History of American–East Asian Relations.*

Books on America's involvement in Vietnam are numerous and still appearing. Generally deemed the best single work is George C. Herring, *America's Longest War.* See also Frances Fitzgerald, *Fire in the Lake;* and William C. Gibbons, *The U.S. Government and the Vietnam War.* For understanding the bureaucratic processes that shaped America's commitment in Vietnam consult Richard Betts and Leslie Gelb, *The Irony of Vietnam: The System Worked.* A masterful analysis of the turn toward sharply increased American participation during the Johnson administration is Larry Berman, *Planning a Tragedy: The Americanization of the War in Vietnam.* The U.S. Army's official history of the war has already produced one well-documented volume: Ronald Spector, *Advice and Support: The Early Years of the U.S. Army in Vietnam, 1941–1960*. Countering earlier works that tended to be highly critical of U.S. actions in Vietnam are recent New Right revisionist works that approve American intervention in Vietnam and argue that the war could have been won. A representative work with this view is Martin Herz, The *Vietnam War Revisited*. See also Harry G. Summers, *On Strategy: The Vietnam War in Context*.

Robert J. McMahon's *Colonialism and Cold War: The United States and the Struggle for Indonesian Independence, 1945–1949* offers an interesting analysis of America's somewhat inconsistent response to the challenge of decolonization in the Dutch East Indies. As such it also stands out as a case study of the U.S. effort simultaneously to mold a Western alliance in Europe and champion decolonization.

South Asia

Studies on American relations with the states of South Asia are relatively few for a region that boasts over one billion inhabitants. Among these few the following can be recommended: Lloyd and Susanne Rudolph, eds., *The Regional Imperative: U.S. Foreign Policy Toward South Asian States* (excellent case studies by experienced South Asian specialists); Norman Palmer, *The United States and India: The Dimensions of Influence;* William Barnds, *India, Pakistan, and the Great Powers;* and W. Norman Brown, *The United States and India, Pakistan, Bangladesh*.

Much of the literature on U.S. relations with India has been concerned with economic development and the role of development assistance. India, in fact, has tended to be singled out as the laboratory for many of the more ambitious developmental theories. Accordingly, it may be useful at this point to mention a few of the studies that treat this larger issue. Two good analyses of development assistance in general are Robert Cassan, *Does Aid Work?* and Roger Riddel, *Foreign Aid Reconsidered*. A short and perceptive review of Western developmental aid to Asia in general is found in John P. Lewis's *Asian Development: The Role of Development Assistance*.

Two short examples of U.S.-Indian relations as seen from India are chapter 6, "United States of America" in A. Appadorai and M. S. Rajan, *India's Foreign Policy and Relations;* and chapter 3, "The Big Powers: India and the United States" in V. P. Dutt, *India's Foreign Policy*.

The Middle East

The Middle East, by contrast with South Asia, has been the scene, time after time, of headline-grabbing news stories from the rise of the state of Israel in the period 1945–48 and the earliest stirring of the Cold War during the same period right down to the more recent Iran-Contra affair, the opening of American official discussions with the PLO, and the chilling actions of Ayatollah Khomeini in imposing a death sentence on novelist Salman Rushdie. Four good general studies of U.S. relations with the region or a major part of it are Seth P. Tillman, *The United States in the Middle East: Interests and Obstacles;* John S. Badeau, *The American Approach to the Arab World;* Robert W. Stookey, *America and the Arab States: An Uneasy Encounter;* and William R. Polk, *The Arab World* (especially Part VII, "The United States and the Arab World").

For U.S. relations with Israel see Nadav Safran, *Israel: The Embattled Ally,* a huge book (over 600 pages) the last half of which treats "Israel and America in International Politics." Note also the book cited earlier by Steven L. Spiegel, *The Other Arab-Israeli Conflict: Making America's Middle East Policy from Truman to Reagan.*

The American involvement in the Arab-Israeli confrontation figures in all of the above books, but two additional books deserve to be singled out. They are William B. Quandt's *Decade of Decisions: American Policy toward the Arab-Israeli Conflict, 1967–1976;* and *Camp David: Peacemaking and Politics.*

Two books that in different ways clarify the first two decades of post-1945 American relations with the Middle East within the Cold War context are Bruce R. Kuniholm, *The Origins of the Cold War in the Near East: Great Power Conflict and Diplomacy in Iran, Turkey, and Greece;* and John C. Campbell, *Defense of the Middle East: Problems of American Policy,* a book that grew out of a Council on Foreign Relations study group in the mid-1950s and well represented what might be called "Establishment" thinking on the Cold War in the Middle East at the time.

Two recent books, both highly critical of American relations with Iran since the 1940s, are James A. Bill, *The Eagle and the Lion: The Tragedy of American-Iranian Relations;* and Richard W. Cottam, *Iran and the United States: A Cold War Case Study.* Two fine books on the long-standing crisis provoked by Iranian seizure of the American embassy and the holding hostage of the Americans captured there until the very end of the Carter administration are Gary Sick, *All Fall Down: America's Tragic Encounter with Iran;* and Warren Christopher, ed., *American Hostages in Iran: The Conduct of a Crisis.*

On U.S. relations with Turkey, which although a member of NATO remains geographically a part of the Middle East, see, in addition to the Kuniholm book, George Harris, *Troubled Alliance: Turkish-American Problems in Historical Perspective;* and Dankwart A. Rustow, *Turkey: America's Forgotten Ally.*

Africa

U.S. relations with Africa have been viewed through a diversity of prisms since the continent began to move into the postcolonial era in the late 1950s. A sampling would include Waldemar A. Nielsen, *African Battleline: American Policy Choices in Southern Africa* and *The Great Powers and Africa;* Rupert Emerson, *Africa and United States Policy;* Donald Rothchild, "Engagement Versus Disengagement in Africa: The Choices for America," in Alan M. Jones, Jr., ed., *U.S. Foreign Policy in a Changing World: The Nixon Administration, 1969–1973;* Fredrick S. Arkhurst, ed., *U.S. Policy Toward Africa;* Helen Kitchen, ed., *Africa: From Mystery to Maze,* Vol. XI in the (Rockefeller)

Commission on Critical Choices for Americans series; David Dickson, *United States Foreign Policy Toward Sub-Sahara Africa*; Jennifer Seymour Whitaker, ed., *Africa and the United States: Vital Interests*; John Stockwell, *In Search of Enemies: A CIA Story*; Helen Kitchen, ed., *Options for U.S. Policy Toward Africa*; Kenneth L. Adelman, *African Realities*; Madeline Kalb, *The Congo Cables*; Henry F. Jackson, *From the Congo to Soweto: U.S. Foreign Policy toward Africa Since 1960*; Helen Kitchen, *U.S. Interests in Africa*; Richard D. Mahoney, *JFK: Ordeal in Africa*; and Gerald J. Bender, James S. Coleman, and Richard L. Sklar, eds., *African Crisis Areas and U.S. Foreign Policy*. A good recent survey on North Africa with a concluding chapter on U.S. policy in that region is Richard B. Parker's *North Africa: Regional Tensions and Strategic Concerns*.

The more recent volumes of *Africa Contemporary Record*, the costly but invaluable annual reference work edited by the indefatigable Colin Legum since 1969, include a chapter on "The United States' Year in Africa." Also of interest is Crawford Young's "United States Policy Toward Africa: Silver Anniversary Reflections," published in the *African Studies Review* (September 1984).

Of special relevance to the continuing debate on U.S. policy toward southern Africa are two articles by Chester A. Crocker (who, as the Department of State's assistant secretary for African affairs from 1981 to 1989, was the architect of the Reagan administration policy of "constructive engagement" and orchestrator of the 1988 Angola-Namibia accords): "South Africa: Strategy for Change" (*Foreign Affairs*, Winter 1980/81); and "Summing Up . . . And Looking Ahead" (*CSIS Africa Notes*, March 1989). Other noteworthy policy-relevant works on the region include *South Africa: Time Running Out*, the report of the Study Commission on U.S. Policy Toward South Africa headed by the Ford Foundation's Franklin Thomas; Gwendolen M. Carter and Patrick O'Meara, eds., *International Politics in Southern Africa*; Richard E. Bissell, *South Africa and the United States: The Erosion of an Influence Relationship*; Mohamed A. El-Khawas and Barry Cohen, eds., *National Security Study Memorandum 39: The Kissinger Study of Southern Africa*; C. Tsehloane Keto, *American–South African Relations, 1784–1980: Review and Select Bibliography*; and *A U.S. Policy toward South Africa*, the report of the Secretary of State's 12-member bipartisan Advisory Committee on South Africa (Department of State, January 1987).

Europe

Since the major focus of American attention in the years immediately after 1945 was Europe, East and West, many of the general studies of postwar American diplomacy already cited concentrate on Europe. Moreover, many of the works cited earlier in discussing the U.S.-Soviet rivalry are directly relevant, for Europe was from the beginning the major field of Cold War confrontation. For these reasons a much more selective listing is given here.

Alan S. Milward has written two excellent volumes on *The Reconstruction of Western Europe, 1945–1951*. See also Michael J. Hogan, *The Marshall Plan: America, Britain, and the Reconstruction of Western Europe, 1947–1952*. Another useful study of this important subject, concentrating on American policy and Franco–German relations, is John Gimbel, *The Origins of the Marshall Plan*.

Studies on NATO include the early (1962) *Nato: The Entangling Alliance* by Robert Osgood; the more recent *Creating the Entangling Alliance* by Timothy Ireland; and Lawrence S. Kaplan's *The United States and NATO*. A general survey is Michael Smith's *Western Europe and the United States: An Uncertain Alliance*.

There are many books on Anglo-American relations. A good sampler of the more important issues and themes can be found in Wm. Roger Louis and Hedley Bull, eds., *The Special Relationship*. A book covering a much longer time period but very relevant in suggesting that the U.S. is following in Britain's imperial footsteps (while being very critical of the U.S., too) is D. C. Watt, *Succeeding John Bull: America in Britain's Place, 1900–1975*. For America's relations with France it might be useful to rely on the perspective of the French scholar, Jean-Baptiste Duroselle, by reading the post-1945 portions of his *France and the United States: From the Beginnings to the Present*. Two multiauthored works on American-German relations are Hans L. Trefousse, ed., *Germany and America*; and Frank Trommler and Joseph McVeigh, eds., *America and the Germans*. On U.S. relations with Italy one can consult H. Stuart Hughes, *The United States and Italy*.

It would be excessive to cite works on U.S. relations with every European country, but given the close (although often stormy) American ties with Greece it may be useful to mention again the Kuniholm book cited in the section on the Middle East as well as Theodore A. Couloumbis and John O. Iatrides, eds., *Greek-American Relations*.

On the early postwar relations with Eastern Europe, see Lynn Etheridge Davis, *The Cold War Begins: Soviet-American Conflict over Eastern Europe*.

Central America

The literature on U.S. relations with Central America has expanded dramatically in recent years along with the increased U.S. involvement and the resulting sharp debate that involvement continues to provoke. For general studies of the region see Morris J. Blachman, William M. LeoGrande, and Kenneth E. Sharpe, eds., *Confronting Revolution: Security through Diplomacy in Central America;* Walter LaFeber, *Inevitable Revolutions: The United States and Central America* (sharply critical of U.S. policy, past and present); James Chace, *Endless War: How We Got Involved in Central America and What Can Be Done;* and Richard R. Fagan and Olga Pellicer, eds., *The Future of Central America: Policy Choices for the U.S. and Mexico*.

On U.S. relations with individual Central American countries the following may be cited: Richard M. Immerman, *The CIA in Guatemala: The Foreign Policy of Intervention;* Robert A. Pastor, *Condemned to Repetition: The United States and Nicaragua;* and Raymond Bonner, *Weakness and Deceit: U.S. Policy and El Salvador*.

The American Approach to Diplomacy

The System at Work

Every state in the global system has its own distinctive machinery of government which necessarily influences its approach to diplomacy. The post-1945 era which inaugurated a greatly expanded American role in the world produced as well many new governmental institutions concerned with foreign policy. The Marshall Plan and Truman's Point Four program for technical assistance both survived in different forms as the idea of foreign aid, or developmental assistance became institutionalized. Two works on this general subject are David Baldwin, *Economic Development and American Foreign Policy, 1943–1962;* and Robert A. Packenham, *Liberal America and the Third World.*

The year of the Truman Doctrine and the beginning of the Marshall Plan, 1947, was also the year of major governmental reorganization in the field of foreign affairs. The military services were combined in a single Department of Defense, the system of the Joint Chiefs of Staff instituted, and the National Security Council established. This year brought as well the creation of an unified intelligence service, the Central Intelligence Agency (CIA). The State Department also greatly increased in numbers. The foreign policy bureaucracy became larger and infinitely more complex. Although the organizational charts looked neat and logical enough on paper, with the summit of the foreign policy pyramid at the White House, the reconciling of these many different bureaucratic claims to formulating foreign policy was no easy task.

Observing this greatly expanded governmental machinery, several scholars developed what has come to be virtually a subfield in political science: bureaucratic politics or the study of how decisions are reached in complex organizations. Useful works on this subject include I. B. Destler, *Presidents, Bureaucrats, and Foreign Policy;* and Morton H. Halperin, *Bureaucratic Politics and Foreign Policy.* A classic case study of bureaucratic politics in action is Graham Allison's *Essence of Decision,* a multifaceted study of American decision making at the time of the Cuban missile crisis. It is noteworthy also that many of the more pessimistic appraisals of American foreign policy in recent years often cite the bureaucratic tangle and the presumed lack of clear lines of authority and decision-making as a major diplomatic flaw. One such example is the book cited at the beginning of this essay, Destler, Gelb and Lake, *Our Own Worst Enemy.*

A good review of the different approaches to foreign policy making in administrations from Truman to Reagan is William F. Bundy, "The National Security Process: Plus ça Change . . . ?" *International Security* 7, no. 3 (Winter 1982–83). Bundy surveys not the substance of policy but the different modalities of coordinating the State and Defense Departments, the National Security Council and other governmental agencies. As such it offers a good insight to the "mechanics" of foreign policy making.

Another characteristic of American government greatly influencing American foreign policy formulation is the distinctive constitutional relationship between the executive and legislative branches of government. Of course, this potentially confrontational situation pitting the president against the Congress did not begin in 1945, but it did become more important as American foreign policy goals became more diverse and infinitely more important. Even since 1945 there have been cycles of interpretation, and it can be safely predicted that scholars and observers will continue to argue that either the president or the Congress has become too powerful in the field of foreign relations. Treating different aspects of this subject are Arthur M. Schlesinger, Jr., *The Imperial Presidency*, Richard E. Neustadt, *Presidential Power*; Francis O. Wilcox, *Congress, The Executive and Foreign Policy*, John Spanier and Joseph Nogee, ed., *Congress, The Presidency and Foreign Policy*; and Goran Rystad, ed., *Congress and American Foreign Policy*.

The international transfer and sales of arms has long been a subject in diplomatic history. Earlier generations of revisionist writers attributed warfare itself to the baneful influence of the "merchants of death." Others have long argued that arms transfers and sales, judiciously applied, can produce a stabilizing balance of power. What cannot be denied is that the United States, for better or worse, has become a preeminent arms supplier. Perhaps the best single book on this issue is *The Global Politics of Arms Sales* by Andrew J. Pierre, for this study places the American role in the larger world context. See also Michael T. Klare, *American Arms Supermarket*.

Many books on intelligence and covert action tend toward the opposite extremes of either polemical exposés or uncritical praise of supposed intelligence coups, but with care the serious student can find thoughtful works in between. Gregory F. Treverton's *Covert Action: The Limits of Intervention in the Postwar World* has the great advantage of growing out of the author's own direct experience as a staff member of the Senate committee in the mid-1970s investigating this very subject. His "Covert Action and American Democracy," chapter 19 in this volume, is a résumé of his findings and recommendations.

Others to be recommended are Ray S. Cline, *Secrets, Spies, and Scholars: Blueprint of the Essential CIA* (an informative and favorable survey by a career CIA official), Thomas Powers, *The Man Who Kept the Secrets: Richard Helms and the CIA;* John Ranelagh, *The Agency: The Rise and Decline of the CIA;* Harry H. Ransom, *The Intelligence Establishment;* and Rhodri Jeffreys-Jones, *The CIA and American Democracy.*

The whole thorny question of what is the proper role of intelligence services in a democracy can, of course, be sharpened if a clear distinction is made between intelligence gathering and analysis on the one hand and covert action or clandestine political action, narrowly defined, on the other. In other words, separating the task of finding out what the enemy or potential enemy is up to (even by secret and "illegal" means) as well as protecting one's own secrets from exposure to the enemy (counterintelligence) is one thing. Acting secretly to destabilize or even overthrow governments is another. For a democracy to openly debate what secret clandestine political actions it will undertake is, of course, a logical absurdity. Yet, to delegate power to others to act secretly, even with one or another form of "oversight," runs into the classical political problem of *quis custodiet ipsos custodes?*—who will guard the guards themselves? A useful way to explore this problem is by studying the actual record of covert action successes (when they are known) and failures (which become known all too readily). An interesting work for the Eisenhower period is Blanche Wiesen Cook, *The Declassified Eisenhower: A Divided Legacy*. More recently, the Tower Commission report on the Iran-Contra affair offers a sobering case study. (John Tower, Chairman, Edmund Muskie and Brent Scowcroft, members, *The Tower Commission Report: The Full Text of the President's Special Review Board*, introduction by R. W. Apple, Jr.)

Theories and Ideology

Every people at every period of time is bound, always more than it realizes, by a limited spectrum of ideas and attitudes which are, quite literally, "thinkable." Beyond lie ideas and attitudes which are "unthinkable." Then, from time to time some intervening stimulus—either a new idea that captures attention or a cataclysmic event that forces reconsideration of the "received wisdom"—provokes change.

Generally speaking, it can be argued that the contours of American questioning and theorizing about diplomacy since the Second World War have revolved around the challenge of those labelled "realists" to what was seen as the earlier American tendency to be excessively idealist or even moralistic in approaching America's role in the world. Foreign policy realism, in turn, has provoked its challengers. This broad theme is the subject of chapter 18 of this volume, "The Realist School and Its Critics" by Richard Falk. Here some of the more influential works that have shaped this ongoing ideological debate will be noted.

Surely the two most important books establishing the essential realist approach are George Kennan's *American Diplomacy, 1900–1950* which first appeared in 1951; and Hans J. Morgenthau's *Politics among Nations: The Struggle for Power and Peace*. Morgenthau's *In Defense of the National Interest: A Critical Examination of American Foreign Policy* should also be mentioned. To these two—Kennan the diplomat-turned-scholar and Morgenthau the scholar of diplomacy—should be added the name of a theologian, Reinhold Niebuhr. His many writings also had a major influence in giving a stamp of approval to a politics of accepting the least evil in an imperfect world as a moral good. Niebuhr's *The Children of Light and the Children of Darkness: A Vindication of Democracy and a Critique of Its Traditional Defense* is perhaps the best example of his work.

Two useful works analyzing and interpreting the realist school are Michael Joseph Smith, *Realist Thought from Weber to Kissinger;* and Robert O. Keohane, ed., *Neorealism and Its Critics*.

To get an appreciation of the various supporters, critics and modifiers of this realist school it is useful to read critically different interpretations of American diplomatic history since 1945. The sharpest debates have been, as noted earlier, on the issue of allotting responsibility for the Cold War. Even here, however, the issue is not clearly divided between realists and others. Many supporters of the early "establishment" American position of placing blame for the Cold War solely on Soviet shoulders may be labelled realists. Many others were idealists determined to shape the world in the best tradition of Wilsonian internationalism. Yet many of America's Cold War critics were just as much idealists in their own way, seeing capitalist America as necessarily a baneful force in world politics. In any case a review of the works cited on pp. 443–448 above while asking the question "where do they fall on the Realist-Idealist ideological spectrum?" can prove a stimulating exercise.

For an even more in-depth venture into the historiography of this period consult Jerald A. Combs, *American Diplomatic History: Two Centuries of Changing Interpretations.* The last two parts, "The Age of Munich, 1939–1965," and "The Age of Vietnam, 1965–?," are directly relevant.

The several thoughtful works of Stanley Hoffmann (e.g. *Primacy or World Order*) should be mentioned. A stimulating work that seeks to link prevailing ideology to changing historical periods from the late nineteenth century to the present is Robert Dallek's *The American Style of Foreign Policy: Cultural Politics and Foreign Affairs.*

Bibliographies, References and Journals

This long bibliographical essay has by no means exhausted the subject. Certain important world areas and a number of important subjects have not even been mentioned. The intention here, however, has been to sketch out the broad lines of American diplomacy since 1945; to suggest that no single issue suffices to organize our understanding of America in the world arena (not the Cold War, not decolonization, not the advent of the nuclear age, but rather all of these and many others as well); and to indicate that we must be sensitive to the changing interpretations of the important period in America's history.

We conclude with a few suggestions on where to find the useful literature on subjects that may have been noted only in passing or even not at all in this essay.

By far the most thorough annotated bibliography of significant books and articles published in English on American diplomatic history from earliest times to 1980 is Richard Dean Burns, ed., *Guide to American Foreign Relations since 1700.*

Most general surveys of American diplomatic history provide bibliographies. The most useful are annotated or classified and not simply long listings of titles. One especially commendable general bibliography is that found in *American Foreign Policy: A History since 1900* by Thomas G. Paterson, J. Garry Clifford, and Kenneth J. Hagan. It provides a good review of basic reference works and bibliographies and a listing of books on American relations with most of the more important countries or regions of the world, arranged alphabetically by country or region. This is followed by an alphabetical listing of American diplomacy by subject.

The *Encyclopedia of American Foreign Policy*, edited by Alexander DeConde provides in three volumes a collection of topical essays treating the major ideas and themes in American diplomatic history.

The best single dictionary for coverage of specific individuals, treaties, etc. is John E. Findling, *Dictionary of American Diplomatic History*.

The official U.S. Department of State series entitled *Foreign Relations of the United States* contains a rich selection of official documents, not only from the Department of State but also from presidential archives, the National Security Council, the Department of Defense, and the Central Intelligence Agency. This series (which goes back to 1861) is now complete for roughly the first decade following the end of World War II.

The Council on Foreign Relations published an annual volume entitled *The United States in World Affairs* during the years 1931–67, with no volumes published in 1968 or 1969 and a final volume in 1970. These annual volumes offer an excellent recapitulation of how things looked at the time. Fortunately, since 1979 *Foreign Affairs* (the journal of the Council on Foreign Relations) publishes a special end of year issue entitled "American and the World" which largely serves the same function as the now defunct *United States in World Affairs* volumes. *Foreign Affairs* is also recommended for the general quality and relevance of its articles written by both statesmen and scholars. Each issue also contains a listing of new books on foreign affairs organized topically.

Two other journals deserve mention: *Diplomatic History*, the journal of the Society for Historians of American Foreign Relations founded in 1967, and *Foreign Policy* (since 1970).

Works Cited

Acheson, Dean, *Present at the Creation: My Years in the State Department*. New York (Norton) 1969.

———, "Random Harvest," *Department of State Bulletin* 16 (June 1946).

Aggarwal, Vinod, *Liberal Protectionism: The International Politics of Organized Textile Trade*. University of California Press, 1985.

Ailleret, Charles, "Directed Defense," *Survival* 10, 2 (February 1968).

Alexander, Charles C., *Holding the Line: The Eisenhower Era, 1952–1961*. Indiana University Press, 1975.

Allison, Graham, *Essence of Decision: Explaining the Cuban Missile Crisis*. Boston (Little, Brown) 1971.

Alperovitz, Gar, *Atomic Diplomacy: Hiroshima and Potsdam: The Use of the Atomic Bomb and the American Confrontation with Soviet Power*. New York (Vintage Books) 1965.

Ambrose, Stephen E., *Eisenhower*. Vol. II, *Eisenhower: The President*. New York (Simon & Schuster) 1984.

Appadorai, Angadipuram, and M. S. Rajan, "United States of America," in *India's Foreign Policy and Relations*. New Delhi (South Asian Publishing) 1985.

Aron, Raymond, ed., *World Technology and Human Destiny*. University of Michigan Press, 1963.

Badeau, John S., *The American Approach to the Arab World*. New York (Harper and Row) 1968.

Baldwin, David, *Economic Development and American Foreign Policy, 1943–1962*. University of Chicago Press, 1966.

Ball, George W., *Diplomacy for a Crowded World: An American Foreign Policy*. Boston (Little, Brown) 1976.

Barnds, William, *India, Pakistan, and the Great Powers*. New York (Praeger) 1972.

Bell, Coral, *The Conventions of Crisis: A Study in Diplomatic Management*. Oxford University Press, 1971.

Beloff, Max, "The End of the British Empire and the Assumption of World-Wide Commitments by the U.S.," in William Roger Louis and Hedley Bull, eds., *The "Special Relationship": Anglo–American Relations since 1945*. Oxford University Press, 1986.

———, *The United States and the Unity of Europe*. Washington, D.C. (Brookings Institution) 1963.

Berman, Larry, *Planning a Tragedy: The Americanization of the War in Vietnam*. New York (Norton) 1982.

Betts, Richard K., *Nuclear Blackmail and Nuclear Balance*. Washington, D.C. (Brookings Institution) 1987.

———, and Leslie Gelb, *The Irony of Vietnam: The System Worked*. Washington, D.C. (Brookings Institution) 1979.

Bill, James A., *The Eagle and the Lion: The Tragedy of American–Iranian Relations*. Yale University Press, 1988.

Blachman, Morris J., William M. LeoGrande, and Kenneth E. Sharpe, eds., *Confronting Revolution: Security through Diplomacy in Central America*. New York (Pantheon Books) 1986.

Bonner, Raymond, *Weakness and Deceit: U.S. Policy and El Salvador*. New York (New York Times Books) 1984.

Borowski, Harry R., *A Hollow Threat: Strategic Air Power and Containment before Korea*. Westport, CT (Greenwood Press) 1982.

Boyer, Paul, *By the Bomb's Early Light: American Thought and Culture at the Dawn of the Atomic Age*. New York (Pantheon Books) 1985.

Brock, David, "Playing the U.N. Game with Gusto," *Insight* (30 May 1988).

Brodie, Bernard, et al., *The Absolute Weapon: Atomic Power and World Order*. New York (Harcourt) 1946.

———, *Strategy in the Missile Age*. Princeton University Press, 1965.

Brown, W. Norman, *The United States and India, Pakistan, Bangladesh*. 3rd ed. Harvard University Press, 1975.

Brzezinski, Zbigniew, "America's New Geostrategy," *Foreign Affairs* 66, 4 (Spring 1988).

———, *Power and Principle: Memoirs of the National Security Advisor, 1977–1981*. New York (Farrar, Straus, & Giroux) 1983.

Buchan, Alastair, *Can International Relations be Professed?* Oxford University Press, 1973.

Buckley, William, "George Kennan's Bomb," *National Review* (4 April 1980).

Bundy, McGeorge, *Danger and Survival: Choice and the Bomb in the First Fifty Years*. New York (Random House) 1988.

Bundy, William F., "The National Security Process: 'Plus ça Change . . . ?'" *International Security* 7, 3 (Winter 1982–1983).

Burns, Richard Dean, ed., *Guide to American Foreign Relations since 1700*. Santa Barbara, CA (ABC–Clio) 1982.

Buzan, Barry, *People, States, and Fear: The National Security Problem in International Relations*. University of North Carolina Press, 1983.

Calder, Kent E., *Crisis and Compensation: Public Policy and Political Stability in Japan, 1949–1986*. Princeton University Press, 1988.

Campbell, John C., *Defense of the Middle East: Problems of American Policy*. New York (Harper) 1958. (2nd ed., 1960.)

Caridi, Ronald J., *The Korean War and American Politics: The Republican Party as a Case Study*. 2nd ed. University of Pennsylvania Press, 1969.

Carr, E. H., *The Twenty Year Crisis, 1919–1939: An Introduction to the Study of International Relations*. London (Macmillan) 1946.

Carter, Jimmy, *Keeping Faith: Memoirs of a President*. New York (Bantam Books) 1982.

Cassan, Robert, et al., *Does Aid Work?: Report to an Intergovernmental Task Force*. Oxford University Press, 1986.

Chace, James, *Endless War: How We Got Involved in Central America and What Can Be Done*. New York (Vintage Books) 1984.

——, and Earl C. Ravenal, eds., *Atlantis Lost: U.S.–European Relations after the Cold War*. New York University Press, 1976.

Challener, Richard D., "The National Security Policy from Truman to Eisenhower: Did the 'Hidden Hand' Make Any Difference?," in Norman Graebner, ed., *The National Security: Its Theory and Practice*. Oxford University Press, 1986.

——, "New Light on the Dulles-Hiss Relationship," *University* (Princeton) 73 (Spring 1973).

Christopher, Warren, et al., *American Hostages in Iran: The Conduct of a Crisis*. Yale University Press, 1985.

Clausewitz, Carl von, *On War*. Ed. and trans. Michael Howard and Peter Paret. Princeton University Press, 1976.

Cline, Ray S., *Secrets, Spies, and Scholars: Blueprint of the Essential C.I.A.* Washington, D.C. (Acropolis Books) 1976.

Clough, Michael, "The U.N.: A Not So Dangerous Place?" in *CIS Africa Notes* 45 (24 July 1985).

Cohen, Warren I., *America's Response to China: An Interpretative History of Sino–American Relations*. New York (Wiley) 1971.

——, ed., *New Frontiers in American–East Asian Relations*. Columbia University Press, 1983.

Collins, John M., *American and Soviet Military Trends*. Georgetown Center for Strategic and International Studies, 1978.

Colville, John, *The Fringes of Power: 10 Downing Street Diaries, 1939–1955*. New York (Norton) 1985.

Combs, Jerald A., "The Age of Munich, 1939–1965," *American Diplomatic History: Two Centuries of Changing Interpretations*. University of California Press, 1983.

——, "The Age of Vietnam, 1965–?" *American Diplomatic History: Two Centuries of Changing Interpretations*. University of California Press, 1983.

Commager, Henry Steele, "Should the Historian Make Moral Judgments?" *American Heritage* 17 (February 1966).

Cook, Blanche Wiesen, *The Declassified Eisenhower: A Divided Legacy*. Garden City, NY (Doubleday) 1981.

Corrigan, Gerald E., "Public and Private Debt Accumulation: A Perspective." Federal Reserve Bank of New York, *Quarterly Review* 10 (1985).

Cottam, Richard W., *Iran and the United States: A Cold War Case Study*. University of Pittsburgh Press, 1988.

Couloumbis, Theodore A., and John O. Iatrides, eds., *Greek–American Relations: A Critical Review*. New York (Pella Publishing Company) 1980.

Cumings, Bruce, *The Origins of the Korean War: Liberation and The Emergence of Separate Regimes, 1945–1947*. Princeton University Press, 1981.

Dallek, Robert, *The American Style of Foreign Policy: Cultural Politics and Foreign Affairs*. New York (Knopf) 1983.

Davies, John Paton, *Dragon by the Tail: American, British, Japanese and Russian Encounters with China and One Another.* New York (Norton) 1972.

Davis, Lynn Etheridge, *The Cold War Begins: Soviet–American Conflict over Eastern Europe.* Princeton University Press, 1974.

DeConde, Alexander, ed., *The Encyclopedia of American Foreign Policy: Studies of Principal Movements and Ideas.* New York (Scribners) 1978.

Deibel, Terry, and John Lewis Gaddis, eds., *Containment: Concept and Policy.* Washington, D.C. (National Defense University Press) 1986.

De Porte, Anton W., *Europe between the Superpowers: The Enduring Balance.* Yale University Press, 1979.

De Santis, Hugh, *The Diplomacy of Silence: The American Foreign Service, the Soviet Union and the Cold War, 1933–1948.* University of Chicago Press, 1980.

Destler, I. M., *Presidents, Bureaucrats, and Foreign Policy; The Politics of Organization Reform.* 2nd ed. Princeton University Press, 1974.

———, Haruhiro Fukui and Hideo Sato, *Managing an Alliance: The Politics of U.S.–Japanese Relations.* Washington, D.C. (Brookings Institution) 1976.

———, and Hideo Sato, *The Textile Wrangle.* Cornell University Press, 1979.

Dickson, Peter, *Kissinger and the Meaning of History.* Cambridge University Press, 1978.

Divine, Robert A., *Dwight D. Eisenhower and the Cold War.* Oxford University Press, 1981.

Donovan, Robert J., *Conflict and Crisis: The Presidency of Harry S. Truman, 1945–1948.* New York (Norton) 1977.

———, *The Tumultuous Years: The Presidency of Harry S. Truman, 1949–1953.* New York (Norton) 1977.

Dougherty, James E. and Robert L. Pfaltzgraff, Jr., *American Foreign Policy: F.D.R. to Reagan.* New York (Harper and Row) 1986.

Dower, John W., *Empire and Aftermath.* Harvard University Council on East Asian Studies, 1979.

———, "The Eye of the Beholder," *Bulletin of Concerned Asian Scholars* 2, 1 (October 1969).

———, *War Without Mercy: Race and Power in the Pacific War.* New York (Pantheon Books) 1986.

Draper, Theodore, "Kissinger Redivivus," *The New Republic* (31 January 1981).

Dulles, John Foster, "A Policy of Boldness," *Life* (19 May 1952).

———, "As Seen by a Layman," *Religion and Life* (Winter 1939).

———, "Peaceful Change," *Atlantic Monthly* (November 1935).

———, "The Road to Peace," *Atlantic Monthly* (October 1935).

Duroselle, Jean-Baptiste, *France and the United States: From the Beginnings to the Present.* University of Chicago Press, 1978.

Dutt, V. P., *India's Foreign Policy.* New Delhi, 1950.

Eden, Anthony, *Full Circle: The Memoirs of Anthony Eden.* Boston (Houghton Mifflin) 1960.

El-Khawas, Mohamed A., and Barry Cohen, eds., *The Kissinger Study of Southern Africa: National Security Study Memorandum 39.* Westport, CT (L. Hill) 1976.

Eisenhower, Dwight D., *Mandate for Change, 1953–1956: The White House Years.* Garden City, NY (Doubleday) 1963.

Emerson, Rupert, *Africa and United States Policy.* Englewood Cliffs, NJ (Prentice-Hall) 1967.

———, *From Empire to Nation: The Rise of Self-Assertion of Asian and African Peoples.* Harvard University Press, 1960 (Beacon Paperback, 1962).

Etzold, Thomas H., and John Lewis Gaddis, eds., *Containment: Documents on American Policy and Strategy, 1945–1950*. Columbia University Press, 1978.

Evans, Peter, Dietrich Rueschemeyer, and Theda Skocpol, eds., *Bringing the State Back In*. Cambridge University Press, 1985.

Fagan, Richard R., and Olga Pellicer, eds., *The Future of Central America: Policy Choices for the U.S. and Mexico*. Stanford University Press, 1983.

Fairbank, John K., *The United States and China*. 4th ed. Harvard University Press, 1983.

Fairlie, Henry, "The Special Senility of the Diplomat: Mr. X," *The New Republic* (24 December 1977).

———, *The Kennedy Promise: The Politics of Expectation*. Garden City, NY (Doubleday) 1973.

Falk, Richard, "Normative International Relations: A General Introduction," in *The End of World Order*. New York (Holmes & Meier) 1983.

———, *The Promise of World Order: Essays on Normative International Relations*. Temple University Press, 1987.

Feldstein, Martin, "Correcting the Trade Deficit," *Foreign Affairs* 65, 4 (1987).

Findling, John E., *Dictionary of American Diplomatic History*. Westport, CT (Greenwood Press) 1980.

Fitzgerald, Frances, *Fire in the Lake: The Vietnamese and Americans in Vietnam*. New York (Vintage Books) 1973.

Foot, Rosemary, *The Wrong War: American Policy and the Dimensions of the Korean Conflict, 1950–1953*. Cornell University Press, 1985.

Fox, Richard, *Reinhold Niebuhr: A Biography*. New York (Pantheon Books) 1985.

Freedman, Lawrence, *U.S. Intelligence and the Soviet Strategic Threat*. Princeton University Press, 1986.

———, "The First Two Generations of Nuclear Strategists," in Peter Paret, ed., *Makers of Modern Strategy from Machiavelli to the Nuclear Age*. Princeton University Press, 1986.

Freeland, Richard M., *The Truman Doctrine and the Origins of McCarthyism: Foreign Policy, Domestic Politics and Internal Security 1946–1948*. New York (Knopf) 1972.

Friedberg, Aaron L., "The Collapsing Triangle: U.S. and Soviet Policies toward China, 1969–1980," *Comparative Strategy* 4, 2 (1983).

Gaddis, John Lewis, "Containment and the Logic of Strategy," *The National Interest* (Winter 1987–1988).

———, "How the Cold War Might End," *Atlantic Monthly* (November 1987).

———, *The Long Peace: Inquiries into the History of the Cold War*. Oxford University Press, 1987.

———, *Strategies of Containment: A Critical Appraisal of Postwar American National Security*. Oxford University Press, 1982.

Galbraith, John Kenneth, *Ambassador's Journal: A Personal Account of the Kennedy Years*. Boston (Houghton, Mifflin) 1969.

Gall, Norman, "The Four Horsemen Ride Again." *Forbes* 138, 28 (July 1986).

Gallagher, Charles F. *The United States and North Africa, Morocco, Algeria, and Tunisia*. Harvard University Press, 1963.

Gallagher, John, *The Decline, Revival and Fall of the British Empire*. Cambridge University Press, 1982.

Gardner, Lloyd, *Architects of Illusion: Men and Ideas in American Foreign Policy, 1941–1949*. Chicago (Quadrangle Books) 1970.

Garnett, John, ed., *Theories of Peace and Security: A Reader in Contemporary Strategic Thought*. New York (St. Martin's Press) 1970.

Garthoff, Raymond L., *Detente and Confrontation: American–Soviet Relations from Nixon to Reagan*. Washington, D.C. (Brookings Institution) 1985.

Gates, Robert, "The CIA and American Foreign Policy," *Foreign Affairs* 66, 2 (Winter 1987–88).

Gellman, Barton, *Contending with Kennan: Towards a Philosophy of American Power*. New York (Praeger) 1984.

George, Alexander, L., ed., *Managing U.S.–Soviet Rivalry: Problems of Crisis Prevention*. Boulder, CO (Westview Press) 1983.

———, Philip J. Farley and Alexander Dallin, eds., *U.S.–Soviet Security Cooperation: Achievements, Failures, Lessons*. Oxford University Press, 1988.

——— and Richard Smoke, *Deterrence in American Foreign Policy: Theory and Practice*. Columbia University Press, 1974.

Gerth, Hans H., and Charles W. Mills, eds., *From Max Weber: Essays in Sociology*. New York, Oxford University Press, 1946.

Geyelin, Philip V., *Lyndon B. Johnson and the World*. New York (Praeger) 1966.

Gibbons, William C., *The U.S. Government and the Vietnam War: Executive and Legislative Roles and Relationships*. Princeton University Press, 1986– .

Giersch, Herbert, "The Age of Schumpeter." *American Economic Review* 74 (May 1984).

Gilpin, Robert, "American Policy in the Post-Reagan Era," *Daedalus* (Summer 1987).

———, *The Political Economy of International Relations*. Princeton University Press, 1987.

———, *War and Change in World Politics*. Cambridge University Press, 1981.

Gimbel, John, *The Origins of the Marshall Plan*. Stanford University Press, 1976.

Goheen, Robert F., "Perceptions of Indo–U.S. Relations," *Darshan* 4, 4 (April 1987). (A monthly publication of the Indian Consulate General in New York.)

———, "Problems of Proliferation: U.S. Policy and the Third World," *World Politics* (January 1988).

Goldman, Eric, *The Tragedy of Lyndon Johnson*. New York (Knopf) 1969.

Goldstein, Judith, "The Political Economy of Trade: Institutions of Protection," *American Political Science Review* 80, 1 (March 1986).

Gourevitch, Peter, *Politics in Hard Times: Comparative Responses to International Economic Crises*. Cornell University Press, 1986.

Graebner, Norman, *America as a World Power: A Realist Appraisal from Wilson to Reagan: Essays*. Wilmington DE (Scholarly Resources) 1984.

Gravel, Mike, *The Pentagon Papers: The Defense Department History of United States Decision Making on Vietnam* (Volumes 1–5). Boston (Beacon Press) 1971–72.

Greenstein, Fred I., *The Hidden Hand Presidency: Eisenhower as Leader*. New York (Basic Books) 1982.

———, ed., *The Reagan Administration: An Early Assessment*. Johns Hopkins University Press, 1983.

Grosser, Alfred, *The Western Alliance: European–American Relations since 1945*. New York (Macmillan) 1982.

Haig, Alexander, *Caveat: Realism, Reagan and Foreign Policy*. New York (Macmillan) 1984.

Haig, Alexander M., Jr., "The Alliance in the 1980s," *Washington Quarterly* (Winter 1980).

Halle, Louis J., *The Cold War as History*. New York (Harper and Row) 1967.

Halperin, Morton H., *Bureaucratic Politics and Foreign Policy*. Washington, D.C. (Brookings Institution) 1974.

Hare, J. E., and Carey Joynt, *Ethics and International Affairs*. New York (St. Martin's Press) 1982.

Harris, George, *Troubled Alliance: Turkish–American Problems in Historical Perspective, 1945–1971*. Washington, D.C. (American Enterprise Institute for Public Policy Research) 1972.

Hastings, Max, *The Korean War*. London (M. Joseph) 1987.

Havens, Thomas, *Fire Across the Sea: The Vietnam War and Japan*. Princeton University Press, 1987.

Healey, Denis, "A Labour Britain, NATO and the Bomb," *Foreign Affairs* 65, 4 (Spring 1987).

Herken, Gregg, *The Winning Weapon: The Atomic Bomb and the Cold War, 1945–1949*. New York (Knopf) 1980.

Herring, George C., *America's Longest War: The United States and Vietnam 1950–1975*. New York (Wiley) 1979.

Hersh, Seymour M., *The Price of Power: Kissinger in the Nixon White House*. New York (Summit Books) 1983.

Herz, Martin, ed., *Decline of the West? George Kennan and His Critics*. Washington, D.C. (Ethics and Public Policy Center, Georgetown University) 1978.

———, *The Vietnam War in Retrospect: Four Lectures*. Washington, D.C. (School of Foreign Service, Georgetown University) 1984.

Hess, Gary R., *The United States' Emergence as a Southeast Asian Power, 1940–1950*. Columbia University Press, 1987.

Hoffman, Stanley, "After the Creation; or, The Watch and the Arrow," *International Journal* (Spring 1973).

———, *Duties Beyond Borders: On the Limits and Possibilities of Ethical Politics*. Syracuse University Press, 1981.

———, *Gulliver's Troubles; or, The Setting of American Foreign Policy*. New York (McGraw-Hill) 1986.

———, *Primacy or World Order: American Foreign Policy since the Cold War*. New York (McGraw-Hill) 1978.

———, "The Sulking Giant," *The New Republic* (3 May 1975).

Hogan, Michael, *The Marshall Plan: America, Britain, and the Reconstruction of Western Europe, 1947–1952*. Cambridge University Press, 1987.

———, "Revival and Reform: America's Twentieth Century Search for a New Economic Order," *Diplomatic History* 8 (Fall 1984).

Holland, R. F., "The Imperial Factor in British Strategies from Attlee to Macmillan, 1945–1963," *Journal of Imperial and Commonwealth History* 12 (May 1984).

Hollander, Paul, "The Two Faces of George Kennan," *Policy Review* 33 (Summer 1985).

Hughes, Henry Stuart, *The United States and Italy*. Harvard University Press, 1953.

Hunt, Michael, *Ideology and U.S. Foreign Policy*. Yale University Press, 1987.

Huntington, Samuel P., "The U.S.—Decline or Renewal," *Foreign Affairs* 67, 2 (Winter 1988/1989).

———, "Coping with the Lippmann Gap," *Foreign Affairs* 66, 3 (1987–88).

———, "Chapter III—The United States," in Michael Crozier, Samuel P. Huntington, and Joji Watanuki, eds., *The Crisis of Democracy: Report on the Governability of Democracies to the Trilateral Commission*. New York University Press, 1975.

Hyland, William G., *Mortal Rivals: Superpower Relations from Nixon to Reagan*. New York (Random House) 1987.

Immerman, Richard H., *The C.I.A. in Guatemala: The Foreign Policy of Intervention*. University of Texas Press, 1982.

Ireland, Timothy, *Creating the Entangling Alliance: The Origins of the North Atlantic Treaty Organization*. Westport, CT (Greenwood Press) 1981.

Iriye, Akira, *Across the Pacific: An Inner History of American–East Asian Relations*. New York (Harcourt Brace and World) 1967.

———, *The Cold War in Asia, A Historical Introduction*. Englewood Cliffs, NJ (Prentice-Hall) 1974.

———, *Power and Culture: The Japanese–American War, 1941–1945*. Harvard University Press, 1981.

Irving, R. E. M., *The First Indochina War: French and American Policy, 1945–1954*. London (Croom Helm) 1975.

Isaacson, Walter, and Evan Thomas, *The Wise Men: Six Men and the World They Made*. New York (Simon & Schuster) 1986.

Jackson, Henry F., *From the Congo to Soweto: U.S. Foreign Policy toward Africa since 1960*. New York (Morrow) 1982.

Jeffreys-Jones, Rhodri, *The C.I.A. and American Democracy*. Yale University Press, 1989.

Jervis, Robert, *The Illogic of American Nuclear Strategy*. Cornell University Press, 1984.

———, *Perception and Misperception in International Politics*. Princeton University Press, 1976.

Jiang, Arnold Xiangze, *The United States and China*. University of Chicago Press, 1988.

Johnson, Chalmers, *MITI and the Japanese Miracle: The Growth of Industrial Policy 1925–1975*. Stanford University Press, 1982.

Johnson, Loch K., *A Season of Inquiry: The Senate Intelligence Investigation*. University Press of Kentucky, 1985.

Kahin, George, *Intervention: How America Became Involved in Vietnam*. New York (Knopf) 1986.

Kahler, Miles, *Decolonization in Britain and France: The Domestic Consequences of International Relations*. Princeton University Press, 1984.

Kaiser, Karl, Winston Lord, Thierry de Montbrial, and David Watt, *Western Security: What Has Changed? What Should Be Done?* New York (Council on Foreign Relations) 1981.

Kaldor, Mary, and Richard Falk, eds., *Dealignment: A New Foreign Policy Perspective*. New York (Basil Blackwell) 1987.

Kaplan, Lawrence S., *The United States and N.A.T.O.: The Formative Years*. University Press of Kentucky, 1984.

Karalekas, Anne, "History of the Central Intelligence Agency," in *Supplementary Detailed Staff Reports on Foreign and Military Intelligence*, Book 4 of *Final Report of the Senate Select Commitee to Study . . . Intelligence Activities*. 94th Cong., 2nd sess. (23 April 1976).

Kattenburg, Paul, *The Vietnam Trauma in American Foreign Policy, 1945–75*. New Brunswick, NJ (Transaction Books) 1980.

Kearns, Doris, *Lyndon Johnson and the American Dream*. New York (Harper and Row) 1976.

Kelly, John B., *Arabia, the Gulf and the West*. New York (Basic Books) 1980.

Kennan, George F., *American Diplomacy, 1900–1950*. University of Chicago Press, 1952. (Expanded ed., 1984.)

———, *Democracy and the Student Left*. Boston (Little, Brown) 1968.

———, et al., *Encounters with Kennan: The Great Debate*. London (F. Cass) 1979.

———, "In the American Mirror," *The New York Review of Books* (November 1986).

———, "Morality and Foreign Policy," *Foreign Affairs* 64, 2 (Winter 1985/1986).

———, *Memoirs, 1925–1950*. Boston (Little, Brown) 1967.

———, *The Nuclear Delusion: Soviet–American Relations in the Atomic Age*. New York (Pantheon Books) 1983.

————, "The Origins of Containment," in Terry Deibel and John Lewis Gaddis, eds., *Containment, Concept and Policy.* Washington, D.C. National Defense University Press, 1978.

————, *Realities of American Foreign Policy.* Princeton University Press, 1954.

————, "The Relation of Religion to Government," *Princeton Seminary Bulletin* (Winter 1969).

————, "The Sources of Soviet Conduct," *Foreign Affairs* 65, 4 (1987).

Kennedy, Paul, *The Rise and Fall of the Great Powers: Economic Change and Military Conflict from 1500 to 2000.* New York (Random House) 1987.

Keohane, Robert O., ed., *Neorealism and Its Critics.* Columbia University Press, 1986.

————, "The World Political Economy and the Crisis of Embedded Liberalism," Chapter 1 in John H. Goldthorpe, ed., *Order and Conflict in Contemporary Capitalism: Studies in the Political Economy of Western European Nations.* Oxford University Press, 1984.

Kirkpatrick, Jeane J., "Dictators and Double Standards," *Commentary* 68 (November 1979).

Kissinger, Henry, *American Foreign Policy.* New York (Norton) 1969. (3rd edition, 1977).

————, "The Meaning of History: Reflections on Spengler, Toynbee and Kant," B.A. Thesis, Harvard College, 1951.

————, *The Necessity for Choice.* New York (Harper and Row) 1961.

————, *Nuclear Weapons and Foreign Policy.* 2nd ed. New York (Norton) 1969.

————, *White House Years.* Boston (Little, Brown) 1979.

————, "The White Revolutionary: Reflections on Bismarck," *Daedalus* (Summer 1968).

————, *A World Restored.* Boston (Houghton Mifflin) 1957 (3rd ed., 1973).

————, *Years of Upheaval.* Boston (Little, Brown) 1982.

Kitchen, Helen, *U.S. Interests in Africa.* New York (Praeger) 1983.

————, "The Making of U.S. Policy toward Africa," in Robert I. Rotberg, ed., *Africa in the 1990s and Beyond: U.S. Policy Opportunities and Choices.* Algonac, MI (Reference Publications) 1988.

————, *Some Guidelines on Africa for the Next President.* CSIS Significant Issues Series 10, 4 (Georgetown University) 1988.

————, and Michael Clough, *The United States and South Africa: Realities and Red Herrings.* CSIS Significant Issues Series 6, 6 (Georgetown University) 1984.

Klare, Michael T., *American Arms Supermarket.* University of Texas Press, 1984.

Kolko, Gabriel, *The Politics of War: The World and United States Foreign Policy, 1943–1945.* New York (Random House) 1986.

————, and Joyce Kolko, *The Limits of Power: The World and United States Foreign Policy, 1945–1954.* New York (Harper and Row) 1972.

Krause, Lawrence B., "The Structure of Trade in Manufactured Goods in the East and Southeast Asia Region," Chapter 8 in Colins I. Bradford and William Branson, eds., *Trade and Structural Change in Pacific Asia.* University of Chicago Press, 1987.

Krauss, Melvyn, *How NATO Weakens the West.* New York (Simon & Schuster) 1986.

Kuniholm, Bruce R. *The Origin of the Cold War in the Near East: Great Power Conflict and Diplomacy in Iran, Turkey, and Greece.* Princeton University Press, 1980.

LaFeber, Walter, *America, Russia and the Cold War, 1945–1984.* 5th ed. New York (Wiley) 1985.

————, *Inevitable Revolutions: The United States and Central America.* New York (Norton) 1983.

————, "Roosevelt, Churchill, and Indochina: 1942–1945," *American Historical Review* 80 (1975).

Lake, Anthony, *The "Tar Baby" Option: American Policy Toward Southern Rhodesia.* Columbia University Press, 1976.

Leary, William M., ed., *The Central Intelligence: History and Documents*. University of Alabama Press, 1984.

Lewis, John Prior, *Asian Development: The Role of Development Assistance*. Lanham, MD (University Press of America)/New York (Asia Society) 1987.

Liddell Hart, Basil, *Strategy: The Indirect Approach*. New York (Praeger) 1954.

Lifton, Robert J., and Richard Falk, *Indefensible Weapons: The Political and Psychological Case against Nuclearism*. New York (Basic Books) 1983.

Linder, Staffan Burenstam, *The Pacific Century: Economic and Political Consequences of Asian–Pacific Dynamism*. Stanford University Press, 1986.

Lippmann, Walter, *U.S. Foreign Policy: Shield of the Republic*. Boston (Little, Brown) 1943.

Lodge, Henry Cabot, ed., *Selections from the Correspondence of Theodore Roosevelt and Henry Cabot Lodge, 1884–1918* 2 vols. New York (Scribners) 1925.

Louis, William Roger, "American Anti-Colonialism and the Dissolution of the British Empire," in William Roger Louis and Hedley Bull, eds., *The "Special Relationship": Anglo–American Relations since 1945*. Oxford University Press, 1986.

——, *Imperialism at Bay: The United States and the Decolonization of the British Empire, 1941–1945*. Oxford University Press, 1978.

——, and Hedley Bull, eds., *The "Special Relationship": Anglo–American Relations since 1945*. Oxford University Press, 1986.

——, and Ronald Robinson, "The United States and the Liquidation of the British Empire in Tropical Africa, 1941–1951," in Prosser Gifford and William Roger Louis, eds., *The Transfer of Power in Africa: Decolonization, 1940–1960*. Yale University Press, 1982.

Lunn, Simon, *Burden-Sharing in NATO*. Chatham House Paper No. 18, Royal Institute of International Affairs. London (Routledge and Kegan Paul) 1983.

Luttwak, Edward, *Strategy: The Logic of War and Peace*. Harvard University Press, 1987.

Maddison, Angus, *Phases of Capitalist Development*. Oxford University Press, 1982.

Mahan, Alfred Thayer, *The Interest of America in Sea Power: Present and Future*. 12th ed. Boston (Little, Brown) 1918.

Mahoney, Richard D., *JFK: Ordeal in Africa*. Oxford University Press, 1983.

Marcum, John A., *Portugal and Africa: The Politics of Indifference: A Case Study in American Foreign Policy*. Maxwell School and Program of Eastern African Studies, Syracuse University, 1972.

May, Ernest R., "Writing Contemporary International History," *Diplomatic History* 8, 2 (Spring 1984).

——, and James C. Thomson, Jr., eds., *American–East Asian Relations: A Survey*. Cambridge University Press, 1972.

Mayers, David, "Containment and the Primary of Diplomacy: George Kennan's Views, 1947–1948," *International Security* 2, 2 (Summer 1986).

——, *George Kennan and the Dilemmas of U.S. Foreign Policy*. Oxford University Press, 1988.

——, "Nazi Germany and the Future of Europe: George Kennan's Views, 1939–1945," *The International History Review* 8, 4 (November 1986).

——, "Young Kennan's Criticisms and Recommendations," *Biography* 8, 3 (Summer 1985).

Maynes, Charles William and Richard Ullman, "Ten Years of Foreign Policy," *Foreign Policy* 40 (Fall 1980).

McCormick, Thomas J., "Drift or Mastery: A Corporatist Synthesis," *Reviews in American History* (December 1982).

McLellan, David S., *Dean Acheson: The State Department Years*. New York (Dodd, Mead and Co.) 1976.

McMahon, Robert J., *Colonialism and the Cold War: The United States and the Struggle for Indonesian Independence, 1945–1949*. Cornell University Press, 1981.

Mearsheimer, John, *Conventional Deterrence*. Cornell University Press, 1983.

Melanson, David, and David Mayers, eds., *Reevaluating Eisenhower: American Foreign Policy in the Fifties*. University of Illinois Press, 1987.

Mendlovitz, Saul H., *On the Creation of a Just World Order*. New York (Free Press) 1975.

———, and R.B.J. Walker, eds., *Toward a Just World Peace: Perspectives from Social Movements*. Boston (Butterworths) 1987.

Millis, Walter, ed., *The Forrestal Diaries*. New York (Viking Press) 1951.

Milward, Alan S., *The Reconstruction of Western Europe, 1945–1951*. University of California Press, 1984.

Minter, William, *King Solomon's Mines Revisited: Western Interests and the Burdened History of Southern Africa*. New York (Basic Books) 1986.

Mojtabai, A. G., *Blessed Assurance: At Home with the Bomb in Amarillo, Texas*. New York (Houghton Mifflin) 1986.

Moore, Barrington, Jr., *Injustice: The Social Bases of Obedience and Revolt*. White Plains, N.Y. (M. E. Sharpe) 1978.

Morgenthau, Hans J., *In Defense of the National Interest: A Critical Examination for American Foreign Policy*. New York (Knopf) 1951.

———, *Politics among Nations: The Struggle for Power and Peace*. New York (Knopf) 1948. (Latest edition 1985, with Kenneth Thompson.)

———, *Scientific Man vs. Power Politics*. University of Chicago Press, 1946.

Morrison, David C., "Slashing NATO's Burden," *National Journal* 30 May 1987.

Nathan, James A. and James K. Oliver, *Foreign Policy Making and the American Political System*. Boston (Little, Brown) 1983.

Nathan, Richard P., Fred C. Doolittle, and Associates, *Reagan and the States*. Princeton University Press, 1987.

National Foreign Trade Council, *Report on the Twenty-seventh National Foreign Trade Convention*. New York (National Foreign Trade Council) 1940.

Niebuhr, Reinhold, *The Children of Light and the Children of Darkness: A Vindication of Democracy and a Critique of Its Traditional Defense*. New York (Scribners) 1944.

———, *The Irony of American History*. New York (Scribners) 1952.

———, *Moral Man and Immoral Society: A Study in Ethics and Politics*. New York (Scribners) 1941.

———, *The Nature and Destiny of Man: A Christian Interpretation* (2 vols.). New York (Scribners) 1941–43.

———, "The Social Myths in the Cold War," in John Farrell and Asa Smith, eds., *Image and Reality in World Politics*. Columbia University Press, 1967.

———, *The Structure of Nations and Empires*. New York (Scribners) 1959.

Neu, Charles E., *The Troubled Encounter: The United States and Japan*. New York (Wiley) 1975.

Neustadt, Richard E., *Presidential Power: The Politics of Leadership from FDR to Carter*. 4th ed. New York (Wiley) 1980.

Nguyen, Gregory Tien Hung, and Jerrold Schecter, *The Palace File*. New York (Harper & Row) 1986.

Nixon, Richard M., *The Memoirs of Richard Nixon*. New York (Grosset and Dunlap) 1978.

———, *1999: Victory without War*. New York (Simon & Schuster) 1988.

Nutter, G. Warren, *Growth of Government in the West*. Washington, D.C. (American Enterprise Institute for Public Policy) 1978.

Nye, Joseph S., Jr., *The Making of America's Soviet Policy*. Yale University Press, 1984.

———, "Neorealism and Neoliberalism," *World Politics* 40, 2 (1988).

Ohmae, Kenichi, *Triad Power: The Coming Shape of Global Competition*. New York (Free Press) 1985.

Osgood, Robert E., et al., *N.A.T.O.: The Entangling Alliance*. University of Chicago Press, 1962.

———, *Retreat from Empire? The First Nixon Administration*. Johns Hopkins University, 1973.

Oye, Kenneth A., Robert J. Lieber, and Donald Rothchild, *Eagle Entangled: United States Foreign Policy in a Complex World*. New York (Longman) 1979.

Packard, George, *Protest in Tokyo: The Security Treaty Crisis of 1960*. Princeton University Press, 1966.

Packenham, Robert A., *Liberal America and the Third World: Political Development Ideas in Foreign Aid and Social Science*. Princeton University Press, 1973.

Palmer, Norman D., *The United States and India: The Dimensions of Influence*. New York (Praeger) 1984.

Parker, Richard B., *North Africa: Regional Tensions and Strategic Concerns*. New York (Praeger) 1984. (Revised and updated, 1987.)

Parmet, Herbert S., *J.F.K.: The Presidency of John F. Kennedy*. New York (Dial Press) 1983.

Pastor, Robert A., *Condemned to Repetition: The United States and Nicaragua*. Princeton University Press, 1987.

Paterson, Thomas G., *Meeting the Communist Threat: Truman to Reagan*. Oxford University Press, 1988.

———, *Soviet–American Confrontation: Post-War Reconstruction and the Origins of the Cold War*. Johns Hopkins University Press, 1973.

———, J. Garry Clifford and Kenneth J. Hagan, *American Foreign Policy: A History since 1980*. Lexington MA (D.C. Heath) 1977. (Rev. ed. 1988).

Patrick, Hugh, and Henry Rosovsky, eds., *Asia's New Giant: How the Japanese Economy Works*. Washington, D.C. (Brookings Institution) 1976.

Pierre, Andrew J., *The Global Politics of Arms Sales*. Princeton University Press, 1982.

Polk, William R., *The Arab World*. 4th ed. Harvard University Press, 1980 (Earlier editions entitled *The United States and the Arab World*).

Powers, Thomas, *The Man Who Kept the Secrets: Richard Helms and the C.I.A.* New York (Knopf) 1979.

Prados, John, *Presidents' Secret Wars: CIA and Pentagon Covert Operations since World War II*. New York (Morrow) 1986.

Pruessen, Ronald W., *John Foster Dulles: The Road to Power*. New York (Free Press) 1982.

Quandt, William B., *Camp David: Peacemaking and Politics*. Washington, D.C. (Brookings Institution) 1986.

———, *Decade of Decisions: American Policy toward the Arab–Israeli Conflict, 1967–1976*. University of California Press, 1977.

Ranelagh, John, *The Agency: The Rise and Decline of the C.I.A.* London (Weidenfeld and Nicolson) 1986.

Ransom, Harry H., *The Intelligence Establishment*. Harvard University Press, 1970.

Reinhart, Uwe E., "Enjoy the Party—For Tomorrow Somebody Will Have to Pay," *Princeton Alumni Weekly* (25 February 1987).

Reischauer, Edwin, *The United States and Japan*. Harvard University Press, 1950. (3rd edition, 1965).

Reiss, Hans, ed., *Kant's Political Writings*. Cambridge University Press, 1970.

Reynolds, David, "The Wartime Anglo-Alliance," in William Roger Louis and Hedley

Bull, eds., *The "Special Relationship": Anglo–American Relations since 1945.* Oxford University Press, 1986.

Riddell, Roger, *Foreign Aid Reconsidered.* Johns Hopkins University Press, 1987.

Ridgway, Matthew B., *Soldier: The Memoirs of Matthew B. Ridgway.* New York (Harper) 1956.

Roberts, John, *Mitsui: Three Centuries of Japanese Business.* Tokyo (Weatherhill) 1973.

Rosecrance, Richard, *The Rise of the Trading State: Commerce and Conquest in the Modern World.* New York (Basic Books) 1986.

Rosenberg, David Alan, "The Origins of Overkill: Nuclear Weapons and American Strategy," in Norman A. Graebner, ed., *The National Security: Its Theory and Practice, 1945–1960.* Oxford University Press, 1986.

Rosenman, Samuel, ed., *The Public Papers and Addresses of Franklin D. Roosevelt, 1940.* New York, 1941.

Rossiter, Clinton, *Conservatism in America: The Thankless Persuasion.* New York (Knopf) 1962.

———, ed., *The Federalist Papers: Alexander Hamilton, James Madison, John Jay.* New York (New American Library) 1961.

Rostow, Walt Whitman, "Beware of Historians Bearing False Analogies," *Foreign Affairs* 66, 4 (Spring 1988).

———, *The Diffusion of Power: An Essay in Recent History.* New York (Macmillan) 1972.

Rubin, Barry, *Secrets of State: The State Department and the Struggle Over U.S. Foreign Policy.* Oxford University Press, 1985.

Rudolph, Lloyd, and Susan Lloyd, eds., *The Regional Imperative: U.S. Foreign Policy toward South Asian States under Presidents Johnson and Nixon.* Atlantic Highlands, NJ (Humanities Press) 1980.

Ruggie, John Gerard, "Another Round, Another Requiem? Prospects for the Global Negotiations," Chapter 3 in Jagdish N. Bhagwati and John Gerard Ruggie, eds., *Power, Passions, and Purpose: Prospects for North–South Negotiations.* MIT Press, 1984.

Rustow, Dankwart A., *Turkey: America's Forgotten Ally.* New York (Council on Foreign Relations) 1987.

Rystad, Goran, ed., *Congress and American Foreign Policy.* Lund, Sweden (Esselte Studium) 1981. (Lund Studies in International History, 13.)

Safran, Nadav, *Israel: The Embattled Ally.* Harvard University Press, 1978.

Sanjuan, Pedro A., "Why We Don't Have a Latin America Policy," *Washington Quarterly* 3 (Autumn 1980).

Sawhill, Isabel V., and Charles F. Stone, "The Economy," Chapter 3 in John L. Palmer and Isabel V. Sawhill, eds., *The Reagan Record: An Assessment of America's Changing Domestic Priorities.* Cambridge, MA (Ballinger) 1984.

Schelling, Thomas C., *Arms and Influence.* Yale University Press, 1966.

———, *Strategy of Conflict.* Harvard University Press, 1960.

Schlatter, Richard, ed., *Hobbes's Thucydides.* Rutgers University Press, 1975.

Schlesinger, Arthur M., Jr., *The Cycles of American History.* Boston (Houghton Mifflin) 1986.

———, *The Imperial Presidency.* Boston (Houghton Mifflin) 1973.

———, *Robert Kennedy and His Times.* Boston (Houghton Mifflin) 1978.

———, *A Thousand Days: John F. Kennedy in the White House.* Boston (Houghton Mifflin) 1965.

Seabury, Paul, "George Kennan vs. Mr. X," *The New Republic* (16 December 1981).

Shawcross, William, *Sideshow: Kissinger, Nixon and the Destruction of Cambodia.* New York (Simon & Schuster) 1979.

Sheed, Wilfred, "The Summer of 1960," *New York Times Book Review* (6 July 1980).

Sheehan, Edward R. E., *The Arabs, Israelis, and Kissinger: A Secret History of American Diplomacy in the Middle East.* New York (Readers Digest Press) 1976.

Shepley, James, "How Dulles Averted War," *Life* (16 January 1956).

Shimbun, Asahi, *The Pacific Rivals: A Japanese View of Japanese American Relations.* Tokyo (Weatherhill) 1972.

Sick, Gary, *All Fall Down: America's Tragic Encounter with Iran.* New York (Penguin) 1986.

Skowronek, Stephen, *Building a New American State: The Expansion of National Administrative Capacities, 1877–1920.* Cambridge University Press, 1982.

Smith, Gaddis, *Morality, Reason and Power: The Foreign Policy of Jimmy Carter.* New York (Hill and Wang, Inc.) 1986.

Smith, Michael, *Western Europe and the United States: An Uncertain Alliance* (Studies on Contemporary Europe, 6). Boston (Allen and Unwin) 1984.

Smith, Michael Joseph, *Realist Thought from Weber to Kissinger.* Louisiana State University Press, 1986.

Sorensen, Theodore C., *Kennedy.* New York (Harper and Row) 1965.

Spanier, John, *The Truman–MacArthur Controversy and the Korean War.* Harvard University Press, 1959.

———, and Joseph Nogee, eds., *Congress, the Presidency and Foreign Policy.* New York (Pergamon Press) 1981.

Spector, Ronald, *Advice and Support: The Early Years of the U.S. Army in Vietnam, 1941–1960.* New York (Free Press) 1985.

Speiser, E. A., *The United States and the Near East.* Harvard University Press, 1947.

Spiegel, Steven L., *The Other Arab–Israeli Conflict: Making America's Middle East Policy, from Truman to Reagan.* University of Chicago Press, 1985.

Spykman, Nicholas John, *America's Strategy in World Politics: The United States and the Balance of Power.* New York (Harcourt, Brace and Co.) 1942.

Stivers, William, *America's Confrontation with Revolutionary Change in the Middle East, 1948–83.* London (Macmillan) 1986.

Stookey, Robert W., *America and the Arab World.* New York (Wiley) 1975.

Stueck, William Whitney, Jr., *The Road to Confrontation: American Policy towards China and Korea, 1947–1950.* University of North Carolina Press, 1981.

Summers, Harry G., Jr., *On Strategy: The Vietnam War in Context.* Carlisle Barracks, PA (Strategic Studies Institute, U.S. Army War College) 1981.

Szulc, Tad, *The Illusion of Peace: Foreign Policy in the Nixon–Kissinger Years.* New York (Viking Press) 1978.

Tatsuro, Uchino, *Japan's Postwar Economy: An Insider's View of Its History and Its Future.* New York (Kodansha International) 1983.

Thompson, E.P., "Notes on Exterminism, the Last State of Civilization," *New Left Review* 121 (May–June 1980).

Thucydides, *History of the Peloponnesian War.* Translated by Rex Warner. London (Penguin Books) 1954. (Revised with new introduction and appendices, 1972.)

Tillman, Seth P., *The United States in the Middle East: Interests and Obstacles.* Indiana University Press, 1982.

Toulouse, Mark, *The Transformation of John Foster Dulles: From Prophet of Realism to Priest of Nationalism.* Macon, GA (Mercer University Press) 1985.

Tower, John (Chair), *The Tower Commission Report: The Full Text of the President's Special Review Board.* New York (Bantam Books) 1987.

Trefousse, Hans L., ed., *Germany and America: Essays on Problems of International Relations and Immigration.* Brooklyn College Press, 1980.

Treverton, Gregory F., *Covert Action: The Limits of Intervention in the Postwar World.* New York (Basic Books) 1987.

Trommler, Frank and Joseph McVeigh, eds., *America and the Germans: An Assessment of a Three-hundred-year History.* University of Pennsylvania Press, 1985.

Tsou, Tang, *America's Failure in China, 1941–1950.* University of Chicago Press, 1963.

Tucker, Robert W., "The Atlantic Alliance and Its Critics," in Robert W. Tucker and Linda Wrigley, eds., *The Atlantic Alliance and Its Critics.* New York (Praeger) 1983.

Turley, William, *The Second Indochina War: A Short Political and Military History, 1954–1975.* Boulder, CO (Westview Press) 1986.

Turner, Stansfield, *Secrecy and Democracy: The CIA in Transition.* Boston (Houghton Mifflin) 1985.

Ulam, Adam B., *The Rivals: America and Russia Since World War II.* New York (Viking Press) 1971.

Ullman, Richard H. and Mario Zucconi, eds., *Western Europe and the Crisis of U.S.–Soviet Relations.* New York (Praeger) 1987.

Vail Motter, T. H., *The Persian Corridor and Aid to Russia.* In the series *United States Army in World War II: The Middle East Theater.* Washington, D.C. (Office of the Chief of Military History, Department of Army) 1952.

Vaky, Viron P., "Hemispheric Relations: 'Everything is part of Everything Else,'" *Foreign Affairs* 59, 3 (1981).

Vance, Cyrus, *Hard Choices: Critical Years in American Foreign Policy.* New York (Simon & Schuster) 1983.

Vasquez, John, *The Power of Power Politics: A Critique.* Rutgers University Press, 1983.

Vernon, Raymond, *Two Hungry Giants: The United States and Japan in the Quest for Oil and Ores.* Harvard University Press, 1983.

Walker, R.B.J., *One World/Many Worlds.* Boulder, CO (Lynne Rienner) 1988.

Walton, Richard, *Cold War and Counterrevolution: The Foreign Policy of John F. Kennedy.* New York (Viking Press) 1972.

Watson, Robert J., *The Joint Chiefs of Staff and National Policy 1953–1954.* Vol. 5 of *History of the Joint Chiefs of Staff.* Washington, D.C. (U.S. Government Printing Office) 1986.

Watt, Donald Cameron, "Demythologizing the Eisenhower Era," in William Roger Louis and Hedley Bull, eds., *The "Special Relationship": Anglo–American Relations since 1945.* Oxford University Press, 1986.

———, *Succeeding John Bull: America in Britain's Place, 1900–1975.* Cambridge University Press, 1984.

Weigley, Russell, *The American Way of War: A History of United States Military Strategy and Policy.* New York, 1973.

Weinstein, Martin E., *Japan's Postwar Defense Policy, 1947–1968.* Columbia University Press, 1971.

Westmoreland, William, *A Soldier Reports.* Garden City, NY (Doubleday) 1976.

Whitaker, Jennifer Seymour, ed., *Africa and the United States: Vital Interests.* New York University Press, 1978.

Wilcox, Francis O., *Congress, the Executive and Foreign Policy.* New York (Harper and Row) 1971.

Williams, William A., *The Tragedy of American Foreign Policy.* 2nd ed. New York (Dell Publishing Company) 1972.

Wills, Garry, *Nixon Agonistes: The Crisis of the Self-Made Man.* Boston (Houghton Mifflin) 1970.

Woodward, C. Vann, "The Age of Reinterpretation," *American Historical Review* 66 (October 1960).

Yergin, Daniel, *Shattered Peace: The Origins of the Cold War and the National Security State.* Boston (Houghton Mifflin) 1977.

Young, Andrew, "The United States and Africa: Victory for Diplomacy," *Foreign Affairs* 59, 3 (1981).

Young, Crawford, "United States Policy toward Africa: Silver Anniversary Reflections," *African Studies Review* 27, 3 (September 1984).

Government Publications

Bretton Woods Agreement. Washington, 1945.

Karalekas, Anne, "History of the Central Intelligence Agency," in *Supplementary Detailed Staff Reports on Foreign and Military Intelligence,* Book 4 of *Final Report of the Senate Select Committee to Study . . . Intelligence Activities.* 94th Cong., 2nd sess., 1976.

U.S. Arms Control and Disarmament Agency, *World Military Expenditures and Arms Transfers.* Washington (annual).

U.S. Central Intelligence Agency, *Handbook of Economic Statistics, 1985.* Springfield, VA (National Technical Information Service) 1985.

U.S. Department of Defense, *Annual Report: Fiscal Year 1979.* Washington, 1978.

U.S. Department of Defense, *Soviet Military Power.* Washington, 1978.

U.S. Department of State, *Bulletin.*

U.S. Department of State, *Foreign Relations of the United States.* Washington, (annual).

U.S. Department of State, *Foreign Relations of the United States.*

U.S. Department of State, *A U.S. Policy Toward South Africa: Report of the Secretary of State's Advisory Committee on South Africa.* January 1987.

U.S. House of Representatives, Committee on Foreign Affairs, *Foreign Assistance for Fiscal Year 1982.* 97th Cong., 1st sess., 1981.

U.S. House of Representatives, Committee on Foreign Affairs, Subcommittee on Inter-American Affairs, *Honduras and U.S. Policy: An Emerging Dilemma.* 97th Cong., 2nd sess., 1982.

U.S. House of Representatives, Committee on Foreign Affairs, Subcommittee on Inter-American Affairs, *United States–Brazilian Relations.* 97th Cong., 2nd sess., 1982.

U.S. House of Representatives, Committee on Foreign Affairs, Subcommittee on Western Hemisphere Affairs, *U.S. Policy Toward Argentina.* 98th Cong., 1st sess., 1983.

U.S. Joint Chiefs of Staff, *Military Posture: Fiscal Year 1988.* Washington, 1987.

U.S. President's Committee on Foreign Aid, *European Recovery and American Aid.* Washington, 1947.

U.S. Senate, Committee on Foreign Relations, *The North Atlantic Treaty Hearings.* Washington, 1949.

U.S. Senate Select Committee to Study Intelligence Activities, *Interim Report of the Alleged Assassination Plots Involving Foreign Leaders in Zaire, Cuba, Dominican Republic, South Vietnam and Chile.* 94th Cong., 1st sess., 1975. Senate Report Number 94–465.

U.S. Senate Select Committee to Study Government Operations with Respect to Intelligence Activities, *Foreign and Military Intelligence.* 94th Cong., 2nd sess., 1976. Senate Report Number 94–755, Book 1.

Japanese Ministry of Defense, *Defense of Japan.* Tokyo, 1976.

Naikaku Sori Daijin Kanbo Kanri Shitsu, *Zenkoku Sensai Shi Jitsu Chosa Hokokusho. (A Survey of the History of Actual Wartime Casualties).* Tokyo, 1979.

Organization for Economic Cooperation and Development, *Japan.* Paris (OECD Surveys) 1969.

Unpublished Papers

Branson, William H., "Capital Flows from Japan to the U.S.: Another False Alarm." 16 March 1987.

Friedan, Jeffrey, "The Economics of Colonialism and Decolonization: American Relations with Underdeveloped Areas, 1890–1950."

Gaddis, John Lewis, "The Eisenhower Legacy and American Grand Strategy, 1960–1968," preliminary paper presented for the U.S. Military Academy Symposium on "The Theory and Practice of American National Security, 1960–1968," 15–18 April 1988.

———, "The Unexpected John Foster Dulles: Nuclear Weapons, Communism and the Russians," paper read at the Dulles Centennial Conference, Princeton University, 26 February 1988.

Johnson, Loch K., "Covert Action and American Foreign Policy: Decision Paths for the 'Quiet Option,'" paper presented to the American Political Science Association annual meeting, Washington, D.C., 1986.

Kennan, George F., *Papers.* (Seeley G. Mudd Manuscript Library, Princeton University.)

Kunz, Diane B., "The Importance of Having Money: The Economic Diplomacy of the Suez Crisis."

Murikami, Yasusuki and Kozo Yamamura, "Technology in Transition: Two Perspectives on Industrial Policy." 1984.

Patrick, Hugh, "The Asian Developing Market Economies—How They Have Affected and Been Affected by the United States–Japan Economic Relationship." 1983.

———, "The End of Eras? Japan and the Western World in the 1970–1980s." 1983.

Serials

Africa Contemporary Record: Annual Survey and Documents. Colin Legum (ed.), New York and London: Africana Publishing Company 1968/69.

"America and the World," an annual issue of *Foreign Affairs.*

Council on Foreign Relations, *The United States in World Affairs.* (Founded 1967).

Diplomatic History.

Foreign Policy.

Notes on Contributors

David M. Bachman is Assistant Professor of Politics at Princeton University. He is the author of *Chen Dyun and the Chinese Political System* and a number of essays on Chinese politics and foreign policy. He has taught at Stanford University and has been a post-doctoral fellow at the Center for Chinese Studies at the University of California, Berkeley. He is an associate editor of *World Politics*.

L. Carl Brown is Garrett Professor in Foreign Affairs and director of the interdisciplinary Program in Near Eastern Studies at Princeton University. A historian of the modern Middle East and North Africa, he is the author of *International Politics and the Middle East: Old Rules, Dangerous Game*.

Kent E. Calder, Assistant Professor of Politics and International Affairs at Princeton University's Woodrow Wilson School, is the author of *Crisis and Compensation: Public Policy and Political Stability in Japan* and co-author of *The Eastasia Edge*. He is currently editing a volume dealing with the domestic implications of Japanese international economic commitments.

Richard D. Challener is Professor of History at Princeton University where he teaches "The History of American Foreign Policy from the Age of Imperialism to the Present." He is the author of *Admirals, Generals & American Foreign Policy*,

1896–1914 and *The French Theory of the Nation in Arms, 1866–1939*. Among his recent publications is "The National Security Policy from Truman to Eisenhower: Did the 'Hidden Hand' Leadership Make Any Difference?" in Norman Graebner, ed., *The National Security: Its Theory and Practice, 1945–1960*. He is working on a biography of John Foster Dulles.

Aaron L. Friedberg is Assistant Professor of Politics and International Affairs at Princeton University where he holds a joint appointment in the Politics Department and the Woodrow Wilson School. His research interests include international relations theory, American national security policy, and the relationship between economics and strategy. The author of *The Weary Titan: Britain and the Experience of Relative Decline, 1895–1905*, his articles have appeared in *Foreign Policy, International Security, The Journal of Strategic Studies, The National Interest, Parameters* and *War and Society*. He has served as consultant to the National Security Council and the Department of Defense.

Richard A. Falk is Albert G. Milbank Professor of International Law and Practice at Princeton University. He has acted as counsel to Ethiopia and Liberia in the South West Africa case before the International Court of Justice, was research director of the North American team in the World Order Models Project, is a senior fellow of the World Policy Institute, and has been vice president of the American Society of International Law. His major publications include: *Revolutionaries & Functionaries, The Promise of World Order, Indefensible Weapons* (co-author), *Human Rights & State Sovereignty, A Global Approach to National Policy, A Study of Future Worlds, This Endangered Planet, Legal Order in a Violent World* and *The Vietnam War & International Law*.

John Lewis Gaddis is Distinguished Professor of History and Director of the Contemporary History Institute at Ohio University. A specialist in the field of United States diplomatic history and national security policy, his publications include *Strategies of Containment: A Critical Appraisal of Postwar American National Security Policy* and *The Long Peace: Inquiries into the History of the Cold War*.

Robert G. Gilpin, Jr. is the Eisenhower Professor of International Affairs at Princeton University. His fields of special interest are theories of international relations, international political economy, and the industrial world. He is the author of *American Scientists and Nuclear Weapons Policy, France in the Age of the Scientific State, U.S. Power and the Multinational Corporation, War and Change in World Politics* and *The Political Economy of International Relations*. He is coauthor and coeditor of *Scientist and National Policy Making*.

Robert F. Goheen is Senior Fellow in Public and International Affairs at Princeton University and Director of the Mellon Fellowships in the Humanities. Born and raised in India, he returned to that country to serve as United States ambassador in 1977–1980. President of Princeton University from 1957 to 1972 he serves as trustee of the American University of Beirut, the Asia Society, Bharatiya Vidya Bhavan (USA), Carnegie Endowment for International Peace, and the United Board of Christian Higher Education in Asia.

Miles Kahler is Professor of Political Science at the University of California at San Diego. He previously taught at Yale and Princeton. His publications include *The Politics of International Debt* (ed.) and *Decolonization in Britain and France: The Domestic Consequences of International Relations* plus numerous articles on comparative politics and international relations. He serves on the Committee on Foreign Policy Studies of the Social Science Research Council and was a Council on Foreign Relations Fellow at the International Monetary Fund in 1983–1984.

Yuen Foong Khong is Assistant Professor of Government and Faculty Associate of the Center for International Affairs at Harvard University. His research and teaching has focused on American foreign policy, the Vietnam War, the impact of nuclear weapons on world politics and cognitive approaches to international relations. He is currently engaged in a National Academy of Sciences project on how American and Soviet leaders have used history in their foreign policy decision-making.

Helen Kitchen has been director of the African Studies Program at the Center for Strategic and International Studies, Washington, D.C. since 1981. In 1974–1976 she directed the Africa Area Study of the (Rockefeller) Commission on Critical Choices for Americans and produced Vol. XI of the Critical Choices series, *Africa: From Mystery to Maze*. Other published works include *Some Guidelines on Africa for the Next President* (1988), *South Africa: In Transition to What?*, *Angola, Mozambique, & the West* (ed.), *The United States and South Africa: Realities & Red Herrings* (co-author) and *U.S Interests in Africa*. She was editor of the journal *Africa Report* from 1960 to 1968 and of *Africa Index* fortnightly from 1978 to 1982. Since 1982 she has published over 90 issues of the *CSIS Africa Notes*, a "briefing paper series for decision makers."

Melvyn P. Leffler is Professor of History at the University of Virginia. His principal areas of interest are twentieth century foreign economic relations of the United States and American national security policies since the Second World War. The author of *Elusive Quest: America's Pursuit of European Stability and French Security, 1919–1933*, he is now completing a study to be entitled *Fear, Power & Preponderance: National Security, the Truman Administration, and the Cold War, 1945–1952*.

John P. Lewis is Professor of Economics and International Affairs at Princeton University. His early work in India as a Brookings Institution Senior Fellow (1959–1960) led to his 1962 Brookings book, *Quiet Crisis in India*. He served as a member of the Council of Economic Advisers under Presidents Kennedy and Johnson in 1963 and 1964. In late 1964 he returned to India to begin a five year term as director of the USAID Mission to India. Lewis was resident chairman of

OECD's Development Assistance Committee in Paris from 1979 to 1981. He has been a member of the UN Committee for Development Planning and a consultant to the World Bank, and Asian Development Bank. He continues to visit South Asia often as an adviser to the Ford Foundation.

David Mayers is Associate Professor of Political Science at Boston University. He is the author of *George Kennan and the Dilemmas of U.S. Foreign Policy* and *Cracking the Monolith: U.S. Policy Against the Sino-Soviet Alliance, 1949–1955* and is coeditor of *Reevaluating Eisenhower: American Foreign Policy in the Fifties.* He is currently writing a book to be entitled *Reporting from Moscow: The U.S. Diplomatic Mission and Policy Toward the Soviet Union.*

Lars Schoultz is Professor of Political Science and Director of the Institute of Latin American Studies at the University of North Carolina at Chapel Hill. His research focuses on United States policy toward Latin America. He is the author of *Human Rights and United States Policy Toward Latin America* and *National Security and United States Policy Toward Latin America.*

Michael Joseph Smith is Assistant Professor of Government and Foreign Affairs at the University of Virginia. He is the author of *Realist Thought from Weber to Kissinger.* His major areas of interest are international relations theory and contemporary American foreign policy. He is currently writing a book, with Stanley Hoffmann, on ethics and international relations.

Gregory F. Treverton is Senior Fellow at the Council on Foreign Relations in New York with responsibility for European and politico-military issues. He served on the staff of the first Senate Select Committee on Intelligence (the Church Committee) and as staff member for Western Europe on the National Security Council during the Carter Administration. He was Director of Studies of the International Institute for Strategic Studies in London and was for six years a faculty member of the John F. Kennedy School of Government at Harvard University before joining the Council. His publications include *The "Dollar Drain" & American Forces in Germany, Nuclear Weapons in Europe, Making the Alliance Work: The United States and Western Europe* and, more recently, *Covert Action: The Limits of Intervention in the Postwar World.*

William H. Weathersby, after a distinguished career in the United States Information Agency served as Vice President for Public Affairs at Princeton University from 1970 to 1978. His last position in USIS was as Deputy Director for Policy and Plans. Earlier he served as U.S. Ambassador to Sudan. He had two tours of duty in India during the 1960s serving the second tour as Minister-Counselor and Consul General at the American Embassy. He had worked as a journalist before joining USIA in 1951.

Mario Zucconi has been associated with the Centro Studi di Politica Internazionale (CESPI) since 1978 and he now serves as director there of United

States & Western alliance studies. He is also visiting professor of political science at the University of Naples and has been a visiting professor at Princeton University. He is coeditor with Richard H. Ullman of *Western Europe and the Crisis in US-Soviet Relations*. Among other recent publications are "Some Aspects of the Problem of Security in Europe" in M. Kaplan (ed.), *Preserving Peace in Europe: A Dialogue Between East & West* and *Il Confiltto Arabo-Israeliano e il sistema internazionale del secondo dopoguerra*.

Index